Fundamentals of Criminal Investigation

(Fifth Edition)

Fundamentals of Criminal Investigation

By

CHARLES E. O'HARA

with

GREGORY L. O'HARA

C H A R L E S   C   T H O M A S   •   P U B L I S H E R
Springfield   •   Illinois   •   U.S.A.

Published and Distributed Throughout the World by
CHARLES C THOMAS • PUBLISHER
Bannerstone House
301-327 East Lawrence Avenue, Springfield, Illinois, U.S.A.

With THOMAS BOOKS careful attention is given to all details of
manufacturing and design. It is the Publisher's desire to present books that are
satisfactory as to their physical qualities and artistic possibilities and
appropriate for their particular use. THOMAS BOOKS will be true to those
laws of quality that assure a good name and good will.

Library of Congress Cataloging in Publication Data

O'Hara, Charles E.
    Fundamentals of criminal investigation.

    Includes bibliographies and index.
    1. Criminal investigation. I. O'Hara, Gregory L., joint author. II. Title.
HV8073,039   1980   364.12   79-21536
ISBN 0-398-04000-1

Printed in the United States of America
M-3

To

LOUIS SATTLER

PREFACE TO THE FIFTH EDITION

THE IDEAS set forth in the present edition are concentrated principally on guiding the serious student to a professional level of effectiveness. The techniques and procedures are presented not merely in relation to a specific offense but rather as part of a coherent theoretical framework applicable to all investigative situations. Since criminal activity reflects all the complexity of the human condition, the investigator will not expect to find "textbook cases" but must be prepared to apply his knowledge to the atypical and the unfamiliar. To this end a theory of investigation is developed in the opening chapter which provides a groundwork for the investigative procedures that follow.

The Fifth Edition has been shortened and, we hope, enriched. The immense growth of investigative literature has rendered impracticable the original concept of encompassing in one volume all the useful recommendations of an introductory nature. Sections describing activities not strictly the work of the investigator have been set aside to make room for the significant scientific and technical innovations which have expanded and further complicated the field of criminal investigation. Again, in recognition of these developments, the authors have provided space for a substantial body of references that will enhance and implement the understanding of the chapters and encourage the reader's own research.

The text has been further oriented toward the development of useful attitudes underlying professional growth so that the student may come away not with a miscellany of procedures and tests but rather with a structured philosophy of criminal investigation.

INTRODUCTION

F ROM ITS INCEPTION, the aim of this book has been to bring the
reader to an intermediate level of attainment in the main
branches of investigation from which he may be able to proceed,
with the help of other literature and his experience, to specialized
fields of crime detection or non-criminal inquiry. It is not presumed
that from mastery of the contents of this book the reader will become
an accomplished investigator. The detection of crime is, after all, not
a science but an art, whose secrets are not likely to be captured in
any great part between the covers of a book. Techniques such as
interrogation and surveillance are acquired mainly through patient
practice and self-criticism. The student can, however, by-pass
months of aimless apprenticeship if he learns at the outset of his
career the significance and application of the basic tools of
investigation, which have been described in Chapter I as the three
"I's"—Information, Interrogation, and Instrumentation.

It is the object, then, of the present book to introduce the student
to investigative work in such a way that he shall, on the one hand,
learn what is meant by a complete investigation and acquaint
himself with the proofs of the most important crimes, and, on the
other, become familiar with the employment of technical methods
and services available to him. The book being thus intended, not as a
compendium, but really, as its title indicates, only as a presentation
of the foundations of investigation, the attempt has been made
throughout to lay a sufficiently broad groundwork to enable the
reader to pursue his further studies intelligently, rather than to
carry any single topic to exhaustive completeness. Since a selection
was necessary, those offenses have been chosen for treatment which
are serious in nature or relatively frequent in occurrence. The
extension to other crimes of the principles elucidated here should be
well within the powers of the attentive reader.

The presentation is directed to the beginning student of the art of
investigation. The experienced investigator and the supervisor may,
of course, find some material that is instructive or interesting. Little

has been said of the administrative practices and problems of a detective division or an investigative agency, and such administrative information as is given is necessarily of a fragmentary and accidental character. The text throughout is addressed to the "investigator," a term chosen in preference to such titles as "detective" and "agent" because of its more general nature. Thus the ideas and precepts have been arranged for practical application by a city detective or plainclothesman, a private investigator, or a federal agent. Military personnel may find the work particularly useful in view of the fact that many of the paragraphs devoted to legal matters reflect the principles of the Uniform Code of Military Justice.

The many recommendations to be found in these chapters are often put in the form of rules and are sometimes permitted to stand unqualified. This manner of presentation does not imply that the recommended method is the only effective procedure for the investigation. The student will understand that, although these precepts are based on accepted practice, they have been interpreted with discretion and a reasonable elasticity. The learner, however, must be guided by rules until he knows enough about investigation to be superior to the rules. He must submit himself temporarily to this discipline, knowing well that there is a freedom beyond the rules and that this freedom is the result of discipline. The rules are the discipline of learning.

This book is based on some fifteen years of practical experience in investigations conducted for municipal and federal law enforcement agencies. It is the development of courses which the author has given through the years for a number of investigative organizations and private universities. During this time he has come to feel that more would be accomplished by his students if they had an introductory treatise adopted to the requirements of the modern investigator. To this end he has compiled his notes in a more finished form. It is recognized that, since investigation is a growing art, the integrity of none of these chapters is secure from either increase or revision.

ACKNOWLEDGMENTS

THE SOURCES of materials used in this text are many and varied: the practical experience during the last generation of detective chiefs of key cities in this country and abroad; the recommendations of federal law enforcement agencies, both civilian and military; the recommendations and suggestions of instructors in universities and colleges offering courses in criminal investigation; the communications of research scientists, both academic and industrial; the reports and counsel of The President's Commission on Law Enforcement and Administration of Justice; and the advice and criticism of colleagues in the Police Commissioner's Office, the Bureau of Technical Services, and the John Jay College of Criminal Justice. In the Fourth Edition the corrections and suggestions of Mr. Harrison C. Allison of the Marion Institute have greatly improved the text. The present edition has profited considerably from the criticisms and recommendations of the recent Rand Corporation Research Study of the criminal investigation process.

Law enforcement officials of other countries have been similarly helpful in the exchange of ideas. From Warsaw, Bonn, Rome, Ankara, Tokyo, Hong Kong, Buenos Aires, and other cities, the encouragement and concern of their responses have emphasized the community of responsibilities as well as the sense of fellowship in the service of criminal justice. Their contributions have aided greatly in the achievement of the authors' objective—the creation of a useful textbook whose point of view is well removed from the parochial or even the provincial attitude.

Charles E. O'Hara
Gregory L. O'Hara

CONTENTS

PART IV

SPECIFIC OFFENSES

PART V

THE INVESTIGATOR IN COURT

PART VI

IDENTIFICATION AND REPRODUCTION

PART VII

SPECIALIZED SCIENTIFIC METHODS

Fundamentals of Criminal Investigation

PART I
GENERAL

Chapter 1

METHODS OF INVESTIGATION

1. Nature of Investigation

A CRIMINAL investigator is a person who collects facts to accomplish a threefold aim: to identify and locate the guilty party and to provide evidence of his guilt. Investigation is an art and not a science; hence it must be discussed in terms of precepts and advice rather than laws and rigid theories. The element of intuition or felicity of inspiration in the choice of methods has its effect on the outcome despite the most methodical and exhausting treatment of a case. Then, too, there is the matter of chance which cannot be omitted from consideration.

In order, however, to provide a basis for a logical discussion of investigation as an applied art, it is necessary to create for ourselves the fiction that it is a science, complete with general principles and special theorems; that, if the investigator operates in harmony with the rules, the case will be inexorably solved; that a failure to solve a particular case is attributable to the employment of unorthodox methods or the neglect of prescribed procedures. With these assumptions, we can proceed to build our structure.

The tools of the investigator are, for the sake of simplicity, referred to as the three "I's," namely, Information, Interrogation, and Instrumentation. By the application of the three "I's" in varying proportions the investigator gathers the facts which are necessary to establish the guilt or innocence of the accused in a criminal trial. The remaining chapters of this book are an exposition of the nature and use of the three "I's."

It should be noted at this point that there are no normative criteria for judging the success or failure of an investigation. The fact that the crime remains unsolved does not indicate a deficiency in the investigation; nor does a conviction of the accused necessarily mean that the investigation was conducted in an intelligent manner. An investigation may be considered a success if all the available information relevant and material to the issues or allegations of the case is uncovered. There is, however, no way of knowing, ordinarily, whether the information was available.

It is a common misconception that every crime is intrinsically soluble; that there is always sufficient evidence available to reveal the identity of the criminal; that the perpetrator always leaves traces at the crime scene which, in the hands of a discerning investigator or technician, will lead inevitably to his door. It is for this reason that a citizen who cannot determine which of his three children opened a forbidden jar of cookies may become indignant at the inability of his police force to locate unerringly the perpetrator of a mysterious robbery among the several million inhabitants of his city.

Many crimes are not susceptible of solution by reason of the fact that the evidence is insufficient. The absence of eyewitnesses, discernible motives, and physical clues will obviously prohibit a solution unless the malefactor confesses. Often, the *corpus delicti* or the fact that a crime was committed cannot be established, and even a confession is of little value.

The concept of "solving the crime" does not satisfy the requirements of a completed investigation. To the general public, this term describes merely the process of discovering the identity of the suspect and apprehending him. These achievements, however, are but two of the objectives of an investigation and leave the investigator far from his ultimate goal of presenting sufficient evidence in a court of law to warrant a conviction. Finding the perpetrator is frequently the simplest phase of the investigation; obtaining the evidence to support the charge in court is often an exceedingly complex task, the difficulties of which are greatly increased by the requirements placed by the court on the character, sufficiency, and mode of introduction of the evidence.

To simplify the presentation of the ideas in these chapters it will be assumed that most crimes can be solved and that the methods described are usually effective in accomplishing the solution. The investigation will be considered successful if the available physical evidence was competently handled, the witnesses intelligently interviewed, the suspect, if willing, effectively interrogated, all logical leads properly developed, and the case comprehensively, clearly, and accurately reported. The verdict of the court in regard to the guilt of the accused will not be considered a necessarily valid criterion of the success or failure of the investigation.

2. Information

The word "information" is used here to describe the knowledge which the investigator gathers from other persons. There are basically two kinds. The first type of information is acquired from regular sources such as conscientious and public-spirited citizens, company records, and the files of other agencies. The second type, which is of particular interest to the criminal investigator and which will receive special attention here, is the knowledge gathered by the experienced investigator from cultivated sources such as paid informants, bartenders, cab drivers, licensed owners and employees in general, former criminals, or acquaintances. The extent to which informants are employed varies widely with law enforcement agencies. The French police, for example, rely heavily on an elaborate network of paid informants. In the English system, however, there is little provision for paid informants. The United States in recent years has drawn away from the English model and is rapidly approaching that of the French with increasingly liberal provisions for paid informants. Many agencies, federal, state, and municipal provide routinely for informant expenditures in any case of more than ordinary importance.

Of the three "I's," information is by far the most important, since it answers the question, "Who did it?" By the marvelous expedient of simply questioning a knowledgeable and often anonymous individual, the identity of the perpetrator, and usually his motive, are revealed. The investigation at once acquires direction, and subsequent steps are meaningful and heuristic rather than merely experimental. The investigator finds himself in a position of working a mathematical problem backwards with the known solution always before him, not in the difficult sense of proving a theorem in geometry but with the mechanical ease of establishing an algebraic identity from a knowledge of the original and the derived forms.

It is commonly held that most cases involving offenses committed by professional criminals are solved in this manner; that a homicide case in which the killer has a previous record is usually broken by a tip from a paroled convict, a hint from a narcotics addict, or a few snatches of conversation gleaned by a curious bartender. The crime of the professional is ordinarily motivated by a desire for economic gain. Larceny, robbery, and burglary share this motive. Assault and homicide are often incidental to crimes of greed or are the by-product of disputes over divisions of spoils or areal rights. The crime of greed, then, when perpetrated by the professional is most frequently solved by information.

When the amateur puts his hand to criminal activity, where the crime is one of passion, sparked by love, hate, or a desire for revenge, or when the offense is "motiveless" by reason of the deranged mind of the perpetrator, information in the usual sense is seldom available. The criminal, as far as the underworld is concerned, is socially trackless; he exists without reference to the milieu of the detective. There are informative sources which may prove helpful but "information" in the second sense is not forthcoming.

The present discussion has been limited to a relatively narrow interpretation of the concept of information. The potential role of modern information technology is far too broad a subject to treat in the limited space available. The systematic storage and rapid retrieval of information by electronic data processing methods have been in operation in some of the larger police departmens for a number of years. Their effectiveness has already been demonstrated in the apprehension process. Plans for an integrated information system for criminal justice have already taken concrete form. Many local police agencies have already availed themselves of computer communication with federal and state systems. The combination of modern technology with information theory has begun to mark a new era in law enforcement.

3. Interrogation

Interrogation, the second "I," includes the skillful questioning of witnesses as well as suspects. The success of "information" depends on the intelligent selection of informative sources; the effectiveness of interrogation varies with the craft, logic, and psychological insight with which the investigator questions a person who is in possession of information relevant to the case. The term *interview* will be used throughout the text to mean the simple questioning of a person who has no personal reason to withhold information and therefore may be expected to cooperate with the investigator; while the term *interrogation* will be used to describe the questioning of a suspect or other person who may normally be expected to be reluctant to divulge information concerning the offense under investigation. The ability to obtain information by questioning is the most prized talent of the investigator.

The novice investigator often overlooks the most obvious approach to the solution of a crime, namely, asking the suspect if he committed the offense. The lesson is so elementary that it is frequently neglected by the beginner in his eagerness to use the more refined techniques of modern crime detection. The guilty person is in possession of most of the information necessary for a successful prosecution, and if he is questioned intelligently, he can usually be induced to talk. A confession, moreover, which includes details that could not be known by an innocent party is a convincing form of proof.

A study of typical homicide cases will reveal the importance of obtaining confessions and admissions. It will be found that if the accused can be induced to "talk" the prospects of a successful prosecution are usually bright. If he remains silent, his chances of being acquitted are inestimably improved. Indeed, the most egregious error committed by clever criminals is that of answering, truthfully or otherwise, the questions of the police. A district attorney in New York City has stated that in sixteen years of dealing with homicide cases he has encountered only two defendants who would not talk to the investigators. The two were acquitted. Of course, the years referred to belong to the pre-*Miranda* period.

The reason for this state of affairs is not difficult to find. In the absence of eyewitnesses and of admissions by the accused, it is only rarely that the available circumstantial evidence is strong enough to support a conviction. The physical evidence may serve to place the suspect at the scene or associate him with the weapon but will contribute little to proving malice, motive, intent, the criminality of the act or, in general, matters relating to the state of mind of the perpetrator. The accused must be asked to supply, directly or indirectly, details from which his actions and intentions can be deduced. He contributes indirectly when by evasive or untruthful statements he gives indications of actions which were not innocently motivated.

It is logical at this point to ask why, if silence so greatly favors the criminal in this system of justice, he is led so frequently to talk to the police even after being properly given the *Miranda* warnings. The reply lies in experience and observation. The normal person is possessed by an irresistible desire to talk. A great deal of his everyday conversation is devoted to justifying his actions or his opinions. He cannot, then, at a time when his reputation and record are being seriously questioned, resist the temptation to come volubly to their defense by stating the truth, if his character and training are so directed, or by resorting to even the most extravagant falsehoods. It must be remembered, too, that a guilty person under questioning by the police is often a very frightened human being who is driven by apprehension to seek comfort, however indirectly, in communication with his fellow man. Only an exceptionally strong personality or a criminal indurated by bitter experience can withstand prolonged, skillful interrogation in silence.

The investigator should look upon a suspect or a reluctant witness as a person who will yield the desired information if he is questioned with sufficient skill and patience. To acquire the necessary proficiency in interrogation is the work of several years. If he is endowed with a fair share of common sense and a capacity for perseverance, he will eventually become reasonably effective in his work. If, however, he possesses insight into personalities and acquires a knowledge of practical psychology by study and observation, he will excel in the art of interrogation by reason of his ability to establish rapport quickly with a wide variety of criminal types. Finally, he must be nimblewitted. Interrogation is an intellectual game that is often won by the player who is mentally faster afoot and who can rapidly take advantage of an opening or an indicated weakness. As in any other game or skill, the art of interrogation must be practiced constantly in order to develop and maintain expertness. It is a common observation of experienced investigators that a period of inactivity of even a few months will result in a marked falling off in their effectiveness as interrogators.

4. Instrumentation

The third "I" is meant to include the application of the instruments and methods of the physical sciences to the detection of crime. Physics, for example, offers such aids as microscopy, photography, and the optical methods of analysis. The role of chemistry is too well known for elaboration here. Biology and pathology are particularly important in crimes of physical violence.

The sum of these sciences insofar as they are applied to crime detection is called criminalistics. Their utility is associated mainly with physical evidence. By their means a part of the *corpus delicti* may be established in certain crimes—the cause of death in a homicide or the nature of the drug in a narcotics violation. They may be used to link the suspect to the scene of the crime by showing that clue materials found at the scene possess the same constituents as materials associated with the suspect. The same procedure is employed in identifying the criminal by tracing a substance found at the scene to a source that can be immediately associated with the suspect.

Instrumentation, however, is taken here to mean rather more than criminalistics. It includes also all the technical methods by which the fugitive is traced and examined and, in general, the investigation is advanced. Thus, fingerprint systems, *modus operandi* files, the lie detector, communication systems, surveillance equipment such as a telephoto lens and detective dyes, searching apparatus such as the x-ray unit and the metal detector, and other investigative tools are contained within the scope of the term.

There has been a tendency in recent years to place too great a relative value on the contribution of instrumentation to the detection of crime. The inexperienced are especially prone to place their faith in technical methods to the neglect of the more basic and generally more effective procedures of information and interrogation. Several reasons may be given to account for this frame of mind. Greater publicity is given the instruments and techniques of criminalistics because they are frequently quite picturesque and attract the attention of the newspapers, feature writers, and popular dramatists. Moreover, many of those assigned to technical duties are scientists accustomed to addressing large groups, reporting new developments in journals, and otherwise publicizing their findings. A small articulate group of persons, such as the medical examiners, by making known their work in correct fashion, will at the same time convey a highly favorable impression of their contribution to investigative work. For example, although the precinct detective may perform 95 per cent of the work in a homicide investigation, it is the remaining 5 per cent contributed by the medical examiner and other technical experts which often receives the publicity and which impresses the uninitiated. The future detective should, then, assign in his perspective of the investigative picture the correct proportions to the contributions of the three "I's" so that proper attention and effort will be given to each.

The most common use of instrumentation is in connection with the physical evidence in the case and the limitations of this tool of investigation are set by the clue materials and other traces found at the scene. In a good percentage of the cases it will be found that there is no physical evidence and that instrumentation is relatively unimportant. Larceny and robbery, for example, are usually committed without leaving physical evidence in the form of traces. In a homicide, however, clue materials and other forms of physical evidence are of paramount importance. The use of information and interrogation is applicable to nearly all cases, but instrumentation is found most effective in cases where physical evidence is abundant.

A thorough training in the resources of instrumentation is of great importance to an investigator. The technical aids are available to him, but unless he understands their applicability to his problems their utility cannot be adequately realized. He should recognize investigative situations in which the physical evidence may be fruitful or where the pattern of the crime suggests a study of the *modus operandi* file. He should be able to anticipate from the character of a surveillance the types of cameras or other optical devices which will be most useful to him. The limitations of technical methods should also be a part of his knowledge, since excessive reliance on instruments may in certain situations result in a neglect of other and more suitable investigative procedures. He may, for example, fall into the error of relying on a lie detector examination to the exclusion of the routine investigative methods.

5. Phases of the Investigation

The objectives of the investigator stated at the beginning of this chapter provide a convenient division of the investigation into three phases: (1) the criminal is identified; (2) he is traced and located; and (3) the facts proving his guilt are gathered for court presentation. This division is made for convenience of discussion, since the three phases are not necessarily separated in time but are usually fused throughout the investigation. The same evidence, moreover, can often be used for all three objectives. Throughout all phases of the investigation, the three "I's" are constantly employed. Although explicit reference to these tools will not be made, their application at each step can be readily seen.

6. Identifying the Criminal

In the first stage the criminal is identified, i.e., some person is identified as the perpetrator of the criminal acts. Ordinarily the identity of the criminal is discovered in one or more of the following ways: confession, eyewitness testimony, or circumstantial evidence.

a. **Confession.** Admission or confession by a suspect is a major objective of every investigation. The confession is, of course, an excellent means of identifying the criminal. From the point of view of proving guilt at the trial, a consideration that will overlap this discussion, it must be supported by other corroborative evidence. The *corpus delicti* must be separately established in order to support a conviction. A confession may be denied in court and unless an affirmative show of voluntariness (*Miranda* warnings and so forth) can be presented by the prosecution, the objections of defense counsel based on charges of duress and coercion may prevail regardless of their falsehood.

b. **Eyewitness.** The ideal identification is made by several objective persons who are familiar with the appearances of the accused and who personally witnessed the commission of the crime. Where the witness and the accused are strangers and the period of observation was limited to only a few seconds, the validity of the identification depends upon the ability of the witness to observe and remember the relative "distinctiveness" of the accused's appearance, the prevailing conditions of visibility and observation, and the lapse of time between the criminal event and the identification.

c. **Circumstantial Evidence.** The identification may be established indirectly by proving other facts or circumstances from which, either alone or in connection with additional facts, the identity of the perpetrator can be inferred. Evidence of this nature usually falls into one of the following classes:

1) *Motive.* It may be inferred from circumstances and from the statements of witnesses that the suspect could have been motivated by a desire for revenge or personal gain. In offenses such as larceny, robbery, and burglary the obvious motive is monetary gain and persons in straitened financial condition may become suspects. In crimes of personal violence such as assult and murder, the existence of a strong personal hatred would be significant, and evidence of quarrels and angry statements would be relevant. Closely related to motive is a desire for criminal action formed by a pathologically disordered mind. Certain types of arson, for example, suggest the work of a deranged incendiary. Some forms of rape and other sexual offenses indicate the work of a deviate. Evidence relating to motive or state of mind is usually obtained by interviewing witnesses. A study of the crime scene and a reconstruction of the occurrence, including the suspect's prior and subsequent acts, may often be helpful.

2) *Opportunity.* It must have been physically possible for the suspect to commit the crime. He must have had access to the area, have been in the vicinity, and have had the means available. It must be shown that the suspect could have been in the vicinity of the crime scene in the sense that it was not improbable for him to have been there. Thus the search is further limited to those who had the opportunity to commit the crime by reason of probable physical presence, knowledge of the criminal objective, and the absence of

alibis. In a crime such as embezzlement the element of opportunity to commit the crime can readily lead to an identification if it is coupled with the desire and need for money. Only a few persons can participate in the financial procedures of a company. A suspect's credit ratings, gambling or investment losses, and style of living can be carefully studied to determine the existence of critical need.

3) **Associative Evidence.** The physical evidence may serve to identify the criminal by means of the clue materials, personal property, or the characteristic pattern of procedure deduced from the arrangement of objects at the crime scene. The perpetrator may leave some clue at the scene such as a weapon, tool, garment, fingerprint, or foot impression; he may unwittingly carry from the scene a trace in the form of glass, paint, rouge, hair, or blood. In offenses of personal gain, the fruits of the crime may be in his possession. Crimes of violence will leave evidence of physical struggle. Where the offense involved the application of force against property, contact with certain materials may be discernible.

7. Tracing and Locating the Criminal

The second phase of the investigation is concerned with locating the offender. Obviously many of the steps previously suggested for identifying the suspect will also lead to his location. Most commonly the answer to the question of the criminal's whereabouts falls easily out of the solution to the problem of his identity. Usually the criminal is not hiding; he is simply unknown. The professional criminal does not operate near his residence, and hence his flight from the scene is merely a return home unless, of course, he has been recognized during the commission of the offense. The amateur usually commits a crime because of the exceptional opportunity. It is to his advantage to remain in his normal haunts, since flight might betray guilt. In those cases, then, the problem is primarily one of identification. In many cases, however, it is necessary to trace a fugitive who is hiding. Tips, interviews, and in general, information as described earlier will be the most useful means. The techniques of tracing the fugitive are described in Chapters 13 and 14.

8. Proving the Guilt

It is assumed that the criminal has been identified and is now in custody. The investigation, however, is far from complete; it has entered the third and often the most difficult phase, namely, gathering the facts necessary in the trial to prove the guilt of the accused beyond a reasonable doubt. The fact that the accused has confessed to the offense and that the investigator has convincing arguments of his complicity, derived from common sense and information, is not sufficient. The court requires that guilt be proved beyond a reasonable doubt and that the evidence be presented in a certain form and in accordance with a prescribed procedure and that it satisfy certain requirements of quality, trustworthiness, and logical sufficiency.

The final test of a criminal investigation is in the presentation of evidence in court. The fact of the existence of the crime must be established; the defendant must be identified and associated with the crime scene; competent and credible witnesses must be available; the physical evidence must be appropriately identified, the chain of its custody established, and its connection with the case shown; and the whole must be presented in an orderly and logical fashion. The complete process of proof is described in the phrase "establishing the elements of the offense."

In order to instruct the investigator in the methods of gathering proof, the treatment of specific crimes has been centered around the key idea of the elements of proof. By reason and tradition a convention has been established as to the essential general facts relating to an offense which must be demonstrated to prove the guilt of the offender and which are contained in the related concepts of *corpus delicti* and elements of the offense.

9. Corpus Delicti

Early in a criminal trial the prosecution must prove the *corpus delicti* or fact that a crime was committed. Unless an offense can in fact be shown to exist, there is little basis for testing the guilt or innocence of the accused and the court may dismiss the case if a *corpus delicti* is not known. The *corpus delicti* is proved by showing (1) there exists a certain state of fact which forms the basis of the criminal act charged, and (2) the existence of a criminal agency which caused the state of fact to exist. In an arson, for example, it must be shown that there was a burning by a criminal agency; in a homicide the death of a person by a wrongful act of another must be shown. Preferably this state of fact should be established by direct and positive proof, but circumstantial evidence will suffice if it is particularly clear and cogent. In a recent case a detective, after stopping an automobile on suspicion of another crime, questioned the driver concerning a mink coat lying on the back seat. The driver confessed to stealing the coat from a restaurant and was duly arrested. Further investigation, however, failed to discover the true owner of the coat, and the case was dismissed for the reason that a larceny had not been established. In general it may be said that a confession in itself is worthless unless proof of the existence of the *corpus delicti* is available.

10. Elements of the Offense

By adding to the *corpus delicti* certain facts concerning the accused, such as his identity as the malefactor, we have the elements of the offense, the necessary and sufficient conditions which must be fulfilled by the evidence before it can be said that the guilt of the accused has been proved. For example, the elements of burglary are: (1) the accused broke into (2) a dwelling (3) in the nighttime (4) in order to commit a crime therein. A charge of burglary can be supported if, and only if, proof of these four elements of burglary is presented.

Normally the organization of the evidence in this form is the responsibility of the prosecuting attorney, but it will be found that the outline presented by the elements provides a convenient framework for the investigator in the development of the case. In addition it offers him the only sound criteria for testing the adequacy of his investigative efforts. Naturally, the investigative procedure does not follow the lines of the elements in its chronological progress. The elements should, however, be kept constantly in mind, even at the outset, so that no evidence essential to the establishment of an element is irrevocably lost and no necessary lead is neglected.

a. **Form.** To acquire a knowledge of the elements of criminal offenses, the investigator must study the penal law of the jurisdiction under which he is operating. It is not to be expected that he will have at ready recall the essentials of all the crimes which he will be required to investigate, but he should possess sufficient powers of analysis to be able to deduce the essential elements from a reading of the penal law. In their most general form the elements of an offense will consist of the following: (1) that the accused did or omitted to do the acts as alleged, and (2) the circumstances as specified. A further study of this form will demonstrate its usefulness despite its generality.

b. **Accused and the Acts Alleged.** In the first general element the identity of the accused must be established and his connection with the acts clearly shown. The methods for establishing the identity of the accused as the perpetrator of the criminal act have been discussed above in connection with the first objective of an investigation. To satisfy this element, however, a close causal connection must be established between the accused and the offense. It is not necessary to show that he willed the particular effect in its final form; it is sufficent to show that his objective in acting was one which could not have been accomplished without violating the law. The accused must be shown as responsible agent, either by physical or moral causation or by omission to perform a legal duty.

c. **Intent.** The investigation must be designed to develop facts which give evidence of the frame of mind of the accused. It must be shown that the accused knew what he was doing. Consciousness of the unlawfulness of the act is not essential, since ignorance of the law is no defense. In some crimes intent is an essential element; in others it is merely necessary to show that the accused was aware of the consequences of his acts. Some crimes include the additional element of malice, the intent to do injury to another. Legal malice does not necessarily imply hate or ill will; it is a mental state in which an act is done, without excuse, from which another person suffers injury. Since malice is not a presumption of law, it must be inferred from the facts developed by the investigation. Motive, or that which induces the criminal to act, must be distinguished from intent. The motive may be the desire to obtain revenge or personal gain; the intent is the accomplishment of the act. Motive need not be shown in order to obtain a conviction, but intent must always be proved where it is an element to the offense. Although proof of motive does not show guilt, the absence of a motive bears on the fact of whether the accused committed the crime. In cases which depend upon circumstantial evidence, proof of motive is especially important. The relative significance of the proof of motive varies widely with the nature of the crime. In homicide, arson, and sabotage, motive is particularly important. In crimes such as robbery, burglary, and larceny, motive is of little or no value since the desire for money is almost universal and need for it quite common. The motives of revenge and hate, however, are only infrequently possessed to such a degree as to be given expression in criminal activity. To establish the motives of revenge, hate, or jealousy the investigator should look into the history of the victim. If the victim is alive he can be requested to give a simple account of his relations with people over the preceding months. If he is an employer, the matter of the promotions and frustrations of employees should be examined. In the victim's social life, the relative stability of his domestic life, his affairs with women, and his drinking habits should be examined. If the victim is dead, this information can be developed through witnesses. The witness should be encouraged to gossip during the interview since a motive is a nebulous matter difficult to detect in a prosaic recital of facts.

11. Role of Reason

Although the investigator is basically a collector of facts, he must also construct hypotheses and draw conclusions relating to the problem of who committed the crime and how it was accomplished. It is expected that his reasoning processes will be logical and that, even when he engages in speculation, good judgment and common sense will be in control. The investigator, faced with a complex crime, may be compared to a research scientist, employing the same resources of reason and resorting, where necessary, to imagination, ingenuity, and even intuition.

Both inductive and deductive reasoning are applicable to investigation. By inductive reasoning, the passage from the particular to the general, the investigator develops from observed data a generalization explaining the relationships between the events under examination. In deductive reasoning, the proceeding from the general to the particular, he begins from a general theory, applies it to the particular instance represented by the criminal occurrence, and determines whether the truth of the instance is contained in the theory. In both processes the passage from point to point must be managed by logical steps, a requirement that is not easily satisfied. The use of correct reasoning processes must be learned by conscious application, and constant vigilance against the pitfalls of false premises, logical fallacies, unjustifiable inferences, ignorance of conceivable alternatives, and failure to distinguish between the factual and the probable.

12. Representative Approach

In considering a crime problem no single method of reasoning may be said to be the only correct procedure for arriving at a solution to the exclusion of alternative procedures. Described below is a suggested approach to the investigation of the more complicated crimes. The steps are related to the problem of determining who committed the crime and how it was done.

a. The criminal occurrence or complaint is critically reviewed to determine its nature.

b. A painstaking and comprehensive collection is made of the data obtained from the crime scene, the witnesses, and observational inquiry.

c. The available information is arranged and correlated.

d. The issues and problems are formulated in terms of the elements of proof required to support the charge.

e. The most likely hypotheses are selected to resolve the problems along lines consistent with the available data.

f. The hypotheses are subjected to the tests of probability considerations, additional interrogation of suspects, and the development of additional witnesses. Various possibilities are eliminated systematically by considerations such as opportunity, motive, past record, observed reactions, and corroboration of alibis.

g. On the basis of consistency with known facts and a high degree of probability, the best hypothesis is selected and given final support.

h. The best hypothesis must be objectively tested and modified or rejected when contrary evidence is uncovered. The investigator must not permit his observations and interpretations to be biased in favor of the hypothesis.

This suggested approach to the systematic use of reason in an investigation may appear to be an unnecessarily abstract and complicated procedure for solving the typical crime. It is, however, given mainly for the more difficult and elaborate crimes. Frequently, it is not possible to determine at first glance whether a particular crime will present a difficult problem. Often an apparently simple crime will go unsolved by virtue of its very simplicity, while a seemingly complex crime may lend itself readily to solution, since its complexity involves parts and organization. The parts naturally supply clues. The organization, or disposition of the parts, presents a pattern to the intelligent observer from which useful conclusions can be drawn.

13. Chance

In many investigative situations reasoning alone will not yield a solution and qualities other than a facility for logic will determine the success of the inquiry. Enterprise, initiative, perseverance, ingenuity, and an insatiable curiosity are among the characteristics which are needed in addition to a rational method of procedure. Consideration must also be given to the fact that chance often plays an important part in the solution of crimes. The element of chance should not be ignored as something strange which may detract from the credit owed to a competent investigation. By training the powers of observation and maintaining a constant vigilance for the unexpected, the investigator will be prepared to take advantage of those slight clues encountered accidentally which sometimes resolve the problem. Chance merely provides an opportunity. An open and observing mind is required to grasp the opportunity and a prepared mind is needed to interpret it.

14. Intuition

Since investigation is essentially an art, consideration must be given in its study to the concept of intuition, the sudden and unexpected insight that clarifies the problem where progress by logic and experiment has been end-stopped. The phenomenon of the detective whose success in many cases appears to be attributable to "hunches" is quite familiar in police work. Some investigators possess a sensitivity to persons and crimes of a violent nature that provides inspiration or illumination when method alone will not yield a solution. The key idea may come suddenly when he is not consciously thinking of the case, or it may arrive dramatically when his mind is weighing the available information or following a routine chain of investigative thought. It may spring involuntarily to the conscious mind from a subconscious that is saturated with the data of a case and is occupied with the many facets of the problem. Intuition, in any event, is not be be despised, particularly in difficult cases where little progress is evident. The conditions of relaxation and even distraction which often encourage this phenomenon should be sought in those situations. Since there is no evidence that crimes are intrinsically soluble, the investigator can expect in many cases to reach a point where sheer plodding work and deductive reasoning are no longer fruitful and where hope would appear to lie in intuition or chance.

15. Summary

This chapter has been devoted to describing the nature of a criminal investigation and the processes by which it is accomplished. For purposes of simplification the tools and methods of investigation were grouped under the three "I's"—Information, Interrogation, and Instrumentation. An investigation was considered as consisting of three phases: (1) identifying the perpetrator; (2) locating the perpetrator, and (3) proving his guilt. To achieve the major objective of successfully presenting the case in court, it was found necessary to gather the evidence in accordance with the pattern which will fulfill the necessary and sufficient conditions for obtaining proof beyond a reasonable doubt. The concept of the *corpus delicti* was introduced as a basic necessary condition to be fulfilled, since it established the fact that a crime has been committed. By considering the *corpus delicti* together with the factor of criminal agency, the final concept of the elements of the offense was reached. The evidence gathered by the investigator must establish the elements. It was found that although many investigators manage to collect the facts to prove the elements, their procedures too often appear to be the result of habit, supervised experience, and even intuition. It was felt that more could be accomplished by a more fully trained investigator, whose conscious knowledge of the nature of the offense would enable him to advert constantly to a schema of the elements, thus providing him with an overall plan of procedure, giving direction and significance to each step, and insuring that the investigation is not concluded without proving each essential act and showing the casual connection between the acts and the accused as their conscious criminal author.

It has been seen, finally, that the terms "solving" and "investigating" a crime are used here in a sense somewhat different from that employed by mystery writers. In the tidy murders of make-believe the crime is considered solved and the investigation completed when the villain has been placed by the author in a plausible framework of guilt and has thrown up his hands in despair before the ingenious exposé by the author's detective. The tedious work of the crime scene, the interviews, tracing, identification, interrogation, assembling of proof, and presentation of testimony are passed over lightly in the world of fiction.

It is not merely a play on words to say that the succeeding chapters attempt to tell the student not "how to solve a crime" but "how crimes are solved." The process is complex and many persons aid in the solution. Notably there is the criminal, who may leave in his path the set of data which will constitute the evidence. Indications betrayed in the planning of the crime, carelessness and bad luck in its execution, admissions or confidences in the *post factum* period—these are the raw materials from which the solution is shaped.

The completed investigation is the end product of teamwork. The patrolman who discovers the crime and protects the scene, the detective who is assigned to the case, the investigators who assist him in running leads, the supervisors who aid administratively, the technical services that preserve, examine, and record the evidence, and the state's attorney who provides overall guidance of the completion of the case and its presentation in court—all of these are members of the team to whom the solution of the case may be accredited.

Finally, it is desirable to avoid the terms *success, failure,* and *accredited* in these matters because of the unfavorable connotation they give to the motive of the investigator. We have described the investigator as a collector of facts relevant to an offense and, by implication, we have described him as gathering these facts impartially. We have not, however, sufficiently stressed this point of the investigator's objectivity, namely, that he has no special interest in establishing the guilt of a particular suspect, that he regards with equal interest facts which may exonerate the accused as well as to those which are inculpating, and that a biased collecting of facts with an exclusive view to the guilt of a designated suspect is destructive of the basic purpose of an investigation, namely, the discovery of the truth concerning the criminal event.

Indeed, a prejudiced investigator is a contradiction in terms, since a biased inquiry cannot remain a comprehensive consideration of all relevant facts but becomes a polarized view of selected, pre-analyzed data. It is no longer an objective search for the truth but a testing of a preferred hypothesis by adducing the most favorable facts and by admitting for examination only the data and materials contributory to its support.

16. The Criminal Justice System

Because of the great variety of criminal investigation units at municipal, state, and federal levels, no attempt has been made to place the investigator in an administrative frame of reference or to give specific treatment to the administrative aspect of his work. As we have seen from the preceding section, he participates in a joint effort of the prosecution team, which includes members of the patrol force as well as the prosecutor and which may include other agencies. The place of the investigator in the total picture, however, can only be understood from a consideration of the criminal justice system as a whole. The reader is referred to the extensive literature that has already grown up around the general subject of law enforcement and the criminal justice system.

ADDITIONAL READING*

Criminal Investigation

Arthur, R.O.: *Scientific Investigator*. Springfield, Ill.: Thomas 1965.

Bozza, C.M.: *Criminal Investigation*. Chicago, Nelson-Hall, 1977.

Dienstein, W.: *Technics for the Crime Investigator*, 2nd ed. Springfield, Ill.: Thomas, 1974.

Gerber, S.R. and Schroeder, O., Jr. (Eds.): *Criminal Investigation and Interrogation*. Cincinnati, Anderson, 1962.

Greenwood, P.W., Chaiken, J.M., and Petersilia, J.: *The Criminal Investigation Process*. Lexington, Mass.: Heath, 1977.

Horgan, J.J.: *Criminal Investigation*. New York, McGraw-Hill, 1974.

Inbau, F.E., Moenssens, A.A., and Vitullo, L.R.: *Scientific Police Investigation*. Philadelphia, Chilton Book Co., 1972.

Jackson, R.L.: *Criminal Investigation*. Toronto, Carswell, 1962.

Kirk, P.L.: *Crime Investigation*, 2nd ed. New York, Wiley, 1974.

Leonard, V.A.: *Criminal Investigation and Identification*. Springfield, Ill.: Thomas, 1971.

Markle, A.: *Criminal Investigation and Presentation of Evidence*. St. Paul, West Publishing, 1976.

McIntyre, D.M., et al.: *Detection of Crime*. Boston, Little, Brown, 1967.

Mettler, G.B.: *Criminal Investigation*. Boston, Holbrook Press, 1977.

Rhodes, H.T.F.: *Clues and Crimes: The Science of Criminal Investigation*. London, John Murray, 1963.

Sanders, W.B.: *Detective Work: A Study of Criminal Investigations*. New York, Free Press, 1977.

*A number of the above books are to be considered as reference works for many of the chapters in the present text. To save space and avoid tedium they will not be subsequently listed.

Schultz, D.O.: *Criminal Investigation Techniques.* Houston, Gulf Pub, 1978.

Sodermann, H. and O'Connell, J.J.: *Modern Criminal Investigation,* 5th ed. Rev. by C.E. O'Hara, New York, Funk & Wagnalls, 1962.

Swanson, C.R., Jr., Chamelin, N.C., and Territo, L.: *Criminal Investigation.* Santa Monica, Calif.: Goodyear, 1977.

International Association of Chiefs of Police: *Criminal Investigation,* 3rd ed. (2 vols.) Gaithersburg, Md.: I.A.C.P., 1977.

Ward, R.H.: *Introduction to Criminal Investigation.* Reading, Mass.: Addison-Wesley, 1975.

Weston, P.B. and Wells, K.M.: *Criminal Investigation: Basic Perspectives,* 2nd ed. Englewood Cliffs, N.J.: Prentice-Hall, 1974.

Criminal Justice

Adams, T.F.: *Law Enforcement,* 2nd ed. Englewood Cliffs, N.J.: Prentice-Hall, 1973.

————: *Introduction to the Administration of Justice.* Englewood Cliffs, N.J.: Prentice-Hall, 1975.

Blanchard, R.E.: *Introduction to the Administration of Justice.* New York, Wiley, 1975.

Brandstatter, A.F. and Hyman, A.A.: *Fundamentals of Law Enforcement.* Beverly Hills, Calif.: Glencoe Press, 1971.

Coffey, A., Eldefonso, E., and Hartinger, W.: *An Introduction to the Criminal Justice System and Process.* Englewood Cliffs, N.J.: Prentice-Hall, 1974.

Edelstein, C.D. and Wicks, R.J.: *An Introduction to Criminal Justice.* New York, McGraw-Hill, 1977.

Germann, A.C., Day, F.D., and Gallati, R.J.: *Introduction to Law Enforcement and Criminal Justice,* rev. ed. Springfield, Ill.: Thomas, 1976.

Gibbons, D.C., et al.: *Criminal Justice Planning.* Englewood Cliffs, N.J.: Prentice-Hall, 1977.

Kalmanoff, A.: *Criminal Justice: Enforcement and Administration.* Boston, Little, Brown, 1976.

McIntyre, D.M., et al.: *Criminal Justice in the United States,* rev. ed. Chicago, American Bar Foundation, 1974.

Radzinowicz, L. and King, J.: *The Growth of Crime.* New York, Basic Books, 1977.

Sullivan, J.L.: *Introduction to Police Science,* 3rd ed. New York, McGraw-Hill, 1977.

Weston, P.B. and Wells, K.M.: *Law Enforcement and Criminal Justice.* Pacific Palisades, Calif.: Goodyear, 1972.

Chapter 2

THE INVESTIGATOR'S NOTEBOOK

1. Purpose

THE INVESTIGATOR who is assigned to a case is charged with the general responsibility of piecing the various parts of an investigation into a coherent whole. He must interview the complainant, search the crime scene, collect and transmit the evidence, interview witnesses, interrogate suspects, and perform the innumerable minor chores attached to an investigation. Although he submits a report of the investigation, many of the details associated with the inquiry which are not essential to the report may well become points of interest to the court when the case comes to trial. The mass of detail is so overwhelming in a major case that very few investigators can successfully rely on their memories. Experienced investigators employ a notebook to record the relevant details of a case. Adequate notes are considered a prerequisite to the future recording, evaluation, and presentation of the information developed in the course of an investigation. The intervention of time affects the quantity and accuracy of the data remembered by the investigator. A few notes taken during or immediately after an interview or a search will serve later to recall the entire interview or the circumstances surrounding a search.

a. **Repository for Details.** Another purpose which the notebook serves is the retention of seemingly inconsequential details that become important in the light of later developments. The press of duties at the time of the occurrence of a major case prevents an objective evaluation of the significance of details. The notebook serves as a repository of data until more leisurely moments permit the assay and placement of such facts or observations.

b. **Basis for the Report.** The notebook contains also the raw material from which the report of investigation is ultimately fashioned. At the outset of the investigation it is not a simple matter to determine what investigative steps will be significant and should consequently be incorporated in the report. The investigator must frequently record data indiscriminately and without adverting to its relevance. Often the identity of the guilty person is completely unknown, and information must be gathered concerning a number of persons who might possibly develop into suspects.

c. **Supplement to Sketches and Photographs.** A complete description of the crime scene must rely on the notebook as much as it does on photographs or crime scene sketches. A photograph is a one-dimensional representation of the scene. Distances between objects are not accurately or even proportionately represented. Despite the advent of color film, chromatic fidelity has not yet been achieved. The crime scene sketch does not purport to be other than merely schematic. The notebook must be employed to describe the true location and condition of objects, the nature and appearance of hidden objects, the texture and inscriptions of various articles, the odor and general atmosphere of the area, and, finally, the inventory of articles of value.

d. **Documentary Evidence.** The investigator's notebook may be used in court by the investigator to refresh his memory while testifying. Defense counsel may under these circumstances subsequently examine the notebook. The possibility of court examination of his notebook should act as a control for the investigator in regard to the care and accuracy which are to be employed in recording notes. Under examination by defense counsel the investigator must be able to account for all entries in the notebook. Cryptic, vague, or illegible inscriptions tend to undermine the validity of the notes and hence militate against the credibility of the witness. One of the conditions sometimes placed on the use of notes in court is that they be original notes which were taken contemporaneously with the phase of the investigation to which they pertain. For example, notes describing the crime scene should have been taken on the scene itself. Of course, exceptions may be made in regard to matters such as moving surveillances or interrogations which by their very nature require that the notes should be made at a later time.

2. Materials

There are ordinarily no official requirements regarding the maintenance of a notebook. Several precautions logically suggest themselves in regard to the manner in which a notebook should be kept. Obviously, ink is preferred to pencil for permanence. A bound notebook creates a more favorable impression in the courtroom than the looseleaf type, since its form does not suggest the possible removal of pages. Ideally, the notebook should contain the notes of only one investigation so that its examination may not involve the unauthorized disclosure of information relating to a separate investigation. This procedure obviates, also, any overlapping or confusion of notes relating to several investigations.

3. Recording Notes

Notes are gathered in chronological order corresponding to the investigative steps or receipt of the information. The sequence is not necessarily in logical order; the notes are first taken and then related to the logic of the investigation in the report. The data of the investigation should be recorded in a complete, accurate, and legible fashion so that, in the event another investigator is required to assume the responsibility for the investigation, he can make intelligent use of the notebook. Improper abbreviations and highly personal, unintelligible locutions should be avoided. In recording an interview of a witness the investigator should preface the notes with the case identification, hour, date and place of interview, and a complete identification of the person interviewed and of any others present. This should be followed by a summary of the interview. Important statements should be recorded verbatim, if possible. The extent of the notes will depend upon the importance of the interview and the ability of the investigator to reconstruct an interview from significant data. The manner in which the notebook is used during an interview will vary. If the matter under investigation is sensitive, the obvious use of the notebook may tend to create a reluctance on the part of the interviewee to be forthright and candid in revealing information. In an interrogation it is poor technique to draw out a notebook as soon as the subject begins to make admissions. The source of information frequently dries up at the sight of a notebook with its connotation of formal procedure. In certain types of interviews, such as those incident to a routine personnel backgound check, there is usually no objection to the open use of the notebook. As a matter of courtesy, however, it is well to request permission of the subject before taking notes.

4. Recording Aids

In a major case the abundance of physical materials to be described, the wealth of potentially relevant data for consideration, and the number of crime-scene interviews that must be conducted suggest the need for ancillary methods of note taking. In the past, some supervisors have solved this problem by dictating to a stenographer as they examined the scene. The use of a portable tape recorder appears to be a simpler solution to the problem. By taping his observations and findings, the investigator can be more comprehensive in his acquisition of information. Subsequently, the relevant taped information can be transcribed to a more permanent form. The tape itself can be retained for a period of time as part of the case record and as a means of refreshing the investigator's memory. In a large office, investigators frequently submit their reports of investigation in taped form to the typing pool.

Chapter 3

REPORT WRITING

1. Importance

THE EFFECTIVENESS of an investigator is judged in large measure by his reports of investigations. If an otherwise satisfactory investigation is poorly reported the reputation of the investigator suffers. The investigator is part of a working team. Unless his information is available to the other members of the organization, proper action cannot be taken in the case. The information is of little use when confined to the investigator's notebook or memory; if it is not communicated to others it fails of its purpose. The report of the finished case provides the necessary basis for action at higher levels; the progress report enables co-workers to take the next logical steps; the initial report establishes the validity of a complaint and indicates the general nature and magnitude of the case. In treating of the subject of report writing the point of view will be that of an investigator who is part of a widespread organization such as a governmental law enforcement agency. In this way the most meaningful type of report can be treated. An agency covering an extensive territory relies heavily on the submission of effective reports by its agents. Often the investigation is nationwide in scope, and as many as ten of the agency's officers will assist the office of origin in covering leads. The only way in which the case can be intelligently managed is through the medium of competent reporting. To a lesser degree the report will be significant in the work of a municipal police department. Here the problem of geography does not interfere with personal communication and extended conferences. Although the report for these organizations is not used as a control mechanism, it is of equal importance as an objective summary of the case findings and as such is an invaluable aid to the district attorney.

31

2. Purpose of an Investigative Report

In order to understand the basis for the report writing requirements that are described below, the investigator must have a clear view of the purpose of an investigative report. The investigator writes his report in order to achieve the following objectives:

a. **Record.** The report provides a permanent official record of the relevant information obtained in the course of the investigation.

b. **Leads.** The report provides other investigators with information necessary to further advance the investigation.

c. **Prosecutive Action.** The report is a statement of the facts on which designated authorities may base a criminal, corrective, or disciplinary action.

3. Nature of the Report

A report of investigation is an objective statement of the investigator's findings. It is an official record of the information relevant to the investigation which the investigator submits to his superior. Since a case may not go to trial until months after the completion of the investigation, it is important that there be available a complete statement of the investigative results. Loss of memory in regard to details, missing notebooks, and possible absence of the investigator are some of the dangers which the report anticipates.

4. Qualities

To be effective the writer of the report should strive toward the basic qualities of expository style: clarity and brevity. Since the investigator is an instrument of justice, his point of view should be objective and impartial. His purpose is not to convict but merely to describe or narrate. Since he is a reporter in the best sense of the word, he must endeavor to achieve accuracy and completeness. The report of investigation is not the place for the investigator's opinions. It should contain only the facts which he has developed. The information given in the report should be relevant. Everything relevant to the proof or disproof of the crime must be included.

a. **Accuracy.** The report should be a true representation of the facts to the best of the investigator's ability. Information both favorable and unfavorable to the suspect should be included. Statements and opinions of the subjects and witnesses should be clearly presented as such. Persons should be completely identified. Information should be verified by statements of other witnesses and by reference to official records or other reliable sources.

b. **Completeness.** The age-old questions of When? Who? What? Where? and How? should be answered. Since the case concerns a crime, the elements of the offense should be established and the additional facts developed should tend to prove these elements. Every lead should be treated, and negative results from leads should be so indicated. Where a lead is not developed, reasons for this lack of action should be given. The report should be documented by appending important statements, letters, findings of other agencies, and laboratory reports.

c. **Clarity.** The report should develop logically. The order of presentation is not fixed but is dictated by the nature of the case. It will be found that the chronological order is best suited to certain parts of the investigation, while others should be associated with the place where the facts were developed.

5. Sequence of Reports

In general all investigative effort should be reported. Obviously, trivial or irrelevant findings should not be included. The report, however, should include negative as well as positive findings in order to remove unwarranted and misleading suspicion. A single report is desirable, but usually this is not possible because of the leads which are involved in a typical case. In a major case a report should be submitted within a matter of a few days. The seriousness of the matter will warrant maximum investigative effort. Headquarters will require assurance that all possible progress is being made and will desire to initiate leads by other offices. The element of publicity attaching to major crimes will require that headquarters be kept in a position to control news releases and protect itself from charges of inactivity or negligence. Routine cases do not require a suspense date or any rapid dispatch of information. There should, of course, be no unjustifiable delay in investigative action. Ordinarily a lapse of ten days may be permitted before the report is submitted. Supplementary reports will be sent out as the information is developed or the leads discovered. In major cases, however, a status report should be made even when no new significant information has been uncovered. The information contained in previous reports should not be repeated. The closing report will be submitted when all leads are developed and the case does not warrant further investigation.

6. Parts of a Report

Many investigative agencies have fixed rules concerning the divisions that will be made in a report. Others provide a form with blocks for administrative data and permit the investigator to arrange the report in logical divisions. In general the report will contain the following parts:

a. **Administrative Data.** In order to properly control cases and file them in an efficient manner, the report must have identifying data on the face sheet. The following information is considered useful:

1) *Date.* The date on which the investigator's dictation or draft of the report was given to the typist will be the date of the report.

2) *File Number.* This is a matter of local custom. Standard decimal classification file numbers can be used.

3) *Subject.* If the Subject is known, his full name and address. He may subsequently be referred to in the same report as the *Subject* or by his last name in capital letters. If the Subject is unidentified a short description of crime should be given. For example: "JOHN DOE, 741 E. 97 St., assaulted with knife in front of 942 14th Ave., 3 December 1979."

4) *Classification.* The specific nature of the case should be given. This may be done by citing the name of the crime and the section of the penal code under which it is punished. If two offenses were

committed the more serious offense will determine the classification.

5) **Complaint.** The name of the complainant and the manner in which the complaint was received will be given. The complaint may have been received directly or from another office. Personal interview, telephone, or mail may have been used. The complaint will form the initial basis for the investigation. The basis and association with the original case will be explained in the first paragraph of the details.

6) **Reporting Investigator.** The name of the investigator assigned to the case will be given. Assisting investigators will be listed in the details of the report. Care should be exercised in identifying each investigative step with the person by whom it was accomplished. This is of particular importance to the prosecutor in preparing for trial.

7) **Office of Origin.** The office, squad, or precinct in which the complaint was received or which has jurisdiction over the area where the offense requiring investigation took place is considered the Office of Origin. This designation may be changed if it is found that all the investigation is to be performed at another office. Headquarters may specify the Office of Origin in some cases. Other offices which assist the case by "running leads" in their territory are termed "Auxiliary Offices."

8) **Status.** This entry should reflect the status of the case within the office or squad submitting the report. The status is either "Pending" or "Closed."

a) PENDING. This term, when used by the Office of Origin, indicates that the investigation is continuing. In effect it often means that the case is not closed. In submitting a pending report an Auxiliary Office implies either that it has developed significant information before completing leads, that it desires to set out additional leads, or that the completion of the leads is delayed.

b) CLOSED. A case can be closed only by the Office of Origin. Ordinarily it is closed for one of the following reasons: the subject has died, the investigation is completed, or further investigation is considered to be unwarranted for some reason such as the failure to establish a *corpus delicti*.

c) AUXILIARY COMPLETION. This designation of status is used by an auxiliary office or squad on completing its assigned portion of the investigation.

9) **Distribution.** The disposition of the original and all copies of the report should be clearly stated. In some organizations, for example, the original will be directed to the Chief of Detectives, a carbon to the District Attorney, where he is interested, another carbon to an interested agency, and the final carbon retained for file. A nationwide agency would have an entirely different distribution, transmitting, for example, two action copies to the office with primary interest in the case.

b. **Synopsis.** Each report should bear on its cover sheet a synopsis or brief description of the actions of the perpetrator as established by the body of the report and a summary of the major investigative steps thus far accomplished. This is done in a single paragraph using narrative style. An estimate of the value of property stolen or damaged should be included. If the perpetrator is known, his name should be used and his present status described. The victim's name and address should be given. The following is an example of a synopsis in a burglary case.

"Investigation revealed that on April 15, 1979, JOHN JONES entered the home of THOMAS BROWN at 6854 Dento Rd. and stole a camera and watch. On 24 April JONES was apprehended at Penn-Central Railroad station in Newark.

Value of property reported stolen: $210.

Value of property recovered: $210.

JONES presently is in George County Jail."

The purpose of the synopsis is to provide a brief, informative summary of the nature and important events of the case. This procedure is of immense value to reviewing authorities and is of assistance in filing the case and facilitating subsequent reference.

c. **Details of the Report.** The "Details" section of the report has for its objective a narrative account of the investigation. It should be arranged logically with an eye to reader comprehension. Each paragraph should normally contain a separate investigative step. Paragraphs and pages should be numbered. All pertinent details uncovered by the phase of the investigation being reported should be related. The investigator should refer parenthetically to all exhibits which support details.

d. **Conclusions and Recommendations.** (Some investigative agencies do not, as a matter of policy, permit the reporting investigator to submit his conclusions or recommendations. Others require such a statement, and to these the subsequent remarks are applicable.) The investigator's opinions, conclusions, and recommendations as to the status of the case and the disposition of physical evidence should be expressed under this heading. Because of his proximity to the sources of information the investigator is in a better position than the reviewing authorities to judge the credibility of statements in his report. Great weight, therefore, is usually given to his conclusions. It is, of course, incumbent upon the investigator to justify or account for any conclusions which are not consistent with his report or not clearly supported by the facts contained there.

e. **Undeveloped Leads.** An undeveloped lead is an "uncontacted" possible source of pertinent information which appears necessary in bringing the investigation to a logical conclusion. Each undeveloped lead known to the preparer of the investigative report will be listed by him under the above heading at the end of the initial and progress reports. The investigator should try to make each lead specific, stating exactly what information is to be expected from the lead.

1) Requests for the development of a lead at a headquarters different from that of the reporting investigator are addressed under "undeveloped leads" to the commanding officer of the office or squad known to be the closest to the source of information. The report describes the character of the lead, the type of information desired, and if possible, the name and address of the source of information.

2) Undeveloped leads at the headquarters of the reporting investigator also are described, together with a recommended course of investigation.

3) If no undeveloped leads exist, the investigator enters "None" opposite this heading.

f. **Inclosures.** Photographs and sketches of crime scenes, identification photographs, and photostats of checks are among the exhibits or inclosures that can aid an assisting office.

1) Each inclosure is assigned a letter of the alphabet and listed. The entry of an inclosure in the report consists of the assignment

of a designated letter for the inclosure followed by a brief description.

2) If the exhibit is suitable for reproduction and inclosure with each copy of the report, the fact of its inclosure is indicated by a parenthetical reference after its description in the Exhibits Section and by its additional listing in the report under the heading. "Inclosures."

3) The value and relation of the exhibit to the case are discussed under an appropriate section in the body of the report.

g. **Style.** Clear, simple language should be employed. The use of confusing pronouns should be avoided. Since many of the items are interviews of a similar nature, care should be taken to avoid stereotyped phrases that are repeated to the point of monotony. There must of necessity, however, be a good deal of repetitious use in a long report, since there are certain common terms which are part of the language of investigation. The past tense should be used. The investigator may refer to himself in the third person. Surnames should be in upper-case letters throughout for purposes of filing as well as for expediting a review of the case.

7. Initial Report

Ordinarily, an initial report should be made after the first few days of the investigation. This should set forth the basis of the investigation, i.e., how the case arose, whether by complaint or observation, and on what authority the investigation was begun. The complainant should be interviewed and the fact of the crime established by noting the presence of the elements. For example, if a larceny is reported the element of true ownership should be established. The evidence found at the scene of the crime and the actions of the investigators in searching and processing should be described. Certain details necessary for an understanding of the physical layout of the scene should be included; other details the importance of which may be later realized should be recorded in a notebook. The interviews which were accomplished on the first day should be described, and finally the proposed leads should be set out at the end of the report.

8. Progress Report

In simple cases the initial report can be the final report. In most cases, however, the investigation will require an extended period of time, from a week to a year. The investigator's headquarters should be kept apprised of the progress of the case by periodic reports describing its status. These reports should be submitted at fixed intervals of time unless developments indicate earlier submission. Another purpose served by the initial report is that of setting out new lines of inquiry. Leads may be uncovered in other areas and the appropriate offices must be furnished the necessary information.

9. Closing Report

When an investigation is terminated a closing report should be submitted. This is done under the following circumstances:

a. On successful conclusion of the case.

b. When all leads are exhausted and there appear to be no further steps to be taken.

c. On orders from higher authority. The submission of the closing report does not preclude the reopening of the case on receiving new information. The closing report should include the results of the entire investigation in summary and should present a picture of the status of the case.

10. Miscellaneous

The information given above for the composition of a report falls far short of covering the many difficulties that may arise in an individual case. The following suggestions are given to assist in reporting certain commonly occurring details.

a. **Informants.** The preservation in secrecy of the identity of the informant is of paramount importance. The informant should be referred to by a symbol such as I-2. The accompanying information should not provide a clue to the informant's identity by revealing occupation, location, habits, or other clues.

b. **Minors.** In interviewing a minor the consent of the parents should be indicated in the report and a remark should be made as to the competency of the witness.

c. **Statements.** A statement of a subject should be set forth verbatim, if practicable. Data should be given concerning the place where the statement was taken and the location of the original statement. Statements of witnesses can be given in substance and a remark made, where applicable, that a written statement was taken.

d. **Records.** Where a record of importance is referred to, the following data should be given: title; location; revealed by whom; date, and content. If the record is to become evidence in the case the name of custodian should be given and a statement should be made concerning the need for a subpoena to obtain the record if necessary.

e. **Events Witnessed by Investigator.** The details of time, place, and identification should be given for significant events witnessed by the investigator.

f. **Description of Persons and Property.** The principles outlined in Chapter 29 should be followed in describing persons or objects such as vehicles, jewelry, or other articles of significance to the report.

11. Conclusion

A report of investigation should not be weighted down by a mass of information that is hardly material or only remotely relevant. Discretion should be exercised, also, in the inclusion of negative material which merely states that certain investigative measures were fruitless and does not prove a point, clarify an issue, or aid the inquiry even by indirection. The report should be consistently functional, designed to prove or disprove the allegations. Some investigative agencies often value the report for its own sake, considering it primarily as a justification of the investigative activity described therein. Every step, whether fruitful or not, is listed to show that no logical measure has been overlooked and to demonstrate as a corollary that the reporting agent is beyond criticism. The system may be commended on a number of counts. It serves to provide reviewing authorities with a ready means of checking subordinates and provides order, method, and routine to investigative activity. In addition it offers supervisors and investigators a sense of security; the investigator knows within fairly exact limits what is expected of him and the supervisor is comforted by the knowledge that his organization may not be reasonably criticized in a particular case on the grounds of obvious omissions or inertia. To the state's attorney and others, however, who must take administrative action on the basis of the report, the irrelevant and immaterial information contravenes the purpose of the investigation by dimming the issues and obscuring the facts that are truly contributory of the proof.

ADDITIONAL READING

Cunningham, D.H. (Ed.): *A Reading Approach to Professional Police Writing.* Springfield, Ill.: Thomas, 1972.

Dienstein, W.: *How to Write a Narrative Investigation Report.* Springfield, Ill.: Thomas, 1964.

Gammage, A.Z.: *Basic Police Report Writing,* 2nd ed. Springfield, Ill.: Thomas, 1974.

Hess, K.M. and Wrobleski, H.M.: *For the Record: Report Writing in Law Enforcement.* New York, Wiley, 1978.

Nelson, J.G.: *Preliminary Investigation and Police Reporting.* Beverly Hills, Calif.: Glencoe Press, 1970.

Patterson, F.M.: *Police Report Writing for In-Service Officers.* Springfield, Ill.: Thomas, 1977.

Patterson, F.M. and Smith, P.D.: *A Manual of Police Report Writing.* Springfield, Ill.: Thomas, 1968.

Romig, C.H.A.: The Improvement of Investigative Reports. 26 *Law and Order,* 3, 1978.

Squires, H.A.: *Guide to Police Report Writing.* Springfield, Ill.: Thomas, 1964.

PART II
INITIAL STEPS

Chapter 4

CRIME SCENE SEARCH

1. General

THE SEARCH of the scene of the crime is, in certain types of offenses, the most important part of the investigation. Obviously, many kinds of crime do not have a "scene" in the sense of an area where traces are usually found. Offenses such as forgery and embezzlement require no vigorous or exceptional physical activity in their commission. There is no impact of the criminal on his surroundings. Crimes of violence, however, involve a struggle, a break, the use of weapons, and the element of unpredictability. In homicide, assaults, and burglary, the criminal is in contact with the physical surroundings in a forceful manner. Traces may be left in the form of clothing, shoe impressions, fingerprints, blood stains, overthrown furniture, disturbed articles in general, and jimmy marks. The scene of the crime must, moreover, be viewed in an active as well as a passive sense. There is not only the effect of the criminal on the scene to be considered, but also the manner in which the scene may have imparted traces to the criminal. The investigator must be able to visualize the way in which the perpetrator may have carried with him the available evidentiary material that may link him to the scene. Flour and coal dust, paint, seeds, soil, and many other traces, depending on the character of the locale, may later be discovered on the clothing or effects of a suspect. Samples of the trace material must also be gathered at the time of the search in anticipation of the finding of these traces on a suspect.

2. Preliminary

Before treating the search itself, it is profitable to consider the actions and duties of the investigator on first arriving at the scene of

45

the crime. The following measures or steps will ordinarily be found necessary:

a. Identify and, if possible, retain for questioning the person who first notified the police.

b. Determine the perpetrator by direct inquiry or observation if his identity is immediately apparent.

c. Detain all persons present at the scene.

d. Summon assistance if necessary.

e. Safeguard the area by issuing appropriate orders and by physically isolating it. All unauthorized persons must be excluded from the crime scene. Spectators, newspaper photographers, reporters, and others who are not officially connected with the investigation should be kept at a distance. Uniformed police stationed at appropriate distances will serve to perform this function. The police should be requested to refer potential witnesses to one of the investigators.

f. Subsequently permit only authorized persons to enter the area.

g. Separate the witnesses so as to obtain independent statements.

h. Do not touch or move any object.

i. Assign definite duties of the search if assistants are present.

3. Assignment of Duties

For a full discussion of the crime scene search optimum personnel conditions must be assumed. As a matter of common experience, however, the investigator will frequently find that he must perform all of the crime scene duties without assistance. It is understood, moreover, that the thoroughness of the search must often be dependent on the relative importance of the case. Where the offense is minor and the work load great, the search cannot justifiably be performed as meticulously as it would in the ideal or isolated situation. For maximum effectiveness, then, a group such as the following should be assigned to the task of the search:

a. **Officer in Charge.** Directs search, assigns duties, and assumes responsibility for the effectiveness of the search.

b. **Assistant.** Implements the directions of the officer in charge.

c. **Photographer.** Photographs the scene and individual pieces of evidence as they are discovered.

d. **Sketcher.** Makes a rough sketch at the scene and later a finished sketch.

e. **Master Note Taker.** Writes down in shorthand the observations and descriptions given by the others. Notes the time of discovery, the identity of the finder and maintains an orderly log of the proceedings.

f. **Evidence Man.** Collects, preserves and tags articles of evidence.

g. **Measurer.** Makes overall measurements of the scene and locates by a coordinate system or otherwise each article of evidence and each significant object present.

h. **Section Leader.** In the search of a large crime scene area, such as the scene of an airplane crash, the size of the searching group will suggest a division of labor into sections consisting of a group of six men headed by a section leader. If a searcher discovers an artifact or object of possible evidentiary significance, he should, before touching the object, call it to the attention of the section leader, who will note the discovery or finding and make the necessary arrangements for its collection, preservation, or transportation. In this way the search of the whole section can be supervised and alternative witnesses to the discovery of evidence obtained.

4. The Survey

At this stage in the investigation, prohibitions and negative advice are most useful. The investigator must initially restrain himself from taking physical action. The natural inclination is to form a quick opinion of what happened and endeavor to verify it by physically examining various articles. The most advisable measure at this point is to stand aside and make an estimate of the situation. Determine what areas bear no foot impressions so that they may be traversed without damage. A place should then be selected for a "headquarters." Notebooks, equipment, and receptacles for evidence can be placed in this designated area. Having formed the estimate, the investigator now determines the number, kind, and views of the photographs he wishes taken. With the photography accomplished, he may proceed with the search. In case of homicide, he should, of course, await the arrival and services of the medical examiner before disturbing the body.

5. The Search

Method rather than intuition should guide the basic search. The examination must, of course, be thorough. It is impossible to predict the vagaries of the criminal mind or to safely imagine all the physical effects of violent action. A plan of search should be formed which will cover all the ground. The scheme must then be doggedly followed. The spirit of the investigation at this point is caught, if the investigator assumes that the physical traces he now uncovers will be the only evidence in the crime. Since every step of an investigation must be undertaken with the thought of ultimate presentation in court, a notebook will be an invaluable aid. Copious methodical notes of appearances and measurements will supplement the crime scene sketches and photographs. In gathering the evidence some principle of selection must be employed since the indiscriminate collection of clue materials is an unscientific procedure which may lead to serious omissions. As a basic guide the investigator should look upon the evidence as serving to establish one or more of the following:

    a. The *corpus delicti* or the fact that the crime was committed.
    b. The method of operation of the perpetrator.
    c. The identity of the guilty person.

6. The Mechanics of the Search

If the crime scene is indoors, the search plan will naturally be dictated by the size of the room and its contents. The unlimited variety of indoor situations precludes systematic discussion. Where the scene is outdoors one of the methods described in Figure 1 can be selected to suit the terrain. The choice of method is not too important since the essential elements of success in implementing any of the suggested schemes are the alertness, knowledge, and experience of the participating investigators. One or more persons can cooperate in an orderly search as long as there is a clearly apparent organization and well-defined leadership. One person must undertake the responsibility of command and he must in consequence dominate the scene. We shall, for convenience, assume in this discussion that three persons are performing the actual search.

a. **Strip Method.** In this method, the area is blocked out in the form of a rectangle. The three searchers, A, B, and C, proceed slowly at the same pace along paths parallel to one side of the rectangle. When a piece of evidence is found, the finder announces his discovery and all halt until the evidence is cared for. A photographer is called for if necessary. The evidence is collected and tagged and the search proceeds at a given signal. At the end of the rectangle, the searchers turn and proceed back along new lanes as shown in Figure 1.

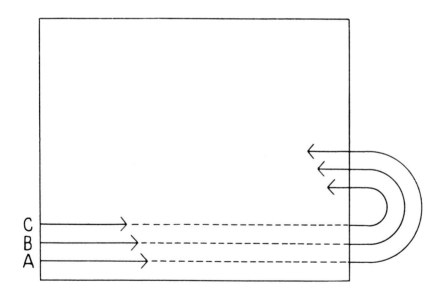

Figure 1. Strip method of search.

A modification of this plan is the *double strip or grid* method. Here, the rectangle is traversed first parallel to the base and then parallel to a side (see Figure 2).

b. **Spiral Method.** The three searchers follow each other in the path of a spiral, beginning on the outside and spiraling in toward the center (see Figure 3).

c. **Zone Method.** One searcher is assigned to each subdivision of a quadrant. Depending on the size of the area, it is divided into quadrants and then each quadrant is cut into another set of quadrants (see figure 4).

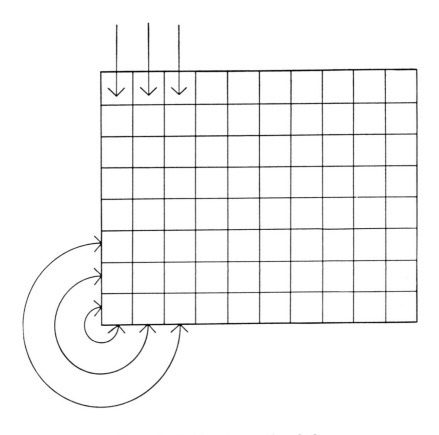

Figure 2. Double strip or grid method.

d. **Wheel Method.** In this method, the area is considered as being approximately circular. The searchers gather at the center and proceed outward along radii or spokes. The procedure should be repeated several times depending on the size of the circle and the number of searchers. One shortcoming of this method is the great increase of relative area to be observed as the searcher departs from the center (see Figure 5).

7. Precautions

The investigator should employ imagination as well as thoroughness in his search. For example, in searches of indoor crime scenes the following are typical of the points that should not be overlooked: cracks in the floor, new paint or plaster, light fixtures, closets,

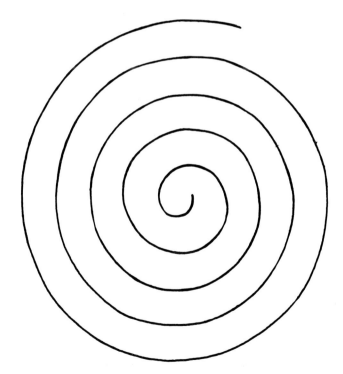

Figure 3. Spiral method.

clothing, shades, draperies, door locks, casings, sills, stairs, banisters, garbage pails, toilets, fuse boxes, asbestos lining of pipes, washing machines, vacuum cleaners, and so forth.

8. Evaluation

During the crime scene search the discovery of physical evidence will be guided merely by the order of path and time. Clues and evidentiary traces will have been collected and preserved without specific regard for their relation to the crime. With the completion of the main search the investigator should devote some time to developing a directive principle to determine the significance of the evidence. Thus far the clue or trace material has been viewed by the discoverer as an abnormality, a thing which is foreign to the scene or simply out of its accustomed place. Its logical position in the

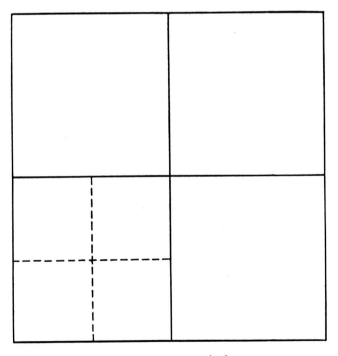

Figure 4. Zone method.

investigative pattern may not as yet be clear. It serves to identify or it belongs to the relation of cause and effect. Blood stains or scuffmarks are examples. The investigator recognizes that these traces are not part of the normal scene. He is aware that their existence is attributable to the human agency in the crime of violence that has taken place. What exactly does the evidence prove or partly prove? What additional evidence must be looked for to supplement the proof—to definitely establish an element or an identity? What norm must be employed to give coherence and pattern to the collected evidence? To answer these questions the investigator must carefully study the materials to determine their significance and probative use. Basically he is searching for two kinds of evidence. In the first category are those facts and materials which establish the elements of proof. These may show that a crime has been committed; that a certain person committed the crime; or that it was committed in a certain manner which indicates the

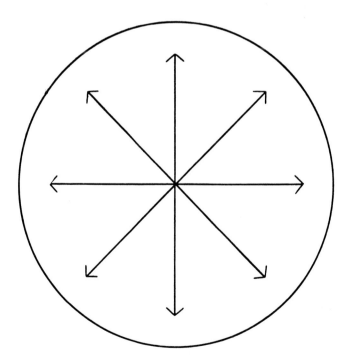

Figure 5. Wheel method.

degree of the crime or the specific offense and also reveals the *modus operandi* of the criminal. Other evidence or the same evidence looked at in a different light may serve to trace the criminal. In the latter category we have as examples the fingerprint or the dry cleaner's mark on a garment. The fingerprint establishes the fact that the criminal was at the scene and assists in tracing the criminal by means of files and comparisons.

9. Reconstructing the Crime

Subsequent to the search of the scene of a crime an effort should be made to determine from the appearance of the place and its objects what actually occurred and, particularly, what were the movements and methods of the criminal, since this latter constitutes part of the *modus operandi*. The process of ascertaining the circumstances of a crime is known as *reconstructing* the crime. It may include a physical reproduction of the positions of articles and persons during the occurrence. From a study of the evidence in this manner it is often possible to make useful inferences which may be synthesized into a reasonable theory.

a. **Physical Reconstruction.** If possible the investigator should reconstruct the physical appearance of the scene from the description of witnesses and the indications of the physical evidence. If the lighting and weather conditions are relevant, the reconstruction should be accomplished at the same time of day and under comparable weather conditions. The witnesses should be requested to reenact their movements while other persons assume the positions of the participants.

b. **Mental Reconstruction.** From the reenacting of the occurrence and the reconstruction of the arrangement of the physical objects some conclusion can now be made concerning the consistency of the accounts of the various witnesses. In reconstructing the actions of the criminal, the investigator should test his theory for logic and consistency. A theory should not be rejected merely because the investigator might not under the circumstances behave in a similar manner. The study should be conducted from the point of view of the mentality of the criminal. No assumptions should be made concerning actions which are not supported by evidence. The theory finally developed by the investigator should provide a line of investigative action but should not be stubbornly pursued in the face of newly discovered facts which are not consistent with it.

10. Equipment

To search and sketch the crime scene and to care for the evidence, a small kit containing a number of the items decribed below will be found useful for each of the designated activities.

a. **Searching.** Equipment for searching the crime scene consists simply of a flashlight and a magnifier.

b. **Sketching.** This equipment consists of (1) measuring devices such as a compass, steel tape, and ruler, and (2) recording implements such as chalk, graph paper, a sketching pad, clip board, and a paper pad for notetaking. The scene will, of course, be also recorded photographically; cameras, however, will ordinarily be contained in a separate kit.

c. **Collection of Evidence.** This will include tools such as a cutting pliers, a knife, a screw driver, and shears as well as tweezers, a scalpel, forceps, and a medicine dropper. Fingerprint equipment, such as powders and lifting tape, should be included.

d. **Preservation of Evidence.** The equipment for this purpose consists essentially of containers such as bottles, envelopes, test tubes, pins, and thumb tacks. To label and seal the evidence there should be provided evidence tags, gummed labels, sealing wax, and grease pencils.

ADDITIONAL READING

Fox, R.H. and Cunningham, C.L.: *Crime Scene Search and Physical Evidence Handbook.* Washington, D.C.: National Institute of Law Enforcement and Criminal Justice, 1973.

Haas, J.E.: The Work of the Crime Scene Unit. *Spring 3100,* Nov.-Dec., 1977.

Jones, J.H. and Peterson, J.L.: *Evidence Technician Program Manual: Optimizing Crime Scene Search Operations.* New York, John Jay College of Criminal Justice, 1976.

Kirk, P.: Criminalistics. *Science*, 357, 1963.

Lurvey, J.B. and Galan, J.I.: *Pocket Guide for Crime Scene Investigators*. Washington, D.C.: American Police Academy, 1978.

Moenssens, A.A., Moses, R.E., and Inbau, F.E.: *Scientic Evidence in Criminal Cases*. Mineola, N.Y.: Foundation Press, 1973.

Osterburg, J.W.: The Evaluation of Physical Evidence in Criminalistics. 60 *Journal of Criminal Law, Criminology and Police Science*, 97, 1969.

Peterson, J.L.: *Utilization of Criminalistics Services by the Police—An Analysis of the Physical Evidence Process*. Washington, D.C.: National Criminal Justice Reference Service, 1972.

Samen, C.C.: Major Crime Scene Investigation—Securing the Scene, Part I. 19 *Law and Order*, 8, 1971. Search Patterns, Part IV. 19 *Law and Order*, 11, 1971.

Schultz, D.O.: *Crime Scene Investigation*. Englewood Cliffs, N.J.: Prentice-Hall, 1977.

Svensson, A. and Wendel, O.: *Techniques of Crime Scene Investigation*, 2nd rev. American ed. by J.D. Nicol. New York, Elsevier, 1965.

Svensson, A. and Wendel, O.: *Sexual Murder and Rape, Techniques of Crime Scene Investigation*, 2nd ed. New York, J. Beck, 1965.

Chapter 5

PHOTOGRAPHING THE CRIME SCENE

1. Use of Photography

Historically the use of maps, models, and sketches preceded the practice of photographing the crime scene. With the acceptance of the photograph, however, and its manifold advantages, the camera has become an indispensable tool of the investigator. Although our interest at present is primarily in the photographic reproduction of the crime scene, it is not irrelevant to consider from a broad view the functions of the camera in scientific criminology. The photographer who wishes to employ the full range of photographic techniques will be versed in the use of 35mm, 4 × 5 press, view, copy, and fingerprint cameras. He will be skilled in the use of filters and in the potentialities of the ultraviolet and infrared regions; orthostereoscopy; photomicrography; microphotography; color work; radiography in the hard and soft regions; gammagraphs; cinematography; and projection work. In practice, however, the investigator ordinarily possesses only sufficient skill to photograph the crime scene and fingerprints. The subsequent discussion is based on this assumption.

2. Evidence Rules Relating to Photographs

A few basic precautions must be observed by the investigator to insure the admissibility of his photographs in court. The following are minimal requirements:

a. The object which is represented should not be immaterial or irrelevant.

b. The photograph should not unduly incite prejudice or sympathy.

c. The photograph should be free from distortion; it should not misrepresent the scene or object which it purports to depict. Distortions ordinarily assume one of the following forms:

1) *Incorrect Point of View.* By selecting a peculiar direction from which to point the lens, the photographer is able to obscure essential objects and emphasize others.

2) *Perspective.* The relationship of distances can be greatly distorted by the improper relationship of the focal length of the lens to the print-viewing distance. Tilting of the plate or lens board in taking the picture or enlarging will also accomplish distortion.

3) *Tone.* Misrepresentation of tones, even to the point of complete obscurity, can result from manipulation of exposure, development, and choice of printing paper.

3. Photographing the Crime Scene

In photographing the crime scene the investigator should endeavor to provide a series of "shots" which supply a maximum of useful information and which will enable the viewer to understand how the crime was committed. The photographer should show the relationships of the various objects to one another. Locations of articles should be clearly seen with reference to recognizable backgrounds. Since at the time the photograph is taken, the investigator cannot be expected to know the significance of all articles of evidence present, he must take a large number of photographs to insure complete coverage. In the suggestions given below the homicide situation has been taken as an example, since it encompasses many of the techniques which are applicable to other crimes.

a. **Overall Photographs.** Several photographs should be taken employing a general view. The camera should be carried clockwise until at least four general view photographs have been taken.

b. **Photographs of the Deceased.** A set of views should be selected to show significant aspects of the body of the deceased. The relationship of the body to surrounding furniture, for example, may be suggestive of action immediately preceding the death.

c. **Photographs of Articles of Evidence.** As the scene is examined, various objects will appear to have a direct relation to the homicide. Weapons, blood stains, hair, fibers, papers, and similar articles should be photographed before they are moved. Two photographs are needed for a significant object which is less than 6 inches in length. The first should be at close range to obtain a fairly large image of the article. The second photograph should be taken with the camera approximately 6 feet from the object in order to bring the background in view and show the object in perspective.

d. **Special Techniques.** Evidence such as a developed fingerprint or a tool mark should be photographed by employing special techniques. Fingerprints should, of course, be photographed with the fingerprint camera. Photomacrography, i.e., the use of an image greater than life size, should be employed for tool marks if the bellows extension of the camera permits.

e. **Photographing the Environs.** The crime scene should not be considered as a physically limited area immediately surrounding the body of the victim or the immediate objective of the criminal. If the homicide took place in a house, for example, the investigator should not consider the single room in which the deceased is found to be the whole crime scene. Any contiguous areas which may have been used in approach, pursuit, flight, or struggle should be considered part of the scene of the crime and should, therefore, be accorded appropriate attention. The nature of the crime will determine the extent to which the environs need be photographed for a fuller understanding of the events that led to the fatal occurrence. For example, the investigator may find that some of the following are significant and therefore suitable photographic subjects: the arrangement of rooms; a passageway; the location of a window; shattered glass; broken furniture; scattered clothes of the victim or his assailant; bullet holes in floors, ceilings, or walls; trail of blood stains; the relation of the house to the street; and the location of street lights. Many other evidence photographs will be suggested by a particular crime scene.

f. **Photographing the Body After Removal.** Additional photographs of the body may be required after the body has been carried from the scene and the clothing has been removed.

1) *Identification.* If the identity of the deceased is unknown,

photographs of the face and of identifying scars or deformities will be important. The face should be photographed from both sides and from the front. The viewpoint should be the same as that used in ordinary identification photographs.

2) **Wounds.** The character of the wounds received by the victim may be of importance in the prosecution of the case. Significant wounds should be photographed to give a true impression of their size and shape. These photographs can be considered as a supplement to the autopsy report.

g. **Photographic Data.** A complete record of each photograph should be made in a notebook so that the following minimum essential information is available if requested in court:

1) Data to identify the photographs with the offense.

2) Data to identify the photographer.

3) Data to orient the camera position with the scene.

4) The date and hour when each photograph was taken.

5) Data reflecting light and weather conditions when each photograph was made, *f/* number and exposure.

6) Data reflecting the type and make of camera, film, and details regarding any special photographic equipment which was used.

7) Focal length of the lens.

8) Data regarding developing, printing, and any special laboratory techniques. This is usually furnished by the laboratory technician, but the investigator should be in a position to present the data and arrange for the appearance of the laboratory technician in court.

9) Data to reflect a complete chain of custody of the photographic film used.

4. Selection of Point of View

The camera should be carefully placed to provide a perspective which is both normal and informative. The incorrect selection of photographic angle (formed by the camera axis and the horizontal) often results in a distorted and false impression of the scene. The height of the camera is normally taken at eye level. This is particularly important if the photograph purports to show what a witness could have seen in a certain position. The location of the camera should be recorded and indicated in the crime scene sketch.

5. Motion Pictures and Videotape

The use of the motion picture and videotape camera is well within the technical powers of the average detective. For certain types of cases the motion picture provides an ideal form as evidence. Insurance frauds, for example, are sometimes proved by this means. Where a person feigns an incapacitating injury and wishes to collect heavy damages, 25 feet of film showing him in active use of the supposedly injured members is sufficient to convince the jury. In criminal cases there are frequent opportunities for the use of motion pictures. Certain criminal activities take place in the street and can be readily photographed in the daytime—for example the consummation of a "buy" in narcotics, breaking into an automobile, or the offer of a bribe. At present the most common routine use of motion pictures is in cases of drunken drivers. In some communities it has been found most economical to photograph the drunk with the motion picture camera at the time of arrest or in the station house. On seeing the film in his sober moments, the defendant is usually quite willing to withdraw his plea of "not guilty." The expense of the film is negligible in comparison with that of the jury trial.

6. "Posed" Photographs and Markers

It is sometimes desirable to illustrate the statement of a witness by means of a "posed" photograph. In this way the inadequacies of verbal testimony can be graphically remedied. To accomplish a posed photograph a person with the same general physical appearance and dress should be employed. Naturally he should be placed in the same spot and positions as directed by the witness, and the camera should be located so as to represent the point of view of the witness. If there is a plurality of witnesses, several photographs should be made to represent the version of each witness. Markers or pointers should be used to clarify important aspects of the photograph. Tire tracks and bullet holes, for example, can be more clearly indicated by delineating chalk marks. Prior to such a procedure, however, photographs should be made of the untouched scene to obviate any objection to the photograph in court on the grounds that it does not purport to show the original scene.

ADDITIONAL READING

Chernoff, G. and Herschel, S.: *Photography and the Law.* New York, Amphoto, 1978.

Dey, L.M.: Night Crime-Scene Photography. 21 *Law and Order*, 4, 1973.

Engel, C.E. (Ed.): *Photography for the Scientist.* New York, Academic Press, 1968.

Fischnaller, J.E., Jr.: Technical Preparation and Exclusion of Photographic Evidence. 8 *Gonzaga Law Review*, 292, 1973.

Katz, J., and Vogel, S.J.: *Photographic Analysis: A Textbook of Photographic Science.* Hastings-on-Hudson, New York, Morgan, 1971.

MacFarlane, B.A.: Photographic Evidence: Its Probative Value at Trial and the Judicial Discretion to Exclude it from Evidence. 16 *Criminal Law Quarterly*, 149, 1974.

O'Hara, C.E.: *Photography in Law Enforcement.* Rochester, New York, Eastman Kodak, 1963.

Poutney, H.: *Police Photography.* New York, Elsevier, 1971.

Samen, C.C.: Major Crime Scene Investigation—Basic Photography, Part II. 19 *Law and Order*, 9, 1971.

Sansone, S.J.: *Modern Photography for Police and Firemen.* Cincinnati, Anderson, 1971.

Scott, C.C.: *Photographic Evidence*, 2nd ed. 3 vols. St. Paul, West Publishing, 1969.

Siljander, R.P.: *Applied Police and Fire Photography.* Springfield, Ill.: Thomas, 1976.

Stilwell, L.: Stereo Photography and Photogrammetry as a Means of Recording Scenes and Measurements of Major Incidents. 85 *Police Review*, 4423, 1977.

Young, P.A.: Night Photography. 28 *Police Research Bulletin*, 21, 1976.

Chapter 6

CRIME SCENE SKETCH

1. General

THE PHOTOGRAPH, ordinarily, is a two-dimensional representation of the scene of the crime and, as such, does not provide accurate information concerning the distance between various points in the scene. The relationship existing between objects present in the scene cannot be clearly understood unless the measured distances are known. Certain objects, moreover, are not visible in a photograph or cannot be clearly identified. A drawing or crime scene sketch is the simplest and most effective way of showing actual measurements and of identifying significant items of evidence in their locations at the scene. Sketches are divided generally into rough sketches and finished drawings.

a. **Rough Sketch.** The rough sketch is made by the investigator on the scene. It need not be drawn to scale, but the proportions should be approximated and the appropriate measurements or dimensions shown. The rough sketch may be used as a basis for the finished drawing. No changes should be made on the original sketch after the investigator has left the scene.

b. **Finished Drawing.** The finished drawing is made primarily for courtroom presentation. It is generally based on the rough sketch and drawn to scale by a person skilled in either mechanical or architectural drawing.

c. **Materials.** A sketch of a crime scene may be accomplished with little more than a pencil, a sheet of paper, and a straight edge. On the other hand, a finished drawing will require more advanced equipment. If the investigator wishes to draw an outdoor crime scene together with the surrounding terrain and achieve a reasonable degree of accuracy, he must possess an elementary knowledge of geometry. The following materials will be found useful although they should not be considered an absolute necessity.

1) **For Rough Sketching.** For a rough sketch it is generally desirable to use a soft pencil. Graph paper is excellent for sketching as it provides a guide for lines and proportions. A clipboard, or a piece of plywood or masonite, of a size which will fit in the investigator's briefcase will serve as a sketching surface. The investigator should have a compass so that he may accurately indicate directions and also a steel tape to insure correct measurements.

2) **For Finished Drawing.** When the finished drawing is to be made in the office, based on the rough sketch, the draftsman will require a drawing set, a drafting board with accessories, India ink, and a good grade of drawing paper. Since the drawing is made to scale, these materials are necessary to insure accuracy. If the finished drawing is to be made at the scene, the equipment of the draftsman should include a compass, steel tape, and alidade.

2. Elements of Sketching

The following considerations apply generally to all sketches:

a. **Measurements.** Measurements must be accurate. In portraying a large area, a sufficient degree of accuracy is obtained by measurements of yards or tenths of a mile; for small areas measurements accurate to the sixteenth of an inch may be required. Measurements should be accomplished by the sketcher himself making the actual measurement while his assistant verifies all readings. Measurements establishing the location of a movable object must be based on an immovable object. While measurements may be indicated between movable objects to establish a correlation, at least one set of dimensions must reach an immovable object.

b. **Compass Direction.** Compass direction must always be indicated to facilitate proper orientation of the sketch. The compass is used to determine "North." A standard arrow of orientation will indicate this direction on the sketch.

c. **Essential Items.** The sketch should portray those items which have a bearing on the investigation being conducted. The inclusion of unnecessary detail will result in a cluttered or crowded sketch and tends to hide or obscure the essential items. Simplicity is essential and sketches should be limited to the inclusion of only relevant material. For example, the sketch will include an outline of the room together with the doors, windows, chimney, and other large fixed objects. The furniture will then be indicated. The dead body or other significant object will be shown in relation to the furniture and other objects. Measurements will be made of the room, fireplace, sink, doorways, etc. The distances of the various parts of, for example, the body from these objects will be measured and recorded.

d. **Scale or Proportion.** The scale of a drawing will normally be dependent upon the area to be portrayed, the amount of detail to be shown, and the size of drawing paper available. It is normally advisable to use the smallest scale practicable. The actual or approximate scale of a sketch should always be shown by words and figures, graphically. If a rough sketch is made, the size of an object may be approximated as correlated to other objects. For example, if one dimension of a room is 30 feet and the other 10 feet, the first line would be approximately three times the length of the second.

e. **Legend.** The legend is an explanation of symbols used to identify objects in the sketch. In sketches portraying a large area, conventional signs or symbols may be used. These should be explained in the legend. If it is necessary to show considerable detail in a sketch covering a small area, the various objects may be lettered and an explanation included in the legend. Excessive lettering in the sketch generally will result in a crowded sketch and obscure essential items.

f. **Title.** The title of a sketch should contain the case identification (case file number and offense); identification of victim or scene portrayed; location; date and hour made; and the sketcher. These data authenticate the sketch.

3. Projection

The normal sketch will show the scene in two dimensions of one plane. When it becomes desirable to portray three dimensions to allow better correlation of the evidential facts of the scene, a projection sketch must be used. This projection sketch of the scene of a room is like a drawing of a cardboard box whose edges have been cut and the sides flattened.

4. Surveying Methods

When portraying large areas, some of the basic surveying methods may be used to facilitate the work of the sketcher and to help insure the accuracy and clarity of the sketch. If the investigator does not have a knowledge of surveying, he should enlist the services of a competent surveyor. The coordinate method, of which there are many simple variations, can be used to meet most of the problems in field sketching.

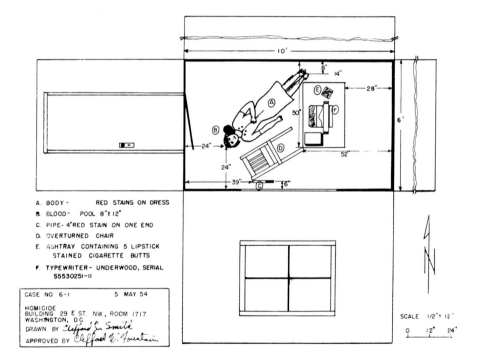

Figure 6. Sketch of homicide scene.

a. **Rectangular Coordinates.** The simplest way to locate points on a sketch is to give the distances from two mutually perpendicular lines. If the crime scene is a room, the objects can be mapped by using two mutually perpendicular walls as the reference lines. A chair, for example, can then be located by measuring its distance from each wall, e.g., 82 inches from the west wall and 43 inches from the south wall. If a graph paper is used for sketching and each unit of the graph paper represents 5 inches (for example) in the room, the chair is located on the graph paper by a point located 16.4 units from the vertical axis and 8.6 units from the horizontal axis, where the two axes are the left hand margin and the lower margin.

b. **Polar Coordinates.** A point can also be mapped by giving its distance from some chosen origin and the direction angle which the distance line makes with a chosen axis of reference. The system is particularly useful for outdoor scenes, being commonly used in daily life. Using a door of a house as the origin, a tree can be located by saying that it is 324 yards away in a direction 42° west of south. The angle is determined by compass using the side of the house as a reference line, and the distance is measured from the door to the tree.

ADDITIONAL READING

Fox, R.H. and Cunningham, C.L.: *Crime Scene Search and Physical Evidence Handbook.* Washington, D.C.: National Institute of Law Enforcement and Criminal Justice, 1973.

Kehl, E.: Sketching the Crime Scene. 4 *Forensic Photography,* 11, 1976.

O'Brien, K.P. and Sullivan, R.C.: *Criminalistics: Theory and Practice,* 2nd ed. Boston, Holbrook Press, 1976.

Samen, C.C.: Major Crime Scene Investigation—Sketching the Scene, Part III. 19 *Law and Order,* 10, 1971.

Chapter 7

CARE OF EVIDENCE

1. Introduction

PHYSICAL EVIDENCE may be defined as articles and material which are found in connection with an investigation and which aid in establishing the identity of the perpetrator or the circumstances under which the crime was committed or which, in general, assist in the discovery of the facts. In order to realize the full probative value of physical evidence it must be intelligently cared for from the point of view of science and the law. A few simple rules can guide the investigator in the protection of evidence from its initial discovery at the scene of the crime until its final appearance in the court. A violation of these rules may lead to a partial loss of the value of the evidence and, in some instances, to the loss of the case.

Physical evidence discovered at the scene of the crime or during the later course of investigation may serve a number of purposes: it may be part of the body or *corpus delicti* of the crime; it may place the suspect at the scene of the crime; it may establish the identity of the offender; or it may enable the investigator to track down the suspect. These categories are obviously not mutually exclusive. In a larceny where part of the stolen money is found, the recovered property is part of the *corpus delicti* and may, through careless spending, leave a trail to the suspect. A fingerprint, by reason of location and through the process of exclusion, may identify the suspect, as well as place him at the crime scene. Finally, careless use of a credit card may describe a pattern of flight, partially identify the suspect, and help guide the investigator to the suspect's ultimate lighting place. Thus, physical evidence can serve several investigative purposes and can be divided roughly into the following categories:

a. Corpus Delicti Evidence. This consists of objects or substances that are an essential part of the body of the crime, i.e., tend to establish that a crime has been committed. For example, in a homicide the corpse or body of the decedent is part of the *corpus delicti* of the offense. The narcotic found in the addict's unlawful possession is part of the *corpus delicti* of a narcotics violation.

b. Associative Evidence. This kind of evidence links the suspect to the crime scene or to the offense. For example, safe lining found in a suspect's shoe may associate the owner with the scene of a safe burglary where an identical type of lining was found on the floor. The headlight glass found at the scene of a hit-and-run motor vehicle homicide can associate the scene with a car having matching glass fragments in a broken lens. Fingerprints and shoe impressions are other common examples.

c. Identifying Evidence. This is associative evidence that tends directly to establish the identity of the perpetrator. This can be exemplified by fingerprints, foot impressions, and quantities of blood found at the place of occurrence.

d. Tracing Evidence. These are articles that assist the investigator in locating the suspect. A laundry mark, for example, found among his effects may assist in tracing a fugitive. Similarly, the credit card mentioned above would provide another tracing clue.

At the risk of repetition, then, these categories are not mutually exclusive; they are simply aspects under which physical evidence may be viewed to serve four main investigative purposes.

2. Evaluation of Physical Evidence

Before an object can become evidence it must be recognized by the investigator as having significance with relation to the offense. He should endeavor to develop an ability to recognize valuable physical evidence through on-the-job experience and by broadening his informational background. The following forms of information and skill will assist his development in this direction:

a. A knowledge of the law of evidence and its application in court procedure.

b. Ability to recreate imaginatively the events preceding, during, and after the commission of a crime.

c. An ability to recognize indications of a *modus operandi*.

d. A knowledge of the substantive law relating to the offense under investigation.

e. A knowledge of scientific laboratory techniques and the conclusions which may be derived from their use.

3. Procedure

The ability to recognize and gather valuable physical evidence must be supplemented by a knowledge of the correct procedure in caring for evidence from the time of its initial discovery until its ultimate appearance at the trial. In order to introduce physical evidence in a trial three important factors must be considered:

a. The article must be properly identified.

b. Continuity or chain of custody must be proved.

c. Competency must be proved, i.e., that the evidence is material and relevant.

The proof of identity implies that the investigator who first found the object can testify that the exhibit offered in evidence is the same as the object he discovered at the crime scene. He should, further, under cross-examination be able to say that another similar article could not have been substituted. Both of these objectives can be achieved by a systematic procedure which would ordinarily consist of the following steps:

a. Protection

b. Collection

c. Identification

d. Preservation

e. Transmission

f. Disposition

4. Chain of Custody

The number of persons who handle evidence between the time of commission of the alleged offense and the ultimate disposition of the case should be kept to a minimum. Each transfer of the evidence should be receipted. It is the responsibility of each transferee to insure that the evidence is accounted for during the time that it is in his possession, that it is properly protected, and that there is a record of the names of the persons from whom he received it and to whom he delivered it, together with the time and date of such receipt and delivery.

5. Protection

The protection of physical evidence serves two major purposes. First, certain types of evidence, such as latent fingerprints, are so fragile in nature that a slight act of carelessness in handling can destroy their value as clues and remove the possibility of obtaining from them any information which would further the investigation. Second, it is necessary that the evidence presented in court be in a condition similar to that in which it was left at the time of the offense. In order that a physical object connected with the commission of the offense be admitted into evidence, it is necessary to show that such object is in practically the same condition, without substantial change, as at the time the offense was committed. Hence evidence should be protected from accidental or intentional change during the period extending from its first discovery after the commission of the offense to its ultimate disposition at the conclusion of the investigation.

a. **Alterations.** The exercise of a reasonable degree of care and the use of common sense will usually minimize the possibility of alteration of the evidentiary object. Special precautions must be employed with certain types of evidence such as articles bearing latent fingerprints. Alterations in the evidence such as contamination, chemical change, alterations of shape, removal of a part, or addition of extraneous characteristics are attributable to the following causes:

1) *Natural Causes.* The initial failure to safeguard evidence from exposure to the elements may result in a deterioration of the evidentiary value of an object. During the period of custody, damage from rain or deterioration from high temperatures may affect certain types of evidence unless special precautions are taken. For example, a vehicle which may bear latent fingerprints should be protected from rain. A blood sample which is not maintained under refrigeration may lose some of its grouping properties on standing in hot weather.

2) ***Negligence and Accident.*** Failure to observe the ordinary precautions for the protection of property may result in breakage, loss, or the acquisition of new characteristics. Examples of this are the careless dropping of a fragile article, pointing to and accidentally marking a document to be used in a handwriting comparison, or opening a box containing fibers in an area exposed to strong drafts of air.

3) ***Intentional Damage or Theft.*** The investigator must keep in mind that in criminal cases there are usually several persons who would prefer that certain items of evidence did not exist. Thus measures should be taken to maintain the evidence secure from destruction, theft, and, in general, access by unauthorized persons.

b. **At the Crime Scene.** Physical evidence which is associated with a crime scene may be exposed to damaging influences prior to the discovery of its significance. Consequently all unauthorized persons should be excluded from the scene to prevent their handling or stepping on objects of evidence. The number of persons who are subsequently permitted to enter the scene should be kept to a minimum. Immediate action should be taken to prevent exposure of the evidence to the elements where there appears to be a likelihood of damage from rain, snow, wind, or sun.

c. **Receiving Evidence.** Where physical evidence is obtained not at the scene of the offense but from some other source such as an informant or from the possessions of a suspect, the investigator should take the necessary measures to protect it from any extraneous contact. For example, if the investigator, away from his office, comes into possession of a narcotics specimen such as a deck of heroin, he should place it in an envelope rather than put it unprotected in his pocket. Often he will acquire evidence when he has no equipment or containers for its protection. In situations such as this he should improvise with envelopes, boxes, or paper. Naturally, the degree of immediate protection required depends upon the physical nature of the evidence. As soon as possible after its receipt, the evidence should be transferred to a suitable container which can be sealed and labeled in the correct manner.

d. **Transporting.** Some risk of damage to evidence is incurred in the process of transporting the evidence. For example, in removing bottles bearing fingerprints from the scene of the offense to the office there is a danger of blurring the prints by contact with the interior surfaces of the vehicle or the sides of an improper container. Similarly if a jar of liquid or a plaster cast is mailed to a laboratory without being properly packaged for protection in transit, the likelihood of breakage is present.

e. **Evidence Not at the Scene.** Much of the physical evidence which is collected in connection with a typical criminal case is not found at the scene of occurrence. Evidence is often delivered to the investigator by a complainant or is found in the course of a search of a suspect's possessions. Moreover, many offenses, particularly those not involving personal violence, are not associated with a definite scene of occurrence. The investigator, therefore, will often receive evidence in circumstances where he does not have the papers, envelope, boxes, labels, and other equipment which he brings to the scene of a crime. In these situations the investigator should improvise methods of collecting the evidence until he has the proper equipment. A little ingenuity will enable him to find containers or envelopes which can serve to hold the evidence safely until he reaches his office. In receiving evidence at places other than the crime scene the investigator should make special note of the circumstances since he may later forget exactly where, when, or from whom he received evidence which was not at the crime scene.

f. **Standards of Comparison.** Known specimens to be used as standards of comparison with the questioned evidence are sometimes needed to aid in establishing a suspect's relationship to the crime under investigation. The character of the articles or materials to be collected for these comparisons is determined by the type of investigation being conducted.

g. **Containers and Packaging.** Articles which can be removed and conveniently packaged should be placed in clean containers such as envelopes, pill boxes, large cardboard boxes, and glass containers. The choice of container will depend upon the size of the specimen; its fragility; its physical state, whether solid or liquid; and whether it is to be transmitted by mail, express, or by hand carrying. Ordinarily there are two phases of the packing of evidence. The first is the transportation of the evidence from the crime scene or place of receiving it to the office. Secondly, if the evidence is to be submitted to a laboratory examination, it must be appropriately prepared for shipping.

h. **Storage.** Adequate facilities for storage of evidence should be maintained by an investigative agency. The evidence room should be so constructed and equipped that physical protection is assured against alteration or destruction from natural causes or unauthorized contacts. Changes of status as to custody of items maintained in the evidence room should be covered by hand receipts. Notations of such changes should be made in the case file. Each instance of deposit and removal of evidence should be recorded by inked entries indicating.:

1) *Date* the evidence was received.

2) *File number* of case.

3) *Title* of case.

4) *Person* or *place* from whom or at which received.

5) *Person who received* the evidence.

6) *Complete description* of evidential items including size, color, serial number, and other identifying data.

7) *Disposition*. The name of the person to whom the evidence was delivered or an indication of any disposition other than delivery to a person. If at the time of receipt of real evidence any information is available as to its intended future disposition, this may be noted; care should be taken to avoid ambiguity in the notation indicating future disposition.

8) *Identify by signature* of the officer in control of the evidence room.

6. Preservation

Evidence in the form of organic matter, such as food, blood, or tissue, may present special problems relating to preservation. Most organic matter changes in character through natural decomposition, and, unless preventive measures are taken, its value for laboratory examination with a view to subsequent use as evidence may be destroyed. In taking measures against such deterioration, the factors of time and temperature should be given special consideration.

a. **Time.** In warm weather there should be a minimum of delay in placing the evidence in appropriate storage.

b. **Temperature.** High temperatures such as 95°F. greatly accelerate the decomposition of matter. Similarly, extreme cold may affect the evidentiary value of a specimen. Blood, for example, will lose some of its value as evidence if it is exposed to high temperatures for a long period of time or if it is permitted to freeze solidly. Ideally, the preserving temperature for blood or other perishable specimens should be between 40° and 50°F.

7. Preservatives

Certain types of perishable evidence require special preservatives to maintain their evidential value. For example, when a specimen of blood is taken for purposes of determining intoxication from alcohol, sodium fluoride may be added to the blood to preserve it for a week at room temprature or indefinitely in a refrigerator. As a general rule, however, no preservative should be used without expert advice. If it appears that the evidence specimen must be retained for a number of days and if refrigeration is not available, the investigator should seek the advice of a chemist or toxicologist concerning the need for any preservative.

8. Collection

Most of the errors committed in connection with evidence take place in the collection of the samples. Insufficiency of sample and failure to supply standards of comparison and controls are the most common errors. These investigative deficiencies are a consequence of a lack of understanding of the principles that should guide the collection from the point of view of the analyst. The employment of improper collection techniques results also in a failure to realize the full probative value of the evidence.

a. **Adequate Sampling.** A generous sample of the evidence should be collected. The analysis of evidence usually requires the consumption of part of the evidence. The laboratory expert can make his determinations with small samples, but the difficulties increase rapidly as the quantity becomes smaller. In analyzing evidence the chemist always endeavors to retain a quantity of the evidence untouched, so that the court may actually see and thus understand the nature of the evidence as well as acquire some knowledge of its original appearance. With a restricted sample the analyst may find it necessary to use almost all of the evidence. Another advantage of the generous sample is that it permits him to perform desirable confirmatory tests. Finally, an adequate sample will more nearly approach the ideal of the "representative sample," i.e., it will provide a sufficient quantity to enable the expert to determine the true nature of the substance, whereas the extremely limited specimen may be an anomalous sample containing extraneous matter not indicative of the true nature of the material.

b. **Standard or Known Samples.** Clue materials such as stains and other traces, particularly those available in only small quantities, are usually found in the presence of a foreign substance which can affect the analysis. In cases of this nature the foreign substance or background material should also be collected in the form of two samples, one bearing the stain or trace and the other free from the stain. For example, if the stain is found imbedded in wood or on linoleum, it should be collected by cutting off part of the wood or linoleum. In this way the analyst can approach his problem with an understanding of the difficulties he may encounter. A sample of the unstained wood or linoleum should also be removed and submitted for the purpose of providing a control that will enable the analyst to determine what impurities are contributed to the stain by the background material. He can, moreover, by means of the control determine what difficulties the background substances will add to the analysis. The control sample should be taken from an area near the stain. For example, if the investigation is concerned with a motor vehicle collision involving a hit-and-run car and a paint smear from the missing vehicle is found on the fender of the victim's car, the collector would proceed by first removing the smear and then taking a sample of the paint of the victim's car from an area approximately 6 inches from the smear. Another control sample would be taken from an area about a foot away. In removing the smear the collector ordinarily cannot avoid scraping some of the paint of the victim's car at the same time.

c. **Integrity of Sample.** An evidence sample should not come into contact with another sample or with any contaminating matter. This error most commonly occurs by initial, superficial comparison of the unknown and known samples. For example, if a tool impression is found on the door of the house during an investigation of a burglary and if a jimmy is found in association with a suspect, there is a temptation for the investigator to experimentally determine whether the blade of the tool fits the impression by placing the tool against the door. The result is a contamination of any paint traces that may have lain on the blade of the tool and which would have served as stronger evidence of its use in the commission of the crime than would the impression alone. A less conscionable error is the placing of the two poorly wrapped samples of known and unknown in the same envelope. To maintain individuality each piece of evidence should be separately wrapped and should not share the same container unless all danger of mingling is removed by the employment of strong protective coverings or partitions.

d. **Types of Evidence.** The simplest division of evidence into categories is that of portable and fixed evidence. If the evidence is readily portable no difficulty exists. The investigator simply removes the whole object. For example, if a fingerprint is found on a cash box, it should be developed and photographed and then the box itself should be brought back to the office or the laboratory. No attempt should be made to lift the print. If the evidence cannot be collected separately because of its size, the removal will often depend on the importance of the case. In a case involving a serious crime the investigator should not, for example, hesitate to remove a bedroom door that bears a good tool impression. Sometimes fixed evidence can also be placed in the same category as evidence not readily portable, since tools can be employed to remove that part of the installation which bears the evidence. A piece of wooden floor should be removed with the appropriate tools, if the importance of the evidence and the gravity of the case indicate the advisability of such a procedure. The decision concerning the removal of evidence will depend upon the individual case. Where it is not possible or practicable to remove the evidence, methods of reproduction such as photography and casting should be employed to accurately represent the condition of the evidence.

1) *Fingerprints.* Articles bearing fingerprints are the most

common forms of physical evidence. Their handling will vary with the nature of the article on which they are found.

a) On Paper. A paper such as a document should be handled with tongs and placed, where the size permits, into a cellophane envelope. It should not be folded unless it is very large and then only along existing fold lines.

b) On Glasses and Bottles. These can be placed over pegs imbedded in a board. Small crates can be built for additional protection.

2) *Firearms, Knives, and Tools.* Articles such as these can be secured to a board by means of strings passing through perforations.

3) *Hairs and Fibers.* The hair or fiber should be picked up with a forceps, wrapped loosely in a filter paper, and placed in a pillbox or envelope.

4) *Dirt, Soil, Particles, Filings, and Fragments.* Material of this nature should be placed in a filter paper and then in a pillbox.

5) *Bullets and Fired Cases.* These should be placed in separate, small boxes and surrounded with cotton.

6) *Clothing.* Stained areas should be widely encircled with chalk to indicate to the laboratory expert the points of interest or places, for example, where preliminary field tests have indicated the probable presence of blood. Unnecessary folding of the garment should be avoided.

7) *Semen Stains.* These will occur in connection with sex cases such as rape or sodomy. If the stain is still moist, it can be collected with a test tube. Distilled water sufficient to just cover the seminal fluid is used to moisten a dried stain prior to collection. The garment should be submitted together with the test tube. The area of the clothing in which the stain was found should be encircled with chalk. If, as is usually the case, the stain is dry the garment is carefully folded, with white paper separating the folds, and placed in a large box for transportation.

8) *Blood.* If the blood is in a fluid condition it should be removed with an eye dropper and placed in a test tube. Physiological saline solution should be added in an amount about one-fifth that of the blood. The remainder of the blood should be treated as a dried stain. If the blood is in the form of a moist stain on clothing, rugs, or fabric, half of the area should be cut out, placed in a test tube, and just

covered with saline solution. The remaining part is permitted to dry, then placed between sheets of white paper and transmitted in an appropriate container. Naturally, where the stain is large, less than half is placed in the test tube. If the stain is dry, crusts should be removed without breaking and placed in a test tube. Additional blood should then be removed by scraping and placed in a separate test tube. Where the dried stain is found on a garment or fabric, the whole should be shipped intact, where practicable, to the laboratory. If the dried stain is quite large, a two-inch square can be cut out, placed in a test tube and just covered with saline. The test tube should be covered with a stopper and sealed. It should be delivered to the laboratory as soon as possible and should not be subjected to extremes of temperature.

9) **Paint on Vehicles.** Wherever possible paint should be removed with a wooden tongue depressor. Wood is preferred to metal as a remover because the latter may leave traces which interfere with spectrographic analysis. However, when a thin paint smear is found on a vehicle it is usually necessary to use metal to remove it. A scalpel of hard steel is preferred. If possible, a paint chip bearing the smear should be removed. Comparison standards should also be taken. A filter paper and pill box should be used to contain the sample. The scalpel itself should also be submitted.

9. Identification

Evidence should be properly marked or labeled for identification as it is collected or as soon as practicable thereafter. The importance of this procedure becomes apparent when consideration is given to the fact that the investigator may be called to the witness stand many months after the commission of the offense to identify an object in evidence which he collected at the time of offense. Indeed, defense counsel may require that the complete chain of custody be established, in which case each person who handled the evidence may be called to identify the object. Obviously such an identification is most easily managed by means of marks or labels which have been placed on the evidence. An additional aid to identification is the investigator's notebook in which should be recorded a description of the evidentiary object, the position where it was found, the place where it was collected or the person from whom it was received, the names of any witnesses, and any serial number which the object may bear, together with the case reference data.

a. **Marking.** Solid objects which have a volume of approximately 1 cubic inch or greater should be marked for identification with the initials of the investigator receiving or finding the evidence. The mark of identification should not be placed in an area where evidentiary traces exist. A sharp-pointed instrument such as a stylus should be used for marking hard objects. Pen and ink can be used for absorbent articles. Special care should be employed in marking articles of great intrinsic value. Objects which are smaller than 1 cubic inch in approximate volume need not be marked. These may be placed in a container such as a pillbox and the container then sealed and labeled. Liquids and pastes should be retained in their

Figure 7. Evidence tape for sealing physical evidence properly and easily. The tape's frangible backing can reveal tampering. Courtesy of the 3M Company.

original containers and appropriately sealed and labeled. If the evidence consists of a large number of similar items, the district attorney should be consulted to determine how many of the items need be brought into court and how many should be marked for identification.

b. **Sealing.** Wherever practicable, articles of evidence should be inclosed in separate containers. Pillboxes, envelopes, test tubes, and bottles containing evidentiary materials should be sealed in such a manner that they cannot be opened without breaking the seal. The investigator's initials (or name) and the date of sealing (in abbreviated form) should be placed on the seal with ink so that the marking extends over to the container from the seal.

c. **Labeling.** After the article of evidence is marked and placed in a sealed container, a label should be affixed bearing identifying case information. This may take the form of paper pasted (gum label) on the container or a tag tied to the object. Thus, a bullet would be marked with the investigator's initials, placed in a pillbox which is then sealed and initialed and finally labeled by affixing a paper sticker to the box. An alleged heroin specimen would be placed in protective paper and inserted in an envelope, which would then be sealed. A paper seal would then be placed across the flap of the envelope and labeled by inscribing thereon the case information. A rifle would be marked and then tagged. The following information should appear on the label or tag:

1) Case number.
2) Date and time of finding the article.
3) Name and description of the article.
4) Location at time of discovery.
5) Signature of investigator who made the discovery.
6) Name of witnesses to the discovery.

d. **Examples.** In the following typical examples of evidence which may be received or obtained, suggestions are made for marking and labeling.

1) *Documents.* A document, like other physical evidence, should be identified by some type of marking. The best method of marking is to initial and place the date where the marking will not affect the examination. The initials and date should be inscribed with a fine-pointed pen. After initialing and dating, the document should

be placed in a cellophane envelope and properly sealed. The envelope can be sealed with gummed paper tape, and the date and initials of the investigator placed thereon. Information concerning the identity of the document should be placed on the outside of the cellophane jacket. A piece of paper bearing the typed information can be stapled to the edge of the envelope for this purpose.

2) *Firearms Evidence.* a) Firearms. A firearm should be unloaded prior to submission to the laboratory. Ordinarily the weapon should be marked with a metal stylus on the right side of the frame. If the firearm is rigidly assembled so that the firing pin or barrel cannot be removed without tools this marking will be sufficient. On the other hand, if the parts which may leave an imprint on the bullet or cartridge case are removable without the aid of tools each part should be marked. Thus, in a .45 calibre semiautomatic pistol the barrel, slide, and receiver should be individually marked. Similarly in a hinge-frame type of revolver the barrel, cylinder, and frame should each be marked. In bolt-action rifles, the bolt and frame should be marked. If the barrel of a shoulder firearm is removable without tools, it should be marked.

b) Loaded Weapons. If the evidence weapon is a revolver containing loaded cartridges or fired cases, the investigator should make a diagram of the rear face of the cylinder to show the position of each cartridge with respect to the firing pin. The cartridges should be numbered to correspond to the numbering of the chambers. To further assist the expert, a mark should be placed on the rear face of the cylinder on both sides of the chamber which lay under the firing pin on original discovery of the weapon.

c) Bullets. In marking bullets care should be taken to avoid scarring an area bearing rifling imprints. The bullet may be marked on the nose or the base. If the bullet is deformed, an area of rifling imprints should be selected. Jacket fragments should be marked on the smooth, inside surface if they bear rifling marks on one side. Core fragments will ordinarily bear no characteristic impressions.

d) Cartridge Cases. A fired cartridge case should be marked inside of the mouth or, if the caliber is too small, on the cylindrical outer surface at a point near the mouth. The case should never be marked on the head, since this area may bear breech-face markings or firing-pin indentations.

e) SHOTGUN SHELLS. If the shell is made of paper, it should be marked with ink; a plastic shell can be marked with a metal scriber. Brass shells should be treated as cartridge cases.

f) SHOTGUN WADS. The wad should be placed in a pillbox, sealed and labeled.

g) SMALL SHOT. Buckshot, birdshot and similar ammunition are too small to be marked. Hence specimens should be placed in a pillbox, sealed and labeled.

h) COMPARISON STANDARDS. In submitting a firearm for examination, an effort should be made to supply ammunition of the same type. For example, if the weapon is owned by a resident of the area, a search of his property should be made to discover similar ammunition. Approximately ten cartridges will suffice as standards of comparison.

3) **Clothing.** Articles of wearing apparel are best marked by an inked inscription on the lining of each garment. A string tag attached to a button or a button hole will serve as a label.

4) **Plaster Casts.** These should be marked on the back before the plaster has dried. When the cast has hardened the marks will be permanent. Subsequently the cast should be placed in a wooden box of suitable size and appropriately labeled.

5) **Photographs.** Each print may be marked for identification on the reverse side in a manner that will reflect appropriate data, including the date on which the photograph was taken, the name of the photographer, and the place where taken; the marking should be carefully made in order not to damage the photograph. Other data of an explanatory nature, generally restricted to technical information regarding the mechanics of making and processing the photograph, may properly be inscribed on the reverse side if the inclusion of such data augments the evidential value of the photograph. If it is found necessary to place supplementary marks (such as measurements, arrows to indicate direction, or lines leading to characteristics of a fingerprint pattern) on the emulsion side of a print, it should be understood that any marking on the front or back of a photograph must be susceptible of explanation by a qualified witness, must not detract from the merits of the picture, and should contribute to expressing a pertinent fact that is devoid of evidential value when considered apart from the photograph. Any abuse of

discretion in this regard may render a photograph objectionable as an exhibit; hence it is generally advisable to have duplicate unmarked prints available for use if needed. Transparent overlays may be utilized when desired.

10. Transmission

If the transmission to a laboratory is desired, the evidence must be carefully packed to prevent loss or damage. In the absence of any local or state laboratory facilities, law enforcement agencies may seek the services of the FBI Laboratory. In communications to the FBI requesting examinations, a letter of transmittal should accompany the evidence, setting forth the essential facts in the case and any information which can be of assistance to the examiner. The communication should indicate that the evidence has not been and will not be examined by an expert other than one of the FBI Laboratory. In transmitting certain types of evidence by mail, cognizance should be taken of current postal regulations. For example, the postal service should not be used in transmitting live ammunition or flammable liquids (see Appendix 3).

ADDITIONAL READING

Fox, R.H. and Cunningham, C.L.: *Crime Scene Search and Physical Evidence Handbook.* Washington, D.C.: National Institute of Law Enforcement and Criminal Justice, 1973.

O'Brien, K.P. and Sullivan, R.C.: *Criminalistics: Theory and Practice*, 2nd ed. Boston, Holbrook Press, 1976.

O'Hara, C.E. and Osterburg, J.W.: *An Introduction to Criminalistics.* Bloomington, Indiana University Press, 1972.

Samen, C.C.: The Evidence Collection Unit. 19 *Law and Order*, 7, 1971.

Svensson, A. and Wendel, O.: *Techniques of Crime Scene Investigation*, 2nd rev. American ed. by J.D. Nicol. New York, Elsevier, 1965.

PART III
OBTAINING INFORMATION

definite markings, serial numbers, or a bill of sale? Can the person who cashed the worthless check recognize the passer? Is the accused the person he claims he is? What personal records are available to identify the accused or to place him in a certain area at a given time? What persons can provide information concerning the activities of the accused on the day of the crime?

b. **Tracing.** If the suspect is missing, the investigator is faced with the problem of tracing. He must know the available sources of information, official and unofficial. Custodians of records and persons dealing in services must be questioned. Police department files, hotel registers, bureaus of vital statistics, employers, associates, and many other sources will yield valuable information if approached in the correct manner. In all of these steps toward building up his case, the investigator must rely mainly upon strangers. Depending upon the technique he employs while interviewing these people, he may come away with all the desired data available or he may obtain only a few scattered facts of doubtful value. He must, moreover, develop in these persons a willingness to testify or make formal written statements if necessary.

2. Definitions

An interview is the questioning of a person who is believed to possess knowledge that is of official interest to the investigator. In an interview the person questioned usually gives his account of an incident under investigation or offers information concerning a person being investigated in his own manner and words.

3. Importance

The greater part of an investigation is usually devoted to interviews. In most cases interviews constitute the major source of information. Because of the apparent simplicity of the typical interview, the novice is inclined to neglect the development of a technique. In his first year in the profession, the investigator should devote his greatest efforts to developing effective methods of interviewing. He should constantly remind himself that the next interview on his schedule may be the only way of acquiring information on a certain aspect of the case under investigation. After each interview he should subject his performance to a critical review by checking the quantity and quality of the information obtained and the extent to which he established rapport with the subject.

4. Qualifications of the Interviewer

The investigator as an interviewer should have the qualities of a salesman, an actor, and a psychologist. He is called upon to subject strangers to extensive questioning on topics of varying sensitivity. He must be measured by the discretion which he employs, and at the same time he may be criticized for a want of perseverance. He must possess insight, intelligence, and persuasiveness. His speech should be suited to the situation, compelling for the educated subject and calculated to strike a responsive note in the subject of little letters. The demands made of the ideal interviewer are too great to be fully met by any individual investigator; nevertheless, the challenge is one that will add interest to the years in which the investigator endeavors to increase his proficiency and ward off the stalemate with routine which often hinders his development.

a. **Rapport.** The relationship existing between the interviewer and the subject usually determines the success of the investigation. By establishing rapport with the subject the investigator may be able to unloose a flood of useful information. On the other hand, if the relationship is strained or marked by mistrust or a feeling of strangeness, the subject may be reluctant to give any of the desired information. The interrogator must endeavor to win the confidence of the subject wherever this is possible, since a completely voluntary offer of information is the ideal result of an interview. Where this is not possible the interrogator may have to rely on the force of his personality, persistence, or other qualities or resources which he may possess. Obviously, the interviewer cannot be a one-sided personality. He must possess a variety of character traits.

b. **Personality.** The primary trait which the interviewer should possess is that of forcefulness of personality. He should instinctively induce confidence by the strength of his character so that the subject trusts him on the first meeting and tends to seek his assistance by confiding in him. There should be no air of superiority in his manner. His demeanor should be sympathetic and understanding. Absence of exaggerated regional traits is desirable to avoid any clash with the subject's prejudices. Tolerance should mark his temperament. He is a person who is aware that prejudice frequently is the name we give to the other fellow's set of convictions.

c. **Breadth of Interests.** To establish rapport with a witness of a complainant, it may be necessary to create a meeting ground of interests. A person tends to regard a fellowman who shares common interests as a sympathetic personality. This is the first step toward placing trust in the interviewer. Obviously, the range of the investigator's interests must necessarily be broad if it is to cover those of many of the witnesses and subjects with whom he will come in contact. It is well known that a good investigator does possess a breadth of practical knowledge. He is acquainted with the habits of working men, the behavior and social life of gamblers, the temperament of storekeepers and the simple business principles by which they operate. On other levels, he knows the habits, prejudices, and modes of thinking of the more prosperous members of the community.

5. The Place and Time

In planning an interview the investigator should, as a general rule, select a place which will provide him with a psychological advantage and conduct the questioning as soon as possible after the occurrence. Naturally this rule must be modified to suit the exigencies and nature of the case.

a. **Background Interviews.** If the interview is concerned with the background of a person being considered for a position of trust, no great difficulty arises in selecting the time and place. References such as individual businessmen and representatives of large companies can be interviewed during normal business hours. Professional men should be interviewed after arranging a suitable time by telephone.

b. **Routine Criminal Cases.** In criminal cases, the interview should be more carefully arranged. In order to obtain a maximum of information, a time should be selected at which the subject can have the leisure to devote his full attention to the matter. If it appears that the subject is under the press of business, the interview should be postponed until the evening. Privacy is another consideration in cases of this nature. An open office with a number of fellow workers present is not conducive to a candid expression of opinion or an accurate recollection of facts.

c. **Important Criminal Cases.** The investigator should arrange to interview witnesses in important cases at places other than their homes or office. Unfamiliar surroundings will prevent the witness from feeling confident and from controlling, through his composure, the amount and kind of information which he gives. The investigator should control the situation. He needs every psychological advantage which can serve to induce candor. The interviewee must respect him to the point where he is extremely hesitant to withhold or color information. Obviously, the investigator's own office is the ideal place.

d. **Time.** As a general principle, an interview should take place as soon as possible after the event. The information is then fresh in the mind of the witness. Moreover, he has had little time to contemplate any untoward consequences of his giving the information. It is seldom possible, however, to conduct the interview at the time set by the investigator. The witness may not be immediately available. Other developments of the case may intervene. Moreover, as a matter of strategy, it may be desirable to place certain interviews subsequent to others.

6. The Approach

On first meeting the subject the investigator should show his credentials and inform the subject of his identity. The point of identity must be stressed, since often the subject misunderstands the investigator with the result that a vague but unpleasant charge of misrepresentation may develop later. In interviewing women in their homes, the investigator should remain at a few paces from the door until the subject is convinced of his identification and invites him in. If at all possible, the investigator should avoid interviews at the threshold. Where necessary, he should return at a later time when the woman is reassured by the presence of a friend.

7. Background Interviews

The simplest type of interview is the one designed to develop information concerning a person who is being considered for a position of trust. The nature of the information desired should be so familiar to the investigator that he can ask the questions without reference to a checklist.

a. **Background Data.** Information on the following points is ordinarily required for a background report:
1) Date and time of the interview.
2) Name, vocation, and address of the interviewee. A request for a letterhead will supply the most accurate information.
3) Subject's full name.
4) Length of acquaintance in years.
5) Type of contact, whether business or social.
6) Degree of association, whether daily, occasional, or rarely.
7) When last seen.
8) Names—parents, brothers, and sisters.
9) Marital status and children.
10) Residence, past and present.
11) Educational background.
12) Personal and financial habits.
13) Personality traits.
14) Membership in organizations.
15) Relatives in foreign lands.
16) Honesty, loyalty, and discretion.
17) Recommendation for a position of trust.
18) Evaluation.
19) References.

b. **Credit Block.** The following additional information is important in a credit check report:
1) Recent changes in address.

2) Place of employment.
3) Name of spouse or parent.
4) Number of account.
5) Date opened.
6) Type of account.
7) Manner of payment.
8) Date closed.
9) Credit rating.
10) Eligibility for futher credit.
11) Other pertinent information.
12) Evaluation.
13) Cross reference.

8. Criminal Cases

The manner in which the interview is conducted will vary with the relationship of the subject to the matter in question. The demeanor of the investigator must be suited to the requirements of the case. The following are the usual stages of this type of interview:

a. **Preparation.** Before interviewing a witness the investigator should mentally review the case and consider what information the witness can contribute. If the importance of the case warrants it, he should acquaint himself with the background of the witness. In this manner he may more easily strike a responsive chord. He should plan his interview, if necessary providing himself with a checklist so that no important point is overlooked.

b. **Warm-Up.** The first few minutes will determine the tenor of the interview. If the investigator permits a clash of personalities or creates a tense atmosphere, the witness may tighten up and be reluctant to divulge all of his information. After showing his credentials, the investigator should open with a few friendly remarks. Conversation on the weather, the difficulties of his profession, and matters of mutual interest will serve to warm up the atmosphere. Although friendly in his approach he should maintain a business-like manner. When he feels that the witness is in a communicative mood, he should turn the conversation toward the witness's knowledge of the case under investigation. The witness should be given every opportunity to give a complete account without interruptions. A mental note should be made of inconsistencies, and other matters requiring clarification. During the witness's recital the investigator should "size him up." Prejudices, educational attainments, moral traits, and intelligence should be assessed.

c. **Questioning.** After the witness has told his story, the investigator should review it with him and request him to amplify certain points. Matters which have not been touched upon by the witness should be treated. The elements of the offense and other points in the case should guide the investigator in his questioning.

1) *Guiding the Conversation.* Many witnesses have a tendency to ramble in giving information. Often their answers are lengthy and not responsive. The investigator must control the interview so that complete and accurate information is obtained.

2) *Corroborating.* Information obtained from one witness should be correlated with that obtained from others. Corroboration of important facts is desirable. The information on such points should be obtained in detailed and specific form.

3) *Inaccuracies.* Discrepancies, falsehoods, and inaccuracies may become apparent during the interview. Questionable points should be treated repeatedly by rewording queries and by additional questions. Honest mistakes should be distinghished from misrepresentations.

4) *Technique of Questioning.* Questions should not be asked until the person appears prepared to give the desired information in an accurate fashion. Direct questions have a restraining effect and will not be suitable until the witness has given his own story and is ready to cooperate in giving additional information.

a) One Question at a Time. A multiplicity of questions tends to confuse the person being interviewed and detracts from the orderly conduct of the interview. The answers can be more easily segregated if a lesiurely, logical procedure is used.

b) Avoid the Implied Answer. The interview becomes futile if the answers are suggested in the questions. The objective is to find out what the person knows. Suggesting the answer defeats the purpose of the interrogation.

c) Simplicity of Questions. Long, complicated, legalistic questions only serve to confuse and irritate. The witness may answer that he doesn't know, when in reality he simply doesn't understand the question. In addition, such questions may embarrass him and cause resentment.

d) SAVING FACE. If his answers tend to give rise to an embarrassing situation by reason of his exaggerations or errors in matters of time, distance, and description, the investigator should cooperate with him and permit him to save face. The investigator should not ridicule his stupidity, poor judgment, or other deficiency. He should assist the subject in order to separate misrepresentation from unintentional mistakes.

e) "YES" AND "NO" QUESTIONS. Any person being questioned should have an opportunity to present relevant knowledge in its entirety. Insisting on "yes" and "no" answers is not only unfair but results in inaccurate answers and prevents a flow of information. Where such responses are concerned, qualification of the answers should be encouraged.

f) POSITIVE ATTITUDE. A common error of interviewers is the use of the negative approach in dealing with witnesses both in questioning and in arranging for the interview. An interviewer who questions a witness by saying, "You couldn't arrange to meet me this afternoon, could you?" is inviting a negative answer. He is unconsciously suggesting that a negative reply will be acceptable and that the interview can be evaded. Similarly, if the investigator puts his question by saying "you didn't see anyone near the house when you arrived, did you?" or "would you care to sign this statement?" he is encouraging a noncommittal answer. The positive approach should always be employed. The investigator should convey by his tone of voice and phrasing that he does not contemplate the possibility of negative or non-informative answers. "I have the interview set for ten o'clock," and "How many persons were at the scene, when you arrived?" are questions that guide the mind of the witness positively. Timidity and lack of confidence are easily detected by the average man. Leadership and firmness are respected and command acquiesence.

g) CONTROLLING THE INTERVIEW. The investigator's confidence and authority communicate themselves to the witness. Hesitancy and doubt encourage evasion; weakness fosters resistance. If the witness appears to be one who will be difficult to control, small psychological gestures will bring him under control. He may be instructed to cease smoking or directed to a chair other than the one he has selected. The difficult witness must learn quickly that the investigator intends to dominate the situation.

9. Techniques for Controlling Digression

After rapport has been established and the subject has been permitted to tell his story in his own words, the most difficult task facing the interviewer is the control of digression. If the interviewer has not mastered the technique of avoiding rambling discourses, his interviewing will tend to be markedly inefficient and he may fail to obtain the desired information. Two principles should guide the interrogator in maintaining control, namely, keeping the subject on the point and preventing him from going into excessive detail in non-essential matters. The following techniques will be found useful in achieving the objective represented by these principles:

a. **Precise Questioning.** Digressions and rambling interviews are often attributable to the ineptitude of the investigator in failing to master his most effective device, namely, precision of question formulation. The question should be constructed as precisely as possible in order to restrict the range of information which the subject can give in answer. For example, to employ the question: "Can you tell me something about the habits of this man?" is encouraging a general discourse in which the subject explains his own principles. On the other hand, "Have you ever seen him intoxicated?" may in its bluntness and precision provide the interviewer with the exact information he is seeking in using the former question.

b. **Shunting.** This technique consists in asking a question which relates the digression to the original line of questioning. This maneuver is preferable to interrupting the subject since the "shunt" appears to rise out of an interest in what the subject is saying. For example, if the subject is relating his occupational history, he may dwell too much on the difficulties of one particular position he held.

The interviewer can then ask quickly, "How much did they pay you for all this work?" When the subject answers, "9,000 a year," the interviewer can ask, "And how much did your next job pay?" and the interviewer has now progressed to another phase of his career.

c. **Skipping by Guessing.** Frequently the interviewer is confronted with a subject whose narration progresses in detailed and obvious steps. To speed up the recital he may ask a question such as "Was he hurt?" which anticipates a conclusion and skips intermediary details. Other such questions are: "How did he finally get home?", "Was he arrested?" A shrewd guess at the probable outcome of the various stages of the subject's recital will encourage the skipping of intervening details. For example, "You met Jones at the bar the next morning, didn't you?" " . . . and that was how you came to meet Brown?" and similar questions will greatly reduce the amount of digression.

10. Types of Interviews

The investigator must suit his techniques of interviewing to the varied personalities that are encountered in life. Some typical classes are discussed here with appropriate recommendations. Within each class one should expect to find wide variations.

a. **Children.** (Wherever possible permission should be obtained before interviewing children. Attempts to use children secretly as informants can cause serious embarrassment through the complaints of the parents.) Young children are given to flights of imagination. The inexperienced investigator will find himself quite bewildered at the turns of thought taken by children in response to questioning. The child may indulge his fancy in an imaginary journey to strange places and relate a series of unreal events. The distinction between truth and unreality may be lost on the child without any intentional desire to deceive. A child under six may invent a story in reply to a question. An older child, from six to ten, may tend to distort the story. The chief advantage of the older child as a witness, however, is the ability to observe, remember, and express himself and the absence of motives and prejudices. Such a child is an intimate of the truth although somewhat at a distance from reality. He is at least a stranger to falsehoods inspired by hate, ambition, or jealousy.

1) **Boys.** Most boys are alert young beings employing their minds in the direct apprehension of reality and instinctively shunning falsehood. The boy will usually describe events and objects as they appear to him. In fact, the intelligent boy can be the best of all witnesses. His perceptions are not dulled by age or preoccupation with cares, and he has a desire to communicate truth.

2) **Girls.** The female when young is intensely interested in the world as it reacts to her. She can be an excellent source of information because she observes with interest events intrinsically boring. She can relate facts concerning the behavior of neighbors, particularly young neighbors. She notices moral traits and psychological dispositions. Unfortunately, a girl improperly motivated can be a dangerous witness. If, in the world which in her mind centers about her person, there are individuals who do not reflect her glory or who have incurred her displeasure, she may permit herself to place fantastic interpretations on their actions. Another fault to be found in the girl witness is the tendency to exaggerate.

b. **Young Persons.** Persons in the prime of their youth are usually living too intensely to pay great heed to others, particularly to those younger or older than they. The intense preoccupation of young people with themselves prevents them from being ideal witnesses. They have not yet begun to reflect on life and to view objectively the behavior of their neighbors. They are inclined to be truthful, but their testimony is not strengthened by any great powers of observation.

c. **Middle-aged Persons.** The person who has reached the middle of his life is keenly aware of his fellow beings at other age levels. Coupled with this perception is the possession of unimpaired faculties and mature judgment. A middle-aged person is often the ideal witness.

d. **Older Persons.** Physical impairment and a tendency to regress into self-preoccupation seriously affect the value of older persons as witnesses. The intelligent older person, however, may be classed as a very effective witness, particularly since he adds maturity of judgment to a leisure for observation.

11. Types and Attitudes of Subjects

The investigator must endeavor to classify the subject as soon as possible after beginning the interview. He must then adjust his method of interviewing to the personality and attitude which he is encountering. Experience with various personality types will suggest to the investigator the best technique to be employed in a particular case. The following is a list of some of the personalities and attitudes which the interviewer will meet:

a. **Know-Nothing Type.** Some persons are reluctant to act as witnesses. This is particularly true of uneducated persons who imagine that any contact with the law means "trouble." An extensive warm-up, followed by persistent questioning, may yield results. Another technique is that of presenting the subject with a great many questions to which he cannot reply that he knows nothing, and then leading into the relevant questions. If the subject persists in his attitude, the investigator should determine whether he is stupid or unobservant before continuing. A few innocuous test questions can reveal the level of intelligence and capacity for observation attained by the subject.

b. **Disinterested Type.** The uncooperative, indifferent person must be aroused. He should be flattered at first to develop a pride in his ability to supply information. His interest should be stimulated by stressing the importance of the information he possesses.

c. **Drunken Type.** Flattery will encourage the drunk to respond to questions and develop an interest. Naturally, it is not advisable to take written statements from a person in this condition. At times the drunk can be the best of all witnesses since he is inspired by his own potent truth serum.

d. **Suspicious Type.** His fears must be allayed. An effort should be made to win him over on the grounds of good citizenship. Failing this, the investigator should employ psychological influence. By implying that he (the investigator) already knows a good deal about the case, the investigator leaves the suspicious witness to infer that this knowledge is sufficient to work against him in the event that he does not cooperate.

e. **Talkative Type.** The garrulous witness merely requires management. The flow of information is there but it requires channeling. The investigator should subtly lead this type back to relevant matters, by interspersing remarks that switch the subject's mind back on the desired track.

f. **Honest Witness.** If the witness possesses useful information and demonstrates honesty and cooperativenss in his attitude, the investigator has found a precious stone that is well worth polishing. Such a person, if he is normally intelligent, can be developed into an ideal witness with a little care and guidance. He should first be convinced of the investigator's mission, namely, the discovery of truth, and disabused of any notion that the investigator is determined to punish or persecute the subject. Secondly, the witness should be given a five-minute talk, with illustrative examples, of the difference between direct evidence and hearsay and the importance of accurate, relevant information.

g. **The Deceitful Witness.** The witness who is obviously lying can often be brought into the investigator's camp by careful maneuvering. He should be permitted to lie until he is well enmeshed in falsehoods and inconsistencies. The investigator can then halt the interview and dramatically announce that he recognizes the witness's statements as falsehoods. He can sustain his point by one or two examples of which he is sure and imply that he knows wherein lies the falsity of the others. A recording of the lies is extremely effective in the playback. Finally, the investigator should refer in vague terms to perjury and false statements and the probability that he may now have to investigate a case of "obstructing justice" with the witness as defendant. The case under investigation should be forgotten for the moment. About five minutes should be spent by the investigator in discoursing with great gravity on the seriousness of the witness's offense, namely false representations to an officer of the law during an official investigation. The average person is unaware that there exists no such offense. He will feel vaguely that he is punishable under the law. Now he has an excellent motive for telling the truth, namely, self-preservation.

h. **The Timid Witness.** Housewives, uneducated, foreign-born people and others may often be unusually timid and stand in awe of law enforcement procedures. The investigator must employ a friendly approach and should spend some time in explaining that the information obtained will be treated as a confidential matter.

i. **The Boasting, Egotistic, or Egocentric Witness.** Patience and flattery are necesary in dealing with the vain or self-centered person. He is potentially an excellent witness because of his drive toward self-expression. Unfortunately, he is prone to color his story and put unwarranted emphasis on his own part.

j. **Refusal to Talk.** The witness who will say nothing is the most difficult of all types. If he is a shrewd criminal with a record, he will probably remain silent. With other types the investigator must persevere. Neutral topics should be chosen to induce the atmosphere of conversation. Motivation should be exhausted before admitting defeat. The witness should be made to feel that he "owes it" to himself, his family, the victim, or even the subject to give whatever information he may possess.

12. Approaches

A direct approach is the most effective with willing witnesses. The investigator should begin in a friendly conversational tone and develop the information naturally. With difficult witnesses such as those who dislike law enforcement officers or who fear retaliation, a direct questioning may be necessary.

a. **Complaint.** The investigator should appear to be sympathetic with the complainant by expressing his interest in the case and assuring the complainant of his gratification by the report of the offense. He should convince him that full cooperation will be given and then proceed to elicit all the facts of the complaint. Privately the investigator should form an opinion of the reliability of the complainant and his complaint. He should determine whether the elements of an offense are present. The records should be checked to discover whether the person is a chronic complainant or has a criminal history. The motivation of the complainant must be considered. The existence of jealousy or grudges may have affected the complainant's point of view.

b. **Persons "Complained of."** Before questioning a person complained of (there being insufficient evidence to consider him a suspect) the investigator should refresh his knowledge of the law, acquaint himself with the facts concerning the elements present, and know the record or reputation of the person. This preliminary questioning should be impartial and probing.

c. **Informants.** The informant should be flattered. Praiseworthy motives should be attributed to his action, such as "duty to society" and "assisting law and order." The informant should be permitted to talk freely and fully. He should then be questioned for details. In concluding, a favorable estimate should be made of the importance of his information.

d. **Victims.** The victim must be treated with some care since his reactions to fancied indifference can be violent and accusations of neglect of duty may be made. The investigator should be sympathetic and listen to the complete story, permitting the victim to offer opinions. The investigator need not support or discourage the suggestions of the victim or offer any of his own at the moment. He should devote himself simply to gathering facts.

13. Evaluation

During the interview, the investigator will be forming a judgment of the credibility of his witness. Physical mannerisms, frankness, emotional state, and content of the statements will form the basis of his evaluation of the worth of the information.

a. **Physical Mannerisms.** Nervousness, evasive facial expression, embarrassment at certain questions, perspiration, and similar signs will give some indication of the trustworthiness of the person.

b. **Frankness.** The person should be tested with questions, the answers to which the investigator already knows. The investigator should compare the subject's account of certain events with the facts that he probably should have knowledge of. Significant omissions should be noted.

c. **Emotional State.** The investigator should observe carefully any unusual reaction to questions. Partial guilt can be detected by unwarranted indignation or excessive protests. Spite, jealousy, and prejudice can be easily detected.

d. **Content of Statements.** The information given by the witness can be compared with statements of other witnesses and with known facts. Discrepancies and misrepresentations can be detected by comparing the information with the known facts.

14. Notebook

The proper use of the notebook is a matter of judgment which will depend on the nature of the interview and the character of the person to be questioned. If the interview is concerned with sensitive matters, the appearance of the notebook at an early stage may instill excessive caution in the subject. After introducing himself and informing the subject of the general nature of the case, the investigator should listen to the subject's story without taking notes. At the conclusion he may request permission to put the pertinent information in writing. If necessary, he should prepare it in the form of a statement, later obtaining the subject's signature. The investigator should carry a sample statement with him to insure covering the important points. Where, however, the interview is concerned with routine matters, such as a background investigation or an interview of a custodian of official records, the notebook should be used at the outset to record the information without loss of time.

15. Hypnosis

The placing of consenting witnesses under hypnosis is increasingly becoming an investigative tool. Some law enforcement agencies, such as the Los Angeles Police Department, have established special units for this purpose. A simple and direct approach is used. After determining the willingness and acceptability of the witness, the subject is placed in a medium-depth trance. An attempt is then made to evoke descriptive details and observed activities associated with an offense, which have thus far not responded to ordinary recall. A number of successes have been recorded by exploring the memory of a witness in this manner. Naturally, the training of police officers in these techniques must be conducted by qualified psychologists or physicans skilled in medical hypnosis.

ADDITIONAL READING

Arons, H.: *Hypnosis in Criminal Investigation.* Springfield, Ill.: Thomas, 1967.

Copinger, R.B., Jr.: Planning the Investigative Interview. 9 *Security World*, 7, 1972.

Dexter, L.A.: *Elite and Specialized Interviewing.* Evanston, Ill.: Northwestern University Press, 1970.

Royal, R.F. and Schutt, S.R.: *Gentle Art of Interviewing and Interrogation: A Professional Manual and Guide.* Englewood Cliffs, N.J.: Prentice-Hall, 1976.

Schultz, J.: Interviewing the Sex Offender's Victim. 51 *Journal of Criminal Law, Criminology and Police Science*, 448, 1960.

Wicks, R.J. and Josephs, E.H., Jr.: *Techniques in Interviewing for Law Enforcement and Corrections Personnel.* Springfield, Ill.: Thomas, 1972.

Chapter 9

INTERROGATIONS

1. A Fundamental Rule

THE SUPREME COURT *Miranda v. Arizona* decision has radically changed the procedural requirements for a lawful interrogation of a suspect or of a person in custody by specifying certain minimal prerequisites to insure the voluntariness of the suspect's responses. Because of its importance the Court's rule is stated at the beginning of the chapter; it will be repeated later in other, and more formal, terms to explain and develop the ideas from which it arose.

Before interrogating a suspect or a person in police custody the investigator should

a. Identify himself to the suspect as a law enforcement officer—this is done orally, together with a show of credentials.

b. Explain to the suspect in general terms the nature of the offense under investigation.

c. Inform the suspect of his wish to question him on matters relating to this offense.

d. Advise the suspect of his rights in substantially the following terms:

(1) You have the right to remain silent; you do not have to answer any questions.

(2) If you answer any questions, your answers may be used in evidence against you.

(3) You have the right to have legal counsel; that is, you may have the services of a lawyer of your own choosing.

(4) If you believe you cannot afford a lawyer, the state will appoint one for you at your request without any expense on your part.

(5) Do you understand your rights as I have explained them to you—namely, your right to remain silent and your right to be represented by a lawyer?

2. Options and Procedure

The fourfold warning of rights, as stated above or its equivalent, must be given by the investigator as a necessary preliminary to the interrogation of a suspect or of a person in custody. The responses of the suspect will determine the investigator's subsequent action.

a. The suspect may choose to remain silent. If before or during questioning the suspect invokes his right to remain silent, interrogation must be forgone or cease. The investigator must respect the suspect's right to remain silent. Threats, tricks, or cajolings designed to persuade the suspect to waive this right are forbidden.

b. The suspect may request counsel. No interrogation must then be attempted until the lawyer of his choosing or a state-appointed lawyer is present. If before or during questioning (assuming that he has waived his right to remain silent) the suspect invokes his right to request and have counsel, the interrogation must cease until a lawyer is procured.

c. The suspect may waive his rights. To forgo these rights an affirmative statement of rejection is evidently required. The burden of proof of waiver is on the State. Withdrawal of a waiver is always permitted. If the interrogation continues without the presence of an attorney and a statement is taken, a heavy burden rests on the Government to demonstrate that the defendant knowingly and intelligently waived his privilege against self-incrimination and his right to retained or appointed counsel. The following points should be noted:

1) Proof of waiver of constitutional rights may take the form of an "express statement that the individual is willing to make a statement and does not want an attorney, followed closely by a statement."*

2) A valid waiver will not be presumed simply from the silence of the accused after warnings are given or simply from the fact that a confession was in fact eventually obtained.

3) "Presuming waiver from a silent record is impermissible. The record must show, or there must be an allegation and evidence

---

*Unless otherwise noted, all of the quotations and much of the formal language used in this chapter are taken from the Supreme Court's decision in *Miranda v. Arizona*, 384 U.S. 436 (1966).

which show that an accused was offered counsel but intelligently and understandingly rejected the offer. Anything less is not a waiver" (*Carnley v. Cochran*, 369 U.S. 506, 516 [1962]).

4) The right to remain silent is not considered waived if the individual answers some questions or gives some information on his own prior to invoking the right.

5) "Whatever the testimony of the authorities as to waiver of rights by an accused, the fact of a lengthy interrogation or incommunicado incarceration before a statement is made is strong evidence that the accused did not validly waive his rights. . . . Any evidence that the accused was threatened, tricked, or cajoled into a waiver will show that the accused did not voluntarily waive his privilege."

3. Matters Unaffected by the Ruling

The warnings must be given when the individual is first subjected to police interrogation while in custody at the police station or while otherwise deprived of his freedom in any way. Thus, the Court's ruling does not affect other modes by which information may be acquired from persons whose freedom has been in no wise restricted by the police.

a. **Confessions without Warnings.** The Court did not purport to find all confessions obtained without warnings and counsel inadmissible. For example,

1) Any statement given freely and voluntarily is, of course, admissible in evidence.
2) There is no requirement that police stop a person who enters a police station and states that he wishes to confess a crime.
3) Similarly, there is no requirement to stop a person who calls the police to offer a confession (or any other statement he desires to make).
4) Volunteered statements of any kind are not barred by the Fifth Amendment and their admissibility is not affected by the *Miranda* decision.

In summary, the fundamental import of the privelege while an individual is in custody is not whether he is allowed to talk to the police without benefit of warnings and counsel but whether he can be interrogated.

b. **Field Investigation.** When an individual is in custody on probable cause, the police may, of course, seek out evidence in the field to be used against him. Such investigation may include

1) Inquiry of persons not under restraint;
2) General on-the-scene questioning as to facts surrounding a crime;
3) Other general questioning of citizens in the fact-finding process.

Questioning of this nature is not affected by *Miranda*, since in these situations the compelling atmosphere thought to be inherent in the process of in-custody interrogation is not ordinarily present.

4. Right to Counsel

After June 12, 1972, no poor person may be sentenced to a term in jail unless he has been offered free legal counsel. This Supreme Court ruling is an interesting development in view of the fact that less than fifty years ago a person could have been tried and sentenced to death without a lawyer in a state court without violating the Constitution. The major historical steps in this evolution were the following:

a. *1932*. The Supreme Court first declared, in the famous "Scottsboro Boys" rape case from Alabama, that the Constitution guarantees the right to counsel in state court trials whenever the defendant's life is at stake (*Powell v. Alabama*, 287 U.S. 45 [1932]).

b. *1963*. The Court extended the rule to all felony cases (in general, those offenses carrying more than a year's imprisonment) by holding that the Sixth Amendment's guarantee of counsel in "all criminal prosecutions" required the states to furnish free lawyers to poor defendants (*Gideon v. Wainwright*, 372 U.S. 335 [1963]).

c. *1967*. In *Miranda v. Arizona* the Court ruled that a person in police custody had a right to legal counsel during interrogation; that is, a suspect must be advised of his right to counsel before interrogation. If the suspect requests counsel, no interrogation must be attempted until the lawyer of his choosing or a state-appointed lawyer is present (*Miranda v. Arizona*, 384 U.S. 436 [1966]).

d. *1972*. The Court saw no reason to limit the Sixth Amendment's right to counsel to felony cases and declared that the defendant is entitled to the "guiding hand of counsel" whenever "the actual deprivation of a person's liberty" is at stake. Thus, judges must now decide in advance of the trial of an indigent defendant if imprisonment is to be considered. Where a jail sentence is possible, the court must offer the defendant free legal counsel. Otherwise, the defendant can be given only a money fine as punishment (*Argersinger v. Hamlin*, 407 U.S. 25 [1972]). A further complication arises out of a 1971 Supreme Court decision to the effect that a poor person could not be put in jail for inability to pay a fine.

e. *The Outlook*. Since fewer than a dozen states provided counsel in all cases involving jail, the 1972 decision affected most communities in the United States. The magnitude of the problem may be grasped by considering the fact that over five million misdemeanor cases are handled annually by the courts as compared with 350,000 felony cases. Since the Supreme Court ruling there have been fewer guilty pleas and more trials and appeals contributing to the swollen backlog and the near breakdown in the criminal courts of some cities. The cumulative impact on the criminal justice system was a matter of conjecture. Some students believed that this new and massive use of defense lawyers would prove too great a weight for the survival of the treadmill system of urban misdemeanor justice that must turn out a defendant every few minutes or be crushed under its growing backlog. By 1975, however, the courts had managed to contain the problem within reasonable proportions. In a five-volume report ("Counsel for Misdemeanants") on this subject by Boston University's Center for Criminal Justice we find the conclusion: "Compliance has generally been token in nature," reform "has been chaotic and uneven at best," and the assurance of legal representation remains "an empty right for many defendants." Judges have availed themselves of the key words of the *Argersinger v. Hamlin* decision permitting "a knowing and intelligent waiver" of the right to counsel. That phrase, says the Center "has resulted in a 95% waiver rate in some lower courts." In Houston and Belle Glade, Fla., according to the report, "it is assumed that a defendant has waived counsel unless he aggressively asserts (the) right." In other jurisdictions "defendants perceive, correctly or not, a tacit rule of court that those who ask for counsel are treated more harshly."

5. Terms

To proceed now from the warning phase to the practical aspect of interrogation, the assumption must be made that the suspect has waived his right to counsel as well as his right to remain silent. As Justice Harlan has remarked (*Miranda v. Arizona*) in his dissenting opinion: "The Court's vision of a lawyer 'mitigating the dangers of untrustworthiness' by witnessing coercion and assisting accuracy in the confession is largely a fancy; for if counsel arrives, there is rarely going to be a police station confession. *Watts v. Indiana*, 338 U.S. 49, 59 (separate opinion of Jackson, J.): 'Any lawyer worth his salt will tell the suspect in no uncertain terms to make no statement to police under any circumstances.'" Nevertheless, the assumption must be made, since the professional investigator accepts with equanimity either decision of the suspect, whether he invokes or rejects his rights.

For the purpose of simplifying the practical aspect of interrogations, special meanings will be attached to some of the terms used. It should be understood that these conventions are not universally accepted.

a. **Interrogations.** An interrogation is a questioning of a person suspected of having committed an offense or of a person who is reluctant to make a full disclosure of information in his possession which is pertinent to the investigation.

b. **Witness.** A witness is a person, other than a suspect, who is requested to give information concerning an incident or person. He may be a victim, a complainant, an accuser, a source of information, an observer of an occurrence, a scientific specialist who has examined physical evidence, or a custodian of official documents. A witness is usually interviewed, but he may be interrogated when he is suspected of lying or of withholding pertinent information.

c. **Suspect.** A suspect in an offense is a person whose guilt is considered on reasonable grounds to be a practical possibility.

d. **Subject.** The term *subject* will be used here most commonly to represent the person, whether witness or suspect, who is being interviewed or interrogated. The subject in this sense is not necessarily the subject of the case under investigation. Where the term is used to refer to the subject of the case, the distinction will be apparent from the phrasing and context.

6. Purpose

The primary purpose of interrogation is to obtain information which will further the investigation. Interrogation is not simply a means of inducing an admission of guilt. It is an investigative tool of far wider application to the effective day-to-day administration of justice. It is a major means of discovering other evidence. It permits the person who appears to be implicated in a crime to present information which can establish his innocence. One of the most important functions of police questioning is that of screening cases where an arrest has been made on probable cause but where a decision to charge cannot or should not be properly made without some further investigation by the police and some evaluation by the prosecutor of the circumstances of the arrest and the availability of admissible evidence. In large metropolitan areas, each day a great number of people will be lawfully arrested for a wide variety of reasons. Routine preliminary questioning may well result in their release prior to the filing of any charge or may result in the filing of a less serious charge.

Some of the other functions served may be found in the following list of the purposes of interrogation:

a. To obtain information concerning the innocence or guilt of a suspect.

b. To obtain a confession to the crime from a guilty subject.

c. To induce the subject to make admissions.

d. To learn the facts and circumstances surrounding a crime.

e. To learn of the existence and locations of physical evidence such as documents or weapons.

f. To learn the identity of accomplices.

g. To develop information which will lead to the fruits of the crime.

h. To develop additional leads for the investigation.

i. To discover the details of any other crimes in which the suspect participated.

7. The Interrogator

The interrogator must be able to impress his subject, not through use of his formal authority but because his personality commands respect. He must be professional in attitude and performance. If he reveals any waivering tendencies the suspect may discover the means of resisting the interrogation. To inspire full confidence, the force of the investigator's personality should be tempered by an understanding and sympathetic attitude. The subject must feel instinctively that he is talking man-to-man with a person who is interested in his viewpoint and problems. The suspect who has been forced to cooperate with hostile organizations may tell his story more readily if he feels that the investigator understands his helplessness and is inclined to take his plight into consideration. The following qualifications and traits are desirable in an interrogator:

a. **General Knowledge and Interests.** To some degree, the efficiency of an investigator is commensurate with his general knowledge. To acquire this breadth of knowldge, the investigator must develop intellectual curiosity and a keen sense of observation. He must cultivate a genuine interest in people and their problems, for such knowledge will help him in determining motives as he deals with many types of personalities in a variety of circumstances. It is highly desirable that he have a wide range of general knowledge concerning professional and technical matters, since his subjects represent nearly every phase of human activity. The background and personality of these individuals, together with the information they provide, can be assessed adequately only if the interrogator is prepared to discuss their major interests intelligently and to analyze their motives in light of environmental factors.

b. **Alertness.** The variety of problems confronting him requires the interrogator to be constantly alert so he can analyze his subject accurately, adapt his technique to the requirements of the case, uncover and explore leads, and alter his tactics when necessary. A sense of logic will not in itself quickly reveal contradictions in a subject's story; it must be accompanied by a ready awareness of the contradictory information. Discovery of gaps in the subject's story after the interrogation is less satisfactory than on-the-spot recognition, because the time interval gives the subject opportunity to reflect upon the matter before questioning is renewed.

c. **Perseverance.** Every interrogation requires a great deal of patience if complete and accurate information is to be obtained. The need for patience is obvious when lack of cooperation is encountered; but perserverance frequently is required even when the suspect is willing to help but is unable to recall precisely the complex ramifications of his story or to explain discrepancies.

d. **Integrity.** If the person being questioned has reason to doubt the integrity of the interrogator, it is physically impossible for the latter to inspire confidence or trust. The interrogator must never make a promise he cannot keep; he should keep all promises he makes.

e. **Logical Mind.** The interrogator must develop the questioning along a logical line. The objectives of the questioning should be clearly defined in his own mind. A plan of questioning should be built around the requirements of establishing the elements of proof of the offense.

f. **Ability in Observation and Interpretations.** He must not only develop the ability to "size up" an individual, but also must learn to observe and interpret his reaction to questions.

g. **Power of Self-control.** He must maintain control of himself at all times. Loss of temper results in a neglect of important details.

h. **Playing the Part.** If it will accomplish the desired results, the investigator may act as though he were angry or sympathetic as the circumstances suggest. Anger, however, should never be simulated to the degree where it might become a coercive factor.

8. Conduct of the Interrogator

The behavior of the interrogator at the outset of the questioning usually creates the atmosphere and sets the tone of the subsequent interrogation. It is of great importance for the investigator to develop an effective personality that will induce in the subject a desire to respond. Personal mannerisms must be controlled wherever they distract or antagonize. The following are some of the more useful reminders concerning attitude and demeanor:

a. **Control of the Interview.** The interrogator must always be in command of the situation. The strength of his personality must constantly be felt by the subject. He must never lose control through indignation, ill temper, hesitancy in the face of violent reactions, or obvious fumbling for questions through lack of resourcefulness.

b. **Distracting Mannerisms.** The subject must be impressed with the seriousness of the interrogator's purpose. Pacing the room, smoking, "doodling," and similar forms of behavior should be avoided, since they tend to convey a sense of inattentiveness or a lack of concentration. The investigator should seat himself close to the subject with no intervening furniture and focus his attention on the subject. The full weight of his personality must be brought to bear on the emotional situation. Distance or obstructions tend to mitigate the effect.

c. **Language.** The speech of the interrogator should be adapted to the subject's cultural level. Profanity and vulgarity should, of course, be avoided, since they diminish the effectiveness of the interrogator by compromising his dignity or antagonizing the subject. The uneducated subject must be approached in his own language. Simple, forthright diction should be employed. It is especially important in sex cases to avoid ambiguities. Slang may be used if it promotes ease of speech or fluency in the subject. The choice of words should be made with a view to encouraging a free flow of speech in the subject. Where the subject may shy away from words such as "assault" and "steal," he may not hesitate to admit that he "hit" or "took." It is a natural tendency for a person to describe his conduct in terms of euphemisms.

d. **Dress.** Civilian dress is more likely to inspire confidence and friendship in a criminal than a uniform. The accoutrements of the police profession should be removed from view. The sight of a protruding gun or billy may arouse an enmity or a defensive attitude on the part of the criminal.

e. **Attitude.** The interrogator is not seeking to convict or punish.

He is endeavoring to establish the facts of the case; to discover the truth, to clarify a misunderstanding; to help the suspect to straighten himself out; to clear up this mess, to simplify matters; to rectify an unfortunate situation; to see what he can do to help the subject to help himself; to get rid of a distasteful task as painlessly as possible; to see that the subject's accomplices are not doing him an injury; and so forth. There is an extensive set of locutions available to the investigator in describing his role in the administration of justice.

f. **Preliminary Conduct.** As stated in the beginning of this chapter, the interrogator should identify himself at the outset and show his credentials to the subject. He should then state, in general terms, the purpose of the investigation. He must advise the suspect of his rights against self-incrimination and inform him that he does not need to answer questions and that, if he does answer, his answers can be used in evidence against him. He must inform the suspect of his right to counsel and of the fact that state-appointed counsel will be made available without cost to him if he so desires. If the suspect requests counsel, the interrogation may not begin until counsel is present. In any event, the interrogator may not question the suspect unless the suspect had definitely waived his right to be silent.

g. **Presence of Other Persons.** Ordinarily, the investigator should be alone with the suspect—and, of course, his lawyer, if he has requested counsel. It is desirable, for several reasons, to restrict the number of persons present at an interrogation. If a confession is obtained the defense may claim the existence of duress because of the presence of five or ten police officers. Moreover, some courts require the prosecution to produce all the witnesses of a confession. A parade of ten detectives to the witness stand creates an unfavorable impression and opens up the likelihood of inconsistencies in the testimony. Ordinarily the interrogator should be alone with the subject. Other parties may be brought in for a specific purpose, such as witnessing the signing of a confession.

9. The Interrogation Room

The room chosen for the interrogation should provide freedom from distractions. It should be designed for simplicity with a view to enhancing the concentration of both the interrogator and the subject on the matter under questioning.

a. **Privacy.** Interruptions dispel an atmosphere of concentration that may have been carefully cultivated by the investigator: hence, the following are desirable:

1) **Restricted Entrance.** A room with a single door is preferable. Several doors suggest possible interruption and destroy the sense of focused attention.

2) Absence of windows or view.

3) Sound-proofing.

4) Telephone without bell.

b. **Simplicity.** Distracting influences should be kept to a minimum. The suspect may strive to avoid the investigator's concentration by focusing his attention on some object in the room which suggests a different train of thought.

1) Medium-sized room.

2) Bare walls. Pictures and charts are distracting.

3) No glaring lights.

4) Minimum furniture.

c. **Seating Arrangement.** The subject and the investigator should be seated with no large furniture between them.

1) **Chair.** Armless, straight-back chair for the suspect.

2) **Table or Desk.** The investigator requires a flat surface on which to place papers and articles of evidence.

3) **Suspect.** Seating the suspect with his back to the door further deprives him of any hope of interruptions or distraction.

d. **Technical Aids.** Although the investigator should be alone with the subject and his lawyer, it is desirable to have facilities for others to observe and hear the suspect during the interrogation. Other investigators may suspect of participation in other crimes. Thus the interrogation room can also serve as a line-up or show-up room. In an important case the investigator will require the assistance of his associates. By their listening unobserved to the interrogation they may be able to make useful suggestions and draw more objective conclusions. Persons such as the prosecuting attorney will find this opportunity to observe the prospective defendant invaluable in preparing his case. Victims and complainants are enabled to make identifications.

1) ***Recording Installation.*** Important interrogations and confessions should be recorded.

2) ***Listening Device.*** A hidden microphone such as a "live" telephone should be installed.

3) ***Two-Way Mirror.*** This device appears to be a plain mirror on one side but permits a person on the other side to see through without being observed. Unfortunately the typical two-way mirror installation is obvious and is familiar to the experienced criminal. A more deceptive arrangement can be devised with a little ingenuity. A framed picture with a mirror strip border is less familiar. A medicine chest with a mirror door will pass unnoticed if a small sink is installed beneath it.

e. **Interrogation Log.** In addition to his regular facilities for taking notes, it is well for the investigator to have available an Interrogation Log. This is esentially a form on which the investigator maintains in chronological order a record of the time periods of interrogation together with a time record of necessities and privileges requested by the accused and granted to him by the law enforcement agents. The interrogation log is a useful addition to the investigator's notes for special reference in answering allegations of duress.

10. Information Sought

The interrogator's primary purpose is to obtain facts or information concerning the offense under investigation for the purpose of determining the identity of the perpetrator and of substantiating a court prosecution. Initially his questions will be designed to learn whether the subject is innocent or whether there is reasonable cause to suspect his implication in the crime. If the responses indicate implication, the questioning will then seek to place the subject at the scene or to develop other associative or corroborative evidence. The identity of accomplices and the location or disposition of any fruits of the crime are, of course, matters of great interest.

To pursue a logical line of questioning, the interrogator should be acquainted with every significant detail of the case so that he is aware of what evidence is available and what evidence is needed, as well as the contributory force of each item of evidence. Thus, he should have a thorough knowledge of the nature of the offense under investigation and a mental outline of the elements of the offense together with the mode of proof required to substantiate each element.

11. Selection of Technique and Approach

In the work of an interrogation, the principle of economy of means should guide the investigator. The simplest approach is best if it achieves the desired result. The interrogator should not be unnecessarily devious. He may outwit himself with his own cleverness or antagonize the subject by creating an unwanted confusion. Ingenuity is desirable when it is required, but it should not be considered as a satisfactory substitute for intelligence. The interrogator must first classify or analyze his subject with the aid of information or criminal records. A preliminary interview will often assist in determining the character and personality of the suspect and in planning the techniques to be used. A detailed exposition of certain techniques of interrogation has been omitted here to avoid any conflict with the spirit of the *Miranda* ruling. Although such techniques may have been accepted as legal, their misapplication or misinterpretation might serve to produce or intensify the inherent pressures of the interrogation atmosphere that the Supreme Court's ruling was designed to overcome. It should be remembered, however, that any colloquy, dialogue, confrontation, or even interview will be surrounded by an atmosphere of varying tensions and pressures arising from the unavoidable differences in status, points of view, and psychological conditions of the participants. An applicant for a position is subjected to pressure when he is interviewed by the personnel director. Similarly, a witness who is subjected to the oppressive but wholly legal cross-examining procedures of a determined lawyer must feel the "inherent pressure" of the courtroom situation.

Knowing that the zero-value pressure condition may be a utopian ideal, the investigator will nevertheless apply his common sense to devise a set of interrogation procedures which are consonant with the spirit of the *Miranda* ruling in that they do not put the accused in such an emotional state as to impair his capacity for rational judgment. His decision to speak and even his decision to make inculpatory statements should be determinations formed in his own will and issuing from a free and rational choice. The interrogation procedures of the law enforcement agent should be informed by the spirit and intent of the Court and not merely constrained by perfunctory formulas and prohibitions.

12. Detection of Deception

Since the interrogator's main objective is to obtain true information—true, that is, in the sense that it accurately reflects what is in the subject's mind—he is necessarily concerned with the methods of distinguishing truth from falsehood. He relies, ordinarily, on his common sense, experience, and knowledge of human behavior to determine whether the subject is giving him true information, is misleading him with evasions and false statements, or is actually ignorant of the facts as he claims. Some conclusion can be drawn from inconsistencies and improbabilities evident in the subject's statements. Often, however, the interrogator must rely on the emotional reactions of the subject discernible in his features and mannerisms or in his unconscious physical behavior.

a. **Physiological Symptoms.** Careful observation of the physical state of the subject as influenced by his emotional reaction to questions has traditionally been considered a source of insight in determining guilty knowledge or deception. Primitive tribes are said to have relied on such methods as sniffing out the guilty person from a group of suspects by detecting an odor arising from an unusually nervous state; or selecting the guilty person on the basis of dryness of mouth as evinced by the relative difficulty experienced in chewing and attempting to swallow a handful of dry rice. The various symptoms observable in a subject are usually consistent with a state of nervousness as well as guilt. The following observation are generalities which can sometimes be useful if they are considered in relation to the known temperament of the subject and other relevant data:

1) ***Sweating.*** Perspiration on the brow may indicate excitement, nervousness, or simply the fact that the room is rather warm for the subject. Sweating palms, however, are indicative of tension and nervousness rather than warm surroundings.

2) ***Color Changes.*** A flushed face indicates anger or embarrassment but not necessarily guilt. An unusual pallor, considered by some a more likely sign of guilt, is often associated with fear or shock.

3) ***Dry Mouth.*** Frequent swallowing, wetting of the lips, and thirst are indications of dryness of the mouth, a common symptom of nervous tension that is sometimes associated with guilty knowledge and deception.

4) ***Pulse.*** An increase in the rate of the heart beat can be caused by the consciousness of deception.

5) ***Breathing.*** Deception is sometimes accompanied by an observable change in the rate of breathing or by an effort to control breathing during critical questions.

b. **The Lie Detector.** In drawing inferences from physiological symptoms, the interrogator is unconsciously serving roughly the purpose of a lie detector, since he is relying on the same principle: the bodily functions of a person are influenced by his mental state. The brain reacts to emotional disturbances by transmitting through the nervous system signals which appropriately affect and regulate the body's vital functions. A suspect's emotions will thus effect certain physiological changes such as a quickened heartbeat; a difference in the rate and volume of breathing; blushing; increased perspiring; and dryness of the mouth. These are autonomic changes, accordingly self-regulating and difficult to control consciously. A number of these changes, moreover, are measurable and can be recorded and interpreted with reasonable accuracy. A mechanical aid for measuring such changes is called a lie detector; if it serves the additional function of recording the changes, it is commonly called a polygraph.

1) ***The Lie Detection Process.*** The lie detector or polygraph does not record lies as such but simply measures changes in blood pressure, pulse rate, breathing, and in the resistance of the skin to a small electrical current. By far the most important element in the process of detecting deception is the qualified examiner, whose

education, training, and experience enable him to determine whether the graphs produced with the instrument present a meaningful pattern. The interpretation of the charts is of critical importance. Without a suitable background in psychology, physiology, and scientific method, the operator of the lie detector may be little more than a shrewd mechanic, using the instrument to support conclusions already half-drawn on the basis of experience and intuition.

In practice the examiner uses both neutral questions (irrelevant to the issues of the case) as well as relevant questions. Neutral questions enable the examiner to establish a norm for the subject's reactions to questions relatively free of emotional content. The relevant questions provide the examiner with some insight into the cause of a subject's fears—the guilty person's fears usually tend to

Figure 8. The Arther III Polygraph: records breathing, blood pressure, pulse, galvanic skin response and plethysmic changes. Courtesy of Scientific Lie Detection, Inc.

increase during a test, his reactions usually become stronger; the fear and nervousness of the innocent person, on the other hand, usually tend to decrease during the test.

2) *Objectives.* Although information obtained by means of the lie detector test is not generally accepted as direct evidence in United States courts of law, the test itself is considered a valuable investigative aid in the achievement of the following objectives:

a) Ascertaining if the subject is telling the truth.

b) Testing and comparing inconsistent statements.

c) Verifying statements made by the suspect before the test.

d) Developing leads to important facts of the crime, such as the whereabouts of a wanted person or the location of stolen goods.

c. **Suitability of Test Subject.** Not all persons are fit subjects for a lie detector test, since certain physical and mental conditions may affect the subject's reactions during the test. The following factors are considered:

1) *Physical Ills.* Permanent conditions such as certain heart conditions and breathing disorders can make a person unfit to take the test. A highly nervous or excitable person may be unfit. Temporary conditions such as drunkenness, sickness, injury, pain, extreme fatigue, and certain respiratory ailments may affect a person's suitability as a test subject.

2) *Mental Ills.* Permanent mental illnesses such as mental deficiency or insanity render persons unsuitable. It may be difficult, or impossible, for them to distinghish the truth from a lie, or even to understand the purpose and procedure of the test. Persons of very low intelligence may display little moral sense or fear of being caught in an offense or a lie. Temporary conditions such as severe emotional upset or the influence of a sedative may also disqualify a person as a subject.

d. **Treatment of Subject.** The success of a test depends in part on how the person was treated before he was asked to take the test, the manner in which he was asked to take the test, and how he was treated while awaiting the test.

1) *Routine Questioning.* A proper interview seldom affects the test results, provided it is not unduly long or rigorous. The investigator should not reveal details of the offense to a person who may be asked to take the test. The interview should be

straightforward, without resort to tricks or bluffs or other ruses which upset the subject or make him suspicious, thereby defeating the purpose of the test at the outset.

2) *Asking a Person to Take the Test.* The investigator should inform the subject of his right to take the test and of the fact that he may have counsel present during the test if he so wishes. He should then explain and discuss the test along the following lines:

a) Describe the test to the person in simple language, removing any misconceptions.

b) Suggest the test as a means for the suspect to indicate his innocence. Do not suggest that a refusal to take the test will indicate guilt.

c) Discuss the capability of the test for indicating, through recorded responses, whether a person is telling the truth. Do not make any false or exaggerated claims for the lie detection process.

3) *Treatment During Detention.* The subject should be treated normally, with food and exercise available at appropriate times. The test, however, should be scheduled promptly to avoid unnecessary delays. Suspects in the same case should not be allowed to communicate with each other.

e. **Planning Text Questions.** The investigator can be of great assistance to the examiner in the preparation of the test questions by giving him detailed and verified factual information about the offense. From a study of representative test questions he can become familiar with the kind of information most useful to the examiner.

1) Whenever possible, the investigator should inform the examiner of the unpublicized facts of the offense, particularly those known only to the victim, the offender, and the investigator. He should inform the examiner of the following:

a) Specific articles or exact amounts of money stolen.

b) Peculiar aspects of the offense, such as a strange or obscene act committed at the scene.

c) The exact time at which the offense occurred.

d) Known facts about a suspect's actions or movements.

e) Facts indicating a connection between suspects, victims, and witnesses, especially when they deny any connection.

f) Exact type of firearm, weapon, or tool used.

g) Results of laboratory tests.

2) The questions to be used are constructed by the examiner to be short, simple, and easily understood by the subject. They are formulated so that only a yes or no answer is required. The examiner is interested in the subject's reaction to the immediate sense of the question and not in the subject's difficulties in understanding the question because of its form or wording.

f. **Test Procedures.** The procedure used will vary somewhat with the person tested and the facts of the case. Polygraph experts will vary, too, in their procedures, some having developed more sophisticated techniques which they have found reliable and sometimes more informative. The following are two basic techniques—the *general question* test and the *peak of tension* test—as described by the Office of The Provost Marshal, U.S. Army, in its technical bulletin (TB PMG 22):

1) *General Question Test.* This test consists of a series of relevant (concerning the offense) and irrelevant (not concerning the offense) questions asked in a planned order. The relevant questions are asked in order to obtain a specific response. The irrelevant questions are asked to give the subject relief after pertinent questions and to establish a normal tracing on the test chart. The questions are so arranged that a specific reaction to a relevant question can be compared with a normal tracing made during the answering of an irrelevant question. The reaction may be strong enough to indicate that the subject either did not tell the truth or that he was unduly disturbed by the question. In the general question test, the subject usually does not know beforehand what questions are to be asked. Repeat tests are used.

2) *Peak of Tension Test.* The second type of test depends on the building up of a peak of tension (emotional disturbance). The subject is usually told beforehand the questions that are to be asked. The series contains one question about a specific detail of the offense. The test chart of a subject who is not telling the truth or who is unduly disturbed usually shows a rise in the tracing up to the relevant question (peak of tension) and a decline thereafter. The rise is due to the fact that the subject dreads the question to which he knows he is going to lie. The decline is caused by the relief of knowing that the dreaded question is past. The peak of tension works best if the examiner knows some unpublicized details of the offense. It is also used when the examiner is probing for a weakness in the subject's testimony. Variations of this test are used as preliminary tests to ascertain if a person is capable of giving a reliable response.

g. **Examples of Prepared Questions.** The questions below are based on a sample case. Allen Rowe was found dead in the day room, killed by a bullet from a calibre .45 weapon. Rowe's wallet, which his friends say contained about five hundred dollars, was found beside his body, empty. Investigation reveals John Simpson as a suspect in the murder and robbery of Rowe. Simpson is promptly brought in for a lie detector test, after being informed of his rights and after giving the necessary waivers. The examiner decides to test him first by the *general question* test and then by the *peak of tension test.*

1) *General Question Test.* The following questions might be used: (Note that questions *c*, *d*, *f*, *g*, and *i* are relevant to the case.)

    a) Is your last name Simpson?
    b) Are you over 21?
    c) Do you know who shot Rowe?
    d) Did you shoot Rowe?
    e) Were you born in Indiana?
    f) Did you take Rowe's money?
    g) Did you shoot a calibre .45 pistol last night?
    h) Is your hair brown?
    i) Have you answered my questions truthfully?

2) *Peak of Tension Test.* If the details of the murder and robbery have not been made public and the investigators have not mentioned specific facts to Simpson, the following peak of tension tests might be used:

    a) First Test.
        (1) Did you stab a man?
        (2) Did you poison a man?
        (3) Did you drown a man?
        (4) Did you shoot a man?
        (5) Did you hang a man?
        (6) Did you strangle a man?

    b) Second Test. [The subject is a member of the military.]
        (1) Did you shoot a submachine gun last night?
        (2) Did you shoot a carbine last night?
        (3) Did you shoot an M1 rifle last night?
        (4) Did you shoot a calibre .45 pistol last night?
        (5) Did you shoot a cannon last night?
        (6) Did you shoot a shotgun last night?
        (7) Did you shoot a calibre .22 rifle last night?

h. **Sources of Error.** It should not be expected that a positive conclusion can be reached in every lie detector test even when properly administered; nevertheless, the investigator should not contribute, through any deficiency of his own, to the inadequacy of a test. Most unsatisfactory lie detector examinations are attributable to two main factors: unsuitable subjects and unprepared examiners.

The lack of preparation of the examiner may be the result of a lack of intelligent cooperation on the part of the investigator. The following precautions will assist the investigator in his contribution to the success of the examination:

1) Do not wait until the last minute to ask a person to take the test. The test should not be used as a last resort after all other methods have failed.

2) Do not tell a suspect everything you know about the offense or about him.

3) Do not fail to investigate the case before you ask a person to take the test. Faulty or incomplete investigation is a pitfall. The background information on each subject should be as complete as possible.

4) Do not depend on mass screening of possible suspects to produce a real suspect or the guilty party. The number of subjects should be narrowed as much as possible.

i. **Post-test Questioning.** A period of skillful questioning by the examiner usually follows every lie detector test. The examiner should select an approach based on the information supplied by the investigator, on the subject's background, and on the results of the test and the effects it seems to be having on the person being tested. The investigator should be available to provide any additional information that might assist the examiner.

13. Psychological Stress Evaluator

This instrument is a form of lie detector that depends on a different principle to detect emotional elements in speech production and to deduce therefrom the relative content of truth or falsity. The objective of the inventors of the Psychological Stress Evaluator (PSE) was to achieve a simpler way of detecting lies, one that would eliminate the use of restraining tapes and cords and the consequent emotional strain that might lead to incorrect readings. The subject merely speaks into the microphone or his voice is recorded by other means on magnetic tape that is fed into a machine as small as a portable typewriter which accomplishes an analysis on the voice pattern.

The key to the successful use of the PSE is the preparation of simple selected questions keyed to the individual and structured to reveal normal or truthful answers and responses that are false. Once the personal pattern has been established, any evasive or false answers reveal stress, that is, if a person is not telling the truth, the analysis of his voice pattern will show it.

The principles underlying PSE and its equipment are best described by their inventors: When one speaks, the voice has two modulations—audible modulation and inaudible. The audible portion is what we hear. The inaudible comes from the involuntary areas (those not directly controlled by the brain or thought processes). Internal stress is reflected in the inaudible variations of the voice. These differences cannot be heard, but they can be detected and recorded by the PSE. Superimposed on the audible are inaudible frequency modulations. The FM quality of the voice is susceptible to the amount of stress that one may be under in speaking. To the human ear, a person may sound perfectly normal, free of tremors or 'guilt-revealing' sound variations. The PSE senses the differences and records the changes in inaudible FM qualities of the voice on the chart. When the chart is interpreted by an experienced examiner, it reveals the key stress areas of the person being questioned.

The advantages of PSE, as suggested by their manufacturers, include simplicity, fewer moving parts, ease of operation, and the provision of a permanent record of the interview which can be reexamined at a later date. One should mention, too, the possibility of surreptitious use, since the PSE can be used to analyze tapes recorded from telephone lines or hidden microphones. Indeed, a voice-stress analyzer called the Hagoth® has already been designed to work directly over the telephone and without the need for a tape recording. The instrument is already on the market with reportedly respectable sales. The ethical and legal questions raised by such an apparatus are formidable. Some indication of official reaction was given by Governor Carey of New York in 1978 when he signed into law a bill that prohibits an employer from requiring, requesting, suggesting, or knowingly permitting a worker or job applicant to be subject to a test on a psychological stress evaluator.

Although it is rather early to discuss the relative merits of this mode of lie detection, polygraph manufacturers consider voice analyzers inferior because they monitor only one supposed indicator of stress where polygraphs typically monitor three (blood pressure, respiration, and the electrical conductivity of skin surfaces).

ADDITIONAL READING

Aubry, A.S. and Caputo, R.R.: *Criminal Interrogation*, 2nd ed. Springfield, Ill.: Thomas, 1972.

Bristow, A.P.: *Field Interrogation*, 2nd ed. Springfield, Ill.: Thomas, 1964.

Burke, J.J.: Confessions to Private Persons. 42 *FBI Law Enforcement Bulletin*, 8, 1973.

Crowley, W.D.: The Interrogation of Suspects. 28 *International Criminal Police Review*, 269, 1973.

Cunningham, C.: Interrogation. *Medico-Legal Journal*, 2, 1973.

Haney, T.D., Jr.: The Need to Repeat Miranda Warnings at Subsequent Interrogations. 12 *Washburn Law Journal*, 222, 1973.

Hirtle, S.: Inadmissible Confessions and their Fruits. 60 *Journal of Criminal Law, Criminology, and Police Science*, 58, 1969.

Inbau, F.E. and Reid, J.E.: *Criminal Interrogation and Confessions*, 2nd ed. Baltimore, Williams and Wilkins, 1965.

Marshall, J., Narqui, K.H., and Oskamp, S.: Effects of Kinds of Questions and Atmosphere of Interrogation on Accuracy and Completeness of Testimony. 84 *Harvard Law Review*, 1620, 1971.

Nedrud, D.R.: *The Supreme Court and the Law of Criminal Investigation.* Chicago, Law Enforcement Pub., 1969.

Pilcher, W.D.: The Law and Practice of Field Interrogation. 58 *Journal of Criminal Law, Criminology, and Police Science*, 465, 1967.

Raciborski, E.P.: On Interrogation of Suspects. 18 *Military Police Journal*, 6, 1969.

Reinhardt, J.M.: The Wish to Confess. 14 *Police*, 50, 1969.

Sable, M.E.: *Miranda* Warnings in Other Than Police Custodial Interrogations. 21 *Cleveland State Law Review*, 135, 1972.

Shapiro, H.R.: *Miranda* Without Warning: Derivative Evidence as Forbidden Fruit. 41 *Brooklyn Law Review*, 2, 1974.

Smith, J.V.: Threshold Questions in Applying *Miranda*: What Constitutes Custodial Interrogation. 25 *South Carolina Law Review*, 699, 1974.

Van Meter, C.H.: *Principles of Police Interrogation.* Springfield, Ill.: Thomas, 1973.

Witt, J.W.: Non-Coercive Interrogation and the Administration of Criminal Justice. 64 *Journal of Criminal Law, Criminology, and Police Science*, 320, 1973.

Detection of Deception

Ansley, N. (Ed.): *Legal Admissibility of the Polygraph*. Springfield, Ill.: Thomas, 1975.

Barland, G.H.: Reliability of Polygraph Chart Evaluations. 1 *Polygraph*, 4, 1972.

Bernstein, P.: Prosecution and the Polygraph. 2 *Polygraph*, 2, 1973.

The Emergence of the Polygraph at the Trial. 73 *Columbia Law Review*, 1120, 1973.

Ferguson, R.J., Jr. and Miller, A.L.: *The Polygraph in Court*. Springfield, Ill.: Thomas, 1973.

Hunter, F.L. and Ash, P.: The Accuracy and Consistency of Polygraph Examiners' Diagnosis. 1 *Journal of Police Science and Administration*, 370, 1973.

Inbau, F.E. and Reid, J.E.: *Truth and Deception: The Polygraph (Lie Detector) Technique*, 2nd ed. Baltimore, Williams and Wilkins, 1978.

Kubis, J.F.: Comparison of Voice Analysis and Polygraph as Lie Detection Procedures. 3 *Polygraph*, 1, 1974.

Larson, J.A.: *Lying and its Detection—A Study of Deception Tests*. Montclair, N.J.: Patterson Smith, 1969.

Polygraph: A Critical Appraisal. 8 *Journal of the Beverly Hills Bar Association*, 35, 1974.

Scientific V. Judicial Acceptance. 27 *University of Miami Law Review*, 254, 1972.

Chapter 10

ADMISSIONS, CONFESSIONS, AND WRITTEN STATEMENTS

1. General

THE ART of interviewing and interrogating is properly supplemented by a knowledge of the procedures for reducing the information acquired to a formal written statement. It is, of course, required that the statement be made knowingly and voluntarily—under the same conditions, in brief, as those which should obtain before a subject is interrogated. If the subject, after intelligently waiving his rights, has brought himself to confess, it may require but a simple additional request by the investigator for him to provide a written version of his statement or to sign a typed version that accurately reflects the information he has given orally. When the spirit of confession has been invoked, the investigator should try to obtain the information in several different forms, of which the written form is considered by many to be the most desirable. It is not sufficient that he, the investigator, knows that the subject has acknowledged guilt. The persons who will prosecute the case find special encouragement in a written confession. Such a statement, freely made and correctly accomplished to include reference to each of the elements of the offense and to indicate that the confession is knowingly and voluntarily given, is a source of reassurance also to law enforcement supervisors, who somehow find such a statement more convincing in a report of investigation than a simple recounting by the investigator of the accused's acknowledgment of guilt and description of the circumstances.

By way of expectancy, the investigator should remember that almost half of all felony defendants make a confession. Defendants accused of property crimes are much more likely to confess to the police than those accused of crimes against the person—presumably because of the persuasiveness of the evidence that can be used to convince the suspect that a denial is hopeless.

2. Relative Importance

There is a tendency on the part of even professional investigators to exaggerate the value of such a confession and to misinterpret its significance. The written confession does not, for example, prove the matters to which it pertains. Often the written statement is not considered admissible and does not become part of the evidence in the case. Moreover, if the written confession is admitted in evidence it will be subjected to the closest scrutiny by defense counsel. Above all, the question of voluntariness is commonly raised by defense counsel and accusations of duress and coercion are brought against the prosecution witnesses. Finally, proof of the elements of the offense should be developed by the investigator independently of the written confession for presentation to the court. He should continue with his investigation and bring it to its completion as though the written confession existed mainly for the purpose of providing guidelines and additional leads for the inquiry as well as a number of details which must be separately proved to supply additional evidence or to serve as a check on the information already acquired.

Confessions have been called "the prime source of other evidence." Often it provides the investigator with information that would be otherwise unavailable—for example, the scope of a conspiracy, the existence and identity of accomplices, additional past offenses attributable to the same person or group, and so forth. Physical evidence that will be later analyzed through a confession or admission: the existence and location of a firearm used in the commission of a crime; the location of an automobile used in an assault; and the location of stolen property are a few examples.

3. Purpose

In addition to providing some of the general investigative advantages described above, the obtaining of written statements can serve the following specific purposes:

a. To provide a written record for the case file.

b. For use by the prosecution at the trial to refresh recollection, impeach witnesses, and, in general, monitor to some extent the testimony.

c. To discourage a witness from wrongfully changing his testimony at the trial.

d. To assist the prosecution in planning its presentation by reducing the element of surprise that unforeseen testimony would introduce.

4. Admissions

An admission is a self-incriminatory statement by the subject falling short of an acknowledgment of guilt. It is an acknowledgment of a fact or circumstance from which guilt may be inferred. It implicates but does not directly incriminate. A simple statement to the effect that the subject was present at the scene of the crime may be an admission. Coupled with such circumstances as the existence of a motive, the admission may provide an inference of guilt. Traditionally, in all courts the prosecution has been permitted to introduce an admission as evidence without first showing that it was made freely and voluntarily. The *Miranda* decision, however, would suggest that admissions and exculpatory statements are to be treated just like confessions:

> The warnings required and the waiver necessary in accordance with our opinion today are, in the absence of a fully effective equivalent, prerequisites to the admissibility of any statement made by a defendant. No distinction can be drawn between statements which amount to "admissions" of part or all of the offense. The privilege against self-incrimination protects the individual from being compelled to incriminate himself in any manner; it does not distinguish degrees of incrimination. Similarly, for precisely the same reason, no distinction may be drawn between inculpatory statements and statements alleged to be merely "exculpatory." [A statement is said to be exculpatory if it is designed to vindicate, to excuse or to free from blame or guilt.] If a statement made were in fact truly exculpatory it would, of course, never be used by the prosecution. In fact, statements merely intended to be exculpatory by the defendant are often used to impeach his testimony at trial or to demonstrate untruths in the statement given under interrogation and thus to prove guilt by implication. These statements are incriminating in any meaningful sense of the word and may not be used

without the full warnings and effective waiver required for any other statement. In *Escobedo* itself, the defendant fully intended his accusation of another to be exculpatory as to himself.

5. Confessions

A confession is a direct acknowledgment of the truth of the guilty fact as charged or of some essential part of the commission of the criminal act itself. To be admissible, a confession must be *voluntary* and *trustworthy*. In addition, the Supreme Court has stated that if a confession is to be used in a federal or state prosecution it must have been obtained by *civilized police practices*. The giving of the fourfold warning of rights is a necessary but not a sufficient condition for the voluntariness and trustworthiness of a subsequent confession. The use of coercion, unlawful influence, or unlawful inducement is obviously outside the limits of civilized police practice. Some examples of circumstances which would render a confession inadmissible are threats of bodily harm or of imposition of confinement; illegal detainment; deprivation of necessities or necessary privileges; physical oppression; promises of immunity, clemency, or of substantial reward or benefit likely to induce a confession or admission from the particular accused.

6. Demonstrating Voluntariness

The prosecution may not use statements, whether exculpatory or inculpatory, stemming from custodial interrogation of the accused unless it demonstrates the use of procedural safeguards effective to secure the privilege against self-incrimination. The investigator, then, must be able to prove, through his own testimony and that of witnesses, for example, that he informed the accused of his right to remain silent and of his right to counsel either of his own choice or appointed by the state if he is indigent. Further, the investigator should be able to make an affirmative showing to the effect that a confession was voluntarily given by evidence of one of the following:

a. The statement was not obtained by urging or by request but was a spontaneous or self-induced utterance of the accused.

b. The statement was obtained without coercion and not during an official investigation nor while the accused was in custody.

c. The statement was obtained during an official investigation after the accused had been informed of the nature of the offense, of his right to remain silent, of the fact that the evidence he might give could be used against him at a trial, and of the fact that counsel would be made available to him if he so requested.

d. The accused knowingly waived his right to remain silent and his right to have counsel before making the statement. (A written and witnessed waiver is preferable.)

7. Illustrative Case

In stressing the need for care in demonstrating voluntariness, it may appear that undue emphasis is being placed on fairly obvious points. It should be remembered, however, that the investigator presenting a written confession of the accused for admission into evidence is often looked upon with skepticism and even distrust. He has, in recent years, been given a bad press. Defense counsel, for example, may for the benefit of the jury suggest that a detective may be described as a person who collects signatures on typed confessions. The magistrate, especially, will have a keen sense of the "heavy burden resting on the Government to demonstrate that the defendant knowingly and intelligently waived his privilege against self-incrimination and the right to retained or appointed counsel." The *Miranda* case will serve to illustrate the fact that ordinary care in obtaining a statement may not suffice. The two police officers in this case, after a two-hour interrogation, "emerged from the interrogation room with a written confession signed by Miranda. At the top of the statement was a typed paragraph stating that the confession was made voluntarily, without threats or promises of immunity and with 'full knowledge of my legal rights, understanding any statement I make may be used against me.' . . . The mere fact that he signed a statement which contained a typed-in clause stating that he had 'full knowledge' of his 'legal rights' does not approach the knowing and intelligent waiver required to relinquish constitutional rights."

8. Depositions

A deposition is the testimony of a witness reduced to writing under oath or affirmation, before a person empowered to administer oaths, in answer to interrogatories (questions) and cross-interrogations submitted by the party desiring the deposition and the opposite party. A deposition is used ordinarily to take the testimony of a witness who will be at a prohibitive distance from the scene of the trial at the time of the trial, or who for some reason would be unable to testify in person at the trial. Ordinarily a deposition should be taken by an attorney and not an investigator.

9. Reducing Statements to Writing

Whenever possible, important statements of witnesses and suspects should be reduced to writing. Specifically, written statements should be taken from:
   a. Subjects and suspects.
   b. Recalcitrant or reluctant witnesses.
   c. Key witnesses.
   d. Any witness who gives an indication of a tendency to change his mind.
   e. Witnesses who will not be available at legal proceedings.

10. Content of the Statement

A lengthy interrogation will develop much information that is unnecessary in the sense of being irrelevant or immaterial. When the subject finally consents to make a written statement, the investigator must then decide what information he wishes to be included in the statement. The exercise of good judgment at this point is important since the subject may subsequently refuse to make an additional statement to remedy any deficiencies in the first.
   a. **Witnesses.** In taking a statement from a witness, the investigator should consider what information the witness may possess and could normally be expected to give in testimony and

second what information is needed for support of the case. The common ground of these two considerations should form the substance of the statement.

b. **Suspects.** The statement of a suspect should substantiate the elements of the charge or contain any information pertinent to the issues of the case. In addition, the statement should include any details of extenuating circumstances or explanations offered by the suspect. Finally, the investigator should apply to the statement the criteria applicable to judging a report of investigation. The purposes of such a report are:

1) Provision of a permanent record of the information.

2) Presentation of clear, direct, complete, and accurate communication.

3) Presentation of information that can form the basis of charges and specifications.

4) Provision of information that can form the basis of additional investigation.

11. Methods of Taking Statements

Although there should be no delay in reducing a confession to writing, the investigator should not interrupt the suspect once he has launched himself into a freely flowing recital. At this point the suspect, although quite willing to speak of his participation in the crime, may be psychologically unprepared to commit his words to the formality of writing. At no time should the investigator weaken his position by appearing excessively eager to put the confession in writing. He should expedite the procedure by having the date line and introductory matter of the statement prepared in advance. The methods which he will employ in reducing the statement to writing will depend on the intelligence and temperament of the suspect; the amount and nature of the information to be recorded; and the availability of stenographic services. The following are some of the methods that may be employed: (The methods are applicable to statements in general.)

a. The subject may write his own statement without guidance. A statement of this nature, which is suficiently comprehensive, is the most desirable form.

b. The subject may dictate to a stenographer without guidance.

c. The investigator may give the subject a list of the essential points to be covered in the statement and suggest that he include these matters and add whatever other pertinent information he may wish.

d. The subject may deliver his statement orally in his own way to the investigator, who writes the statement.

e. The subject may deliver his statement orally to the investigator or a stenographer in response to questions put to him by the investigator. The responses are recorded verbatim.

f. The investigator may assist the subject in dictating his statement by suggesting words and locutions which will express the subject's intended meaning. Naturally, great caution must be exercised by the investigator to protect himself from a charge of influencing the subject. A taped recording is useful.

g. The investigator may prepare the statement by writing his version of the information given by the subject. He should try to use expressions employed by the subject and submit the statement to him for corrections and changes.

12. Form for Statements

Although different law enforcement agencies will employ varying formats, the following outline of a statement will be found common to many of them and generally satisfactory.

a. **Identifying Data.** The first paragraph of a statement should contain the date, place, identification of the maker, the name of the person to whom the statement is made, and a declaration by the maker that the statement is being made voluntarily, with any necessary waivers.

b. **The Body.** The body of the statement can be given in expository or narrative form. It is of great importance, particularly in a confession, that the statement include all the elements of the crime and the facts associating the subject to these elements. The words of the subject should be used, but the scope of the confession should be guided by the investigator. The investigator may write the statement himself to insure the inclusion of all the necessary details.

The subject should afterwards be requested to read the statement and sign each page at the bottom. In order to establish more firmly the fact that that subject read the statement, it is well to include several errors—typographic or otherwise—and request the subject to correct any errors in reading and to initial the corrections in ink. If the subject fails to recognize the errors, they should be called to his attention. Each page should be numbered by writing in the lower right corner: "Page__of__Pages."

c. **Conclusion.** The concluding paragraph should state that the subject has read the document of so many pages and that he has signed it. The subject should then be requested to sign the statement on each page and initial corrections as described above.

13. Witnesses to a Confession

The presence of witnesses will provide a defense in rebutting claims that duress in the form of threats or promises was employed by the investigator. After the investigator has prepared the statement for signature, witnesses may be introduced so that they can later testify to the following:

a. That the subject read and revised the entire statement with the investigator.

b. That the subject objected to certain words, phrases, or statements.

c. That he corrected certain words and phrases and initialed the corrections.

d. That he evidently understood the contents of the confession.

e. That he was in his right senses, knew what he was doing, and acted voluntarily.

f. That he acknowledged the statement to be true and correct. Each person witnessing the signature should sign as a witness. The signatures should show their names and addresses. If the witness is a member of the law enforcement agency, his signature should be accompanied by his grade, title, and assignment.

14. Swearing to the Statement

If it is desired to have the subject sworn to the statement, all persons should stand. The investigator should instruct the subject to raise his right hand. The investigator should also raise his right hand and proceed to recite the oath. Although there is no fixed form for the oath, the following will be found generally applicable:

"Do you (state name of subject) solemny swear that the statement which you have made and to which you are about to affix your signature is the truth, the whole truth, and nothing but the truth? So help you, God."

After the subject is sworn, the statement is signed by the subject, the investigator administering the oath, and the witnesses.

15. Investigation Subsequent to the Confession

At the conclusion of a successful interrogation, the investigator, although he is in possession of a written confession, should not yield to a feeling of complacency. The investigation should not be considered complete until the confession has been critically reviewed in relation to the charge. The following points should be considered:

a. On the information available, can it be said that the elements of proof have been established?

b. What substantiating evidence is needed to sustain the facts which are contained in the statement or which have been developed in the interrogation?

c. Is there sufficient evidence, independent of the confession, which can be presented in court to show that the offense charged has probably been committed by someone? The significance of the question lies in the fact that, normally, an accused cannot be convicted upon his confession or admission unless his statement is substantiated by other evidence. Moreover, the court may not consider the confession as evidence against the defendant unless there is in the record of trial other evidence, either direct or circumstantial, that the crime charged has probably been committed. Additional confessions by the accused cannot be used to corroborate information found in any one of the confessions.

16. Statement Forms

The following representative forms have been found acceptable in courts:

a. STATEMENT OF SUSPECT

Personally appeared before me, the undersigned authority for administering oaths, ... who has been advised that he need not make any statement, and any statement he makes may be used against him in any proceeding, civil or criminal, and that he may, at his request, have the benefit of free legal counsel before making any statement; and who declares that the following statement is given freely and voluntarily, and without promise of benefit, or threat or use of force or duress; does proceed, under oath, to state as follows:

I, ..., have been advised that I need not make any statement and that any statement I make may be used against me in any proceeding, civil or criminal. I . . .

(BODY OF STATEMENT)

I have read the foregoing statement consisting of . . . . pages which I have initialed and signed and I state that it is true and correct to the best of my knowledge and belief. (DECLARANT HANDWRITING)

....

(Signature)

Sworn and subscribed to before me this . . . . day of...........................

/s/..

....

OFFICIAL TITLE /t/..

WITNESSED:.. ....

(Signature) (Address)

....

(Signature) (Address)

b. STATEMENT OF A WITNESS

Dated............................

I,.. ,having been duly advised that I need not make this statement and that it may be used against me in any proceeding, civil or criminal, declare that the following statement is given freely and voluntarily, without promise of benefit, or threat or use of force or duress, do proceed to state as follows:

(BODY OF STATEMENT)

I have read the foregoing statement consisting of . . . . pages which I have initialed and signed, and I state that it is true and correct to the best of my knowledge and belief. (DECLARANT HANDWRITING)

....

(Signature)

WITNESSED: ....

(Signature) (Address)

....

(Signature) (Address)

17. Admissibility of Confessions

A confession which is obtained under duress or by compulsion or without the continuous presence of the prescribed constitutional safeguards is inadmissible in court. The investigator who obtains a confession through the employment of illegal practices renders inadmissible not only the suspect's statement but very likely the evidence which might subsequently be developed from the leads contained in the statement. Hence great care and sound judgment must be exercised in obtaining a confession to avoid casting a shadow on its legality. The investigator must have a thorough knowledge of the court requirements for admissibility and of the procedural safeguards and standards of conduct by which it is insured.

a. **Tests for Admissibility.** The test employed by state and federal courts for the admissibility of a confession is the following: *A confession must be voluntary and trustworthy, and it must have been obtained by civilized police practices*. The Supreme Court requires more than the voluntary-trustworthy test in demanding that the police methods should not be "inherently coercive" and should be attended continuously by the prescribed protective devices. Regardless of the actual effect of the police behavior on the accused in giving the confession, the Supreme Court requires that this behavior should not even have a *tendency* to compel a confession. Further, the Court considers the susceptibilities of the individual defendant in these cases rather than the police methods in general.

b. **Meeting the Tests.** In the present and the preceding chapter a number of the procedural safeguards for meeting the test of admissibility have been treated. They are summarized and referenced below:

1) *Fourfold Warning.* The foremost requirement, upon which later admissibility of a confession depends, is that a fourfold warning be given to a person before he is questioned (see p. 105).

2) *Proof of Waiver.* To forgo these rights an affirmative statement of rejection is required. No conclusion can be drawn from a suspect's silence after the warnings have been given. An express statement, preferably written and witnessed, that the suspect is willing to make a statement and does not wish an attorney may constitute a

satisfactory waiver. In any event, a positive showing should be made to meet "the high standards of proof of waiver of constitutional rights required by the Court." (see p. 106.)

3) ***Proof of Voluntariness.*** "The voluntariness doctrine . . . encompasses all interrogation practices which are likely to exert such pressure on an individual as to disable him from making a free and rational choice." Again, the investigator should be prepared to make a positive showing to the effect that the statement or confession was voluntarily given (see p. 133).

4) ***Record of Conduct.*** The record of the interrogation, including the investigator's notes and the interrogation log (p. 117), should reflect the continuous availability of protective devices for the suspect's rights, the absence of any threats, tricks, or cajolings to obtain a waiver of rights, and the absence of all forms of duress and coercion in the conduct of the interrogation as described below. The testimony of witness is part of the record.

18. Forms of Duress and Coercion

Police behavior which would adversely affect the admissibility of a confession may be classified into three types of restraint: *Coercion, Duress,* and *Psychological Constraint.*

a. **Coercion.** The term *coercion* connotes the idea of physical force; it is the direct application of illegal physical methods. This obviously refers to beatings or forms of assault such as hitting with a rubber hose or newspaper, punching, using glaring lights, administering cathartics, placing a man in a brace, forms of torture, and so forth. The threat of such abuse is also included in this category.

b. **Duress.** Duress is taken here in the legal sense to mean the imposition of restrictions on physical behavior. This includes prolonged (six hours, for example) detention in a dark cell; privation of food or sleep; imposing conditions of excessive physical discomfort; and continuous interrogation over extraordinarily long periods such as twenty-four hours. If arrangements are made for appropriate intervals of rest, the investigator may interrogate over reasonable (reasonable, that is, in relation to the amount of information that is required in the case) periods of time, several days or weeks, for example, without violating this prohibition against duress provided, of course, the protective devices are continuously available to the accused—that is, the accused should at all times be able to invoke his right to remain silent and his right to have counsel present. In considering the probable effects of indirect physical abuse in the form of duress, the age, sex, temperament, and physical condition of the subject must be considered.

c. **Psychological Constraint.** The free action of the will may be unlawfully restrained by threats or other methods of instilling fear. Moral restraint by means of threats can destroy the voluntariness of a confession. Obliquely suggesting the prospect of harm to the suspect, his relatives, or his property can be interpreted as psychological abuse even though these suggestions do not assume the form of explicit threats. A susceptible person could, under these circumstances, be induced to give a false confession. It is sufficient that the subject reasonably thought he was placed in sufficient danger. To tell the subject that he will be hanged or given over to a mob unless he confesses or to state that he will be sent to jail for more serious crimes is sufficient to affect admissibility. Some courts have gone so far as to hold that the use of the following statements constitutes a threat: "You had better confess"; or "It would be better for you to confess"; or even, "You had better tell the *truth*." However, it is permitted to employ the following techniques: to tell the subject that the police will discover the truth anyway; that the subject may tell what he wishes and run the risk of imprisonment; to display impatience with the subject's story; and to give the underlying impression that the investigator considers the subject guilty.

19. Deception and Promises

No deception, promises, threats, tricks, or cajolings may be used to obtain from the suspect a waiver of his rights. If we assume, now, that waivers have been properly obtained and the suspect has submitted to interrogation, to what extent may the investigation use deception and promises in his questioning without jeopardizing the legality of a confession or statement? The safest policy and, no doubt, the one more consonant with the character of the investigator is to avoid all deception and promises, thereby obviating misunderstandings and misinterpretations that can later render a confession inadmissible.

a. **Employment of Trickery and Deception.** The working rule traditionally applicable in state courts is the following: Trickery and deception may be used if they are not of such a nature as to be likely to lead the subject into a false confession. The following are examples of deceptions that have been considered permissible by the state courts: (1) informing the subject that his accomplice has confessed; (2) pretending that cogent evidence such as additional witnesses or documents exists. Although the use of these ruses has not been specifically prohibited by the Supreme Court, implied disapproval could be deduced from the *Miranda* decision, which was devoted to the provision of safeguards to protect the overly susceptible from even the minor subtleties of interrogation tactics.

b. **Employment of Promises.** The use of promises may render a confession inadmissible. The following test should be applied: Is the promise of such a nature that it is likely to cause the subject to make a confession?

Examples of the substance of promises which can render a confession inadmissible are:

1) Release from custody.
2) Cessation of prosecution.
3) Pardon.
4) Lighter sentence.
5) Grant of immunity or remission of sentence.
6) Prosecution for only one of several crimes.

20. Other Uses of Confessions

a. **Confessions of Several Crimes.** It is not desirable to permit a number of crimes to be included in the confession. In a trial for one crime it is ordinarily not permissible to bring in evidence which shows that the defendant committed another crime except where the additional crimes tend to establish:

1) Intent.
2) Guilty knowledge.
3) Identity of the defendant.
4) The scheme used in the commission of the crime being tried.

Actually, if the additional crime is part of the same transaction, the confession is admissible. A written confession, however, should be drawn up with one offense in view.

b. **Use of One Defendant's Confession Against Another.** A confession of a defendant may be used against his accomplice if the latter, when first knowing of the confession, fails to deny it. The confession cannot be used unless the confessor himself so testifies in court or unless the confession had previously been made in the presence of the accomplice and he failed to deny it. Thus, the investigator, on receiving such a confession, should have the confessor confront the accomplice with the accusation. In many states, the silence of the accomplice may be used as evidence of his guilt.

21. Summary

It should be apparent that the matter of a confession must be approached by the investigator with great caution. The subject must be advised of his constitutional rights. Threats or other forms of duress should be avoided. Oral confessions are valid, but written ones are obviously preferable. Witnesses should be present to the confession and its circumstances. An accused should be taken before a committing magistrate within the time limit provided by statute. Finally, if wrong police methods have been used in interrogation, it is possible to later obtain a valid confession by showing that the threats or other abusive influences had been removed and that their effect could no longer be reasonably said to exist.

ADDITIONAL READING

Inbau, F.E. and Reid, J.E.: *Criminal Interrogation and Confessions,* 2nd ed. Baltimore, Williams and Wilkins, 1965.

Inbau, F.E.: Legally Permissible Criminal Interrogation Tactics and Techniques. 4
   Journal of Police Science and Administration, 249, 1976.
Invergo, M.: Questioning Techniques and Written Statements. 5 *Police Law
   Quarterly*, 3, 1976.
Schafer, W.J.: *Confessions and Statements*. Springfield, Ill.: Thomas, 1968.
Van Meter, C.H.: *Principles of Police Interrogation*. Springfield, Ill.: Thomas,
   1973.

Chapter 11

RECORDING INTERVIEWS
AND INTERROGATIONS

1. Methods of Reproduction

A INTERVIEW or an interrogation may not be considered a success unless it is faithfully reproduced in its significant parts. The retention of information received in a sensitive interview is a recurring problem of investigation which may be solved in a number of ways.

a. **Mental Notes.** Relying on simple memory has the advantage of permitting an uninterrupted flow of information without inspiring caution by the appearance of pencil and paper. The disadvantages are obvious. The untrained memory may come away from an interview with little more than a general impression and a few phrases.

b. **Written Notes.** Although a great improvement over mere memory, written notes must necessarily be sketchy. They suffice to record significant data. As a tool of the routine interview, they are satisfactory. An interrogation, which may be accompanied by an oral confession, requires more exact reproduction. A flood of information may overwhelm the interrogator when dealing with a subject who suddenly becomes willing to speak freely.

c. **Stenographic Notes.** The presence of a stenographer may deter a hesitant subject. Moreover, the investigator seldom has stenographic facilities at his disposal.

d. **Sound Recording.** The disc, tape, or wire recording has been found to be the simplest and most practical means of reproducing the interview or the interrogation. It requires, of course, physical preparation and a moderate degree of technical facility.

e. **Sound Motion Picture.** The ideal solution is the sound motion picture or videotape, that combination of sound and sight which most nearly represents to the senses the event itself. In important cases where the subject confesses and agrees to re-enact the crime, a sound film will provide the most convincing evidence for presentation to the jury. The surreptitious use of sound films for the purpose of obtaining evidence has been admirably exemplified by the techniques employed in a well-known spy ring case. In this investigation, trained agents elaborately prepared a room for shooting a sound film. A table was prepared under light of an intensity sufficient to permit film exposure without arousing suspicion. The meeting room adjoined a bathroom providing a line of sight from the medicine chest through the door to the table. Behind the specially prepared half-silvered (two-way) mirror of the door of the medicine chest, a motion picture camera was set up. For this arrangement, the wall behind the medicine chest had been knocked down so that the camera could be set up in the adjoining room with the lens behind the mirror. Relatively intense illumination was used on the conspirators. The resulting film provided impressive evidence and indubitably identified the participants of the conference.

2. Recording

One of the characteristics of modern criminal investigation is the extensive use of recording devices for the production of a transcript of interviews and interrogations. Obviously, the best evidence of an interview is the recorded voice. The words themselves are there; the tones and inflection provide the true meaning; the author of the statement is identifiable. For these and other reasons, wherever it is possible and practicable, an effort is made to record an important interview. Although the recording of a conversation appears at first glance to be a fairly simple process, the investigator who attempts a transcript without training and preparation usually must learn by the embarrassing deficiencies of his initial efforts that there is both an art and a science associated with this branch of investigative work. Because of the wide variety, both in size and quality, of the recording systems on the market, no attempt at a treatment of the technical aspects of these instruments would be feasible in this compass.

3. Types of Recording

There are two general types of recording: the overt and the surreptitious, the use of each being suggested by the nature of the case.

a. **Overt Transcripts.** Often there is no need to conceal the fact that a recording is being made of an interview. The suggestion to record the conversation may be made by the investigator or the interviewee. Some men occupying important positions make a practice of recording such interviews for their own protection. The nature of the interview will determine whether the investigator should suggest that a recording be made. If the witness is "friendly to the prosecution" and the information which he has to offer is somewhat complicated in nature, the most practical procedure is to request permission to record. A courtesy copy of the record may be given to the interviewee if he so requests. The advantage of this solution to the reproduction problem is the relative ease with which the recording can be made with the cooperation of both parties. Recordings of telephone conversations can also be more simply made with permission of the subject. Arrangements can be made with the telephone company for the necessary apparatus. A fifteen-second signal is imposed on the line to inform the subject that a recording is being made.

b. **Surreptitious Transcripts.** More commonly, the recording of an interview or an interrogation will be made without the knowledge of the subject. Sensitive interviews and interrogations should always be recorded in important cases. The following embrace most of the situations which will be encountered by the investgator:

1) *Interrogation Room.* The room set apart for interrogations or for interviews in the offices of the law enforcement agency should be equipped with a permanent recording installation. The live telephone (the mouthpiece is rewired to bypass the hook switch and transmit sound) is the preferred instrument. The microphone

disguised as a calendar pad may prove adequate with inexperienced subjects.

2) *Rooms Prepared on Short Notice.* If the subject must be interviewed at some place other than the investigator's office, it will be necessary to make an installation in a relatively short time. The telephone can be made into a live microphone or the calendar pad can be used. A microphone can also be installed in a desk. Whatever arrangements are made, they should be carefully tested beforehand. Failures are quite common as a result of the work of inexperienced technicians.

3) *Unprepared Meeting Places.* If the interview must take place in a room, automobile, or restaurant without previous technical preparation, a pocket recorder can be used or one which is concealed in a briefcase. The investigator can be *wired* for the occasion, i.e., a microphone and small recorder can be attached to his person and concealed beneath his clothes.

4) *Telephone Conversations.* In recording interviews which take place over the telephone, special equipment must be used. In some communities, the legality of the procedure must be considered.

4. Purpose of Recording

The techniques and care exercised in making a recording will vary with the purpose of the interview or the interrogation.

a. **Interview.** If the purpose of the interview is merely to obtain information, no special technique is required. Where the information is to be used as evidence, as in the case of a witness who may later refuse to testify, the precautions described below must be observed.

b. **Interrogation.** The purpose in recording an interrogation may be one of the following:

1) *Evidence for Court Presentation.* Admissions and confessions should be reproduced. If the subject later refuses to make a formal confession or changes his "story," the recording can serve as evidence.

2) *Contradictions.* During the interrogation the subject may deny guilt or knowledge of the crime and may offer elaborate alibis

and excuses. If he is persistently interrogated, he may contradict himself or fall into inconsistencies. By recording the interrogation and playing it back to the subject, he may be brought to appreciate the futility of deception.

3) *Implication of Associates.* The information supplied by the subject may tend to show the guilt of associates or accomplices. The record can later be played for the associates for the purpose of inducing them to confess.

4) *Assisting Later Interrogations.* In the first interrogation of the subject, a long and relatively complicated story or recital of facts will often be given. At the moment it may be difficult for the interrogator to detect the weak points or the inconsistencies in the subject's statement. To further question by wild guessing or improving with the data at hand may weaken the position of the interrogator and give confidence to the subject. If the interrogation is interrupted after the first recital of the story, the investigator can leisurely listen to the statement, analyze it for consistency and credibility, and check certain points for trustworthiness. After determining the weak points, he can then plan the strategy and tactics to be employed in the next interrogation session.

5. Techniques

The mechanics and physical principles of recording are described in textbooks and manuals. Additional instructions can be obtained from the manufacturer's directions for the equipment used. The present section deals with the tactics that must be employed by the investigator in order to obtain an effective recording of an interview for the purpose of evidence.

a. **Radio Techniques.** The methods of recording are those of radio broadcasting and not television. The investigator must put himself in the position of the future listener. A recording made by an untrained investigator may result in a meaningless jumble of voices and unintelligible references. The investigator must imagine himself as a radio director. The performance must be managed so that the listener can understand *what* is being said; by *whom* it is being spoken; and *what object* is being referred to at any given moment. In a surreptitious recording, the investigator is at the disadvantage of being restrained from giving explicit directions; he must avoid by obvious mannerisms divulging the fact of the recording.

b. **Identifying Persons.** The interview may involve two or three persons. Since many persons have voices which are not readily distinguishable, for the recording to serve as evidence the voices must be identified as being those of specific individuals. To achieve an identification of voices, the investigator should refer to the interviewees as often as possible by name. This can be conveniently accomplished under the guise of excessive courtesy. A statement may be associated with a definite person by tagging the conclusion with a remark addressed to the author such as, "Was that on Tuesday, Mr. Smith?" or "Was that the same check, Mr. Jones?" The statement can also be associated by a leading question such as "What did Brown say to you, Mr. Smith?"

c. **Identifying Objects.** If the recording is made by an inexperienced investigator, sentences such as the following may be heard: "I gave him this other check"; or "He made this entry in the book." Such statements are not effective for evidence purposes because the object to which reference is made cannot be identified by the listener from the recording alone. The investigator should follow such a statement by an identifying question of his own, such as "You mean check number four, Mr. Smith?" or "That is, he wrote these words 'No Sales' on line 14 of page 24. Is that correct, Mr. Jones?" Although these statements may appear stilted on paper, to the interviewee they will seem to be the normal plodding methods of the mediocre investigator. The investigator may not impress the interviewee with these tedious, repetitive questions, but he will rescue the recording from becoming a meaningless recital of untagged pronouns.

d. **Describing Physical Action.** If the interviewee's statements involve the simulation of some physical act, the investigator must manage to include a description of the action in the recording. For example, the victim of an assault may, as part of his narrative, imitate the motions of his assailant in delivering a blow and accompany the action with some non-descriptive sentence such as "He hit me here like this. . . . " The investigator can then follow such a statement with a few clarifying sentences. "Let me get this straight, Mr. Brown. You were standing sideways, 2 feet from Black when Black swung his right fist and hit you on the back of the neck just below the left ear. Have I got it right?"

e. **Overt Transcripts.** If the recording is being made with the knowledge and consent of the interviewee, more elaborate precautions can be made to clarify the identity of the speakers and the objects to which reference is made. If there are a number of persons present, the speaker may be identified before he begins. If several speakers overlap, a request can be made to repeat the statements separately. At various points in the interview, it may be necessary to make statements which are not properly part of the recording. Agreements can then be made to "go off the record." The investigator should then make specific oral statements such as "Going off the record." and "Back on the record."

f. **Surreptitious Recordings by the Interviewee.** It has been previously stated that persons occupying positions of importance often protect themselves from possible future complications such as misquotations by secretly making their own recordings. Whenever an investigator conducts an interview in the office of such a person, he should assume that such a recording is being made and guide his own conversation accordingly. He should make the supposition that the interviewee has thrown a switch and that a concealed microphone is recording his conversation. In this way he can avoid statements or remarks that are susceptible to later misinterpretation to the detriment of the investigation or the investigator's reputation.

ADDITIONAL READING

Gebhardt, R. H.: Video Tape in Criminal Cases. 44 *FBI Law Enforcement Bulletin*, 5, 1975.

Rifas, R. A.: *Legal Aspects of Video Tape and Motion Pictures in Law Enforcement.* Evanston, Ill.: Traffic Institute, Northwestern University, 1972.

Chapter 12

INFORMANTS

1. General

THE TRADITIONAL shortcut to the solution of a crime or to the location of a wanted person is the informant. In recent years the informant has figured significantly in a number of prominent cases, from the trials of the Chicago Seven, The Seattle Eight, and the Harrisburg Seven to most of the trials of the Black Panthers. Major police forces rely heavily on informants. One informant in the San Francisco area is responsible for an estimated 2,000 arrests a year, mostly in narcotics offenses. In consensual crimes, such as narcotics cases, there are rarely complaints from the victims. The use of informants by the Federal government is quite common. The Internal Revenue Service employs them to uncover tax frauds. In 1970 FBI informants accounted for over 14,000 arrests and the recovery of more than $50 million in money and merchandise.

The practical investigator who is pressed by a heavy case load must perforce rely heavily upon this source of information. A good proportion of important cases are solved by means of informants. The social level of the informant will vary with the nature of the offense or inquiry. The investigator must know his way about the taverns, bowling alleys, pool halls, and other hangouts of his area. He must fraternize with people at all levels of society: bartenders, cab drivers, doormen, bootblacks, waiters, maids, janitors, window cleaners, security personnel, night watchmen, milkmen, and, in general, all those who see their fellow citizens from a special point of vantage. These are the persons who will constitute the cadre of informants that may aid the investigator's work immeasurably. Often information will be voluntarily offered by those whose motives spring from good citizenship. In general, however, the motives of the informant should not prohibit the enjoyment of his confidence. At times it will be necessary to repay the informant by favors or by cash. In any case, the payment should take a form in accordance with professional ethics. For convenience we may make the following distinction between informants:

a. In general an *informant* is a person who gives information to the investigator. He may do this openly and even offer to be a witness, or he may inform surreptitiously and request to remain anonymous.

b. A *confidential informant* is a person who provides an investigator with confidential information concerning a past or projected crime and does not wish to be known as the source of the information. The investigator must take special precautions to protect the identity of such an informant since his value as a source is lost on disclosure.

2. Motives

The motives for revealing information are numerous and it becomes the investigator's responsibility to evaluate the informant and the information given in order to arrive at the truth. Some of the more common motives are:

a. **Vanity.** The self-aggrandizing person who delights in giving information to gain favorable attention from the police authorities.

b. **Civic-mindedness.** The public-spirited person of good standing in the community who is interested in seeing that justice is done.

c. **Fear.** The person under an illustion of oppression by enemies or of other impending danger.

d. **Repentance.** The person, usually an accomplice, who has a change of heart and wishes to report a crime that is preying on his conscience.

e. **Avoidance of Punishment.** The person who is apprehended in the commission of a minor offense and seeks to avoid prosecution by revealing information concerning a major crime.

f. **Gratitude or Gain.** The person who gives information to express appreciation or obtain a privilege, such as one who is arrested and desires cigarettes or other items or a former prisoner who wishes to repay the police officer's interest in the welfare of his family during his detention.

g. **Competition.** The person (usually one earning a living by questionable means) who wishes to eliminate his competitor.

h. **Revenge.** The person who wishes to settle a grudge because someone else informed against him, took advantage of him, or otherwise injured him.

i. **Jealousy.** A person who is envious of the accomplishments or possessions of another and wishes to humiliate him.

j. **Remuneration.** The person who informs solely for the pecuniary or other material gain he is to receive.

3. Obtaining Confidential Informants

An effective investigator of criminal offenses in a localized area usually has a number of confidential informants drawn from various classes and occupations. He has developed their friendship and cooperation over the course of years. In the investigation of a suspect he can sometimes find in his group of informants one or two who are in a position to observe the subject. When operating in other than his usual area the assistance of another investigator can be sought in obtaining informants.

4. Protecting the Informant

The investigator should compromise neither himself nor the informant in his pursuit of information. He should make no unethical promises or "deals," and should not undertake commitments which he cannot fulfill. He should safeguard the identity of his informant, first as a matter of ethical practice and second because of the danger of undermining the confidence of his sources. Wherever possible he should accept the information on the terms of the informant. The identity of informants should not be disclosed unless absolutely necessary and then only to the proper authorities. To preserve this secrecy, each confidential informant may be assigned a number, symbol, or fictitious name, and should be referred to by such designation in reports. To avoid discovery of identity of the confidential informant, great care must be exercised when a meeting or communication is contemplated. Confidential informants should not be called to testify in court. Such action would reveal their relationship and would terminate the informant's sources of information or invite vengeance upon him. Nevertheless, in extraordinary circumstances it may be practicable and desirable to summon a confidential informant as a witness in court. The general rule governing the safeguarding of the identity of confidential informants by law enforcement officers on the witness stand in trials has been announced in *Wilson v. United States* 59 F2d 390, 392 as follows: "It is the right and the duty of every citizen of the United States to communicate to the executive officer of the government charged with the duty of enforcing the law all the information which he has of the commission of an offense against the laws of the United States, and such information is privileged as a confidential communication which the courts will not compel or permit to be disclosed without the consent of the government. Such evidence is excluded, not for the protection of the witness, but because of the policy of the laws; . . . however, . . . a trial court must dispose of the case before it. If what is asked is essential evidence to vindicate the innocence of the accused or lessen the risk of false testimony, or is essential to the proper disposition of the case, disclosure will be compelled."

5. Treatment of Informants

After the investigator has been stationed in an area for a period of time, he has developed numerous sources of information, including persons from all walks of life. The treatment of the informant in the investigator-informant relationship is an individual problem based upon personality, education, and occupation. The investigator's sources of information are only valuable if they are able to obtain desired information or if they are willing to volunteer known information. To aid the investigator some general rules regarding this relationship with informants are listed:

a. **Fair Treatment.** The informant should be treated considerately, regardless of his character, education, or occupation.

b. **Reliability.** The investigator should be scrupulous in the fulfillment of all ethical promises which he has made. Any other policy results in distrust and a loss of the informant.

c. **Control.** The informant should not be permitted to take charge of any phase of the investigation.

6. Communicating with the Informant

In order to avoid revealing the status of the informant, careful judgment must be used in communication. The following points should be observed:

a. Meetings should be held at a place other than the investigator's office.

b. The circumstances surrounding the meetings should not be repeated to the extent that a recognizable pattern is created.

c. The proper name of the informant should not be used in telephoning. Designation by code is advisable for obvious reasons.

d. The investigator's organization should not be identified in any correspondence with the informant.

7. Dismissal of Informants

If after a period of time an informant becomes undesirable, the investigator should advise his supervisor of the situation and arrange for a debriefing of the informant. In accomplishing the debriefing, the investigator should avoid antagonizing the informant or otherwise creating a reaction unfavorable to the organization. If a record of the informant is maintained, the reasons for or the circumstances surrounding his dismissal should be also placed in writing, since the question of his usefulness may arise in the future. Among the more common reasons are ineptitude, compromise of identity, security risk, criminal record or act, and submitting false information. Often an informant will be dismissed without prejudice when he requests such action or when his services are no longer required.

8. Evaluating Informants

The investigator should continually evaluate his informants and form an estimate of their reliability. The information received should be tested for consistency by checking against information obtained from other persons. The motives and interests of the informer should be considered in the evaluation. The reports or leads from either known or unknown informers should be considered potentially valuable and should be developed by the investigation according to their significance until their true value is determined. Often these "tips" will prove to be groundless. The investigator should not, however, become excessively skeptical in the face of disappointments and should be receptive to future information. Finally, in dealing with anonymous persons who voluntarily offer information by telephone, he should remember that such persons ordinarily do not call back once they have delivered their message. Hence he should endeavor to draw out all relevant information before the anonymous caller ends the conversation.

9. Potential Informants

The following is a partial list of persons who because of their occupations may be in a position to supply useful information, depending upon the nature of the investigation:

Barbers
Bartenders
Beauty shop operators
Club and association secretaries
Dry cleaners, laundry delivery-
    men
Employment agency clerks
Garagemen
Grocers
Gunsmiths
Hotel managers, bellboys, tele-
    phone operators
Household servants
Insurance investigators
Janitors, charwomen, window
    cleaners
Locksmiths
Milkmen and home delivery-
    men
Money lenders
Neighbors
Newspaper reporters, editors
Parking lot operators
Postmen

Prostitutes
Public utility employees
Race track employees and
  bookmakers
Rental agency clerks and
  agents

Restaurant employees and en-
  tertainers
Tailors
Waiters and waitresses

10. Informant's Status

The informant belongs to the organization and not to the individual investigator. Hence, the information concerning the identity of the informant should be maintained in a central file. The following points are important:

a. The supervisor should *personally* maintain the file.

b. The classification of the file should be at least confidential.

c. The informant should be assigned a code designation consisting of the local office number and his number. Thus an informant in squad office 31 might have the designation 31-9.

d. The informant's name should never be used in reports. It should be referred to by symbol only.

e. Copies of the informant's file should be prepared on index cards for filing at the local office and at headquarters.

11. Methods of Private Investigators

It is appropriate at this point to discuss briefly the operations of the private investigator, who has in recent years developed to an art the work of obtaining information. Naturally the methods of the private investigator are not greatly restricted. Unembarrassed by public scrutiny, his activities can exceed the bounds that delimit the acceptable scope of the operations of the law enforcement agent. Much of the work of private investigators is devoted to credit and background reports designed to uncover insurance, security, and general personnel risks. About one-fourth of the private agency cases are concerned with domestic problems such as divorces and missing persons. Only 5 per cent are criminal defense cases. It may be said that private investigative work requires two major talents: the ability to conduct surveillances and ingenuity in developing information. Some of the methods used are listed here but it is not suggested that they may be conscionably used in law enforcement work.

a. **Contacts.** Deprived of the authority that permits law enforcement agents to have access to official records and other sources of information, the private detective must rely for his intelligence on "contacts" and "cooperation." In some situations the desired information can be bought; in others it can be obtained in exchange. Thus, some private investigators by enlisting the clandestine aid of an employee can obtain unlisted telephone numbers, telephone toll calls data, telegram messages, address records of utility companies, and hotel registrations. Through a "connection," such as an unscrupulous clerk, he can obtain from federal, state and municipal agencies many types of records: civil service histories, military and social security records, automobile registrations, income tax payments, and mail covers. Even members of law-enforcement agencies are sometimes willing to become sources of information, expecting in turn to be assisted by the private detective in the same manner.

b. **Other Methods.** The ingenuity of the private detective enables him to develop temporary sources in a short time to suit the needs of a case. Trades people, such as utility service men, milk delivery men, and mailmen, owners of grocery stores, pharmacies and newsstands, disgruntled employees, unfriendly neighbors, business competitors, and many others respond to the knowing tactics of the experienced investigator. He may pose as a federal investigator or an insurance representative depending on the layman's credulity for the acceptance of his "credentials." He may manage to obtain the office trash of a company or subject by an arrangement with the collector, by renting his own trash removal truck, or by renting an office in the same building and substituting his own trash container for that of the subject. The list of ruses employed by the private investigator would, perhaps, require several chapters for adequate treatment. The following may serve as an example: One detective pursuing matrimonial cases obtains hotel registration records by requesting permission of the manager under the guise of investigating a bad check. The pretense is supported by a check, made out by the detective, bearing the subject's signature which is to be compared with the registration.

ADDITIONAL READING

Earhart, R.S.: *A Critical Analysis of Investigator—Criminal Informant Relationship in Law Enforcement.* Washington, D.C.: International Association of Chiefs of Police, 1964.

Gutterman, M.: The Informer Privilege. 58 *Journal of Criminal Law, Criminology and Police Science*, 32, 1967.

Harney, M.L. and Cross, J.C.: *The Informer in Law Enforcement*, 2nd ed. Springfield, Ill.: Thomas, 1968.

The Informer Privilege: What's in a Name? 64 *Journal of Criminal Law and Criminology*, 56, 1973.

McCann, M.G.: *Police and the Confidential Informant.* Bloomington, Indiana University Press, 1957.

McClean, J.D.: Informers and Agents Provocateurs. *Criminal Law Review*, 527, 1969.

Rissler, L.E.: The Informer-Witness. 46 *FBI Law Enforcement Bulletin*, 5, 1977.

Chapter 13

TRACING AND SOURCES
OF INFORMATION

1. Introduction

A GREAT PART of investigative work is devoted to "finding" missing or wanted persons. The solving of a case frequently depends upon locating the perpetrator. The proper presentation of a case in court involves the discovery and identification of witnesses. The search for a person is frequently a simple matter of a few telephone calls or a visit to a house. At other times, however, the hunt can become a lengthy and complicated ordeal.

The search for persons commonly requires a concomitant search of records and an application to various sources of information. The term *tracing* is used here to describe all of these procedures. A patient study of records and the acquisition of information from official sources and private agencies are frequently required in order to obtain additional evidence as well as to locate or to identify a person.

One of the most hackneyed aphorisms of investigative work is the maxim, "An investigator is no better than his information." Ordinarily this principle is used in reference to unofficial sources of information such as confidential informants. In a very true sense, however, it is applicable to *all* the sources of information, official as well as unofficial, which are available to the investigator. The detective who depends exclusively on tips and personal interviews to the exclusion of the official sources hinders himself in his work. He is inefficient and is, in fact, operating at only a fraction of his true capacity. Often a vital point of information can be readily obtained by a reference to so obvious a source as the telephone book or by a simple visit to the public library, but instead many investigators will spend weeks clarifying this point by personal interviewing of witnesses. This neglect of informative sources is usually attributable to the tradition in which many detectives are nurtured. Newspaper reporters and private investigators are trained to habits of research. The police, however, because of their ready access to the confidence of private persons, have a tendency to deal with these exclusively and, since they are usually pressed for time, to remain in ignorance of the methods of the research type of investigation. In the following discussion many of the available official sources are listed.

2. Tracing a Missing Person (witness, victim, or other)

In searching for a person, the aim of the investigator is first to obtain the information necessary to identify him beyond question. His pedigree, social, business, and criminal history will form the basis of the identification. The facts uncovered through informants should be verified by an examination of informative records. The investigator, in locating a missing or wanted person, should use the simplest facilities first. An example of this direct procedure is given below.

a. **The Telephone.** The investigator should telephone the home of the missing person (unless, of course, the request for a search has come from the home). Ask simple direct questions. Is he home? Where has he gone? What is his present address? Naturally, for the latter questions the investigator will be required to identify himself. Telephone the employer of the missing person and ask a series of similar questions. Telephone friends and relatives and make inquiries. Obviously the investigator should follow up any leads he obtains from these sources.

b. **Visit the Home.** If telephone inquiries are fruitless, the investigator should visit the house. He can question the family; or, if the family has moved, he can make inquiries of the neighbors and discover the habits and haunts of the missing person. He should endeavor to learn as much as possible concerning the habits, haunts, and social life of the missing person. Since the average person is strongly ruled by habits, we should expect him in his new surroundings to do the things that he likes to do and to which he is accustomed. The state of mind of the missing person is important. Some conclusions can be reached concerning this by questioning the family. Was he worried or nervous? What were his plans or ambitions? Were his home and vocational conditions satisfactory? Did he draw any pay or any money from the bank? What was the condition of his room? Who saw him last? What was the conversation? How did he behave when last seen? The superintendent, landlord, or realty agent can be interviewed to find the name of the mover or to examine the lease for references. The local tavern, drug store, filling station, and stationery store should be visited.

c. Record of Change of Address. The following sources may have a record of the change of address:

Post Office
Board of Education
Board of Elections
Motor Vehicle Bureau
Tax Assessment Lists
Bank
Census
Haulers and Movers

(The other sources listed below should then be consulted for possible leads.)

d. Mail Covers. The post office can be particularly helpful in many cases. A request can be made of the post office inspector to have a mail cover placed on the homes of relatives. A copy will then be made, including the mailing place and date stamp, return address if any, and all other markings present on the front and back of each piece of mail sent to the address being covered. A cover is usually placed on mail for two weeks or a month. The post office does not open the subject's mail. It simply maintains a list of postmarks and names of return addresses on mail cover. Consideration should be given to the work involved. A request should be made only when useful results can be reasonably expected. The request should state the specific period of time for which the mail cover is needed. It should not run in excess of sixty days. If the desired information is obtained before that, the cover should be canceled. An investigation office should maintain an index of all current mail covers. Even though no obvious lead is obtained, attention should be paid to typewritten letters, especially if several are sent from a particular mailing point and no return address is given, for they undoubtedly are not business letters. If specimen handwriting of the missing person is obtained it can be compared with the copies made while the mail cover is in operation. If the writing on any piece of mail appears similar, it merits further investigation.

e. **Mail Ruse.** A useful ruse employed in tracing by mail is that of sending a special delivery or registered letter bearing the subject's name to the address of a friend or relative who may know the subject's hideout. The mail supervisor is instructed not to deliver the letter, but to say that it must be sent or called for at the post office by the addressee. Since the relative will imagine that the letter contains an important message or document, he will get in touch with the fugitive. The mail of the fugitive and the friend should, of course, be covered in this situation.

3. Tracing the Fugitive

The technique employed in tracing a fugitive will vary with the character of the subject. In the case of an astute fugitive, discreet methods must be employed. With the inexperienced criminal a more direct approach is permissible. The methods described in the preceeding sections will be found useful. The following checklist is given as an example of a typical, routine trace. Naturally the order of these steps is not fixed and in some cases various steps can be omitted.

a. **Routine Information.**
1) Full name and alias.
2) Physical description.
3) *Modus operandi*.
4) Motive.
5) Associates past and present including girlfriends.
6) Habits, hangouts, and resorts he is known to frequent.
7) Criminal record, photograph, and fingerprints.
8) Residence, last known and previous locations.
9) Employment, last known and previous employers.
10) Relatives, names and addresses of all available.

11) Close friends, names and addresses.

12) Physical condition.

13) Motor Vehicle Bureau, check for operator's, chauffeur's, or owner's license.

14) Social Security number.

15) Selective Service history, records from local boards.

16) Handwriting for comparison with mail cover, hotel registrations, etc.

b. **Immediate Action.** The following steps can be taken with reference to law enforcement agencies, when prompt action is required:

1) Teletype.

2) Police circulars.

3) Police journals; FBI bulletins.

4) Wanted card at local and state Bureau of Criminal Information.

5) Wanted Persons File at FBI (Washington, D.C.).

6) Local Bureau of Information for information on summons and arrest cards, aid and accident cases.

7) Bureau of Motor Vehicles for accident reports or reports of lost plates.

8) Chief Magistrates Court or equivalent for fingerprint file with regard to arrests on minor charges.

9) If a parolee, the Parole Board concerned should be notified.

10) If the fugitive is known to frequent the race tracks, notify the Pinkerton Detective Agency.

11) Notify former arresting officers.

12) Place a notice or consult the monthly bulletin of the American Hotel Association, published by Wm. J. Burns International Detective Agency.

4. Scope of Federal Information Gathering

Records maintained by elements of the federal government will reflect the particular function of the agency involved as well as its responsibilities and security requirements. The scope and volume of the information contained will depend on the purpose of the record and will vary also with the agency. In general, the records can be placed in one of the following categories:

a. **Civilian Personnel Records.** This is a basic class of records for a government that is the employer of millions of persons. The typical employee dossier will contain the following information: name, date of birth, social security number, educational background, professional qualifications, job assignments, and so forth. Ordinarily the dossier will include employment applications, proficiency reports, and information relating to the person's security clearance status.

b. **Military Records.** Information similar to the above is included in the personnel folders of present and former members of the Armed Forces. Data pertinent to service personnel having current duty or standby status is maintained in the active files of the Department of Defense or other appropriate agency. Records of former military personnel are maintained in several records repositories in various parts of the country and, in limited form, in the files of the Veterans Administration. Finally, as will be seen below, combined Department of Defense files contain investigations and security clearance status and include military personnel who have been the subject of actions relating to these matters.

c. **Information on Private Individuals.** The federal government maintains millions of records on private persons. Some are related directly to criminal activity; some are concerned with security matters, identifying persons and specifying the reasons why a certain level of security clearance was granted or withheld; still others—a far larger class of records—contain highly detailed information on individual citizens without any specific relation to crime or security. Examples of this last category are the records of the Census Bureau, the Bureau of Internal Revenue, and the Social Security Administration. The list of agencies and their files given below is not intended to be comprehensive—omitted are records of such departments as Agriculture, Labor and the Post Office, as well as records maintained by regulatory agencies such as FCC, FTC, SEC, and AEC among others. It will serve, however, to suggest some of the more fruitful sources of personal information together with their relative accessibility.

5. Civil Service Commission

a. **The Security Investigations Index.** This consists of index cards listing every personnel investigation made by the Commission and other agencies since 1939. Cards show, for the person named, when an investigation was made, what agency made it, and where the investigative file is located. Information is derived from agencies making the investigations listed; information from the index is available on request to any personnel or security official having bona fide employment or investigative interest in the individual.

b. **The Security File.** This consists of index cards containing lead information to persons who might be proved ineligible for government clearance because of questioned loyalty or subversive activities. The file primarily involves private citizens and is developed from published hearings of federal and state legislative committees, public investigative bodies, reports of investigation, publications of subversive organizations, and various other newspapers and periodicals. The file is used extensively by investigative and intelligence officials of various federal agencies, particularly in connection with national agency checks, inquiry cases, and full field investigations in connection with federal employment.

6. Commerce Department

In addition to census information and a data bank on departmental personnel, the Commerce Department maintains several non-intelligence–oriented compilations of records on individuals:

a. **Seafaring Personnel.** Data on seafaring personnel of various ratings, including 32 items of information on the graduates of the Merchant Marine Academy to reflect current employment status.

b. **Decennial Census.** The Bureau of the Census maintains on microfilm all census records from 1900 to date, ranging in growing increments from 76 million persons enumerated in 1900 to more than 220 million counted in the 1980 census. The scope of information has varied over the years. The most comprehensive census undertaken from the standpoint of personal information gathered was that completed in 1980. Individual information is available only to the individual concerned or to his legal heirs.

7. Defense Department

The departmental records include Army investigative files relating to security, loyalty, or criminal investigations concerning various classes of personnel.

a. **Military Service Records.**

b. **Civilian Personnel Files.**

c. **Defense Central Index of Investigations.** This is a locator file, presently being computerized, which identifies by individual name the location of files concerning an unspecified number of present and former service personnel, civilian employees, and contractor personnel.

d. **Defense Supply Agency File.** This is an index of personnel cards detailing security clearance information for persons employed by contractors engaged in classified work for the Department of Defense and eleven other federal agencies. Information includes vital statistics, clearance sought, investigation conducted, and action taken; where adjudicative action has been taken, reason for issuance or denial of a clearance as well as information on the individual's background, personal life, personality, habits, etc., are included. Information in the file is made available on a need-to-know basis by the above user agencies; clearance status information only is made available to cleared contractors concerning persons actually or potentially in their employ.

8. Department of Health, Education and Welfare

Among the extensive records on individuals maintained by component agencies of HEW, two groups are considered major information systems: the National Center for Health Statistics (NCHS) and the Social Security Administration's (SSA) data systems. Additionally, the Department provides financial support to a number of computerized data banks operated by state and local governments, public school systems, colleges and universities, and health and welfare organizations.

a. **National Center for Health Statistics.** The NCHS, considered a key component of the federal statistical system, provides statistical intelligence on vital events, health, injury, illness, impairments, dental, hospital and other health care services. HEW reports that, while much of the input into the system is individual oriented, with persons identified, confidentiality is maintained by authorizing release of information only in summary or statistical form which does not identify individuals by name.

b. **SSA Data Systems.** These are so extensive as to render statistics concerning their scope largely meaningless. Data banks maintained contain information on all individuals issued a Social Security number, on all beneficiaries of major social welfare programs conducted under authority of the Social Security acts, and on all those subject to Social Security taxes, among other categories of data.

9. Justice Department

In addition to the files maintained by the FBI and other subdivisions, the Justice Department retains several files for its direct use in support of the following systems:

a. **Civil Disturbance System.** This is used as an intelligence aid for planning purposes as well as on-the-scene information for use in police operations during a disorder. The system consists of two fully automated files: The Subject File contains information on persons involved in civil disturbances; the Incident File contains records of events that have developed into civil disorders. The Incident File contains descriptions of the event without listing names. The Subject File contains name, age or date of birth, sex, race, home city and state, aliases, and criminal record. A code number cross-indexes the Subject File with the Incident File, which does not contain personal data. Only the Justice Department has direct access to the files. Information is made available on a need-to-know basis to other federal agencies and law enforcement bodies. The system is utilized to respond to requests for information by the Attorney General or his principal assistants in connection with either prosecutive functions or for intelligence evaluation. Additionally, information is provided any concerned federal official on a need-to-know basis about potential disorders so that adequate preparations can be made to prevent or contain such activity.

b. **Organized Crime Intelligence System.** A computerized file and card index, the system includes financial information, participation in illegal organizations, business connections, associations, habits, or any other data on the individual listed of possible future value in investigations, prosecutions, or intelligence analysis.

c. **Federal Bureau of Investigation.**

1) *National Crime Information Center.* The NCIC is the FBI's computerized index containing information on wanted persons, criminal histories, and stolen and/or missing property. Information concerning individuals for whom warrants have been issued is retained in the Wanted Persons File, which contains records of warrants and descriptive data on the persons wanted. The file is completely computerized with extensive communications networks among local, state, and federal law enforcement agencies, who may enter records directly into the index from typewriter-like terminal devices in their respective departments. Such records are immediately available in response to query by other agencies participating in the system.

Information in the Wanted Persons File relates to individuals for whom federal warrants are outstanding or for individuals who have been identified with an offense classified as a felony or serious misdemeanor for whom the jurisdiction originating the entry has been issued a warrant. Probation or parole violators with outstanding warrants are also entered in the NCIC. Law enforcement agencies in the federal government, the fifty states, the District of Columbia, Puerto Rico, and Canada have direct on-line access to the computer records; the system is used to identify suspects and apprehend fugitives.

Descriptive data recorded includes name, sex, race, nationality, date of birth, height, weight, hair color, FBI number, NCIC fingerprint classification, miscellaneous identification numbers, Social Security number, driver's license data, offense for which warrant was issued and date of warrant, and data identifying license plates and automobiles associated with the wanted person.

2) *Fingerprint and Criminal Identification Files.* A national

clearinghouse for such records, the files contain over 200 million fingerprint cards—at present visually classified, manually searched, and divided into criminal and civil sections. The civil file is comprised of cards on federal employees and applicants, Armed Forces personnel, civilian employees in national defense industries, aliens, and persons wishing to have their fingerprints on file for identification purposes.

Fingerprint cards contain the name, signature, and physical description of the person fingerprinted; information concerning the reason for fingerprinting; identity of contributing agency; date printed; and, where applicable, the charge and disposition or sentence. Some cards contain the residential address, occupation, and employment of the person fingerprinted.

Identification records, compiled from fingerprint cards, contain the identity of the contributors of the cards; names and aliases of the subject of the record; agency identifying numbers; dates of arrest and/or incarcerations; charges; and dispositions. No other information concerning an individual's background, personal life, personality, or habits is included in these records.

Fingerprint cards are submitted by over 14,000 contributors representing local, state, and federal law enforcement agencies, including penal institutions, the federal government, and organizations authorized by state laws to contribute fingerprints for official purposes.

The FBI's records are furnished to authorize officials of the federal government, the states, cities, and penal or other institutions for their official use only. Written record is maintained of each dissemination of an identification record, including the date disseminated and the identity of the receiving agency.

The FBI began computerization of federal criminal offender identification records on May 1, 1970. Later that year the Attorney General directed the FBI to establish a nationwide computerized system for the exchange of criminal history information between the FBI and the states for the benefit of all law enforcement arms—police, prosecutions, courts, probations, and corrections. The goal of this project was a computerized national index of criminal history records concerning serious offenders which could be queried over communication lines by remote law enforcement computer terminals, utilizing computer and communication facilities presently serving the National Crime Information Center. The result of this project was the Computerized Criminal History (CCH) file containing the personal descriptions of those arrested for serious offenses, the nature of the charge, and the disposition of the arrest.

The FBI is presently nearing completion of its Automated Identification Division System (AIDS) which will eventually provide for automatic fingerprint searching of the criminal name indices and computer storage and retrieval of arrest record data.

3) **Known Professional Check Passers File.** The FBI's PRO-CHECK is a tape storage of records containing information on prolific bad check passers. Information includes a description of the person (age and appearance), his method of operation, and the check format (how his checks are customarily filled out). Information is collected from existing FBI investigative records and is accessible only to FBI personnel involved in official investigations concerning bad checks.

d. **Immigration and Naturalization Service.**

1) **Alien Reports File.** This file is maintained in the district offices and suboffices of I&NS, and contains reports submitted by aliens in the United States each year during the month of January. The records contain the person's name, date and place of entry, length of time for which admitted, and U.S. and foreign addresses. The file is designed to serve mainly as a locator. Only security and enforcement agencies of the federal government have access to information from this system. Its major use is to answer inquiries relating to a person's immigration status and location of any relating files.

2) **Master Index.** Maintained in the central offices of I&NS, this index contains names and other identifying characteristics of those persons admitted to or excluded from this country since 1952, as well as sponsors of record. The record contains the person's name, date and place of birth, country of nationality, date and place of entry into the U.S., immigration status at the time of entry, case file number, and location of the office holding the individual's file. The file is designed primarily as a locator, used solely by security and enforcement agencies of the federal government.

3) **Nonimmigrant Index.** This index contains names and other

identifying characteristics of those persons admitted to the United States for temporary periods of time, and who must eventually depart from this country. Only security and enforcement agencies of the federal government have access to information from this index, whose primary function is to assist in the control of aliens during the periods of their temporary stay in this country.

e. **Drug Enforcement Administration.**

1) *Addict Files.* These identify persons reported by federal, state, and local agencies as illicitly using a narcotic drug. Information includes name, criminal identification number, city and state of birth, date of birth, sex, race, drug cures, drug used, length of use, original reason for use, reporting agency and city, and date reported. Information is obtained from arrest records maintained by law enforcement agencies at all levels. Data is available on request to federal, state, and local enforcement agencies for law enforcement purposes in the form of statistical data only. Identifying data are available only to those agencies which originated the file. Data are made available in statistical form to the Congress and other federal agencies as well as state and local enforcement and health agencies.

2) *Defendant Statistical Program.* These records identify persons arrested by the Drug Enforcement Administration for violations of drug laws. Information is obtained from the person following his arrest and includes particulars of his arrest, past criminal and/or drug record, and related data. Information is published in statistical form only for the use of Congress, other federal agencies, and the public.

10. State Department

The Passport Office of the State Department maintains a "Look-out File" to check eligibility in passport applications. The Lookout File is a completely computerized record of those persons who have been placed in the file for a variety of reasons: defectors, expatriates, and repatriates whose activities and background demand further inquiry; persons wanted in connection with criminal activity; persons on whom there is an outstanding court order restricting travel or involvement in a custody or desertion case; indebtedness to the United States; Organized Crime and Rackets list; known or suspected communist or subversive; loss of U.S. citizenship; delinquent or suspected delinquent in military obligations; not U.S. citizen and not clear that they ever possessed U.S. citizenship; previous passport issued on insufficient evidence; miscellaneous or reason unknown and there is a lookout.

The principal use of the Lookout File is to identify those passport applications which require other than routine adjudication in determining eligibility. In addition, whenever an application is *flagged*, the original source of the lookout is notified that the individual has applied for a passport. Requests for additions to the file are received from various sections of the State Department, other government agencies, and, in the limited category of child custody cases, from an interested parent or guardian. Direct access to the file is limited to personnel in the State Department involved in passport matters whose official duties require access. When an individual whose name is in the file applies for a passport, this fact is provided to the requesting agencies.

11. Treasury Department

a. **Customs Bureau.** This office maintains a computerized data bank of information on suspects, which is available on a 24-hour basis to Customs agents and inspectors throughout the United States. The file is used to identify suspect persons and vehicles at various ports of entry into the U.S., and includes name and address, social security number, citizenship, race, sex, date of birth, physical description, driver's license, suspect category, vehicle information, aliases, known associates, and "remarks." Information in the file is available on a need-to-know basis to law enforcement agencies.

b. **Internal Revenue Service.** A comprehensive data bank is maintained by IRS in the form of tax returns filed by every tax-liable individual and corporate entity in the United States. Among the files maintained by IRS the following are of special interest:

1) *Tax Returns.* A comprehensive data bank is maintained by IRS in the form of tax returns filed by every tax-liable individual and

corporate entity in the United States. IRS data can be made available to:

a) Certain federal agencies by written request and in accordance with rules which vary with the agency.

b) States, the District of Columbia, Puerto Rico, and U.S. possessions when requested by the chief executive official of such jurisdiction to assist in the administration of local tax laws. Tax information concerning all citizens of a given state has been made available in recent years on magnetic tape to facilitate comparison of returns and identification of non-filers.

2) *Firearms.* Another compilation of personal data maintained by IRS is a list of persons who have registered firearms in compliance with federal law as well as licensed dealers and others required to be licensed under Title I (State Firearms Control Assistance) of the Gun Control Act of 1968. Information from this file is considered in the public domain and is available on written request.

c. **Secret Service.** Information files are maintained on persons and incidents involving counterfeiting of U.S. or foreign obligations (currency, coins, stamps, bonds, U.S. Treasurer's checks, Treasury securities, etc.), as well as forgery, alteration, or fraudulent negotiation of U.S. Treasurer's checks and U.S. Government bonds. The Service also has an extensive collection of information affecting its responsibility for protecting the President and other designated persons. At present the information of the Secret Service is maintained on a partially computerized basis. The scope of such data banks is not made public but includes information derived from other federal agencies on a continuing basis in areas of concern to the Secret Service.

12. Department of Transportation

The National Highway Safety Bureau maintains a National Register Service. This is a computerized record of the names of persons whose license to drive has been denied, terminated, or temporarily withdrawn by a state or political subdivsion thereof. They are identified by name, alias, physical characteristics, social security number, date and place of birth.

Information comes from voluntary reports submitted by state officials from their files. Access to information in the Register is limited to Federal agencies, states, and political subdivisions of states, and only with respect to an individual applicant for a motor vehicle operator's license. The brochure describing the Register, however, envisions its use by other than driver's license administrators. Examples given include police, prosecutors, judges, school administrators, insurance firms, and transportation companies.

A printout on each name requested by an authorized agency will include the personal information noted above, as well as the reason for license revocation, the date the license was withdrawn, the date the person is eligible to have it restored, and the date of restoration (where reported).

13. Veterans Administration

The VA maintains two data banks affecting an unspecified number of the estimated 30 million veterans now living. The first of these contains data on beneficiaries of various VA benefits, with special reference to eligibility for benefits and location. The second consists of data on veterans who are patients, and includes relevant medical records and information on eligibility for medical care. Such records are available only for use of the Veterans Administration.

14. Data Banks and the Threat to Privacy

a. **A New Industry.** The acquisition of data on individuals has become a major activity of a number of Federal agencies. In recent years a new era of gathering and distributing information was entered with the development of high-speed data retrieval systems, many based on computer technology. Some public officials have been led to predict the ultimate establishment of a national computerized data bank incorporating dossiers of *cradle-to-grave* information on every United States citizen. Advances in the field of communications have led to the development in some Federal agencies of so-called *data banks*—mechanized or computerized files of instantly available information which can be rapidly transmitted, upon request, to authorized agencies and individuals throughout the country.

b. **The New Technology.** The governmental process of gathering, storing, retrieving, and disseminating data on individuals has always existed and has been recognized as a significant threat to the functioning of a free society. In the last ten years, however, incredible advances in technology have enabled government agencies to achieve surveillance capability undreamed of only a short time before. Where once methodical persistence could maintain a surveillance on a number of persons, we are now entering an era where surveillance capability is achieving the quality of inevitability. Electronic and photographic developments now permit the collection of vast amounts of data on day-to-day activities of all citizens, without so much as an inkling that the data collection is taking place. Innovations in computer technology have made possible the storage, retrieval, and dissemination of personal dossiers on millions of persons.

c. **The Threat to Privacy.** The marriage of sophisticated information-gathering techniques with computer information storage and dissemination systems has created for the first time a very real danger that the sense of privacy which has traditionally insulated Americans against the fear of state enchroachment will be destroyed and be replaced, instead, by a pervasive sense of being watched. Since the protection of the sense of privacy is essential to the preservation of individuality which characterizes a democracy, legislators and a government advisory committee have proposed a number of safeguards against this new enchroachment:

1) *Statute of Limitations.* We can no longer start life anew by moving to another town. A shrinking world has destroyed that procedure. An informational statute of limitations should be an integral part of any surveillance system, automatically expunging stale information after a given period.

2) *Individual Access.* The surveillance process must be hedged with rigorous safeguards. Every person about whom data is being stored by the government should be permitted access to his dossier to check its accuracy and propriety. Upon receipt he should be permitted challenge.

3) **Dissemination Notice.** Prior to its dissemination, notice should be given an individual of a request for information.

4) **Transmission.** There must be a way for an individual to prevent information about him that was obtained for one purpose from being used or made available for other purposes without his consent.

5) **Reliability.** Any organization creating, maintaining, using, or disseminating records of identifiable personal data must insure the reliability of these data for their intended use and must take precautions to prevent misuse.

6) **Secrecy.** There must be no personal data record-keeping systems whose very existence is secret.

15. Rapid Transmission of Information

a. **Incidents.** The power of the computer as a tool of police service in field investigation can be seen in the following incident reported by the Oakland, California, Police Department. As he pulled his police cruiser into a drive-in hamburger stand, patrolman Raoul Martin observed a late-model Volkswagen. The furtive behavior of its occupants aroused Martin's suspicions, prompting him to run a check on the car. He ran his hand quietly over the keyboard of a computer. There was no need to speak to the dispatcher. Within seconds the requested information appeared on a small video screen. The Volkswagen had been stolen in Monterey several weeks earlier. Martin moved in quickly to make the arrest.

In another incident, a Pennsylvania State Police officer on stopping an auto for a traffic violation noticed that the vehicle identification number had been altered and decided to check the legal serial numbers through the NCIC vehicle file. The response showed that a Michigan police department had reported the vehicle stolen. As a result the two occupants of the car were taken into custody. A search of these persons revealed that one was armed with a .38 caliber revolver. A check through NCIC on the serial number of the gun showed that it had been reported stolen. After obtaining a warrant, the police searched the vehicle and found a quantity of narcotics and assorted jewelry.

b. **Equipment.** The communications equipment used in the first of these cases was a high-speed, digitalized computer, the Digicom® system of GTE Sylvania. The patrol car contained a terminal with a keyboard the size of a portable typewriter, a radio transmitter, and an electronic city map. The other parts, at Oakland Police headquarters, included a small computer, another keyboard terminal and a large screen map. To run a check on a car, the patrolman simply typed the letters and numbers of the license plate on the keyboard mounted on the transmission hump before the front seat. These symbols are converted into the binary code and radioed back to headquarters, where the small computer processes the request and passes it along to the Police Information Network (PIN), a computer facility serving nine counties in the San Francisco area. The computer scans its memory bank and in less than a minute transmits the requested information to the video screen of the patrol car terminal: the license number; the year, make, and color of the vehicle; the owner's name and address; warrants outstanding against the owner; and the facts of the car's theft if it had been stolen. For vehicles from outside the San Francisco area and even from out of the state, the patrolman can check the license at Sacramento or at the FBI's National Crime Information Center in Washington, D.C., by pressing other buttons on his keyboard.

c. **Applications.** There are, of course, a great number of practical applications of the computer to law enforcement. By shortening the time lapse between the request for information and the transmission of data, computer technology permits the investigator to avail himself of ongoing opportunities by rapidly providing a legal basis for apprehension. Thus, the computer can facilitate on-the-street investigations by quick delivery of information about targets of opportunity. At headquarters, computer information can greatly assist in the control and direction of an extensive surveillance, a moving search, or a wide-area pursuit by giving the supervisor current information on the exact location of police vehicles. The effectiveness of many police operations relies heavily on shortening the time span between information request and appropriate police action.

ADDITIONAL READING

Emerson, V. J.: Information in Forensic Science. 15 *Journal of the Forensic Science Society*, 257, 1975.

Harris, D.R., Maxfield, M., and Holladay, G.: *Basic Elements of Intelligence: A Manual for Police Intelligence Units*. Washington, D.C.: U.S. Government Printing Office, 1976.

Miller, A.R.: *The Assault on Privacy: Computers, Data Banks and Dossiers*. Ann Arbor, University of Michigan Press, 1971.

Murphy, H.J.: *Where's What?; Sources of Information for Federal Investigators*. New York, Warner, 1976.

Murphy, J.J.: *Arrest by Police Computer*. Westmead, Farnborough, England: Heath, Ltd., 1975.

The National Crime Information Center. A Special Report. 43 *FBI Law Enforcement Bulletin*, 1, 1974.

O'Brien, K., Boston, G., and Marvin, M.: *Directory of Criminal Justice Information Sources*. Washington, D.C.: U.S. Government Printing Office, 1976.

Reider, R.J.: *Law Enforcement Information Systems*. Springfield, Ill.: Thomas, 1972.

Tobias, M.W.: *Police Communications*. Springfield, Ill.: Thomas, 1974.

Westin, A.F.: *Privacy and Freedom*. New York, Athenaeum, 1967.

Chapter 14

MISSING PERSONS

1. General

ALTHOUGH the problem of finding and identifying missing persons is hardly the most exciting branch of detective work, it is a routine task of the first magnitude in importance. In a large city, a considerable fraction of the cases of the detective division is concerned with Missing Persons. In New York, for example, approximately 17,000 such cases are handled annually by the Missing Persons Bureau. Nearly 13,000 prove to be young runaways who return home on their own within a few days. The Missing Persons unit is ordinarily concerned with three classes of persons: (a) missing persons under about nineteen years of age; (b) unidentified dead, and (c) unidentified persons. Missing persons over eighteen years of age who are in full possession of their faculties are not ordinarily the concern of the police. Private investigators, however, are usually hired for cases of this nature.

2. Definitions

The following definitions, although not in widespread use, will serve to simplify the treatment of this subject.

a. The term *missing person* is often confused with "wanted person." The latter is a person who is sought by the police in connection with a crime. We may use for our definition the following: a missing person is anyone reported missing who is under eighteen or who, being eighteen or over, is: (1) seriously affected either mentally or physically, or (2) absent under circumstances which would indicate involuntary disappearance.

b. *Unidentified dead* will include those whose true identity is unknown and those whose relatives or friends cannot be immediately located.

c. An *unidentified person* is one who has been physically or mentally affected to a degree or in a manner requiring the attention of the police and who cannot be readily identified, or whose friends or relatives cannot be immediately located.

3. Crimes and Conditions Associated with Missing Persons

a. **Homicide.** In the disappearance of many thousands of people annually in this country, it is to be expected that personal violence should play a significant part in some of the cases. Murder, the unspoken fear of the relatives and the police, must always lie in the back of the investigator's mind as a possible explanation. The suspicions of a shrewd investigator have not infrequently uncovered an unsuspected homicide. The two most popular motives for this type of homicide are money and love. As an example of the love motive, the Feldt case is fairly representative. George Feldt walked into a police station one morning and reported his wife, Selma, age 47, missing for two days. Detective John Brandt of the Missing Persons Bureau was assigned to the investigation. In the first interview, Detective Brandt permitted Feldt to talk at considerable length. Feldt attributed various motives to his wife's disappearance. Before many minutes had passed he was accusing his wife of adultery with some unknown man. Subsequent interviews convinced the detective that Feldt was much more interested in the gratuitous vilification of his spouse than in her prompt return. In the course of these diatribes, it dawned upon Brandt that Feldt was speaking as though his wife's death were an accomplished fact. Brandt pursued the inquiry to Feldt's home. There he questioned Feldt's stepdaughter, age 18, and well-endowed by nature. The girl obviously was shaken by some fear. She confessed to an intimacy with Feldt and revealed her own suspicion of foul play. The cellar of Feldt's home was then searched for evidentiary traces. A newly cemented area attracted immediate attention. Digging in this spot, the detectives uncovered the body of Mrs. Feldt. She had been almost decapitated by a blow from a sharp instrument. The discovery of a blood-stained ax in a corner completed this part of the inquiry. Confronted with this evidence, Feldt confessed to the homicide. His infatuation with the stepdaughter had led him to conceive this violent plan to dispose of his wife. The methods employed were quite crude; nevertheless, carelessness on the part of the police might have insured Feldt's success. An intelligent investigation and a routine search had uncovered the crime.

b. **Suicide.** To the layman the suicide theory is one of the first to suggest itself in a disappearance case. Statistically, however, it can be shown that the odds are greatly against the suicide solution. Approximately one out of 2,000 missing persons cases develops into a suicide case. Suicides are ordinarily motivated by financial difficulties such as business failures, domestic troubles, or incurable disease. In the investigation of a case the detective should endeavor to discover the motive for the disappearance. A voluntary disappearance is motivated by a desire to escape from some personal, domestic, or business conflict. If the motive is founded merely in boredom or the desire for a change, suicide can be readily eliminated. A disappointment in love seldom results in self-inflicted death.

c. **Simulated Suicide.** These are usually planned by persons wishing to defraud insurance companies or to arrange for a change of spouse. The scene of this prefabricated demise is most commonly a watery one, such as a boat, bridge, or beach. This selection is obvious, since the perpetrator must leave clothing as a means of identification under circumstances which would make plausible the absence of the body. In general, no conclusion should be made concerning suicide unless the body is recovered. A drowned person will ordinarily be washed ashore within five to ten days. After twenty days, it may be concluded that the body has been carried out to sea (or that the person is still alive). A search for motives should include an inquiry into insurance policies. Naturally, the insurance company will promptly bring this matter to the attention of the police. The following are representative cases:

1) A bath house cleaner pursuing his Monday morning duties found a set of men's clothing in one of the lockers. A few hours later, detectives called at the home of Mrs. Sol Stern to inform her that her

husband's clothes had been left unclaimed at a bath house on a local beach. Mrs. Stern became hysterical and was of little assistance to the detectives. A $50,000 insurance policy on the life of Sol Stern was of more interest to them. Two months later, a report from the Montreal police informed the detectives that a man answering Stern's description had been knocked unconscious in an auto accident. The only identification was a newspaper clipping describing the disappearance of Stern at the beach. Stern later confessed to the fraud.

2) The technique of feigning suicide can be more highly developed if the perpetrator is an exceptional swimmer, as was Alfred Jones, another frequenter of beaches. Jones disappeared into the water during a heavy storm and before the eyes of several witnesses. Mrs. Jones, however, had greater faith in her husband's aquatic prowess. She insisted that he was still alive and had merely swum into some other woman's arms. This theory was vindicated two years later, when Jones was discovered living with another woman in a town fifty miles away.

d. **Extortion.** The extensive publicity which accompanies the disappearance of a person of some means usually stimulates the more unbalanced element among newspaper readers. The police department and the relatives of the missing person are besieged by crank letters suggesting false clues and absurd motives. Sometimes, however, the relatives become the target of an extortionist who pretends that he is holding the missing person in custody. The ransom note usually suggests that a large sum of money be forwarded to the writer by some means which may involve an innocent messenger or even the employment of homing pigeons. Needless to say, the writers of these letters in some cases know nothing of the location of the missing person. They are merely exploiting the disturbed emotions of the relatives. Naturally, an effort should be made to trace the extortion letter. A dummy package or some other ruse should be employed to trap the extortionist.

e. **Amnesia.** Loss of memory and with it knowledge of identity is a rare occurrence even among missing persons cases. Amnesia has its highest incidence in the confections of scenario writers. Of the authentic cases, the most frequent cause is battle shock.

f. **Psychoses.** The insane person of unknown identity is a more common type of missing person. A person of this sort is brought to the city or county hospital for examination. If he is adjudged insane, he is committed to a state hospital. The unidentified insane should form a separate file in a missing persons bureau. Psychoses which most frequently result in a missing persons case are dementias caused by organic changes in the cortical brain cell. The presenile psychoses—Alzheimer's disease and Pick's disease—are relatively rare forms of dementia which occur in the forties; the arteriosclerosis dementias may be seen from fifty upward; while uncomplicated senile dementias seldom appear before the age of sixty. The onset of these psychoses is ordinarily gradual. There is an uninterrupted deterioration of mental powers accompanied by defective memory, disorientation, and confusion. Members of the family are well aware of the condition and will readily describe the symptoms to the investigator.

g. **Abandonment.** Unhappy marriages account for a large percentage of disappearances. The voluntary disappearance of a married adult can in itself become a crime when it assumes the form of abandonment, e.g., the abandoning of a pregnant wife in destitute circumstances. Abandonment is a criminal offense and, as such, is a matter for police action.

4. Investigative Steps

The following procedure is suitable to a large city. The steps can be readily telescoped to fit the exigencies of a more limited personnel.

a. **Unidentified Dead.** The following steps are ordinarily followed in cases where the dead person is unidentified:

1) The report is received at the local detective squad.

2) The squad detective visits the scene, fills out a form with a full description of the deceased.

3) The squad detective notifies the Missing Persons Unit by telephone, giving a description of deceased. At the same time, he forwards the official form.

4) The Missing Persons Unit consults its records.

5) The Missing Persons Unit sends a detective to the morgue to see the victim.

6) Three sets of fingerprints are made to be transmitted to the local department's identification bureau, to the state's identification bureau, and to the Federal Bureau of Investigation.

7) Photographs are made as a permanent record. Particular attention is given to scars, tattoos, deformities, and other outstanding characteristics.

At the morgue, the following procedure is customary:

1) The body is immediately examined.

2) The clothing is searched for dry cleaner's and laundry marks and clothing labels.

3) The property is recorded. Documents are examined for identification.

4) An examination is made for scars caused by accidents or operations; tattoos; birth marks; moles; and other superficial characteristics.

5) Appliances, such as a truss, elastic stockings, artificial limbs, etc., can be traced through a manufacturer of prosthetic apparatus.

6) A complete description of the body is made.

7) Fingerprints of the deceased are recorded.

8) X-rays can be made to provide a more accurate description of bone structure anomalies.

9) The teeth should be described by a dentist.

b. **Missing Persons.** The steps which are to be followed in locating a missing person are quite similar to those given in the preceding chapter for tracing a wanted person. Ordinarily, however, there is one important difference between the two types of cases, namely, the motive. If the wanted person is the perpetrator of a crime, his motive for escape is quite clear; it is simply the evasion of justice. The typical missing person, on the other hand, is endeavoring to escape his present circumstances; he wishes to re-establish himself in new surroundings rather than simply to lie in hiding. The investigator should first complete the routine steps in official procedure:

1) *Notification.* A full description which places emphasis on peculiarities of the body or dress should be transmitted to other law enforcement agencies. A teletype alarm should be sent to the

neighboring states. Later a general alarm should be transmitted. Circulars with a complete description and a photograph should be distributed for placement in public places such as hotels, railroad stations, and post offices. Inquiries are made at hospitals and morgues.

2) *Background Investigation.* The investigator should interview the relatives and friends of the missing person in order to establish a motive. Information concerning the following should be developed.

a) Domestic background.
b) Personal habits.
c) Business history.
d) Associates—social and business.
e) Medical history.
f) Educational background.
g) Family history.

The methods described in the preceding chapter for tracing wanted persons will guide the investigator subsequently.

5. Illustrative Cases

Two 1952 Chicago cases will illustrate the effectiveness of these techniques in a typical large city.

a. One case involved the body of a man recovered from Lake Michigan. The fingerprints were not adequate since there was no general file. The only other clues were a pair of red swimming trunks and a red stone ring bearing the initials "T. B." and a manufacturer's marking. A visit to the manufacturer revealed that this latter was a class ring, specifically made for Wendell Phillip's High School. The school register listed a Timothy Bradley as a graduate of that class. Bradley's father denied this identity of the body. On questioning, it was found that the young Bradley had maintained a post office savings account. The prints were compared with those of the postal record and proved to be those of Timothy Bradley.

b. In another case, a man identified as Lawrence White was found dead in the street. The identification had been made by White's brother. When it was discovered that the family had no funds for burial, a further police investigation followed to save the body from a potter's field burial. Since White had been a World War II veteran, the prints were sent to Washington for verification with the hope that a burial could be achieved through the Veterans Administration. Washington reported that the prints belonged to a man named Stanley Michael Hochrek, another war veteran. Hochrek's sister visited the morgue and identified the body as that of her brother. It was learned that Lawrence White had left town the day of Hochrek's death to take a railroad job.

6. Misconceptions Associated with Missing Persons

A great deal of the statistical and conceptual information about missing persons is unreliable and inaccurate. There are no reliable nationwide statistics on missing persons. Among the more common myths popularized by magazines and other media are the following:

a. **Number of Missing Persons.** A number of journalistic sources have maintained that one million persons voluntarily absent themselves each year. The fact of the matter is that there is no way of demonstrating how many people disappear. There is no central clearing house for such information. Even if there were a source for a reliable statistic, this would still remain a "dark figure," since it would be unduly raised by the premature alarms of parents and spouses and would be lowered by the large number of people too proud, too poor, too depressed, or too indifferent to report.

b. **Clearance Rate.** It is widely believed that the police solve 95 percent or more of missing person cases. In practice the police do not have jurisdiction to look for everyone reported missing. The great majority of the cases that are handled by the police are solved by the voluntary return of the missing person.

c. **Difficulty of Disappearance.** "It is practically impossible to disappear in today's society." This is held to be true by reason of the efficiency of the police, the claims of private investigators, and the mass of documentation that accumulates in the average person's life. The notion of the difficulty of disappearing probably has its origins in the movies and television dramas which for the past fifty years have exploited the theme of the inevitable discovery of the fugitive, the lost, and the strayed. On any television night there is some film illustrating the futility of hiding from the Mafia. In reality it is quite simple for a person to disappear in a large city without a trace. In New York he would move five miles away or take a subway to Newark. To begin his new life he would acquire a new name and would "repaper" accordingly, e.g., a new Social Security card and driver's license. His behavior must, of course, be guarded and his activities moderately restricted, since changes of identity are most commonly discovered in the course of a routine ID check in connection with some trivial offense.

7. Sources of Information

There are no sources of information about missing persons who have changed their name. If the person has retained his own name then the Motor Vehicle Bureaus of the area and the credit bureaus are the most likely sources. The following comments suggest the usefulness of these and some other sources:

a. **Motor Vehicle Bureau.** Since a license is issued to any requesting adult who can pass the test, this source is useful only if the name is unchanged.

b. **Credit Bureaus.** This is the largest private source of alphabetized information on American citizens. The Associated Credit Bureaus of America number over 2,000 interconnected bureaus which exchange information among themselves and their 400,000 clients based on the 130-million customer reports on file.

c. **Federal Bureau of Investigation.** The FBI does not conduct searches for missing persons. It will, however, post a "missing persons" notice in its Identification Division files when a request is made by an authorized law enforcement agency or by an immediate relative of the individual whose location is sought. On receipt of pertinent information regarding the whereabouts of the missing person the interested party is notified immediately.

d. **Social Security Administration.** This agency annually receives more than 2,000 requests for information concerning the whereabouts of its clients. Most of the requests come from state and federal officials and relate to tax investigations, immigration problems, national security, and the Aid to Families with Dependent Children program. The Social Security Administration does not accept private requests. It should be noted that a Social Security card can be obtained simply on request. The card is designed for social security and tax purposes, not for identification. Since 1937 more than 150 million people have registered. At least 4 million have signed up more than once.

e. **Insurance Companies.** Although these companies conduct investigations of death claims related to missing persons, they do not reveal their information to the police or to private persons. That is, even after they have discovered a missing person these companies will not inform the relative. They consider the policy holder as a client whose confidence and wish for privacy they must respect. A company such as the Prudential receives annually close to 2,000 death claims based on legal declarations of presumed death, i.e., the court has decided there is reason to concede the demise of an individual even though no corpse has been found.

f. **Private Investigators.** The resources of the private investigator are limited since he must proceed on the assumption that the missing person will not change his name from Reginald Smith to Alonzo Jones. The investigator writes letters to the state motor vehicle bureaus in the area, requesting information about the issuing of a license to anyone named Reginald Smith. If the results are negative he then writes to credit bureaus, enclosing the appropriate fee and requesting a file check by name and date of disappearance. If the missing person has not changed his name, the investigator has a good chance of finding him.

ADDITIONAL READING

Bontly, T.: Missing Persons, 100 *McCalls*, September, 1973.

Gallagher, R.S.: *"If I Only Had It To Do Over Again . . ."* New York, Dutton, 1969.

Goldfader, E.: *Tracer. The Search for Missing Persons.* Los Angeles, Nash, 1970.

Krauss, T.C.: Forensic Odontology in Missing Persons Cases. 21 *Journal of Forensic Sciences*, 959, 1976.

Pileggi, N.: *Blye, Private Eye.* New York, Playboy Press, 1976.

Weitzman, L.J.: Social Studies; A Study of Missing Persons, Ph.D. dissertation, Columbia University, 1970.

Chapter 15

SURVEILLANCE

1. General

I~N~ MANY investigations a point is soon reached where little or no advantage can be obtained by further questioning of the complainant or the friendly witnesses. It is time, then, for the detective to go into the field to locate the criminal or, if he is known, to study his habits. At this juncture, the investigator must resign himself to the tedious but essential task of observing the activities of witnesses or principals in the case. The nature of the observation may be such that it is necessary to "put a tail" on certain persons or to maintain a fixed surveillance of a particular place. To the amateur these matters may appear relatively simple and readily accomplished by the use of ordinary common sense. The experienced investigator, however, is well aware of the value of a systematic procedure and the methodical employment of certain precautions. There is, in other words, a *technique* of observation. There are certain principles underlying this technique, which have been established by experiment and experience. There are pitfalls and errors which lead readily to a predictable failure. A surveillance which has failed may carry a double misfortune: the investment of time has been dissipated in the space of a few minutes, and the situation is often immeasurably worse than before because the subject of the surveillance is now alerted and will increase his precautions tenfold.

2. Definitions

Surveillance is the covert observation of places, persons, and vehicles for the purpose of obtaining information concerning the identities or activities of subjects. The surveillant is the person who maintains the surveillance or performs the observation. The subject is the person or place being watched. Surveillance may be divided into three kinds: surveillance of places; tailing or shadowing; and roping or undercover investigation. The objectives and methods will vary with each type of observation.

3. Surveillance of Places

In criminal investigations the crimes which usually require this kind of surveillance are gambling, prostitution, acting as a fence, and the illegal sale of drugs or alcohol. Private investigators will ordinarily watch a place to uncover evidence of dishonesty among the employees or of infidelity in a divorce case. In general, the objectives of place surveillance are:

To detect criminal activities.

To discover the identity of persons who frequent the establishment and to determine their relationship.

To discern the habits of a person who lives in or frequents the place.

To obtain evidence of a crime or to prevent the commission of a crime.

To provide a basis for obtaining a search warrant.

a. **Preliminary Survey.** A careful survey of the surrounding area should precede any surveillance of a place. The character of the neighborhood, the residents and the transients should be noted. The observation point should be selected after careful study. Two types of place surveillance will suggest themselves:

1) Using a room in a nearby house or business establishment and remaining undercover.

2) Remaining outdoors and posing as a person who would normally conduct his business in such an area, i.e., a laborer, carpenter, street vendor, or an employee of the building under observation.

b. **Equipment.** Whenever possible, a photographic record of visitors to the place should be obtained. A motion picture camera and a 4 × 5 still camera with telephoto lenses can be used. A

Figure 9a. Photograph of a street scene taken with a 35mm camera using a 50mm lens. Note the encircled areas which appear in (b) and (c).

Figure 9b. Surveillance photograph. This is the left encircled area of (a) photographed with a 35mm camera using a 40-inch reflector lens. Both photographs were taken at the same distance.

Figure 9c. Surveillance photograph. This is the right encircled area of (a) photographed with the same conditions as (b). Shortening the object distance by approximately 50 yards has improved the defintion. All photographs were enlarged to the same degree of magnification. The advantages of the 40-inch telephoto lens for surveillance work are obvious.

ten-power telescope or pair of binoculars is especially useful. If permission has been obtained, wire taps and recording apparatus can be employed. A night-viewer can be used in dark, unlit areas.

c. **Report.** A complete "log" of the activities taking place in the establishment under surveillance will form the basis of the report. The time of arrival and departure of each person should be carefully noted. Photographs and motion picture film footage should be numbered with reference to time. In addition to, or in lieu of, photographs, descriptive notes of visitors should be taken.

d. **Movements.** A certain degree of activity will be necessary to set up the observation post, move in equipment, relieve surveillants, and terminate surveillance. This should be accomplished as unobtrusively as possible. Surveillants should enter and leave separately. If it is necessary to take into confidence the residents of the observation point, the number of confidants should be held to a minimum and the purpose of the installation should not be revealed.

e. **Closed-Circuit Television.** The application of television to the work of law enforcement has proved fruitful in improving ongoing crime detection, decreasing response time to police incidents, and increasing the efficiency of surveillance personnel. Television installations for the protection of department stores, banks, and other institutions are familiar sights. The following are some more interesting illustrations of the use of this tool:

1) *Hidden Television Camera.* On August 22, 1972, three men were apprehended in the act of stealing $360,000 in negotiable bonds from a New York brokerage house where one of them worked. A separate batch of securities worth more than $400,000 was found in their getaway car. Federal and city law enforcement officers, acting on information, had watched over a closed-circuit television system as one of the defendants, a head messenger, handed a 2-inch-thick manila envelope to another defendant, who then proceeded to the waiting car.

2) *Video Patrol.* In Mount Vernon, N.Y., two remote control television cameras were placed in operation on the city's main business street. The cameras are capable of a legible image of a license plate at a distance of two blocks from the lens.

3) *Campus Security Surveillance.* A laser television communica-

tions installation is used at Case Western Reserve University as part of a remote surveillance system, linking television cameras by laser beams to the monitor in a police station nearly a mile away. The University police watch a 2-mile square area by television over two

Figure 10a. Closed-circuit television system used to detect criminal activity in the 2-mile square area of Case Western Reserve Campus and University Circle. Courtesy of A.C. DiFranco.

laser beams night and day. The two cameras were installed on top of the tallest buildings on the campus. The University Circle police force has reported a significant decrease in crime in the area.

4. Requirements and Appearance of Surveillant

The following are the conventional requirements for an investigator selected to shadow a person:

a. Average size, build, and general appearance.

b. No noticeable peculiarities in appearance or mannerism.

c. No conspicuous jewelry or clothing.

d. Perseverance and capacity to wait for hours at a time without showing any signs of impatience or irritation, since these attract attention.

e. The appearance of attending strictly to his own business and of not being interested in what others may be doing.

f. Resourceful, versatile, and quick witted, so that he can readily conceive reasons or excuses for being in any given place.

Figure 10b. Monitoring the surveillance cameras by remote control from the police station. Courtesy of A.C. DiFranco.

g. A fluent speaker, able to talk his way out of embarrassing situations without arousing suspicion.

h. Trained in one or two good standard *covers*, such as canvassing for the city directory or a trade publication or selling hosiery, brushes, or other common articles. In this connection he should carry with him the necessary forms, data, or identification to give his pretense an appearance of authenticity.

5. Shadowing

Shadowing or *tailing* is simply the act of following a person. The purpose of shadowing will depend upon the nature of the investigation. In criminal work the objective may be:

a. To detect evidence of criminal activities.

b. To establish the associations of a suspect.

c. To find a wanted person.

d. To protect a witness.

In the work of the private detective we may have an objective of the following nature:

a. To discover the associates, amusements, and habits of an employee who has been proposed for a position of responsibility.

b. To check the loyalty of employees in an establishment where thefts have occurred.

The objective of the surveillance will determine the character of the tail:

a. A "loose tail" will be employed where a general impression of the subject's habits and associates is required.

b. "Rough shadowing" or shadowing without special precautions may be used when the criminal *must* be shadowed and is aware of this fact; or where the subject is a material witness and must be protected from harm or other undesirable influences.

c. A "close tail" or surveillance in which extreme precautions are taken against losing the subject is employed where constant surveillance is necessary. For example, such a procedure would be recommended where the subject is suspected of impending criminal activities; or where the subject is suspected of past criminal activities and it is expected that these subsequent movements will yield the desired evidence; or where it is thought that the subject will lead the investigator to the hideout of the criminal.

6. Preparation

The investigator should, as always, make a preliminary survey of his task to prepare himself for contingencies that may suddenly arise:

a. Before undertaking a surveillance mission, the surveillant, assuming that he does not know the subject to be shadowed, should obtain a complete description of him and, if possible, arrange to have someone who does know the subject point him out to the surveillant. This description should particularly emphasize those details which are visible from *behind* the suspect, since that is the angle from which the surveillant will generally be watching him. It should include the type of headgear, overcoat, suit, and shoes that he ordinarily wears, the general carriage of his head and shoulders, whether his walk is fast or slow, his step short or long, and whether he acts as though he knows where he is going and goes there, or is hesitant and erratic in his pace and direction.

b. The investigator should learn as much as possible about his subject—his habits, haunts, and social life. In what areas will he be active? Are his tastes expensive? Will he dine at an expensive restaurant?

c. In the light of this information the investigator should accordingly prepare himself. He should endeavor to dress and act as though he belonged to the milieu in which he expects to find the subject. In preparation for a possible confrontation by the subject, he should have a plausible "story" which he can support with documents and knowledge.

d. He should comport himself as one belonging to the neighborhood. His manner should be casual and his interest apparently centered on matters other than the subject. Nervousness and haste should be studiously avoided. His dress should conform to his surroundings. In a commercial area he would wear a business suit; in a factory neighborhood, rough clothing would be in order; in suburban sections an informal costume would be found suitable.

e. He should study the neighborhood carefully in order to become familiar with the transportation lines and the likely pedestrian routes between certain points. In the event he loses his subject, the investigator will thus be better prepared to pick up the trail again.

f. The subject should be identified at the outset of the surveillance. Mental notes should be taken of the physical description, clothing, and the behavior of the subject.

7. Shadowing by Foot

The technique of shadowing by foot will vary with the number of men available. From one to six men can be usefully employed on a foot tail. The private investigator with a limited budget may be forced to do the shadowing by himself. A police agency should assign at least three persons to a foot tail. The purpose of using two or more persons is to minimize the risk of detection by falling into the subject's line of view too often or by being forced to make abrupt changes of direction.

a. A three-man tail is described here as typical of shadowing technique. The three men will be referred to as A, B, and C. A is closest to the subject S. He follows S at a distance which depends upon the conditions of pedestrian traffic. B follows A, at about the same distance from A as A is from S. C may precede S or, if vehicular traffic is moderate, may be approximately opposite him on the other side of the street. B and C take turns in occupying the position, thus preventing A's becoming a familiar and noticeable figure to S.

b. A number of advantages recommend this ABC method of shadowing. If the subject becomes suspicious of any of the operators, that person can quickly drop out of the tail. If S suddenly turns a corner, A may continue straight ahead, instead of hurrying to the corner and anxiously looking for the subject. C may then cross the street and follow S, thus taking up the A position. C, moreover, has been in a position to view any sudden disappearance into a building.

c. Prearranged signals should be employed. For example, if A feels that he has been "made," he can signal that he is dropping out of the tail by adjusting his hat.

8. Tactics

In general, the subject should be kept unaware of the shadowing operation. The investigator should be inconspicuous. He should not be detected looking directly at the subject. He should shift from left to right, never remaining for long directly behind the subject. Both sides of the street should be used. If he suspects that the subject has become alerted to the tail, he should request immediate removal from the assignment. A number of situations will arise that will test the resourcefulness of the investigator. A few of these are described below.

a. **Turning Corners.** If the subject turns a corner, the surveillant should not hurry. If the subject is lost, the nature of the neighborhood will determine the subsequent procedure. In most cases it is preferable to lose the subject than to alert him to the tail.

b. **Entering a Building.** If the building is a store, the operator should wait until the subject comes out. Naturally, in cases of a department store or an establishment with a number of exits it will be necessary to follow into the store. If the subject enters the elevator of a building, the surveillant should board the same elevator. If the elevator boy requests a floor number, he should give him the same one that the subject gave or else the top floor with the intention of alighting at the subject's floor. When two investigators are present, one should alight at the subject's floor but proceed in a different direction. The other investigator can then return to the first floor and wait for the subject.

c. **Taking a Bus.** The surveillant should board the same bus; sit behind the subject and on the same side. If he misses the bus, he should, of course, hire a taxi and board the bus at a point ahead.

d. **Taking a Taxi.** When the subject takes a cab, the surveillant should record the time, place, name of the taxi company, and license. He should endeavor to follow in another taxi. If this results in failure, he should trace the taxi by means of his recorded information and ascertain the destination from the taxi driver.

e. **Taking a Train.** If the subject shows his intention of buying a train ticket, the surveillant should endeavor to get in line behind him with one person intervening. If he hears the destination requested by the subject, he may buy a similar ticket. In the event he is unable to hear the destination, he should ask the agent the destination requested by the subject. If the surveillant does not intend to purchase a ticket, he should merely request a time table.

f. **In a Restaurant.** The surveillant should allow a few minutes to elapse before following the subject into a restaurant. He should then take an obscure seat and arrange to finish his meal at the same time as the subject.

g. **In a Hotel.** An inquiry can be made concerning the room of the subject. If he is registered, the surveillant can take an adjoining room.

h. **In a Telephone Booth.** The surveillant should either go into the next booth or stand near enough to hear. He should note the telephone book used and the page at which it is left open.

i. **In the Theater.** The surveillant should sit behind the subject and take note of the various exits which are available.

9. Recognition of Surveillant

There are two risks constantly incurred by a shadower—the risk of being "made," or recognized as a shadow by the subject, and the risk of being "lost," or eluded by the subject. Not even the most experienced shadow man can avoid these contingencies. He should, however, be prepared to take intelligent counter-measures.

There is a tendency among inexperienced surveillants to become easily convinced that they have been uncovered or "made" by the suspect—that the latter has found out that he is being shadowed and knows the identity of his follower. Rarely is there a real basis for the belief; it arises merely from the self-consciousness of the inexperienced shadow man. If the suspect does "make" the shadower, the latter will be left in no doubt about the matter from the actions of the suspect, who will often take a malicious pleasure in demonstrating that he is aware of the shadow. When the surveillant knows he has been recognized as such, he should drop the surveillance at once, but must exercise care in his subsequent actions. Although the suspect may have had several good views of the surveillant and has been convinced that the latter is following him, he will still be unaware of the identity of the shadow and will wish to satisfy his curiosity. Hence he is quite likely to turn shadower himself and follow the surveillant. Should the surveillant return to his home or office, followed by the suspect, the latter would then know who had been shadowing him and would be aware that the authorities had knowledge of his illegal activities. Thereafter, the suspect would either desist entirely from the pursuit of his objective or render the surveillance difficult if not impossible. The surveillant, therefore, must be quite certain that he has thrown off a shadow, either by the suspect or by someone else, before he goes to any place where the association might tend to identify him.

10. Testing a Tail

A favorite trick of suspects "testing for a tail"—ascertaining whether or not they are being shadowed—consists of boarding a public conveyance, such as a bus, streetcar, or subway train, waiting until the last possible second before the door closes and then jumping off the vehicle. The subject then looks about quickly to determine if any other person jumped off. If the shadower alights too, the suspect will study him closely to facilitate future recognition. On finding himself in this predicament, the surveillant's best tactic is to remain on the vehicle until the next stop, alight, and board the next car or train. Often he will find his subject and can continue the surveillance. To avoid being caught in this manner, the experienced surveillant will arrange to be the last passenger to board the vehicle, and will remain just inside the door until it is closed. Under these conditions if the suspect starts toward the door, the surveillant can immediately step off and appear to be waiting for another car or train.

11. The "Convoy"

When engaged upon a surveillance mission, the investigator must keep in mind that a shrewd subject is often guarding against a shadow by having one of his men follow him at a reasonable distance to observe whether or not the same person is constantly in the rear. Therefore, the shadower must keep a lookout *behind* himself to guard against this. If it is determined that the subject does have a follower or "convoy," the shadower must get behind the "convoy" and follow him instead of the subject.

12. Tailing by Automobile

The suggestions which have been offered for tailing by foot are applicable in large part to surveillance by means of the automobile. The number of persons and cars assigned to the task will be a function of the importance and difficulty of the assignment. Two cars can be used more effectively than one. By steadily interchanging positions, the risk of detection can be greatly lessened. At least two persons should follow the subject at a distance of about 100 yards. The distance of operation will become greater on highways and less in crowded traffic. If a second car is used, it should follow at an equal distance behind the first. The chief difficulty in tailing a vehicle will be encountered at night, since a great many cars will look quite similar at a distance from the rear. The subject car can be easily lost against a background of city traffic with its puzzling patterns of neon signs, traffic signals, and the taillights of other autos. The simplest solution to this problem is to mark the subject car beforehand so that it is identifiable at night. A pellet gun or even a .22 caliber revolver wrapped in a cloth can be used in an emergency to put a hole in one of the rear lights. A quick spray of a small area on the rear fender with an aerosol can of liquid glass will provide a less obtrusive means of identifying the car, since the reflective material is clearly seen from a position on a line perpendicular to the fender but is practically invisible from any other angle.

In an important case, where two or more surveillance cars are used, the movements of the cars should be closely coordinated through radio intercommunication. Depending on the radio facilities available, control can be maintained by one of the surveillance cars or by the communications center.

13. Disguising the Car

A car of popular type and color should be used. If possible, a change in vehicles should be made each day. The following precautions are sometimes useful:

a. **License Plates.** If the suspect uses a car, the surveillant, naturally, must also use a vehicle. He must be careful that the license plates cannot be identified as those of an investigator or his organization. He cannot, in general, use his own personal plates, since a check by the suspect would lead directly to the surveillant. There are three solutions to the problem:

1) Use tags borrowed from someone who is trustworthy, but who has no official associations.

2) Use rented cars.

3) Use special unregistered (dead) plates issued through the cooperation of motor vehicle authorities.

b. **Use of Rented Cars.** For an extensive surveillance job the use of rented cars is perhaps most satisfactory, since the surveillant can often change not only the license plates, but the cars themselves as the circumstances indicate.

c. **Appearance.** It is possible to alter the appearance of the car by various devices such as the use of removable stickers or other windshield adornments; changing license plates; shifting the headlights from dim to bright; using a multiple contact switch to eliminate one of the headlights; rearranging the seating of the occupants; changing the occupant's clothes, e.g., changing or removing hats; changing the number of the occupants.

14. Techniques

The manner of driving should be changed often. The driver should, for example, alternate between right and left lanes of his side of the road. A suspicious subject will suddenly stop his car to observe whether the surveillance car passes by. Obviously, to avoid detection, the surveillance car must proceed at the same speed until an opportunity is afforded to halt unobstrusively and permit the subject car to pass. Where two tail cars are employed, the stopping of the subject's car can be signalled from the first tail car to the second by flashing the brake lights in rapid succession an agreed number of times. A good part of tailing by vehicle consists in parking and awaiting the emergence of the subject from a home or business establishment. It is well to park as far away as is compatible with satisfactory observation. A car parked in the same block as that on which the subject resides will usually cause suspicion. The surveillant car should be parked in the next block, if at all possible. The building exits and the subject's car can be kept under close observation by means of binoculars. The occupants of the surveillant's car should sit in the back seat and remain inconspicuous. If they must wait a considerable time, it is advisable to leave the car and walk up and down the street casually.

15. Precautions

Among the most common errors made by inexperienced surveillants are the following: staying parked in the same spot too long; using a conspicuous car; having both surveillants in the front seat for an extended period of time; approaching the parking position furtively; parking in a prohibited zone, thereby attracting attention; operating a shortwave radio with excessive volume; failing to manage the changeover to a relieving team unobtrusively; telephoning repeatedly from the same store or filling station.

16. Notes

Since the activities observed during a surveillance may later become part of the evidence in a trial or perhaps become the basis of a subsequent interrogation, it is highly important that a record of the day's observations should be made. This should take the form of a log—a chronological record of the activities of both the surveillant and the subject. The reason for recording the movements of the surveillant lies in the importance of definitely establishing his movements for the purposes of cross-examination in a trial. An accurate knowledge of the subject's activities will prove of great value in an interrogation of the subject. By making shrewd guesses as to the purpose of the subject's movements, the interrogator can often lead the subject into the belief that his knowledge is quite detailed and intimate. The subject may more easily be persuaded into a confession. Moreover, a written record can be objectively studied in retrospect for the purpose of evaluating the results of the surveillance. By integrating the separate reports of each surveillant, the investigator may be able to construct a logical pattern of the subject's behavior which can serve as a criterion for the validity of the hypothesis that led to the surveillance. The following is a suggested log form:

Notes on a Surveillance
Case No......................

Investigator's Name
Date:..................

1. Operator's arrival—time and place..
2. Exact time of all items...
3. Description of premises—exits and entrances................................
4. Data on auto...
5. First observation...
6. Telephone calls..
7. Conversations...
8. Persons contacted by subject...
9. Places visited by subject..
10. Period covered..
11. Time of relief..

17. Conclusion

It is not assumed that the treatment of this subject which has been given above will provide the investigator with an unfailing method of dealing with every surveillance situation. A surveillance is a minor form of conflict. No fixed pattern can be prescribed. General principles should be studied with the prevailing reservation that the strategy will depend for its success upon an intelligent implementation by tactics. Thus, procedures must be frequently improvised to suit the requirements of the situation; the nature of these will, of course, depend upon the resourcefulness of the surveillant. When should he run the risk of being "made?" Is the time element sufficiently liberal that he may safely drop the suspect at this point to obviate the danger of recognition? When should the obviously fruitless surveillance be terminated? It should be apparent that the successful surveillant is the end product of training, experience, and

native intelligence. Rigid adherence to rules and dogged perseverance alone will not suffice.

18. Methods of Private Investigators

The very nature of private investigative work requires intense
concentration on the art of surveillance. As a result of extended
study, exceptional ingenuity, and impressive expense authoriza-
tions, private agencies have developed a number of excellent
instrumental techniques for surveillance.

a. **Automobile Surveillance.** One agency simplifies the problem
of tailing a vehicle by attaching to the understructure of the vehicle a
miniature transmitter with a mercury battery as the power supply.
The investigator's car, equipped with a receiver and a direction-
finding antenna, can then follow at a distance which precludes
detection.

b. **Wiretaps and Bugs.** A *wiretap* is an electronic device that
picks up both ends of a telephone conversation. A *bug* detects voices
in a defined space. Protection from wiretapping is based on the
Federal Communications Act of 1934, while protection from
bugging relies on the Fourth and Fourteenth Amendments.
Federal law authorizing both is based on Title III of the Omnibus
Crime Control and Safe Streets Act of 1968. The short description of
some of these eavesdropping devices given below overlooks the
technical difficulties associated with their use:

1) **Wiretaps.** The telephone can be tapped at a number of places
along the line, either in the building, along the street lines, or even
at the telephone exchange. The tapped line is monitored by
earphones or run into a recorder. Instruments are available that
record only when the line is in use. The more common forms of
tapping are the following:

a) Direct Tap. This is the most common form. A direct tap is
placed right on the phone pair in the phone company's bridge box,
usually located in the basement. A set of wires is attached to the
specified pair in the box and run into a tape recorder or a headset
concealed nearby.

b) Parasite Tap. This is a miniature transmitter wired into and drawing power from the telephone line. A variant of this device is the so-called *parallel tap*, which includes a small microphone as well as a transmitter. It has a self-contained battery but can draw auxiliary power from the telephone itself.

c) Induction Coil. Various types of coils and pick-up loops can be used in coupling to an active telephone line for the purpose of monitoring the conversations.

2) **Bugs.** The bug is a sophisticated radiating device in the form of a self-contained receiver and transmitter. In size some of these instruments are no larger than a fingernail and thus can be readily concealed in some part of a room. The listener can be in an adjoining room or even outside the building, depending on the nature of the instrument. Another device in this category is the body-worn transmitter. The capacities and limitations of concealed microphones in general can be studied in the references at the end of this chapter.

c. **Recorder.** The problem of surreptitiously recording conversations has been greatly simplified by the development of small instruments such as the pocket-sized recorder. These instruments are tape recorders of the approximate size of the 35 millimeter camera. They may be readily concealed in a pocket and will record for two hours. Other recorders, with longer running time, are concealed in suitcases and briefcases.

d. **Television.** The television camera and receiver have been added to the resources of the private investigators. By means of a closed circuit television system the activities of the subject can be observed by the surveillant at a distance. A number of private companies have installed these circuits to watch the activities and general behavior of their employees. In one factory four concealed cameras were installed to visually monitor the production line. A receiving set, connected to the cameras by a coaxial cable, was installed in the office of the plant manager. The employees of any section of the production line could then be observed by the manager surreptitiously and leisurely.

e. **Cameras.** The technological possibilities of surveillance in the future are suggested by *Time* magazine (Feb. 6, 1978) in its description of the supersonic SR-71:

The plane carries high-powered cameras that can map most of the U.S. in three passes, as well as three-dimensional filming equipment that can cover more than 150 sq. mi. so precisely as to locate a mail box on a country road.

Concerning spy equipment for monitoring persons and conversations, the article continues:

If a spy wants pictures to go with the dialogue he has bugged all he needs is an unobstructed view of his target, a little quiet, and either a Starlight Viewer with a camera adapter or an Intensifier Camera, both made by Law Enforcement Associates Inc., a New Jersey electronics firm. Compact hand-held devices, they retail for about $3,000 and can be operated along with earphones and a parabolic reflector or "dish" that can pick up normal speech up to 800 yds. away in an open space or in a room across a noisy street. The Starlight Viewer amplifies light 50,000 times and is perfect for nighttime surveillance; the intensifier needs some light but produces more sharply detailed photographs.

A bare outline of surveillance capabilities has been presented here. In the age of the reconnaissance satellite, the laser beam, and similar devices, it is difficult to place a limit on future possibilities. The legal problems associated with the use of such a technology are formidable.

19. Eavesdropping and the Law

The increased use of wiretapping and the rapid development of microphones and transmitting devices in miniature form have aroused concern in the courts and among lawmakers for the protection of individual privacy. Responding to this need Congress passed Title III of the Omnibus Crime Control and Safe Streets Act of 1968, 18 U.S.C. 2510—2520 prohibiting the interception of wire and oral communications by federal law enforcement officers except in one of the following circumstances:

1) Where one party consents;

2) Where a court order authorizing the interception is granted;

3) Where an officer determines that an emergency situation exists involving national security or organized crime, under the condition that he later obtains judicial authorization.

Except in cases of consent of one party, state officers do not have the right to intercept communications unless a state law authorizes it. To be admissible in court, all evidence must be obtained according to the provisions of this federal law.

20. Surveillance and Society

The scientific revolution of the past few decades has provided a technology that vastly increases the potential scope and effectiveness of technical surveillance. The threat to individual privacy has grown in proportion, while the problem of imposing protective controls on the use of technical surveillance has become equally formidable in size and complexity. Since the investigator is closer to the base of the problem, he should acquire an appreciation of its true scope and a sense of his personal responsibility to contribute to an ethical solution consistent with his claim to professional status. After all, the essential element in the definition of a professional man is this—he is a person who answers to himself for his own conduct.

a. **Categories of Surveillance.** Three broad categories of surveillance have been suggested to correspond respectively to what a person is doing, what he is thinking, and what he has done and thought in the past:

1) *Physical Surveillance* is concerned with what a person is doing or saying; hence it embraces those activities which can be apprehended by the senses, mainly sight and hearing. The methods described in this chapter belong in this category. Included, also, are eavesdropping, wiretapping, picture-taking, and spying. The technological facilities for accomplishing these forms of surveillance are impressive in variety and sophistication.

2) *Psychological Surveillance* is concerned with what a person is thinking and feeling. It is concerned with man's mind—his thinking, beliefs, opinions, feelings, and reactions. The tools of this form of surveillance include lie detectors, employment forms, personality tests, and the use of mind drugs. The areas of interest may include sex, religion, ethics, politics, and the normative references of behavior in general.

3) *Data Surveillance* is concerned with what a person *has* done or *has* thought. It consists, therefore, of the innumerable records man leaves behind in his journey through life—birth certificates, church records, school records, records of offenses, of credit and debt, of employment and of employers' estimates of character, of military service, and so forth. The major tool is, of course, the giant computer, centralized, comprehensive, infinite in appetite, instant in response, and forever faultless in memory.

b. **Applications.** The uses of these forms of surveillance are too many and too familiar to enumerate. Many of these applications are well intended but most of them can be adapted to questionable purposes and worse. The businessman, for example, may in good faith conceive the notion of researching customer reaction by means of hidden microphones, but subsequently he will find it difficult to resist the temptation of taping a sample of his employees' conversations, especially if his industrial psychologist supports his inspiration with a suitable label, such as "Employee-Attitude Sampling," or if his security chief seconds the recommendation on the grounds that it may provide a clue to the perpetrators of a series of inside merchandise thefts. Thus, the steps leading from legitimate inquiry into unjustified snooping are insensibly graduated to suit the spiritual gait of all but the most scrupulously honorable.

Together these three categories of surveillance with their highly sophisticated supporting apparatus represent a massive threat to the individual as such. They menace that aspect of the person which makes him, in his own mind, an individual—namely his privacy. The acknowledgment of human dignity takes the primary form of conceding the individual the privacy of his thoughts and converse.

c. **Supervision and Control.** Ordinarily we should look to the Supreme Court for protective rules against the invasion of privacy. In recent years the Court has tended to lay down objective standards for law enforcement conduct designed to permit close judicial supervision, despite the cost of such control in terms of convictions. The problems presented by the immensely broadened field of surveillance, however, cannot be solved by federal controls or restrictive rules similar to those prescribed for testing the legality of wiretapping. The Supreme Court cannot police the policeman by means of exclusionary rules issued and enforced by Washington. It must inevitably bow to the reality that the people of each community must shoulder much of the responsibility for enforcing the Constitution in their own area. The local law enforcement agencies, as the key representatives of the community in these matters, must assume major responsibility for the proper conduct of surveillances and the lawful use of the resources of the various categories of surveillance. The ultimate determinant in this area, however, must be the ethical judgment of the individual investigator, guided by the spirit of the law as interpreted through court decisions and by the policy statements of his organization.

In this connection, we should recall that the investigator is selected for three major qualities—character, judgment, and the ability to deal with people—and that the most important of these is character, the habit of acting on principle. The efficacy of any policy or set of rules will depend on the character of the investigator to whom they are issued. In this sense the law enforcement agencies constitute the propylon of the temple of justice. And in this spirit, too, we can understand Justice Oliver Wendell Holmes's observation that the law of the land may be the United States Constitution but to most of us it's whatever the policeman on the beat says it is.

ADDITIONAL READING

Physical Surveillance
Degarmo, J.W., Jr.: The Nature of Physical Surveillances. 42 *Police Chief*, 2, 1975.
Kornoff, J.J.: Police Helicopter Surveillance and Other Aided Observations. 11 *California Western Law Review*, 505, 1975.
Siljander, R.P.: *Applied Surveillance Photography.* Springfield, Ill.: Thomas, 1975.
————: *Fundamentals of Physical Surveillance.* Springfield, Ill.: Thomas, 1978.

Electronic Surveillance
Afferback, L., et al.: *Vehicle Tracking and Locating Systems.* Bedford, Mass.: Mitre Corp., 1974.
American Bar Association Standards Relating to Electronic Surveillance. Chicago, American Bar Association, 1971.
Carr, J.G.: *Law of Electronic Surveillance.* New York, Clark Boardman, 1977.
Courtney, J.: Electronic Eavesdropping-Wiretapping and Your Right to Privacy. 26 *Federal Communications Bar Journal*, 1, 1973.
Dash, S. (Ed.): *Eavesdroppers.* New Brunswick, N.J.: Rutgers University Press, 1959.
Jones. R.N.: *Electronic Eavesdropping Techniques and Equipment.* Washington, D.C.: National Institute of Law Enforcement and Criminal Justice, 1975.
Lapidus, E.J.: *Eavesdropping on Trial.* Rochelle Park, N.J.: Hayden Book Co., 1974.

Mason, J.F.: Designers Compete for that Snug Automatic Bug in the Rug. 21 *Electronic Design*, 20, 1973.

Neville, H.C.: Foiling the Electronic Eavesdroppers: a Survey of Available Countermeasures. 12 *Security World*, 4, 1975.

Oliver, B.M. and Cage, J.M. (Eds.): *Electronic Measurements and Instrumentation.* Inter-University Electronic Series, vol. 12. New York, McGraw-Hill, 1971.

Pollock, D.A.: *Methods of Electronic Audio Surveillance.* Springfield, Ill.: Thomas, 1973.

Saunders, E.F.: Electronic Eavesdropping and the Right to Privacy. 52 *Boston University Law Review*, 831, 1972.

Schwartz, H.: Comment—the Watergate Wiretapping. 9 *Criminal Law Bulletin*, 635, 1973.

————: Six Years of Tapping and Bugging. 1 *Civil Liberties Review*, 26, 1974.

Chapter 16

UNDERCOVER ASSIGNMENTS

1. Information

UNDERCOVER work or "roping," as it is sometimes called, is a form of investigation in which the investigator assumes a different and unofficial identity in order to obtain information. It may be classed as a method of surveillance. In its most effective form the investigator wins the confidence of the subject and induces him to reveal the desired information. The investigator, by adopting an identity compatible with the surroundings in which he will work, places himself in a position where he will be able to observe and gain the confidence of the subject.

Undercover work is a useful technique in crimes which require organization. "Selling crimes" involving drugs, alcohol, pornographic literature, stolen goods, frauds, contraband, or black market operations will constitute a large part of undercover work. In the investigation of subversive activities and systematic thefts undercover operations are almost indispensable. Undercover work is most successfully used when there is knowledge that certain persons are engaged in criminal activity but proof that may be used in court is lacking. It is especially effective in the investigation of ongoing offenses, such as blackmail or extortion. In such cases the undercover agent must gain the confidence of a criminal whose identity is known but against whom more evidence must be gathered. Verbal admissions may be obtained if the acquaintance is sufficiently developed, or better, a microphone can be placed surreptitiously in the rooms occupied by the suspect so that a recording can be made of any conversations concerning the blackmailing operations.

An investigator of the same ethnic background is sometimes

placed in the cell of a criminal. The undercover agent is selected, among other reasons, because he speaks the foreign language used by his "cell mate." The common national background and language compatibility, sympathy, reticence, or other assumed attitude needed to gain the confidence of the criminal has frequently been the means of gathering information about a particular crime or the activities of an organized mob which could not be obtained in any other way.

The undercover agent who has infiltrated into a criminal gang is in a position to learn the operations, feelings, past activities, and future plans of his "confederates." This information coupled with that obtained by intercepting telephone conversations among gang members can lead ultimately to the building of a successful case against the gang or any individual in it. An excellent illustration of this is the investigation of Al Capone on charges of income tax evasion by Elmer L. Irey of the Treasury Department. Evidence against organized groups dealing in contraband (narcotics), smuggling (gold, diamonds, etc.), or scarce items under government priorities or controls (resulting in hijacking trucks carrying these items) may in some cases be obtained using this technique.

2. Objectives

The general objective of an undercover investigation is the obtaining of information. Usually the information is desired for the purpose of evidence. There are situations, however, where the information is sought simply to lay the groundwork for a separate and major investigative step. The following objectives comprehend most of the investigative situations in which undercover work is employed:

a. **Obtaining Evidence.** The undercover worker places himself in an excellent position for obtaining evidence, either direct or physical. He can observe criminal activities, listen to conversations, photograph documents, and perform many other useful services.

b. **Obtaining Information.** The undercover worker is close to the most reliable source of information—the criminals themselves. He may find himself in the position of having the criminal explain to him the very details of the crime.

c. **Checking Informants.** If it is suspected that an informant's reports are prejudiced, misleading, or inaccurate, an undercover check can be made.

d. **Fixed Surveillance.** The most effective position for a surveillance is in the bosom of the criminal family. The undercover worker can even become a friend of the subject so that he is aware of every move made by him. He can also assist in the installation and maintenance of investigative equipment.

e. **Preliminary to Search.** The investigator can lay part of the legal basis of the search by determining the presence of contraband, for example, or by observing criminal activities. In addition he can assist the surreptitious approach of the searchers.

3. Selection of the Undercover Worker

Since the undercover assignment is the most sensitive type of investigative work, the selection of the operator must be made with great care. The ideal undercover agent is a combination of an actor and a good investigator. The selection should be made with consideration of the following elements:

a. **Background.** If the assignment places the agent in a special milieu, he must fit into the environment. His physical and other racial characteristics should not stand out. He must be able to suit his speech and line of thinking to that of his associates. His educational and technical background must rise to the required level. His conversation, knowledge of hobbies, and sports, as well as general information should suit the particular social stratum in which he will find himself.

b. **Temperament.** A calm, affable, enduring personality is required. He should have the necessary self-confidence to carry him through the more trying moments and the resourcefulness to adjust to a change of plans or situation.

c. **Intellect.** The undercover agent must above all be intelligent. He should have a clear view of the objective of the mission and the overall strategy that must be employed in its accomplishment. A retentive memory and keen imagination will serve him in good stead. Finally he should be an excellent observer and a person of sound judgments. Major decisions may be required during the course of the assignment. A mere tactical adjustment may be insufficient in a crisis. A critical situation will require the judgment of a good mind to avoid jeopardizing the whole investigation.

4. Assignment

The nature of undercover work can vary widely. A given assignment may require the investigator to place himself in several different social settings, testing to the fullest his resourcefulness, adaptability, and endurance. As a general rule the more complex assignment is more demanding in the completeness and flawlessness of the cover story which is employed. An assignment, for example, to perform undercover work with a group of competent racketeers entails serious hazards and requires the utmost attention to details. Among the more common types of assignment are the following:

a. **Neighborhood Assignment.** Here the investigator must move into the neighborhood of the subjects. In some situations it may be necessary to move into the rooming house of a subject. The assimilation of the undercover agent into the neighborhood background must be gradual and natural. A long period of time is required before the agent is accepted and his comparatively recent accession to the neighborhood is forgotten.

b. **Social Assignment.** In this type of work the investigator must frequent clubs, taverns, or other social meeting places visited by the subject or known to be centers of illegal activity.

c. **Work Assignment.** In the investigation of systematic thefts in a place of business it is usually necessary for the investigator to assume the role of a fellow employee. The work assignment can also be employed in place of the neighborhood type. The part of the employee is one of the simplest of undercover roles. The agent is not required to explain or justify his presence. If the job which the agent fills is a sales or clerical position, the assignment is relatively simple. Professions and trades require some experience or training prior to engagement in the assignment.

5. Preparation for the Assignment

If an investigator is working under the control of a superior, he should not undertake an undercover assignment without the express authorization of his superior officer. The type of character which the investigator should assume will be determined by the subject of the investigation. The following preparations for undercover work are recommended:

a. **Study of the Subject.** Unless the investigator has a thorough knowledge of his subject, he will find himself frequently at a disadvantage. The investigator should, as a first step in the preparation, draw up a checklist of the details of the subject's character and history.

1) *Name.* Full name, aliases, and nicknames. If he holds public office, then the title and the name of the department.

2) *Addresses.* Past and present, residential and business.

3) *Description.* A portrait parlé as given in Chapter 29.

4) *Family and Relatives.* An acquaintance with members of the family may suggest another source of information.

5) *Associates.* This knowledge is essential to an understanding of the subject's activities.

6) *Character and Temperament.* The strengths and weaknesses of the adversary should be known. Likes, dislikes, and prejudices are particularly helpful.

7) *Vices.* Drug addiction, alcohol, gambling, etc.

8) *Hobbies.* Suggest a simple way of developing acquaintance. A common interest of this nature creates a strong bond of sympathy.

9) *Education.* This knowledge suggests the limitations of the subject and will indicate the desired level of education in the investigator.

10) *Occupation and Speciality.* These suggest, again, a possible meeting ground and are also indicative of the character of the subject.

b. **Knowledge of the Area.** The investigator should make a thorough study of the area in which he is to operate. If he is to pretend previous residence there, he should possess an intimate knowledge of neighborhood details. The following checklist can be used.

1) **Maps.** The general layout and features of the area can be learned from a street map. Bordering areas should be included in the study.

2) **National and Religious Background.** The predominant racial characteristics of the inhabitants can be learned from a resident or from police officers assigned to posts in the area.

3) **Transportation.** The routes of surface lines and subways should be known together with their service schedules.

4) **Public Utilities.** A knowledge of matters such as the type of current available will assist in setting up a plant for technical surveillance.

c. **Cover Story.** A fictitious background and history for the new character of the investigator should be prepared, including the names, addresses, and descriptions of the assumed places of education, employment, associates, neighborhoods, trades, and travels. The investigator's background story should seldom, if ever, be wholly fictitious. It is usually advisable for the investigator to maintain that he is from a city in which he has lived and with which he is well acquainted. If it can be avoided, the home town of one of the subjects should not be selected as the origin of the investigator. Arrangements should be made to have principals in the fictitious history ready to corroborate the assertions of the undercover investigator, as the criminals may investigate his claims. It is good practice to select corroborating principals who are engaged in occupations which will not cause suspicion or arouse too much interest on the part of the subjects. It is imperative for the successful undercover investigator to possess all of the requisites for the assignment, such as appropriate personality, ability, background story, and attention to details.

Provisions should be made in the cover story for some of the following:

1) Frequent contact with the subject.

2) Freedom of movement and justification for actions.

3) Background that will permit the investigator to maintain a financial and social status equivalent to that of the subject.

4) Mutual points of interest between agent and subject.

5) Means of communication with agent's superiors.

6) Alternate cover story in the event that the original cover story is compromised, i.e., "Plan B."

7) A method of leaving the area quietly at the conclusion of the mission.

d. **Physical Details.** Personal possessions should be obtained for the undercover investigator which are appropriate to the character assumed in quality, price, age, fit, degree of cleanliness, laundry marks, and manufacturer's design; and ostensibly obtained from the place which the undercover man will claim as his origin. Personal possessions may include clothes, a pocketbook, a watch, a ring, a token, a suitcase, stubs of tickets from amusement places and transportation agencies, a brand of tobacco, matches, photographs, letters, certificates, or amounts of money. The undercover investigator must not possess any articles which will suggest his true identity. Badge or credentials must never be found on the person of an undercover agent; and a firearm or other weapon may be carried only where compatible with the investigator's background story.

e. **Testing.** The investigator should memorize all details in connection with his assumed role and the fictitious portions of his biography. He should be tested by prolonged questioning and surprise inquiries.

f. **Disclosure of Identity.** The investigator should be instructed whether to disclose his identity or remain undercover if arrested by other authorities. A plan or act should also be laid out against the contingency of accidental disclosure of identity.

6. Conduct of the Assignment

a. **Demeanor.** The undercover man must in every respect live the part which he plays. His appearance, language, attitude, opinions, interests, and recreations must support the assumed role. He should speak little, but let his actions carry conviction. When required, he must speak and act with assurance regarding his assumed past and trade, as he may be called upon to demonstrate his knowledge of the assumed trade. An undercover man should not ask questions except as part of the assumed identity, because inquiries usually attract attention. Bragging or showing too much knowledge may also invite unwanted attention.

b. **Approach.** Making contact with the subject or subjects is normally the first hurdle for the undercover investigator. As a general rule, the undercover man should create a situation where the subject or subjects become interested in and approach him, thinking he is what he purports to be. Many a subject has become interested in an undercover man who lived in the same rooming house, one whom he encountered frequently in the neighborhood or at a club or business house, or one who supposedly was vacationing, hunting a job, or a reputed expert in a matter which was a hobby of the subject.

c. **Entrapment.** It is against public policy for an officer of the law to incite or participate in the commission of a crime; the undercover man must, therefore, take care not to get involved as an accessory to a crime. He may pretend to fall in with their plans, but should never make any suggestions or promises, or render any real assistance with regard to the perpetration of crime. He should not be guilty of planting the criminal idea into the mind of the subject. At the trial the subject may plead entrapment and fix the responsibility for his actions on the agent.

Narcotics undercover work is particularly suceptible to entrapment charges. The accused may assert that the police provided the money, motivation, and connections to make the deal or that the police forced him to supply heroin. The undercover agent can protect himself from these charges by making several buys from the same dealer and also by obtaining testimony relating to the character and reputation of the accused. As a general rule the undercover worker can avoid such a charge if he maintains a restrained and passive role and does not engage in "creative activity" with respect to the commission of the offense.

7. Taking Notes

Written notes should be made by an investigator only when they are of unusual importance and when they cannot otherwise be remembered. They should be written in such a manner as to be unintelligible to anyone else. Numbers may be written as parts of a mathematical problem or as a telephone number. They may be written on inconspicuous materials such as chewing gum or cigarette wrappers, toilet paper, paper napkins, match boxes and covers, magazines, or on the wall paper in certain types of dwellings. Exposed film should not be kept in the agent's possession. It should be sent in immediately even though there is only one exposure on the roll.

8. Communication with Headquarters

a. **Telephone.** Communication between headquarters and the undercover investigator must be accomplished by secret methods. In calling headquarters by telephone it is best to use a dial telephone in a public booth not connected with a PBX or local switchboard operator. To lessen the possibility of wiretapping, the investigator should use a different telephone for each call.

b. **Written reports** may be addressed to a fictitious girlfriend at a prearranged general delivery address which is under the control of officials from headquarters. It is best not to put the undercover investigator's return address on the envelope as the post office department might return it to the investigator's dwelling for insufficient postage or other reason, in which case it might fall into improper hands. Since criminals usually have little correspondence, the investigator should not become conspicuous by the posting of numerous letters. To preclude the possibility of the reports falling into improper hands before mailing, they may be written in the post office and mailed there.

c. **Meetings** at secret, prearranged rendezvous may be held with representatives from headquarters, but this method of communication is dangerous, as the investigator may be tailed to the rendezvous. If the investigator, en route to the rendezvous, discovers he is being followed he may "lose" his follower in such a manner as not to show a deliberate attempt, or he may forgo the rendezvous and pursue a course which would appear natural to the "shadow."

d. **Emergency.** The possibility of making telephone reports to one's superiors while in the presence of the subjects should not be overlooked when it is imperative that headquarters be notified immediately of the latest developments. This communication may be accomplished by calling an unlisted number at headquarters or at the home of an associate investigator, under the pretext of calling a friend or business person on some routine matter. In such cases, the investigator should be sure that the person telephoned knows the alias with which he is addressed, understands the situation, and will cooperate.

9. Arrest of the Undercover Investigator

If the investigator is arrested by the police he will act in accordance with his orders. If he has not received orders regarding the disclosure of his identity in case of arrest by other law enforcement officers, he must act according to his judgment. In such a case, if retaining his assumed character does not serve a useful purpose, the investigator should refuse to make a statement except to a member of his own organization.

10. Departure

The undercover investigator should not "vanish." A plausible reason for departure should be invented. Discharge from employment, family illness, and fear of local police are among the many reasons that can be offered. The agent should leave open the avenue of return; otherwise a resumption of the assignment becomes too difficult.

11. Large-Scale Operations

Undercover work varies widely in the period of time consumed and the extent of the cover. The simplest activity is the buy and bust operation in which the undercover agent, on finding an unwary narcotics seller, tries to make a deal and thereafter arrest the dealer. Recently, more sustained and elaborate operations have been set up by a number of police agencies in the form of illegal "fences"—a rented warehouse and several plainclothesmen posing as criminals, one of whom, of course, is "Mr. Big." The purpose of the operation is to recover stolen property and to identify and arrest the thieves and fences responsible.

The Law Enforcement Assistance Administration, which has helped finance some twenty-two such projects ("Operation Sting") in fifteen cities, reported that these activities have recovered property valued at $44.4 million and have been responsible for more than 1,500 arrests. Most charges relate to the stolen goods unwittingly sold to the police before hidden cameras and microphones, but these operations have led also to arrests for murder, rape, bank robbery, arson and other offenses. The buying and selling of stolen property permits the development of close relationships with suspects who think they are dealing with fellow criminals.

ADDITIONAL READING

Hicks, R. D. II: *Undercover Operations and Persuasion.* Springfield, Ill.: Thomas, 1973.

Motto, C. J.: *Undercover.* Springfield, Ill.: Thomas, 1971.

Schiano, A. and Burton, A.: *Self-Portrait of an Undercover Cop.* New York, Dodd, Mead, 1973.

PART IV
SPECIFIC OFFENSES

Chapter 17

ARSON

THE GRAVITY of the arson situation in this country can be measured by the increased attention being devoted to the investigation of this offense. A National Fire Academy with provision for training arson investigators has been established as part of the Federal Government's National Fire Prevention and Control Program; several U.S. Attorneys have set up arson task forces for their areas; the larger cities have instituted arson squads and greatly increased the number of fire marshals; insurance companies have similarly increased their arson investigative units and training programs.

This impressive law enforcement response is in porportion to the steady rise of arson statistics during the past ten years. Because of the difficulty of determining how many of the fires of "unknown causes" are in fact deliberately set fires, there are no accurate figures for the number of arson incidents in a given year. Nevertheless, the extent of the problem nationwide is reflected in the rough estimates offered by experts for the year 1976:

Deliberately started fires..................... more than 100,000
Deaths caused by such fires................ more than 1,000
Injured persons................................ more than 10,000
Insurance claims costs........................ $2 billion

Characteristic of this increased arson activity is its growth as a commercial enterprise, complete with entrepreneurs, brokers, middlemen, and agents. The lone fire setter has in some areas been replaced by a conspiracy—a group of persons organized to accomplish the offense in a professional manner. The case of Suffolk County in Massachusetts is a good illustration of this trend. In one morning, as part of a state police raid, twenty-two persons were arrested, among them six attorneys, eleven real estate operators, four public insurance adjustors, one police officer, and a retired fire chief. A total of twenty-six men were ultimately arraigned on charges as varied as fraud, bribery, and murder—and all were alleged to have committed arson. In general, they were accused of contracting with landlords, financially troubled shopkeepers, warehouse owners, and others to burn down their buildings for insurance with a provision for sharing in the claim.

Smaller-scale operations are, of course, more common. For some landlords arson is seen as a means of profitably liquidating otherwise unprofitable assets. The following pattern has been discerned in areas such as the South Bronx: the tenants are driven out by cutting off the heat or water; the fire insurance is paid up or even increased with a promise of improvements; finally the firesetter is hired. From one point of view the landlord is selling his building to the insurance company because no one else will buy it.

The traditional problem in the investigation of arson is that of proof—the fire too often consumes the evidence and the clues. The traces of the arsonist's activity are burned with the property. In the choice of method the arsonist can still rely on the simple approach of matches, fuses, and gasoline. There are, however, expert firesetters whose ingenuity is impressive. In one case the arsonist deactivated the sprinkler system by building a wooden collar around the main pipe, filling it with dry ice, and thereby freezing the water in the pipe. In the subsequent blaze this clever contrivance disappeared and it was only through other investigative bypaths that its use was discovered. Recently investigators have tended to reach out farther than the fire scene for means of proof, since the arsonist may be part of a conspiracy. For example, federal prosecutors have begun to use the federal mail fraud statutes (the mails are used for false insurance claims) because it is often easier to prove mail fraud than to establish the perpetrator at the scene or to prove interstate travel to plan arson. The U.S. Attorney for western Pennsylvania has won twenty arson convictions based on the federal crime of mail fraud.

The formidable difficulties encountered in proving arson are best shown by insurance company records. Although the companies bring only ten per cent of these questionable fire cases to civil court, they still lose eight out of ten such suits.

I. BURNING OF BUILDINGS

1. Arson Defined

Arson is the malicious burning of another's house. The gravity of the offense lies in the danger to the lives of persons who may be dwelling in the house at the time of the fire. The spirit of the common law implies that arson is a crime against the security of a dwelling house as such and not against property. Various state statutes, however, provide for the punishment of burning property as such under the law of arson. A "Model Arson Law" has been proposed and is in effect in many states. The elements of proof required in the aggravated form of arson are concerned with the "burning," "malice" and "dwelling" aspects of the offense:

a. **Burning.** A structure is not burned within the meaning of an accusation of arson until some part of it is heated to the point of ignition. Any appreciable burning is sufficient. It is not necessary that there be a flame or that the structure be consumed or materially injured. The ignition satisfies the requirement of burning.

b. **Inhabited Dwelling.** If the structure is used exclusively or in part specifically for dwelling purposes it is classed as an *inhabited dwelling*. The essential consideration is the use which is made of the building; it is not essential that a human being be actually present in an "inhabited dwelling." Thus a trailer, tent, church, or theater can be the subject of an aggravated arson. The value and ownership should be proved even in aggravated arson, since they provide an additional method of identifying the dwelling or structure. Facts related to the identity of the actual occupants should be obtained.

c. **Malice.** Unless there is a malicious intent to burn, no crime of arson exists. Malice is the intent to do injury to another. Fires caused by negligence or accident do not constitute arson. The intent is to be inferred from the facts. The conditions surrounding the act such as threats, quarrels, expressions of dislike, applications of fire insurance, and so forth, may supply a basis for inferring intent. The prosecution must show that a burning was accomplished with criminal design. The law presumes that a fire is accidental in origin; hence the criminal design must be shown beyond a reasonable doubt.

2. Attempted Arson

Attempted arson is an act done with specific intent to commit arson which, except for the intervention of some preventing cause, apparently would result in the actual commission of the offense. The attempt, consequently, must be accompanied by some overt act designed to carry out the intent. The mere gathering of incendiary materials with malicious intent to burn a structure is not an attempt to commit arson. If, however, a lighted match is applied to the structure or other property, the act is an attempt to commit arson even though the match may be immediately extinguished by the elements or otherwise.

3. Methods of Proof

The investigation of arson often presents a complex problem because the methods employed by incendiaries and the manner in which they operate are far greater in number and more varied in aspect than those employed by most other types of criminal. Proof of the commission of the offense is rendered more difficult because the physical evidence, normally providing material assistance in an investigation, is often destroyed by the criminal act itself. The same basic elements of all criminal investigations, however, are required of arson inquiries, namely, the establishment of the *corpus delicti* and the identification of the perpetrator.

a. **Corpus Delicti.** Since in law every fire is presumed to be of accidental origin until proved otherwise, this presumption must be overcome before an arson charge can be established. Evidence must be adduced to show the *corpus delicti* of the offense, that is, the existence of the essential facts demonstrating that the offense had been committed. It must be emphasized that the unsupported confession of a person with respect to the burning is insufficient and inadmissible in the absence of a substantial and independent showing of the *corpus delicti*. To establish the *corpus delicti* the following two facts must be established:

1) *Burning.* It must be shown that there was a fire, i.e., a burning or charring as distinguished from a mere scorching. The burning of

the property and its location can be established by the direct testimony of the complainant, fire department personnel, or other eyewitnesses. Physical evidence in the form of burned parts of the building may also be offered as proof.

2) **Criminal Design.** It must be shown that the fire was willfully set by a person criminally responsible. This may be established directly by the discovery of an incendiary device or plant such as a candle or mechanical arrangement, by the unexplained presence of accelerants such as kerosene or gasoline, or by eyewitness testimony. Negatively, the incendiary nature of the fire can be shown by the elimination of accidental and natural causes such as those previously described. The testimony of technical experts, expressing the opinion that the fire was not of an accidental or natural origin, can be used. Electrical, heating, or structural engineers, for example, can, if properly qualified, testify to the absence of wiring deficiencies, structural defects, or other conditions which could cause fire. The evidence should be sufficient to exclude every reasonable hypothesis other than that the property was feloniously burned.

b. **Other Evidence.** Once the *corpus delicti* is established, any legal and sufficient evidence, direct or circumstantial, may be introduced to show that the act was committed by the accused and that it was done with criminal intent. In arson cases direct evidence is ordinarily lacking with respect to the connection of the offender with the crime and great reliance must be placed on circumstantial evidence. The following general types of evidence will usually be encountered in addition to those discussed in the preceding paragraphs.

1) **Evidence Associating the Suspect with the Scene.** Clue materials such as tools, matches, and articles of clothing may be found at the scene and sometimes traced to the suspect. Similarly, the suspect may have carried on his person or clothing traces which link him to the scene.

2) **Evidence Showing Intent.** The actions of the suspect can frequently offer evidence of criminal intent. For example, anticipation of a fire may be shown by such circumstances as the removal of valuable articles or the substitution of inferior articles. Ill feeling or unfriendly relations between the accused and occupants of

the burned building may be shown. The absence of any effort to extinguish the fire or to turn in the alarm in the presence of an opportunity is significant. The flight of the suspect may be incriminating.

4. Motives

Although it is not absolutely necessary to establish a positive motive, the fact that the element of intent is essential in proving arson suggests the importance of showing a motive. In cases where great dependence is placed on circumstantial evidence it is especially important to prove a motive. Experience has shown that five motives predominate in arson cases, namely, economic gain, concealment of a crime, revenge, intimidation, and pyromania. Since government property is not insured the importance of economic gain as a motive in fires on government-owned property is greatly diminished.

A significant number of arson cases involve juveniles who are hired by landlords, contractors, salvagers, or dissatisfied residents to set fires, sometimes for as little as ten dollars a job. Some terrorist groups are suspected of employing arson as a tactic to further their political aims. Riots are usually accompanied by random incendiary acts. The possibility of fires being set out of a pure sense of mischief should also be considered.

a. **Economic Gain.** The burning of property can profit the assured directly or can provide a means of gain for the perpetrator indirectly without regard to the insurance.

1) *Insurance Fraud with Assured Directly Benefiting.* The business motives which underlie the defrauding of an insurance company are often complex and not readily apparent to the investigator. Although reference is made here to business establishments, the motives described are applicable to such simple cases as the housewife who burns a sofa or some clothes for the purpose of replacing the property with new articles. The following are among the more common motives attributed in the past to businessmen:

a) DESIRE TO MOVE. The premises may no longer be desirable

because of the condition of the building, the fact that the quarters are outgrown, or because of the locality.

b) DISPOSING OF MERCHANDISE. The stocks on hand may have lost value by reason of the seasonal nature of the business, obsolescence, scarcity of materials necessary to complete contracts, overstock in the absence of expected orders, or a changing market.

c) PROPERTY TRANSACTION. The business itself may no longer be desirable because of impending liquidation, settlement of an estate of which it is part, the need for cash, prospective failure, the comparatively greater value of the land, or the comparatively greater value of the insurance benefits.

2) *Profit by a Perpetrator Other Than the Assured.* Although the beneficiary of the insurance on the business or the premises may be innocent, the perpetrator may achieve economic gain. Offenders of this type can usually be placed in one of the following categories:

a) Insurance agents wishing more business.

b) Insurance adjusters desiring to adjust a loss by securing a contract.

c) Business competitors.

d) Persons seeking jobs as protection personnel.

e) Salvagers or "strippers" who are interested in stealing the copper pipes, the boiler, or the plumbing fixtures.

f) Contractors wishing to rebuild or wreck. In the longstanding practice of "fire-chasing," the contractor rushes to the scene of a house fire to obtain a repair contract. In the agreement the contractor arranges for the insurance settlement to be sent to him. He inflates the cost of the damages and makes only the minimal repairs. Eventually the contractor may resort to arson to increase his business, often in collusion with the owner who in return receives a kickback.

g) Apartment residents who are dissatisfied with their housing may arrange for a fire to be set. Fire victims often can collect special cash benefits from the city as well as priority in new public housing.

b. **Concealment of a Crime.** The arsonist may set fire to a building in order to conceal a projected or past crime. He may, for example, wish to divert attention in order to loot the burning premises or burglarize others. Another motive is the desire to break out of confinement in the confusion caused by the fire. The most common of these motives, however, is the desire to destroy evidence. For example, a person whose office records would not pass inspection may conceal mismanagement by burning the documents. Supply personnel can conceal a stock shortage by arranging a fire in the supply room. Finally, it is not uncommon for a criminal to attempt to conceal crimes such as larceny or murder by burning the building in which the crime was perpetrated.

c. **Punitive Measure.** An arsonist may use fire as a means of punishing another person for reasons of jealousy, hatred, or revenge. For example, a military person suffering a real or imaginary grievance may set fire to a barracks or a chapel.

d. **Intimidation and Economic Disabling.** Fire is a favorite means of warfare, both private and international. It can be used as a weapon of the saboteur, the unscrupulous striker, or the racketeer to intimidate or to disable economically as a step toward forcing submission to certain demands.

e. **Pyromania.** Strictly speaking, pyromania, an uncontrollable impulse toward incendiarism, is a mental affliction and not a motive. Indeed, pyromania is a term used to describe a condition of mind leading to an act of arson that is not rationally motivated. This type of person has a passion for fire that can be satisfied only by watching flames. Ordinarily the pyromaniac works alone. He may not run from the scene, turn in an alarm, or do anything observable which could associate him with the fire. Among the various types of pyromaniacs are the following:

1) *The Abnormal Youth.* Included in this group are mentally deficient persons of both sexes who set fire without any realization of the seriousness of the act. Their enthusiasm and rapture at the sight of the blaze, together with their general conduct, which is easily recognized as that of a mentally disturbed person, can make them noticeable even in the throng that gathers at the scene of a fire.

2) *The "Hero" Type.* Occasionally cases occur in which the person sets a fire, subsequently pretends to discover it, and turns in the alarm. Persons of this type wish to appear as "heroes" to the public. A person who desires to be a fireman, for example, or a watchman, may set fire to a building and endeavor to achieve spectacular rescues in order to attract the attention of spectators.

3) *Alcoholics and Drug Addicts.* Persons who subject themselves

to intense artificial stimulants such as alcohol or narcotics sometimes develop a strong urge toward incendiarism. In their normal condition these persons do not evince any sign of pyromania. Under the influence of the stimulant, however, they become victims of an uncontrollable desire to see a fire.

4) *Sexual Deviates.* This type of pyromaniac, usually a male, is said to derive sexual stimulation from setting a fire and watching the flames. He is thought to be a person given to chronic self-abuse, whose sexual gratification is enhanced by acts of arson.

5. Factors Influencing Burning

Most ordinary combustible substances are compounds of carbon and hydrogen, often containing mineral matter and oxygen. When they burn freely and completely in the air, the carbon reacts with the oxygen to form carbon dioxide; the hydrogen combines with the oxygen to form water; and the mineral matter remains behind as ash. In the first stages of a fire the building structure and the materials, such as wood and cloth contained in building, are merely heated and give off gases and vapors. With increased heat and exposure to flames these materials finally reach the ignition point and burst into flame. The rate and extent of the spread of fire depend on a number of factors, chief among which are the following:

a. Wind velocity and direction.

b. Relative humidity, dryness of the materials, and the absence of rain.

c. Air temperature.

d. Nature and condition of any vegetation surrounding the building.

e. Nature of the building construction; in particular the presence of wood and the arrangements for drafts. Partitions, laths, eaves, roofs, and shingles which are constructed of wood will aid the spread. Drafts created by stairwells, elevator shafts, and open doors and windows will obviously hasten the conflagration.

6. Causes of Fire

A fire originates intentionally or accidentally. One method of proving that a fire was intentionally set is to eliminate systematically the possibility of accident. An accidental fire may arise from the working of certain forces of nature or from negligence in the use of equipment or materials. The following are the most common accidental causes:

a. Carelessly discarded cigarettes and matches.

b. Careless disposition of readily combustible materials such as oily waste and painting equipment.

c. Poorly managed or defective heating systems. This includes overheated and overturned stoves; clothes dried too close to a fireplace; lint from fabrics coming in contact with open fires or radiant heaters; faulty chimneys and flues; explosions resulting from kerosene stoves; and leaks in pipes of gas stoves.

d. Spontaneous combustion arising from the storage of oily or chemically saturated materials such as cloth, paper, or cotton waste deposited in poorly ventilated places.

e. Sun rays focused by bubbles in window panes, shaving mirrors, or by some other peculiarly shaped glass article which may serve as a convex lens.

g. Lightning. If a thunderstorm took place in the vicinity of the fire at the time of occurrence, an examination should be made for traces of lightning. Metal parts of the building may exhibit melting. Paint will be streaked with burned areas. Cracks in the walls, broken bricks, and soot driven into the rooms from the chimney are among the other signs. Lightning usually strikes a high point of the building and may be traced in its path to the ground.

h. Electrical mishaps. As a subdivision of accidental causes of fire, electrical sources deserve more extended treatment because of the frequency with which such accidents arise. Modern buildings are heavily equipped with electrical wiring to operate fixtures, machines, and heating apparatus. Defects in any part of the system may result in fire. Specifically, the cause is either an arc or sparking or excessive heat. A combination of these may also be found as the cause.

1) Arc or sparking. These will be discussed together since an arc may be considered as a sustained sparking. When an inductive circuit is suddenly broken, the electromotive force induced in the inductive coil may rise to a very large value causing a current to jump across the opening contact points in the form of a spark. The

breaking of the circuit may be caused by the opening of a switch or the loosening of a contact. If an electric circuit is carrying a current larger than that for which the switch was designed, the spark, when the switch is opened, may vaporize sufficient metal to cause an arc across the mains and so open the circuit breaker or destroy the switch. On high potential circuits, switches are immersed in oil to prevent this danger. The presence of combustible material in the area surrounding the arc may readily provide fuel for a fire.

2) Overheating. One effect of current flowing through a wire is the production of heat, which is proportional in quantity to the resistance multiplied by the square of the current. The smaller the diameter of the wire, the greater the heat produced. A short circuit may lead to a greater current through the circuit than the wire can maintain. The result is a melting of the insulation and the ignition of nearby combustible materials. The National Electric Code pre-scribes maximum current loads for various sizes and kinds of wire. Among the other causes of overheating are faulty wiring, improper voltage, low line capacity, neglected electric motors, soldering, curling, and flat irons. Other appliances such as vacuum cleaners and refrigerators can overheat if they are neglected.

7. Methods of the Arsonist

The techniques, devices, and materials employed by the arsonist vary with his mentality and with his emotional condition immediately prior to the commission of the offense. A person who plans an incendiary fire for an insurance fraud or to conceal a series of embezzlements will ordinarily plan his crime carefully and employ ingenuity in its execution. A pyromaniac of the mentally deficient type or a person concealing an unplanned crime of violence usually acts in haste and is indifferent to the need for cleverness. It may be noted that excessive ingenuity frequently betrays the arsonist, since the fire is often under control before the incendiary device is destroyed by the flames.

a. **Incendiary Materials.** Obviously to create a fire there must be present combustible material. The burning material or fuel may be already present or later introduced. It may be a solid, liquid, or gas.

Strictly speaking, only gases burn. The solids and liquids must be heated to liberate flammable gases. The gases in turn must be raised to the proper temperature before ignition occurs. Hence there must be present the material to burn and a source of heat to raise the temperature of the fuel to the kindling point. Finally there must be a supply of oxygen, since burning is an oxidation process. If the supply of oxygen is only 17 per cent of the atmosphere present, the flame is extinguished and the fire cannot be supported. Oxygen may be supplied from the air or from oxidizing agents.

1) **Liquids.** Liquids such as gasoline or ether with low flash points do not require open flame for ignition. In the presence of a spark, rapid and explosive fires may result from the mixture of these vapors with air. The following liquids possess excellent incendiary properties and as a consequence are often used by the arsonist as accelerants:

Liquid	Flash Point (Fahrenheit)
Alcohol (grain)	61°
Benzol	40°
Petroleum ether	24°
Gasoline	45°
Kerosene	100°
Naphtha (safety)	100°
Turpentine	95°

2) **Gases.** Certain gases when mixed with air possess excellent ignition properties and when present in an enclosed area can lead to an explosion. In an arson investigation, however, it should be remembered that a slow fire, poorly ventilated, will often provide its own explosive gases. The following are the more common gases resulting in fires from explosions.

Gas	Explosive Limits
Acetylene	2.6%-55.0%
Butane	1.6%-6.5%
Carbon Monoxide	12.5%-74.0%
Ethylene	3.0%-35.0%
Hydrogen	4.1%-75.0%
Natural Gas	4.8%-13.5%
Propane	2.3%-7.3%

3) **Solids.** When solids exist in finely ground or powdered condition they form an excellent combustible substance. Coal dust,

grain, metals, and other materials will burn rapidly when combined with air and ignited. Some substances generate intense heat on contact with water. Notable among these are sodium, sodium peroxide, potassium, and calcium carbide. Certain solids, called oxidizing agents, give off oxygen on decomposition thus aiding combustion. Incendiary pencils, for example, can be made with potassium chlorate, an oxidizing agent, and sugar separated from a fragile capsule of concentrated sulfuric acid. When the capsule is broken, the acid extracts water from the sugar, leaving charcoal and giving a sufficient heat reaction to liberate the oxygen from the chlorate and ignite the charcoal. The following are typical families of oxidizing agents:

> Chlorates
> Perchlorates, including Perchloric Acid
> Chromates, including Chromic Acid
> Bichromates
> Nitrates, including Nitric Acid
> Permanganates

b. **"Plants" and Other Contrivances.** The "plant" is a device which is designed to ignite combustible material sometime after the initiating action. During this period of time the arsonist has an opportunity to escape from the premises or leave the neighborhood. With a sufficient time delay the criminal may establish an alibi by being present at another place at the time of the fire. Exceptionally clever arsonists employ remote control devices to accomplish ignition thus obviating the necessity of being at the premises to start the fire. The following methods are used in conjunction with the combustible materials described previously:

1) *Heating Appliances.* Gas and electrical appliances can be employed to supply the heat necessary to ignite a combustible material. The following have been used by arsonists:

a) *Heaters* such as flat irons, toasters, soldering irons, hot plates, and lamps. The heater is placed in contact with a combustible material, switched on, and abandoned. The arsonist thus has sufficient time to leave the scene.

b) *Sparkers* such as electrical switches, door bells, short circuits, and telephone boxes. If the vapor of a volatile fluid such as gasoline is present in high concentration, the spark may be sufficient to set off an explosive flash. It can be seen that a plant of this nature permits the criminal to be at another place when some other person innocently performs the initiating action.

2) *Mechanical Devices.* These are usually time delay arrangements such as the following:

a) *Clock mechanisms* which can be arranged so that the alarm movement starts the action.

b) *Altered equipment* such as broken pipes on oil burners or sprinkler systems in which combustible fluids have been placed.

c) *Magnifying glasses* focusing sunlight on a combustible material.

d) *Animals* tied to ignition devices.

3) *Trailers.* A favorite device of the criminal is a slow burning initiating arrangement constructed in one of the following ways:

a) *Streamers* may be made out of candlewick, rope, or cloth saturated with an inflammable liquid such as kerosene. They are strung from room to room to provide a path for the fire.

b) *Cigarettes* can be employed for this purpose by lighting and placing them on a book or box of matches.

c) *Candles* can be placed in straw, excelsior, or paper. Often a piece of the candle may be recovered from the neck of the supporting bottle.

4) *Inflammable Gases.* The combination of a plant and an inflammable gas is a particularly dangerous arson technique. The result is usually an explosion followed by a fire. The more common gases employed for this purpose are the following:

a) *Illuminating gas* may be made to fill the interior of a building by sawing off a low-lying pipe or by simply turning on a jet. A spark or pilot light will ignite the gas.

b) *Sewer gas* may be caused to seep into a structure in certain city areas by removing the water from a toilet, sink drain, or trap.

5) *Chemical Devices.* These became well known as offensive weapons in World War II.

a) *Thermite bombs* are found exceedingly difficult to control. The main body of the bomb consisted of powdered aluminum and titanium oxide.

b) *Phosphorous* can be used to impregnate cards, so that, on drying, the cards burst into flame.

c) *Molotov Cocktails* in the crude form of a soda bottle filled with gasoline and a streamer of cloth or paper have become the favorite incendiary device of rioters.

6) **Explosives.** Bombs are ordinarily used to cause physical damage to machinery or personnel. Any ensuing fire is usually not intended. However, since fire is one of the common consequences of such an act, the use of explosives can become an act of arson. Nitroglycerin, TNT, mercury fulminate, gunpowder, and gun cotton are the common explosives employed for this purpose.

8. Investigation During the Fire

Since there is much valuable evidence and information to be gathered during the fire, the investigator should respond to any serious or suspicious fire affecting property within his assigned area of responsibility. By maintaining appropriate liaison with the fire department servicing the area, it is possible to arrange for prompt notification in the event of such a fire. It will be assumed throughout the following discussion that the burning property includes a building.

a. **Observations During the Fire.** The extent to which the investigator can conduct a preliminary investigation during the actual burning will vary with the nature and severity of the fire. General observations can, of course, be made from an appropriate distance and certain examinations of the peripheral area can sometimes be made at this stage. Much of the information suggested below can also be obtained later from eyewitnesses.

1) *Smoke and Vapors.* The characteristics of the smoke, steam, or other vapors which emanate from the fire are useful indications in determining the nature of the burning substances, including the accelerants used. In the following list the color of the smoke is related to the most common incendiary agent which may emit it.

a) STEAM AND SMOKE. The presence of steam indicates that humid substances have come in contact with the hot combustible substances. The water present in the humid substance is evaporated before the substance begins to burn.

White smoke is given out by the burning of phosphorus, a substance that is sometimes used as an incendiary agent.

Grayish smoke is caused by the emission of flying ash and soot in loosely packed substances such as straw and hay.

Black smoke is produced by either incomplete combustion or the preponderance in the burning material of a product with a petroleum base such as rubber, tar, coal, turpentine, or petroleum.

Reddish-brown or yellow smoke indicates the presence of nitrates or substances with a nitrocellulose base. Thus, smoke of this color can be emitted from the burning of nitric acid, nitrated plastics, film, or smokeless gun powder. A number of these substances are suitable as accelerants.

2) **Color of Flame.** The color of the flame is indicative of the intensity of the fire and sometimes of the nature of the combustible substances present. The temperature of the fire may vary from 500 to 1500 degrees Centigrade with the color of the flame ranging from red, through yellow, and finally becoming a blinding white. Some accelerants may give a characteristically colored flame. For example, burning alcohol is characterized by a blue flame. Red flames may indicate the presence of petroleum products.

3) **Size of Fire.** The size of the fire should be noted at the time of arrival and at subsequent intervals thereafter. This information may be significant in relation to the time at which the alarm was received. An unusually rapid extension of the fire is indicative of the use of accelerants or some other method of physical preparation. Naturally the opinion of the experienced firemen present at the scene is of value in this matter. A knowledge of the type of construction, the ventilation facilities, and the normal contents of the building will enable a professional observer to form an opinion as to whether the fire has traveled abnormally fast.

4) **Direction of Travel.** Since hot gases rise and fire normally sweeps upward, the direction of travel of a fire is predictable from a knowledge of the construction of the building. It will be expected that the flames will tend to rise until, on meeting obstacles, they project horizontally to seek other vertical outlets. The extent and rate of travel in the horizontal direction will depend primarily on the direction of the wind and on ventilating conditions such as open doors and windows. The spread of fire in an unusual direction or at

an exceptional rate should arouse suspicion as to the presence of accelerants or a prepared arrangement of doors and windows.

5) *Location of Flames.* The investigator should note carefully whether there is more than one apparent point of origin and should try to estimate the approximate location of each. Unrelated fires in different places are indicative of arson. The incendiary may, for example, arrange timing devices in different places with the result that the separate outbreaks of flames will be apparent.

6) *Odors.* Many substances which may be used as accelerants emit a characteristic smell. Naturally the odors detectable at the scene of a fire are determined mainly by the substances which are stored, manufactured, or used on the premises. The smell of a highly inflammable substance in an area where it is not normally used should arouse suspicion. Turpentine, alcohol, kerosene, and gasoline are among the accelerants which emit characteristic odors.

b. **Examinations During the Fire.** In addition to his observations of the flame and smoke, the investigator can at this time make many important examinations of the building and the scene.

1) *Exterior Openings.* The investigator should note the condition of the windows, doors, or other openings. Locked outside doors and obstructed entrances may indicate an intent to impede the firemen in their efforts to extinguish the fire. Open windows and interior passageway doors may suggest an arrangement for ventilating the fire and promoting its rapid progress. Drawn shades or windows covered with blankets where such arrangements are unusual indicate an effort on the part of the arsonist to conceal his preparations and work.

2) *Preliminary Examination of the Scene.* A limited search of the area surrounding the fire may be made at this time. The attention of the investigator should be directed to two types of evidence: first, equipment that may have been used by the arsonist such as containers, matchbooks, and tools; and secondly, traces which may lead to the perpetrator, such as shoe and tire impressions.

3) *Photography.* The progressive stages of the burning should be photographed from various angles. Photographs of the spectators are sometimes made in the hope that the incendiary may be present in the crowd and that in the event of a series of criminal fires the face of the arsonist may be revealed by his repeated presence in the

photographs of the spectators. Such a procedure is advisable if it is thought that a pyromaniac is operating in the area.

4) *Observation of the Spectators.* Some types of arsonist, such as the pyromaniac, remain at the scene to watch the fire. By observing the spectators the experienced arson investigator is occasionally able to identify the incendiary. An exceptional appearance of personal satisfaction or excitement is sometimes indicative of the pyromaniac. If the fire takes place during normal sleeping hours, the arsonist may be sometimes distinguishable by being one of the few fully clothed persons among the spectators.

9. Investigation of Scene After the Fire

The difficulties that may be encountered in the search of the suspected arson scene depend primarily on the extent to which the building or other property has been consumed. If the fire has been promptly reported and quickly extinguished, the discovery of incriminating evidence may be a relatively simple matter. On the other hand, where the fire has gone beyond control and has reduced a considerable portion of the property to ashes, it may be exceedingly difficult to uncover traces of value. Whatever the condition of the scene, however, it will be found that a patient, methodical study of the area will often reveal indications of criminal design and sometimes will permit a logical reconstruction of the arsonist's method of operation. It is of paramount importance in arson cases to know what type of evidence is significant.

a. **Safeguarding the Scene.** In order to preserve and safeguard the evidence prior to a search the investigator must prevent unnecessary disturbance of the debris and the intrusions of unauthorized persons. This may be achieved by liaison with the fire department and uniformed police. An agreement should be made with the firemen in the case of suspected incendiarism to postpone clean-up operations until the investigator has completed his examination of the premises. It will, of course, be necessary for the firemen to perform a certain amount of washing down and overhauling, but it may be requested of their commander that extreme care be exercised in this activity to prevent excessive disturbance of potential evidence. The senior police officer may be requested to issue orders excluding from the scene all persons not officially concerned with the extinguishment of the fire or the investigation of its origin.

b. **Order of Searching.** The area immediately surrounding the burned property should now be more thoroughly examined for evidentiary traces and clues. The doors and windows of the building should be studied for evidences of a break, particularly if the premises are normally locked during the period in which the fire took place. Tool impressions, broken window panes, and forced locks are the obvious marks of such a break. The investigator should now progress to the interior, directing his observations to the charred remains of the fire primarily for evidence of the use of accelerants or other incendiary devices. Assuming that the burning has been extensive, the following order will normally be followed: the outer shell of the remains, the first open area or floor from the point of entry, the first inner shell or wall of an inside room, and the general area suspected of being the point where the fire first broke out.

c. **Locating the Point of Origin.** One of the major objectives of the search is the location of the point of origin, since it is in this area that the physical evidence of criminal design is most likely to be discovered. The region in which the fire originated may be determined by information obtained from witnesses and by an examination of the debris. In searching for the exact point of origin the investigator should follow the path of the burning to its source by observing the intensity of the destruction and the charring of the uprights. Fire that envelops a wooden beam tends to round the edges of the side away from the source of the flame. The surface of the charred wood bears a pattern of crevices that is similar in appearance to the skin of an alligator. The probable point of origin is the place where the small checks in the "alligator pattern" and the deep charring are found. Thus as the investigator draws closer to the point of origin he will find that the charring becomes deeper and the segments of "alligatoring" become smaller. The relative depth of charring can be determined with the aid of a metal probe such as an ice pick.

d. **Examining the Point of Origin.** The debris at the point of

Figure 11. Arson scene. The cluttered area suggests the difficulties of determining the point of origin.

origin should be studied carefully for the purpose of determining the cause of the fire, whether accidental or incendiary. A search should be made for traces of combustible materials. Substances such as peculiarly colored ashes, soot, unusual formations of clinkers, and impregnated materials should be collected for laboratory examination. In conducting his search the investigator should recall the nature of the materials ordinarily stored in the area so that he will be able to detect extraneous or misplaced objects such as fuel and oil cans. Peculiar odors should be noted. The remains of streamers or other plants should be observed and protected. The degree of burning, general appearance, carbonization, and oil content of burned objects should be noted.

e. **Traces of Accelerants.** The investigator should give special attention to any evidence of the use of a liquid accelerant such as gasoline, kerosene, or turpentine. Often the point of origin may be located by tracing such substances to the place of spillage. Since a fluid will flow downward to lower levels, the search for traces of an accelerant should be extended to the floors or cellar below the level of the fire, in the hope that some of the substance may still remain there in an unburned state. A study of the manner in which wood is charred sometimes reveals indications of an accelerant. If wood is soaked with a petroleum product, such as gasoline or kerosene, prior to burning it, it will acquire a distinctive appearance in charring. The "alligator effect" will be more easily observed. The char marks will be deeper where the liquid has seeped into the wood. Thus, the charring will follow the pattern of the spilled liquid. If a soaked trailer was used, the charring will follow the outline since the burning will be deeper in the area occupied by the impregnating substance. Sometimes the burning pattern will indicate the removal of certain objects after the fire had begun.

f. **Altered Protective Devices.** To insure destruction the arsonist sometimes tampers with the sprinkler system or the alarm devices, rendering them ineffectual. For example, he may pour paraffin into the main sprinkler line or mute the water flow alarm. The investigator should arrange to have the fire protection system of the building inspected. The condition of the supply valves should be carefully checked. The water flow should be examined for signs of tampering. Abnormal conditions of fire doors, transoms, and windows should be observed.

10. The Physical Evidence and Its Collection

The task of collecting physical evidence in an arson case is complicated by the delicate condition of the materials. Any piece of evidence that appears to have unusual significance should be photographed and located on a sketch before it is moved since the act of collecting the evidence sometimes results in an alteration. The following are typical of the significant articles of evidence that may be present in a fire of incendiary origin.

a. **Containers:** The arsonist uses bottles, cans, barrels, pails, or boxes to hold the combustible liquid. Any residual gasoline or similar fluid should be poured into a glass container, such as a mason jar, covered, and sealed with paraffin. This may be the most important piece of evidence; it should not be permitted to evaporate by placing it in a container with a loose cover. The original container should be collected and preserved in a similar way if possible. Wrapping paper, cardboard boxes, string or cord, or similar articles which may have been used to cover the substances in transporting it, should also be collected. These articles may sometimes be traced to the perpetrator of the offense.

b. **Ashes and Debris.** If it is found that the ashes or debris contain traces of accelerant or some other significant clue, these materials should be collected for transmission to a laboratory. Where straw or excelsior has been used in a "plant," the ashes will retain their characteristic shape. The burned remains of clothing are sometimes significant. The degree to which cloth will burn is normally limited. Wool, for example, is ordinarily not completely consumed unless it is soaked with an inflammable liquid. In the collection of debris the investigator should not overlook materials which have fallen to lower floors or to the cellar since these sometimes contain valuable evidence such as the remaining parts of a "plant."

c. **Fingerprints and Impressions.** A search for fingerprints should be made in the usual manner, giving special attention to such objects as containers for accelerants. A fingerprint should be developed, if necessary, and photographed. The object bearing the print should, if its size permits, be transported to the office for preservation. Impressions made by tools, shoes, or tires should be photographed and cast.

d. **Incendiary Devices.** The investigator should be alert during the search for suspicious articles such as wires, fuses, straw, or candles which could have formed part of an incendiary device. Since the arsonist may arrange for several points of origin, the search for such devices should be extensive. Closets and obscure corners should be searched for heating appliances.

e. **Stoves and Fireplaces.** The arsonist sometimes insures the destruction of clothing, records, and papers by first burning them in one of the ordinary heating devices. The ashes remaining in stoves and fireplaces should be observed to determine if they are hot and should then be examined for evidence of burned materials that may be significant in the case.

f. **Tools.** A careful study should be made of all tools present in the building. They may have been brought there and abandoned by the arsonist, thus providing a tracing clue, or they may have been employed by a resident arsonist in his preparations. Wax on knife blades; sawdust and chips on saws, augers, and bits; and metal particles on axes are important, depending on the materials used to set the fire. If tool marks are present on door jambs or window sills as a result of forcible entry, the blades of the screwdrivers and crowbars should be examined for a comparison of size and for paint particles.

g. **Documents.** In certain types of incendiary fires such as those designed to conceal evidence of embezzlement or other irregularities of records, the arsonist will attempt to arrange the incriminating documents so that they will be exposed to the flames. For example, he may arrange ledgers in tented fashion on a table to aid the burning. Since, however, masses of paper, such as books, do not burn as well as the novice arsonist imagines, often incriminating documents which were intended for destruction are left by the fire in salvageable condition. In the examination of such documents, the absence of certain papers, such as insurance policies, which are normally kept in the area, should be investigated.

11. Interior Arrangement

The condition and contents of various areas in the building should be noted. An occupant planning a fire will be tempted to remove certain items such as articles of value or sentimental significance. Fur coats and jewelry, for example, may have been removed before setting fire to a dwelling house. The insurance policy and the inventory may be removed from a commercial building. A movement of a large part of the more valuable contents may be accomplished. Sometimes certain articles may be placed in a more exposed position in order to accomplish their destruction before the fire is placed under control. The closet door in a dwelling will often be purposely left open to insure the burning of other clothing ordinarily placed with the fur coat. An account book may be arranged in tented fashion on a desk to accomplish the destruction of evidence of financial irregularities.

12. Witnesses

The gathering of physical evidence is merely the first phase of the investigation, and is primarily concerned with establishing the *corpus delicti* and, secondarily, with the discovery of traces leading to the identity of the perpetrator. Additional evidence can be obtained by carefully questioning the various persons associated with the discovery and control of the fire, the security personnel, the occupants of the building, and the owner. Suggested checklists of important points of information are given in paragraph 16.

a. **Persons First Arriving at the Fire.** Every effort should be made to locate and question the person who first saw the fire. Passersby, watchmen, and policemen are among those who may have made important observations. The identity of the person who turned in the alarm should be learned. These persons should be questioned concerning the exact place where the fire began, the number of places where they have seen flames, and the manner in which the fire spread. Their opinions should be sought on the probable origin of the fire, the color of the smoke, and the general appearance of the conflagration. An inquiry should be made about suspicious actions on the part of anyone near the premises, such as hastily leaving the scene on foot or in an automobile.

b. **Firemen.** The most reliable information concerning the fire can be obtained from the firemen, who are professional observers of these occurrences. They should be questioned concerning the nature of the fire, the color of the flames and smoke, and the perceptible odors. Information can also be obtained concerning the condition of doors, windows, and shades. The firemen may also have observed the arrangements of stock, packing cases, and furniture.

c. **Watchmen.** If a watchman is employed in the building, he should be able to provide detailed information concerning the condition of the building prior to the fire. He should be questioned at great length concerning the building and the fire. In addition, inquiries should be made concerning the occupants of the building in regard to their recent behavior and movements of stock or furniture. He should be asked about his suspicions and his theory concerning the origin of the fire. Finally, he should be asked to identify the last person to leave the building.

d. **Occupants.** The occupants and employees of the building should be interviewed separately. They should be encouraged to give their own accounts, theories, and suspicions of the fire. The identity of the last person to leave the building should be determined. Was it customary for him to be last? Who ordinarily locked the premises?

e. **Owner.** The owner of the damaged property should be questioned concerning his activities at the time of the fire. Any aliases which he may have employed should be determined. He should be questioned also regarding prior arrests, apprehensions, convictions, previous fires, financial standing, businesses, domestic conditions, and hobbies or amusements that could have caused reverses in his financial situation.

13. Photography and Sketching

A photographic record should be made of the destruction accomplished by the fire and of physical evidence uncovered by the search. The photographer should follow the order of the search, photographing each area of significance to the investigation prior to the search. When the point of origin is located it should be thoroughly photographed to show such points as the type and extent of "alligatoring" and charring and the remains of any incendiary device. As each important piece of evidence is discovered it should be photographed in its original condition and in its position when it is completely uncovered. In addition to the photographs a sketch of important areas should be made showing the location of the various articles of evidence. As an aid in the construction of his sketch the investigator will find that the blueprints of buildings maintained in the files of housing and building departments are particularly useful in giving the dimensions and other details of the structure.

14. Packaging and Forwarding of Evidence

Articles of physical evidence which have been collected to determine the possible presence of an accelerant or which, in general, may contain traces of an inflammable substance should be placed in airtight containers, such as mason jars, in order to prevent the evaporation of volatile components. The containers should be packaged to provide adequate protection and forwarded or hand-carried to the laboratory as soon as possible. Postal regulations should be carefully observed in forwarding through the mails. The post office facilities should not be used to ship flammable evidence. Couriers or other means of delivery should be employed in such instances. In the examination of debris samples the laboratory expert can be greatly assisted by the provision of certain information relating to the fire. The following data are usually found of assistance and should be included in the letter of transmittal in addition to the regularly required information:

a. An itemized list of the evidence being submitted with information concerning the means by which it is being forwarded.

b. The date and time of burning.

c. A brief description of the type and construction of the burned building or object and the extent of damage or destruction caused by the fire.

d. A list of the chemical agents used in extinguishing the fire. Water, carbon tetrachloride, and carbon dioxide are the most common agents employed.

e. Photographs and scaled sketches on which are indicated the points where the various articles of evidence were collected.

15. Sources of Information

The identification files should be searched for the names of any persons associated with the building or with the fire. The local fire department may be consulted for records of previous fires. Depending on the nature of the fire the following may be consulted: local police records of known incendiaries; records of recent repairs or alterations in the building; records such as inventories, financial statements, and bills of sale where it is suspected that the fire was designed to conceal embezzlement or theft; personnel rosters of persons employed and of persons recently discharged where the fire is thought to be inspired by hatred. In addition to these records the investigator can, where appropriate, avail himself of the following central indices:

a. **Material Files.** Reference collections of incendiary materials such as match folders, rope, and celluloid are useful. A discarded match found near the scene of a fire can offer a valuable tracing clue in an arson case. In some cases the type of matchbook from which the match was taken can be identified and the match itself associated with a matchbook found on the person of a suspect. Some match folders contain advertising of places such as taverns and restaurants. Since the places of distribution for such folders are limited in number, these establishments can often provide an identifying eyewitness. Similar tracing can be accomplished with cord and string that have been used to wrap incendiary materials.

b. **Central Index.** The National Board of Fire Underwriters located in New York maintains a central index file of the names of all persons suspected or convicted of arson.

c. **Insurance Companies' Files.** Because of the tremendous financial loss that results from arson, insurance companies are prepared to offer active cooperation to law enforcement agencies in their investigation of this crime. For example, the Mill Mutual Fire Prevention Bureau, Chicago, provides information for arson investigators in behalf of the midwestern underwriters. It should be noted that these sources of information are most useful where a peculiar *modus operandi* has been repeatedly observed. For example, cases involving pyromaniacs can usually be investigated with the characteristic pattern of the outbreak of the fires a starting point.

16. Checklist

The list found below is given as an aid to the investigator in an arson case. The list does not purport to be comprehensive, nor are the points covered applicable to every case. It will be found, however, that in the investigation of an arson involving a building many of these points are relevant and their coverage by means of interviews, observation, or search of records will make for a more complete report.

a. **Official Data**
1) Address, location, and description of the building.
2) Date and time of burning.
3) Time of receipt of alarm by the fire station.
4) Fire station receiving the alarm.
5) Fire units responding.
6) Time of arrival and departure of fire units.
7) Designation of the building in terms of construction, material, size, age, and materials stored there.
8) Designation of type of fire by the fire department records.
b. **Date of Ownership, Occupancy, and Property Value**
1) Owner of the building.
2) Tenants of the building.
3) Occupants.
4) Value of the property.
5) Insurance coverage.
6) Name of insured.
7) Name of insuror.
8) Loss of property through fire.
c. **Discovery of the Fire**
1) Who reported the fire?
2) When was the fire reported?
3) How was the fire reported? Verbally, telephone?
4) Did the person who reported the fire have any motive for doing so?
5) Who discovered the fire?
6) When was the fire first discovered?
7) Under what circumstances was the fire first discovered?
8) What was the time interval between discovery and report? How was the time interval accounted for?
d. **Conditions Surrounding Fire**
1) Initial observations of the fire.
2) Point of origin of fire. In what building? In what room?

3) Direction of winds; weather conditions such as temperature and humidity; electrical storms.

4) Type of fire—flash or otherwise.

5) Explosion.

6) Speed of travel.

7) Odors—gasoline, kerosene, etc.

8) Appearance of smoke—shape and color.

9) Appearance of flames—size, intensity, color, and area of spread.

10) Hissing or crackling noises.

11) Direction of spread.

12) Were any windows or doors, normally closed and locked, left open?

13) Evidence of forced entry.

14) Chemical agents used to extinguish fire—water, foam, CO_2.

e. **Condition of Building**

1) How was the room or building furnished? Was there a stove of any kind? Was there a fire in the stove? What fuel was used? Was the stove well insulated? When were ashes last removed? Where were they placed?

2) Check for changes in building while occupied by present tenant, such as partitions, electric wiring, stoves, etc.

3) Was any electric wiring exposed? What was its condition? Were they ever repaired? When? By whom? What was the load carried by these wires? Was there ever any heat observed in the wires or terminals?

4) Number and kind of electric motors in the room or building. Provisions for safeguarding against dust.

5) Were there any machines in the room or building? What type? When were they last used? What power did they consume? When were they last tested and lubricated?

6) Location and condition of pipes, particularly gas pipes.

7) Location and condition of all electric lights, appliances, and wiring, including the condition of fuses.

8) Existence of devices for focusing sun's rays.

9) Degree of care exercised in storing inflammable materials.

10) Condition of fire-fighting equipment.

f. **Persons Associated with the Building**

1) Persons present in building at time of fire. Last person in the building. Persons in and around in the last 24 hours. Loiterers in the area.

2) Possessors of keys to the building.

3) Persons responsible for the security of the building.

4) Names and addresses of all occupants, tenants, employees, and all persons frequently around premises.

5) Last person to leave the building—were his actions customary?

g. **Motive**

1) Description of all property on premises; when it arrived, value, and amount of insurance.

2) Recent movements of property.

3) Possible substitutions of less valuable property.

4) Financial condition of owners of the property.

5) Impending inspections, investigations, inventories, and audits.

6) Relations between property owners—friendly or inimical. Recent defections from partnerships or severance of employment.

7) Possibility of concealment of a crime.

8) Existence of previous criminal record on the part of any of the occupants.

9) Existence of a record of confinement to a mental institution.

10) Possible association of any persons with other mysterious fires.

h. **Evidence of Intent**

1) Failure to summon the fire unit within a reasonable time.

2) Tampering with warning devices or communications systems.

3) Doors, windows, transoms, and ventilating systems left in an other than normal position.

4) Placement of incendiary materials, such as gasoline, oil, candles, matches, timing devices, and cans containing residual inflammable material, in the building.

5) Tampering with fire-fighting equipment or fire-control systems.

6) Removal of property of value prior to the fire.

7) Bringing personal property into the building.

II. AUTOMOBILE FIRES

17. Motive

Occasionally, a car is set on fire to conceal a crime. Sometimes the burning of a car may be incident to another crime. Most commonly the deliberate setting fire to a vehicle is done to defraud the insurance company. The increasing sale of automobile insurance has led to a sharper rise in the number of such fires each year. In Boston, during the year 1973, insurance investigators paid out 2.7 million dollars in burned-car claims after only routine investigation. The cars destroyed were usually those with a high market value for which the owner either could not make the payments or afford the expense of the high consumption of fuel. The owners would pay $100 to $150 for a "torch" job and receive $3,000 to $4,000 in insurance claims. The time and zeal which the law enforcement investigator brings to these last-mentioned cases should be tempered by the reflection that he is not employed by the insurance company. Moreover, the insurance company can usually make available to him the services of an expert, trained and experienced in the investigation of automobile fires. Among the more common motives for this offense are the following:

a. **Financial Difficulties.** These are similar to those encountered in other arson cases with the following additions:

1) Inability to meet the payments on the car or to return it to the dealer.

2) Demands by the finance company that payments be made or the vehicle surrendered.

3) Inability to sell the equity in the car.

b. **Domestic Problems.** A divorce may be pending or one of the spouses may object to the ownership or improper use of the car.

c. **Dissatisfaction with the Automobile.** The car may have a long history of mechanical trouble. Excessive depreciation and unsuitability for the owner's needs are additional reasons.

18. The Burning of Automobiles

It is extremely difficult to accomplish the total loss of a vehicle, since an automobile is mainly composed of noninflammable materials. With the exception of the upholstery, wires, and tires, there is very little that can be burned. Experiments have shown that a short in the wiring will almost always burn itself out without setting fire to the other parts of the automobile. When the upholstery is set on fire it will smolder for hours without breaking into open flame.

19. Examination of the Burned Car

The burned automobile should be examined before the owner is interviewed. The point of origin should be located and the manner in which the fire spread should be determined. The following areas should receive special attention:

a. **The Electrical System.** The owner may claim that the fire started because of a short. A total fire loss from this cause is extremely rare.

1) Locate the wiring area where the short was first suspected.

2) Look for melted strands of wire with beaded ends at the broken points.

3) Burned out head lamps indicate a battery short.

4) Check the battery charge. A short will usually lead to a run-down battery.

5) Examine the distributor points for fusing due to a short while the motor was running.

b. **Gas Tank and Gas Line.** Gasoline may have been obtained from the tanks, gas line, or the fuel pump.

1) Examine the *gas line* for breaks or other tampering such as disconnection.

2) Examine the *gas cap* for signs of fire. If there are no signs it may have been placed on after the fire. If an explosion took place the cap will bear signs of this occurrence.

3) The *fuel pump* should be examined for missing parts or tampering. Determine whether the line from the fuel pump was disconnected to obtain gasoline.

c. **Under the Hood.** The possible points of origin under the hood are the fuel pump, carburetor, and wiring. The use of incendiary substances is indicated by lead melted from the lower or outside seams of the motor, burned fan belt, and burned rubber cushions in the front of the motor. Another indication is the presence of burned spots on the paint. When the perpetrator pours gasoline over the motor he sometimes spills a few drops on the front fender. These areas will burn even though they are not in the direct line of the fire.

d. **Body.** Often an excess of inflammable fluid is used to burn a car with the result that the fluid seeps through the floor of the car and the fire produces oil or gasoline soot on the underside of the car. Similarly, soot deposits on the underside of the frame and springs indicate the use of inflammables.

e. **Other Indications.** Often the criminal commits the error of making small economies. The investigator should check the accessories to determine whether any of the extra equipment has been recently removed. Heater, radio, air horn, fog lights, spare tires, and similar equipment may have been first removed from the car. In fact, the complete set of tires has been removed in some cases. Where total burning has taken place the tires may be completely consumed but wires will remain on the metal rims. An inspection should also be made for the substitution of inferior equipment prior to burning.

20. Interviewing the Assured

After the car has been examined the investigator should obtain a statement from the assured, permitting him to give his account of the burning without interrupting. Subsequently the assured should be questioned in detail along the following lines:

a. **Purchase.** All data concerning the sale of the car and its financing should be obtained, including such details as the name of the salesman.

b. **Conditions.** Amount of extra equipment on the car at the time of fire; mileage; defects; name of service station to which the car was customarily brought.

c. **Movements.** The assured should be questioned in detail concerning his movements during the hours preceding the loss. Information may be developed in this way to establish motive or deception.

d. **Observations.** The assured's recital of the discovery and progress of the fire are often revealing. Most persons have never observed the accidental burning of a car. If the assured has no experience in these matters, he will describe details that are peculiar to a fire contrived with an inflammable material.

e. **Assured's Theory.** The investigator should display a great interest in the owner's explanation of the cause of the fire and his opinion on the point of origin. These statements should be compared with the results of the physical examination.

f. **Subsequent Movements.** The manner in which the owner left the scene is significant. If the fire is arranged to take place in an isolated place, the perpetrator makes prior arrangements for transportation.

g. **Other Witnesses.** Other persons who observed the fire should be interviewed separately. The lines followed in interviewing will be dictated by the nature of the fire and the statement of the owner.

h. **Subsequent Checks.** The complete investigation should include a check of the following items:

1) Dealer's records; reconditioning records before sale; prior owner's reason for sale.

2) Chattel mortgage records; issuance through local agency or bank; records including those associated with a second mortgage.

3) Assured's title to determine if he has an insurable interest.

21. Law

In common law and in most jurisdictions the malicious and willfull burning of an automobile is not considered arson but is prohibited under statutes relating to the malicious destruction of property. In some jurisdictions, however, the term *simple arson* is used to describe the criminal burning of property other than a dwelling and the term *aggravated arson* is used for the burning of an inhabited structure.

ADDITIONAL READING

Barlay, S.: *Fire*. London, Hamish Hamilton, 1972.

Barracato, J. and Michelmore, P.: *Arson*. New York, Norton, 1976.

Battle, B. and Weston, P.B.: *Arson*. New York, Arco, 1960.

Bradley, J.N.: *Flame and Combustion Phenomena*. Scranton, Pa: Barnes and Noble, 1969.

Brown, R.: The Purpose and Importance of Written Reports in Arson Investigation. 25 *Fire and Arson Investigator*, 1, 1974.

DeArmond, H.T.: Automobile Arson Investigation. 25 *Fire and Arson Investigator*, 3, 1975.

Ettling, B.V. and Adams, M.F.: *Study of Accelerant Residues in Fire Remains*. Washington, D.C.: National Criminal Justice Reference Service, 1968.

Fitch, R.D. and Porter, E.A.: *Accidental or Incendiary*. Springfield, Ill.: Thomas, 1968.

Hurteau, W.K.: Arson Investigation and the Collecting of Evidence. 11 *Security World*, 3, 1974.

Inciardi, J.A.: The Adult Firesetter: A Typology. 8 *Criminology*, 145, 1970.

Kirk, P.L.: *Fire Investigation*. New York, Wiley, 1969.

Levin, B.: Psychological Characteristics of Firesetters. 27 *Fire and Arson Investigators*, 3, 1977.

Lewis, B. and Von Elbe, G.: *Combustion, Flames, and Explosion of Gases*, 2nd ed. New York, Academic Press, 1961.

Macdonald, J.M.: *Bombers and Firesetters*. Springfield, Ill.: Thomas, 1977.

Mach, M.H.: Gas-Chromatography-Mass Spectrometry of Simulated Arson Residue Using Gasoline as an Accelerant. 22 *Journal of Forensic Sciences*, 348, 1977.

Nicol, J.D., and Overley, L.: Combustibility of Automobiles: Results of Total Burning. 54 *Journal of Criminal Law, Criminology and Police Science*, 366, 1963.

Quinan, D.J.: Coordination on Fire Investigation. 24 *Fire and Arson Investigator*, 1, 1973.

Scott, L.G.: Arson the Perfect Crime. 4 *Washington Law Enforcement Journal*, 3, 1974.

Soothill, K.L. and Pope, P.J.: Arson: A Twenty-Year Cohort Study. 13 *Medicine, Science and the Law*, 127, 1973.

Vliet, A.R.: The Fire Investigator and Electrical Fires. 26 *Fire and Arson Investigator*, 1, 1976.

Chapter 18

NARCOTICS VIOLATIONS

1. Introduction

THE PROBLEMS ASSOCIATED with narcotics and other dangerous drugs are too well publicized to require elaboration here. It is the common belief that the illicit trade in narcotics is centrally controlled by a few powerful criminals who exercise an extraordinary influence over large sections of the country. This chapter does not pretend to establish the truth or falsity of this belief. The extent to which propositions of this nature are true and the reliability of the associated statistics will not be treated here. The subject of narcotics is a land of dark figures, myths, and unprovable propositions. We shall content ourselves in this chapter with activities within the ken and scope of the operations of the individual investigator. He should understand the nature of the drugs he is dealing with, the probable nature of the addict, the typology of sellers at various levels, and the action he can take to circumvent criminal activities connected with narcotics and other dangerous drugs.

2. Drug Addiction

The state of addiction may be described as a condition in which a person through repeated use of a drug has become dependent on it for his sense of well-being and, if deprived of the drug, suffers a psychic craving usually manifested by characteristic withdrawal symptoms due to an alteration of certain physiological processes.

a. **Causes.** Most commonly it is found that drug addiction is attributable to the availability of an addicting drug coupled with the existence of a personality disorder such as a psychoneurosis or a constitutional psychopathic inferiority. Initially the future addict makes his acquaintance with the drug through another addict or a criminal seller. It is only rarely that his introduction to the drug will be in the form of a prescribed medical treatment or self-medication. The psychoneurotic individual will take drugs to relieve an emotional or physical distress, while the psychopathic person resorts to them for their intoxicating effect. The first experiment, however, will usually be prompted by curiosity or a desire for adventure. The beginner feels confident that he will avoid addiction but continues to experiment until he is a victim of the habit. Although an initial venture into the use of drugs may have been prompted by a pleasure-seeking curiosity, a quest for euphoria or excitement, the narcotics addict, after he has fully acquired the habit, is definitely pursuing neither pleasure nor dreams—he is simply easing the pain. The condition is summed up in the words of a heroin addict to a reporter: "You don't even know what I'm talking about; *you* feel okay all the time. *Me,* it costs me $100 a day just to stop hurting so much."

b. **Addict.** The Controlled Substances Act defines an addict as follows: "The term 'addict' means any individual who habitually uses any narcotic drug so as to endanger the public morals, health, safety, or welfare, or who is so far addicted to the use of narcotic drugs as to have lost the power of self-control with reference to his addiction."

c. **Physical Dependence.** Through continued use the addict gradually reaches a state where he finds the drug necessary to maintain his normal sense of physical well-being. The need is an actual physical one, which is attributable to physiological changes, particularly in his nervous system. It is more than the mere psychological craving that attends a habit. If deprived of the narcotic, the addict becomes physically ill to such an extent that he will resort even to criminal methods to obtain the source of his relief.

d. **Tolerance.** The body adjusts itself to repeated use of narcotics so that the addict soon finds his customary dosage failing to give the expected reaction. Increased quantities of the drug are required to give the needed stimulation or even to maintain a feeling of physical normality. The increase in dosage is inevitably followed by correspondingly increased tolerance as the body seeks to develop relative immunity to the toxic effects of the drug. In a short time the addict finds himself able to absorb quantities of the narcotic which formerly would have been fatal.

e. **Moral Degeneration.** Social disapproval of drug addiction demands that the use of narcotics be surrounded by secrecy. Deceit, subterfuge, and evasion must be employed by the addict to disguise his condition. The source of drug supply, moreover, is associated with the criminal element of society and the addict finds himself dealing and even associating with the underworld. The great cost of the drug may create a serious problem. The addict of limited means finds himself in financial straits and is driven to petty larceny and worse in his efforts to support the habit.

f. **Drug Dependence.** In addition to developing a physical dependence the addict also acquires a psychic dependence on the drug. From repeated usage he begins to associate a sense of satisfaction and mental well-being with the periodic administration of the drug. The two concepts—physical and psychic dependence—are closely related and their various aspects are not readily distinguishable. For this reason the World Health Organization introduced the broader concept of *drug dependence*, a state which may include either or both the physical and psychic dependence. In this connection WHO recommended that the nature of the dependence be identified by specifying the nature of the drug, such as drug dependence of the morphine type, of the barbiturate type, of the amphetamine type, and so forth.

3. Definitions

The following definitions are used in the Controlled Substances Act:

a. **Narcotic.** The term "narcotic" drug means "opium, coca leaves, and opiates" or "any compound, manufacture, salt, derivative, or preparation" of them, or any substance chemically identical with any of these substances.

b. **Opiate.** The term "opiate" means any drug or other substance having an addiction-forming or addiction-sustaining liability similar to morphine or being capable of conversion into a drug having such an addiction-forming or addiction-sustaining liability.

c. **General.** Several points should be noted in the definitions given above. The term "opiate" is not used here in the customary sense of an "opium derivative" but rather as a catch-all designed to include synthetic drugs which have a similar addicting effect as morphine. Modern chemistry periodically synthesizes drugs which may be used medically as a substitute for morphine and hence should be placed under legal control. The Attorney General may declare these new drugs to be within the meaning of the term "narcotic" and thus subject to the same regulations. Other drugs with abuse potential are similarly placed in the appropriate schedules of the Controlled Substances Act.

4. Legal Provisions

In general, federal and state laws forbid the unauthorized manufacture, sale, use, or possession of narcotics. Since the laws are quite lengthy and technical, they may be described only briefly here.

a. **Federal Law.** The following are some of the important federal laws in effect prior to the Controlled Substances Act which initially regulated the sale and use of drugs:

1) *Harrison Act (1914).* Taxed the importation, manufacture, distribution, and sale of narcotics and gave them a legal definition.

2) *Narcotic Drug Import and Export Act (1922).* Limited the importation of opium and coca leaves to that required for medical and scientific needs. The importation and manufacture of heroin and smoking opium were prohibited.

3) *Marihuana Tax Act (1937).* Controlled the distribution of marihuana by a system of registration and taxation, making it difficult to obtain illegally.

4) *Drug Abuse Control Amendments (1965).* Placed amphetamines, barbiturates, and hallucinogens under repressive controls.

b. **Controlled Substances Act (1970).** Laws relating to narcotics and dangerous non-narcotic drugs were incorporated in the Comprehensive Drug Abuse Prevention and Control Act. This act is divided into four titles. Title II, which is concerned with control and enforcement, is called the Controlled Substances Act. This act is the

COMPARISON OF THE SCHEDULES OF THE CONTROLLED SUBSTANCES ACT (CSA) IN TERMS OF CONTROLS IMPOSED

SCHEDULE*	TYPES OF SUB-STANCES COVERED (PARTIAL LIST)	RECORD KEEPING	MARKETING QUOTAS	DISTRIBUTION RESTRICTIONS
I	Heroin, LSD, mesca-line, psyilocybin-psilocyn, MDA, mari-juana, hashish, hashish oil	Records must be kept sep-arate from all other rec-ords of the handler (for easy audit)	Yes	DEA order form required prior to transaction
II	Opium, morphine, meperidine, metha-done, methaqualone, cocaine, phenmetra-zine, methyl phenidate			
III	Glutethimide, some amphetamines, nar-cotics, stimulants, and depressants, DCP	Records need not be separated but must be kept in a readily re-trievable form	No, but some drugs limited by Schedule II Quotas	DEA registration number required
IV	Chloral hydrate, meprobamate, some stimulants, and de-pressants			
V	Over-the-counter drugs containing co-deine and certain narcotics			

*Registration is required with DEA for handlers of substances in all schedules.

	DISPENSING LIMITATIONS	IMPORT EXPORT	SECURITY REQUIRED	MANUFACTURER SUPPLIER RE- PORTS TO DEA	CRIMINAL PEN- ALTIES FOR TRAFFICKING (FIRST OFFENSE)
I	For research only	Permit re- quired from DEA	High secur- ity (i.e., spe- cial vault, 24-hour alarm)	Yes	Narcotic: 15 years/$25,000

Nonnarcotic: 5 years/$15,000 |
II	Written, signed, unrefillable pre- scription required				
III	Written or phoned-in pre- scription refillable up to 5 times in 6 months if so authorized by physician	Permit re- quired from DEA for nar- cotics; prior notice to DEA of planned transporta- tion involv- ing nonnar- cotics	Special security (i.e., surveil- lance)	Yes, for narcotics	5 years/$15,000
IV				No	3 years/$10,000
V	I.D. required— cannot be a minor	Permit re- quired for import of narcotic prepara- tions; prior notice re- quired for export of narcotics and import/ export of nonnar- cotics		Yes, for manufac- turers of narcotic preparations	1 year/$5,000

SOURCE: Drug Enforcement Administration: *Fact Sheets* Washington, D.C.: U.S. Government Printing Office, 1973).

controlling federal statute, superseding all other federal narcotics laws. It divides narcotics and other dangerous drugs into five schedules according to medical usage and abuse potential. Responsibility for enforcement is shared by the Drug Enforcement Agency and the Food and Drug Administration who monitor production, procurement, and sale of the controlled substances. Criminal penalties for violations are based on the classification of the drug, the nature of the offense (possession, sales, or manufacture) and whether it is a first or subsequent offense.

c. **State Laws.** Because state laws are not always consistent with federal law, a violation in one state may not be a violation in another. The federal government encourages each state to adopt similar drug laws not only to facilitate enforcement but also to benefit manufacturers, pharmacists, doctors, and their patients. To assist states in making their drug-control laws consistent with federal legislation, the Uniform Controlled Substances Act was developed, which many states have adopted with only minor revisions.

5. Opium

Opium is derived from the oriental poppy plant (*papaver somniferum*) which is grown chiefly in Asia but is found in other areas such as Mexico and the Balkans. The plant is usually 3 or 4 feet high with smooth, dull foliage and flowers approximately 4 inches wide. The opium itself is a latex or milky substance obtained by slitting open the capsules of the plant and scraping the sides. The small cakes thus obtained are pressed into a larger mass, the shape of which will depend on local custom. Raw opium is dark brown or black in color and is bitter to the taste. A number of alkaloids are derived from this substance, the most important of which are morphine, heroin, and codeine.

a. **Prepared Opium.** By a process of boiling, fermentation, and roasting, a dark brown extract of the raw opium is obtained which may be smoked, chewed, or eaten. This is the opium which is offered to the market for consumption. Opium for medicinal purposes is obtained in powder or granulated form or in solution. In powder form medicinal opium is light brown or dark yellow in color.

Solutions of opium such as laudanum were popular analgesics in Europe during the eighteenth and early nineteenth centuries when they could be readily purchased without prescription.

b. **Smoking Opium.** The use of the opium pipe is largely confined to Asians and persons of Asian origin in this country. The pipe consists of a long stem and a detachable bowl with an extremely narrow opening. It is usually smoked in a prone position because of the requirements of the operations. The opium is heated by means of a small lamp employing peanut oil as a fuel to avoid smoking and unpleasant fumes. The lamp is covered by a cone-shaped device to direct the heat. The opium is heated until it is viscous fluid. A long metal needle (yen hock) is dipped in the opium and a small pellet is gathered with a twirling motion. The pellet is cooked over the flame, kneaded against the lamp to express moisture, and placed over the opening of the pipe. The addict draws in the smoke with slow, deep inhalations. After the opium has been smoked, a usable residue remains in the pipe in the form of a charcoal-colored mass. This is called opium dross or yen shee and contains carbon, unburned opium, and morphine. After soaking in water, draining and evaporating, the yen shee can be smoked again. It may also be mixed with tea or wine and is even injected into the body by some addicts. Because of the narcotic potential of yen shee the possession of the opium pipe itself is considered illegal.

c. **Effects.** The use of opium produces a feeling of well-being and relieves bodily pains. The drug is absorbed slowly into the body, gradually renders the smoker drowsy, and finally induces a deep sleep accompanied by fantastic dreams of a pleasant character. Continued use of opium results in addiction. The user acquires a physical dependency on the narcotic and suffers severely if it is withdrawn.

6. Opium Derivatives

The consumption of opium by smoking or other means is relatively uncommon in the United States. The use of opium derivatives constitutes the major narcotics problem. These are far more powerful in their stimulating effect and in the addiction which they produce. The opium derivatives are a group of some twenty alkaloids which possess complex organic structures. Their general appearance is that of a white powder. The alkaloids most commonly used illegally are morphine, heroin, and codeine.

a. **Morphine.** Morphine in the form of morphine sulphate, morphine hydrochloride, and morphine tartrate is widely used by the medical profession as an analgesic. It is the most important of the alkaloids and constitutes about 12 per cent of the use of raw opium. For legitimate use it is found in the form of a small white cube or tablet approximately one gram in weight. Illegally it is usually sold as a white powder, a small quantity of which is wrapped in a glassine paper. In this form the quantity is referred to as a "deck." Almost invariably the morphine is "cut" or diluted by the sellers to obtain greater profits. The actual amount of morphine present in a deck may be as low as 3 per cent; the remainder is a harmless white substance such as milk sugar.

1) *Method of Use.* Although morphine may be taken orally, the method is considered wasteful. Ordinarily the addict injects it into his body by means of a hypodermic needle or its improvised equivalent. For medical purposes the drug would be injected under the skin or into the muscles. To achieve a more rapid and stimulating effect, however, the addict usually injects it directly into the blood stream. A user employing this method is called a "mainliner." The investigator should become familiar with the apparatus characteristically employed by the addict. A bent spoon, medicine dropper, needle, and rubber band constitute the user's "kit." The drug is dissolved in water placed in a bent spoon. A match is applied to the bottom of the spoon to accelerate the dissolving by heat. The medicine dropper is used in place of the conventional hypodermic syringe. The needle, attached to the dropper by the rubber band, is used to penetrate the skin. Still cruder methods may be employed by the addict. In place of the needle, the end of the dropper may be broken to present a jagged edge to the skin. Again, the user may simply incise the skin with a sharp blade and insert the end of the dropper.

2) *Effects.* With the injection of the drug the addict experiences an extraordinary stimulation. A sense of euphoria pervades his being. His spirit is invigorated, his mind becoming keener and his

self-confidence increasing greatly. The effect lasts for several hours, after which he gradually subsides into his former state. With prolonged use of the drug the addict will develop great tolerance and require a daily dosage many times more than that which originally supplied a stimulus.

3) *Identifying the Addict.* When in possession of his normal supply of the drug, it is difficult to distinguish an addict on the basis of his appearance. Experienced narcotics investigators are unable to detect the addict by merely looking at his face. His conduct will appear quite normal since he ordinarily has adjusted himself to the use of the drug. There will be no irrational or otherwise exceptional behavior beyond a possible excess of enthusiasm. When the effects of the drug have worn off, however, the addict may be betrayed by an unusual drowsiness; prolonged abstinence may also result in identifiable symptoms. With the lapse of twenty-four hours after withdrawal, the addict will begin to experience severe pains in his back and legs. He may be overcome by nausea and suffer pains in his stomach. His eyes and nose begin to run in continuous lachrymation.

4) *Physical Marks.* Under the influence of morphine the eyes of the user will be characterized by a contracted pupil which does not react normally to changes of intensity of illumination. Since the addict must inject the drug quite frequently, his arms will be marked by punctures and scabs. The recent application of the needle will be shown by a small red spot on which a small drop of blood has coagulated. The scab formed over this mark will remain for approximately ten days. Dark blue scar tissue may be seen where the vein walls have broken down through repeated punctures. Some addicts, especially women, will inject in the area in back of the thighs.

5) *Sources of Supply.* The use of morphine as a sedative or an analgesic is quite common in the medical profession; hence the drug can be legally manufactured. The illegal trade is supplied by smuggling, clandestine manufacture, or theft from legitimate users such as hospitals or pharmacies. Morphine has for the most part been supplanted by heroin as the drug of choice in the illicit trade.

b. **Codeine.** Methylmorphine or codeine is similar in many respects to morphine, but its effects are very much weaker in intensity. It is a natural alkaloid of opium and is in common medical use as a sedative in cough mixtures and an analgesic in tablet form. Its physical state in its pure form is that of a crystalline powder or of long, slender, white crystals. Although codeine, like all psychoactive drugs, represents a certain hazard for dependence-prone individuals, the problem of drug abuse with codeine does not remotely approach that of morphine or heroin. Primary codeine dependence can occur, but because of its rarity is considered to be a medical curiosity, and vast clinical experience supports the view that the danger of inducing drug dependence with the usual therapeutic dose is slight. Instances of abuse of codeine cough syrups, particularly by juveniles, have at times been publicized by the news media, leaving the impression that the problem is widespread. There are no adequate statistical data on the true incidence of this type of abuse, but the opinion of authorities in the field of drug abuse, after reviewing what data are available, has been that abuse of codeine-containing cough syrups is minimal and sporadic, and of little significance with respect to the general drug abuse problem.

c. **Heroin.** Heroin is a synthetic drug made from morphine as a diacetyl derivative. It is by far the most common drug occurring in cases of narcotic addiction. In appearance it is usually a white, crystalline powder; occasionally it is found in cubes or tablets. The method of use is similar to that of morphine. Rarely the user absorbs it by sniffing or rubbing into the gums. The effects of heroin are the same as those of morphine but greatly magnified in intensity. "Four times more powerful" is a phrase commonly used in comparing these two drugs. The withdrawal symptoms are qualitatively identical. Heroin differs from morphine and codeine in that it may not be legally manufactured in the United States. It is not recognized as an authorized drug by the U.S. Pharmacopoeia. Thus, the licenses granted to possess other narcotics do not extend to heroin, and its possession by persons other than law enforcement officers acting in performance of duty may ordinarily be considered illegal. The drug is, however, used legitimately by members of the medical profession in certain foreign countries. It is considered a particularly effective analgesic for use in the terminal stages of such diseases as tuberculosis and cancer. Large quantities of heroin are manufactured abroad for illicit traffic in this country. Perhaps one reason for its popularity in the illegal market has been the desire of narcotic dealers to increase their sales through the medium of a drug which can easily obtain a grip on the victim and produce an addiction most difficult to conquer.

7. The Heroin Problem

a. **The Magnitude of the Problem.** The worldwide American war on opium growing and heroin smuggling promises to be at least as protracted, and perhaps as inconclusive, as the conflict in Vietnam. As awareness of the dimension of the effort spreads, officials are beginning to scale down their expectations. There is less talk of burning the world's poppy fields. The emphasis is now on disrupting supply routes by pinching off the flow of heroin into this country and by reducing availability on the street. Fifty-seven nations have been selected for diplomatic attention—either as producing or trans-shipment areas. The combination of furious diplomatic activity abroad and the continuing ravages of addiction at home often gives the impression that American addicts have a corner on the world opium market. Yet, in fact, they are the marginal consumer. The annual illicit world production of opium is estimated at 100 to 1,500 tons and the illicit American consumption is 60 to 100 tons—that is, 6 to 10 tons of heroin. And the American market, it is reckoned, can be supplied through the cultivation of little more than 5 square miles of arable up-country land. The task of stopping the flow of heroin into this country is overwhelming. In a typical year approximately 250 million people enter the United States in 65 million vehicles, 306,000 planes and 157,000 ships. Obviously, the most scrupulous search could discover only a minute fraction of the innumerable sites where illicit narcotics might be secreted.

b. **The Problem of Addiction.** Although there is no doubt that using certain psychoactive drugs predisposes a person to repeat the experience, opinion is divided on whether this results from a biochemical change or from a purely psychological or behavioral response. Whether addiction results from a biochemical change or from an unconsciously learned behavior pattern, or both, there is no doubt among researchers that certain chemicals have a molecular structure capable of inducing varying degrees of pleasure in the user. Psychological dependence is a response in behavior patterns that leads a person to want to take the drug again and again, often simply because it feels so good. Depending on the individual's personality, almost any drug can produce a psychological dependence. One indication of its strength is the difficulty tobacco smokers have in quitting the habit. Physical dependence, on the other hand, involves actual biochemical changes in the body so that the brain cells appear to function normally only in the presence of the drug. A phenomenon often confused with physical dependence is tolerance. This is an adaptation of the brain cells in which they become able to function normally in the presence of the drug but do not require the drug. Increasing tolerance makes it necessary to increase the dose to achieve the same effects.

c. **The Problem of Contagion.** One of the hardest-dying myths is that the dope pusher is the person most responsible for spreading addiction among the young. By now we know that the biggest culprit is not the pusher, who plays an indispensable backup role, but the youthful, enthusiastic addict who thinks he's onto a good thing and wishes to share it with his friends. This applies to many different drug addictions, but when it comes to heroin, initiation in the use of the needle is an important ritual that requires one addict to teach another. Hence, heroin maintenance is no solution as long as there are young, enthusiastic users constantly enlarging the addict population.

A number of studies have been made of this phenomenon of contagion, of which the Nils Bejerot experiment is particularly informative. Bejerot plotted the explosion of amphetamine mainlining from a tiny group of Stockholm poets and Bohemians in 1949 to a runaway epidemic claiming 12,000 addicts twenty years later. Drug epidemics, Bejerot finds, are spread by "personal initiation from established addicts"; they begin within certain defined class or ethnic boundaries, and then spread outward into a larger society. The debut age is low; there are usually 3 to 6 male addicts for every female addict and, most alarmingly, epidemics spread "by geometric progression if other conditions remain unchanged." The one factor that correlates most highly with the epidemic spread of addiction is the availability of the drug in question. Heroin may be fairly available today; as it is made more available there will be more junkies—many more.

d. **Institutional Response.** Those who look for a cure, e.g., for heroin, through methadone or heroin antagonists (or through law enforcement) must constantly be reminded that for every drug eliminated ten can be found to take its place that will produce nearly equivalent euphoria, addiction, and trouble. The problems of addiction are not the problems of an isolated drug, whether alcohol or methaqualone, but rather are symptomatic of sociological and economic conditions.

8. Synthetic Analgesics

Modern medical research has developed a series of drugs designed to be used as substitutes for the opium derivatives. These chemically synthesized drugs produce the same effects as the narcotics previously discussed. They are prescribed as analgesics, that is, substances which relieve pain. Since their effects are similar to those of morphine they have been declared opiates and their manufacture, sale, and use are strictly regulated by the Controlled Substances Act. Among the more important of these synthetic analgesics are the following: meperidine, methadone, Dilaudid®, and Percodan®.

a. **Meperidine.** Meperidine hydrochloride is also known by the following names: Demerol®, Dolantin®, Dolantol®, Endolat®, and the international generic name, pethidine. For relief of pain this drug lies somewhere between morphine and codeine in its effects. Opinions vary in regard to its capacity to develop physiologic dependence. The drug does have a moderate degree of addiction liability. Mild withdrawal symptoms are observable. These are qualitatively similar to morphine but considerably milder.

b. **Methadone.** Methadone hydrochloride is also known by the following trade names: Methadon®, Amidone®, Amidon®, Dolophine®, and Adanon.® Its pharmacologic action is like that of morphine, except for its failure to produce a "high." Methadone can definitely produce an addiction. The withdrawal symptoms are more gradual in their appearance and are less severe than those of morphine. In treating addiction to heroin, physicians commonly substitute methadone to alleviate withdrawal pains. A number of cities have instituted programs of methadone maintenance to care for their heroin addicts.

c. **Dilaudid (Dihydromorphinone Hydrochloride).** This substance is closely allied to morphine in its chemical nature and in its physiological effects. It is effective in doses considerably smaller than are necessary with morphine. The withdrawal symptoms are qualitatively identical with and just as severe as those attending abstinence from morphine.

d. **Percodan (Oxycodone Hydrochloride** and other analgesic ingredients). An effective and widely used pain reliever, Percodan has achieved great popularity in the illegal market among youths. It is a semisynthetic opium derivative sold in yellow or pink pills. Percodan is similar to codeine in its effects and is somewhat greater in its addictive potential. Under the trade name of Percobarb® this substance is offered in combination with a barbiturate in the form of a blue-and-white or blue-and-yellow capsule.

9. Cocaine

This drug is a sparkling white crystalline powder which is obtained from the leaves of the coca shrub, *Erythroxylon coca*, a plant cultivated by Andean Indians before the Spanish occupation. The raw coca leaves are either chewed or brewed as a tea by the Indians to deaden pain, allay fatigue, diminish hunger, and relieve altitude sickness. Cocaine is derived from the coca leaves either as an alkaloid powder or a more water-soluble hydrochloride. It has a legitimate medical use as a surface anesthetic. Illegally, the drug is taken through the nose by sniffing or is injected in the vein. The initial effect is stimulating, pleasurable, and productive of self-confidence.

a. **Source.** The legitimate medical needs of the world are met by 200 to 500 tons. The annual yield of Bolivia and Peru alone, however, is estimated to be about 15,000 tons, most of which is consumed by the native Indians. Importation of coca leaves and the manufacture of cocaine are under the strict control of federal narcotics laws. Only a single chemical company is licensed by the Justice Department to import leaves and produce pure cocaine.

b. **Illegal Traffic.** During the last few years there has been a marked increase in the flow of illegal cocaine into the United States. The Drug Enforcement Administration has reported an enormous increase in the official seizure of cocaine being smuggled into this country. "Body carriers," who a few years ago brought only 5 to 10 lb. of cocaine concealed on their persons or in their baggage, are now found to carry from 80 to 100 lb. The mountains of western South America are the leading source of cocaine smuggled into this country.

The first step in processing coca leaves into cocaine is performed by the highland Andean Indians who pluck the leaves from the small bushes. To a gasoline drum filled with the leaves they add kerosene and one or more solvents, leaving the mixture to soak. After the fluid is drawn off and the soggy leaves removed, the residual thick, coffee-colored paste is ladled into small containers and sold to laboratory agents. These clandestine laboratories then refine the paste into white cocaine, sometimes pressing it into small pills. There are many such clandestine laboratories presently in operation. Some of these are mobile units, thus presenting an additional police problem.

c. **Ingestion.** The typical price to the cocaine dealer is several hundred dollars an ounce. Ordinarily, the pure cocaine will be diluted with lactose, dextrose, or quinine and sold at an exorbitant price to the customer. The user takes the substance either by sniffing or by injection. Oral ingestion is ordinarily confined to the coca leaf chewing or brewing by Indians.

1) *Sniffing.* It is still a common practice to administer the drug by sniffing. A small amount is placed on the back of the hand and snuffed up. This direct application, however, can result in the destruction of body cells and the consequent erosion of the septum or middle part of the nose. Excessive use is accompanied by a characteristic deformity—the so-called "rat's nose."

2) *Injecting.* Injecting is done as with heroin: a water solution of cocaine is drawn into a hypodermic (or its equivalent) and injected into the vein. "Mainlining" is preferred because of the intense, quick-acting, and longer-lasting effect.

d. **Physical Effects.** Cocaine is an intense central nervous system stimulant, affecting the higher brain centers to render the user alert, restless, and apparently more energetic. The sense of fatigue is diminished and the appetite suppressed. In extreme cases, paranoia and psychosis may appear with nausea and hallucination. Although relatively rare, cardiac failure and subsequent death can result from an overdose of cocaine in the blood stream.

e. **Mental Effects.** Following an injection, the cocaine user experiences great exhilaration and even a sense of ecstasy. He becomes restless and garrulous. With heavy use hallucinations and illusions of a paranoid nature may develop; the user may become an irresponsible victim of his imagination. The chief evil in the immoderate use of cocaine is thought to be an excessive freedom from inhibitions and a consequent predisposition to reckless action, aggressive behavior, and confusion.

f. **Dependence and Withdrawal.** Neither tolerance nor physical dependence develops with the continued use of cocaine. It is not addicting in the sense in which the opiates are addicting; that is, there is no characteristic abstinence syndrome. Although withdrawal is normally uneventful, the heavy user may experience severe depression, great fatigue, and a confused state of mind. The continued use of cocaine can develop a strong psychic dependence, leading to a profound and dangerous type of abuse. It should be kept in mind that there is a dearth of scientific knowledge about the abuse of cocaine and very little experimentation on its effects is being performed.

g. **Law.** Cocaine is classed as a narcotic under federal law and its unauthorized sale, use and possession are prohibited by the same laws that proscribe the opiates. The state laws controlling cocaine are also characterized by harsh penalties—heavy fines and sentences up to life imprisonment. The classification of this drug under the same laws as the addicting opiates is a historical fact of a less sophisticated age, since medically and pharmacologically cocaine, a stimulant, has been found to be the opposite of heroin and morphine, which act on the sense as depressants. In the absence of any clear knowledge of the dangers of cocaine, the prospect of placing it under new and separate legislation is not bright.

h. **The User.** There is no typical cocaine user, and the range of personalities covered by the term is quite broad. The user may be a young adult in search of a new experience or a depressed person seeking to recapture his interest in life. As a hallucinatory drug, cocaine has an attraction for the rock-drug culture, in which mind-expansion and the atmosphere of illusion have a special value. As a stimulant, cocaine appeals to the imaginative but unsure person looking to acquire a feeling of self-confidence. Among the regular users of cocaine are said to be a sizable number of well-known public personalities who wish to project an enthusiastic and energetic image. In brief the cocaine user can be described as a person who wishes to change an impression—either his impression of the world about him or the impression he gives to the world.

10. Marihuana

Marihuana or *Cannabis saliva* is the most widely used of the illicit drugs. The smoking of marihuana cigarettes is especially popular among adolescents, who experience a mild intoxication in this manner. The hemp plant from which the drug is obtained is a hardy weed which can be grown in a variety of climates. In warm regions the plant develops a resinous substance which has a strong narcotic effect. The hemp plant grows wild or is cultivated in Turkey, Greece, Syria, India, Africa, Brazil, Mexico, and the United States. The appearance of the plant varies widely with the region in which it is found. Most commonly it is approximately five feet in height; green in color with stalks fluted lengthwise; compound palmate leaves usually containing seven leaflets; flower (in the male plant) like greenish yellow sprays about 6 inches in length; fruit or seed (in the female plant) in the form of a brown or greenish yellow moss enclosed in a green, sticky hull.

a. **Preparation and Use.** Marihuana is made from the female hemp plant. As the plants ripen, their flower and seed heads exude a resin that contains the highest natural concentration of active cannabis chemicals. The pure resin is hashish, a combination of powerful chemicals that rarely reaches the United States. The typical seizure of marihuana is a variable combination of female cannabis seed heads with leaves, chopped-up stalks, flowers, and hulls. Marihuana is illegally imported into this country, mainly from Mexico, either loose or in the form of a pressed brick, called a "key" because of its one kilo (2.2 lb.) weight. Marihuana is usually consumed by smoking it in cigarette form *(joint)*. The potency of the cigarette will depend on the region in which the plant is grown and the amount of resin used. At best, it is only one-tenth as strong as hashish. Marihuana may also be eaten when mixed with foods such as sweetmeats and it may be consumed as a beverage by steeping it in the same manner as tea.

b. **Identification.** The hemp plant itself may be readily recognized by the serrations and vein structure of the leaf. Familiarity with the appearance of the plant is essential. Prepared marihuana has the general appearance of catnip. In this form it may be recognized by an experienced microscopist. Several chemical tests are available. One of these, the Duquenois test, can be applied by the investigator as a corroborative measure prior to a seizure. Although not conclusive it is a fairly reliable indication of the presence of marihuana. A small amount of the suspected material is placed in a test tube. Two cubic centimeters of the Duquenois reagent are added to the substance and shaken for thirty seconds. One cubic centimeter of concentrated hydrochloric acid is added. If marihuana is present, the solution will turn pink, change to violet and finally become a deep blue. A supply of the Duquenois reagent can be obtained from a chemist or pharmacist.

c. **Effects.** The pattern of behavior induced by smoking marihuana will vary widely with the individual and the quality of the cigarette ingredients. Most physicians agree that the only physical effect of marihuana smoking is a temporary impairment of visual and muscular coordination. As for mental effects, the Medical Society of the County of New York has classified marihuana as a mild hallucinogen, although hallucinations are only one of many effects the drug can produce. It can impair judgment and memory and can cause anxiety, confusion, or disorientation. It does not appear to cause any severe mental illness (psychosis)—in contrast with the frequency of such breakdowns among persons taking LSD. However, when pre-psychotic people take marihuana, there can be a serious psychotic reaction, with marihuana serving as a catalytic rather than a causative agent.

Figure 12. Marihuana leaf.

There is a substantial difference of opinion on the relationship of marihuana use to criminal behavior and violence. One view is that marihuana is a major cause of crime and violence. Another is that marihuana has no association with crime and only a marginal relation to violence. The 1972 report of the National Commission on Marihuana and Drug Abuse found no evidence to substantiate the reputation of marihuana for inciting people to antisocial acts. Marihuana does have a tendency to release inhibitions, but the effect of the drug appears to depend on the individual and the circumstances. Thus, with regard to sexual acts, marihuana might predispose the user to friendlier relations but could hardly be considered an aprodisiac. Similarly, with regard to acts of violence, the response will depend more on the individual than on the drug.

Some members of the medical profession take a more severe view of the effects of marihuana. To present this point of view it should suffice to quote Doctor Nicholas A. Pace, President, New York Affiliate, National Council on Alcoholism: "Scientific studies worldwide have shown that chronic marijuana use causes inhibition of cellular growth, reduction in sperm production, development of abnormal sperm cells, interference with the synthesis of important genetic material in the cell, interference with the immune system, destruction of chromosomes, abnormal embryonic developments and birth defects in experimental animals, and, above all, brain damage." (*New York Times,* Letters, May 16, 1977)

d. **Tolerance and Withdrawal.** Marihuana is not an addicting drug. No tolerance is developed with continued use; that is, no increase in quantity is required to produce the desired effect. The use of marihuana does not develop a physical dependence nor does sudden abstinence from the drug result in anything resembling the severe withdrawal syndrome with its intense physical suffering and uncontrollable craving that characterizes the opiates or narcotics. At worst withdrawal may leave the habitué depressed and irritable, since marihuana can lead to a psychic dependence as can many other substances, especially those which alter the state of consciousness.

e. **The Marihuana User and the Law.** Although the smoking of marihuana is a habit and not an addiction, its use and possession are prohibited by most state laws. Under the Uniform Narcotic Drug Act, in force in most states, marihuana is defined and controlled as a narcotic drug. The controlling federal statute, although ostensibly a tax law, in practice is simply a criminal law imposing sanctions on persons who sell, purchase, or possess marihuana. These legal prohibitions with respect to marihuana are based on the drug's supposed liability to lead to petty offenses and even serious crime through underworld associations and, in particular, on the supposed tendency of the habitué to experiment with heroin in search of more intense excitement.

Responding to a considerable increase in the number of marihuana users and an even greater increase in the number of those who consider the laws controlling this drug excessively severe, some states have passed laws to "decriminalize" the possession of small quantities of marihuana or to institute non-criminal treatment for those who use marihuana. This view looks upon marihuana as a substance similar to alcohol—not especially harmful when used in moderation and, even when in excess, attended by evil effects attributable to the individual rather than the drug.

The opposite view is held by many reputable physicians and public officials, who consider the alcohol analogy a weak argument since it seeks to justify the adoption of a new vice by trying to show that it is no worse than a presently existing one. This group indicts marihuana on three counts: 1) it builds up an addictive need for continued use; 2) it impairs mental functioning at least temporarily and may damage the mind permanently; 3) it leads often and almost inevitably to the use of "hard" narcotics such as heroin.

Those who seek relaxation of the rigor of present marihuana laws deny the truth of all three charges. With respect to the first charge they point out that marihuana use leads to a habituation and not an addiction—that marihuana is not a narcotic in the medical sense, since it is not physiologically addicting as evidenced by the absence of withdrawal pains and by the absence of any buildup of tolerance that would lead to increasing doses. The second charge, too, is rejected on the grounds of insufficient supporting evidence and because of the existence of a significant body of evidence to the contrary, namely, that no physical damage and no permanent mental impairment have been linked to the use of marihuana.

Greater difficulty, however, is encountered in dealing with the third charge, namely, that marihuana habituation "leads" to the use of heroin. It is denied in the sense that marihuana has any intrinsic quality that results in a heroin liability. There is evidence that a majority of the heroin users who come to the attention of public authorities have in fact had some prior experience with marihuana. Nevertheless, there are too many marihuana users who do not graduate to heroin, and too many heroin addicts with no known prior marihuana use to support the theory that there is any special quality in the drug that leads to heroin use. There is sufficient evidence, however, to permit the conclusion that some people who are predisposed to marihuana are also predisposed to heroin use, and the further conclusion that through the use of marihuana a person forms personal associations that later expose him to heroin.

In summary, it would appear that the third charge is rejected here by requiring rigorous scientific proof, a much higher order of proof than is ordinarily available in sociological areas. The practical investigator would readily and instinctively concede that there is no pharmacological causal connection between the continued use of marihuana and an ultimate heroin addiction. He would, nevertheless, point to the need for a closer examination of the economics of the illegal drug trade—the likelihood, in view of the equivalent sanctions, that the marihuana seller is also a seller of the far less bulky and considerably more profitable heroin and that ordinary business sense would encourage the sale of heroin, particularly in the presence of a predisposed market. Finally, since the third charge presents a problem that is not academically soluble within at least the next decade, he would suggest that a meeting ground of the two groups be found in a consideration of the desirability of separating the marihuana dealer from the heroin dealer by a modification of the marihuana laws which would establish a penalty for selling this substance markedly less than the sanctions imposed on the sale of heroin.

f. **Identifying the User.** It is not possible for the investigator to identify definitely the marihuana user in his normal state, but certain indications will be found helpful. The confirmed user may develop a yellowish skin particularly about the eyes. In addition the eyes may appear exophthalmic, i.e., "pop-eyed." During a period of use a characteristic odor, resembling that of cubeb cigarettes, is detectible on the breath. The general behavior of a suspect may be compared with the typical pattern previously described.

11. Dangerous Non-narcotic Drugs

Certain drugs, although not prohibited under federal narcotics laws, deserve extended treatment because of their popularity and the deleterious effects attending their misuse. Some of these drugs—the tranquilizers and stimulants—are obtainable only on prescription; others, such as the hallucinogens, cannot be obtained even in this manner. For the illegal sale of both classes of drugs a considerable market exists and an illicit traffic has developed accordingly.

a. **Laws.** A series of federal enactments that had been found inadequate to deal with the traffic in dangerous non-narcotic drugs was replaced by the Controlled Substances Act of 1970. This, the principal federal law in the field, limits manufacture, sale, and distribution of any controlled drug to designated classes of persons, such as registered wholesale druggists and licensed physicians. It requires that inventories be taken and records of receipts and dispositions be maintained. It also places restrictions on the refilling of prescriptions. Criminal penalties are provided for violations, including manufacture, sale, or distribution by unauthorized persons. The first offense is a misdemeanor; the second, a felony. Possession of drugs for personal use is not an offense under this statute.

All of the amphetamines and the barbiturates are controlled by specific language in the statute. In addition, any other drug with potential for abuse because of its depressant, stimulant, or hallucinogenic effect may be placed under control by designation. The statute is enforced by the Bureau of Drug Abuse Control, an agency within the Food and Drug Administration.

b. **Addictions, Tolerance, and Withdrawal.** Opinions vary with respect to the addicting properties of the dangerous non-narcotic drugs. The medical profession generally considers the confirmed use of these drugs to be a habit and not an addiction. Except perhaps in the case of the barbiturates no physical suffering follows withdrawal. Very little tolerance to these drugs is developed even by prolonged use. While these drugs may not be considered addicting in the strict sense, it must be noted that a great psychic dependence can be developed and hence that users may in some cases require medical care in their efforts to break the habit.

12. Barbiturates

By far the most commonly abused of this class of drugs are the barbiturates or derivatives of barbituric acid, which are prescribed by physicians as soporifics or sedatives. In correct dosage the barbiturates are a harmless and invaluable aid to the treatment of insomnia, nervousness, and related conditions. They are readily obtainable, and their use is common at institutions such as hospitals. An excessive dose is toxic and may result in death. In fact an overdose of barbiturates is the most fashionable and one of the most common methods of suicide. The drug was once prescribed by many physicians without the exercise of any exception forethought. With some doctors it had replaced the old-fashioned placebo. Drugstores are the ordinary source of supply. A few unscrupulous pharmacists sell them under the counter. Operators on the criminal fringe peddle barbiturates in lodging houses, poolrooms, and bars.

a. **Identification.** Barbiturates are usually found in the form of white powder. Occasionally, they are dispensed in solution. For the most part, however, they are sold as tablets or capsules. The names of the various barbiturates would form a long list which could, according to frequency of usage, be headed by phenobarbital, sodium Amytal®, Seconal®, Nembutal®, and Tuinal®. The nomenclature is variable, different terms being used in England and Japan, for example. The various barbiturates are distinguishable by the color series employed by the manufacturers in their gelatin capsules: sodium Amytal is usually found in a blue capsule, Seconal in red, Nembutal in yellow, and Tuinal in a capsule with a blue body and an orange cap. Phenobarbital is usually manufactured in the form of a white tablet.

b. **Effects.** The barbiturates vary widely in the duration and the speed of action. Phenobarbital acts slowly but is effective for a long period of time. Seconal is felt within fifteen minutes but its effect is short-lived. Tuinal is rapid in the onset of its effects and is relatively long lasting. All of the barbiturates affect the higher cortical centers, partially removing control over learned behavior and inhibitions governing instinctive behavior. The user loses consciousness as the intermediate centers are reached, and in the final stages the respiratory and circulatory systems may be affected by the action of the drug. Death may ensue if the depression of the central nervous system is sufficiently severe. Because of the wide latitude of dosage, the margin of error is sufficiently great to preclude accidental death except under circumstances of unusual ignorance. The fatal dose is considered to be fifteen times greater than the sleeping dose. This estimate must be drastically modified, however, if an alcoholic drink is taken in connection with the drug. As with many other poisons, the effect of barbiturates becomes more toxic with alcohol. The synergistic action of alcohol and the barbiturates is well known to habitués and it is a common practice among them to drink whiskey together with two or three capsules of Seconal.

c. **Identifying the User.** According to the President's Commission on Violence there is no reliable evidence to the effect that tranquilizers (including barbiturates) are associated with antisocial behavior. "Behavior may change and some observers may disapprove of the changes, but crime itself has not been shown to occur." Although the use of barbiturates is not illegal, the identification of the user is sometimes helpful in the investigation of an illegal sale. The habitué is usually a maladjusted person who seeks escape from reality through the medium of the drug. Occasionally, he is a narcotic addict who is deprived of his opiate supply and seeks relief from the withdrawal symptoms. The barbiturate user enjoys a mild sense of well-being on taking the drug. He appears intoxicated and lapses into mental confusion. His speech is slurred, reflexes are diminished, and muscular control is seriously affected. Sleep supervenes after a period of time which depends on the type of the barbiturate and the extent to which alcohol has been taken. Even after awaking the effects are still felt and the user may still be recognized by his "out-of-focus" eyes, imprecise movements, and difficulty of articulation particularly with respect to distinguishing the dentals. Tests are available for the detection of barbiturates in the urine. The confirmed addict sometimes suffers from amnesia and may incur serious injuries from falls. Tranquilizers can result in an impairment of driving ability.

d. **Withdrawal Symptoms.** Usually there are no physical symptoms following the abstinence from barbiturates. Some medical authorities, however, have observed that, if a person has been taking as much as one gram of a powerful barbiturate daily for a period of two months, the abrupt withdrawal of the drug may be followed by epileptiform seizures within two to seven days.

e. **Illegal Use.** Although a serious attempt to control the use of barbiturates was made by the Controlled Substance Act of 1970, great quantities of these substances are apparently diverted from the enormous supply used legally by the medical profession. Some barbiturate supplies are illegally manufactured in laboratories in

Mexico and California. Some quantities are acquired by forged prescriptions and drugstore burglaries. The main sources, however, would appear to be those supplies which are manufactured for legal use but which somehow are diverted to illegal sales by an organized black market or by unscrupulous retailers. Among illegal users the most popular of the barbiturates is Seconal.

13. Amphetamine (Benzedrine)

The use of amphetamines has become prevalent in the United States and is one of the more common complications of opiate addiction. This drug is representative of a broad class of stimulants known as "pep pills." Ephedrine and epinephrine may also be placed in this category. The drugs in this group (sympathomimetic agents) are aromatic compounds, all of similar chemical structure, which affect the sympathetic nervous system, stimulating certain nerve impulses and inducing a primary action on the cortex of the brain. They uplift the spirit, dispel fatigue, and impart a sense of great work capacity. Their use without medical supervision is disapproved because of the danger of overwork attending the removal of the normal signals of fatigue. During World War II they were used to instill energy and confidence in the troops and to assist pilots in long bomber missions.

a. **Appearance.** Amphetamine may be found as a colorless liquid with a burning taste and a strong odor or in the form of white, crystalline powder. At one time amphetamine was readily available in the form of an inhalant. The paper strips containing the amphetamine could be removed by addicts and swallowed. The drug is now found in the form of orange-colored, heartshaped tablets. Other tablet colors such as the green, heartshaped Dexamyl,® are found as well as other shapes. Benzedrine® and Dexedrine® are the common trade names.

b. **Effects.** Amphetamine has been called the modern cocaine, since the effects are similar although milder in degree; it is used widely by narcotic addicts, prisoners, and maladjusted adolescents. Users experience increased muscular efficiency, exhilaration, sleeplessness, and a loss of appetite. Persons with unstable personalities may experience untoward reactions. Habituation and excessive use can result in overexertion and collapse. Little tolerance is developed. It has been observed by the President's Commission on Violence that research done to date contradicts the claims linking amphetamine use either to crimes of violence, sexual crimes, or to accidents.

c. **Sources.** The most common illegal sources of amphetamine are the unlicensed and unscrupulous manufacturers who supply the drug to unauthorized distributors. The retail outlets are too many and too varied to permit any useful description.

14. Sedatives and Hypnotics

There are other drugs besides barbiturates that act as behavioral depressants reducing the level of alertness and activity, and these may be conveniently grouped under the heading of sedatives and hypnotics. Sedatives are drugs used to decrease anxiety and motor activity by depressing the central nervous system. Hypnotics tend to depress the system even further, thus inducing a state resembling a normal sleep. Usually both kinds of drugs can be used for either sleep or sedation by increasing or decreasing the dosage. Included in this group are the minor tranquilizers, glutethimide, methaqualone, and chloral hydrate.

a. **Minor Tranquilizer.** This is a pharmacological classification for those drugs which are used to relieve the less severe psychological disorders. They are commonly prescribed for relief of anxiety, sedation, and as a muscle-relaxant. Included in this group are meprobamate (Miltown®, Equanil®), chlordiazepoxide (Librium®, Librax®), and diazepam (Valium®). Although these drugs are less powerful than barbiturates, abrupt withdrawal after an extended period of overuse may cause comparable ill effects.

b. **Glutethimide.** Sold under the trade name Doriden®, this drug is used as a sedative and as a hypnotic with effects similar to barbiturates, useful in treating various types of insomnia.

c. **Methaqualone.** This is a powerful sedative-hypnotic sold under various trade names, the most familiar of which are Sopor® and Quaalude®. This drug is used medically in the treatment of insomnia or for daytime sedation. Recommended dosages for sleep are between 150 and 300 milligrams. Large overdoses of the drug may lead to delirium and coma, progressing to convulsions. The effect of the drug is heightened when used with other sedatives or with alcohol. Thus, the danger of overdose is greater for students, who tend to use the drug while drinking alcohol.

d. **Chloral Hydrate.** This drug deserves special mention because it is sometimes put to criminal use. In planning a larceny the criminal may administer a heavy dose of the drug to his victim in the form of "knockout drops." Chloral hydrate is found in the form of colorless, transparent crystals, strong in odor and sharp in taste. Since it is highly soluble in water and alcohol, it may be readily mixed in the victim's drink. On ingestion the central nervous system is depressed, and pulse and respiration slowed, and the victim quickly sinks into a deep sleep. When combined with alcohol the effect of the drug is considerably enhanced; hence the name "knockout drops." An overdose may paralyze the respiratory center or the heart and result in death. Chloral hydrate has a legitimate use in the field of medication, where it is prescribed as a sedative or soporific. It is dispensed in the form of tablets or capsules.

15. Hallucinogens

This group of drugs named for their capacity to cause hallucinatory effects includes several natural chemicals, mescaline and psilocybin, and a number of synthetics, LSD, STP, and DMT. Although marihuana can also be placed in the class of hallucinogens, it has been treated separately because of its long established use and the special legislation which it has attracted.

a. **Natural Hallucinogens.** These are considered relatively mild in comparison with the synthetics. Their use was discovered from observation of the practice of Indians.

1) *Mescaline or Peyote.* This drug has religious and cult associations in northern Mexico and the southwestern United States. Studies of the effects of mescaline gave rise to the present research into the use of synthetics for *mind-expanding* purposes. Mescaline is taken from the spineless peyote cactus in the form of a

flower or *button* which resembles a dried brown mushroom, about the size of a half dollar and a quarter-inch thick. The button is eaten or brewed in a concoction for drinking. Narcotics agents have recently reported that the use of peyote, alternately sipped with orange juice, has grown in popularity among the young. The drug produces hallucinations, described by some as an appearance of geometric figures against a kaleidoscopic background of colors. Although bitter in taste and tending to produce nausea, the drug does not appear to have any serious after effects. The user experiences a sense of well-being but is not incited to violent action. The chemical name is 3,4,5-trimethoxyphenethylamine.

2) ***Psilocybin.*** This substance is extracted from Mexican mushrooms. It is considered far more powerful than mescaline. This drug may be obtained in capsules containing either spores or dried, ground mushrooms.

b. **Synthetic Hallucinogens.** This group of drugs is presently the subject of considerable controversy, with its proponents extolling its "mind-expanding" capability and its potential for research while its opponents decry the use of such dangerous substances in our present state of knowledge.

1) ***LSD, STP, and DMT.*** Of these three well-known synthetic hallucinogens, LSD (d-lysergic acid diethylamide) is considered the most important in several respects—first, LSD appears to be the most widely used (and abused) and second, it is by far the most powerful hallucinogen yet developed. The ingestion of as little as one quarter-millionth of an ounce can cause hallucinations that last for four hours. In addition to causing hallucinations and distortions of perception, LSD may also give rise to psychological reactions, such as, feelings of panic, violent impulses, suicidal tendencies, and even what might be termed acts of insanity. Long-term physical damage is also suspected by biochemists. Abnormal chromosomal patterns have been observed in persons who have taken LSD. Although not as powerful as LSD, STP (also known as DOM [dimethoxymethylamphetamine] and DMT (dimethyltriptamine) have equally dangerous psychological sequelae.

2) ***Use and Abuse.*** The hallucinogens have no recognized medicinal use, although LSD is being used experimentally in the treatment of alcoholism and certain forms of mental illness. Against

the questionable promises of inconclusive research and the dubious claims of enhanced creativity and widened scope of spiritual sensitivity must be set the known dangers associated with the use of these drugs and the dangers of the unknown. In the rapidly expanding world of psychopharmacological knowledge the "dangers of the unknown" cover a sizeable area of formidable contingencies. In addition to the hazards of brainwashing or mind control, there is the possibility of "mind dulling" and a picture of a society of people "manipulating their central nervous system by the use of psychoactive agents. . . . Different individuals, using different drugs to achieve different conditions of heightened stimulation or tranquilization, may be unable or immotivated to question existing social thought and standards of behavior and thus become a conforming mass. . . . Because such frightening conditions as mind controlling or conforming may be possible, it is imperative that we recognize (that) the threat of our exploding knowledge in biochemistry and behavior lies precisely in the abuse of this knowledge to coerce, to control and to conform." (Dr. Eiduson, *Science Journal*, May, 1967)

3) *The Drug Culture.* The use of LSD and other hallucinogenic drugs, such as marihuana, hashish oil, and cocaine, is fostered in drug-oriented religious cults, particularly in the California area. In 1972 a task force of federal, state, and local narcotics agents conducted a raid on a ranch of the Brotherhood of Eternal Love, an offshoot of O'Leary's League of Spiritual Discovery (LSD). The raid, said to be one of the largest coordinated police efforts against illegal narcotics traffic, revealed an operation that smuggled 1,000 pounds of hashish into the U.S. every month. A seizure was made of more than one million pink LSD tablets. As fronts for the sale and distribution of drugs the Brotherhood used popular counter-culture businesses such as health food stores, juice bars, psychadelic shops, record stores, surf equipment stores, used car lots, a rug company, and a beach club.

4) *PCP or "Angel Dust."* Phencyclidine (PCP) is the most dangerous drug to appear on the streets since LSD became widely available a decade ago. There are few specific controls over PCP. At present it is synthesized in home factories—an investment of $100 can produce a quantity of PCP worth $100,000 in retail value. The

drug, a white, crystalline substance, is a hallucinogen that can be snorted, swallowed, injected, spread over comestibles or taken with marihuana. PCP or angel dust has proved to be a very potent psychoactive drug capable of causing convulsions and violent behavior and occasionally producing death. During 1976 PCP was responsible for 214 deaths in the Detroit area alone. Unpredictable and irrational behavior is typical of chronic users. The rapid proliferation of PCP is attributable to the difficulties of control. Specific legislation is still under study. The manufacture of PCP is a simple, relatively odorless process that can be managed in the average home. The possible control of PCP suggests another, more formidable and more general problem in legislation, namely, the possibility of home manufacture from easily obtainable materials of an indefinite number of hallucinogenic drugs. The investigation of drugs like PCP depends on information from disgruntled users, fires from unexplained causes, and mysterious explosions.

16. Investigative Methods

The proof of a narcotics violation usually consists in establishing the following elements: (a) that the accused did or failed to do the acts as alleged and (b) the circumstances as specified. The act to which reference is made is the possession or use of a habit-forming narcotic drug or marihuana. In establishing these elements the investigator will usually be required to place emphasis on the points which are developed in the succeeding paragraphs.

a. **The Nature of the Substance.** A basic but essential step in the investigation is the establishment of the fact that the substance in question is a prohibited narcotic or marihuana. A *corpus delicti* must be proved independently of any confession. Occasionally the trial of a user is permitted to take place before the receipt of the laboratory report because the accused agrees to plead guilty to the charge of possession, and subsequently the laboratory analysis fails to reveal the presence of a narcotic. The accused is deceived in this matter by the unscrupulous "pusher" who sells a harmless white powder instead of a narcotic. The accused's admission should not be accepted as proof. The laboratory analyst must testify to the chemical contents of the substance. Some courts will accept a written affidavit from the chemist; others require the court appearance of the expert since his written report, being only hearsay evidence and not an official record or business entry, may not be admitted into evidence on the grounds that its admission would be prejudicial to the rights of the accused. If the chemist occupies an official position, however, his affidavit is usually accepted in the absence of any objection by defense counsel.

b. **The Unlawful Act.** The investigator must prove that the accused's relation to the narcotic was without legal authorization, i.e., that he illegally possessed, sold, or used the drug. Since the three acts are never completely separable, the following discussion will overlap in some areas.

1) *Possession.* The most common act is that of possession since it is assumed at some phase of the use or sale of the narcotic. It is necessary to prove that the narcotic was in the possession of the accused. Possession of a narcotic is presumed to be wrongful unless the possessor can prove otherwise. The possession is innocent if the drug has been duly prescribed by a physician or when it is possessed in performance of duty or when it is in his possession through accident or mistake. The subject should be searched in the presence of witnesses if any are available. If the narcotic is found on the person of the subject he should be confronted with it in order to induce an admission. Often the investigators will discover the drug in a cache. The confirmed user or experienced seller will usually have several places where he may hide his narcotics. The problem of the investigator is to associate the subject directly with the hidden drug. He should not under ordinary conditions remove the substance from the cache; a surveillance should be maintained for the purpose of observing the subject's return to the hiding place to recover the narcotic. Naturally the surveillance should be terminated after a reasonable period of time, but every effort should be made to prove that the subject had personal, conscious, and exclusive possession of the substance. To show merely that the accused had access to it is not sufficient to establish possession.

2) *Use.* Proving use of the drug is important chiefly in cases conducted for organizations which have requested an investigation of an employee as a possible drug user. In addition, proof that the

accused is a user may corroborate a charge of possession. The subject may claim that his possession is attributable to accident or mistake or that the drug was prescribed by a physician and was obtained with a legitimate prescription. A number of steps can be taken by the investigator to test these claims. Incident to apprehension he may obtain a statement from the subject concerning his intent to use the narcotic. The accused should be interrogated extensively concerning all the details of any explanations he offers. If the name of the prescribing doctor or a dispensing druggist is given, verification of these facts should be obtained. If the subject admits the use of drugs he should be questioned concerning such details as the frequency of injections, methods of administration, amount of dosage, cost of the drugs, circumstances under which the drug was first used, growth of the habit, sources of supply, and identities of sellers.

a) APPARATUS. The subject's person and dwelling should be searched for hypodermic needles, medicine droppers, bent spoons, and other instruments that are used in administering narcotics. These should be submitted for laboratory analysis to determine the presence of any residual narcotics. It should be noted that possession of the apparatus cannot by itself support a charge of use of an opiate unless some residue of a narcotic is present in the instrument.

b) WITNESSES. Information concerning the habits of the accused may be helpful. It is possible that there may be an eyewitness to the actual administration of the drug. Again, witnesses may be developed to whom the accused has confided his addiction.

c) MEDICAL TESTIMONY. The accused should be examined by a physician for physical marks, conditions, and symptoms which indicate addiction. Analysis of the urine and blood will reveal the presence of narcotic if the specimens are taken soon after administration. The withdrawal syndrome is the most reliable indication of addiction.

3) *Selling.* The illegal sale of narcotics is a more serious offense than possession or use; hence the chief objective of a narcotics investigation should ordinarily be the location of the source of supply or at least the immediate seller of the drug. The proof of a drug sale is established by testimony of the investigator or other

eyewitness who has observed the exchange of money or other thing of value for a narcotic substance. In some states the proof of a selling charge is less demanding. Several states have enacted legislation under which the illegal possession of drugs in excess of specified amounts creates a presumption of intent to sell. The law also permits the prosecutor to establish a presumption of possession by all persons present in a motor vehicle wherein drugs are found. Although both presumptions are rebuttable, the shifting of the burden of proof considerably lightens the task of the prosecution. Moreover, the necessity of employing informants to make purchases of drugs for the purpose of establishing the fact of a sale no longer exists, since the mere possession of certain amounts is *prima facie* evidence of intent to sell.

a) LOCATING THE SELLER. Intensive questioning of a user will usually lead to the identity of the seller. In most cases the user knows the seller only by nickname and is able to give only the addresses of places frequented by the seller. The user should be taken to the identification division and requested to study the photographs of convicted narcotic sellers.

b) UNDERCOVER ASSIGNMENTS. An investigator can be assigned to work undercover, posing as an addict. After locating the seller he should arrange to make a "buy." This operation, of course, is not a simple matter and the assistance of informants and others may be required. The investigator may make the purchase himself but it is preferable to have a confederate make the purchase with the investigator as a witness to the sale. It may be possible for the investigator to witness a sale to a user who is not a confederate. This latter arrangement has the advantage of avoiding the complication of a charge of entrapment.

c) SURVEILLANCE. Fixed and moving surveillances are sometimes needed to witness the sale and to gather other evidence. Binoculars should be used in fixed surveillances in order to observe the details of the purchase. Photographic methods provide excellent corroborative evidence. In order to obtain identifiable images, while working at a discreet distance, a telephoto lens should be used. A 16 millimeter motion picture camera and a 4×5 still camera will provide a satisfactory film record.

d) OTHER TECHNICAL AIDS. The investigation will often be greatly assisted by the use of imagination. Certain scientific techniques will aid in connection with proving the sale. For example, marked money should be given to the seller in making the purchase. If the serial numbers of the bills are recorded, they can be later identified when recovered incident to a search of the seller. Another valuable technique is the employment of tracing powders. A fluorescent powder may be lightly dusted on the bills or on the envelope in which the bills are passed. Particles and smears of the powder will be transferred to the hand and clothing of the seller. Although the powder is relatively invisible, it will fluoresce brilliantly under the ultraviolet light. Thus it will be possible to identify the seller even after he has disposed of the money and detect also any confederates who have subsequently handled the money. Tracing powders of this type are especially useful in a surveillance conducted to trail the seller to his employers and, perhaps, to the ring leaders of the local narcotics trade. In one case, for example, it was possible to locate the headquarters of a narcotics ring by following a seller until he disappeared into a multiple dwelling house. A portable ultraviolet light was then directed on the door knob of the entrance of each apartment until the characteristic fluorescence of the tracing powder was observed (see Chapter 40).

e) SEARCHING. A thorough search of the suspect's person and clothing should be made incident to an apprehension in order to discover any narcotic substance or apparatus for the administration of drugs. Since the narcotic is usually small in quantity and the apparatus readily hidden, exceptional care and considerable ingenuity must be employed in the search. The following suggested places of concealment have been gleaned from case histories: The shipment and possession of narcotic drugs are hidden in every conceivable and bizarre manner. Grooved plants, hollow bedposts, false-bottomed stoves, hollow heeled and soled shoes, false-backed water closets, hidden compartments in various articles of furniture, the inside of stereo speakers, the backs of cuckoo clocks, sealed tubes or pockets in automobile tanks, whiskey, fish and pickle barrels, coffee, gypsum, and flour sacks, hollowed-out tombstones and grindstones, tins in blocks of wax, hollowed-out candles, specially constructed corsets and other underclothing, belts tied to various parts of the body beneath clothing, rolled-up magazines and newspapers, falsely manifested packages, and hollowed-out staves in shipped barrels, are some of the methods which have been used. Heroin has been stuffed inside a live boa constrictor and in a toy llama. Prisoners have obtained narcotics tied to cats' bellies, and in Egypt drugs have been transported by camel under an excised flap of hide. The various body orifices, the toes, underarms and fingernails are places where drugs may be hidden. As a mode of concealment the inconspicuousness of the obvious should not be forgotten; carrying drugs openly in the guise of familiar and legitimate objects is perhaps the most subtle means of avoiding detection in some circumstances.

f) ORGANIZED SMUGGLING. On the organized-crime level (particularly in Europe) the most popular method of smuggling opium and morphine base is the use of specially constructed compartments or *traps* built into passenger cars, commercial trucks, and touring buses. Much of the morphine base is concealed in trucks carrying bonded consignments of legitimate cargo, which has been sealed with a customs band. These sealed trucks, operating under international customs arrangements, will ordinarily be allowed to travel across various national frontiers with little or no controls. The great number of such trucks traveling into western Europe precludes any systematic inspection.

g. MARIHUANA SEA-SMUGGLING. Airplanes have been used extensively in marihuana smuggling, landing in remote fields or through air drops. However, the hazards of low-level flying without lights across unfamiliar mountainous terrain have led smugglers to look for a more practical method to deliver their cargo. As in the days of Prohibition, marihuana smugglers have now taken to the sea because of its relative safety as well as the greater capacity of the ship. The following is the typical *modus operandi:* A freighter, flying a foreign flag and loaded with bales of marihuana, sails from South America to rendezvous outside the 12-mile limit with schools of shuttle craft. These latter will carry cargoes as far as 100 miles to shore. Some, capable of 50 miles an hour, can outrun everything but a helicopter. It is estimated that there are about 32 foreign freighters lying outside the 12-mile limit to serve as motherships for approximately 200 shuttle ships. Serving as protective organizations, in 1976 the Coast Guard, Customs Service, and the Drug

Enforcement Administration seized 26 ships and 315,000 lb. of marihuana. In 1977 these figures had risen to 54 ships and 1.2 million lb. Enforcement, however, depends on old-fashioned police work on shore: long hours of day and night surveillance, infiltration of drug operations, and the buying of drugs, as well as the constant development of informants. The use of informants is the mainstay of the Drug Enforcement Administration According to one former deputy director of the Administration, "The life-blood of any enforcement agency is information. We would not get very far without informants. The majority of cases are initiated by information developed from informants."

With the increased demand for cocaine in the United States, more cargo space is required and thus similar sea-smuggling techniques are employed. A Columbian freighter coming into New York will dock in the East River to conduct normal business. Sometime during the course of its stay crew members will lower packages of cocaine into the water. Swimmers are hired to carry the floating packages ashore to contacts in the city streets. Intercepting the drugs is difficult because they are brought ashore at night under cover of darkness. Searching a freighter effectively is a formidable task because of their great size (almost a block long and 5 stories high) with hundreds of recesses which require special mirrors to examine.

17. Laboratory Examination

In order to conclusively identify a substance as being a narcotic, it should be submitted for analysis by a qualified chemist. The admission of an accused as to the nature of the substance bears no weight in proving that a narcotic is present in the substance. Several tests have been developed for the identification of certain narcotics in the field; since, however, the tests are not conclusive or entirely reliable, they should not be attempted by the investigator. In addition to diminishing the quantity of available narcotic, the employment of these tests incurs the additional risk of misinterpreting the results in cases involving synthetic narcotics. If the charge brought against the suspect is a violation of the federal law, the evidentiary substance should be forwarded directly to the nearest District Supervisor of the Drug Enforcement Administration, Department of Justice. State, county, and municipal laboratories may be used for violations of laws committed within the corresponding jurisdictions. In connection with some laws, it may be desirable to obtain quantitative analysis. Often, however, the quantity of substance available is insufficient for this purpose.

a. **Letter of Transmittal.** The evidence forwarded to the laboratory should be accompanied by a letter of transmittal containing, in addition to the usual data, a statement concerning the circumstances under which the evidence was seized, any statement of the suspect regarding the nature of the substance, and any other information which the investigator may possess as to the type of drug suspected. Such information is particularly valuable when the evidence sample is small. It is customary for peddlers to adulterate the narcotic by the addition of an innocuous substance such as milk sugar or aspirin. This adulteration adds to the difficulty of analysis. If the chemist is provided with a hint concerning the nature of the narcotic, he can eliminate from consideration a number of drug groups and concentrate on one or two indicated groups, thus conserving that part of the evidence which would necessarily have been consumed in more exhaustive tests.

b. **Disposition.** Since narcotic drugs are placed in the category of contraband, they must be disposed of in accordance with the laws and regulations of the Drug Enforcement Administration. When retention of the evidence is no longer required it may be transferred to the Drug Enforcement Administration or disposed of in accordance with local laws.

18. Care of Evidence

The handling of narcotics evidence requires exceptional care because it is usually limited in quantity and an accounting must be made for weight and the number of items of evidence. All of the available evidence should be forwarded to the laboratory in a manner that insures freedom from contamination.

a. **Original Container.** Ordinarily the evidentiary material should not be removed from its original container. It may be removed for purposes of inventory, but subsequently it should be returned to the container. It is important to preserve any boxes, cans, bottles, envelopes, or wrappers connected with the evidence, since these may serve as additional clues to a removed source. These containers should be marked for identification. In addition, in the case of a purchase the wrapper may identify the establishment of the seller. In one case, where a narcotic user confessed to obtaining the substance from a drugstore, it was possible in the face of the druggist's denials to show by means of glue spots and paper cutter marks that the glassine envelope had been removed from the top of a pile of such envelopes found in the store.

b. **Inventory.** All suspected narcotics should be accurately weighed or counted by the investigator in the presence of a witness. When the evidence is in the form of tablets or capsules it should be both counted and weighed since it is possible to remove some of the drug without altering the number of items present. A record of the inventory should be made in a notebook.

c. **Packaging.** When the inventory is completed the evidence should be placed in a suitable container. Tablets, pills, capsules, and powders can ordinarily be placed in a small envelope or a pillbox; liquids should, of course, be placed in a bottle. Seals should be placed across the flap of the envelopes and the edge of the bottle cap. The seal should bear the investigator's name. If the evidence is to be shipped to the laboratory, it should be placed in an appropriate box, with precautions taken to prevent breakage or loss.

d. **Labeling.** A label should be affixed to the container of the evidence before packaging. This label should bear the following information:

1) Case number.
2) Name, rank, and title of the investigator.
3) Weight and substance or number of items.
4) Time and date when seized.
5) Place of seizure.

19. Medical Examinations

A medical examination of a suspect often provides corroborative evidence of the use of a narcotic. Such a procedure should be accomplished in accordance with the laws of the jurisdiction and with due consideration of the rights of the accused. A physician experienced in narcotics cases should be employed.

a. **Use and Addiction.** By observing such signs as contracted pupils and especially the abstinence syndrome, the physician can give an opinion as to the use of drugs. Needle scars and ulcerations on the arms and legs may indicate addiction.

b. **Body Fluids.** A urine analysis or blood examination will provide the best evidence of recent use of a narcotic. The physician or a qualified medical technician should draw the samples of the suspect's blood and urine, which should then be transmitted to a toxicological or pathological chemist. Approximately thirty milliliters of blood should be taken. The test tube containing the sample should be corked and sealed with a piece of white tab tape, covering part of the cork and tube. The accused's name, the time and date of taking the sample and the name of the physician or technician should be written on the top. Although 30 cubic centimeters of urine are adequate for a test, a more generous sample should be taken. A witness of appropriate sex should be present when it is voided. A screw-top jar may be used and labeled in the manner previously described.

c. **Nalorphine.** One of the methods used to detect a narcotics user is the administration of nalorphine, followed by observation of the subject's eyes. If the pupils dilate, the person has been using narcotics. Nalorphine (Nalline) is a substance which affects the same part of the central nervous system as the narcotic analgesics but which does not achieve any marked degree of euphoria or pain killing. That is, nalorphine, although it affects the same receptors and has even a greater receptor affinity than heroin, morphine, or methadone, does have enough intrinsic activity to be considered useful as an analgesic. Because of this very high receptor affinity, nalorphine will displace previously administered heroin, morphine, or methadone molecules from the receptors and will precipitate a classic morphine abstinence syndrome. This explains why in cases of narcotics overdose with opiates the administration of nalorphine is a potentially lifesaving diagnostic therapeutic measure. It also explains why nalorphine testing is used in the State of California for testing narcotics abuse in parolees. The administration of nalorphine to a *clean* subject usually results in pupillary constriction. However, as predicted from the theory, the administration of nalorphine to someone whose CNS morphine receptors are occupied will result in pupillary dilatation as part of the precipitated abstinence syndrome.

The nalorphine test is not foolproof and the results of the test should be considered as circumstantial medical evidence. In general, nalorphine testing is correct in about 85 per cent of the cases.

20. Narcotics and Crime

The exact relationship between drug addiction and crime is not known. The fact that drug addicts are crime prone is well accepted. Certainly the drug addict is associated with drug offenses, that is, violations of the various narcotics laws, especially those relating to possession and use. The extent of the drug addict's responsibility for non-drug offenses cannot be estimated with any great degree of accuracy. In any discussion of the subject, however, a clear distinction must be made between drug offenses (violations of narcotics laws) and non-drug offenses.

a. **Drug Offenses.** Although addiction in itself is not a crime under either federal or state law, it is a condition which easily, if not inevitably, leads to violations of the narcotics laws. To maintain his habit, the addict must necessarily buy and possess the drugs before he can use them. Unauthorized purchase and possession are violations of both federal and state laws. Moreover, to finance his expensive habit the addict frequently becomes a seller, thus greatly increasing his liability to arrest. Finally, in many states the non-medical use of narcotics is an offense, as well as the mere possession of a hypodermic needle or the equivalent paraphernalia such as a needle and syringe. Since a habit must be ministered to daily, the addict must violate each day a number of narcotics laws and run to some degree the concomitant risk of arrest.

b. **Non-Drug Offenses.** "Criminals become addicts, but opiate addicts do not become criminals through the maddening or deteriorating effects of drugs." This finding of the 1962 addiction

DRUG	CHEMICAL or TRADE NAME	DESCRIPTION	HOW TAKEN	TYPICAL DOSE	DURA-TION OF EFFECT	INITIAL SIGNS	RISKS OF ABUSE	PHYSICAL DEPEND-ENCE
Narcotics								
OPIUM	*Papaver somniferum*	Dried milk of opium-poppy pod	Smoked or swallowed	Varies	6 hrs.	Euphoria Drowsiness	Loss of appetite Painful withdrawal symptoms	Yes
MORPHINE	Morphine sulphate	Derivative of opium	Injected	15 mg	6 hrs.	Euphoria Drowsiness	Loss of appetite Painful withdrawal Impaired breathing	Yes
HERION	Diacetyl-morphine	Derivative of morphine	Injected	Varies	4 hrs.	Euphoria Drowsiness	Loss of appetite Painful withdrawal Constipation	Yes
METHADONE	Dolophine Amidone	Synthetic analgesic	Swallowed or injected	10 mg	4-6 hrs.	Less acute than opiates	Loss of appetite Painful withdrawal Constipation	Yes
Depressants								
BARBITURATES	Phenobarbital Seconal Nembutal	Barbituric acid derivative	Swallowed	50-100 mg	4-12 hrs.	Drowsiness Muscle re-laxation	Incoherence Depression Withdrawal difficulty	Possible
MEPROBAMATE	Miltown Equanil	Non-barbiturate sedative	Swallowed	Varies	4 hrs.	Drowsiness Muscle re-laxation	Incoherence Deresssion Withdrawal difficulty	No
METHAQUALONE	Sopor Quaalude	Non-barbiturate sedative	Swallowed	75-100 mg	4 hrs.	Drowsiness Muscle re-laxation	Delirium Coma	No

Stimulants

	Chemical name	Description	Method	Dose	Duration	Effects	After-effects	
COCAINE	Methyl ester of benzoylecganine	Isolated alkaloid of coca leaf	Sniffed or injected	Varies	Varies	Excitation Talkativeness Tremors	Loss of appetite Irritability Insomnia	No
AMPHETAMINES	Benzedrine Dexedrine Methedrine	Synthetic central-nervous system stimulant	Swallowed	2.5-5 mg	4 hrs.	Alertness Talkativeness Activity	Irritability Confusion Agressiveness	No

Hallucinogens

	Chemical name	Description	Method	Dose	Duration	Effects	After-effects	
MARIJUANA	*Cannabis sativa*	Flowering resinous top of female hemp plant	Smoked	1 or 2 cigarettes	4 hrs.	Relaxation Europhia Vagueness	Altered perception Impaired judgment	No
PEYOTE	3,4,5-trimethoxyphenethylamine	Dried cactus buttons containing mescaline	Swallowed	350 mcg	12 hrs.	Exhilaration Anxiety Gastric distress	Visual hallucinations Paranoia Possible psychosis	No
LSD	d-lysergic acid diethylamide	Synthetic compound 400 times more powerful than mescaline	Swallowed	100 mcg	10 hrs.	Excitation Exhilaration Vagueness	Visual and auditory hallucinations Possible psychosis	No
DMT	Dimethyltryptamine	Synthetic compound similar to mushroom alkaloid psilocybin	Injected	1 mg	4-6 hrs.	Excitation Exhilaration	Possible psychotic reaction	No
PCP	Phencyclidine	Synthetic compound	Sniffed, Swallowed or injected	Varies	Varies	Euphoria Irritability Irrationality	Irrational violence Convulsions Coma	No

study of Lawrence Kolb is increasingly confirmed by the proliferating literature on addicts—most addicts are definably deviant, delinquent, or criminal before becoming addicted. Most addicts have a greater tendency than their socioeconomic peers to be delinquent.

Addicts as a group do not specialize in violent crime. There is a clear and highly significant tendency for heroin users to be charged with property crimes as opposed to crimes against the person. Non-users appeared, on the basis of the charges against them, to be more violent in their criminal behavior. James M. Markham, in an article appearing in the *New York Times Magazine*, March 18, 1973, summed up the current expert opinion on the relation of heroin to crime in the following words:

> Given the current state of ignorance, it is impossible to answer with any pretense of precision the question—"If I am mugged, what are the chances that my mugger is an addict?" But, as we have seen, we do know this much: The image of the decent young fellow suddenly plunged into a desperate economic struggle to "feed his habit" is far too simplistic. Typically, an addict was deviant or criminal before addiction; the onset of addiction tends to continue, not create, a pattern of antisocial behavior. Getting hooked and "taking care of business" may in fact increase the new addict's level of criminality. But available evidence suggests strongly that addiction thrusts our hypothetical addict into property crimes, not muggings or other crimes of violence. Some addicts may have been violent criminals before they were addicts—and may continue to be violent. But there are some indications that the over-all rate of violence in the junkie population decreases slightly after the onset of addiction.

c. **The Cost.** The average heroin addict requires 5 grams a day at a cost of about sixty dollars. Obviously, the typical addict cannot afford the expense of his drug supply and, because of the nature of drug addiction, he must supplement his income by any available means. Thus he finds himself drifting into a career of small-scale crime—larceny, burglary, selling narcotics, procuring, prostitution, and other offenses which will yield the increment necessary to support his habit. For the most part he concentrates on theft of cash or of property which can be converted to cash.

No doubt, if we were to total the number of addicts and the cost of the crimes attributable to them in their efforts to obtain the price of each day's drug supply, we should obtain an impressive set of figures. With the value of the property loss running into many millions of dollars, we should be drawn to the conclusion that the drug addict is responsible for a great part of the country's crime burden. We must, however, set against this array of statistics the overriding consideration that the heroin addict is a special kind of offender—his criminal acts are directed toward the support of an addiction of which he is usually the unwilling captive. There is also the consideration that the nature of his crime is not assaultive or violent; the offenses rarely betray a personal malevolence or capricious cruelty. The element of malice seems to be missing from his criminal conduct, so that his behavior, and even his life, is better described as extrasocial rather than antisocial. Indeed, the great loss to the nation is not in the stolen property or cash but in the usufruct of citizens whose lives have lost all major direction and purpose other than the acquisition of the day's drug ration.

ADDITIONAL READING

Andrews, G. and Solomon, D. (Eds.): *The Coca Leaf and Cocaine Papers.* London, Harcourt Brace, 1977.

Baridon, P.C.: *Addiction, Crime, and Social Policy.* Lexington, Mass.: Heath, 1977.

Brecher, E.: *Licit and Illicit Drugs.* Boston, Little, Brown, 1972.

Brown. F.C.: *Hallucinogencic Drugs.* Springfield, Ill.: Thomas, 1972.

Cull, J.G. and Hardy, R.D.: *Types of Drug Abusers and Their Abuses.* Springfield, Ill.: Thomas, 1974.

Cushman, P., Jr.: Relationship between Narcotic Addiction and Crime. 38 *Federal Probation*, 3, 1974.

De Faubert Maunder, M.J.: The Rapid Detection of Drugs of Addiction. 14 *Medicine, Science and the Law*, 243, 1974.

Fuqua, P.Q. *Drug Abuse—Investigation and Control.* Hightstown, N.J.: McGraw-Hill, 1978.

Gorton, S. and Carr, T.: How the Uniform Controlled Substances Act Works. 2 *Washington Law Enforcement Journal*, 24, 1972.

Green, T.: The *Smugglers*. New York, Walker, 1969.

Greenberg, S.W. and Adler, F.: Crime and Addiction: An Empirical Analysis of the Literature, 1920-1973. 3 *Contemporary Drug Problems*, 221, 1974.

Greene, M.H. and Dupont, R.L.: Heroin Addiction Trends. 131 *American Journal of Psychiatry*, 545, 1974.

Gupta, R.C. and Andkofoed, J.: *Identification Guide—Tablets and Capsules.* Toronto, Canada Law Book, 1967.

Harney, M.L. and Cross, J.C.: *The Narcotic Officer's Notebook*, 2nd ed. Springfield, Ill.: Thomas, 1973.

Heroin Paraphernalia: Breakdown of a Fix. 10 *Criminal Law Bulletin*, 493, 1974.

Hider, C.I.: The Rapid Identification of Frequently Abused Drugs. 11 *Journal of the Forensic Science Society*, 257, 1971.

Hutton, G.W.: Marijuana Problems: A Legal Problem. 42 *Police Chief*, 5, 1975.

Kempton, R.J. and Kempton, T. Methaqualone Abuse: An Epidemic for the Seventies. 3 *Journal of Drug Education*, 403, 1973.

McLaughlin, G.T.: Cocaine: The History and Regulation of a Dangerous Drug. 58 *Cornell Law Review*, 537, 1973.

Moore, M.H.: *Buy and Bust*. Lexington, Mass.: Heath, 1977.

Nakamura, G.R. and Thorton, J.I.: The Forensic Identification of Marijuana: Some Questions and Answers. 1 *Journal of Police Science and Administration*, 102, 1973.

Oteri, J.S., Weinberg, M.G., and Pinales, M.S.: Cross-Examination of Chemists in Narcotics and Marijuana Cases. 2 *Contemporary Drug Problems*, 225, 1973.

Pace, N.A.: The Marijuana Health Hazard. 9 *Law Officer*, 3, 1977.

Pascarelli, E.F.: Methaqualone Abuse, the Quiet Epidemic. 224 *Journal of the American Medical Association*, 1512, 1973.

Phillips, C.R.: Drug Testing Procedures in Crime Laboratories. 8 *Valparaiso University Law Review*, 655, 1974.

Power, D.J.: Illicit Drug Taking. 14 *Medicine, Science and the Law*, 250, 1974.

Rangel, C.B.: Heroin Paraphernalia: Accessories of Death. 2 *Journal of Drug Issues*, 42, 1972.

Shellow, J.M.: The Expert Witness in Narcotic Cases. 2 *Contemporary Drug Problems*, 81, 1973.

Sidle, A.B. and Widdop, B.: Nitrate Test for Methaqualone. 6 *Forensic Science*, 135, 1975.

Stephens, R.C. and Ellis, R.D.: Narcotics Addicts and Crime: Analysis of Recent Trends. 12 *Criminology*, 474, 1975.

Tarshis, M.S.: *The LSD Controversy: An Overview*. Springfield, Ill.: Thomas, 1972.

Williams, J.B. (Ed.): *Narcotics and Hallucinogenics*. Beverly Hills, Calif.: Glencoe Press, 1967.

Wilner, D.M. and Kassenbaum, G.G. (Eds.): *Narcotics*. New York, McGraw-Hill, 1965.

Chapter 19

SEX OFFENSES

1. Introduction

THE TERM *sex offenses* is used here to include rape, carnal knowledge, sodomy, and deviant sexual practices related to the condition of homosexuality. An investigation of these offenses is particularly demanding of the investigator because of the discretion and tact which must be employed. This is especially true of homosexuality cases which can have a serious effect on the security of an organization. Moreover, since the accusation of a sex offense, although easily made, is often difficult to substantiate or disprove, the investigator has a special responsibility to protect the reputations of innocent subjects of such charges.

Sex offenses may be divided into two groups. The first, and generally more serious, involves physical aggression against unwilling victims, as in forcible rape, violent homosexual attack, or indecent assault. The second involves such acts as illicit intercourse or voluntary homosexual relations, acceptable only to the immediate participants but offensive to relatives, neighbors, or a substantial part of the community. This latter group presents distinctive problems in law enforcement. Fortunately, the authorities receive few complaints from voluntary participants in prohibited sexual behavior, and since the offenses are ordinarily committed in private, only a relatively small proportion of this activity is brought to the attention of law enforcement agencies.

One important result of employing the penal law to suppress behavior that is condemned primarily because it affronts the moral sense of non-participants is the great variety of laws and enforcement policies that ensue. Nations and states, as well as groups within states, differ widely in the gravity with which they view violations of sexual mores and in their estimates of the seriousness of the associated police problem. The discussion given in this chapter has been restricted to those offenses on which the law is fairly uniform and basically uncontroversial. Included, too, are certain sexual deviations (such as practices related to homosexuality and sadism) whose expression may carry implications (such as security considerations) having a far-reaching social effect.

I. RAPE

2. Nature of Rape

The act of having sexual intercourse with a female (other than the offender's wife) without her conscious and voluntary permission is traditionally forbidden by law. If the act is committed without the consent of the female, regardless of age, it is considered rape. Special provision is made for the protection of those females who are considered incapable of giving consent. Thus, if a woman is of unsound mind, unconscious, or in an advanced state of intoxication and the accused is aware of this condition, the act is rape. Similarly, if the victim is a female child who is not old enough to understand the nature of the act, the accused may be charged with rape. The act of sexual intercourse with females below a certain age under circumstances not tantamount to rape is called carnal knowledge or statutory rape. The elements of proof required to support a conviction on a charge of rape are discussed below.

a. **The Accused Had Sexual Intercourse with a Certain Female Not His Wife.** Penetration, however slight, is sufficient to complete the offense. It must be shown beyond a reasonable doubt that the private parts of the male entered at least to some extent those of the female. It is not necessary to prove emission. Corroboration of the victim's testimony with respect to penetration is not required. Finally, penetration can be established in the absence of the victim's testimony by circumstantial evidence such as expert medicolegal opinion.

b. **The Act Was Done by Force and without Her Consent.** The force required is simply that used to effect the act of penetration. If the woman is in normal condition the act must be committed against the utmost reluctance and resistance which she is capable of making at the time. Since the degree of resistance is a relative matter, it must be judged in the light of all of the circumstances of the occasion such as the degree of force employed by the assailant and the apparent uselessness of the resistance. In the case of females too young to understand the nature of the act or women of unsound mind or relatively unconscious (to the offender's knowledge), the absence of consent is considered to exist regardless of the actions or statements of the victim.

c. **Legal Changes.** Recent changes in state laws reflect a growing national trend to view rape not as a deviant sexual offense but as a violent crime of assault. Rape is considered the major crime least reported to the police—the FBI says only one offense in five is reported. To encourage women to come forward to report a rape case prosecutors have sought legislation to spare them embarrassing questioning at the trial. Many states have changed the rules of evidence in a rape case to limit the introduction of materials about a victim's personal sex life, either current or in the past, except in limited circumstances. Changes have been made, too, in the corroboration requirement, which in the past has made it extremely difficult to put a rapist behind bars unless he had also committed a more easily provable robbery or assault along with the rape. Forty per cent of sex cases were dismissed even under the eased corroboration law that went into effect in New York on July 1, 1972. The main revision was that the new law did not require a witness to the act of rape itself. But it did require evidence of the attempt (torn clothing, fluids present internally or externally) and of the woman's lack of consent (bruises, a neighbor who heard screams).

3. Characteristics of the Offense

One source of information on the offense of rape is a study by the Israeli sociologist Menachem Amir *(Patterns in Forcible Rape)* based on the investigation of 646 cases in Philadelphia. The study shatters, again, several popular myths, e.g., that black men go after white women. In 77 per cent of the cases victim and offender were both black; in 18 per cent both were white. In this urban study, rape was found to be an overwhelmingly intraracial event in which the victims were mostly black. Other findings from this study are given below.

a. **Characteristics.**

1) *Alcohol* was a factor in only one-third of the cases.

2) *Acquaintanceship.* In two-thirds of the cases the offender and victim were hitherto unknown to each other.

3) *Place.* Most rapes are committed indoors; one-third take place in the victim's homes. The dark-alley event is rare.

4) *Time.* Most rapes are committed on weekends; the peak time is Friday evening.

5) *Age.* Offenders tended to be under 25; victims tended to be under 20. Both offenders and victims tended to be unmarried.

6) *Occupation.* Only 10 per cent of the offenders were in occupations above the level of skilled worker.

7) *Resistance.* More than 50 per cent of the victims failed to resist.

b. **The Offender.** The rapist is usually described as an emotionally immature person, with deep feelings of inferiority and a sense of inadequacy with respect to social relations. Some psychologists distinguish two general classes of offenders—criminal and psychiatric. The distinction has been found useful, medically and legally, in the treatment of sex offenders. In a few states a sex offender must be examined by a board of psychiatrists. In New Jersey, for example, if he is diagnosed as a "repetitive/compulsive offender," an indeterminate sentence (with an upper limit of 30 years) is prescribed at a specialized treatment center. If he is otherwise diagnosed, he is sentenced as a criminal. The following are some of the characteristics of the two groups:

1) *Psychiatric Offenders.* Compared with the criminal offenders, the psychiatric offenders have a higher average IQ, have a broad range of educational and achievement levels, and vary widely in social position. The typical psychiatric offender is said to be gentle and even naive about sex, living on fantasy and retreating from normal life out of a sense of inadequacy. Many are latent homosexuals who overcompensate by the overt, aggressive heterosexual act of rape. The psychiatric rapist knows that he is sick

and typically feels tremendous guilt and shame, and even concern for his victim.

2) *Criminal Offenders.* In contrast, the criminal rapist feels no guilt, has no concern, and does not accept the idea that anything is wrong with him. He is a sociopath, of course, but he is not *sick* in the psychiatric sense. His action is frequently motivated by a contempt and hostility toward females.

4. Interview of the Victim

The victim should be interviewed as soon as possible after the occurrence. Another female should be present during the interview. The victim should be questioned thoroughly concerning the occurrence, the circumstances surrounding it, and her movements before and after the commission of the offense. Questions should be asked concerning her acquaintance with the suspect. Since charges of rape are easily made, the necessity of close scrutiny of the victim's complaint is evident. Logical inconsistencies in the victim's story may indicate the falsity of a charge. Sometimes when the girl is a consenting party, she becomes frightened after the act and, to save her reputation, brings a charge against her escort. Young girls may bring a false charge through fear of their parents' knowledge of their consent to the act. The following special points should guide the investigator in his questioning.

a. **Fresh Complaint.** The victim should be questioned concerning the manner and time in which she complained about the attack. In prosecutions for sexual offenses, such as rape and sodomy, evidence that the victim made complaint a short time thereafter is admissible. Under this rule evidence that the complaint was made, the offender identified, or other details may be given. The sole purpose of receiving the fresh complaint in testimony is the corroboration of the victim's story. The investigator should verify this information through witnesses such as the person who first heard or received the complaint.

b. **Consent.** To establish lack of consent, it must appear that the victim resisted to the extent of her ability at the time and under the circumstances. Useless or perilous resistance is not required. In regard to the acquiescence of a female child, the question of her ability to understand the nature of the act arises as a question of fact to be determined by the court. It has been held by some courts that a child under the age of ten years is presumed incapable of consenting to the act.

c. **Chastity of the Victim.** Ordinarily the defense may not introduce evidence showing the unchaste character of the victim, but, if she testifies as a witness, such evidence as specific prior sexual acts with the accused or others is admissible on the issue of the possibility of her having consented to the act charged and thus on the question of her credibility.

5. Medical Examination of the Victim

The victim of an alleged rape should be requested to submit to a medical examination as soon as possible after the occurrence. No delay should be permitted because of special physical conditions claimed to have been brought on prematurely by the act. The fact of the menstrual flow does not negate the suspicion of deception on the part of the woman since some females will engage in sexual intercourse during the menstrual period. The examination should be accomplished by a qualified doctor of medicine, preferably a pathologist or a physician with medicolegal experience in these matters.

a. **Consent.** If the victim is an adult, permission for the examination must be obtained. With regard to persons under the age of sixteen, permission should be obtained from a parent or guardian, since those under that age may not be considered sufficiently adult to give permission. The object of the examination should be explained to the victim and the examinee informed that the findings will be embodied in a medical report. Another female should be present during the examination.

b. **Significance of Signs of Physical Resistance.** Physical signs of rape will vary in different cases and may even be absent although the offense was in fact committed. Hence the medical examiner may not affirm in the absence of physical evidence that rape was not accomplished. Where evidence does exist, the range of physical signs will usually vary according to the capacity for physical resistance. In the case of young children or unconscious females, the evidential results of resistance will probably be absent, while the local signs of accomplishment of the act may be well marked, this latter condition varying with the previous experience of the victim. A distinction must be made between the general signs of resistance and the local physical evidence. Where a vigorous woman alleges ravishment, it is to be expected that signs of violence such as wounds, bruises, and scratches will be present and their absence should induce a moderate degree of skepticism, unless the girl avers that she fainted from fear, became panic-stricken, or was otherwise rendered incapable of physical resistance. The acts and demeanor of the female immediately after the alleged commission should be subject to very critical investigation in these cases.

c. **Findings.** In his report the physician will ordinarily include the results of the following types of examination:

1) The general physical appearance and demeanor of the female.

2) The presence or absence of marks of violence on the body; their character and position, when present.

3) The presence or absence of marks upon the clothing, when the offense is alleged to have taken place in the open.

4) The condition of the affected parts with respect to bleeding, bruising, and previous experience.

5) Secretions obtained for microscopic examination.

6) Examinations of stains on garments for semen.

7) Examination of fingernail scrapings for traces such as blood, hair, human tissue and fibers, which may have been acquired while resisting the assailant.

6. Medical Examination of Suspect

An examination of the suspect by a physician, if conducted soon after the occurrence, may provide valuable evidence. In addition to medical evidence of recent sexual activity, the physician may discover traces such as pollen granules and foreign hair and fibers on the body which may link the suspect to the crime. Fingernail scrapings should be taken as in the case of the victim. In addition the hands should be carefully examined for traces of cosmetics which may have been acquired by contact with the victim.

7. Examination of Clothing

Since in a sexual assault intimate contact takes place between the clothing of the assailant and that of the victim and, in some cases between the garments of both and the ground, a careful examination of the clothing of the suspect and the victim should be made for traces of grass, weeds, seed, and soil. If traces are found which correspond to similar materials found at the crime scene, this evidence may serve in the case of the suspect's clothing to associate him with the scene or, in the case of the victim, to partially corroborate her story. The examination of clothing for other than biological stains should be accomplished by a law enforcement laboratory expert rather than the medical examiner or other physician.

8. Examination of the Crime Scene

If there are no eyewitnesses and little direct evidence, the investigator must rely on circumstantial evidence. The scene of the crime should be carefully examined as soon as practicable after the reporting of the offense. Described below are some suggested investigative steps and types of evidence found at outdoor scenes. For indoor scenes and automobiles the same general principles are applicable with appropriate modifications.

a. **Photography.** Photographs of the crime scene are sometimes useful in verifying or disproving statements of the victim or suspect concerning their activities at the scene. These should include an overall photograph of the area, a close-up of the immediate locale of the activity, and photographs of special points of interest to the case such as approaches, broken branches, and so forth.

b. **Tire Impressions.** The approaches and surrounding area should be examined for tire impressions. These should be photographed and cast if they appear helpful.

c. **Shoe Impressions.** The shoe impressions of the suspect at the crime scene can constitute valuable evidence, particularly if he later denies having been at the place. Photographs and casts of male shoe impressions should be made. Shoe impressions of the female victim may also be of importance under certain circumstances.

d. **Clothing and Other Personal Belongings.** Personal articles such as clothing, handkerchiefs, papers, or jewelry should be carefully collected and preserved.

e. **Matches.** Used matches and match booklets discarded at the scene sometimes provide valuable clues. The match, for example, may fit a match booklet later found on a suspect. The match booklet may bear the advertisement of an establishment patronized by the suspect.

f. **Fingerprints.** Surfaces capable of bearing latent fingerprints should be appropriately processed.

g. **Soil, Seeds, and Pollen.** Particles of soil and excrescences of the flora sometimes adhere to the person or clothing of the perpetrator. The investigator in his search of the crime scene should be alert for any characteristic material which might be used to identify the suspect. Samples of soil, seeds, and pollen should be collected from the immediate scene and preserved for possible comparison with similar material that may be later found on the person of a suspect.

9. Neighborhood Inquiry

Persons living in the neighborhood of the crime scene should be interviewed to ascertain whether there are any witnesses who heard outcries or who saw the suspect or the victim during the broad period of time including the occurrence. Particular attention should be given to any spontaneous exclamations which may have been heard. A notable exception to the hearsay rule of evidence is the admissibility of utterances concerning the circumstances of a criminal act made by a person without deliberation or design while he also is in a state of excitement caused by participation in or observation of the event. The utterance may be an exclamation, statement, or oral manifestation of pain and suffering.

10. Abettor as a Principal

An accused may be found guilty as a principal in rape, attempt to commit rape, and assault with intent to commit rape, even though he had no intercourse with the alleged victim, if he shared the criminal intent or purpose of the active perpetrator of the crime, and, by his presence, aided, encouraged, or incited the major actor to commit it. There must be an intent to aid or encourage the person who actually commits the crime; the aider or abettor must be shown to have associated himself in some manner with the venture, and it must be shown that he participated in it as something that he wished to bring about, and that he sought by his action to make it successful. For example, one who stands guard while his companions commit a rape is guilty as a principal even though he did not have intercourse with the victim.

11. Carnal Knowledge or Statutory Rape

The absence of consent is an essential element of rape, whereas in carnal knowledge the victim assents to the act. If the consenting victim is of unsound mind or so young as to be unable to understand the nature of sexual intercourse, the act is one of rape since such a female is considered legally incapable of consent. Carnal knowledge can, however, be made a lesser included offense of a charge of rape when there is evidence pointing to consent by a victim under sixteen years of age (or other age given in the statute) rather than the application of force by the accused. The techniques employed in the investigation of carnal knowledge are similar to those of rape with the added requirement of proof of age. Documentary proof of the child's age is desirable. In view of the youth of the victim, the investigator should obtain the consent of the parents prior to such investigative steps as the arranging for a medical examination.

12. Attempt to Commit Rape

Charges of attempts to commit rape and assaults with such intent are common occurrences in criminal investigative work. They deserve special study on the part of the investigator both for their frequency and their relative complexity. An attempt to commit rape is a lesser included offense of the crime of rape. To constitute an attempt to commit rape, there must be a specific intent to commit rape accompanied by an overt act which directly tends to accomplish the unlawful purpose.

a. **Elements of Proof.** The following matters must be proved in order to establish the offense of attempted rape:

1) That the accused did a certain act.

2) That the act was done with specific intent to commit rape.

3) That the act amounted to more than mere preparation and apparently tended to effect the commission of the intended offense.

b. **Specific Intent.** The specific intent required is the accomplishment of unlawful sexual intercourse with a woman not the wife of the accused, by force and against her will. This may be established, either by direct evidence, such as statements proved to have been made by the accused at the time of the alleged offense, or by circumstantial evidence, such as an inference as to intent drawn from the nature of the act committed. A statement of intent may be proved by the testimony of anyone who heard it being made, or by other competent evidence.

c. **Overt Act.** An overt act is one that amounts to more than mere preparation to commit an offense, and must be one which in the ordinary course of events would result in the commission of the offense. To constitute an attempt to commit rape, the overt act must have proceeded far enough so that the crime would have been completed but for extraneous intervention.

d. **Consummation of Offense.** An accused may be convicted of an attempt to commit an offense although at the trial it may appear that the offense was consummated.

13. Assault with Intent to Commit Rape

In some cases specific provision is made in the criminal statutes for the punishment of assaults with intent to commit rape. The offense is discussed here in order to distinguish it from an attempt to commit rape. An assault with intent to commit rape is not necessarily the equivalent of an attempt to commit rape, for an assault can be committed in furtherance of the intended act without thereby achieving that degree of proximity to the consummation of the act which is essential to constitute an attempt to commit the act. An "assault with intent" differs from an "attempt" in that it lacks the element of the overt act which would have led to the accomplishment of the crime except for some unlooked for interference. The procedure followed in the investigation of an assault with intent to commit rape is similar in many respects to that employed with respect to rape itself. Additional points requiring special attention are the following:

1) *The Assault.* The victim should be interviewed to obtain a complete and detailed description of the assault. Where physical force was not actually applied, the nature of the threats or menacing gestures becomes of critical importance and must be thoroughly explored. If a weapon was employed, the investigator should obtain a detailed description of it from the victim. In the event that he is successful in finding the weapon, he should endeavor to establish its ownership. Where the weapon is a gun, it should be submitted for laboratory examination.

2) *The Intent.* The purpose of the assailant to have sexual intercourse can be established by statements made at the time, by indecent expressions suggestive of sexual preoccupation, by gestures or by the intimate nature of the application of hands, and by the obvious, demonstrable absence of any other rational motive. A thorough interrogation of the accused can often establish the absence of any rational motive other than rape even though the questioning may not succeed in obtaining an explicit admission of the intent.

3) *Use of Force.* The accused must have had a purpose to carry out the plan with force and against the will of the female. This purpose cannot be proved by direct evidence unless the accused had been overheard to make a statement to this effect. However, it will suffice to establish the intent by circumstantial evidence, that is, by facts and circumstances from which, alone or in connection with other facts, the existence of the intent can be inferred on the basis of the common experience of mankind.

14. Indecent Assault

Provision has been made under criminal statutes for the punishment of men who satisfy their desire for erotic pleasure by touching females in a sexually intimate manner. Indecent assault is the term used to describe the action of a male in taking indecent, lewd, or lascivious liberties with the person of a female without her consent and against her will with the intent of gratifying his lust or sexual desires. More simply stated, the offense consists of an intimate caressing or fondling of a female against her will. The investigation of a complaint of this nature should include a complete and detailed description of the occurrence by the female, an interview of witnesses, and an interrogation of the suspect. In questioning the suspect particular stress should be placed on the activities and location of the suspect before, during, and after the time of the occurrence of the alleged offense. The details of any alibi which the accused offers should be thoroughly explored. An effort should be made to find witnesses who can offer information concerning the accused's actions during the broad period of time that includes the occurrence. A search should be made for any past record of a similar offense on the part of the accused. The background and history of the female should also be investigated to detect any record of involvement in sex crimes or a propensity for placing similar complaints.

15. Indecent Acts with a Child Under the Age of Sixteen Years

More vigorous provisions are usually found in the criminal code for the protection of girls under sixteen years of age from the dangers of indecent assault. In addition, the law is equally applicable to cases involving youthful male victims. The offense comprises the taking of any immoral, improper, or indecent liberties with the body of a child of either sex under the age of sixteen years. It differs basically from indecent assault in that consent by the victim is not an element and does not constitute a defense. The investigation of this crime is similar to that of indecent assault. An interview of the parents should, however, be conducted with a view to determining the child's credibility. Ordinarily the major difficulties encountered in the investigation of this offense lie in the unreliability of the child's account. If the child is quite young, it is not a simple matter to obtain an accurate relation of the events in specific detail. In addition, the identification of the offender is sometimes a problem. The investigator should permit the child to give an account of the occurrence without interference or suggestion and should then explore ways of eliciting other necessary information without stimulating any latent tendency towards fantasy.

16. Checklist for Rape and Lesser Included Offenses

In addition to the usual who, when, what, how, why, and where questions the following points should be covered where they are relevant:

a. Employment, marital status, and family relationships of the victim.

b. Previous history of similar occurrences or related offenses in which the present complainant was the victim.

c. Exact location of the commission of the offense.

d. Locations where preparations may have been made.

e. Places visited prior to the occurrence.

f. Persons seen prior to the occurrence.

g. Road followed in arriving at the place of occurrence.

h. Location of rooms, houses, or other establishments from which the occupants could have heard or seen the events. Names and addresses of occupants.

i. What physical force did the accused employ?

j. Detailed description of any weapon used by the accused.

l. Statements or utterances of the accused at the crime scene.

m. Nature and degree of resistance offered by the victim.

n. Duration of efforts at resistance.

o. Utterances of the victim at the time of the offense.

p. Screams or outcries of the victim.

q. Movements of the accused and the victim subsequent to the offense. Paths followed, roads used, places passed, and persons seen.

r. To whom did the victim make the first report of the offense?

s. Was the victim's report made voluntarily or was it the result of persuasion?

t. Exact time of the victim's report.

u. Was the report made as soon as possible after the act took place? What reasons are given for any delay?

v. Results of the medical examination: Do they offer proof of the use of violence? Resistance? Penetration? Was the victim pregnant at the time of the offense? How long had she been in this condition?

w. Reputation of the victim: Chastity? Had she engaged previously in sexual acts? If so, with whom and when? Has she previously made similar complaints? Does she have any motive for false accusation?

x. Victim's relation to the accused: Were they previously acquainted? How long were they acquainted? How often did they see each other? What were the typical circumstances of their meetings? When did the accused make the first advance? How often did he make advances? What were the victim's overt reactions to these advances?

y. Statement of the Accused: Accused's responses to those inquiries listed above which are applicable to his actions, viz., movements at the scene, utterances, relationship with the victim, and so forth. Details of any alibi of the accused. Detailed log of accused's movements during the broad period of time including the occurrence. Verification of details concerning his alibi and movements.

z. Reputation of the accused: Criminal record; military record; social history; marital status; previous involvement in similar or related offenses; associates.

II. SODOMY

17. Elements

Sodomy has traditionally been known as the "crime against nature." The term *sodomy* as it is used here includes sodomy proper, which is the carnal copulation of human beings in other than the natural manner, and bestiality or carnal copulation by a human being with an animal. Although sodomy is usually practiced by homosexuals, it may take place between male and female, as well as between two males or two females. Both parties are guilty of sodomy if they participate willingly. Proof in the offense of sodomy consists in showing that the deviant act took place as alleged. The sexual connection in a deviant manner is the essence of the offense. Penetration of the body must be shown, but it need not be any particular distance, since any sexual penetration, however slight, is sufficient to complete the offense. The fact of penetration may be proved by circumstantial evidence. It should be noted that emission is not a necessary element and need not be proved to make out a consummated offense.

18. Investigative Procedures

The proof of sodomy is by no means a simple matter, since the act is usually performed in circumstances designed to insure great privacy. Ordinarily a sodomy case develops as an outgrowth of an investigation into homosexuality. A number of the investigative methods employed in rape and homosexuality cases are applicable to the investigation of sodomy.

a. **Eyewitnesses.** The investigative problems are greatly simplified if an eyewitness, other than the participants, can be found. The witness should be questioned in detail concerning the action he observed. The specific anatomical detail of the act is of great importance and the witness should be encouraged to describe the occurrence fully. He should also be asked to describe the participants and to state the significant points by which he would be able to identify them. Finally, he should be requested to account for his presence in the vicinity of the place of occurrence at that time or, where this is not applicable, the reason why his attention was drawn to the activity.

b. **Participants.** In the absence of eyewitnesses the interrogation of the other witnesses is of vital importance to the success of the case. Although both participants are guilty of the offense of sodomy, a different approach is usually employed in the interrogation of the active party as distinguished from the passive. In difficult situations the one should be played against the other in order to induce a confession. The passive participant or pathic is usually the weaker of the two and should be interrogated accordingly. It should be noted that in certain cases no clear distinction can be made between active and passive parties since the nature of the occurrence may have been such as to involve reciprocation or mutual and equally active participation. Naturally, where the crime is one of bestiality the distinction is of no value. It is understood here that the rights of a suspect are scrupulously protected during any interrogation (see Chapter 9).

1) *Active Participant.* The investigator should, as far as practicable, acquaint himself with the background of the accused prior to the interrogation. Some knowledge of the reputation, record, and associates of the accused should be required to enable the investigator to form an estimate of the suspect's character. Since in the interrogation the first approach is usually one designed to induce admissions, the investigator should employ euphemisms in referring to the offense. Terms such as "sodomy," "bestiality," "unnatural act," or "crime against nature" should be avoided. In the preliminary phases words such as "contact," "caress," and "connection" will serve to create an atmosphere conducive to frank discussion. After admissions have been obtained the interrogator can shift gradually to a restatement of the nature of the occurrence in terms of explicit, anatomical detail. In the preliminary stages it is often useful to follow the lines of the suspect's history. The interrogator can ask a series of questions relating to the following data:

a) Participation in similar offenses prior to present occurrence.

b) Arrest record for similar offenses.

c) Marital status: single; married (no children); married (children); divorced (no children); divorced (children).

d) First act in which subject participated: Active oral, passive oral, active anal, passive anal, bestial, mutual masturbation, or other.

e) Principal cause of first act: experimentation; compelling inner urge; intoxication; submission to force; or other.

f) Usual case of subsequent acts, particularly recent ones:

continuing experimentation; compelling inner urge; intoxication; or other.

g) Frequency of acts.

h) Partners in such acts, viz., whether the acts are performed promiscuously or are confined to one or several partners.

2) *Passive Participant.* The pathic or passive party in a sodomy case is usually the more vulnerable of the suspects. In many cases, particularly if he is not confirmed in the sex habit, he will be under the impression that he is relatively innocent by comparison with his partner. As in dealing with the active party, the investigator should not impart by his reactions any sense of the gravity of the offense. Expressions of shock or abhorrence in the initial stage of the interrogation may strengthen the suspect's resolve to remain silent. Restraint on the interrogator's part leads the passive suspect to believe that he will be receptive to any admissions which would indicate that he, the passive partner, was practically an unwitting victim. From the opening wedge of an admission of this type the interrogator should endeavor to work toward a full confession. An inquiry into the subject's personal history along the lines described in the previous paragraph may develop the spirit of clinical candor. It should be noted, however, that the suggestions given here represent the simplest line of approach to the problem of interrogation. Different types of subjects with varying degrees of experience will require different treatment. The interrogator should be sufficiently resourceful to try several different approaches where one has failed. Corroboration of admissions by the pathic must be shown in those cases where he consented to the act, since, being a willing participant, he must be regarded as an accomplice.

c. **Physical Evidence.** The scene of occurrence should be examined for evidence of the criminal act, such as stained handkerchiefs, and if necessary, for traces or clues which will associate the suspects with the place. In addition, arrangements should be made for a physical examination of the suspects by a medical examiner. When the offense is based on penetration of the anus, a medical examination can also provide corroboration founded on the abnormal condition of the anal region. On young persons the examination may disclose great tenderness around the anal sphincter, accompanied by signs of bruising, and laceration. In the older subject or in habitual offenders the anus becomes dilated, loses its natural, puckered orifice and develops a thickened, hardened skin. If the examination takes place soon after the act, the physician may discover seminal stains on the person of the passive offender or victim and fecal soiling on the active participant. Bestiality or sodomy committed with an animal is usually difficult to prove because of the lack of direct evidence. Medical examination is ordinarily successful only in demonstrating the presence of animal hair on the accused. Occasionally, semen may be found on the coat of the animal.

III. HOMOSEXUALITY

19. The Nature of Homosexuality

Homosexuality is the sexual propensity for persons of one's own sex. Normal behavior, the sexual attraction to a person of opposite sex, is termed *heterosexuality*. In homosexuality the person is subject, with varying degrees of compulsion, to sexual fixations or erotic attachments to persons of the same sex. The condition may be latent or may be overtly manifested. It is with the latter type that the investigator must be concerned. Male homosexuals often commit sodomy, particularly in the form of fellatio, and sometimes practice mutual masturbation. Female homosexuals, also called *lesbians*, may engage in cunnilingus and tribadism. Both types may engage in fondling, embracing, and kissing as a means of achieving sexual satisfaction.

20. Recognizing the Homosexual

It is a popular belief that the male homosexual can be identified by his feminine mannerisms and physical characteristics. This theory, however, is by no means generally true, not even in regard to the great majority of homosexuals. Many male homosexuals are virile in appearance and athletic in physical demeanor. Similarly the lesbian, while disliking men, may attract them strongly by her feminine beauty. On the other hand, there are many males possessing a feminine appearance and females with a mannish face and manner who are not in the least homosexual. Finally, to add to these difficulties of recognition, there is the phenomenon of bisexuality. Many homosexuals are married and conduct normal sexual relations with their spouses while practicing their preferred mode of deriving erotic stimulation in secrecy with another of their own sex. As a general rule, then, the investigator cannot trust his unaided observation of a person to deduce that a condition of homosexuality exists, but rather must rely on eyewitness testimony and other evidence to support such a judgment. The investigator should, in fact, as in other types of investigations, make no conclusions but simply describe the facts and amass evidence.

21. The Homosexual Problem

The condition of homosexuality is not a crime. Although overt manifestations of the condition, such as sodomy with a person, are otherwise punishable under criminal statutes, these considerations are, in the strict sense, irrelevant to the question of homosexuality itself. Although there is no specific penal provision for homosexuality in view of the fact that it is only a condition or tendency, the homosexual frequently creates a security or a morale problem which is of investigative interest. Homosexuality among members of large oganizations is looked upon as highly undesirable in that it serves to impair efficiency and *esprit*. Further, such individuals are considered security risks because of the influence that may be exerted upon them through a homosexual relationship with a person desiring "sensitive" information. Moreover, homosexuality tends to be epidemic: the hard-core homosexual, frequently unable to control his inclinations or desires, will usually look for a sexual partner, and, unless he can find another homosexual, he will tend to recruit some other person for his purpose. It will be found that the discovery of one homosexual in the course of an investigation often leads to the uncovering of a number of others.

22. Lesbianism

Homosexuality among women is tolerated more readily by society, attracting far less attention than its male counterpart and arousing less antipathy. Indeed, lesbianism is heeded so little that it is difficult to find anywhere in the United States a record of conviction or prosecution of a female under state sodomy laws. This is partially explained by the fact that the character of the female homosexual is less aggressive, her activities less overt, and her efforts at recruitment less obvious. Further explanation is offered by the statistics of the Kinsey research, which indicated that only one-third to one-half as many females as males were primarily or exclusively homosexual at any age.

While lesbianism poses no general police problem, it does, however, represent a danger to security and morale in organizations such as the armed services in which large numbers of women are employed. The nature of military life, with its necessary sharing of accommodations and close association during and after working hours, provides a satisfactory arrangement for the unscrupulous female homosexual who wishes to recruit from the innocent or the ignorant.

23. Initiating and Controlling Homosexual Cases

An investigation of an allegation of homosexuality should not, ordinarily, be initiated except on specific information. The informational basis of the case should not consist of non-specific facts such as mere acquaintance, neutral correspondence, past residence, or the presence of the subject's name in a homosexual's address book or letter. Moreover, an investigation founded on specific information should be carefully controlled to prevent unnecessary extension. Leads should be carefully evaluated for relevancy and materiality. If it is necessary to interview supervisors or associates of the subject the questions should be limited to reputation and character. The element of homosexuality should not be introduced unless information of this nature is first proffered by the interviewee. Minor children who are victims in sex offenses will present special interviewing problems. It is essential that a tactful approach be employed to preclude any subsequent serious psychological disturbance in the child. The interview should be conducted in the presence of a parent, guardian, or juvenile authority. A slow, friendly, manner should be used to avoid exciting the child. Allegations and statements made by a child should be evaluated on the merits of the child's maturity and tendency to indulge in fantasy.

24. Investigative Steps

Witnesses such as associates and supervisors, both past and present, should be interviewed if the information available to the investigator indicates that these persons are logical sources of additional evidence. Valuable clues may sometimes be obtained by means of a trash cover and a discreet search of quarters in which special attention is given to diaries, letters, and other written material. Because of the tendency of some homosexuals to commit their thoughts and feelings to writing and to employ certain characteristic terms of endearment and other locutions, their communications are often fruitful sources of information. Other articles which should be noted in a search are items ordinarily associated with females such as cosmetics and feminine garments.

25. Interviewing the Homosexual

In suggesting techniques of interviewing persons suspected of homosexual tendencies or practices it is not possible to prescribe fixed rules or even widely applicable principles, because of the variety of personality types which is encountered in these cases. The recidivist homosexual whose sex habits are confirmed by years of indulgence will by dint of experience be able to resist the moral pressure of prolonged and vigorous questioning. On the other hand, the immature person who has under the influence of alcohol and without full volition committed an isolated homosexual act may be impelled by remorse to a ready confession of his lapse. Since the majority of unknown homosexuals are relatively young and inexperienced, the simplest assumption that can be made for the purposes of discussion is that they will more readily yield to an initial display of interest on the part of the investigator that is free from manifestations of animosity or hostility. The suggested techniques described in some of the subsequent paragraphs can be abandoned without difficulty in favor of more effective tactics when the course of the questioning indicates the necessity of such a shift.

a. **Qualifications of the Interviewer.** The investigator who is assigned to interview a homosexual should be carefully selected on the basis of maturity, experience, and criminological knowledge. He should understand the various aspects of sex and marital relations and should be able to maintain rapport with the various types of offenders in discussing these matters. Finally, he should be well versed in the terminology of sex discussions so that he can word his questions in a manner calculated to elicit candid and accurate responses.

b. **Establishing Rapport.** To win the confidence of the subject the interrogator should convey the impression that his mission is not one of prosecution and that he is sincerely desirous of discovering the origin and causes of his sex problem.

c. **Diction.** The choice of words and phrases will directly affect the investigator's success. Initially the interrogator should form his questions so that they carry an assumption that the subject has participated in abnormal sex acts. For example, the question "When did you first do this?" should be used rather than "Did you ever do this?"

d. **Order of Question.** If the suspect is shy or guilt-ridden, the order in which the questions are arranged will be important. Embarrassing questions about sex habits should not be asked too early in the interrogation. Preparation should be made for critical questions by a series of neutral inquiries concerning schooling, physical health, and relations with parents.

e. **Introduction.** Initially the interview should not suggest too strongly a criminal investigation. The investigator should appear to be conducting a personnel background inquiry. At first the conversation should be casual and related to everyday affairs, common acquaintances, or recreational interests. The experienced investigator will be able to establish rapport without conveying to the subject the impression that he is making an exceptional effort to put him at ease. After devoting an appropriate length of time to the introduction, the investigator should shift smoothly to more pertinent questioning. He may state that a situation has arisen that requires him to obtain information concerning the background of certain persons. He should further state that the inquiry may make it necessary for him to ask a number of questions of a personal nature. The following information should then be obtained as a means of "warming up" to the sexual topics:

1) *Background history* including the subject's birthplace, the family income during his boyhood, parents' educational background and compatibility, number of children, class of neighborhoods, type of dwellings, and other factors relating to his boyhood.

2) *Educational history* including the types of schools attended, the courses pursued, relative academic success, relationships with instructors, and extracurricular activities.

3) *Social life* including general background of friends, extent and nature of social activities, and club memberships.

4) *Recreational interests* including types of sports, names of athletic clubs, extent of athletic interests, and summer camp activities.

5) *Military history* including circumstances of separation from the service.

6) *Medical history* including any consultations with a psychiatrist or psychologist.

f. **Body.** Naturally the most important part of the interrogation will deal with the subject's homosexual activities and the commission of substantive sex offenses. Little practical guidance can be given in regard to inquiries concerning sex offenses since the techniques to be employed will vary widely with the character of the subject. The questioning should, however, develop the following information, which, in addition to furthering the inquiry, will serve to supply useful data for use by reviewing authorities:

1) Arrest record for sexual offenses.

2) History of homosexual activity (if he divulges this readily many of the subsequent topics will be covered at this point).

3) Circumstances surrounding the first act of homosexuality—

age, cause, initial desires, degree of urges and desires, submission to force, inducement, exact physical nature of the act.

4) Exact physical nature of subsequent acts.

5) Nature of present sexual life; include any tendencies toward bisexuality.

6) Associates in homosexual activities—character of persons and manner of developing acquaintanceship.

7) Efforts to cure the condition, such as psychiatric treatment or change of social habits.

8) Identity of associates in homosexual activities.

9) Identity of places frequented for the purpose of associating with homosexuals.

10) Marital history including number of children, compatibility, and desires for normal domestic life.

IV. OTHER FORMS OF SEXUAL DEVIANCE

26. Significance

In the interests of public decency, law enforcement must take cognizance also of those forms of sexual deviance, other than sodomy, which directly affect persons other than the deviant himself and his partner. This effect is usually an affront of sensibilities or an outrage of personal dignity, but occasionally it may be bad example and constitute a deleterious influence on the conduct of others. No attempt will be made here to treat the subject of sexual deviance comprehensively, since a complete listing of the various forms would require a book in itself and would be, in large part, a treatise of chiefly academic interest. It is not possible to give a strict definition of the term *sexual deviance*. The generalized psychiatric acceptance of this term has in recent years been broadened to include any sexual act which constitutes a deviance from the heterosexual act of coitus. A convenient division of deviant acts may be made into those which constitute a misuse of the parts of the body designated by nature for normal sexual union and those which indicate a deviance from a normal sexual aim. In the first class would lie fellatio, cunnilingus, and anilingus; while the second class would embrace those acts which use a substitute object in place of the normal one, such as fetishism, voyeurism, and sadism.

27. Indecent Exposure

Indecent exposure is the exposure of the genitalia to one of the opposite sex under other than the conventionally lawful circumstances. Usually this offense is committed by a male in the presence of one or more females. In psychiatry this compulsive neurosis is termed *exhibitionism*. The personality of individuals given to this practice is characterized by timidity and lack of aggressiveness and there is in them little desire and often no psychological capability for the normal sexual act. In exposing himself the exhibitionist irrationally hopes that the woman will be attracted to him and will likewise expose her own person. The manner in which the exhibitionist operates will vary considerably. Some expose themselves at windows to female passersby. Others frequent parks and reveal themselves to individual females by rapidly drawing aside their overcoats or a covering newspaper. Still others accomplish their objectives while seated in automobiles and even in public conveyances.

28. Voyeurism

A voyeur (from the French word meaning a "looker" or "viewer" is a "Peeping Tom." Voyeurism is the derivation of sexual excitement and satisfaction from viewing the genitalia or naked body of another. Ordinarily the voyeur prefers to remain unseen and finds particular pleasure in watching the disrobing of women. His activities are frequently followed by masturbation. In general the voyeur does not constitute a danger to society. Indeed his viewing activities do not even constitute an offense other than in some cases the incidental trespass of property. If the Peeping Tom remains in his own quarters and views the undressing of a woman in another building he commits no substantive offense although his conduct, if it is commonly observable by his associates, is reprehensible as having a deleterious effect on the morale of others and he may be classed as a public nuisance.

29. Sadism and Masochism

The sadist achieves sexual excitement by inflicting physical punishment on another. The masochist, on the other hand, derives his pleasure from submitting to physical ill treatment at the hands of a sadist or another. In some persons both of these deviances are mingled. The most common forms of punishment employed are those of whipping and biting. Although these deviances are practiced by both male or female, it is found that the female is seldom a sadist, her nature being more inherently passive. While the masochist will derive sexual pleasure only from submitting to punishment by one of the opposite sex, the sadist may derive lascivious excitement from inflicting torture on a member of either sex.

30. Fetishism

This deviance involves the use of an object, usually intimate wearing apparel, of a person of the opposite sex to derive sexual satisfaction. The fetishist's mind is such that he can conduct most of the acts of lovemaking with this over-evaluated object with the exception of the sexual act itself. Pure fetishism is not uncommon among men but is a rarity in women. Fetishists sometimes break into houses to remove a certain type of article, such as shoes, lingerie, stockings, or other feminine wearing apparel.

31. Transvestitism

The practice of wearing the clothes of the opposite sex with the erotic desire of simulating attributes thereof is termed *transvestitism*. Male homosexuals occasionally dress up in feminine garments and solicit attention openly. At homosexual parties some of the members may array themselves in female costumes. Transvestitism is considered offensive in males and is explicitly forbidden by the laws of many states. The same offense among females, although more common, is considered socially acceptable, since this action does not appear in females to possess the deviant interest which it provides for males.

32. Frottage

This is a sexual deviance in which excitement is aroused and satisfaction achieved by rubbing against the clothing or anatomical parts, usually the buttocks, of a person of the opposite sex. The frotteur is almost invariably a male, the deviance being practically unknown in females. *Toucherism* is closely allied to frottage. The toucheur is subject to an irresistible impulse to touch the body of another person. He is encountered most commonly in large crowds, deriving sexual excitement from intimately touching women, apparently inadvertently. Such acts as pinching or caressing are made to appear like a casual contact.

33. Tribadism

Tribadism, the mutual vis-á-vis friction between women, is a common and effective method of achieving sexual excitement between female homosexuals. The tribadist is often bisexual; that is, she practices intercourse regularly with a person of opposite sex and yet derives intense pleasure in physical contact with members of her own sex.

34. The Social Problem

A change in public attitude toward the homosexual has taken place during the last decade in the direction of a broader understanding of his problem and his need for protection in certain areas of social life. The homosexual represents a problem that will not disappear by the public's looking the other way. The experts do not understand the causes of homosexuality. Family background, cultural environment, and even genetics are looked upon as key factors influencing the development of this condition. It is generally agreed that an adult homosexual will probably always be a homosexual. Since the number of hard-core homosexuals is estimated at more than 4 per cent of the male population, society cannot ignore their existence and should permit them to achieve a *modus vivendi*. At present a great many homosexuals live in fear—fear for their jobs or fear of blackmail, knowing that their vulnerability increases as they rise in their fields. The following case vividly illustrates the dangers that beset the career and peace of mind of the sexual deviate.

In early 1967 the New York City police and FBI agents broke up an extortion ring of 70 persons that had blackmailed over 700 homosexuals for a profit running into hundreds of thousands of dollars. According to the *New York Times*:

> The victims included men from the heights of eminence: two deans of Eastern universities, several professors, business executives, a motion picture actor, a television personality, a California physician, a general and an admiral, a member of Congress, a British theatrical producer and two well-known singers. Another victim, a high-ranking military officer, committed suicide the night before he was to testify to a New York County grand jury investigating the racket.
>
> All were shaken down by crooks posing as police officers after decoys from the ring got the victims into hotel rooms. In every case the extortionists made the same threat, to expose the homosexuals unless they paid up.

As a remedy for the plight of the homosexual, a number of organizations are endeavoring to make sexual acts between consenting adults an issue of morality not law. They point to the example of Great Britain, where, as a result of the Wolfenden Report, the sex law regards that which consenting adults do in private as a matter of private conscience rather than public law. Public solicitation, however, and sexual acts between minors still carry severe penalties. The American Law Institute has urged reform of the United States law along these lines, stating in its 1955 report that "no harm to the secular interests of the community is involved in atypical sexual practice in private between consenting partners." In 1967 The American Civil Liberties Union took a similar position, stating that "the right of privacy should extend to all private sexual conduct and should not be a matter for invoking the penal statutes." The policy statement added, however, that "the state has a legitimate interest in controlling, by criminal sanctions, public solicitation for sexual acts and, particularly, sexual practice where a minor is concerned."

The homosexual, too, argues that the abolition of sodomy laws would change his status from "that of covert criminal to open deviate, thereby putting the blackmailers out of business." Further, he believes that a change in policy regarding public employment of homosexuals would remove the major threat of the blackmailer and that as a result he would no longer be a security risk. "He would be different but trustworthy," they argue.

The argument, however, is unsound. A change of laws or regulations would have little effect on the point of view of society, and it is the attitude of society and not the law that determines the vulnerability of men in high position to extortion and blackmail. The homosexual's susceptibility as a security risk would be negligibly affected by a change of legislation. Moreover, in the absence of sodomy laws the police would still invoke nuisance and loitering statutes to control homosexuals as public attitude indicated.

Finally, it should be noted that the laws penalizing homosexual conduct are honored more in the breach than in practice. Although forty-nine states have sodomy statutes, the application of these laws is an unusual occurrence. Police attention is ordinarily directed toward the suppression of public solicitation and the molestation of minors. The homosexual's plight can hardly be attributed to police harassment or excessive zeal in specialized application of the law. It may more accurately be considered a reflection of public attitude, the ultimate determinant of public policy.

ADDITIONAL READING

Amir, M.: *Patterns in Forcible Rape.* Chicago, University of Chicago Press, 1971.

Bard, M. and Ellison, K.: Crisis Intervention and the Investigation of Forcible Rape. 41 *Police Chief,* 5, 1974.

Batelle Human Affairs Research Centers: *Forcible Rape: Medical and Legal Information.* Washington, D.C.: National Institute of Law Enforcement and Criminal Justice, 1977.

Benedict, J.N.: Homosexuality and the Law. 38 *Albany Law Review,* 84, 1973.

Brodyaga, L., et al.: *Rape and Its Victims.* Washington, D.C.: National Institute of Law Enforcement and Criminal Justice, 1975.

Bryant, G. and Cirel, P.: *A Community Response to Rape: An Exemplary Project.* Washington, D.C.: National Institute of Law Enforcement and Criminal Justice, 1977.

Chappell, D., Geis, R., and Geis, G. (Eds.): *Forcible Rape: The Crime, the Victim and the Offender.* New York, Columbia University Press, 1977.

Cottell, L.C.: Rape—the Ultimate Invasion of Privacy. 43 *FBI Law Enforcement Bulletin,* 5, 1974.

Geis, G. and Chappell, D.: Forcible Rape by Multiple Offenders. 11 *Abstracts on Criminology and Penology,* 431, 1971.

Guttmacher, M.: *Sex Offense: The Problem, Cause and Prevention.* New York, Norton, 1961.

Hall Williams, J.E.: The Neglect of Incest. 14 *Medicine, Science and the Law,* 64, 1974.

Hibey, R.A.: The Trial of a Rape Case. 11 *American Criminal Law Review,* 309, 1973.

International Association of Chiefs of Police. *Interviewing the Rape Victim: Training Key #210.* Gaithersburg, Md.: IACP, 1974.

Macdonald, J.M.: *Indecent Exposure.* Springfield, Ill.: Thomas, 1973.

Parker, T.: *The Hidden World of Sex Offenders.* Indianapolis, Bobbs-Merrill, 1969.

Rosen, D.H.: *Lesbianism.* Springfield, Ill.: Thomas, 1974.

Rossman, P.: The Pederasts. 10 *Society,* 28, 1973.

Schultz, L.G. (Ed.): *Rape Victimology.* Springfield, Ill.: Thomas, 1975.

Schur, E.M.: *Crimes Without Victims: Deviant Behavior and Public Policy.* Englewood Cliffs, N.J.: Prentice-Hall, 1966.

Walker, M.J. and Brodsky, S.L. (Eds.): *Sexual Assault. The Victim and the Rapist.* Lexington, Mass.: Heath, 1977.

Chapter 20

LARCENY

I. LARCENY IN GENERAL

1. Definition

A PERSON who wrongfully takes, obtains, or withholds, by any means whatsoever, from the possession of the true owner or any other person, any money, personal property, or article of value of any kind is guilty of larceny if he intends to permanently deprive or defraud another person of the use and benefit of the property or to appropriate the same to his own use or the use of any person other than the true owner. If the intent is simply to temporarily deprive another person of the use or benefit (and so forth) the offense is sometimes called *wrongful appropriation*.

2. Elements

The elements of larceny and the points of proof which must be established by the investigator are the following:

a. That the accused wrongfully *took, obtained, or withheld* the property described in the specification.

b. The *ownership* of the property, i.e., that such property belonged to a certain person named or described.

c. The *value* of the property.

d. The *intent* to deprive.

3. Taking, Obtaining, or Withholding

Generally the taking is accomplished by the thief so that he can acquire actual possession of the property, but this specific action is not necessary. A person may take constructive possession by employing an agent or by other means. For example, a person may steal electrical energy by fraudulently adjusting the electric company's wiring so as to bypass the meter. He may steal an animal by enticing it through food to leave the owner's premises. He may have funds of another transferred to his own bank account. Examples of *withholding* are a failure to return, account for, or deliver property to its owner when a return, account, or delivery is due. Again, a person may devote property to a use not authorized by its owner. It should be noted, however, that a debtor is not guilty of larceny because he refuses to make payment to a creditor, since he is not withholding specific property.

4. Ownership

The taking must be from the possession of the true owner or any other person. Care, custody, management, or control are forms of possession. Unless an owner of the property can be found the charge of larceny cannot be supported. Ownership is commonly shown by a bill of sale or a record of continued possession. The following points should be noted in connection with ownership.

a. A *true owner* is a person who at the time of the taking had the superior right of possession, i.e., the organization as against the custodian of the funds or as against a member; the estate as against a trustee.

b. The term *"any other person"* refers to an owner of the property by virtue of his possession or right to possession, who is other than the one who takes the property.

c. A *general owner* is a person who has title of the property.

d. A *special owner* is a person who has not title but who has the care, control, custody, management or use of the property.

e. The word *person* includes a government, corporation, estate, and so forth.

5. False Pretense

Property can be larcenously obtained by a false representation of a fact. For example, a person can collect money by representing himself as an agent of some creditor. A person may misrepresent the extent of his funds in a bank and utter a check without intending to meet payment.

6. Intent

The intent to steal must be present to constitute larceny. This intent may exist at the time of the taking or may be formed afterward. For example, a person may drive off in a car with the intent to ride a short distance and return. After driving a while he may conceive the intent to keep the car. The intent must in most cases be inferred from the circumstances:

a. If a person takes property, hides it, and denies that he knows about the property, the intent to steal can be inferred.

b. Conversely, if he takes the property openly and returns it, his actions would tend to disprove intent.

c. A proof of subsequent sale of the property is strong evidence of intent to steal and can be introduced to support a charge of larceny.

d. A person may be guilty of larceny even though he intends to return the property ultimately, if his intent to return it is made to depend on some future condition or happening, such as an offered reward.

e. A person who pawns the property of another, intending to redeem it at a future date and return it to its owner, may be guilty of larceny.

f. Once a larceny is committed, a return of the property or a payment is no defense.

7. Value

The investigator must not only show that a thing of value was taken but he must be able to establish the approximate value of the item. This element is important also in establishing the degree of larceny and in fixing punishment. The general rule is that value in larceny is the local, legitimate market value on the date of the theft. The following points should be noted:

a. In thefts of government property serviceable items are

deemed to have values equivalent to the prices listed in official publications such as catalogues of the military services.

b. Market value may be established by proof of the recent purchase price paid for the article on the legitimate market. The testimony of a person who has ascertained the price of similar articles by adequate inquiry in the market will be accepted.

c. With certain kinds of property the value is clearly apparent and can be inferred by the court from its own experience. An automobile in fairly new condition or a collection of precious stones is known to the court to have a value in excess of five-hundred dollars.

d. An owner may testify to market value if he is familiar with the quality and condition of the object.

8. Miscellaneous

Since the circumstances that surround a larceny can be infinitely varied, it is not possible to treat this offense comprehensively. The following are some of the more common questions that may arise:

a. **Finding Property.** A person finding property and taking it away with an intent to keep it is guilty of larceny, if there is a clue to the identity of the owner or if the owner may be traced by the character, location, or marking of the property.

b. **Theft of Several Articles.** If a number of articles are stolen at substantially the same time and place, a single larceny is charged even though the articles may belong to different persons. When several articles are stolen at the time and the accused is found in possession of some of the articles, this fact tends to show that he stole them all.

c. **Total Value of Separate Larcenies.** If several larcenies are committed at different times from different owners, the value of the stolen items cannot be summed up for the purpose of presenting a charge of grand larceny.

d. **Unexplained Possession.** The facts that the accused cannot explain possession of stolen property; that it has been in his possession since it was stolen; and that he had an opportunity to steal it are sufficient to support conviction of larceny. Possession of stolen property normally raises a presumption that the accused stole it.

e. **Flight.** The fact that the accused absconded at the time of the larceny is a circumstance tending to establish his guilt, but it is, by itself, not sufficient to support a conviction.

9. Motives

Obviously, the most common motive of larceny is economic gain. Kleptomania, an obsessive impulse to steal, is not uncommon. A person suffering from this mental peculiarity will usually have a long history of similar thefts and will not have any definite plan for converting the property to his own use. Revenge and malicious mischief are other motives of larceny. A person will sometimes steal solely for the purpose of exposing another to a serious inconvenience.

10. Investigative Procedure

The techniques to be employed in a particular case will be determined by the type of thief involved. The remainder of this chapter is devoted to a discussion of the different kinds of thieves and the *modus operandi* employed by each. As a general basis of procedure, however, the investigator will find it worthwhile to record the following data in the initial states of the inquiry. Many of the suggestions can be disregarded in minor or uncomplicated cases.

a. Date and hour of the theft. If this is unknown the period between the time when the stolen object was last seen and the discovery of the theft should be established.

b. A complete list and description of the missing property. If there are several witnesses who can offer this information, it should be obtained independently from each as a means of checking.

c. The location of the property immediately prior to the larceny; other places in which the property had been previously located; places searched for the property.

d. Reasons for placing the property in the location described above. The investigator should reflect on the logic of placing the property in this location. Safeguards employed or the absence of safeguards where logically indicated.

e. Identity of person who first discovered the loss. How did it come to his attention? Was he the logical person to make the discovery? Who should have ordinarily made the discovery? Other witnesses to the discovery.

f. A list of persons who knew the location of the property.

g. A list of persons who knew of the existence of the property.

h. A list of persons who had access to the property.

i. Movements of persons having access prior and subsequent to the loss in cases where the time interval is reasonably short.

j. List of absentees in commercial establishments.

k. Ownership of the property: true owner, person having possession at the time of theft, person responsible for the property.

l. Proof of ownership, custody, or responsibility.

m. Estimated value of the property. Bills of sale. Where documentary evidence is absent, the approximate date of purchase and the identity of the vendor.

n. Suspects named by the owner or others. Reasons for their suspicions. Employees exhibiting unusual behavior within the last month.

o. Suspects in financial straits, faced with future money problems, or maintaining a standard of living inconsistent with their incomes.

p. Reconstruction of the larceny; *modus operandi* of the thief; means of access; selection of time; method of concealing the larceny; in larceny by false pretenses, the conversations and transactions which took place between the perpetrator and the victim or other parties.

q. Character of property; saleability; uses; convertibility.

r. List of possible markets for the property.

s. Interrogation of each suspect: activities prior and subsequent to the larceny; time at which he last saw the property; time at which he was last near the location of the property; persons who can verify his alibi; financial circumstances; present indebtedness; contemplated investments or purchases; relations with the owner.

t. Records: previous larceny complaints made by the victim; history of periodic or systematic thefts; employees with police records; background of suspects.

u. Interviews of building employees, and others who may have observed persons approaching the area containing the property at unusual times or in a peculiar manner. Complete physical descriptions of any suspects developed in this manner.

v. Physical evidence such as latent fingerprints, shoe prints, articles of clothing, or similar traces left at the scene.

II. AUTOMOBILE LARCENY

11. Automobile Thefts

Approximately one million automobiles are stolen in the United States each year. Many of these stolen cars are recovered because a high percentage of auto thefts are perpetrated for temporary use rather than for resale. However, in urban areas where professional car thieves operate, less than half are recovered. To combat auto theft activity special measures have been adopted for its prevention and trained groups of investigators are assigned to the problem. The annual monetary loss from the larceny of cars is so great that insurance companies have established the National Auto Theft Bureau to assist local law enforcement agencies in the recovery of cars and the apprehension of the criminals. Another agency set up for the same general purpose is the recently established Federal Interagency Committee on Auto Theft Prevention. Large municipal police departments have organized Auto Squads or Auto Theft Details to counteract this criminal trend. These squads consist of detectives who have received special training in the methods of operation of automobile thieves and who have an intimate knowledge of the identity of known auto thieves and the organization of their gangs. Every state has a special law relating to larceny of automobiles. These laws are not uniform; at present, there appears to be no immediate possibility of the enactment of a uniform law. Section 408 of Title 18, U. S. Code, provides for the punishment of persons who transport in interstate or foreign commerce a stolen motor vehicle, knowing it to have been stolen. In addition, this law relates to the receiving, storing, selling, or disposing of such a motor vehicle, knowing it to have been stolen. These offenses are investigated by the FBI. In considering the larceny of automobiles, a distinction should be made between wrongful appropriation and true larceny. A large number of thefts of automobiles are temporary appropriations. Vehicles in this category are frequently recovered. Obviously there are two distinct classes of auto theft.

a. **Temporary Appropriation.** Many cases of automobile larceny fall in this category. The motive is temporary use. The car is stolen, remains missing for a few days, and is abandoned. Later, it is observed for a period of days unattended in the street. A resident of the neighborhood or the patrolman assigned to the post makes the report. The license is checked against the registrations of vehicles reported stolen and the auto is returned to its owner. The following are the more common types of this offense.

1) *Juveniles and Joy Riders.* The most serious aspect of auto theft is represented by the statistics relating to the age of the typical offender. Many auto thefts are committed by juveniles—in 1977, 53 per cent of the persons arrested for auto theft were under eighteen years of age and 71 per cent were under twenty-one. In addition, auto theft is a common statistical starting point of a criminal career—in an FBI sample of juvenile auto theft offenders 41 per cent had no previous arrest record. A substantial contribution to crime prevention can be made by adults by removing the ignition key and otherwise securing their unattended automobiles.

2) *Professional Criminals.* In perpetrating a "big job" (usually robbery) the professional criminal is faced with the problem of obtaining transportation and at the same time avoiding the danger of exposing a license plate as a clue. The obvious solution to this problem is to steal a car, use it in the commission of the crime, and abandon it in an unpopulated neighborhood. The larceny is committed as near as practicable to the time of perpetration of the major crime in order to avoid the danger of a pickup by local police through teletype or radio transmission of the license plate. In planning a robbery, the criminals arrange to use the stolen car at the scene of the crime, drive to a secluded spot, and then switch to their own car. Since the stolen car is readily recovered, the investigator is concerned with the major crime rather than the car theft.

3) *False Report by Owner.* Occasionally the owner will falsely report the theft of his vehicle in order to cover up a serious accident.

While driving he may have injured a pedestrian and left the scene without stopping. On reflection he becomes aware of the seriousness of a hit-and-run charge and of the probability that a witness may be able to recognize the car. He then forms the plan of simulating a car theft. He may damage the car door or side window in order to give the appearance of a forced entry. He then abandons the car and proceeds to report the "theft" to the police. Naturally the investigator should be suspicious of any "theft" where the recovered car shows signs of an accident. An inquiry should be made into all hit-and-run cases which took place during the pertinent period in order to determine whether the vehicle reported stolen is implicated.

b. **Professional Automobile Thieves.** The true automobile thief steals a car so that he can profit by its sale. Subsequently the car may be resold as a unit or stripped for the sale of its parts. Frequently the thief belongs to a well-organized group that is set up to steal cars, disguise them, obtain fraudulent registration, and sell them in a prepared market.

1) *Stealing the Car.* The actual work of stealing a vehicle is carried out by a professional within the space of a few minutes. The following are representative steps in the operation:

a) TARGETING. The thief selects a car on a street where he thinks he can work for a short time without drawing attention.

b) OPENING THE DOOR. In the absence of a key the problem of the locked door is attacked through the window by means of a *snake*, a sharp-bladed tool that is passed between the top of the window and the rubber insulation to catch the lock button and raise it.

c) THE IGNITION CYLINDER. With the door open the thief may jump the ignition behind the dash or under the hood by means of a set of alligator clips. The more professional approach uses one of the following methods:

i. Master Keys. Although it is time-consuming, the thief may use a set of keys, one of which is sure to work for any given line of cars.

ii. Code Cutter. This is a punch device for cutting blank keys according to a car's ignition code number.

iii. "Slapper." This is a tool (also known as the "slam hammer") originally designed to pull dents out of auto bodies. It can be adapted to pulling out the ignition cylinder in three or four good whacks. The thief then slips in a standard replacement cylinder (a "deadlock"), which is equipped with keys.

d) Steering Column. With the advent of locking devices on steering columns, the simple breaking into a car and jumping the wires to drive it off has become rare. Auto thieves now use long, thin saws that can be inserted into the steering column to break the lock. After this operation the ignition lock is managed by one of the methods previously described.

e) Towing Away. Some thieves employ the simple method of using a tow truck to take the car away. Still others employ vans and cranes to lift the auto from the ground, place it into a truck, and drive off.

f) Copying the Key. Another common procedure of auto thieves is to establish a connection at a car wash, parking garage, or restaurant with a parking service and then make copies of the keys of selected cars, noting down their tag numbers. Later, after locating the car on the street, the thief uses his stolen copy of the key to drive off.

g) Neutralizing Alarms. Although the professional thief would rather steal a car without an alarm system, he is prepared to neutralize the standard systems if necessary with a special key to turn them off or by cutting the right wire or bypassing them with a pair of alligator clips. Most alarm systems and locks can be neutralized by so innocent-appearing a mechanism as a tow truck.

2) *Disguising the Car.* Automobiles can be identified by means of the Vehicle Identification Number (VIN). A visible VIN will be found on a plate on top of the dash for police inspection. A hidden VIN is stamped on a part of the car which varies from model to model and which is changed each year. The auto industry has entrusted the looseleaf binder filled with VIN location diagrams from each manufacturer only to the FBI and the private National Auto Theft Bureau, rather than to local or state police departments. The NATB owes its privileged status to the International Association of Chiefs of Police, which has designated NATB as the national clearing house for stolen cars and as a source of expert witnesses to answer auto-identification questions. The professional car thieves will locate VIN stampings on new cars by buying a Cadillac, for example, and removing the body to examine the chassis. At least a dozen car theft rings in the United States buy or steal the latest models as soon

as they appear and make a microscopic examination of the auto frames to find the hidden VINs. Knowing the locations, the car thieves can quickly have the true numbers abraded and new ones inscribed. Often the dies which are used to punch in the new numbers are defective and a recovered car can be linked to a set of tools. About a third of the cars stolen are renumbered and usually repainted for resale.

3) *Fraudulent Registration.* The car-theft organization must provide apparently legitimate papers for the stolen vehicle, if they wish to sell it. To accomplish this a study is made of the various state laws and regulations controlling registration and transfer of ownership. For example, the thieves are aware that most states have a "certificate-of-title" law and that it is less difficult to transfer stolen cars in the others. A certificate of title is a history of the car's ownership. A New York registration stub, however, may be used to transfer a car with no more information about the owner than his name. The thief can alter the information on a faded and tattered but bona fide stub to fit a car he wishes to sell.

4) *Market.* The outlet chosen by the car thief for his merchandise will depend on the thief's specialty and his *modus operandi.* The following are some of the usual outlets:

a) "Car Clouts" and "Boosters" are persons who steal parts and property out of cars. Articles such as hub caps, CB units, or tape decks will be brought to second-hand dealers.

b) Saleable Parts. A car can be cut up into parts for sale within a few hours after it is stolen, while the identifiable parts with VIN stampings—chassis, engine, and transmission—are destroyed. Complex parts such as a *nose clip* with front fenders, grill, hood, and bumper will fetch up to $2,000 per set for a new Cadillac. The operation is highly professional. A short time after the vehicle is stolen it disappears into a well-equipped junkyard where a team of specialists or "cutters" proceeds to cut off the saleable parts and destroy the remainder.

c) Selling "to order". Professionals who steal and sell to order are the most skillful and systematic of all. In one scheme they recruit car wreckers who will sell them the identification plates and registration papers of late-model wrecks. They then repaint stolen cars to match the wrecks in all but color.

d) Export. In recent years an export market for stolen cars has been developed in places such as Mexico, Puerto Rico, Brazil, and the Dominican Republic. One type of export operation is well illustrated by a ring uncovered in the New York area after stealing more than 300 automobiles for export from 1969 to 1972. The stolen vehicles were General Motors cars specified by officials of the government in Santo Domingo. The ring operated by hiring persons to steal late-model cars in return for $200 to $300. Stolen identification plates were then purchased from a General Motors employee at $75 each. With the stolen plates substituted for the originals, the ring paid other persons $25 each to drive the cars to the piers in New Jersey and New York. At the piers proper shipping documents were obtained, and fees of about $500 were paid to ship the cars to the Dominican Republic, where officials would arrange to have the cars passed through customs without payment of import duties. The cars were then sold at twice their value. Members of the ring in New York received about $1,500 for each car. Two of the ringleaders, Dominican aliens, were arrested in the Bronx and charged with criminal possession of stolen property, unauthorized use of a vehicle, forgery, criminal possession of a forged instrument, criminal possession of forgery devices, forgery of vehicle identification numbers, and illegal possession of identification numbers.

12. Illustrative Cases

a. **Steal-to-Order Car Ring.** The following case appeared in the April 26, 1968, issue of *The Long Island Press* under the headline, "Smash Multi-Million $$ 'Steal-to-Order' Car Ring."

The case presents a number of special facets of professional interest. First, there is a detailed account of the *modus operandi* of an urban auto theft ring. Second, an interface with organized crime on a much larger scale is indicated. Third, an interface with a corruptible aspect of officialdom is shown. Finally, the police operation is well planned and efficiently executed; the groundwork for the raid is prepared by months of painstaking investigation. The account of the case is given here in the words of reporters Fred Carpenter and Edward Kulik:

The arrest yesterday of 21 alleged members of a nationwide multi-million-dollar auto theft ring may spark a full-scale probe of state Motor Vehicle Department operations, The Press learned today.

Two of those arrested in 25 predawn raids on Long Island and in Brooklyn were a Springfield couple employed at the department's Jamaica branch (the husband as a security officer and the wife as an inspector.

Police attributed more than 400 thefts of Cadillacs in the past year to the "steal-to-order" ring which maintained private and "master" garages in Queens and Brooklyn containing piles of license plates.

Police said the fatal shooting of Michael Marino, 29, of Rosedale, who was found with two bullets in his head last Feb. 23 in the Sheepshead Bay section of Brooklyn, was linked to the ring and indicated he was rubbed out because of a dispute over a profit split.

The brains behind the operation, police said, was 23-year-old John Carneglia of Brooklyn.

Detectives Donald Leadbetter and Edward Carol of the Queens Burglary Squad and Detectives Nicholas Panarella and Patrick Walsh of Brooklyn's 75th Precinct worked on the case for months before joining about 50 other police yesterday in simultaneous raids.

Police said the ring, operating in wholesale business fashion with mass-production techniques, employed order-takers, salesmen, inventory clerks and managers in addition to car thieves, and maintained a stock inventory. It also paid a $500 "tax" to a Manhattan Mafia representative for each stolen car sold.

Police gave the following account of the ring's operations:

When a customer asked for a certain type and color of car, usually a Cadillac, a clerk would check the inventory of stolen cars stored in private, rented garages on Long Island or in Manhattan.

If the particular type or model was not in the inventory, the clerk would check the "available" list. This list consisted of cars, not yet stolen but whose location and description had been noted by a "spotter" who was paid $25 for each auto he scouted. Often a car would be in the process of being sold even before it had been stolen.

Orders would go out to a "stealer," who received $175 for each auto he brought in. He would go to the location where the "spotter" had indicated the auto would be at a particular time, according to the owner's habits, and drive the car to one of the ring's garages, using master keys provided by the ring. The "stealer" was also permitted to keep anything of value in the car when he stole it.

To avoid a possible arrest from a random police roadcheck between the site of the theft and the gang's garage, a properly registered car was driven over the route minutes before the stolen car was taken.

Once in the garage, "number men" would change a digit in the metal strip bearing the auto's identification number. They even had a technique with the plastic strips used for identification numbers in some later models.

The car, worth perhaps $8,000 was sold for about $3,000. If the customer was from out of state, the vehicle would be turned over to a "transporter" for delivery.

The "transporter" would receive $300, even more than the "stealer," because he had to take the vehicle over state borders and this automatically constituted a federal offense.

The "transporter" would deliver the car, perhaps to Miami, Fla., using stolen gasoline credit cards, then fly home using stolen credit cards. In some cases he would return with the customer's old car, which the gang accepted for trade-ins at "book value."

The Motor Vehicle Department's MV-50 sales forms were usually obtained from burglaries of car dealers and the ring paid from $50 to $100 for each.

Presumably, the dealer would report the forms stolen and the department would alert all of its branches to be on the lookout for the code number, but if the ring had help from an MVD employee in the branch, it could bypass that problem.

Police said the raids began at 5 a.m. yesterday morning at the homes of the suspects and at three "master" garages.

Police said six cars were recovered and that several hundred wigs were found at the home of John Carneglia together with a large assortment of watches.

According to the police, the gang never mentioned automobiles in all their dealings but referred to them as "flowers" or simply "merchandise."

It will be noted that one of the more vulnerable areas in organized car theft is that of obtaining a suitable registration for the stolen vehicles. One of the methods used in this case involved stealing the registration of a similar car in another state—in Massachusetts, for example, where the state requires that the registration be kept in the vehicle. After the ringleader had "pre-sold" a luxury car to a buyer who had specified make, model, year, and color, another member of the ring would go to Boston and, sometimes in collusion with an airport parking lot attendant, steal the registration and vehicle identification from a matching car. Copying the buyer's signature, the leader would forge a bill of sale and use the registration certificate and tag to file a registration in New York State. Subsequently, a car matching the fraudulent registration would be spotted in New York and stolen. After the plates had been switched, the car would be delivered to the buyer.

The use of the computer in tracing the stolen cars presents one of the more interesting aspects of this case. The cars were traced by borrowing the computer tapes recording Massachusetts registrations and using them in the computer system that records the New York Registrations. The computer sifted out 5,500 duplicate Cadillac registrations, of which 312 were traced and 115 found to be legitimate, involving cars leased in Massachusetts and used in New York or cars leased in New York and used in Massachusetts. Eighty-four cars were recovered as stolen and 32 others, with fictitious addresses, were still being sought. Eighty-one were still being investigated.

  b. **Frauds.** A variety of frauds, many of them connected with insurance, are practiced by car thieves. It will be noted that a number of these schemes require for their success an elaborate organization, sometimes extending over several states. The following are representative of frauds that have come to the attention of law enforcement agencies:

  1) ***The Phantom Car Fraud.*** An insurance fraud ring based on "phantom cars" was uncovered recently by the Pennsylvania State Police. The ring, centered in Philadelphia, apparently operated with inside information from the General Motors Corporation and the State Motor Vehicle Bureau. The massive fraud involved inventing a registration number for a non-existent car, reporting the car stolen and collecting the insurance. The operation, which began in 1969, involved 450 phantom General Motor cars and millions of dollars in claims unwittingly paid by 13 insurance companies. As many as 250 persons using 1,200 false names were involved. The following is an example of how the fraud worked:

  A person using an alias registered five late-model Pontiacs over a period of two years, receiving properly stamped titles verifying ownership at a fictitious Philadelphia address. The person somehow received the titles by mail at the address, insured the cars, reported them stolen, and then collected thousands of dollars in insurance claims. In the State Motor Vehicle Bureau at Harrisburg, a computer checks the vehicle identification number on each auto title application to determine if such a number is already registered. If it is, the computer rejects the application. Hence the number is a key factor in making the fraud work. Every car has an identification number containing a coded description of the car and a six-digit identifying number. The persons engaged in the fraud were sufficiently familiar with the VIN system to know the coded prefix.

2) **Insuring a Wreck.** This is another form of the phantom car fraud. The perpetrator first buys a late model, completely wrecked car from a salvage yard. At the same time he will obtain a title and the vehicle identification number. With this identification he will register and insure the car without even taking possession of the vehicle. Several months later he will report his "car" as stolen. By that time what was once a car will have disappeared as scrap. Under state law, however, the insurance policyholder must receive the market replacement value of the car. Thus the policyholder makes a profit on the insurance and the salvage dealer receives payment for a car that did not exist.

3) **Duplicating from Salvage.** In this operation the thieves buy a wrecked car to obtain the identification papers that go with it. Subsequently they steal an identical car in good condition. The stolen car is then taken apart and the parts put back together again on the frame of the wrecked car. They have now duplicated the car for which they have legal papers and can sell it.

4) **Stripping the Car.** The perpetrator of this fraud strips his car to the frame, stores the parts, and dumps the skeleton in a lot. After reporting the car to the police as stolen, he subsequently informs them anonymously of the location of the frame. The insurance company pays for the loss of the car.

5) **The "Erector Set" Fraud.** As a continuation of the previous fraud, the owner will buy the frame from the insurance company for a few hundred dollars and take it to the garage for reassembly with the dismantled parts.

6) **Changing the VIN.** After the theft of a car, the VIN is abraded and a new number is impressed with a set of steel stamps. The numbers are changed also on other parts, such as air-conditioners, which manufacturers have lately been stamping with identification numbers. Ostensibly, the vehicle is now a new car. Papers are obtained for it, often from another state. After a series of resellings, the car comes back to the New York market with an apparently genuine pedigree.

13. Indications of a Stolen Automobile

The investigator sometimes encounters an automobile which is not listed in the alarms or notifications as stolen but which arouses his suspicions in connection with its ownership. Certain indications are helpful in confirming or dispelling these suspicions:

a. **Tags.** New tags found on a used automobile in the middle of the tag year are suspicious. The auto thief sometimes buys new tags for a stolen vehicle for the purpose of registering the car in the name under which it is to be sold. The tag bolts should be examined for rust and other signs of age. New bolts with an old tag suggest that the tag was stolen. In estimating the time when the bolts were placed on, it should be remembered that bolts will usually show signs of rust after a month's exposure.

b. **Registration.** Recent registration of a used car indicates the possibility of preparation for the sale of a stolen car, since lawful owners do not ordinarily re-register a car prior to selling.

c. **Bill of Sale.** A notarization on a bill of sale for a used car is suspicious since, in most cases of used cars, the bill of sale is not notarized.

d. **Keys.** Are the keys original factory keys or are they duplicates? A duplicate key will ordinarily be imprinted with some identifying data such as a small number or the name of the locksmith.

e. **Vent Glass.** In stealing a car the thief frequently forces open the vent window or breaks it. The vent area should be examined for tool marks and the vent glass should be studied to determine whether it is a replacement. Vent glass which is original equipment will ordinarily have a trademark in the lower corner. On the replacement glass the open edge will be found rough as compared with the corresponding surface of factory glass.

f. **Ignition.** Is there evidence of tampering with the ignition switch? Among the signs of such tampering are the following: Coil wire stripped of insulation near the points where it enters the coil; a new switch with wire taped in the area of previous stripping; and the presence of extraneous wires.

14. Prevention

It is difficult to defeat a determined professional car thief. If his heart is set on a particular car, the experienced thief will find some way of entering it or, as a last resort, he may tow the car away or remove it bodily into a van. The car owner can, however, improve his chances for continued possession by adopting sound security habits with respect to ignition keys, safeguarding of registration, and strategic parking. In addition, a growing industry of car-theft prevention has made available a wide range of devices for further security, e.g., burglar-alarm systems, some of which lock the hood and cut off the ignition; horn and light flashers; mercury switches; gas-line cutoffs; four-digit ignition switches; and locks that join the gas pedal and steering wheel. The list is endless; the devices actually delay or discourage the thief but in the end the owner is left with the sobering reflection that what man can devise the thief can bypass.

In the past decade auto manufacturers have assisted greatly in this problem by developing and installing devices that significantly increase the difficulty of car theft. These include less accessible ignition system locations, increasing the number of ignition key combinations, and making the ignition system connector cable more difficult to remove from the ignition lock. Recently the auto industry introduced a combination ignition, transmission, and steering column lock on all new cars. It far surpassed the security of the old locks which could be easily defeated by *hotwiring*, i.e., crossing ignition wires in back of the dash or under the hood.

15. Deterrents in Car Theft

Throughout this section the various deterrents against car theft have been mentioned—alarm systems, ingenious locking devices, legislation such as "certificate-of-title" laws, and improvement of drivers' car-security habits. All of these measures have their value since they contribute to the difficulties which the thief must surmount. After the car has been stolen, however, there are few restriction's on the thief's behavior, since there is no consciousness of being watched and little danger of detection and apprehension. Since the number of cars stolen is so great—100,000 annually in New York City alone—any scheme for surveillance would necessarily be computer based. It has been proposed that the state institute an automatic license plate scanning system (ALPS). Electronic cameras mounted as strategic points along the highway, such as toll booths, would scan all passing vehicles, record and recognize all numbers and letters on license plates. The data would be sent by leased phone lines to a computer containing a list of all wanted license plates. If a scanned plate checks with a number on the wanted list, this fact together with other relevant information on the crime involved would be sent back to the scanning station within two seconds. The local operator would then radio a patrol car parked downstream along the highway to intercept the vehicle bearing the wanted plates. To operate ten ALPS scanners in a large urban area for five years would cost about $11-million. Such a system would be expected to cut the cost of all damages from car theft by an impressive $100-million per year. Within a few years we should expect to see a nationwide link-up of computers maintaining up-to-the-minute lists of stolen cars, tied at strategic points to license-plate scanners. Mobility and speed of transportation, which characterize a good part of the modern criminal's activity, must be countered by law enforcement with an equally modern tool—the rapid transmission of information.

16. Bicycle Theft

a. **The Problem.** The nationwide rise in the popularity of bicycle riding has been accompanied by an equal rise in the incidence of bicycle stealing. The increase is attributed to two factors: 1) The sudden burst of popularity of bicycling in many parts of the country has produced both a market and a supply for the thieves.

2) The value of bicycles has increased greatly. The problem has changed from a situation of "a few kids stealing bikes" to one where organized groups sweep through the city, fill a truck with stolen bikes and take them to a factory where they are sandblasted to remove the paint and serial numbers and then repainted and sent out to be sold as new bikes. Some 10-speed models cost as much as $500 and can be sold by thieves for as much as $200.

b. **Prevention.** The need for special enforcement efforts has become apparent during the last few years. Pittsburgh, New Orleans, Chicago, and Dade County, for example, have instituted mandatory bicycle registration programs. There is, however, a growing demand in some states for a computerized master registration system for all bicycles sold in the state to permit a rapid check of the ownership of a questionable bicycle.

c. **Investigation.** The method of investigating bicycle thefts will vary with the nature of the case. A single, casual theft is best handled by the patrol force. Where it appears that a ring of bicycle thieves is involved, a full-scale investigation is required.

1) *Description.* The investigator should obtain the necessary information on the make, model, year of purchase, cost of the bicycle, and most important of all, the serial numbers. The color of the paint, the nature of the accessories, any marks of personal identification, defects, and marks of damage are additional data to be recorded.

2) *The Factory.* In the investigation of an organized group of bicycle thieves the investigator should endeavor to locate the factory where the processing takes place. Since this can become a fairly big operation—one group, operating in central California was processing 100 bicycles a week—floor space, equipment, and materials are required. Precinct business files should be examined and the assistance of members of the patrol force should be enlisted to determine the character of any suspected business operations which could lend themselves to this work. Automobile body shops are an example of a business which can be diverted to bicycle conversion work. Sources of materials such as quality enamel paints should be explored. Consultation with bicycle manufacturers may prove useful in ascertaining the nature of the equipment and the types of paint that would be used on the bicycles.

3) *Field Investigation.* The patrol force is best suited to the field investigation of smaller operations. Bicycle riders should be questioned concerning ownership. This procedure is, of course, much simpler in cities which require registration of bicycles or encourage property registration with the police. Places where bicycles are sold should receive police attention. Sometimes stolen bicycles show up in bicycle stores. More commonly they are sold to bargain hunters on the street, in parks, or in flea markets.

17. Pleasure Boat Theft

The theft of pleasure boats and marine equipment has shown a remarkable increase in recent years. In 1976 the insurance companies estimated their loss for that year at over $61 million—over 13 per cent of all claims. The American Institute of Marine Underwriters plans to establish a national theft bureau similar to the National Auto Theft Bureau, which is sponsored by the insurance industry. At present the Coast Guard is responding to the complaints of the boating public by expanding its duties to include the search and rescue of stolen boats. A file on stolen boats will be maintained by the Coast Guard to enable it to issue vessel lookouts and coordinate action with other law enforcement agencies.

Some of the problems in this operation are the ease with which hull identification numbers can be altered and the confusion created by boat registration methods that differ in states and are distinct from federal yacht documentation. The major difficulty, however, is the lack of any existing system of stolen boat information. The insurance industry plans to solve this problem by the creation of a computer tracking system similar to that being used for cars. The use of model and hull identification numbers will form the basis of this system. Transmission of information will probably be handled by marine radio telephones.

III. PICKPOCKETS

18. Pickpockets

The pickpocket is a species of criminal indigenous to large cities. An urban population with its many places of congregation and its crowded transportation systems provides unending opportunity for the pickpocket. This type of criminal is, however, restricted in number because of the great skill that is required for successful operation. Moreover, his skill in itself is a handicap because it endows him with a reputation and thereby makes him known to the police. In the criminal argot, he is known as a "cannon." There are numerous other slang terms employed in this branch of crime which will not be used here since, despite their picturesqueness, they belong to a dying dialect. In the age of the checkbook and the credit card the pickpocket is becoming less common. Few of the younger generation have either the patience or the professional pride to devote years to an apprenticeship in this demanding art.

a. **Operational Techniques.** The equipment and preparation of the pickpocket are of extreme simplicity. Given a crowd of moderate dimensions, he can ply his trade with his bare hands. He may work alone or with one or more confederates. The purpose served by the confederates is that of distracting the attention of the victim. The element of *modus operandi* is of great importance in detecting pickpockets. Most pickpockets employ the same technique throughout their criminal careers. In studying the methods described below, the investigator should make the assumption that the pickpocket is a person of great skill. Some of these techniques may be seen on the stage. The performer, while talking to his voluntary victim, can remove his suspenders, belt, or watch without the victim's knowledge. The techniques of the professional magician are employed by the pickpocket. Distraction of the victim's attention and swiftness of operation are the most important elements of the pickpocket's success. A pickpocket is known by his style. His designation is derived from the clothing area in which he operates.

1) *Fob Worker.* Although the pickpocket who takes money from the fob pocket is fast disappearing along with the type of garment from which his name was derived, he is worth discussing because his equivalent, the operator who works in the front of the victim, is still current. This operator is held in low esteem by his professional colleagues. His method consists in abstracting money from the most accessible place—the fob pocket. Usually he gathers only small change. The fob worker is usually also a tailpit worker, i.e., he steals from the side pocket of a man or woman's jacket. The fob worker is ordinarily an old man who, through hebetude or age, has lost his nerve or his touch. He employs a handkerchief or "wipe" to cover his operations. The "wipe" serves also to hide the coins. On observing an approaching detective, the fob worker will raise the handkerchief to his mouth and, if necessary, swallow the coins. Since many of these criminals have five or six felonies in their

records, they fear an additional conviction for grand larceny, which would, in some states, be constituted by the taking of so little as twenty-five cents from the person of another.

2) **Inside Worker.** This is a more advanced operator. Considerable skill is required to remove a wallet from the inside pocket of a man's coat. To cover his operations, an inside worker usually employs a "stiff," i.e., a newspaper which he places against the victim. Very few pickpockets resort to inside work.

3) **Pants Pocket Workers.** The pickpocket who operates in the trousers is considered the cleverest of this class of thief. A highly developed skill is necessary to abstract a wallet from a man's side pocket without his knowledge. The pants pocket worker uses only two fingers—the index and middle finger—to perform this operation. Sometimes this type of worker employs as many as two assistants. One of the assistants—the "stall"—distracts the victim by jostling him and excusing himself. A newspaper may be employed in these motions. The other assistant receives the wallet in a quick pass from the operator. The "mechanic" or "tool" performs the actual picking of the pocket. The whole operation is accomplished with the dispatch and precision of a football play. As the victim boards a subway train or other vehicle, the "stall" will fall or push against him from the front and mutter regrets or muffled curses. Simultaneously, the "mechanic" will have lifted the "poke" or wallet from the victim and passed it to his assistant. If the victim feels the operation and turns suspiciously, the pickpocket will run away. Since he no longer has possession of the "poke," his apprehension is of little avail for police purposes, for there can be no case unless the money is found in his possession. The person who receives the "poke" remains in the same position to avoid arousing suspicion. This person is usually a man without a previous conviction. Thus, he will at most receive a suspended sentence under the current court customs.

4) **The Lush Worker.** Probably the lowest form of pickpocket is the criminal who steals from a drunk or a sleeping passenger in a train. Lush workers operate in trains, buses, street cars, waiting rooms, and parks. They observe a prospective victim who is apparently sleeping or unconscious. Sometimes they test their victim by gently kicking his foot as they pass by. If the victim does

not react, the lush worker proceeds to take his money and other valuables.

5) *Bag Stealers.* A woman's handbag suspended from her arm is an inviting target for the petty thief. In crowded areas such as department stores or trains, the thief may remove the bag or its contents without attracting attention. There are several forms of this theft. The *bag opener* surreptitiously opens the bag suspended from the woman's arm and then removes the change purse or wallet. The *bag clipper* cuts the strap by which the bag is suspended, removes the wallet, and throws the bag away. The *bag snatcher* jerks the bag away from the woman's grasp.

b. **Apprehending the Pickpocket.** If the pickpocket is a professional, he will undoubtedly have a record. The crime can then be solved by means of the *modus operandi.* The techniques of pickpockets are well known. The detective can restrict the number of suspects by paying close attention to the victim's story. By consulting the known pickpocket file and showing photographs to the victim, he may be able to obtain a preliminary identification. The difficulties of finding a lush worker are much greater. Where the lush worker confines his activities to a certain neighborhood or a particular transportation line, the outlook is somewhat brighter. The great weakness of the lush worker is his tendency to take such valuables as fountain pens and watches. Strong proof of his guilt is provided if he is apprehended with these in his possession. The apprehension of pickpockets is considered specialized work in large cities. Some police departments have pickpocket squads or details consisting of a few detectives who are well acquainted with the appearance and habits of known pickpockets. These detectives are assigned to subways, railroad and bus terminals, and racetracks. In a city such as New York, the transit police are assigned to the task of apprehending lush workers.

IV. MISCELLANEOUS THIEVES

19. Miscellaneous Thieves

a. **Automobile Baggage Thieves.** This form of theft, though little publicized, accounts for larceny losses amounting to hundreds of thousands of dollars each year in a large city. The thieves usually operate in pairs and work in the hotel section of the city. Visitors to the city, frequenting the hotels, theaters, and restaurants in the area, often park their cars with clothing and suitcases in the rear seat part of the vehicle. One of the pair of thieves acts as a lookout and also serves as a shield. This part is sometimes played by a woman to lend a natural air to the proceedings. The other member opens the car or breaks into it by means of the ventilator. The clothing and baggage, usually valued at several hundred dollars, are removed and the thieves walk away with the loot. If the thieves wish to perform their work rapidly, they break the glass and push the handle down. To prevent any noise of the shattering, they may first fix a sheet of flypaper over the windows. The apprehension of this type of thief is best accomplished by means of a plainsclothesman plant. A casual patrol of an area may reveal suspicious activity on the part of two persons. Discreet surveillance from a distance will enable the plainclothesman to observe the actual theft. A panel truck equipped for viewing from within is useful.

b. **Package Thieves.** There are a number of forms of package thievery. All of them can be classed as minor operations. The success of these thieves depends upon the carelessness of the agent in guarding or delivering the property. Since the theft is a minor one, it does not warrant extensive investigation. It will suffice to periodically caution merchants and their associations of the prevalence of this form of crime and to instruct them in precautionary measures. The following are some of the techniques employed by the package thief:

1) *Fraudulent Receiving.* The thief acquires knowledge of the identity of the consigned. He places himself at the entrance of the consignee's residence or place of business. When the delivery boy approaches, he advances to meet him and chides him on his tardiness thereby convincing the delivery boy that he is the consignee. He takes the package, signs the receipt, and sends the boy on his way. Some thieves employ a confederate to learn the address of the consignee by striking up a conversation with the delivery boy. In a variation of this type of offense, the thief telephones an order to the company in the name of an old customer and waits outside of the address.

2) *Packages from Vehicles.* Deliverymen tend to be careless in the protection of their vehicle while they bring the package from the vehicle into the building occupied by the consignee. Often they leave the ignition key in the vehicle. A pair of thieves will study the habits of the driver along his route. Waiting until the driver enters a building, they hop into the vehicle and drive away. Another type of thief simply steals a package from the unattended vehicle. The thieves may drive up in their own vehicle and transfer the merchandise.

3) *Sidewalk Thieves.* Parcel post packages left on top of a full mailbox; packages left by express deliverers in front of the building; garments hanging on small trucks in front of factories; and similar unattended property may be observed in the business streets of a larger city. Opportunities such as these are quickly noted and exploited by the "small-time" package thief.

4) *Senders.* The delivery boy is accosted and requested to carry a message to a fictitious person while the thief guards his package. The boy is rewarded with fifty cents for his service. This type of thief is rapidly becoming extinct, partially because the old-fashioned delivery is also rapidly disappearing. Occasionally, this petty trick is perpetrated on a boy carrying a musical instrument.

c. **Dishonest Employees.** The systematic larceny of merchandise by collusion of dishonest employees can result in serious losses. Prevention of this type of theft is accomplished by careful background investigations of applicants prior to employment. Detection of the thieves usually is the result of intelligent surveillance. Undercover work or roping by an investigator posing as an employee will ordinarily yield results in the space of a few weeks. The following techniques may be used by the criminal:

1) *Checkers and Order Clerks.* By arranging for the shipment of merchandise in excess of the actual order these thieves can transfer a considerable amount of property before the loss is discovered.

2) *Drivers.* The truckman leaves the unattended vehicle in the street with the ignition key in the lock. His confederates steal the truck while he is making a telephone call or eating in a restaurant.

3) *Express Loaders.* Express companies frequently report losses of merchandise apparently delivered in a regular manner. In one form of this type of larceny the loader changes the address on the

carton and the driver delivers the package to the loader's confederate unwittingly. The investigation should center around the fact that a knowledge of the truck routes is necessary for the success of the operation. Spot checking the loaded merchandise may reveal the existence of an altered or obliterated address on a package.

4) *Waterfront Pilferage.* In the past the losses through thefts attributable to dock workers, longshoremen, and other waterfront workers have been estimated in the millions. The unloading of a ship involves the transfer of property of enormous value. A conspiracy to systematically divert such property into the hands of thieves can result in overwhelming losses. This form of larceny can be so great in magnitude and so intricate in the details of its accomplishment that the subject cannot be treated in this limited space. Waterfront pilferage, moreover, is usually a racket centrally managed by criminals who also directly control the hiring of waterfront personnel. The investigation of this offense must be undertaken by a fairly large squad of detectives. In the New York area a Waterfront Commission was established for this purpose. Surveillance and undercover work are required. It is not sufficient to apprehend one or two workers in the act of diverting merchandise. The investigation should lead to the discovery of the drops, fences, and bosses. In recent years investigators in this area have been increasingly successful. Pilferage, as reported by terminal operators, totaled less than $500,000 in 1977. It was nearly ten times as high as recently as 1970. A guaranteed annual income, born of automated shiploading and containerization, assures all 14,000 registered longshoremen in the New York area a living wage and considerably reduces the temptation to larceny. Seniority has replaced favoritism, and the risk of losing licenses has discouraged loansharking and other swindles. On the docks themselves, the efforts of the Waterfront Commission and the rapid displacement of bulk cargo by prepacked containers, too big for easy stealing, have combined to wipe out many of the old rackets.

d) **Sneak Thieves.** The term *sneak theft* is used to include a number of forms of petty larceny involving unattended property.

1) *Baggage Thieves.* Travelers in railroad and bus terminals frequently have occasion to place their baggage down while they

attend to some business such as purchasing a ticket. The baggage
thief takes advantage of the unguarded moment, swiftly picks up the
bags and walks calmly away. The detection or apprehension of this
type of thief is ordinarily the responsibility of the railroad police.

2) **Shoplifters.** Department stores annually suffer considerable
losses from the operation of store thieves. Female shoplifters are in
the majority since their presence in a store is more likely to pass
unnoticed. The techniques employed by shoplifters are many and
varied. The department stores usually have their own methods and
even their own detective personnel for dealing with this problem.
Larger department stores have a definite policy in dealing with the
apprehended store thief. The possibility of a suit for false arrest is
often present and, therefore, special measures are taken to obviate
such a danger. The kleptomaniac, or person who suffers from a
psychological disturbance impelling him to steal, sometimes finds a
convenient area of activity in shoplifting. The shoplifter working in
collusion with a dishonest employee presents another obstacle to
retail security. The emergence of well-organized rings composed of
trained full-time shoplifters has added an element of dedicated
professionalism to this offense. The major problems with respect to
shoplifting, however, are its rapidly increasing incidence and the
fact that the majority of offenders are teenagers.

a) STATISTICS. There are no accurate figures for the incidents of
shoplifting in the United States. However, one can safely say that
the loss to American merchants from this offense amounts to several
billion dollars a year. Costs include not only the loss of merchandise
but also the expense of hiring full-time security personnel. Most
experts agree that more than half of these thieves are teenagers—
the great majority of them white and from middle-class suburban
families.

b) PREVENTIVE MEASURES. The full technology of visual surveillance
is brought to bear on the shoplifter: telescopes, binoculars,
television cameras, two-way mirrors in fitting rooms, convex
mirrors to widen the field of vision—in brief, the paraphernalia of
the spy and *voyeur*. Indeed, practically every means of preventing
shoplifting is used except the obvious one, namely removing the
portable and concealable goods from the reach of the thief. In the
words of Bill Davidson (*Saturday Evening Post*, May 18, 1968):

In most stores, there has been a long-standing conflict between security people and merchandising people. The security specialists would like to see everything chained down or behind glass; the merchandising experts insist that customers won't buy anything unless they can handle it freely. The merchandising people usually win.

c) THE PROBLEM. The police cannot be expected to become greatly exercised over the loss of property which the merchant prefers to leave unprotected. From the merchant's point of view the loss is not necessarily real, since it is calculated to be offset by the profit increment flowing from point-of-sale advertising and display. However, against this dubious advantage of a marginal increase in business, we may set the very real and often tragic effect on thousands of young people of an arrest for larceny, with its consequent social obloquy and the liability of a police record. The existence of a police record may seriously affect the direction of these young lives: it may prevent the juvenile from entering a college; it may debar him from desirable areas of employment; it may prevent his entering a profession, such as that of lawyer; or it may prohibit his engaging in a business, such as real-estate brokerage, for which a special license is required. The penalties can be many and harsh; certainly they are a high price to pay for a five-dollar theft, particularly by a juvenile who may have been taught little about the moral meaning of theft and even less of the sanctions that can be routinely imposed by society. In the face of these consequences, the merchant's permissiveness in the display of his goods would seem to warrant serious examination from the point of view of culpability. The merchant's contribution to the offense may lie this side of entrapment, but in the spectrum of culpability it does not place him in the region of clear innocence. Permissiveness for profit, with its calculated inducement to possess, carries an unconscious but implicit invitation to the weak willed to practice petty larceny.

e. **Pennyweighting.** One or two thieves engage a jeweler in a discussion of a prospective sale. The jeweler's goods are displayed. In the course of the discussion, the attention of the jeweler is drawn away from the goods, and false, imitation jewelry is substituted for it. The operation must be "cased" and planned so that a reasonably similar substitute can be acquired.

f. **Hotel Thieves.** This type of thief steals jewelry, furs, or money from hotel rooms. He sometimes works in collusion with bellboys or hotel clerks who advise him concerning the guests' property and habits. Entrance to the room may be achieved without the cooperation of the hotel employees in the following ways: stealing the key from the desk; obtaining a duplicate key by previous rental of the room; skeleton keys; picking the lock; forcing the lock with a piece of celluloid or similar material. Hotel thievery in past few years has grown to great proportions. The owners of hotels are often reluctant to install effective locks or lock systems. Recently, however, a number of hotels in New York, where the problem is most severe, have begun to take advantage of modern technology to protect their residents. At a cost of more than $1 million the Americana installed a computerized system designed to protect guests against burglars. After the guest unlocks his door with his regular key, he has about thirty seconds to insert a special card into a box on his television set; otherwise a light flashes on a console summoning a security man. The Algonquin Hotel spent about $200 a room to replace its keys with a computerized system that uses individually programmed cards to unlock doors. When a guest checks out, the electronic combination is changed. Other hotels are expected to follow the Algonquin lead.

g. **Credit Card Thieves.** For a number of years the fraudulent use of stolen or lost credit cards was a source of worry to credit men and financial officers throughout the nation. The thief, after acquiring the credit card by taking one from an unguarded counter or by stealing a wallet or pocketbook, would apply it to making a great number of small purchases from stores or in a series of larger purchases at widely separated places. Unless checked in time, the thief could acquire a sizeable amount of goods, services, and money.

Remedial measures have been devised to discourage the use of stolen or lost credit cards by rapidly transmitting the appropriate information to those authorized to grant credit. Countertop data processing units have been introduced into the retailing industry and in service stations and airline reservation desks to link up with computers storing the required information. A clerk can now punch the numbers of a credit card into the unit and receive a rapid response regarding the current status of an account, charge plate, or credit card.

The larceny involved in credit-card loss does not represent a serious law enforcement problem, since the corrective measures of stricter controls of distribution and use lie well within the resources and administrative capabilities of the businesses concerned. Clearly the profits resulting from this freedom of distribution of credit cards and permissiveness in their use more than compensate for any losses, and the expense of introducing stricter controls would not be offset by the amounts of the larcenies prevented. Moreover, as the credit-card system becomes permanently embedded among our purchasing habits, businesses will not be reluctant to consider losses incident to their misuse a part of their overhead, warranting an appropriate adjustment of prices. There are, however, those who would look upon this degree of permissiveness and resilience in business policy as an implicit subsidy of larcenous conduct.

V. CONFIDENCE GAMES

20. Confidence Games—Swindles

The obvious reader interest in the subject of "con" men or swindlers is an open invitation to an author to dwell extensively on this aspect of criminal activity. It is difficult to touch even lightly on this topic without allotting to it a space in the crime world far out of proportion to the small number of people who practice professionally the art of swindling. We must, of course, omit from our discussion a number of aspects of this crime, since swindling is defined in general as the art of obtaining money or property from another by fraud or deceit. Such a definition would readily lead us into embezzlement, stock manipulation, and other high level commercial operations that depend for their effectiveness on a background of a stable and substantial business structure. Our concern is chiefly with confidence games, and this type of fraud is a short-term operation that is equivalent to a one-night stand in business.

The distinguishing characteristic of most confidence games is the fact that the victim is knowingly engaging in a dishonest act. It is in the very act of perpetrating a larger fraud upon another that the victim is himself defrauded.

a. **The Spanish Prisoner.** The Spanish (or Mexican) prisoner is a mail fraud which depends for its success on the victim's romantic view of life in the Latin countries. The victim receives a letter requesting money to obtain the freedom of the sender, who claims to be falsely imprisoned. In return, the sender promises on his release to share a hidden treasure with the victim. After sending the money the victim hears no more from the prisoner.

b. **The Sir Francis Drake Swindle.** The victim receives a letter or a visitor informing him of the pleasant discovery that he is one of the descendants of Sir Francis Drake and as such is entitled to a share in the fortune left by that famous adventurer. Since the estate is not completely settled, a certain sum will be required for litigation. The victim agrees to put up the money. A few months later, he is informed that the court proceedings will be more protracted than first estimated. An additional sum is requested. The mulcting continues until the victim is exhausted in either finances or credulity. In the 1910s this swindle was practiced throughout the midwest with extraordinary success. In common faith, the victims banded together to form a Sir Francis Drake Club to advance their interests in the estate and even to support the defense of the swindler against the government's prosecution. Needless to say the swindle is still practiced today with success.

c. **The Money-Making Machine.** The victim is shown a machine which will literally make money for him. The con man demonstrates its efficiency by showing the production of several bills. The machine is then sold to the victim at an appropriate price. The money-making machine may appear in different forms, either as small as a cigar box or as large as a peanut roaster. As recently as 1966, money-making machines were being sold in this country.

d. **Stock Swindles.** The sale of worthless stocks in Canada oil wells, for example, is still a staple of the swindler. According to the Better Business Bureau, approximately one million dollars is lost each week through frauds of this kind.

e. **Wallet Dropper (Dropping the Leather).** This is another "short con" played by two men, A and B. The victim, V, is walking peacefully along the street when A walks past him rapidly and drops a wallet. Before V can reach down to pick it up, B comes from behind and seizes it. Since the wallet contains no means of identification, B pretends to recognize V's claim to a share and agrees to divide the contents. A is now well out of calling distance. The wallet contains a few small bills and a counterfeit one-hundred dollar bill. If V can change the bill, B will walk away with the fifty dollars leaving the wallet to V. When V cannot produce the change, B consents to settle for security in the form of money or jewelry. He leaves the wallet in V's possession and agrees to meet him tomorrow to arrange a proper division.

f. **The Smack Game.** This is a small con game which is worked by two men, the roper and the insideman. The roper develops a chance acquaintance with the victim at a railroad station or a bar. The insideman accidentally encounters the two men and joins their company on some pretext. The roper suggests that they match coins for drinks or for cigars. Money bets are finally suggested. The game is played by tossing coins in the air. The odd coin is the winner. While the insideman is absent for a few moments, the roper, feigning a dislike for the insideman, suggests to the victim that they arrange to fleece the third player. The scheme is described in which the roper will always call opposite to the victim. Thus, if the victim calls "heads" the roper will call "tails." In this way they continue to always have one or the other winning the play. They agree to divide the spoils later. The scheme, of course, is highly successful. The bets mount until a substantial sum has changed hands. The insideman manages to lose all the large bets to the roper, who thus acquires a considerable amount of the victim's money. When the insideman finally concedes defeat, the roper and the victim walk off together. At this the insideman expresses vehemently the suspicion that he has been fleeced by professional sharpers. He threatens to call the police unless they show evidence of the absence of conspiracy by departing in different directions. The roper suggests to the victim that he will meet him later at a designated point to divide the money. Naturally, there is no later meeting and the victim is left to meditate upon his experience.

VI. EMBEZZLEMENT

21. Embezzlement

A study of the penal law of a state will reveal the fact that the crimes of larceny and fraud occupy many more pages than the serious offenses of murder and robbery. The obvious reason for this is the ingenuity of the criminal in devising new schemes of illegally obtaining money. In the present treatment these forms of theft, frauds, and cheats have been placed under the general heading of "larceny," since they are all methods of depriving an owner of his property against his will. The difference between the various forms of larceny lies ordinarily in the title or type of ownership or custody which the criminal enjoys at the time of the offense. Since only the most important of these "white-collar crimes" can be touched upon in this text, an effort is made to stress the general principles which govern investigations of this type so that the reader can extend the application of appropriate techniques to other forms of larceny. Certainly one of the most lucrative and popular of the "white-collar crimes" is embezzlement, the fradulent appropriation of money or goods by a person to whom they are intrusted. It is an obvious crime in the sense that it is committed by a person confronted with a combination of opportunity and temptation. The motivation is simple—profit. Beyond the immediate prompting of a desire for profit are the proximate motives of financial straits and a desire for power. It is the crime of the unfaithful steward, a larceny possible only in an office of trust.

a. **Statistics.** Since the offense of embezzlement involves no violence, does not affect the person of another, and is committed at the expense of a fairly wealthy organization, no great odium attaches to the criminal. The embezzler is simply dishonest in the least disreputable sense of the word. The terms "clever" and "master mind" are applied to his "defalcations" by newspaper reports. The embezzler's deeds are sometimes recounted with ill-concealed admiration as though he were a Robin Hood of the land of file cabinets and computing machines. It is little known that several thousand embezzlers are arrested each year and that the loss from this crime amounts to millions of dollars annually. To a considerable degree the financial damage is absorbed by surety companies and is reflected in the adjustments of fidelity bond insurance. In 1975, an estimated 189 million dollars was lost by banks alone through embezzlement, more than five times the amount lost through bank robbery during that same period. The tolerance of society toward the embezzler is reflected in the comparison of sentencing patterns for both crimes—91 percent of those convicted of bank robbery serve time in jail, compared with only 17 percent of those convicted of embezzlement of bank funds.

b. *Modus Operandi.* The methods employed by the embezzler depend upon the nature of the transactions over which he has control in the performance of his duties. In the banking business the employee may have control of the recording of accounts and may manipulate several accounts so that the loss cannot be detected except by a complete audit. The criminal has a thorough understanding of the financial operations of the organization. In some instances, where the criminal is the firm's accountant or bookkeeper, he may be the only person in the organization with a comprehensive knowledge of the working of the company's finances. His criminal operations may take place over a period of months or years. In a recent case a bank cashier was found to have been embezzling over a period of eighteen years.

c. **Investigation.** An inquiry into a charge of embezzlement often requires the services of an accountant. The investigator who does not possess such a knowledge should avail himself of the services of an experienced accountant who is not an employee of the company. Before proceeding with the case it is well for the investigator to ascertain the company's policy in these matters. Many companies do not choose to prefer charges against the dishonest employee. Their policy is to avoid unfavorable publicity by simply discharging the guilty person. If it is the intention of the company to press charges, the investigator should carefully note the documentary evidence which will be needed to substantiate the charges. Photographs of the documents can be made as the case progresses. These photographs will aid in the preparation of the case until the records are formally offered in evidence.

d. **Discovery of the Loss.** The first notice of the defalcation may be in one of many ways:

1) *Disappearance.* The embezzler may suddenly flee his surroundings. He will leave town and take up residence in another city. The disappearance of an employee entrusted with large sums of money gives rise to natural suspicions. In a recent New York case a bank official left the city with over $400,000. The discovery of the loss was made after his departure. After spending a few days in Florida he voluntarily surrendered.

2) *Inspection.* The annual audit of the company's records may reveal the loss. In some cases the embezzler devises covering methods which will withstand the scrutiny of the auditors.

3) *Information.* If the criminal is not clever and particularly if he is quite young, a sudden display of prosperity will arouse the suspicions of neighbors or friends. Jealousy may motivate them to notify the company or bank of their suspicions. Rival employees, an abandoned wife, a trusted consort, or disgruntled accomplices are other likely sources of information.

4) *Accident.* Some unusual circumstance of business operations may require a review of certain accounts. In such a situation another employee may stumble over the irregularity.

e. **Establishing the Loss.** Before taking any serious action with respect to any suspect, the investigator should first satisfy himself that a crime has in fact been committed. To this end he should have an accountant examine the "books" and make a record of the financial irregularities.

f. **Suspects.** The number of suspects is usually quite small. The guilty person must first have access to the funds and the accounts. Often there is only one logical suspect. In more complicated cases the investigator may have to conduct background investigations. The following points should be noted.

1) *Office Behavior.* Was there anything unusual in the behavior of the suspect during office hours? Did he appear nervous or worried? Did he take his annual vacation at the regular time? In some forms of embezzlement the criminal may not risk a day's absence for fear of detection.

2) *Living Habits.* Does the suspect live within his means? Who are his associates? Does he drink? Frequent night clubs? Are his social aspirations inconsistent with his income? A discreet neighborhood check will reveal this information.

3) *Financial Status and Credit.* Is the suspect solvent? What is the extent of his debts? What is the state of his bank account? Does he keep a number of accounts? Do these accounts show great activity even though the total value is not large. Does he have accounts in other states? Does he have a safe deposit box? Credit investigating agencies can assist in this phase of the investigation.

g. **Checklist.** The following points should receive special attention.

1) The relation of trust and confidence should be proved.

2) It must be shown that property was entrusted to the accused as agent, bailee, or trustee to keep for the owner or to treat in accordance with the owner's instructions.

3) The property was received by the accused.

4) The property is accurately described.

5) A fraudulent intent was formed.

6) The property was appropriated by the accused for some use other than that intended by the owner. The fraudulent intent and appropriation are often established by one or more of the following facts:

7) The disposition made of the property or money such as deposits in a bank.

8) Failure to perform the assigned duty relating to the property.

9) Failing to return the property after a demand for the return was made subsequent to the dereliction of duty.

10) Denial of having received the property.

11) False entries in documents or ledgers recording the transaction.

h. **Computer Abuse.**

1) *Introduction.* There is a noticeable lag between the advance of technology and the development of new methods of detection of crimes resulting from the application of that technology. Obviously, the computer is suited to the purposes of the embezzler. Indeed, the computer can take on the aspect of a silent partner of the embezzler while the employers look upon it as a witness to their employees' integrity. The following article (*Saturday Review*, July 13, 1968) illustrates this trend:

> An even more disquieting aspect of the dependence on computers is that these machines are printing less and less information onto sheets that can be

audited by humans. In fact, computers are often sold as being so 'honest' that they eliminate the expense of auditors. While computers *are* as honest as cash registers, they do what skilled programmers tell them to do and, unfortunately, are controlled by individuals such as the quiet man formerly in charge of computer cards at a brokerage firm in New York. He went to the office on weekends and programmed the computers to gradually transfer $250,000 from the corporation's account to accounts for him and his wife by showing that it had been used to purchase stock. Not only did the scheme go undetected for eight years, but the company's management was so impressed with the computer programmer that they promoted him to vice president before accidentally discovering the mythical account. Yet, after the programmer confessed, nobody could determine how he manipulated the computer to steal the $250,000. He had to tell the auditors.

Stock firms, banks, and wholesalers are repeatedly embezzled by two methods that computer operators find ridiculously simple: (1) have computers deduct a few, seemingly inconsequential cents in excess service charges, dividends, interest, or income taxes from thousands of customers' accounts and channel the total to themselves; (2) manipulate computers to systematically report portions of an inventory as normal "breakage" or "loss" and then divert the merchandise to accomplices. In both schemes, the embezzlers eventually remove the rigged cards, insert the genuine tape onto the computer, and conceal who did it and how (and sometimes if) the embezzlement transpired.

An example of the susceptibility of the computer was displayed in a case involving an extensive embezzling operation uncovered in Westinghouse Corporation's appliance-sales division in Greenvale, New York. Billy Howard Hudgins, an operations manager, had manipulated a computer system, which he had set up, so as to embezzle nearly $1-million. He had issued forged corporation drafts to be cashed by co-conspirators, who would subsequently return the bulk of the proceeds to him. The co-conspirators were charged with falsely representing that they were legitimate creditors and payees of Westinghouse and sharing in the illegal booty. Hudgins was able to avoid detection by destroying the canceled checks before the auditors became aware of them. The auditors began to suspect the system when they did not recognize the name of a creditor on a $1,000 company draft that had cleared while Hudgins was on vacation. Hudgins had violated a number of the rules for successful embezzling: First, he had taken a vacation; second, he had changed his life-style, lavishing expensive gifts on a number of friends; and third, he had permitted too many co-conspirators. In a conspiracy, the probability of detection increases exponentially as the number of co-conspirators grows greater.

Experts in data processing security maintain that crimes such as these could have been prevented by the use of standard auditing practices that would have been routinely applied if the business system involved anything but the "mysterious" computer. Too many businessmen seem to consider the computer as something special and beyond ordinary understanding. The computer is a piece of hardware technology that is amenable to countervention and will yield to attack just as a window lock will yield to a jimmy. The computer is no more to be blamed for these thefts than forgeries are to be blamed on pens.

2) *Definition.* Computer fraud is simply larceny by embezzlement, using the advanced technology provided by computers. Its success depends frequently on the absence of any regular checking or auditing system, a condition arising from the natural reluctance of superiors to master the procedures of computer operation.

3) *Losses.* The annual loss attributable to computer fraud in the United States is estimated to be about $300 million. By the very nature of the offense the correct amount must remain a dark figure.

4) *Extent of Use.* Approximately 150 thousand computers are currently used in the United States to facilitate such tasks as banking; credit transactions, including those involving credit cards; maintaining records of corporate sales; inventories and payrolls; trading securities; and maintaining Social Security, health, welfare, and tax records. The 150 thousand computers in current use do not constitute an accurate measure of the true extent of computer operations. One large computer, for example, may serve several thousand persons or corporations who, on a time-sharing basis, feed their particular programming data into it by telephone connection from remote keyboard terminals or other devices and receive, through telephone lines, printouts and other records of processed information. Thus, the number of Americans now directly involved in computer operations is estimated at more than two million.

5) *Protective Measures.* Steps to insure the integrity of computers include installing them in protected areas and permitting only limited physical access. Further protection will rely on the

rapidly expanding capability of auditing the financial activities of electronic data processing systems. The long-term solution, however, must rely on the development of computers with security principles as part of their fundamental design specifications. The secure computer system would allow operators to perform only specific tasks directed and monitored by the computer itself. Little or no maintenance would be required over the life of the system. Required maintenance would take place only in the presence of company executives and government inspectors, and the computer system would be thoroughly audited before being placed in operation. Under these conditions the incidence of computer abuse should diminish.

VII. THE CRIMINAL RECEIVER

22. Receiving Stolen Property

The thief's problem of converting the stolen goods into cash is solved by finding a suitable fence, i.e., a receiver of stolen property. The choice of a fence will depend on a number of factors, chiefly the character of the stolen goods and the underworld connections of the thief. In 1970 the New York City police arrested over 12,000 persons on charges of criminal possession of stolen property (as compared with only 1,800 arrested in 1966). The increase stems partly from the general growth in criminal activity and partly from the increased efforts of the police, particularly against hijackers. Moreover, the upsurge of crime by addicts in recent years and other shifts in crime patterns have wrought changes in the multi-million dollar fencing trade. Some addicts have taken to selling stolen property such as jewelry on the streets. The purchase and sale of goods stolen from airports has become in itself a business of some magnitude. Robert Cudak, of New York testifying in a Senate hearing in 1971, stated that fences had paid him $1 million in a four-year period of 200 thefts at John F. Kennedy and other airports—thefts largely of furs and jewelry.

A larceny investigation will often branch out into a case of receiving stolen property. On locating stolen property the investigator should exercise great care in conducting the search and exhaustively interviewing the criminal receiver, the thieves, and other persons. The elements of receiving stolen property are described below together with the usual methods of proof. It should be noted that this crime is difficult to prove and consequently all the suggested avenues of approach should be explored. The evidence in cases of this nature is largely circumstantial. The accused usually hides behind a legitimate business front and the testimony of the thieves is looked upon with skepticism by the jury. The activities of the receiver should be investigated in minute detail. His responses under extensive questioning should be checked carefully for discrepancies as to detail.

a. **The property was stolen.** The testimony of the thieves will prove this element. Since the thieves are not considered accomplices to this offense, they may be induced to give a statement as to the stolen character of the property.

b. **The property was received by the accused.** Again, the thieves can offer testimony to this fact. Proof is also offered by the fact that the property was found in the possession of the accused. If the room wherein the property is found is occupied only by the criminal receiver, no difficulty exists. If there is more than one occupant, each must be interviewed to eliminate all but the guilty. The investigator should endeavor to develop additional evidence such as the fact that the stolen goods were located in immediate association with other property of the accused or the accused was observed in physical possession of the property.

c. **The receiver knew that the property was stolen.** Testimony that the thieves informed the receiver of the theft would prove this fact indirectly. Other evidence includes the absurdly low purchase price; the fact that the person from whom it was received could not have been the legitimate owner; and the fact that it was not bought from a responsible person or from an established business concern.

d. **The accused had the intent to convert the property to his own use.** Evidence should be obtained of any effort to dispose of the property. During the search particular attention should be given to any arrangements for concealment of the stolen goods.

23. "Operation Sting"

A new approach to the apprehension of burglars and their associates was initiated with the establishment of "Operation Sting," a method whereby the police, posing as fences, would buy the stolen property from the burglars. In conjunction with and financed in part by the Justice Department's Law Enforcement Assistance Administration, forty-seven such operations were set up in thirty-five cities during the last three years.

Typically the strategy called for undercover detectives to rent stores and warehouses in neighborhoods where burglaries and street thefts were common and pass themselves off as prospective buyers of stolen goods. The building would be refitted to meet the requirements for surveillance, communications, and safety. An appropriate "front" would be devised in the form of a small cleaning business or trucking operation. About six officers were required to man the operation. One officer dealt with the sellers of stolen property. Another, hidden from view, operated surveillance equipment. Other surveillance officers were stationed in a building across the street from the store to record license plates, make other observations, and provide additional protection.

The site of the fencing operation was selected with a view to accessible parking and inconvenience with respect to public transportation to induce the sellers to use their cars. Transactions were videotaped and clean-surfaced objects were available for accidental fingerprints from handling. Negotiations were managed so that the seller would find it convenient to leave the phone number of a location where he could be reached. In the course of casual conversation the client would sometimes be led to reveal the identity of other fences or the general nature and approximate date of the burglary offense.

The effectiveness of "Operation Sting" is difficult to evaluate. As a strictly business enterprise the venture in New York City ("Operation Fence") cost about $800,000 in police salaries (at eight sites) and another $345,000 for equipment and "buy money." It is estimated, however, that a "gross" of $8.3 million in recovered property was achieved, ranging from stolen government checks (purchased for 10 cents on the dollar) to brand new automobiles

($250 apiece). Also recovered were two original bronze statues by Frederic Remington, valued at $100,000.

Some of the police aspects of the operation were favorable. About 480 persons were arrested for illegal possession of stolen goods, including a man reputed to be the biggest underworld fence in Queens. Most of them pleaded guilty on being shown the videotapes of their selling stolen goods to the undercover officers. The arrests were made after the operation had been closed down.

VIII. LOAN SHARKING

24. Introduction

Loan sharking is the lending of money at exorbitant rates of interest. A fuller definition would include the threat of violence that is later brought to bear on the debtor in the event he defaults. The victim, of course, is a person in serious financial straits. The loan shark himself is usually an underworld character. The importance of loan sharking lies in the fact that it is considered one of the largest sources of revenue in organized crime. (Gambling is the largest.)

Although loan sharking is ordinarily a violation of the laws relating to usury and extortion, it is placed in this chapter partly for convenience, partly because a loss of money is involved, and partly because of its kinship with confidence games in that the victim of the offense is also a victim of his own self-deception in money matters. The typical victim, short of credit and collateral and attempting to discharge a heavy, short-term money obligation, undertakes another and more formidable financial burden.

25. The Offenders

As a highly lucrative branch of organized crime, loan sharking is controlled by well-organized units, each divided into about four levels of operating personnel and headed by a chief or boss.

a. **The Boss Loan Shark.** At the top of a unit is the "boss loan shark," a high-ranking man in a well-organized crime group.

Although he may also be the head of a legitimate business (such as the underworld-owned First National Service and Discount Corporation in New York) as an avocation, his loan sharking operation is conducted without any established headquarters and without the bookmaker's corps of runners or banks of telephones. Since he seldom carries less than $5,000 on his person, he is not susceptible to a vagrancy charge. An Assistant District Attorney of New York has testified: "We have known a loan shark who lent a million dollars in the morning and another million in the afternoon." One boss loan shark is known to have turned a half-million dollars into 7.5 million dollars in about five years. In Manhattan alone there are at least ten men comparable to him.

b. **Organization.** There are about four levels of operation in the organization of a big loan shark.

1) *At the top level* is the boss loan shark himself, providing the financing and the overall supervision. For example, at the beginning of the year he will distribute a million dollars among his ten lieutenants with the simple instruction: "I don't care what *you* get for it, but *I* want one per cent per week."

2) *Second Level.* Each of the ten lieutenants must now farm out $100,000 among his subordinates with similar instructions, requiring however, 1.5 to 2 per cent interest per week.

3) *Third Level.* Each of the lieutenants may have about thirty subordinates who may themselves do the lending, if the loan is large enough, or may farm out the money in turn to their own subordinates for lending. Again the interest requirement will be raised.

4) *Fourth Level.* Most of the actual operations are conducted at this level, which may consist of working bookmakers and streetcorner hoodlums. The interest rate at this level is usually 5 per cent of the principal per week and may be higher. This interest is known in the business as "vigorish."

c. **Operation.** The basic operation of loan sharking has already been outlined: a pyramid of distributors or lenders, at each (descending) level of which a higher interest rate is used so that ultimately the customer is being charged 260 cents per dollar per year, and ultimately, at the top, the million dollars outlay by the boss loan shark should show a half-million dollars in profit at the end of the year. The two objectives of the operation are the acquisition of money and the acquiring of legitimate businesses. The means by which they are achieved may be summed up by the word "enforcement," a term covering the truly criminal aspect of loan sharking, namely, extortion.

26. "Enforcement"

Since a successful business must be based on a sound policy, calculated to yield predictable results, loan sharking has developed a reliable procedure for dealing with the critical matter of default.

a. **"Lender Makes the Rules."** The arbitrary manner in which the loan shark determines the rules is illustrated by a case which began with a $6,000 loan to a businessman. The borrower made three payments and then missed two. As a penalty, the loan shark declared that the debt was now $12,000, with the 5 per cent interest per week now on this larger sum. Again, the businessman failed to pay and the declared principal was increased to $17,000. Finally, the debt had grown to $25,000 and the debtor was called to account. The loan shark declared himself a half-partner in the victim's business. Now he was to collect half of the business profits *and* the weekly payments on the old loan. Eventually the situation became hopeless and the loan shark issued his final declaration: "You forget about the business and we'll forget about the loan. It is now all mine."

b. **"The Sit Down."** When it appears that the victim is in serious trouble and can no longer meet the payments, a "sit down" is called. This is a meeting presided over by a recognized underworld chief and called to decide what lump sum the loan and the accumulated vigorish can be settled for. It is a court from which there is no appeal. As an example, we may consider the case of an optical company whose chief executive received a loan of $22,000 with interest payable at $1,100 per week. Later another $6,500 was lent, and the total interest payments became $1,425 per week, without diminishing the amount owed. Soon the executive was convinced that he couldn't maintain the payments. Although he had already paid $25,000 in interest, he still owed the entire principal of the loan, $28,500 and was still faced with the prospect of continuing the interest payment of $1,425 per week. A "sit down" was called, with Chief Frank Eboli presiding. It was ruled that Don Ferraro should take over the optical company and operate its plant. In a few months the company had been looted of its assets and driven into bankruptcy.

   c. **Sanctions.** Failure to meet payments is met with grave disapproval and followed usually by the imposition of severe sanctions. Depending on the nature of the case and especially on the victim's assets, a decision is made,—unilaterally, as we have seen—and a penalty imposed which may take the form of assault, murder, or expropriation of the customer's property.

   1) *Assault and Murder.* Depending on the amount of his indebtedness, the defaulter may be punished by a beating or by killing. The underworld-owned First National Service and Discount Corporation employed two "enforcers" for this purpose, Anthony Scala, "The Leg Breaker," and Anthony (Junior) Franco. A victim who had borrowed $11,600 unable to meet his payments for a number of weeks found that he now owed $16,898, with diminishing prospects of meeting future payments. He was subsequently found murdered.

   2) *Appropriation of Property.* If the victim still possesses business assets, the presiding chief at the "sit down" frequently rules that the loan shark should take over the property in discharge of the indebtedness. In this way the loan shark can become an invisible partner, if not the outright owner, of a legitimate business. Using this procedure, members of the underworld have acquired a controlling interest in nightclubs, optical stores, brick companies, and even Wall Street brokerage houses and banks.

   3) *Exploitation of Services.* It may be decided that the services of the victim can be made to compensate for his debt. Thus, in the case of a well-known sports announcer who could no longer meet his payments it was decided that, because of his reputation and wide range of acquaintances, he would prove valuable as a "steerer." When the sports announcer would come in contact with persons in financial difficulty, he would recommend the services of a friend who liked to lend money. The friend, of course, would be the loan shark.

27. The Victim

An interesting aspect of loan sharking is the character of the victim. One would suspect that a person agreeing to take on a hard obligation to pay 5 per cent interest per week for an unpredictable term must be short of business acumen and bereft of any vestige of prudence. Actually, the victim is typically a man of common sense and experience, and not infrequently he is intelligent and well educated. In fact, substantial business and professional men appear to be the preferred victims of the loan shark. The Marcus Case of 1968 was not atypical. James Marcus, New York City's Commissioner of Water Supply, Gas and Electricity, was an intelligent, experienced person who, finding himself in financial difficulties, had resorted to the loan shark and found himself a few months later in deeper financial trouble. He also discovered that when he was in trouble with the loan shark he was in trouble with the underworld. Subsequently, he was accused of accepting an alleged bribe of $40,000 on a city contract worth $840,000 for the cleaning and repair of a reservoir. Like other victims, swept up by the pressures of the moment and the optimism of the sudden, solitary hope afforded by the loan shark, he had committed himself irrevocably to a spiraling financial obligation.

28. Investigation

Loan sharking is a difficult crime to investigate because it is a personal transaction to which there may be no witnesses other than the principals. Some loans are negotiated under circumstances which the victim is reluctant to reveal. For example, gambling losses are a common source of the financial difficulties we have spoken of. There is usually a loan shark at a floating crap game. In fact, the people who run the game may be more interested in the loan sharking than in the gambling. One of the gamblers in the dice game may run short of money. He feels that another $500 would enable him to recoup and accordingly applies to the loan shark in the corner of the room. Since the loan shark knows his customer—indeed, he may have already checked his credit ratings—he lends him the $500. If the gambler wins, he returns $600 for the $500 he has just borrowed. If he loses the money, he will have to come up with $600 within twenty-four hours. In the victim's mind the circumstances of such a loan preclude the confidence of the police.

a. **Evidence.** Even though the victim does talk to the police, there is little evidence beyond his uncorroborated statements. Occasionally (as in the case described in the next section) the enforcers make the mistake of telephoning their threats and intentions, and the investigators may obtain more convincing evidence. A search of the loan shark or of the place where he is thought to keep his records is ordinarily not fruitful. Even when the records are seized, they are usually found to be too meager or to cryptic to serve as evidence. In one case, a search yielded a typical record sheet bearing a list of sums ranging from $13,000 to $43,000, after which were placed a set of initials to represent the client. Sometimes mnemonic devices or substitute names are used, but even if the real names are used, the records do not constitute adequate supporting evidence.

b. **Undercover Men.** The use of an undercover man is probably the best, if not the only, solution to the problem of proof in loan shark cases as it is in many other criminal activities of organized crime. The harvest reaped from the activities of Herbert Itkin, a Manhattan labor lawyer who for six years served as an undercover agent for the FBI, is impressive proof of the effectiveness of a well-placed informer. From his testimony in the 1968 federal bribery conspiracy trial known as the Marcus Case it appeared that Itkin infiltrated the world of organized crime in 1962 and faithfully mapped it for the FBI until "his cover was blown" with the arrest of his friend Marcus. By the time Itkin left the witness box, his disclosures as the Government's star witness had implicated a number of people in corrupt and criminal schemes including persons reputed to be well-known members of the underworld.

29. Remedial Measures

Because of the formidable difficulties encountered in obtaining evidence against loan sharks as compared with the obvious effectiveness of employing undercover agents such as Itkin, the latter appears to be the logical course for law enforcement. There is, however, a peculiar reluctance on the part of law enforcement officials to approach the problems of loan sharking and other aspects of organized crime in this manner. In part this reluctance can be attributed to the unfavorable reaction of the public to the use of undercover men and informers, with its European connotation of police spies prepared to extend their surveillance over other citizens. Part of it, too, is caused by the difficulty involved in recruiting satisfactory agents, since the unfavorable reception given by the public to their work and the patent dangers of such employment are not offset by any great personal reward. Another remedy proposed for the control of loan sharks is the passage of special legislation. In most states, however, the legislation would appear to be adequate. In New York, as in many other states, there are laws to control usury. All states have statutes covering extortion and conspiracy. At present, then, it would appear that the best remedy would be a program of education of the prospective victims (through the general public) in the methods of the loan shark and the dangers inherent in such borrowing. In particular, potential victims should be encouraged to enlist the cooperation of the police if they find themselves the subjects of threats and extortion. The importance of this step was seen in the recent case of a defaulter who, after receiving a number of threatening telephone calls, went to the local detective squad. While he was explaining his situation to the detectives, the "enforcers" called his wife to tell her that they would be there that night to break her husband's arms and legs. This, of course, was a poor tactic on the part of the criminals, since the investigators and the state police arranged to be present when the enforcers appeared at the door, repeating their threats and demanding payment. They were arrested for assault and extortion. The victim was not molested further—again, a matter of good business policy: why bother with a victim under police surveillance when the city is filled with customers ready to pay 5 per cent per week?

ADDITIONAL READING

Larceny

Basham, D.L.: Larceny: The Investigator's Dilemma. 18 *Military Police Journal*, 6, 1968.

Jackson, B.: *A Thief's Primer*. New York, Macmillan, 1969.

Pratt, L.: *Bank Frauds*, 2nd ed. New York, Free Press, 1975.

Schima, K.: *Expressung und Nötigung, Eine Kriminologische Studie*. Vienna, Springer-Verlag, 1973.

Winfrey, C.: Hotels Trying to Stem Rise in Theft. *New York Times*, Sept. 7, 1977.

Automobile Theft

Achord, B.: Detection and Identification of Stolen Vehicles. 22 *Texas Police Journal*, 9, 1974.

Brickell, D. and Cole, L.S.: *Vehicle Theft Investigation*. Santa Cruz, Calif.: Davis Pub., 1975.

Chilimidos, R.S.: *Auto Theft Investigation*. Los Angeles, Legal Book Corp., 1971.

Colombell, W.E.: Examination of Vehicle Identification Numbers. 46 *FBI Law Enforcement Bulletin*, 6, 1977.

Fraser, G.: *Modern Transportation and International Crime*. Springfield, Ill.: Thomas, 1970.

Hoover, J.E.: Ignition Key to Crime. 41 *FBI Law Enforcement Bulletin*, 4, 1973.

Lawless, T. and Peterman, J.: Autotheft and the Uniformed Officer. 40 *Police Chief*, 6, 1973.

National Automobile Theft Bureau. *Passenger Vehicle Identification Manual*. Downers Grove, Ill.: NATB, 1974.

Nelson, A.T. and Smith, H.E.: *Car Clouting*. Springfield, Ill.: Thomas, 1958.

Northwestern Traffic Institute. *Locating and Identifying Wanted Vehicles*. Evanston, Ill.: Northwestern University, 1972.

Scott, R.D.: Arkansas Shows How to Keep the Pressure on Car Thieves. 39 *FBI Law Enforcement Bulletin*, 9, 1970.

Serial Number Location Guide for Construction Equipment. Oak Brook, Ill.: A.E.D. Research and Services, 1976.

Shoplifting

Alexander, A. and Moolman, V.: *Stealing*. New York, Cornerstone Library, 1968.

Curtis, S.J.: *Modern Retail Security*. Springfield, Ill.: Thomas, 1972.

Edwards, L.E.: *Shoplifting and Shrinkage Protection for Stores*. Springfield, Ill.: Thomas, 1974.

Goldman, E.H.: Security and Technology of Loss Prevention. 9 *Security World*, 44, 1972.

Griffin, R.K.: Behavioral Patterns in Shoplifting. 8 *Security World*, 9, 1972.

Meyers, T.J.: A Contribution to the Psychopathology of Shoplifting. 15 *Journal of Forensic Sciences*, 295, 1970.

Post, R.S.: *Combating Crime Against Small Business.* Springfield, Ill.: Thomas, 1972.
Shoplifting: Observations and New Data. 10 *Security World*, 16, 1973.
Williams, H.E.: Shoplifting. 14 *Colorado Policeman*, 4, 1977.

Credit Card Theft
Credit Cards: Distributing Fraud Loss. 77 *Yale Law Journal*, 1418, 1968.
Dodge, R.L.: Credit Card Fraud Investigation. 8 *Security World*, 24, 1971.
Lipson, M.: Crime and the Credit Card. Part I. 39 *FBI Law Enforcement Bulletin*, 6, 1970. Part II. 39 *FBI Law Enforcement Bulletin*, 7, 1970.
Paul, P.: Credit Cards. 32 *International Criminal Police Review*, 307, 1977.
Westermeier, J.T., Jr.: The Privacy Side of the Credit Card. 23 *American University Law Review*, 183, 1973.

Confidence Games
Blum, R.H.: *Deceivers and Deceived.* Springfield, Ill.: Thomas, 1972.
Carey, M. and Sherman, G.: *A Compendium of Bunk or How to Spot a Con Artist.* Springfield, Ill.: Thomas, 1976.
Glick, R.G. and Newsom, R.S.: *Fraud Investigation.* Springfield, Ill.: Thomas, 1974.
Hancock, R. with Chetz, H.: *The Compleat Swindler.* New York, Macmillan, 1968.
Maurer, D.W.: *The American Confidence Man.* Springfield, Ill.: Thomas, 1974.
Rosefsky, R.S.: *Frauds, Swindles and Rackets.* Chicago, Follett, 1973.

Criminal Receiving
Cappell, D. and Walsh, M.: "No Questions Asked": A Consideration of the Crime of Criminal Receiving. 20 *Crime and Delinquency*, 157, 1974.
Klockars, C.B.: *The Professional Fence.* New York, Free Press, 1975.
Klose, K., Lewis, A.B. and Shaffer, R.: *Surprise! Surprise! How the Lawmen Conned the Thieves.* New York, Viking, 1978.
Law Enforcement Assistance Administration. *Strategies for Combatting the Criminal Receiver.* Washington, D.C.: U.S. Government Printing Office, 1976.
Walsh, M. and Chappell, D.: Operational Parameters in the Stolen Property System. 2 *Journal of Criminal Justice*, 113, 1974.

Computer Crime
Bequai, A.: Computer Crime: A Growing and Serious Problem. 6 *Police Law Quarterly*, 1, 1976.
Jacobson, R.V., Brown, W.F. and Browne, P.S.: *Guidelines for Automatic Data Processing Physical Security and Risk Management.* Washington, D.C.: U.S. Government Printing Office, 1975.
McKnight, G.: *Computer Crime.* New York, Walker, 1974.
Parker, D.B.: *Crime By Computer.* New York, Scribner's, 1976.
Whiteside, T.: Dead Souls in the Computer. Part I. 53 *The New Yorker*, Aug. 22, 1977. Part II. 53 *The New Yorker*, Aug. 29, 1977.
_____. *Computer Capers.* New York, Crowell, 1978.

Chapter 21

BURGLARY

1. Importance of Burglary

B URGLARY IS CONSIDERED by many to be the most important form of
theft. The frequency, expense, and difficulty of controlling this
crime place great demands on law enforcement personnel.
Moreover, a burglary is usually the average citizen's only contact
with crime, and hence, as a taxpayer, he demands attention. The
importance of the burglary problem is recognized, too, by detective
commanders at every level, since their efficiency records and their
career progress frequently—and often unfairly—depend on the
fluctuations of the burglary statistics for their areas of operation. It is
not expected, of course, that the incidence of burglary can be made
to approach zero in any large urban district, and the failure of a
detective command to achieve this millennial objective is of little
significance. What can, however, be reasonably expected in the way
of efficiency is the apprehension of criminal groups employing
definite crime patterns which are indicative of organization and
method. For example, the operations of a safe mob using a torch
should be curtailed after the first five jobs. Similarly, it should not be
too difficult to apprehend a mob that specializes in jewelry stores or
liquor shops. The use of plants, information, tails, *modus operandi*
files, and physical evidence can be effectively focused, if a
meaningful pattern of target selection and technique is apparent.

2. Definitions

a. **Burglary.** The definition of burglary varies in different states.
In some jurisdictions degrees of burglary are defined in the law to

take care of the distinction between burglary of a dwelling house at night, which is considered a serious crime, and housebreaking. For present purposes, a definition taken from the common law will suffice. Burglary is the breaking and entering in the nighttime the dwelling house of another, with intent to commit a crime therein. The "crime therein" is usually taken to mean larceny or an offense which is a felony against the person such as rape or assault.

b. **Housebreaking.** This offense is simply the unlawful entering of the building of another with intent to commit a crime therein. The elements of "dwelling house," "nighttime," and a specification of the crimes are absent. All of these elements must be present in order to constitute the crime of burglary. It is apparent that a discussion of burglary will necessarily include the lesser crime of housebreaking; the present treatment will be restricted to the major offense, since its investigation includes the techniques and procedures applicable to housebreaking.

3. Proof

The following elements must be established in proving the offense of burglary:
a. Breaking and entering.
b. Dwelling house of another.
c. Nighttime.
d. Intent to commit a crime therein.

4. Elements of the Offense

a. **Breaking and Entering.** There must be a breaking either actual (physical force) or constructive (trick or ruse). Entering a hole in the wall, an open skylight, door, or window will not constitute breaking. The essence of the break is the removal or putting aside of some material part of the house on which the dweller relies for security against intrusion.

1) *Actual Breaking.* This term describes the application of physical force to effect entry. Opening a closed door or window;

unlocking or unlatching a door; lifting a fastening hook; pushing open a closed transom or trapdoor; removing a fastened screen; cutting a pane of glass or the netting of a screen are examples of physical force. If a guest, lodger, or servant, already lawfully in the building, forces an inner door, he has committed a break.

2) **Constructive Breaking.** The use of collusion, trick, ruse, intimidation, or impersonation to gain entry constitutes a break. Thus, a person who gains entry by impersonating a repairman has accomplished a break.

3) **Entry.** The insertion of any part of the body into the building constitutes entry. The insertion of a long pole or hook into the building is considered sufficient entry.

4) **One of Two Accomplices.** To support a conviction of two persons for burglary it is not necessary that both enter. If one enters, the other also commits burglary by being present and aiding in the entry.

b. **Dwelling House of Another.** The term *building* as used in defining housebreaking refers to a structure having four sides and a roof which is used by man to shelter himself or his property. Thus, a *building* includes freight cars, booths, tents, warehouses, a watchman's shanty, and a tool house. The term *dwelling house* means a building used as a residence. Thus, a store is not a subject of burglary unless part of it is used as a dwelling house. Temporary absence of the occupant does not deprive a dwelling house of its character as such. The house must be in the status of being occupied at the time of the breaking and entering. This does not mean that someone must be actually present in the structure. If the occupant leaves it temporarily with the intention of returning, though he may remain away for some time, the house remains a dwelling house. Hence, a dwelling used only during vacation periods and over weekends can be the subject of a burglary. The test lies in the occupant's or owner's intention to return.

c. **Nighttime.** Both the breaking and the entering must be in the nighttime, which is the period between sunset and sunrise, when there is not sufficient daylight to discern a man's face. It is not necessary that both the breaking and the entering occur on the same night.

d. **Intent.** To constitute burglary, there must be an intent to commit a specific offense within the dwelling house. The fact that the actual commission of the felony was impossible is immaterial. The breaking and entering are, ordinarily, presumptive evidence of an intent to commit a crime therein. The crime intended by the burglar is in most cases larceny.

e. **Proof on a "Plant."** The detective who is assigned to a tail or a plant detail should keep constantly in mind the requirements of proof. On observing the criminal, the first impulse is to make an arrest. Often, this is done while the burglars are occupied with the preliminaries of forcing entrance. An arrest at this time permits the criminals to escape the onus of the full crime, since they can be charged only with attempted burglary or illegal entry by reason of the overt act. A patient investigator will permit the burglars to enter and apprehend them *in flagrante delicto* or while making their exit.

5. Criminal Type

Traditionally the burglar, and in particular the safecracker, has been portrayed as a masked, bewhiskered, burly individual whose daring was matched only by his ruthlessness in disposing of interference. This legend undoubtedly had its origin in the facility with which the safecracker could be caricatured by cartoonists. His safe, mask, blackjack, and flashlight have come to be the picturesque symbols of the professional criminal. By this intimate association, the safe burglar has acquired in fiction the attributes of character corresponding to the physical properties of the safe itself—steely toughness of fiber and impregnability to moral suasion. Historically, this picture may, indeed, have been true, but modern criminal society is far more democratic. The safecracker category, for example, includes all races, colors, and creeds: the skilled craftsman and the bungler; the timid and the bold; the lone wolf and the pack member; the professional criminal and the young amateur trying his wings; the local thug and the strong boy from a distant city. The occupation of safecracker has proved so remunerative to some practitioners that its membership has swollen beyond the limits imposed by any of the restrictions of qualifications in the form of skill.

6. Safe-Breaking

Since the most important burglaries usually involve breaking into a safe, special consideration will be given to this type of offense.

a. **Safe-Breaking Methods.** The skill of the safeman can be judged by the method which he employs to open a safe. A number of procedures are currently in practice; however, the most picturesque method—the use of nitroglycerin—has disappeared from the safeman's repetoire. The great risks which were run in the use of nitroglycerin led to the introduction of newer but more prosaic methods which were adequate for the exigencies of the average job. As a consequence the high-explosive technique has become almost obsolete as a practical procedure of safe burglary. The following methods are currently in use:

1) *Rip Job.* The greatest number of safemen employ the rip technique. The required tools include an electric drill (or a brace and bit) and a sectional jimmy or a crowbar. A hole is made in the upper or lower left-hand corner of the door. The jimmy is placed into the hole and the door is pried up until exposed to a point just beyond the dial.

2) *Punch Job.* The punch job is, at present, the second most common method of opening safes. When performed by an expert this operation is clean, rapid, and not unduly noisy. For its successful execution, there are four requisites: a moderate degree of skill and experience; a reasonable portion of luck; the correct selection of a safe; and the simple tools, viz., a sledge hammer and drift pin or center punch. The technique is relatively simple. The dial is first knocked off the safe with the hammer. The punch is then held against the spindle of the safe and hit sharply with a mallet or hammer. If the safe is one in which the tumblers are on the end of the spindle, the small sockets will be broken when the spindle is forced back and the lock will be released. Some safes, however, are "punch-proof," the tumblers being set off from the spindle. The typical burglar is successful in only a small percentage of punch jobs and usually must resort to additional techniques.

3) *Chopping.* The chop job is crude in method, but its effectiveness is not modified by its lack of esthetic appeal. The operator simply turns the safe upside down so that the bottom is

exposed. The bottom of many safes is the weakest section, and a hole can be made in it with a reasonable amount of force. The application of a jimmy further simplifies the process. Once the hole has been effected through the bottom of the safe, the burglar has access to its contents.

4) *Burning.* At one time, it was thought that the "burn" or "torch" technique was obsolescent. The last ten years, however, have witnessed a recrudescence of its popularity. In part, the revival is attributed to the wider dissemination of manual skills. This training can be acquired in schools, shipyards, and other places where welding is performed. Unfortunately, an acetylene tank can be quite dangerous in the hand of the amateur. It is necessary, moreover, to intelligently control the relative amounts of oxygen and acetylene in order to obtain the proper temperature. Hence the operator of the torch must be a reasonably skilled workman. The size of tank which is carried to the job is variable. Small tanks are available which are suitable for inconspicuous conveyance. The burner is applied to the central area of the safe and a circle is burned about the dial which is then removed to permit opening the safe door.

5) *Carry-Out.* In this operation, the safe is simply physically removed from the house. Most commonly, this method is used in private dwelling houses, in which the safe is usually quite small and movable. A passenger car is used to transport the safe from the house. Stores and other establishments which are located near the street level are also likely places for this type of job. A dolly cart and a truck must be used for a larger safe.

6) *Touch or Combination.* The Jimmy Valentine type, beloved of mystery addicts and hapless bookkeepers is, as far as the police are concerned, without any real-life counterpart. A few highly skilled employees of safe manufacturers purport to be able to open safes by the sense of touch applied to the dial. The fiction of the safecracker listening to the tumblers is maintained by careless office employees who neglect to close the safe properly or who leave the combination hidden in some fairly obvious place. The experienced safeman is well acquainted with the habits of the office-worker species in his native haunt. He is aware, for example, of the evening custom of careless employees of giving the dial only a half turn to lighten the burden of their morning labors. The safe is not actually locked. The

burglar has merely to reverse the half turn to make his night's work profitable. Similarly, he is privy to the common secret of cashiers who hide the combination on the inside cover of a ledger or paste it on the side of a drawer. He is aware, too, of the tendency of office personnel to employ multiples of the number five in selecting a combination.

b. **How Safe Is a Safe?** It is an almost daily experience of detectives in some sections of large cities to be summoned to the scene of a safe burglary. The proprietor will usually be striding about the office, a dazed look in his eyes, exclaiming, "Look what they did to my safe! Is it possible?" The scene before the detective's eyes will indeed be depressing. The safe will be lying on its back, the door pried open, and the carefully maintained records scattered about the room. A thin coat of white powder covers the documents. Tools and miscellaneous debris are strewn about the safe. "Is it possible?" the proprietor asks. The detective knows that not only is it possible, but it is a fact discouragingly repeated in his daily experience. The proprietor of the safe has spent his years of ownership in a pleasant but unfounded sense of security. A safe (i.e., a metal container with a combination lock) means to the proprietor a burglarproof iron box. He fancies it an impregnable fortress resisting valiantly the night-long ministrations of six masked men with acetylene torches and nitroglycerin. The possibility of a theft of the combination always exists, but mere physical assault will, he feels, avail nothing against these steel barriers. Safe manufacturers, however, take a different view of this matter. They do not think (nor do they intend that the proprietor should so consider) the average safe to be burglarproof. To them, it is a strongbox, a deterrent to casual larceny and a protection in the event of fire. That it will not resist the determined efforts of a moderately skilled cracksman is a fact of which they are keenly aware. The heavy doors, which appear to the layman as an eight-inch wall of steel, are in reality relatively thin metal layers containing an insulation of fireproofing material. The safe manufacturers (and the insurance companies) have endeavored to make safe owners aware of the nature and limitations of their safes. There are *burglarproof* safes. The problem has been met by the safe companies and they offer for sale, at a higher price, a safe which they consider proof against the average burglar. The construction of such a safe is entirely different from that of the fireproof strongbox. Naturally, no safe is completely "burglarproof," since time and equipment will eventually prevail over the strongest construction.

c. **Safe Construction.** The ordinary safe is simply fire resistant. It is constructed of sheet-steel boxes separated by several inches of insulation. It serves also as a deterrent to the thief, since it is equipped with relocking devices and burglar-resistant locks. The burglar-resistant safe, on the other hand, is built with thick, laminated steel to withstand the efforts of an experienced burglar for a period of approximately seven hours. As a protection from fire, this safe is imbedded in concrete or placed within a larger fire-resistant safe.

7. Breaking into Commercial Establishments

Most burglars are unskilled; a few, such as the loft burglar, described in the following section specialize and develop suitable skills for their selected work. For the most part, then, the selection of the point of entry and the method of breaking in can be considered choices made after a quick survey of the opportunities and weaknesses of the building and its condition. The findings of the President's Commission on Crime in the District of Columbia shed some light on the representative methods used in breaking into commercial establishments: In 21 (7 per cent) of the 313 commercial burglaries surveyed, burglars entered through unlocked doors and in 70 cases (22 per cent) through unlocked windows. In 111 cases the burglars broke windows to gain entry, and in 95 cases locks were forced. A total of 105 of the commercial establishments burglarized were reported to have burglar-resistant locks; 65 of these establishments, however, were entered by means other than by tampering with the lock. Sixty-four per cent of the burglarized commercial establishments were located on the first floor.

8. Loft Burglars

This type of burglar specializes in stealing merchandise from lofts. He may, as part of his loft work, open a safe if one is available. Indeed, loft burglars carry practically the same tools as a safe burglar. A loft burglar, however, is something more than a crude mechanic. He must possess some knowledge of the worth of merchandise; he must be a judge of different kinds of material. For example, if the loft mob is stealing bolts of cloth, one of them should be able to select the most expensive goods. In addition, the loft burglar must be acquainted with a receiver who will dispose of the goods.

a. **Planning.** A loft job is usually elaborately "cased." The leader has accurate knowledge of the plant layout, the protection system, the amount of merchandise on hand, and the habits of the personnel. This information may sometimes be obtained through a dishonest employee. More often, it is acquired by ruse, observation, and personal inspection.

b. **Gaining Entry.** The entry into the chosen premises usually takes place at night, preferably over the weekend when the area is relatively quiet. A common point of entrance is the skylight. The burglars have knowledge of ready access to a nearby building. From the roof of this building, they may reach the roof of their objective. They may then kick in the glass of the skylight and let themselves down by means of a rope. If the windows are not wired or barred, they may descend the fire escape ladder and break a window. In deserted streets, the burglars are emboldened to make a more direct entry by forcing open the main door or by pulling down the swinging ladder of the fire escape. Another means of entry is an open delivery chute. Still another kind of loft burglary is represented by the "lay-in-mob." Members of a "lay-in-mob" will acquire the confidence of a legitimate businessman, visit him in the late afternoon on an apparently honest mission, and subsequently secrete themselves in another part of the building until the personnel has departed at the close of business.

c. **Removing the Goods.** The loft mob usually employs a truck to remove the merchandise; since the burglary takes place in a business section of the city, the presence of a truck passes unnoticed. The goods are then brought to a "drop-off" to be later inspected by the receiver.

9. Apartment House Burglars

Large multiple dwelling buildings offer many advantages to the burglar who operates in a large city. Ordinarily, the majority of the tenants are unknown to each other, and consequently the appearance of a new face on the premises will not arouse suspicion. Similarly, when the burglar has once gained entrance, his activities within the apartment will seldom attract the attention of the neighbors. The following are among the techniques commonly employed:

a. **Gaining Entry.** This type of burglar usually selects the target by observing the lights from the street and noting apartments with darkened windows. Entry may be gained to the buildings by ringing the doorbell of a resident who is home at the time, opening the front door, and jamming the locking mechanism with a thin piece of wood such as a toothpick. A period of time is permitted to lapse while the tenant is convinced that his bell was sounded by mistake. The burglar then enters the building and frees the lock. Entry into the apartment is accomplished by means of a strip of celluloid applied to the lock or by jimmying a window accessible from a fire escape. If the building is guarded by a doorman, the burglar may enter an unguarded entrance, proceed to the roof, and select the apartment of choice. By using the roof he may "hit" four or five apartments in one night. Finally, it should be noted that many apartment dwellers are careless about locking their doors—a fact which is well known to the "door shaker," a burglar with minimal technique who simply goes through a big apartment building or a hotel, usually between 9:30 A.M. and noon, trying doors until he finds one unlocked or ajar. In a New York Police Department survey of apartment houses in the borough of Queens, 25 out of 150 apartment doors were found unlocked.

b. **Procedure.** The burglar searches the closets and dressers for valuables such as jewelry and furs. Sometimes he empties the drawers of the dresser on the bed or floor to facilitate the search.

c. **Leaving the Building.** On departing, the burglar may leave the loot in the hallway and emerge empty-handed to see if a tail is waiting to pick him up. If the road appears clear, he returns, picks up the loot, and departs.

10. The Suburban Burglar

Dwelling houses in middle-class suburbs are considered simple and staple targets for the burglar. The houses are sufficiently detached to enable him to operate unnoticed, and the target can be selected without difficulty by driving about and observing the familiar signs—the absence of any lights in the early evening and the doors flung open to reveal an empty garage. For reassurance the burglar will approach from the rear to try the bell. Failing any response or other signs of activity, he will break a pane on the door or window to let himself in. In a few minutes he will have made the evening rewarding. Should he decide not to break and enter, he can still turn a tidy profit by picking up the bicycle, the lawn mower, and a few power tools from the garage. A moderately industrious burlgar can, in this way, average over $500 a week. His success as a burglar is attributable to the carelessness of the householders rather than to any specially developed skills. Although he may eventually be picked up through a neighbor's phone call or as an incident of patrol, the long series of depredations could be easily prevented by a few common-sense precautions.

11. The Hit-and-Run Burglar

The suburbs have proved such an inviting target that a number of variations in daytime burglary technique have been introduced, which in turn have led to the adoption of new protective measures.

a. **The Commuter Burglar.** Where the suburban burglar tends to work alone and operates not far from where he lives, the *commuter* burglar is definitely a city dweller, will travel as far as 30 miles for his target, and spends very little time in its selection. These burglars present an even more difficult problem to the police, since they operate in a much greater area and are rarely seen twice in the same locality. Working in pairs, the commuter burglars drive out from New York City or Newark, for example, drop off the Garden State Parkway into a residential development and cruise about until they find a house that appears to be unoccupied. While one drives around the block, the other rings the doorbell. If the homeowner answers, the thief asks directions to a fictitious address. If no one answers, he smashes in the glass of a rear window or door and quickly goes through the house, picking up small appliances, cameras, money, and jewelry, leaving when his confederate returns in the car.

b. **Delivery Trucks.** Some of these burglars drive up in a delivery van to cart away heavy items such as color television sets, expensive high fidelity equipment, and similar appurtenances of an affluent community. Delivery trucks are too common in these areas to attract special attention. Another ruse is to pose as a television repairman and pull up at the selected house in an appropriately marked truck. In one case, the burglar was a genuine repairman, half of whose calls were legitimate. In other calls he would choose a likely house and, if the occupant was away, enter by the rear, quickly remove any money and jewelry and leave in his van.

c. **Dinner-time Burglars.** The wealthy suburbs of New York, such as the North Shore communities and Westchester County, have recently become the targets of "dinner-time burglars." While the family and guests are collected in one area of a large house preoccupied with dinner, the burglar busies himself in the relatively remote bedroom area, searching the rooms for jewelry and cash. The early evening hours are propitious for this sort of activity, since it is too early for the burglar alarms to be switched on. Obviously, a sensible protection against this type of intruder is the possession of an intelligent dog.

d. **Alarm Installations.** The frequency of daylight hit-and-run burglaries in the suburbs has resulted in a demand for burglar-alarm installations connected with police headquarters. In an affluent community, such as Scarsdale in Westchester County, New York, several thousand burglar alarms have been installed in residences. When triggered, the alarm automatically dials the Scarsdale police headquarters number and transmits a recorded message saying that the identified house is being burglarized. Unfortunately, these automatic burglar alarms tend to be hypersensitive, giving rise to an inordinate number of false alarms. The New York City Police Department, for example, states that its 911 emergency telephone number system, already overloaded with thousands of unnecessary calls, is being strained even further by calls set off by malfunctioning or misused burglar alarms. More than 7,000 calls triggered by automatic burglar alarms flow into the 911 system every day. Nearly 98 per cent of these are what officials categorize as "unfounded"— meaning that the alarms did not involve a crime and that they were set off by some accident such as a pet tripping over the wires, the vibrations of a passing truck, or even a thunderstorm.

12. Summer Home Burglary

The breaking and entering of vacation homes in the off-season is becoming a relatively common offense in rural and resort areas. Thousands of vacation homeowners throughout the country are discovering that their rural havens have become targets for off-season burglars and vandals. The sharp increase in these offenses has followed the growing resort population. Each year more vacation homes are built and each year they become more elaborate in their furnishings and equipment. With the burgeoning population these homes are scattered over a much wider area, presenting a serious problem to a police force that is geared to the local population. Many of these houses are located on the farther side of a lake or are hidden away in the mountains at the end of a road that is little used in the summer and is impassable in the winter. The normal patrol of the sheriff's department or of the state troopers is not suited to burglary protection in these areas.

13. Physical Evidence

On arriving at the scene of a reported burglary, the investigator should first search the building for the burglar. This may appear to be an odd piece of advice, but experience has shown that the burglar is sometimes interrupted in his work and finds his path of escape blocked. This is particularly true of loft buildings where the area is so large that the burglar deems it safer to conceal himself than to risk dashing out of the building. It is assumed that police officers responding to the call will search the neighborhood for the burglar. The next investigative step is the search for physical evidence.

a. **Heelprints.** The most common clue left at the scene of a safe burglary is a heelprint on paper. The burglar, after opening the safe, throws the papers on the floor and carelessly steps on them. In wet weather, the prints may be exceptionally good. If a sufficient number of defects are observable in the heels, an excellent identification can be made.

b. **Fingerprints.** The complainant in a burglary case always relies heavily on the discovery of a fingerprint for the solution of the crime. Experienced investigators, although they do not neglect this investigative technique, understand that relatively few burglaries are solved each year through the medium of fingerprints. If the importance of the case warrants a photographic record, pictures should be taken of the affected room and the point of break and entry before processing for fingerprints. In the development of latent fingerprints, the following area and objects will receive attention:

1) *Area of Break.* If this is on the outside, weather effects usually prevent the deposit of good prints. Immediately inside of the area of the break, however, prints may be found. This is especially true if it has been necessary for the burglar to climb through a window. The inside of the window and the sill are good surfaces for prints.

2) *Closets.* Prints are often found on door and jamb of a closet. Naturally, most of the prints will be those of the occupants.

3) *Door Knobs.* Fingerprints are practically never found on door knobs. The manner in which the knob is handled ordinarily prevents the retention of fingerprints.

4) *Dressers.* In a house burglary, the dresser is searched by the burglar. The color of the wood and the presence of furniture polish usually prevent developing prints. Polished boxes and glass covers may bear prints.

5) *Furniture.* The chairs, bed, and tables are not likely sources.

6) *Bottles and Glasses.* Burglars often drink the owner's liquor. The glasses and bottles are ideal surfaces for receiving prints. It may be safely said that bottles and glasses are the most likely of all sources of prints in a burglary investigation.

7) *Cartons and Crates.* Objects found in a loft, such as wooden containers, seldom bear prints.

8) *Safe.* If the safe is "crinkled" or if the paint is old and quite worn, the search for prints will usually be unsuccessful. A new, smooth, enamel surface will yield prints. A particularly good source is the cash box. The bottom of the change shelf of the cash box should receive special attention.

9) *Walls.* Success depends primarily on the nature of the paint.

The areas near light switches and in back of the safe should be processed.

10) *Tools.* Although it is possible to find a print on a tool, such a discovery is quite rare.

11) *Papers.* Again, there is a possibility, but small probability. Sized paper and heavy smooth stock can be powdered at the scene. Other papers should be removed to the laboratory for silver nitrate treatment.

12) *Desks.* It is seldom that a print is found on a plain wooden desk, either on the top or in the fronts of the drawers.

c. **Clothing.** In a house burglary, the criminal sometimes exchanges his own jacket or suit for that of the owner of the house. Dry cleaner's marks present on the clothing will offer an invaluable clue.

d. **Glass.** If a window was broken in effecting entry, glass particles may be present in the pockets of the suspect. Samples of the broken glass should be collected for possible future comparison in the event that a suspect is picked up.

e. **Paint.** If a jimmy has been used to force the door or window, paint may adhere to the tool. Paint samples should be taken for future comparison.

f. **Tool Marks.** In jimmying a door or window, tool impressions are left by the criminal. These should be photographed from a distance of a few feet and also in a one-to-one shot. Impressions in wood serve only to indicate the size of the jimmy. Marks in metal may sometimes be positively identified as having been made with a particular tool. In safe burglaries, excellent tool marks are left on the dial in "knocking" it off with a cold chisel and hammer or with the hammer alone (see Chapter 36).

g. **Tools.** The preceeding two paragraphs have assumed that the burglar departed with his tools. In most instances, however, the criminal leaves his tools behind him. The reason for this is his fear of being picked up with the tools in his possession. In some states, it is a crime for a person to be found at night with burglar tools in his possession. Consequently, the experienced burglar purchases his equipment before the job and leaves it at the scene. In the case of an "inside job" in a factory, the burglar may use the tools present on the premises. An effort should be made to trace the tools to the store in

Figure 13a. Safe burglary. A combination of a "rip" and a "punch" job.

which they were purchased. If the subject of the burglary is a factory or garage, the burglar may depend on finding the instruments in the building. This is particularly true if the burglary is an inside job or if it has been "fingered" by a former employee. Certain types of tools, such as sectional jimmies or very fine drills, suggest a special *modus operandi* and may limit the suspects to a small number.

h. **Peculiar Habits.** Some burglars are given to odd behavior such as defecation on the floor, stealing desk ornaments, eating candy, or drinking excessively from bottles found on the premises. Peculiarities of behavior should be noted and checked against the *modus operandi* index.

i. **Safe Insulation.** Samples of safe insulation should be taken for possible future comparison. Since the typical safe is of the

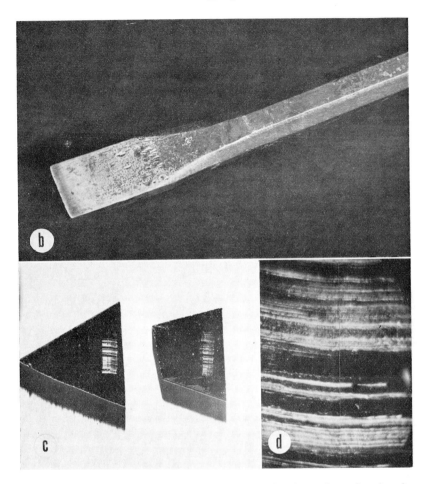

Figure 13b. Blade of the jimmy used to open the safe. This tool was found in the possession of a suspect and was later shown, by the methods described below, to be the jimmy used on the safe. c. Two pieces of metal bearing tool impressions. The piece on the right was part of the safe; the impression was made with the suspect's jimmy. D. A photomicrograph of the tool impressions made with a comparison microscope (magnification × 18). Note the fine vertical line dividing the photograph at the center. The tool impression the right half of the picture is that on the metal piece taken from the safe; that on the left is the test impression. The concurrence of a great number of the lines indicates that both impressions were made with the same tool. Courtesy of James Osterburg.

fire-resistant kind, it contains insulating material. The burglar, in breaking into such a safe, scatters the insulation on the floor. In some burglaries, so much of this material is strewn about the room that the layman is under the impression that an explosion has taken place. The insulation material falls on the clothing of the burglars and is picked up by their shoes. Sometimes, the insulation material can be found in the nail holes of the heels weeks after the commission of the burglary.

1) *A Clue Material.* Safe insulation material can serve as excellent clue material. Some safe manufacturers make their own insulation material; others order it from outside firms according to certain specifications. It has been found that the materials differ sufficiently to constitute a medium of identification. Thus, if a suspect is found with safe insulation material on his clothing which on spectrographic comparison is found to be chemically the same as the sample of material from the broken safe, there is a strong indication of guilt.

2) *FBI File.* The FBI Laboratory maintains a Petrographic File, one section of which consists of safe insulations and data concerning such substances. Specimens have been obtained from the products of the major safe companies of the United States. This file has assisted often in the solution of safe burglaries. As an example of the usefulness of the file, a case of the Kentucky State Police may be cited. In the course of a series of burglaries, a drug store in Albany, Kentucky, was broken into and the safe containing money and narcotics was removed to an isolated area where it was broken into. The Kentucky State Police picked up a suspect near Albany and on searching him found light grey material in his trouser cuffs. The trousers, evidence material, and samples of insulation from the safe were sent to the FBI Laboratory for comparison. Under the microscope, the material from the trousers appeared to be the same as that from the safe. It was found, by reference to the Petrographic File, that the insulation material was relatively rare. Thus, it could be concluded with a high degree of probability that the sample in the cuff was acquired at the scene of the burglary.

ADDITIONAL READING

Alth, M.: *All About Locks*. New York, Hawthorn Books, 1972.

Barnes, R. and Sarro, R.: *Are You Safe from Burglars*. New York, Doubleday, 1971.

Conklin, J.E. and Bittner, E.: Burglary in a Suburb. 11 *Criminology*, 206, 1973.

Dussia, J.: Safe Burglary Investigation. 36 *FBI Law Enforcement Bulletin*, 11, 1967.

Green, E.J. and Booth, C.E.: Cluster Analyses of Burglary M/Os. 4 *Journal of Police Science and Administration*, 382, 1976.

Klotter, J.C. and Cusick, R.I., Jr.: *Burglary Prevention, Investigation and Prosecution*. Louisville, University of Louisville, n.d.

Matias, G.J.: A Better Criminal "Mousetrap." 40 *FBI Law Enforcement Bulletin*, 9, 1971.

Murphy, R.B. and Horton, S.: Focus on Burglary: A Management Approach to Prevention of Crime. 42 *Police Chief*, 11, 1975.

Safe Insulation and its Value in Crime Detection. 43 *FBI Law Enforcement Bulletin*, 11, 1974.

Scarr, H.A.: *Patterns of Burglary*, 2nd ed. Washington, D.C.: U.S. Government Printing Office, 1973.

Shover, N.: Structures and Careers in Burglary. 63 *Journal of Criminal Law, Criminology and Police Science*, 540, 1972.

Webb, D.B.: *Investigation of Safe and Money Chest Burglary*. Springfield, Ill.: Thomas, 1975.

Chapter 22

ROBBERY

1. Introduction

Rᴏʙʙᴇʀʏ is perhaps the most glamorous of the major crimes. We speak of "robber knights" and "robber barons," of "bold robbers" and "daylight robbery." The element of reckless courage is usually associated with robbery, since the criminal often declares himself in the most forthright manner imaginable. He stands with his weapon bared and demands from his victim the property on which he has set his heart. There is present in this situation the imminent possibility of resistance, of a chase and a vigorous pursuit by the police. The daring character of the typical robbery does not imply that the planning of the crime is without ingenuity or that the executants are devoid of finesse. On the contrary, a truly first-rate robbery is as much an achievement of timing and precision as a skillfully executed play of a professional football team. At the other end of the scale we have the truly low class robber—the common "mugger" who employs all the subtlety and delicacy of a pile driver.

There is considerable confusion in the mind of the layman concerning the meaning of the term *robbery*. The average citizen uses it as a synonym for burglary and for larceny. There is a fundamental difference; indeed, from the point of view of the criminal it is a vital difference, since the offense of robbery may mean a few additional years in jail. Robbery is considered a very serious crime because it involves immediate personal danger to the victim. Robbery is the taking of property from another in his presence and against his will. Larceny is simply the taking of someone else's property. (Thus robbery implies the additional but lesser crime of larceny.) Burglary is the breaking into a building with the intention to commit a crime—any crime, be it larceny, murder, or simple mischief.

2. The Offense and the Offender

The FBI in the Uniform Crime Reports estimates a total of 417,038 robbery offenses committed in the United States in 1978. Nearly half of the robberies were committed on the street. On account of the number of unreported street offenses, this figure should be considered as only a useful approximation. Many robberies, especially muggings in major cities, are not reported because the victim believes that the difficulties in identifying, locating, and apprehending the offender are too formidable and that the chances of recovering the lost property are too remote. Nevertheless, a special interest attaches to the statistics of robbery, since this offense is considered by criminologists to be the bellwether of violent criminality: Robberies indicate a tendency to use violence on a stranger and, in general, most robberies are reported to the police.

It is difficult to draw meaningful conclusions concerning the robbery offender on the basis of the available statistical information, since these data quickly become dated and their applicability varies from region to region. For example, a large number of persons responsible for robbing banks today tend to be youths and amateurs, whereas in the past they were often mature professionals. Consequently, this trend directly affects such key factors as the targets of the robber, his control over potential violence, and the effectiveness of traditional police deterrent and control measures. The following are a few of the observations that have been made on the offender and his habits.

a. **Age.** Young offenders are responsible for a very large proportion of robberies that occur in the United States. About 75 per cent of all persons arrested for robbery are under the age of 25; 55 per cent are under 21; and 33 per cent are juveniles. Most of the juveniles involved in robbery were arrested on charges of mugging or strong-arm robberies. Youths, in general, tend to operate in groups.

b. **Firearms.** According to the Uniform Crime Reports, 60 per cent of all robberies are committed with a weapon and about 40 per cent of all robberies are committed with a firearm as the weapon. There is reason to believe that measures which could effectively limit the availability of firearms, especially handguns, or otherwise deter persons from using a gun to commit a robbery would reduce significantly the number of armed robberies.

c. **Violence.** Armed robberies tend to result in little injury, apparently because the overwhelming threat of the weapons discourages and minimizes resistance. Most injuries that are suffered are incurred in strong-arm robberies or muggings where contact is more likely to elicit victim resistance and where the offender tends to be more youthful and consequently more prone to employ physical force. The majority of robbers, however, rarely cause physical injury to their victims. Although they are professionally prepared to use violence to achieve their ends, they are not otherwise given to assaultive behavior. For them violence is a tool to be used with discretion when it is the unavoidable means to a professional end. They belong to the subculture of thieves rather than the subculture of violence.

Nevertheless, the pattern may be changing. As the average age of the robber becomes younger, the non-violent nature of robberies may change. The last few years have witnessed a marked increase in the level of violence. Finally, despite the generally non-violent character of the robber, a most important consideration is the formidable nature of the threat of violence in the offense of robbery. The violence and danger inherent in this threat are intolerable. The public sense of security requires that the threat of deadly force and serious bodily harm associated with robbery must be taken into account when assessing the gravity of the crime even though the frequency and level of violence are relatively small.

3. Law

Robbery is the unlawful taking of personal property from the person or in the presence of another against his will, by means of force, violence, or fear of injury, immediate or future, to his person or property, or the person or property of a relative or member of his family, or of anyone in his company at the time of the robbery. Robbery is similar to larceny with the element of violence, actual or threatened, added. It includes some of the elements of larceny plus the taking of the property from the person by force or fear.

a. **Proof.** The following elements must be established:

1) The taking of the property.

2) That the taking was from the person or in the presence of the person.

3) That the taking was against his will, by force, violence, or putting in fear.

b. **Taking of the Property.** The reader is referred to Chapter 20 for those elements relating to the property involved.

c. **From the Person.** The words "from the person" are not to be taken in a literal or strict sense. If the property is taken in the presence of the owner it is, in the contemplation of the law, taken from his person. For the condition "in the presence" to be satisfied, it is not necessary that the owner be within a certain distance of his property. If the victim is left tied up in one room, while the robber takes his money in another room, the taking is considered to have been done in his presence.

d. **Force or Violence.** The force must be actual violence, but the amount is immaterial. The violence is sufficient if it overcomes the actual resistance of the person robbed, or puts him in such a position that he can make no resistance. If resistance is overcome in snatching the article, there is sufficient violence. If, however, an article is merely snatched from the hand of another or if a pocket is picked by stealth, the offense is not robbery.

e. **Fear or Threats.** Putting the victim in fear of bodily injury is sufficient intimidation to sustain a charge of robbery. Actual fear need not be proved, since a legal presumption of fear will arise from facts clearly indicating the cause. The fear may be aroused by word or gesture where the victim is threatened with a gun or knife.

f. **Bank Robbery.** The Federal Bank Robbery Statute (Section 2113, Title 18, U.S. Code) provides, as a penalty for bank robbery, a maximum fine of $5,000 or a maximum sentence of twenty years or both. If, in the course of the robbery, an assault is committed or a person's life is placed in jeopardy by the use of a dangerous weapon, the penalty becomes $10,000 and/or twenty-five years. Penalties are prescribed for burglaries and larcenies committed against certain banking institutions. The statute also provides penalties for knowingly receiving stolen property acquired in a bank robbery, burglary, or larceny. The Federal Bank Robbery Statute applies to any member bank of the Federal Reserve System, member banks of the Federal Deposit Insurance Corporation, and any bank organized and operated under the laws of the United States. The statute also covers federal savings and loan associations and any banking institution insured by the Federal Savings and Loan Corporation.

4. Bank Robbery

For an adequate understanding of the crime of robbery, we shall focus our attention on the robber *par excellence,* the bank robber. The most highly skilled professional criminals concentrate on bank robbery. The reason for this is fairly simple. At one time, the rewards of safe burglary tempted the professional criminal. Before the development of the time lock, an expert burglar could steal a half-million dollars by opening a bank safe. In modern times, the bank has become almost invulnerable because of the time lock, which can be set to jam the bolt mechanism for a period of time during which the vault cannot be opened even by an employee possessing the combination.

The safes of business firms yield little to the burglar in the way of cash since business is carried on by means of checks and securities which are ordinarily not negotiable. Stolen jewelry will realize less than 20 per cent of its true value. Hence, the modern criminal who is in search of the big "score" must resort to bank robbery. "Scores" running into hundreds of thousands are made each year.

5. The Bank Robber

Persons who rob banks cannot be placed in simple categories. They range in background from all walks of life; they may be of any age from eight to sixty; color, creed, and sex do not prescribe boundaries. The most practical division of bank robbers would yield two general classes: individuals and groups.

a. **Individuals.** These are persons who operate singly. He (or she) may be motivated by greed, want, the desire for a thrill, or the need for extreme self-testing. Most commonly he is a person who enters a bank, passes a note to the teller demanding a large amount of cash and informing the teller that he is armed with a pistol or an explosive device. He may be armed or unarmed; since the weapon is concealed, the teller is instructed to make the safe assumption and to surrender conveniently available cash without further questions. Wishing to avoid injury to clients or employees, banks ordinarily issue standing instructions for the teller to concede to the robber's wishes. This policy, in turn, has encouraged robbers in the commission of twenty or more offenses before they have been caught. The robber's confidence is such that he may periodically revisit the same bank and successfully use the same technique for many months.

b. **Groups.** This class consists of criminals whose records include several serious offenses. They operate in small groups of three or four persons. They are serious-minded, fairly competent, and often dangerous. The methods of procedure described in the succeeding paragraphs will give additional insight into the character of the professional bank robber.

6. Patterns

The method of operation of the bank robber varies widely with the individual criminal. The target he selects, for example, may be located in the center of a populous area and protected by all the approved safety devices and measures; or it may be an isolated bank far from the nearest policeman. The bank may never have been previously robbed or it may have been robbed several times within recent years. The preparation given to the robbery may be a matter of months or even years, or the perpetrator may have conceived the plan on the spur of the moment. Despite these wide variations, however, a number of trends are apparent. The following generalizations will provide a rough picture of the typical robber.

a. **Selection of Target.** The small branch bank or savings and loan association is preferred. Larger institutions involve a greater hazard because of the number of employees and customers.

b. **Time.** Wednesday and Friday are favored slightly over the other days. If the job is closely cased, the day selected may be one on which large payroll deliveries are expected. The time of day is selected so that the least number of people will be present. Opening time, lunch hour, and closing hour are preferred. As an example of time selection one should consider the Bank of Manhattan Company Robbery in Queens, New York City, in which $305,243 was lost. Three men escorted a young bank clerk as he left his home in Queens, ushered him at gunpoint into his Ford and drove with him fourteen blocks to his office, one of the thirty-five branch banks of the Bank of Manhattan Company in Queens. They waited on the sidewalk until the manager arrived and showed him their submachine gun. At 8:52 A.M., with all the bank employees accounted for, the bandits entered, herded eleven people into a vault, locking the inner gate with a chain and padlock which they had brought for that purpose. Within eight minutes they had gathered the money. At 9:00 A.M., they quietly drove away with the most money ever taken in a U.S. bank robbery. During the holdup one of the bandits said: "We've been casing this joint for six months." They knew the bank employees' names and faces. They also knew that the vaults contained an extra $200,000 that day to meet local payrolls.

c. **Disguises.** Hoods and masks are increasingly worn. Sunglasses are the most common disguise. Most robbers wear hats or caps, frequently for the purpose of concealing the color of their hair.

d. **Weapons.** In the majority of cases guns are carried; in others they are simulated. Toy guns are used in about 10 per cent of the cases. The weapons are frequently disposed of by throwing from the window of the getaway car, by burying, or by hurling into a body of water. The weapons are not often discharged, the trend being away from unnecessary brutality and murder. Each year, however, the records show a sufficient number of fatalities to discourage foolhardy resistance.

e. **Escape Methods.** The typical bank robber uses a rented or stolen car to make his getaway from the bank and later transfers to his own car. A popular make such as a Ford or Chevrolet is chosen to avoid attracting attention. The robbers may use their own car for a getaway and equip it with stolen license plates, which will be discarded later. It is found that the vehicle and articles left in the vehicle provide the most useful clues in tracing the criminal.

f. **Criminal Group.** The typical robbery is perpetrated by a pair of criminals. Approximately 75 per cent of the robbers have records of previous arrests for crimes such as robbery, burglary, and larceny. In an FBI study of 100 robberies it was found that in the large majority of cases persons from the local area were involved. In seventy-eight of the cases the robbers lived within a radius of approximately 100 miles from the scene of the robbery. In thirty-three of the seventy-eight cases at least one of the robbers resided in the city or town where the crime took place.

7. Modus Operandi of the Professional

Since the criminal type in robbery varies so widely, a narrow selection must be made in treating *modus operandi*. In the description found below the techniques of skilled professional robbers are given. These methods represent "best practice"; they are the product of experience and mature planning. Although this discussion of the methods of operation of robbers is concerned mainly with bank robbery, it will be found that the same techniques are applicable to other forms of this crime.

a. **Fingering the Job.** Professional thieves do not leave the selection of the target to chance or a good guess. Some of their marks (targets) are "dug up," that is, discovered by the criminals themselves. Experience coupled with shrewd observation and surveillance will suggest profitable and practicable targets to the thief. Often, the robbers are tipped off to a target by "small-time" criminals. Pickpockets, gamblers, and ordinary "grifters" will tip off the robber with an agreement for a 10 per cent share in the proceeds. Legitimate business people will also tip off "heist" men. A truck driver or parking lot attendant may finger a truck as a hijack target for a share in the proceeds. A bank manager will tip off a criminal, supplying all the necessary information for the safe and profitable accomplishment of the robbery in order to cover up embezzlements which he has perpetrated. An unscrupulous jeweler will encourage a robbery of his own shop in order to put in an excessive claim with the insurance company.

b. **Casing the Job.** The professional robbers do not attack the bank at random and improvise their tactics to suit the needs of the situation. The mob must equip itself with a plan. The initial step, then, is reconnaissance or "casing." Experience has shown that there are no limits to the extent of the mob's preparation. The mob obtains information on the layout of the bank building; the surrounding terrain; avenues of approach; location and movements of bank personnel; fixed police posts; location of bank guards. One famous bank robber would spend weeks in casing a bank, extending his study even to an examination of the "Bankers' Directory" for information concerning the bank, its officers, and other personnel. Often, the bank robber will employ ruses to gather information concerning the interior of the bank, its operations, and its personnel. The following are a few of the ruses employed:

1) *Loitering.* A member of a mob may simply loiter about a bank in order to obtain information. He may appear to be waiting for someone inside the bank or may stand outside and observe at a distance. This form of casing is, however, likely to draw suspicion.

2) *Feigned Business.* The caser may enter the bank on the pretext of cashing a check, changing large bills, opening an account, or making a small deposit.

3) *Salesman Pretext.* One ingenious bank robber obtained considerable information about a bank in one of the southern states by posing as a salesman for an aluminum screen firm. The vice president of the bank escorted him on a tour of the bank ostensibly for the purpose of surveying the bank's need for screens. The spurious salesman obtained a signed contract for the screens after closing time. He followed the bank official into a vault, pulled out a gun, and obtained $17,000. He was apprehended within five hours after the robbery. It should be noted that this example illustrates an operational technique as well as a method of casing.

c. **The Group.** The "heist mob" is usually a group of three or four experienced criminals. Ordinarily there is no leader or "mastermind." The members of the group act as equals with an authority to which their knowledge and experience entitle them.

d. **Assignments.** Each member of the mob may have his own special activity in which he has acquired experience through previous "jobs." The following are some of the specifically designated functions:

1) **The Wheelman.** The wheelman or driver undertakes to solve all the problems relating to the transportation of the mob from the scene of the stick-up. He must undertake, first, to obtain a car for transportation at the scene. He usually steals this car and provides it with another set of license plates. The car selected is fairly new, inconspicuous, and capable of rapid acceleration. It is not the only car employed in the job. At a distance from the scene, the criminals will shift from the stolen or getaway car to the "front" car, which is owned by one of the mob.

2) **The Rodman.** One person is assigned to the task of gathering and transporting the guns which are to be used. He is usually a good marksman and is expected to specialize in gunplay if the situation demands. Submachine guns are avoided.

3) **Insidemen.** These persons must perform the actual work of the robbery. The rodman is also an inside man, and occasionally the wheelman may be called upon to go inside a building.

e. **Planning.** The details of the robbery are planned with scrupulous attention even to seemingly trivial matters. The wheelman studies the geography of the area, together with its streets and traffic conditions. The getaway route is carefully laid out. The mob assembles at a "meet" shortly before the appointed time for the job. The plan or layout is once again studied in a general briefing. The mob changes clothes if necessary. For example, in a factory district, they would don overalls. The members leave the "meet" separately and go to the mark by separate routes. They gather within a few blocks of the mark and "rod up." They proceed on foot to the bank, the wheelman driving up and parking near the entrance. If it is practicable, the inside men occasionally work with masks on their faces. (Rubber masks were used in the Brink's case.) One of the mob is assigned to do the talking. He speaks evenly and avoids dramatics, since he is the center of attention and most likely to be identified. After obtaining the money, the robbers depart in the getaway car and drive to the "front" car. If they are not being pursued, they shift to the front car. During the journey, they change their clothes and transfer the money to paper bags. Some of the mob take the money and guns in the front car to the place selected for the "meet." The wheelman goes to another part of the city with the getaway car. Sometimes, the front car is changed for a third car.

8. Reactions at the Scene

There are many points of view from which the bank is regarded during a holdup.

a. **Executives.** A decreasing number of executives choose to look upon their bank as a beleagured fortress whose flag, the greenback, must be preserved at whatever cost and whose vaulted heart of gold must be contested by bitter inches. The robber, of course, brings a different philosophy of the situation. He views the banker as an intransigent misanthrope suffering from an overvaluation of his responsibility to the insurance company. He considers himself a just aggressor whom society has grieviously wronged in denying him an access to a reasonable share of its riches.

b. **The Bank Employee** is guided by mixed motives. In his loyalty he is keenly aware of the traditional heroism of fictional and factual bank cashiers. The cinematic *coup de main* may endear him to his superiors and win him the lavish attention of the television cameras. On the other hand, his instinct for clerical order rebels against any procedure as untidy as resistance by physical violence.

c. **Bank Guard.** The special case of the bank guard is difficult to analyze. After years of incredulous expectancy that poor unfortunate may be left helpless in trauma or given over to a panicky self-sacrifice. However, if he is a trained professional or a retired police officer, he may be the only one present whose behavior is intelligent and effective.

d. **Customers.** The state of mind of the customers is ordinarily the least involved. Their concern is usually simple and primal—the preservation of their own invaluable persons. There are, of course, the unpredictable few; but the courageous and the panic-stricken alike can aggravate the danger.

e. **Police.** Apart from all these groups and occupying a middle ground of motives are the police. They are sensible of their responsibilities for the protection of life and property and the apprehension of the criminals, but they prefer the event to be uncomplicated by homicide.

9. Instructions for Employees

a. **During the Robbery.** The behavior of the employees and customers during the robbery should have safety as its objective.

1) The persons present should follow the instructions of the robber. Since the criminals are extremely nervous, an unexpected action on the part of an employee may precipitate gunfire.

2) Employees instructed to hand over money should endeavor to keep the loss of money at a minimum. In other words, while obeying an order to hand over money, they should not volunteer to reach for money not visible to the robbers.

3) The employees should observe the robbers carefully. Physical descriptions, peculiarities of behavior, method of operation, voice, and exact words are invaluable aids to the investigators. If an employee has a view of the street he should note any accomplices standing outside and also try to remember details of the getaway car.

4) When the robbers are leaving, the employees should remain until the danger is removed.

5) Employees should be conscious of the presence of physical evidence and should avoid obliterating evidence such as fingerprints.

b. **After the Robbery.** As soon as the robbers have gone, an employee should put into action the "robbery plan." He should first telephone the police and keep the telephone line open. The following information should be given:

1) The fact that the robbery has occurred.

2) The exact time of the departure of the robbers.

3) The number of robbers.

4) An accurate description of each robber, referring to them as "Robber No. 1," "Robber No. 2," etc.

5) The make, year, color, style and license plate of the getaway car and direction in which it departed.

After giving this information, the employee should keep the line open and monitor the telephone. Another employee should request the customers to remain until the police arrive. If the customers are sufficiently composed, he should take down their names and addresses. Cooperative customers should be requested to write down descriptions of the robbers and their behavior. The customers should be discouraged from comparing notes and endeavoring to arrive at a common denominator in their descriptions. An effort should be made to find witnesses in the street.

10. Investigation

a. **General.** There are several major obstacles to the solution of the crime of robbery. First, there are usually very few traces left behind by the criminals. The actual physical work of robbery as compared with burglary is of such a minor nature that the criminal scarcely leaves any impress on his surroundings. Secondly, the time allotted to the work is of such short duration that the victim is not sufficiently composed to note the exact appearance of the robbers. In addition, the probability of interruption becomes quite small in an operation that occupies the space of only a few minutes. Finally, the violent manner of the robber dismays the victims and prevents civilian cooperation.

Robbery belongs to that category of crimes in which the criminals are perfect strangers. There is ordinarily no one remaining at the scene of the crime who would be suspected. It is seldom that an inside accomplice is employed to provide information concerning the physical layout or the habits of the personnel. The motive of robbery is simple and uncomplicated and hence can yield no clues.

The physical clues, although they should by no means be overlooked, are ordinarily of little value in the original detection of the perpetrators. Their true worth is later realized in the additional proof which they may offer. The solution of a robbery will most often be reached through "information." Intelligent use of stool pigeons and a friendly association with known criminals constitute the most valuable key to the crime. In subsequent arrests for other serious crimes, the detective should closely interrogate the criminal concerning his activities at the time of the robbery in question. The list of daily arrests should be scrutinized for persons who have a robbery conviction in their records. These persons should then be checked against the recorded descriptions of the wanted robbers. If the physical descriptions and the interrogation justify such a measure, the detective should personally check the criminal's story concerning his location, occupation, working hours, friends, and residence during the time of the robbery.

b. **Interrogation.** If the suspect waives his right to be silent, he should be interrogated by a person thoroughly familiar with bank robbery operations. Since the suspect may be a professional bank robber, special techniques of questioning may be required. For example, in questioning such a suspect it may be found useful for the interrogator to refrain from showing his special interest in the robbery actually under investigation. Without in any way violating his rights, the suspect may be permitted to assume that he is being interrogated concerning a different crime. A burglary, or better a homicide (fictitious or factual), which took place at a distant town will serve the purpose. The crime selected should have taken place at the same time as the robbery. The suspect will then feel quite free in establishing his alibi and may even risk an alibi in which he is placed near the scene of the robbery. If he is guilty and somewhat naïve, he may even suggest the names of his confederates as a substantiation of his alibi. The investigator should not reveal his true intent until he has exhausted the possibilities of this line of inquiry. Later, the direct accusation of the true crime should be brought in with the full impact of the existing evidence—eyewitnesses, knowledge of subsequent activities, and other identifying elements. A sudden psychological onset of this sort frequently results in utterly confusing the suspect. He has been picked up for one crime, has presented an alibi for a second, and finds himself maneuvered into a third. The prospect of a confession is now at its brightest.

c. **Interviewing Witnesses.** On receiving a telephoned report of a robbery, the proprietors of the establishment should be immediately instructed to detain all witnesses. When the police arrive, the witnesses should be quietly separated and instructed not to discuss the crime with anyone until they have been interviewed. Each witness should then be individually interviewed concerning the event and the appearance of the participants. This procedure is of great importance since, if the witnesses are permitted to congregate and engage in random conversation, the value of their subsequent descriptions of the criminals will depreciate. Listening to other opinions will dissuade the witness from his original impression. He will be tempted to follow the "party line." His description will then share the consensus and will not have the value of an independent observation. Witnesses should subsequently be taken to the local bureau of identification to look at the photographs of known robbers. If possible, they should also be shown the FBI bank robbery album.

11. Clues and Investigative Techniques

a. **Vehicle.** One of the best tracing clues in the crime of robbery is the getaway vehicle. The amateur may sometimes use his own car. The professional will usually employ a stolen car and switch later to his own car. At other times, the robber may use his own car with a stolen license plate or with no license plates. Quite often, the car has been rented from an agency. As a starting point, the investigator should obtain detailed descriptions of the car from as many witnesses as possible. Naturally, if one of the witnesses noted the license plate number, the investigator is at a marked advantage. The alarm should be sent out immediately with this information. The registration should be obtained as soon as possible from the state bureau of motor vehicles. The list of alarms for stolen cars should be checked both for the license plate and the type of car. Local car rental agencies should be canvassed to determine whether a car answering to the description of the robbery vehicle has been recently rented. The combination of a rented car and a stolen license plate has a strong appeal for the ingenious burglar. In checking the car rental agency, the investigator may further assume that the witnesses have erred in their descriptions of the vehicle and should obtain a list of cars rented since the day preceding the robbery together with the exact times of checking out and returning. The manager of the agency may be able to give a good description of the person renting a car resembling the getaway car.

A robbery which took place in Carlisle, Iowa, offers a good illustration of this latter technique. After holding up the bank and obtaining $4,500, the two robbers were seen departing in a dark green Plymouth with no license plates. The car was going in the direction of Des Moines. The police of that city canvassed car rental agencies. At one agency, it was found that a dark green Plymouth had been checked out at 9:42 A.M. on the day of the robbery and had been returned at 12:15 P.M. The man who rented the car was described by the owner of the agency. Working with this description, the police succeeded in apprehending the criminals.

b. **Latent Prints.** The counters and other furniture touched by the robbers should be processed for latent prints. Occasionally, the robber may handle papers, checks, or currency. These should be processed with silver nitrate. In one recent case, the robber, observing that a bank employee was watching him with great care, picked up some advertising circulars, threw them to the employee, and ordered him to write his name on one of them. The robber placed the signed paper in his pocket. Subsequently, the circulars were processed for latent prints. On one of the circulars a print of value was developed. A search of the FBI Identification Division files yielded a successful comparison. The witnesses were requested to study photographs in the FBI bank robbery album. A positive identification was made with one of the photographs. The criminal in the identified photograph was found to be the possessor of the fingerprint developed on the circular. He was subsequently apprehended and convicted. The getaway car, which is usually recovered shortly after the crime, is an excellent source of fingerprints. The rearview mirror, front doors, and side windows are the most fruitful areas for processing. Each year, one or more robberies are solved by means of a print deposited on the rearview mirror by a robber adjusting it to his sitting height.

c. **Restraining Devices.** In order to restrain the victim or his employees, the robbers frequently tie them up with rope, towels, sheeting, or adhesive tape. The robbers may bring the tying materials or ligatures with them in anticipation of the need or will use the materials at hand when the emergency arises. For example, in a robbery involving the theft of narcotics from a hospital, the criminals, on encountering resistance, may resort to the use of adhesive tape. The persons finding the victim tied up should endeavor to release him without disturbing the knots. A characteristic type of knot may offer a clue to the identity of one of the criminals. Similarly, in removing adhesive, care should be taken to avoid obliterating fingerprints on either side of the tape. In addition to the significance of the knots and the fingerprints, the restraining material may sometimes be traced to its source, if it has been brought to the scene by the criminals. The cord, for example, may have been removed from a Venetian blind. The edge of the adhesive tape may match the end of a roll of tape found on the suspect.

d. **Stolen Property.** The robbers are not always careful in the selection of loot. Money bags, paper bags, and small traveling bags are used to hold the loot. In addition to cash, they may take securities and traveler's checks. The latter are excellent tracing clues. In one recent robbery, the stolen traveler's checks were traced for several months as they were passed by the criminals. The trail led through a number of eastern cities. The investigators were able to construct a pattern from these peregrinations and finally made a shrewd forecast of the next stop in the criminals' itinerary. Plants were staked out in the city and the criminals were apprehended as they were about to cash another traveler's check.

e. **Other Physical Evidence.** Footprints may be left on the bank floor by the robbers if the streets are wet or snowy. A discarded newspaper may provide a clue to the area which they have passed through. The newspaper should, of course, be processed for latent prints. Discarded garments such as gloves, hats, or jackets may bear dry cleaners' marks or tags. A gun or other abandoned weapon may provide a tracing clue after it has been processed for prints.

f. **Voice.** An important part of the *modus operandi* of the crime of robbery is the manner of speech of the criminals. The opening and closing speeches of the robber are highly characteristic. The criminal in his planning has usually determined a set of orders which he will give the victims, e.g., "This is a stick-up, keep your hands down and walk to the back." Some criminals will repeat this without modification at each job. While intimidating his victim, the robber may employ the language of violence and vulgarity that is closest to his fancy and hence is part of his character. It is important, then, for the detective to obtain an exact statement of the language used by the robber.

12. Illustrative Case

The case of "Dashing Dan," the Tunisian immigrant who held up twenty banks in the New York area in three months, illustrates, among other things, the consistency of the robber in his *modus operandi* and the ease with which banks can be robbed in a large city. On June 1, 1970, Raphael Pavia was arrested as he was about to enter his home after having completed his twentieth job. In his possession the FBI agents found $1,910—the exact amount of the last holdup. The authorities had known for some time what the suspect looked like; pictures taken of the robber by hidden cameras during nearly all of the twenty bank holdups had made him one of the most photographed suspects in history. In nearly all of the robberies Dashing Dan used the same methods, handing a note to the teller demanding only large denomination bills. The notes always said the holdup man had a gun pointing toward the teller, but none of the tellers ever saw him holding a gun or any other weapon. On six occasions the tellers denied having large bills, and the robber walked out quietly. When he was not turned down, he always said "thank you" for the money. The holdups all occurred on Mondays, Wednesdays, or Fridays. The suspect was given the name Dashing Dan by the FBI because of his politeness and because of the speed with which he moved from one bank to another on days when a teller turned him down. The FBI in announcing the arrest said it had been brought about "as a direct result of Federal and city police cooperation" and "the assistance of news articles, which have appeared recently publicizing his activities."

13. *Modus Operandi*

In the investigation of the crime or robbery, the *modus operandi* file is of great importance. In the absence of physical clues, the techniques and mannerisms of the robbers are often the most valuable clues to the identity of the robber.

a. **The *Modus Operandi* File.** The robbery index can be arranged profitably along the following lines:

1) *Type of Robbery*

Bank	Gasoline Station
Bank Messenger	Warehouse
Payroll at Premises	Hotels
Payroll Messenger	Dentists and Doctors
Armored Car	Gambling Games
Cab Driver	Residences
Store (with subdivisions according to type of store)	Mugging
	Private Cars
Theater	

2) **Method of Attack**
Threatening
Assault

Binding
Drugging

3) **Weapon**
Mugging
Blackjack
Brass Knuckles

Revolver or Automatic (Specify size and type)

4) **Object**
Money
Clothing

Jewelry
Goods

5) **Vehicle**

6) **Voice and Speech**
(Characteristic orders, threats, or phrases)

7) **Peculiarities**
Takes clothes of victim
Cuts telephone wires

Slashes tires

14. Armored Truck Robbery

Although the robbery of armored trucks can often be classified as a hijacking, the more characteristic features place it in the class of bank robbery. The money itself is quite portable and is removed at the scene or transferred to another vehicle within a short distance. The armored truck, moreover, is never a target of opportunity; its schedule, pattern of deliveries, and security precautions are carefully studied before a detailed plan is drawn up. The large amounts of money carried by armored trucks in receipts or for payrolls make them prime targets for robbery. Two robberies in Long Island City will serve to illustrate a typical *modus operandi*. In each case the truck was captured during a coffee break.

In November, 1969, gunmen held up a Wells Fargo armored car during a meal stop of the guards and escaped with $1.37-million in receipts from the Aqueduct Race Track. The details are similar to those of a robbery which took place two years later, in November, 1971, in which three gunmen, taking advantage of the guards' coffee break, held up an armored car and escaped with over $525,000 in payrolls. Shortly after 6 A.M. two guards went into a diner for coffee during a layover period in their schedule. The third guard remained in the truck. The men had already made payroll deliveries at Kennedy and La Guardia Airports and had to wait for the payroll office of the Bulova Watch Company to open. While one of the two guards paid the check, the other guard went to the truck and banged on the door. As the driver opened the door and the guard entered, three men who had been hiding on the left side of the truck quickly followed him in and hit him with the butt of a gun. At gunpoint the driver was ordered to pull away. The remaining guard emerged from the restaurant in time to see the door close and the truck drive away. The truck was driven two blocks to a nearby expressway, where the money, in sealed sacks, was transferred to two waiting cars. The three gunmen then made their escape.

15. Payroll Messengers

Chain stores, theaters, insurance company branch offices, and similar businesses require messenger protection in transferring their receipts to the bank. Factories and other business establishments with large numbers of employees who are paid in cash request protection in bringing the money from the bank. The term "covering the payroll" is used by the police in referring to both types of protection. With the increased use of paychecks, the latter service is slowly disappearing as a police function. Before the platoons of police are "turned out" from the station house, payroll covering assignments are given to designated patrolmen. In large cities, the demand for payroll coverage far exceeds the capacity of the police force to provide this type of service. Consequently, a considerable number of payrolls are not protected.

The planning of a messenger robbery may be as meticulously detailed as that of a bank holdup. The messenger robbery, in fact, is similar in every respect to the bank job. The payroll or receipt bag is an even more inviting target than the teller's cage. The "take" may run from $100 to $100,000. The crime may be executed in an isolated area or in a crowded street. One successful group of robbers in an Eastern city used the building elevator as the scene of their operations. By obtaining information from a dishonest employee, the robbers can know the exact time and path of the messenger and also the value of the haul. Casing over a period of several weeks will reveal the messenger's routine.

The messenger robbery often yields a higher return than the bank job. In 1945, two bank messengers in California were entrusted with $111,000 for delivery to a local check-cashing agency which provided service for employees of a large manufacturing plant. Two bandits, one dressed as a military policeman, abducted the messengers at gunpoint, removed the money, and left them trussed up.

16. Payroll Protection

The loss of payrolls through robbery is often attributable to carelessness. By taking extra pains and using imagination, company officials can keep payroll losses to a minimum. The money-handling habits of the employees should be periodically reviewed. "Habit" provides the criminal with a timetable. With the assistance of local police a variable system of transporting payrolls to and from the bank should be devised. Most police departments will provide an armed guard for escort purposes. The following points should receive attention in formulating a plan.

a. **Personnel.** The person who is assigned to carry the money should be changed frequently.

b. **Time.** The time of transferring the money should change every day or week, depending on the frequency of transfer of money.

c. **Exit.** Multiple exits should be available.

d. **Route.** The same route to or from the bank should not be used everyday. A set of five or even ten routes can be laid out. If necessary, the route may involve travel in the opposite direction from the true destination in order to confuse the criminal.

e. **Armed Escort.** By arrangement with local police an armed guard can be obtained for each trip. If the guard is delayed, the messenger should wait for his arrival and not venture the journey without him. The escort should not ride or walk with the messenger. In a large crowd he should walk from 10 to 15 feet behind the messenger. In sparsely populated areas this distance should be increased to 50 feet. The escort should be alert for the possibility of the messenger running off with the money, since he is the one with the best opportunity for stealing. As an added precaution the identity of the escort should not be revealed to the messenger. This measure is necessary only when the messenger is not an employee of long standing and the sum of money is quite large.

17. Loan Companies and Savings Associations

These organizations are similar to banks except for the fact that the building is relatively weak in structure and permits a forced entry. Thus, the robbers can enter at night, await the arrival of employees in the morning, and force them to open the safes. In a recent robbery of this type the robbers approached the savings association building from an empty lot in the rear. Using a spread jack they forced apart the bars protecting a window. One robber jimmied open the window, entered, and hid in the toilet. At 8:45 A.M., the manager "opened up" the building, preparatory for business. As he entered the back room, the robber met him with his gun in hand. He ordered the manager to crawl out, below eye level, to the small, burglarproof safe in the front room. The manager opened the safe and handed $2,500 to the robber, who escaped through the rear.

18. Jewelry Stores

The robbery of jewelry stores is usually practiced in large metropolitan shops where the value of the stock may run into the hundreds of thousands of dollars. In the typical jewelry job the robbers dress exceptionally well in order to appear as customers during the first few minutes of the operation. Various ruses are employed. The "gentleman robber" has become popular in recent years. This type of criminal has all the appearances of a wealthy customer. He is fastidious in his tastes and requests the jeweler to show him the best of his stock in a certain line, preferably diamonds. At the opportune moment, when a big "take" is on the trays before him and the road appears relatively clear, the robber displays his gun and takes the jewels.

Other types of bandits use a more direct approach, but still rely on initially gaining the confidence of the salesman. In stores which are not visible from the street, the robbers will avoid all formalities and conduct the operation in the manner of a bank robbery. Methods of detecting jewelry store robbers rely heavily on locating the fence. A market is needed in order for even 20 per cent of the value of the jewelry to be realized. Tips are obtained from jewelers and pawn brokers who recognize the exceptional value of the merchandise and question its origin.

19. Closing-Time Shop Robberies

Chain stores, haberdasheries, druggists, restaurants, and many other kinds of business establishments usually have a fairly large sum of money at hand in the evening, especially on Saturday night. A gang of three robbers may attack a series of these shops in an evening. One of the criminals will remain in the getaway car while the other two proceed to hold up the store. The employees are herded into the back room, the money taken from the cash register, and the bandits disappear. Since the employees have an excellent opportunity to observe the robbers closely and listen to their voices, effective clues can be derived from physical descriptions and the *modus operandi*.

20. Liquor Stores, Gasoline Stations, and Delicatessen Stores

These are three very popular targets for the modern robber. The liquor store usually has several hundred dollars in cash on hand and is attended by only one or two persons. The delicatessen store is a likely objective because of the late hours kept by the employees on Saturday and Sunday nights. This is particularly true in New York City (Manhattan) where periodically there is a wave of robberies of delicatessen stores. Gasoline stations, because of their isolation and all night service, are also obvious targets.

These three targets have been grouped together because they form part of the *modus operandi* of the robber. A criminal will "specialize" in liquor stores alone, for example, on one evening robbing two or three. The apprehension of this type of robber depends upon the likelihood that he will pull the same kind of job in the near future. Thus, the "plant" or "stake-out" is the technique sometimes used by the police. The operation of a stakeout unit is described in Section 28.

21. Bill Collectors

In poor neighborhoods, collectors for insurance, milk, and similar companies are common victims of robbery. The operation takes place in a hallway. Ordinarily, the bill collector has been fingered by someone in the neighborhood who is acquainted with his habits. The robbers are usually strangers to the area. A canvass of the residents may yield a physical description of the criminals and occasionally an identification.

22. Taxi Drivers

Robbery of a cab driver on Saturday nights is still a crime of some proportions. Typically, two robbers enter a cab as passengers, direct the driver to a lonely spot and proceed to rob him of the day's receipts. In other instances the robbers may take the money as soon as they are in the cab. In New York the taxi robbery problem was brought under control by the introduction of bulletproof shields and lock boxes for cash receipts and by the activity of the Police Department's taxi and truck surveillance unit.

In the workings of the unit police officers pose as cab drivers, cruising and picking up fares. One of the tactics employed is the following: One officer will drive while two others, also in civilian clothes, will act as passengers. They will pretend to pay the cabbie and walk a short distance away. The driver will then fake an engine failure and put up the cab's hood. If a mugger makes a move, the two "passengers," who are observing, close in and make the arrest.

23. Robbery of Individuals

The term "individual" is used here to mean a person not at the time representing a business. The form of robbery is a "small time" operation practiced by a criminal wanting the imagination or daring required for the robbery of an establishment. Although the perpetrator may lack the courage for larger endeavors and may be armed with only a blackjack or a knife, he may possess a viciousness and savagery that make him exceedingly dangerous.

a. **Mugging.** The term *mugging* is derived from the assailant's technique of seizing the victim from behind with one arm locked around his neck or head and the other being used to frisk his valuables from him. Muggers may act alone or in concert. They attack men and women. A person, preferably one intoxicated, returning home at night from a social engagement is the ideal victim. The mugger may operate with a female accomplice whose function it is to entice the victim into a building.

1) *The Offense.* Mugging may be described as the robbery of an individual accompanied by an assault. The offense usually takes place indoors—in hallways, elevators, stairways, and apartments. Thus, more than half of the muggings occur outside of the purview of the patrol force. Many of the victims are chronic drunks or men seeking the company of prostitutes or homosexuals. The habits of these persons obviously render them especially vulnerable to the mugger. On the average, the mugger strikes many times before he is arrested, and even when arrested and convicted, he will usually be on the streets again in a relatively short time. Because of an overloaded judiciary system, the desire to avoid a costly and time-consuming trial or deficiencies in the evidence, the defendant is permitted to plead guilty to a lesser offense (plea-bargaining) than

the armed robbery and assault charge for which he was originally arrested. Parole further reduces the time served in prison for an offense. Many offenders are juveniles and are often treated leniently with suspended sentences. Hence, the time served is minimal and there are many repeat offenders.

2) *Plea-Bargaining.* The judiciary and the prosecuting attorney have often been criticized, perhaps unfairly, for the number of repeat offenders preying on the public. A recent study conducted by the Vera Institute of Justice explains in good part the apparent indulgence shown by judges and prosecuting attorneys in plea-bargaining. An arrest-to-disposition examination of fifty-three randomly selected robbery cases showed that fifty-two were plea-bargained or dismissed outright and only twenty-seven went to jail. Of the twenty-seven jailed only eleven were imprisoned for more than a year.

A closer study of the cases, however, indicated that simple logic rather than misplaced magnanimity directed these court decisions. In nineteen of the fifty-three robbery cases the defendant and victim were known to each other, i.e. they were "non-strangers." Robberies by non-strangers have a high clearance rate, since the offender is identified and located by the victim. Convictions, however, are not necessarily forthcoming because of the later reluctance of the victim to press charges. Thus, fifteen out of the nineteen non-stranger arrests resulted in no jail sentence and the few jail sentences were for periods of less than a year.

Of the thirty-four robbery cases not involving a relationship between defendant and victim, i.e. "stranger" robberies, twenty-three resulted in jail sentences of five years or more. The arrests that did not result in jail terms were cases in which the victim failed to testify or proved to have questionable reliability. In some cases the defendant's lack of criminal record suggested judicial clemency.

3) *Investigation.* The investigation of a "stranger" mugging requires prompt action. Ordinarily, the patrol force is more effective in this kind of case. The local police officer has some knowledge of the neighborhood, its inhabitants, and the sources of information. Personal inquiry of possible witnesses and the owners of taverns and restaurants is the most helpful beginning. In the absence of a struggle, few traces may be found at the scene or on the

victim. Since in the mugging of a female the criminal usually puts his hand over the mouth to prevent an outcry, the investigator should examine the palms of suspects for lipstick stains. Sometimes a mugging case can be solved by spectrophotometric comparison of a female victim's lipstick with a red stain removed from the hand of a suspect.

4) *Decoy Units.* The use of a disguised police officer to pose as a potential victim of a mugger has proved a successful technique in an increasing number of cities. The project requires a person experienced in amateur theatricals, including make-up procedures. In larger cities like New York and San Francisco, decoy street crime units are broken down into full-time day and night decoy teams. One male or female officer in each team is designated as the decoy with two to five other members acting as backup. Through the police department's property clerk an impressive array of disguises was made available to the unit. Dressed as clergyman, little old ladies, cabbies, tennis players, bums, and sometimes Santa Claus, these policemen pretend to be innocent bystanders and likely victims in areas of high street crime. In a typical case, a policewoman arrested two men who had tried to rob her as she sat on a park bench, wearing a shabby dress and a gray wig. She was a seemingly helpless decoy, but hidden nearby were several "backup men"—plainclothesmen who were ready to come to her aid. The 250-member New York City unit, which was started in 1971, has long been considered one of the most successful in the country. It has made more than 20,000 arrests since 1971, most of them on felony charges, and 90 per cent of the arrests have resulted in convictions.

b. **Lovers' Lane.** A particularly vicious type of robber is the criminal who selects as his victims couples sitting in parked cars in secluded spots. Quite frequently, after taking the man's money, the robbers will force him to witness the rape of his female companion. These robberies are difficult to solve because of the victim's desire to withhold information and avoid publicity.

c. **Hitchhikers.** Probably the most fruitful of all robbery fields is that of hitchhiking banditry. Indeed, if he is disguised by a military uniform, the robber cannot fail to be successful in soliciting a ride on the highway. The masquerading soldier thumbs a ride, seats himself alongside of the driver, and pulls out a gun. He alights and is picked up by a confederate who is driving nearby on a different road. Alternatively, he may order the driver out of the car and drive to a place near his own vehicle.

d. **Doctors and Dentists.** Professional men such as dentists and doctors are likely subjects for robbery since their offices are open to prospective patients. Selecting a time which will permit him to be the last patient, the robber "sticks up" the dentist and takes whatever money is available. The victim is usually too intelligent to offer resistance but can often give an excellent description of the criminal.

Twenty such robberies were attributed to Martin Nicholosi, a former convict who allegedly gained entry by deceiving dentists into believing he needed root-canal work. In 1975 he was arrested and charged with the armed robbery of more than twenty dentists and physicians in Brooklyn. In the words of Sgt. Emidio Ponzi of the Brooklyn Robbery Squad: "He pulled off a couple of jobs in the offices of physicians where he complained of chest pains. When the coast was clear, he whipped out his revolver and said, 'This is a stickup.' " The robberies had netted the suspect thousands of dollars in money and jewelry over a period of six months.

e. **Residence.** The homes of certain types of wealthy business-men are targets for the robber. The typical victim lives in an area which is on the outskirts of the city without being isolated. Thus, the robber is afforded to some degree the "cover" of a populated neighborhood, and his presence does not attract unusual attention. Often, the owner of the house is professionally engaged in a business which falls somewhat short of the respectable. Income tax evaders who must conceal large sums of money in their houses are representative of this class of victim. The job is usually fingered. The most important lead in a case of this type is frequently the servant. Obviously, former employees should also be investigated. The victim is usually the housewife or the maid, who is tied up with rope or sheeting. Adhesive tape is sometimes used to prevent an outcry. Since the robbers must handle the furniture and other objects in their search for the loot, an examination for latent prints may be profitable.

In house robberies which also involve rape, the crime is usually committed haphazardly without any previously conceived plan. In a recent case of the author's, a single fingerprint developed on the middle of a closet door led to a conviction. The robber forced his way into the apartment by threatening the housewife with a knife. After raping her, he stole some jewelry and money. The robber was described as a small, young man in rough clothes. The area was canvassed within a radius of a mile for errand boys until one answering the description was discovered. Although the victim was doubtful of his identity, having fainted during the assault, the fingerprint on the closet door served to substantiate the suspicion.

f. **Elderly.** One development in the rising crime pattern of New York is the marked increase in the number of assaults and robberies of elderly people. Young men, teen-age boys, and even young women are known to be preying on the elderly. The favorite method of operation is to induce the elderly people to open the apartment door and then, rushing in, to threaten and rob them. Various ruses are used. One team of two men and a young woman employ the following procedure: the young woman informs the elderly person that she has mistakenly received her (or his) mail. When the door is opened, her two male companions rush into the apartment, overpower the elderly person, and remove the valuables.

24. Illustrative Cases

a. **Team Work in Investigation.** One of the most important factors in the success of the bank robber is his ability to move with great speed away from the scene of the crime. In a matter of a few hours he may be many miles from the scene of the crime. The efficiency of the police in apprehending the criminal depends to a great extent on the rapidity and methods used to prevent escape. Since the radius of police operations is quite extensive, different jurisdictions become involved. A successful investigation of a robbery will rely heavily on cooperation between the different law enforcement agencies involved.

In the following case, the solution to two robberies in a large eastern city depended on close cooperation between the FBI and local law enforcement agencies. In the first robbery, two armed men held up the bank at noon and fled with $28,000 in cash. The FBI and the local police department interviewed bank employees, and customers, and street witnesses to obtain descriptions of the criminals and details of their *modus operandi*. The witnesses were shown the FBI bank robbery album and pertinent sections of the local rogues gallery. The suspects selected from the photographs were screened by checking their activities on the day of the robbery.

Ten months later, three armed men held up another bank in the same area and left with $35,000. The FBI and the police repeated their investigation procedure and concluded from the similarity in *modus operandi* that the same criminals were involved in both robberies. The additional information provided by the witnesses enabled the investigators to further narrow down the list of possible suspects. Within a week, the three robbers were apprehended and $33,000 was recovered.

b. **"Phony Guards Get Bank 198G"—May 15, 1968.** At 11:30 A.M., two men wearing the uniforms of Wells Fargo armored car guards walked into a branch of the First National City Bank in Brooklyn. After signing the apparently proper releases, they walked out with $198,000 in bills.

At 2:45 P.M. two other men wearing the uniforms of Wells Fargo armored car guards walked into the same branch bank, and asked for the same $198,000. They were the legitimate Wells Fargo men.

"It was a bewilderment," said Leon Boher, the branch bank manager. "It certainly points up one of our control problems." We didn't even know about it, of course, until the other two fellows showed up."

The bogus guards calmly carried the money in a cloth bag from the bank, while the branch was bustling with business.

The two legitimate Wells Fargo men had to produce their identification cards. A call to the Wells Fargo Armored Car Company confirmed their identification, Mr. Boher said, and the police were summoned.

Mr. Boher said that when the money was given out, "everybody signed what they thought were the right papers, and the money was handed out." It was to be transported to the Federal Reserve Bank in Manhattan.

The two bogus guards were wearing uniforms that were very similar, if not identical, to Wells Fargo uniforms. These, in turn, are similar to New York City police uniforms, except for the Wells Fargo badges. At least eight agencies in New York associated with law enforcement or security wear this same uniform.

It should be noted that the offense involved here is not robbery but simply larceny using false pretenses. Nevertheless, the risk, the target, the daring, and other elements suggest that the perpetrators should be placed in the category of bank robbers.

c. **"Phony Guards Get Bank 93G"—Aug. 16, 1968.** One would assume that the preceding "robbery-by-impersonation" initiated a great deal of follow-up action in the way of notifications, special precautions, identification procedures, and similar barn-door closing activities. Nevertheless, three months later, in Elyria, Ohio, the same trick was used to steal another fortune from a bank. Two men wearing the uniforms of Brink's Inc. walked away from a branch of the Lorain County Savings & Trust Co. with $93,000 intended for the real armored truck guards, who arrived ten minutes later.

The manager of the bank, Owen Workman, said the men picked up the cash, at an outside window of the bank, which is in an enclosed shopping mall. The men were wearing what looked like Brink's uniforms.

d. **The White Helmet.** The Japanese police have reported a robbery more impressive in its expertise than either Britain's Great Train Robbery or America's Brink's Robbery. On Dec. 20, 1968, a young Japanese staged a single-handed robbery of a bank delivery car and escaped with 294 million yen—$817,000. The bank car, an unmarked passenger vehicle, was delivering the money from a downtown bank to the Toshiba Electric Company's plant in Fuchu, a suburb of Tokyo. The money was intended for the year-end bonuses of Toshiba employees. En route to the factory, the car was halted by a motorcycle rider dressed to resemble a Japanese highway patrolman. He wore the white helmet of the Japanese police and the lower part of his face was concealed by a white scarf, a common practice of the motorcycle police in the winter.

The supposed highway patrolman told the four bank employees he was investigating a report that a bomb had been placed in the car. He ordered the four men out of the car and crawled under it. "I've found it," the robber shouted. Smoke gushed forth beneath the vehicle from a smoke bomb ignited by the robber. The four employees drew away from the car in response to the waves of the robber, who then calmly sat down in the driver's seat and drove off.

To date the Japanese police have found no clue to the identity of the robber or the whereabouts of the money. The motorcycle, it was learned, had been stolen a month earlier. The money, for the most part, was in small denominations with serial numbers unrecorded.

e. **The Elevator Bandit.** This man specialized in robbing tenants of luxury Manhattan apartment buildings, pulling as many as forty separate elevator holdups in a space of three months. In some instances he would don a green doorman's uniform and politely greet his victims as he passed them into the elevator where they would be robbed. At other times he would work with a young woman accomplice as the two posed as well-dressed residents. As the elevator rose with the potential victims trapped inside, the man would ask the young woman for "the keys to the apartment" and then reach in her purse and pull out a gun. The Elevator Bandit was finally identified by his victims through mug shots and through an informant's tip. He was observed coming out of a building that had been staked out. He pleaded guilty to eighty-four robberies.

25. Deterrents, Control, and Tactical Measures

The study by the Bureau of Social Science Research on the deterrent value of crime prevention measures indicates that insofar as traditional police "deterrents" (such as maximizing police presence and employing aggressive patrol) are concerned, they are not very effective. Presumed deterrents depend on the perceptions of the robber as to the likelihood and severity of punishment, as well as on his capacity to act rationally, that is, in accordance with his perceptions. Unhappily, those who commit serious crime do not tend to be highly rational; either they do not fear the consequences or else they block out the fear during the commission of the crime. The traditional deterrents, in short, assume a rationality in criminal behavior that is not found in practice.

In discussing bank robbery recommendations were made for the development and improvement of robbery response and apprehension capabilities by cordoning off escape routes and assigning police manpower according to predetermined apprehension plans. A number of cities have developed effective criminal apprehension systems, such as "Operation FIND" in Philadelphia and "Operation Barrier" in Kansas City.

Often communities must develop protective measures suited to their peculiar problems. In New York, for example, the problem of taxicab holdups was solved by equipping cabs with fixed strongboxes for receipts. Other communities have sought to reduce or eliminate the opportunity factor in robberies by requiring exact change, or using scrip systems. The use of inexpensive vaults in commercial establishments and delivery trucks has reduced the vulnerability of these targets.

The following are examples of tactical measures that have been used in some cities:

a. **The Stakeout Unit.** In some cities the off-street robbery rate is sufficiently high to justify a special unit to deal with the robbery of stores—a stakeout unit, i.e., an arrangement for a fixed surveillance of a targeted premises to interdict an attempted robbery. In New York City, for example, where approximately 40,000 in-premises armed robberies occur each year, a stakeout unit was established in 1968 and in four years had conducted 182 such operations, in which 24 armed robbers had been killed, 19 wounded, and 53 arrested. Although these operations had affected only a minute fraction of the robbers, it was thought that news of the events would have a marked deterrent effect. After a critical review of its cost-effectiveness with relation to deterrence, the New York unit has been discontinued. A description of the unit's procedures has been retained, however, since it represents an example of a fixed-surveillance system for store robberies that is applicable to high-probability targets.

1) *Personnel.* The New York Stakeout Unit consists of forty men, four sergeants and one lieutenant. Men selected for this assignment are skilled marksmen, currently trained in combat shooting. They are persons of stable temperament, patience, judgment, and the capacity to take quick decisive action. Ordinarily, a stakeout team consists of two men, but in larger stores, such as supermarkets, a three-man team is required. Instructions are given in tactics, the use of deadly force, and combat shooting. In addition, the unit's activities are evaluated in

detail at monthly meetings. Because of the nature of the task, work tours are limited to five hours. Usually the man at the viewing spot is spelled in thirty-minute periods.

2) *Locations.* On receiving a request for a stakeout, a supervisor should examine the premises to determine whether the physical layout is suitable for such an operation. The store should offer facilities for concealment of the stakeout team. A simple partition or a curtain is a minimum. If the layout of the store does not permit safe firing (i.e., an exchange of fire under the anticipated circumstances that would not entail any special hazards to store personnel, customers, or street pedestrians), the supervisor should decide against an interior stakeout plan. If a decision is made in favor of a stakeout, the storeowner or manager should be briefed in the essentials of the operation. An arrangement should be made for viewing the front area from a concealed position. In a typical setup, such as a liquor store, viewing can be arranged by hanging a see-through mirror in front of a hole cut out of the partition. The stakeout team can thus remain in the rear stockroom while maintaining a full view of the store. A transmitter should be placed near the cash register so that the team can hear what is going on. This is necessary because some robbers speak so softly that a robbery can take place with literally no one aware of it but the man handing over the money and the robber.

3) *Tactics.* The layout of the store and the immediate neighborhood should be studied. Fields of possible gunfire should be plotted. Contingency plans should be drawn up according to the positions that may be occupied by the store owner or the clerk, or in the event a customer enters the store while the robbery is in progress. Consideration should be given to paths of fire which may include pedestrians on the street. A guiding principle in determining tactics should be the avoidance of any great danger to innocent bystanders. Escape routes, both on-foot and vehicle, should be studied, since the robber may escape for any one of a number of reasons. The unpredictable must be taken into account. The proprietor may accidentally, in a mixture of fear and surprise, reveal the fact of the stakeout and even the whereabouts of the concealed policemen. In short, the stakeout team must anticipate and visualize the possible outcomes, formulating a response, either

positive or negative, and thereby minimizing the number of chance or unanticipated happenings.

b. **Anticrime Units.** Some cities have found an effective response to the threat of muggers in the establishment of special units of undercover men who pretend to be innocent bystanders and likely victims in areas of high street crime. A city-wide analysis of street crime patterns is first drawn up. Whenever an unacceptable pattern is discerned, an effort is made to saturate the area with anticrime personnel. A plainclothes patrol of this nature is considered more efficient in producing arrests than uniformed patrolmen on post. The use of the decoy unit is the principle tactic employed (p. 440).

c. **Electronic Stakeouts.** The improved capabilities of small transmitters and receivers has led to their extensive tactical use in robbery prevention and robber apprehension. Philadelphia's Tac II system is an excellent example of a wireless alarm system adapted to this purpose. It consists of a base receiver with the capacity of receiving electronic signals from as many as 20 miniature transmitters. A bank or store in a high robbery area is selected to house the base station receiver, which is manned by two trained stakeout policemen. A series of stores or businesses in the nearby area that are probable targets is then selected to have individual transmitters and activators placed in them. To activate a Tac II unit, any action such as lifting a particular object or opening a specific drawer can be arranged to trip the alarm. The stakeout receives the signal and takes action.

ADDITIONAL READING

Bellemin-Noel, J.: Combatting Armed Attacks on Financial Establishments. 31 *International Criminal Police Review*, 296, 1976.

Carlson, E. R.: Hostage Negotiation Situations. 25 *Law and Order*, 7, 1977.

Conklin, J. E.: *Robbery and the Criminal Justice System.* Philadelphia, Lippincott, 1972.

Daniels, M. R.: The Police Role in the Bank Protection Act of 1968. 40 *FBI Law Enforcement Bulletin*, 6, 1971.

Dunn, C. S.: *The Patterns of Robbery Characteristics and their Occurrence among Social Areas.* Washington, D.C.: U.S. Government Printing Office, 1976.

Einstadter, W.J.: The Social Organization of Armed Robbery. 17 *Social Problems*, 64, 1969.

Feeney, F. (Ed.): *Prevention and Control of Robbery*, 5 vols. Davis, University of California Center on Administration of Criminal Justice, 1973.

Lamson, P.A.: A Concentrated Robbery Reduction Program. 40 *FBI Law Enforcement Bulletin*, 12, 1971.

Macdonald, J.M. and Brannan, C.D.: The Investigation of Robbery. 4 *Police Chief*, 1, 1974.

Maher, G.F.: *Hostage: A Police Approach to a Contemporary Crisis.* Springfield, Ill.: Thomas, 1977.

McCormick, M.: *Robbery Prevention: What the Literature Reveals.* La Jolla, Calif.: Western Behavioral Science Institute, 1974.

Ozenne, T.: The Economics of Bank Robbery. 3 *Journal of Legal Studies*, 19, 1974.

Sagalyn, A.: *The Crime of Robbery in the United States.* Washington, D.C.: U.S. Government Printing Office, 1971.

Ward, R.H. and Ward, T. J.: *Police Robbery Control Manual.* Washington, D.C.: Law Enforcement Assistance Administration, 1975.

Chapter 23

TRUCK ROBBERY

1. Introduction

ONE OF the most interesting aspects of modern crime is the renaissance of highway robbery in the form of hijacking. Caravans, stagecoaches, merchant ships, beer trucks, and other conveyances have in their time been subjected to the depredations of highwaymen. The modern hijacker has, however, surpassed his predecessors in both perfection of technique and amount of earnings. In a single cargo theft several hundred thousand dollars worth of marketable merchandise is often available to him. These impressive losses are made possible by the great capacity of the modern trailer truck. The loss usually takes the form of consumer goods of an easily disposable nature, such as liquor, cigarettes, lingerie, stockings, television sets, refrigerators, washing machines, and so forth. Thus, without any exceptional risk, the hijacker may realize a good deal more in one such venture than he would in the typical bank robbery. Often, it is easier to steal a trailer truck than a bicycle. The success of this type of operation depends upon the popular assumption that "nobody would steal anything that big."

The hijacking gang has no fixed form of composition. It may be a loose alliance formed for a particular job or it may be an established gang of considerable size. Ordinarily, the hijacking gang is a well-organized group of relatively competent criminals. The hijacking of a truck that has been left for a few hours by the driver is an act that requires little daring or forethought. This is merely a form of larceny. Hijacking in its true sense is highway robbery and, hence, is a much more complicated task.

Hijacking of this latter type consists of a series of integrated operations that require skillful planning, precise timing, and bold execution. Various skills are required: fingermen, spotters, gunmen, drivers, jumpers, drop men, and fences. At its highest level of organization, the hijack gang works in the following fashion: the fingerman, usually a dishonest employee of the trucking firm, informs the gang of an impending shipment—the nature of the merchandise, the truck, its itinerary, schedule, make, plates, and so forth. Where a spotter is employed, the fingerman will point out the truck to him. The gunmen stop the truck at a chosen point and either remove the driver to their car or bind and gag him in the back of the truck.

The goods are sometimes removed from the truck by backing another truck against it and shifting the load. At other times, the truck is driven directly to a garage or warehouse and unloaded there. The merchandise is placed in the hands of the fence, who has previously made arrangements for its sale and disposal.

An elaborate procedure is ordinarily required for trucks traveling long distances over main highways. In the city, more direct methods may be employed. The truck is simply stolen in the driver's absence, while he is eating, making a delivery, or drawn away on a ruse. Very often the trucks are left by the driver with the key somewhere in the cab, even in the ignition. This carelessness is in great part attributable to the knowledge that the truck is insured. The indifference of various types of employees to the protection of insured merchandise has led to thefts remarkably simple in execution. In one case, a truck containing $50,000 worth of merchandise was unloaded at night at a parking lot in the heart of a large city.

2. Trucking Procedure

For a systematic inquiry into a hijacking or a theft from a truck line the investigator should be familiar with the procedure normally used in documenting, loading, shipping, and unloading a shipment by motor truck. The following list of steps will provide a number of check points in tracing a shipment. It is assumed that a carton of clothing is being shipped from A company in Chicago to B company in Philadelphia.

a. **Packager.** At the shipper's the goods are carefully packed in four fiberboard containers which are then steel strapped. The name and addresses of B company are stenciled on each carton. The order number is also inscribed.

b. **The Traffic Manager.** A company prepares a bill of lading in triplicate, describing the shipment and giving the order number.

c. **The Shipping Clerk.** The shipping clerk of A company calls the trucking company requesting that they make a pickup.

d. **The Dispatcher.** The dispatcher of the trucking company orders one of the drivers in the neighborhood to make the pickup.

e. **The City Pickup Driver.** The driver makes the pickup after first checking the packaging and stenciling of the cartons. He then proceeds to the motor freight terminal. Best practice requires him to close and lock a canvas-covered steel folding gate after each pickup.

f. **Freight Terminal Action.** At the terminal the shipment is unloaded on a platform. A manifest is made up for the numbered trailer to which the cartons are assigned. The traffic and billing department of the transportation company receives the bill of lading. A waybill number is assigned to the shipment.

g. **Terminal Loading.** The shipment is placed on the trailer, the doors are closed and a transportation company lock is affixed together with a seal, the number of which is recorded by the dispatcher. The seal number is also placed on the manifest and the road driver's dispatch order.

h. **Alarm System.** The trailer is assigned to a numbered tractor. Ideally it is equipped with an automatic alarm which will sound a warning if it is disturbed at any time while in transit or unattended. The alarm is set by the dispatcher at the terminal by means of a master key. It can now be turned off only by the dispatcher in Philadelphia with his master key.

i. **Drivers.** The driver receives instruction from the dispatcher. He is to be relieved by two other drivers in relay along the route. In compliance with the Interstate Commerce Commission's regulations, he maintains a driver's log showing the times of driving and rest. As an additional check some tractors are equipped with an instrument that records automatically the periods of driving and stopping as well as recording the speed of the vehicle.

j. **Arrival.** On reaching the Philadelphia terminal the driver checks in with the dispatcher and gives him a report of the trip, a copy of the logs, and a pouch containing bills and instructions concerning the load. The shipment is unloaded and checked against the manifest.

k. **City Delivery.** The cartons are checked and loaded into a city delivery truck, which in the course of its stops arrives at the clothing warehouse. The doors are unlocked and the cartons placed on the platform where they are checked by a receiving clerk who signs the waybill. He may mark the cartons with the date and time of delivery and a symbol to indicate that they were in acceptable condition.

3. The Hijack Mob

Since organized hijacking is a fairly complicated procedure, each crime will present certain structural weaknesses, namely, the operations of the personnel. These will be dealt with in the order of probability:

a. **The Fingerman.** This is probably the weakest point in the plan. Where a series of robberies has been perpetrated against a single trucking concern, the employees of the company who have access to the necessary information should be thoroughly investigated. A fingerman supplies information on the truck marked for hijacking. He gives the gang a description of the truck and its cargo, the license plate number, and road route, time of departure, schedule of stops, and time of arrival. At the selected time of hijacking he surreptitiously points out the target truck to a spotter.

b. **The Fence.** A hijacker without a reliable fence is at a serious disadvantage. In most cases, the fence plays a major role in the success of the crime. He can be traced either directly, by means of the known criminal file, or indirectly, by means of the merchandise. A complete description of the merchandise should be obtained for this purpose. The usual survey of pawn shops and secondhand dealers should be made. Many fences specialize in a particular type of merchandise such as textiles, liquor, or cigarettes. They maintain warehouses, act as wholesalers, and sell merchandise in small lots to legitimate retail outlets. Frequently the retailers are not aware that the goods which they are receiving have been stolen. Some fences will handle all types of merchandise. A notorious example of this was Arthur "Fish" Johnson of Chicago, who was imprisoned for receiving stolen property. When Johnson's premises were searched, the police found $500,000 worth of merchandise of varied types: automobile seat covers, cameras, outboard motors, bales of sponges, clothing, and so forth. Johnson's hijacking connections operated in all parts of the country. They received 40 percent of the retail price for merchandise, if they were regular suppliers. Occasional suppliers received from 10 to 25 per cent. Johnson also maintained his own retail store, which was located at the back of a confectionery shop. Here he sold his goods for 50 per cent of the legitimate retail price.

c. **The Spotter.** In a well-organized mob the spotter has several duties. His first locates and points out the truck for the hijack mob. After the truck is stolen he follows it in his car. At convenient intervals he stops at a telephone booth and communicates with the headquarters of the mob to learn if the theft has been discovered by the police. If the alarm has been sent out and the situation appears grave, he overtakes the truck and instructs the driver to abandon it. Otherwise, he follows the truck to the "drop," a warehouse, garage, or, in the country, a barn.

d. **The Driver.** The driver of the truck should be the first suspect, both because of his availability and because of the frequency with which drivers, as a matter of police experience, are discovered in collusion with hijack mobs. The lie detector can be used to excellent advantage to determine whether the driver possesses any guilty knowledge. The direction toward which subsequent investigative efforts can be pointed will depend on the outcome of the deception test. If the results of the test are positive in the sense of indicating that the driver was in collusion with the hijack mob, weeks of fruitless investigation can be avoided. If the lie detector is not in recommended use by the law enforcement agency having jurisdiction, the investigator must rely heavily on the interrogation of the driver.

1) *Investigation of the Driver.* A background investigation of the driver should be made to obtain the following information:

a) Does the driver have a police record?

b) Who are his associates?

c) Do they have police records?

d) What are the driver's personal habits? Has his style of living changed? Is it logically compatible with his income?

e) Was he a "shaper?" That is, was he a driver who takes odd jobs in place of the regular driver?

f) Was it customary to entrust cargo of this value or a tractor of this condition and quality to such a driver?

g) Did he draw his expense money at the beginning of the trips?

h) Did he fill out the tax withholding slip?

i) Did he report to the shop steward to have his union card checked?

j) Did he ask for the route? Where to stop for gas? The terminal address?

k) Was the distance he had traveled at the time of the holdup consistent with the schedule?

l) Were the stops that he made the usual ones for a driver on that route?

2) *Interviewing the Driver.* In questioning the driver, great emphasis should be placed on the details of his journey. By going back and forth over this itinerary, it may be possible to develop inconsistencies in his story. The approximate time elapsing at each rest stop should be ascertained. Whom did he speak to at gas or rest stops? Did he make any telephone calls? If he spoke to any other driver, an effort should be made to ascertain the identity of the driver, since such a person could have been used to communicate with the gang. The second phase of the interrogation of the driver should deal with the *modus operandi* of the hijackers. The information desired is listed below under the appropriate heading. In the third phase of the interrogation, the investigator should seek to develop information concerning the driver's activities on the days preceding the crime. Where did he go? At what time? To whom did he speak? What telephone calls did he make? Much of this information can be later checked for possible inconsistencies.

3) *Itinerary.* The investigator should interview personnel at rest stops along the route. Times of arrival and departure, conversations, telephone calls, and similar information should be developed.

e. **Organized Crime.** The requirements of planning, teamwork, coordination, and resources suggest that we should expect to find organized crime as a major participant in hijacking activity. In New York City, for example, social clubs have been observed by the police to be focal points for organized crime's truck hijacking network. The clubs serve as recruiting stations and testing grounds for future members of the organization. A series of successful hijackings can provide the stepping stones whereby a man on the fringes of organized crime can move closer to the inner network and up in the scale of responsibility. Most of the hijackings are "steal-to-order" jobs. A target truck is selected because of the existing market need for the cargo, with due consideration for the truck's vulnerability. Often the hijacked loads are sold even before they are stolen. During a recent gasoline shortage, for example, there was a wave of gasoline truck hijackings.

Police investigators believe that organized crime has spotters throughout the trucking industry who may be drivers or simply have access to truck yards. The information is conveyed at social clubs to sources with ties in the upper echelons of organized crime, where contact is made with a prospective buyer. Often legitimate retailers are buyers who are looking for a bargain and prefer not to ask questions. The expenses for running the hijack operation are not great since the hired men are paid between $500 and $1,000, depending on whether they are drivers or gunmen. The hijacked truck is unloaded by men who are paid $150 for a few hours work. The cost of a drop, usually a warehouse where the hijacked cargo is stored until it is resold, is about $300 a day. Other expenses include the spotter's fee and a sum set aside for legal fees in the event the hijacker is caught.

4. Charges in Hijacking

One of the difficulties to be met in the prosecution of hijacking is in the nature of the charge to be brought. Since the state penal code does not ordinarily have a formal charge of hijacking, the arresting officer must consider related offenses such as kidnapping, robbery, or possession of a gun. Most commonly the offender is charged with criminal possession of stolen property. The officer must then concern himself with proving that the cargo—cigarettes or jewelry, for example—was actually stolen and that the offender knew that the property in his possession was stolen. Whatever the charge brought, it is of great importance for the investigator in his interviews to note and record the actions of each offender during the hijacking.

5. *Modus Operandi*

Since hijacking is a specialized form of crime, the method of operation files will be helpful. The professional hijacker, since he is after a specific truck, can select the place where he will strike and knows the approximate time of arrival. The place is usually one at which the truck must slow down or stop, such as a road feeding into a main highway. Ordinarily, the hijacker climbs on the running board with his gun drawn and then enters the truck at the seat next to the driver. It is common practice for the hijacker to demand the driver's chauffeur's license. The driver is then informed that his family will be in danger if he gives the police a description of the perpetrator. The threat is real since the hijacker now has the home address of the driver. The method of operation of the hijack group will be developed through an interview with the driver. The questioning should be detailed and reported several times to check for inconsistencies. Queries such as the following should be used:

a. How many men were there?

b. What were their appearance and dress? (A physical description should be obtained for each member of the gang.)

c. Who first spoke and what did he say?

d. What other statements were made?

e. What were the movements of each individual?

f. What orders did they give you?

The questions should then go over the individual actions of each of the hijackers, their conversation and final orders. A full description of their vehicle should be obtained. Other points of the *modus operandi* are the following:

g. **Nature of the Goods.** Liquor, cigarettes, nylon stockings, and other forms of cargo attract particular gangs who have established methods of profitable disposal of such goods.

h. **Technique.** Is it larceny or robbery? How was the ignition jumped? Was the key in the cab?

i. **Disposal.** Was the truck unloaded in a garage or was the load shifted to a switch truck?

j. **Ruse Employed.** Among the common ruses are the following:

1) An independent driver drops a legitimate load in the terminal and then uses the tractor to steal another load.

2) A fake solicitor accosts the driver in the street and hurriedly instructs him to pick up a load in a congested area, thus inducing him to abandon the truck at a distance from the address given. While the driver is in the building the truck is stolen.

3) A spotter follows a delivery truck as it makes its rounds. When the driver enters a store to make a delivery, the spotter telephones him from a pay booth. By impersonating the dispatcher of the trucking firm, he instructs the driver to make a pickup on the fifth or sixth floor of a loft building in the neighborhood. The truck is stolen as soon as the driver enters the loft building.

4) A truck driver appears at the delivery gate of a manufacturing company. Posing as an employee of a trucking firm, he shows orders to pick up one of the company's trucks that had been left there previously to be loaded. After signing receipts he departs with the truck.

6. Examination of the Vehicle

Since the vehicle is usually driven away by the hijackers, it may contain physical evidence. The following are the types of evidence that are sometimes found:

a. **Fingerprints.** Rearview and side mirrors; windows; cab door ledges and handles areas, side and rear doors. The most likely places for finding prints of value are the areas adjacent to the sills of the cab doors.

b. **Soil on Clutch Pedal.** Soil from the shoe of a criminal driver may be characteristic and can be compared with soil found on the shoe of suspects.

c. **Used Matches.** These may fit match booklets of suspects.

d. **Match Booklets.** These may bear inscriptions of local

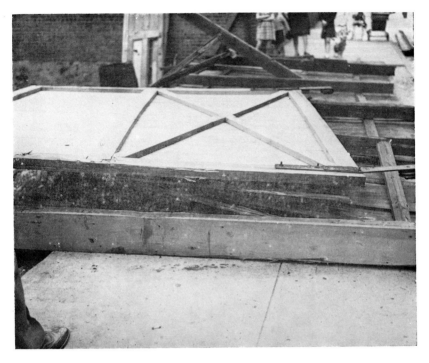

Figure 14a. The fence shown here was pushed over by a hijacked truck while it was being backed out of the yard by an inexperienced driver.

restaurants, taverns, or shops and thus indicate a locality the gang had visited.

e. **Heel and Shoe Prints.** Torn cartons may be found in the body of the truck which bear heel and shoe prints made by the criminals in climbing over the merchandise.

f. **Distance Traveled.** By estimating the distance which the truck has traveled, a clue can be obtained in regard to the neighborhood of the "drop." The odometer reading can be taken and compared with the mileage recorded when the tank was last filled with gas. The amount of gasoline in the truck is a good indication of the upper limit of the radius of operation.

g. **Top of Cab.** An examination of the top of the cab may reveal scratches, paint, or tar particles. These clues are acquired when the truck enters a garage or other "drop" in which the entrance ceiling is

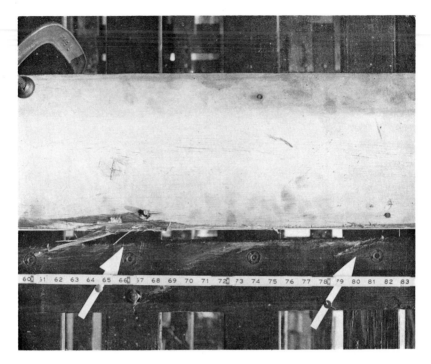

Figure 14b. The white arrows indicate the significant points of correspondence between the damaged board and the scraped truck.

too low. Suspected drops can then be examined for similar traces. If a side of the truck is freshly damaged or scraped, it can be expected that a side of the entrance of the drop bears exchange traces.

h. **Tires.** The truck tires sometimes pick up characteristic traces such as dirt, rock, clay, or similar material. These traces are an indication of the terrain over which the truck traveled when it was driven off the road to the drop. They should be carefully scraped out and preserved for comparison.

i. **Unloading Time.** An estimate of the time required for unloading the truck should be obtained with the assistance of an experienced truckman. The element of time elapsed in the hijacking operations assists in determining the radius of the area in which to search for the "drop."

Figure 14c. A board from the edge of the fence which came in contact with the side of the truck.

7. Informants

A hijacking job is not undertaken haphazardly. It is often the work of highly trained personnel. In addition the mob must be associated with a fence and perhaps with other specialists. Because of the interdependence of the criminals the probability of obtaining "information" is quite high. Consequently the detective should rely heavily on his informants in a case of this nature. Garage workers, warehouse employees, gas station attendants, and former criminals are the most likely sources of information.

8. Preventive Measures

The following is a partial list of measures that have been found helpful in the prevention of hijacking and cargo theft:

a. **Law Enforcement Agencies.** An impressive array of public and private agencies has joined forces in the war against hijackers. At the federal level, the Department of Transportation has established a Division of Transportation Security. The FBI, of course, regards hijacking as one of its special problems. If goods borne by truck are consigned to another state, their theft becomes a federal matter. The local law enforcement agencies benefit by the concurrent jurisdiction, since the FBI lends its forces and facilities to the search and monitors the investigation where several states are involved. Large municipal police departments have organized special squads or details of detectives for this work. Insurance companies and trucking associations have also taken special measures for dealing with hijacking. Notable among these is the Trucking Industry Committee on Theft and Hijacking (TICOTH) of the American Trucking Associations. Various other security councils and security committees of state and city motor truck associations are available for assistance in hijacking and theft problems.

In Philadelphia, for example, a theft-prevention bureau has been set up for the local chapter of the Pennsylvania Motor Truck Association. Armed guards are placed to watch the busiest terminals; unmarked cars equipped with radio maintain a night patrol; and known fences are kept under surveillance. Associated Transport, the largest trucking concern in the United States, has arranged for armed guards to follow valuable cargo. The organization maintains hundreds of miles of leased telephone lines for transmitting to the police instantaneous reports of the occurrence of a hijacking.

b. **Surveillance.** In New York the Safe, Loft, and Truck Squad spends a good deal of its time investigating hijack complaints, interviewing drivers, and tracing stolen merchandise. Some of the men are assigned to prevention work. This team practices "scientific selection" or "targeting" with the aim of identifying persons with possible ties to organized crime who may participate in hijacking. A target might be a person with a record of truck robbery who has no steady employment and who is living beyond his ostensible means. The targeted person is kept under surveillance until an attempt is made to hijack a truck. A surveillance operation of this kind recently led the team to a hijacked truck containing $750,000 worth of tin ingots and to the arrest of six men.

c. **Protective Systems.** Companies such as Babaco Alarm Systems, Inc. provide systems for protection against package thefts, truckload losses, and hijackings. The following are representative:

1) **Anti-theft Protection.** In the one-key control alarm system the truck's ignition lock is superseded by a lock which is keyed the same as the alarm lock. One key operates the truck and the alarm on the cargo compartment, which is *always on* even while the truck is in motion. With the ignition off a *Parker* alarm is set to detect unauthorized movement of the vehicle. The driver cannot remove the alarm key from the body lock while the alarm is off. After loading or unloading he must close the doors and turn the alarm on again to regain possession of the ignition key.

2) **Anti-hijacking Devices.** A *sealed cab ignition immobilizer* is effective against hijacking. The alarm on the cab doors is *always on* and is set by the dispatcher when the vehicle leaves the trucking terminal. A duplicate of the key is retained at the point of destination so that the alarm can be turned off when the driver arrives. Any opening of the cab doors (even by the driver) while the vehicle is en route will result in immediate stalling of the motor. The truck cannot be started again until such time as someone from management arrives at the scene with the alarm key. Modifications of this system are available to suit varied stopping schedules.

3) **Trailer Protection.** A self-powered unit can be installed to provide a siren warning signal if the cargo doors are opened or if the trailer is moved. Babaco features a dual control arrangement: a *Parker* device to protect against door-opening and unauthorized movement and a *sealed load* unit to protect the doors between terminals and warehouses. The driver has no control over the *sealed load* lock.

4) **Movement Tracers.** A miniature transmitter can be installed in the truck and trailer to emit a reasonably powerful signal and thus permit tracing and pursuit by a vehicle equipped with an appropriate receiver. Another useful device is the so-called Service Recorder, which can be used (after the vehicle has been recovered) to check the movements of a vehicle that has been hijacked. By means of a pendulum mechanism, this instrument records the time

periods during which the vehicle is in motion. By examining the chart, the time at which the truck was stationary or moving can be determined. The driver's account of his movements can be verified and some useful knowledge concerning the hijacker's operation can be deduced.

d. **Procedural and Other Measures.** The following are some of the recommendations that have been made to motor carriers to reduce the losses from thefts and shortages:

1) *Hijacking.*

a) STRICT SUPERVISION of personnel. Careful screening of job applicants by comprehensive background checks.

b) IMPOSITION OF PENALTIES for leaving the key in the cab.

c) STRICT RULES to prevent drivers from leaving trucks anywhere except in designated protected areas.

d) "ROLLING PLANTS" in areas frequented by hijackers. This measure is simply a plainclothes radio motor patrol. Additional patrols are required on weekends, when hijackings are more frequent.

e) MARKING THE TOP of the metal container with reflective paint so that it can be readily identified from the air in the event of a helicopter pursuit.

2) *Shortages and Theft.* The control of losses from shortages and theft is initially an internal problem. The following are the basic recommendations for this purpose:

a) ACCOUNTABILITY. Institute a program requiring a count of each shipment each time it is handled, from receipt to delivery. Insist that each employee who handles a shipment sign his name or his initials certifying the count.

b) CARD FILES. Maintain a card file on the shipper, consignee, product, and persons handling the freight up to the point where the shortage was noted. Review the accumulation of these shortage cards at one-month, two-month, three-month, and six-month intervals for patterns. The results of the previous steps will suggest problem areas and point to corrective measures within the carrier's control.

c) EMPLOYEE ASSISTANCE. Seek the help of the employees by soliciting information on stolen cargo and loopholes in the operating system. Establish and advertise the phone number of a responsible company official to receive calls from employees who may want (on an anonymous basis) to advise management of operational defects and *soft spots* in the system.

d) PLANT SECURITY. A survey of the physical installation should be made to check the adequacy of the lighting, fencing, and so forth.

e) REPORT LOSSES. Each theft or suspected theft should be reported to all law enforcement agencies having jurisdiction. This will establish a complaint history, thus justifying the future assignment of investigators to cargo thefts in the areas in which losses are occurring.

f) CAUSES OF CARGO THEFT. An informed and effective response to cargo theft should be based on a general understanding of certain elementary facts about cargo theft:

(1) *Circumstances.* For all transportation modes except rail, 85 per cent of cargo theft losses occur at terminal locations during normal operating hours in less than carload quantities and involve persons and vehicles authorized by management to be on the facility premises.

(2) *Commodities.* Thirteen commodity categories account for 90 percent of total theft losses. These are items with "instant" marketability.

(3) *Collusion.* Most cargo offenses are perpetrated by one or two employees working in concert with an outside buying source—in some cases the very retailers being serviced by the victim trucking firm. Cargo thefts are, for the most part, collusive acts which require employee assistance to achieve success.

9. Illustrative Case

The following case, which was investigated by the FBI, illustrates a number of useful techniques. When the abandoned truck was found in Baltimore, an empty bottle and two chewing gum wrappers were discovered in the cab. The side seal of one of the cargo doors was broken. An experienced truckman estimated the unloading time at forty-five minutes. The gasoline remaining in the tank was measured and the truck was driven back to the terminal, a distance of 5.6 miles. To refill the tank four and a half gallons were required.

Since the truck averaged four miles to a gallon, it was estimated that it had been driven 12.4 miles in addition to the 5.6 miles required to return to the terminal. The truck had departed from the terminal at 10:30 P.M. and had been abandoned at 12:15 A.M. It was concluded that the truck could not have traveled beyond the environs of Baltimore. Thus the search area was conveniently restricted.

The agents found that the missing driver, Ralph Williams, was relatively unknown. He was a "shaper," taking work where he could find it. Thus it was surprising that he had been assigned to Tractor 275, a vehicle recently turned out of the shop and loaded with a valuable cargo. A regular man had been passed up for the shaper. Although the shaper had drawn six dollars for expenses and filled out a tax withholding slip, he had not reported to the shop steward to have his union card checked.

By examining the handwriting on the tax withholding slip and comparing it with handwriting in the FBI files, the agents discovered that the missing driver was Edward R. Linthicum, a criminal who had served seven terms for embezzlement and fraud. The attention of the agents was now turned to the dispatcher, John C. Road, who had hired Linthicum. Road stated that Linthicum had applied by phone and had not been investigated. Although a new driver, he had not asked for the route, the address of the New York terminal, or the places for obtaining gas.

Linthicum was captured in New Jersey. He confessed to the larceny and attributed the plan to William N. Bedsworth, an assistant agent of the freight drivers' union. Bedsworth had planned the hijacking and coordinated with Road. They had realized $12,000 on the cargo, of which $3,750 each went to Bedsworth and Linthicum with only $880 going to Road. Seven other persons had participated in the conspiracy and had shared in the profits. Among them were a druggist, a grocer, a war-plant worker, and a contractor, a brother of a trucking company official, whose home had been used as the drop. Of the ten persons involved only Linthicum was a professional criminal.

ADDITIONAL READING

Clyne, P.: *An Anatomy of Skyjacking.* London, Abelard-Schumann, 1973.

Cooke, M.: Looking Ahead: Freight Theft Prevention. 8 *Security World*, 93, 1971.

Dunley, R.J.: Protecting Commercial Vehicles and Their Loads Against Theft. 16 *Security Gazette*, 4, 1974.

Evans, A.E.: Report on Aircraft Hijacking in the United States Law and Practice. 10 *Criminal Law Bulletin*, 589, 1974.

Fraser, G.: *Modern Transportation and International Crime.* Springfield, Ill.: Thomas, 1970.

Keller, E.J.: Truck Hijacking. 22 *Law and Order*, 4, 1974.

Chapter 24

FORGERY

1. Introduction

" IT WAS wonderful what could be done with a piece of paper."
These words are attributed to Ivar Kreuger, a remarkably
clever manipulator of securities, whose forgeries at one time
threatened the stability of international finance. The words are
unfortunately true today as they have been for hundreds of years.
Forgery, as we know it today, the alteration of documents that
impose a financial obligation, dates from the days of the merchants
who first instituted the procedure of transferring money by means of
a piece of paper. This measure, taken to thwart the robbers who
harried the highway shipments of gold and silver, introduced a new
and even greater evil than that which it was intended to cure. In
place of the armed thug, forthright, brutal, and direct, there arose
the penman, a person of education, talent, and imagination, whose
crime affected only property and hence did not incur popular
odium.

Since forgery attacked the landed and the moneyed classes it was
not viewed with equanimity by the law. Financial transactions in
business depend on credit and in turn on the paper which
represents credit. Negotiable instruments, bills of lading, bills of
hand, checks, and similar documents are the tools of commerce.
Destroy their trustworthiness and the transactions of finance suffer
accordingly. So serious did the threat of forgery become that the
English instituted the death penalty for this offense. In 1819 an issue
of one-pound notes consisting of simple pen and ink inscriptions on
ordinary white paper proved irresistible to a great mass of the
populace. During the succeeding seven years, 94,000 persons were
arrested for the crime of forgery. Of this number 7,700 were
sentenced to death.

468

Forgery has kept its pace with the growth of business. At present it is a flourishing crime growing at a steady rate. There has, however, been a tendency to exaggerate the annual loss from forged and fraudulent checks, placing it somewhere between 400 million dollars and 1 billion dollars. According to the American Bankers Association, "It is generally acknowledged by most authorities on the subject, however, that no factual data or experience statistics are available to substantiate these astronomical figures. At best, any statistics on the total annual loss through forged checks can only be qualified estimates which may have been projected from the results of limited surveys. . . . Regardless of the absence of verified statistics, there seems to be little evidence in banking to support the estimates of those who claim the total losses on forged and fraudulent checks have exceeded 70 million dollars in any recent year."

Using the figure 70 million dollars as an upper limit of losses, we may make some interesting observations:

a. In 1972, about 20 billion checks were used for $8,000 billion in regular transactions.

b. The total losses sustained by banks on *forged* checks have ranged from 4 to 6.5 million dollars annually in recent years. The bankers' forgery losses thus range somewhere between 5 to 10 per cent of the total. Allowing an additional 5 per cent of the total loss figure as a liberal estimate of the bankers' share of other fraudulent check losses, it would appear that their total is about 15 per cent of the check losses.

c. The remaining 85 per cent of the losses are shouldered by businessmen who operate stores, hotels, and other commercial enterprises. The reason for their sustaining the bulk of the loss is associated with their willingness to risk honoring checks without reliable proof of the identity, financial responsibility, or title of the presenter. Businessmen are not fully aware of the resourcefulness of the sophisticated check operator, who can always prove *some* identity and who can circumvent the magnetic identification tape bands put on checks supplied to depositors as safeguards against fraudulent use.

d. Over 15,000 persons are arrested annually on charges relating to forged or fraudulent checks.

e. The average value of the fraudulent check is about eighty dollars.

f. Eighty per cent of fraudulent checks are lost or stolen checks with forged endorsement.

g. Five per cent of the forgeries are "raised" checks, i.e., checks with the amount increased.

h. The remainder are "bad" checks because of non-existent accounts or insufficient funds.

i. Forged checks account for 70 per cent of the forgeries; wills, prescriptions, and bills are among the other forged documents.

2. The Forger

Forgery in the early twentieth century was a much more complicated procedure in which a variety of false instruments such as bank notes, drafts, bills of exchange, letters of credit, registered bonds, and post office money orders as well as checks were manufactured or altered and foisted off. A knowledge of chemicals, papers, inks, engraving, etching, lithography, and penmanship as well as detailed knowledge of bank operations were prime requisites for success. The amounts of money sought were relatively large and often they had to be obtained through complex monetary transactions. The technological characteristics of this kind of forgery made planning, timing, specialization, differentiation of roles, morale, and organization imperative. Capital was necessary for living expenses during the period when preparations for the forgeries were being made. Intermediates between the skilled forger and the passers were necessary so that the latter could swear that the handwriting on the false negotiable instruments was not theirs and so that the forger himself was not exposed to arrest. In short, professional forgery was based on the technology of the period. The forger of extensive knowledge and highly developed skills is rapidly becoming a figure of history. The universal prevalence of checking accounts and credit cards has greatly simplified the forger's task. He is now a "loner" following one of the types described below:

a. **General Type.** Forgery is practiced by a wide variety of types, male and female, young and old. Elderly women have plied the forger's trade successfully. Prisoners have produced forgeries during their confinement. It is of little use to enumerate the endless number of types except to illustrate the element of variety, the range of social levels, and the differing backgrounds. The most useful conclusion to be drawn from such a study is the existence of two prerequisite qualifications: a degree of clerical skill and elementary business knowledge and an exceptional amount of that type of courage which is best described as "nerve." A high-school education would seem to be indicated by the former qualification. In the nineteenth century, when such academic training was far less common, this degree of knowledge and skill would have served to screen out a great number of adults from the domain of suspects. The compulsory education of modern times has equipped most of the population with the technical facility and basic knowledge of the forger. At present the most practical way of studying the forger is to classify him by his *modus operandi*.

b. **The Habitual Check Passer.** This type has spent many years in passing checks. Often he spends a year or two in jail between short periods of freedom. One well-known check passer has spent a good part of fifty years in prison. His profits have been meager, barely sufficient to offer a comfortable living. He is typical of the mediocre check passer who has not had any great degree of success in passing even small checks. He has become familiar to the police and his chances of future success naturally diminish with each arrest.

c. **The Successful Check Passer.** A small group of forgers manage to make a distinguished success of their criminal careers. They are the "gentlemen" of the profession, the aristocrats who manage to evade the law for many years. They are characterized by an unusually "honest" appearance, which borders on distinguished prosperity. Their apparent good character and honesty quickly hurdle the first barrier, the suspicions of the person cashing the check. This type of forger is professional in his operations. His manner, story, dress, face, and his check are calculated to avoid raising the slightest suspicion. It is as simple for him to cash a fraudulent check as it is for the honest person to change a fifty-dollar bill.

d. **The Roving Check Passer.** This type of forger passes several checks in one community and moves on to another. He goes from one jurisdiction to another often leaving the state before his checks have been found to be fraudulent. He presents a great problem to the police, since he is an exceptionally clever criminal and his true identity is difficult to determine.

e. **The Disguised Check Passer.** By changing his appearance this check passer is able to escape arrest for long periods of time. He may employ such simple tricks as horn-rimmed glasses, mustache, or dyed hair. Recently one check artist enjoyed great success by disguising himself as a clergyman. He would pass five or six checks for a total of $200 in one evening in the same community and then would pass on to another area. Finally he came to a city were police had been expecting him and had alerted the merchants. His error lay in working the same disguise too often.

3. Techniques of the Forger

To pass a forged check, the criminal must first obtain blank forms on which to write the forgery, or he may obtain checks meant for another person and merely add the endorsement. He may use equipment to make the check look more genuine. Finally, he must have identification papers to support the story.

a. **Obtaining Blank Forms.** The following are the most common methods:

1) *Exchange Offices.* Military bases and other large organizations sometimes operate check cashing services. Blank check forms with the name of a local bank are placed out on the counter for use. Many of these facilities now require identification numbers on checks.

2) *Theft.* The forger may steal blank checks from an office. Posing as a salesman, telephone repair worker, or window cleaner, he will await an opportunity to steal a number of checks from the back of a book. Another method is to pilfer mail and thus obtain cashed or uncashed checks.

3) *Printing.* Using a stolen check as a model, the forger can have facsimiles printed. Alternatively, he may print a check bearing the name of a fictitious company.

b. **Equipment.** The professional check passer will equip himself with mechanical devices for practicing his trade: Checkwriters, protectographs, typewriters, rubber stamps, date stamps, and even printing equipment. With these he can produce the perforations in a check that convince the bank cashier of its authenticity. He can stamp *certified* on the check to remove any residual doubts of the passer. Finally, he can print the names of reputable companies such as General Electric or Exxon.

c. **Identification Papers.** Supporting papers are necessary for a successful forgery operation. Documents such as Social Security cards, automobile registration, driver's license, ID card, and service discharge papers can be used by the forger to identify himself to the check casher. The following, a more refined technique, is currently being employed throughout the country. The passer poses as a former employee of a motor company. He uses motor company forms and offers as identification a letter from his former employer addressed to him and stating with appropriate regrets that his employment is terminated and the enclosed is his final check.

d. **Official Papers.** The business of selling a variety of official identification documents has broadened out to include a much wider market than that of supplying supporting identification papers for forgers. The largest market now accommodates persons with no criminal connections. Driver's licenses, for example, are bought by non–English-speaking persons who are not able to pass the written parts of license examinations. Persons without qualifying high school or college education buy blank diplomas and degree certificates on which their own names will be filled in. Professional criminals are able to obtain birth certificates, licenses, car registrations, diplomas, armed forces discharges, Social Security cards, and even passports. Some of these documents are counterfeit, but most are genuine document blanks stolen from government offices and printing houses. Gangsters concentrate primarily on the wholesale end of this business. They arrange to buy blocks of documents from inside contacts and then sell them to retailers. In turn, the retailer sells them to individual customers at a great markup. Normally, he will assist the customer in filling out the document or form to insure its correct appearance. A diploma, for example, may require calligraphy or special lettering in affixing the customer's name. For New York driver's licenses the name and serial number must be typed in using an IBM 1428 OCR typewriter ball, the one used on authorized licenses. For an additional fee, a truck driver's license can be stamped with a red "1" on the upper left side, indicating that the driver is qualified to drive a tractor truck.

4. Examples of Forgery Techniques

The techniques and methods which have been described above are shown below in the actual operations of successful forgers.

a. **Using a New Account.** The check operator often opens a new account with a bank with the objective of defrauding unsuspecting bank customers or of obtaining a supply of checks for the purpose of defrauding banks. Using the passbook for identification as a bank-approved customer, the swindler attempts to capitalize on his status as a depositor by presenting worthless checks at the bank, often in split-deposit or cash-back transactions. Thus, he simply presents a worthless check together with a deposit slip indicating that part of the amount of the check is to be credited to his account and the balance to be returned in cash. Another method used is the duplicate deposit slip swindle, in which the operator presents duplicate deposit slips listing worthless checks for deposit to an account. If the teller accepts the worthless items and returns the receipted duplicate deposit ticket without verifying the account, the check operator will return and present a worthless check, requesting that it be cashed.

b. **The Wednesday-to-Monday Scheme.** During the 1970-1971 period a number of banks in the New York area were defrauded of a total of about $2 million by means of the following scheme: The ringleader would recruit someone, typically a gambler or an unemployed person, to open a checking account, using his own name and address. The initial deposit would be small, $10 to $15. A few days later, but always on a Wednesday, the recruit would be supplied by the ringleader with a counter check—easily available in any bank or even in a stationery store—made out for an amount between $2,000 and $2,700. The counter check would be made out to the depositor, signed with a false name and would bear a fictitious account number. The bogus check would be deposited on

Wednesday, and early Monday morning the recruit would return to the bank and withdraw all but $100 of the money in his account. The Wednesday-to-Monday time frame was necessary to take advantage of the three or four days needed by banks to process checks drawn on other banks. The money would be divided between the recruit and the ringleader. On discovering that the counter check was worthless, the bank would question the depositor about the source of the check. The story would follow a pattern: The recruit had met a fellow at the race track who wanted to pay back an old gambling debt. He had no idea where the fellow lived. He was sorry, but the money was already spent. The bank had no recourse than to absorb the loss unless it could be proved that the depositor knew the check was fraudulent. Eventually the ring was penetrated by a patrolman assigned to the district attorney's squad who, acting as an undercover agent, became a recruit. His disclosures led to the indictment of twenty-two men on charges of conspiracy to commit

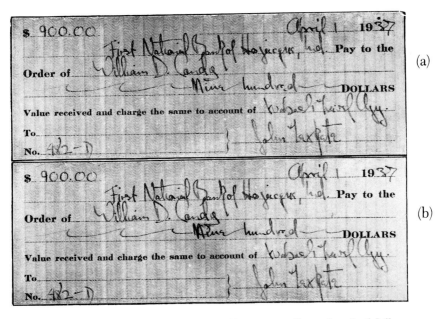

(a)

(b)

Figure 15. The amount of the check shown in (a) was originally one hundred dollars. By chemical processing it was possible to show (b) that the "O" of the word "One" had been eradicated and "Ni" written in its place. Courtesy of Francis Murphy.

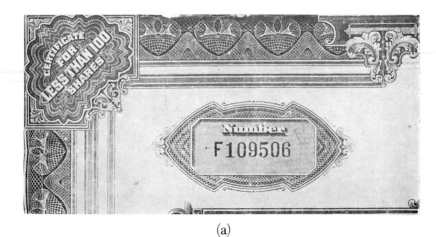

(a)

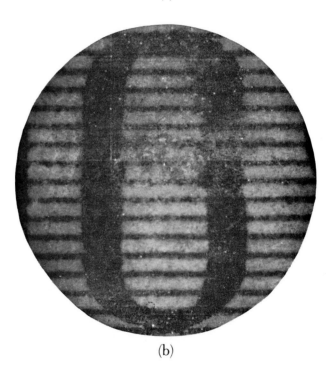

(b)

Figure 16. The stock certificate, of which the upper left corner is shown in (a), appears to bear the number F 109506. Microscopic examination, however, revealed that the second "0" had been changed from a "9." The photomicrograph (b) shows the disturbance of the fibers. Courtesy of Edward Palmer.

grand larceny, forgery, and criminal possession of forged instruments.

c. **Using Checks in Excess of Purchases.** One passer of fraudulent checks successfully pursued his career of forgery for a half century by limiting his gain from each illegal transaction to a small sum such as ten or twenty dollars. His method consisted of purchasing several hundred dollars worth of merchandise and giving a forged check slightly in excess of the bill. He would receive in change the small excess and would avoid receiving the goods by stating that he would pick them up at a later time or by having them delivered to a fictitious address.

d. **Use of Elaborate Credentials.** Another accomplished forger, Courtney Taylor, selected as victims jewelry and department stores. Posing as a representative of one of the well-known firms whose names were printed on his checks, he successfully passed the bogus instruments in twenty-eight states. In eighteen months he obtained $55,000 in this manner. Entering a store and leisurely selecting an item for purchase he would offer in payment a "salary" check or "bonus" check from the concern whose name was printed on the face. For identification he would display company credentials, selective service cards, Social Security cards, operator's licenses, and similar papers, all fraudulent. While waiting for the check to be approved he would discuss the product of his concern and even produce samples. The preparation which Taylor made for his career of forgery is of particular interest. While serving a prison term, he devoted his reading time to a study of the literature relating to printing. Eventually he became the possessor of such printing equipment as a hand printing press, trays of type, printer's ink, and a trimmer. A search of Taylor's apartment at the time of his arrest revealed 172 completed checks for amounts totaling in excess of $16,000, fifty-seven Selective Service cards, assorted fraudulent identification cards, railroad and airline ticket stubs, a stamp-making kit, assorted stamps, a checkwriter, and a typewriter. Apparently Taylor had extensively applied his knowledge of printing. In one particular month he printed up check forms of thirty-two widely known business establishments and divisions of state and city governments. Typical of Taylor's operations was the use of the "voucher system." He would first obtain a photograph of a widely known trademark such as that of Smith Brothers Cough Drops® and have a cut prepared. At a legitimate printing concern he would pose as the District Sales Manager for Smith Brothers, present the cut and order the printing of a number of new sales contracts. He would lay the basis for the order by explaining that he had encountered a shortage of promotional-type sales agreements. The form which the printer was requested to prepare consisted of a sheet of paper, the upper portion of which bore the same design and printing that would be found on a legitimate check. The lower part contained an agreement for the signature of the merchant whereby for a sum of money he contracted for a 25 per cent increase in his purchases of Smith Brothers products. By detaching the upper part, Taylor would have a typical check form. Naturally, precautions were taken before calling for the completed printing order to determine whether the printer's suspicions had been aroused. Using the check portion, Taylor would prepare an apparently genuine check by using a numbering machine, a date stamp, a typewriter for the payee's name, a checkwriter for the amount, and the signature of a fictitious officer of the company. With the support of appropriate credentials, Taylor successfully passed a great number of such checks drawn on a number of companies.

e. **The Dual Signature Scheme.** Probably the most accomplished forger of this century was Alexander Thiel who was active from 1930 to 1943, cashing four-figured checks at New York banks several times a year. Thiel is noteworthy also because of his association with the Campbell case. Bertram Campbell, an innocent stockbroker, was arrested and convicted for forgeries committed by Thiel on the testimony of eyewitnesses, the chief point of identification being his small mustache. After serving three years in prison, Campbell was released after Thiel's confession. In his statement Thiel confessed to forgeries amounting to $250,000 and described in detail the schemes he used so successfully.

Blank checks were obtained by committing a burglary in the offices of a businessman. After removing the checks from the book Thiel would write on the check stubs "void, imperfect" or "checks removed, defective printing." If a checkwriter was used in the office, he would stamp the blank checks. Next, Thiel would break into the office of a second individual—the person whose name he intended to use in forging the checks—and appropriate necessary papers for identification such as letters and office letterheads and canceled checks with model signatures. Equipped with these papers he would open a bank account in the name of the latter person and deposit a forged check for several thousand dollars, drawn on the account of the first individual. Thiel would now test both persons to determine whether either had become suspicious. He would telephone the first man, stating that he was a person of the same name and was inquiring about another person of that name. If the victim had discovered the loss of the blank checks, he would at this time indicate this knowledge. In addition Thiel would learn in this way whether the bank had communicated with the impersonated man to verify the fact that he had opened an account. With these assurances the stage was satisfactorily set. Allowing time for the clearance of the deposited checks through the bank on which they were drawn, Thiel would then cash checks on the account which he had opened under the assumed name. The whole operation would be completed within a given month, before the victim received his monthly bank statement.

Thiel's success was attributable mainly to his "dual signature" scheme and his remarkable facility for simulating signatures. The key to his method lay in the authenticity of his references. On opening an account he would use an assumed name and give as a reference the bank in which the true owner of the name had an actual account. In addition he would write the signature of the impersonated man in the presence of the bank official. This signature would be forwarded to the reference bank where invariably it would be declared genuine.

f. **Credit Card Schemes.** The proliferation of credit card systems and the growing variety of goods and services to which they may be applied have inevitably inspired schemes for their larcenous misuse. Since the credit card itself represents considerable buying power, counterfeiters have addressed themselves successfully to the problem of producing fraudulent specimens. In addition to their intrinsic purchasing power, credit cards can be used also as a means of personal identification for the purpose of cashing checks.

In 1966 more than $300,000 worth of traveler's checks were cashed by an alleged underworld syndicate. The case began with the theft of $407,000 in blank American Express traveler's checks at Kennedy Airport from a truck in transit from aircraft to hangar. Prior to the theft, the syndicate had counterfeited American Express credit cards for identification use by the passers and had recruited a number of persons to cash the checks.

Immediately following the theft, American Express informed the FBI and quickly distributed to banks, hotels, and gambling casinos a "hot list" containing the numbers of the stolen checks. Three days after the checks had been stolen, one of the passers cashed $200 worth in San Juan, Puerto Rico. He then moved on to Las Vegas and cashed $20,000 in checks at the gaming casinos. Subsequently, more than $300,000 worth of the traveler's checks were cashed in banks and hotels. The checks were passed with the help of the credit cards especially counterfeited for the operation.

Within a year after the theft of the checks some thirty persons had been arrested in connection with this case. Most of these had been apprehended while attempting to pass checks. Several, however, were arrested as co-conspirators. One of the latter, who had apparently been cooperating with the police, was murdered before the trial, presumably by members of the syndicate.

g. **Collusion by Bank Officers Check-Kiting Scheme.** Special difficulties are presented by cases in which the forgers are aided in their scheme by an employee of the bank. In a recent case two bank officers and their brothers were arrested on a 50-count indictment charging them with using a check-kiting scheme over a period of 27 months to embezzle $887,000 from the Bankers Trust Company and the National Bank of North America. The two bank officials (one in each bank) had instructed their employees to treat the checks of Salvatore Giordano, one of the brothers, as cash deposits, thus permitting funds to be withdrawn immediately. This enabled them to circumvent the usual two or three-day waiting period for writing checks against deposits. The conspiracy came to light when a bank messenger neglected to deliver on a Friday a bundle of checks approved for cash deposit to the main offices of the Bankers Trust. On the following Monday a shortage of $440,000 was discovered at the Bank of North America. When the previously forgotten checks were presented for payment at Bankers Trust they were marked "insufficient funds" because of the shortage. When the $440,000 in checks were not honored, Giordano persuaded the collaborating bank officer to certify four checks totaling that amount to be deposited. But Bankers Trust refused to honor the certified checks. A subsequent audit and suits by the banks against each other for refusing to make good on the checks led to the uncovering of the scheme and the indictment of the five conspirators.

h. **Forgery of E Bonds and Money Orders.** As a result of a long investigation conducted by the Brooklyn special strike force of the Justice Department, seventeen persons were recently indicted in Federal Court in Brooklyn, accused of cashing stolen United States Treasury bonds and postal money orders valued at almost $500,000. The indictment charged conspiracy and the forgery of Series E savings bonds and United States postal money orders ranging in value from $25 to $1,000. The defendants were accused of cashing them at banks in the New York metropolitan area. The bonds and money orders were said to have been the proceeds of burglaries of homes, offices, and post offices throughout the country. The Brooklyn gang let it be known that they would buy these items at about 10 per cent of their face value. Members of the gang were provided with forged identification kits that included driver's licenses and Social Security cards matching the names on the bonds and postal orders. It was then a relatively simple matter to cash them at one of the hundreds of banks locally available.

5. Law

Forgery laws are quite lengthy and vary with states. Only the basic parts of these laws are discussed below.

a. **Definition.** Forgery is committed by a person who, with intent to defraud, knowingly makes or utters (passes, offers, or puts in circulation) a false writing that apparently imposes a legal liability on another or affects his legal right or liability to his predjudice. The term *false* as used here refers to the making of the writing and not to the content of, or the facts contained in, the writing. For example, a check which bears the signature of the maker and which is drawn with intent to defraud on a bank wherein the maker has no credit is not a forgery but is simply a bad check. Signing the name of another to an instrument without authority and with intent to defraud is forgery since the signature is falsely made. The distinction here is that the falsely made signature purports to be the act of another. Although forged checks are the most common, other instruments such as railroad tickets, wills, pari-mutuel tickets, and receipts are also subject to fraudulent alteration and making.

b. **Elements of Proof.** To support a charge of forgery the following elements must be established.

1) *False Making.* It must be shown that a writing was falsely made or altered. The writing concerned is usually a signature or a number on a check. An alteration may be shown by the document examiner using physical methods. A false signature can be established by a comparison with the true signature which it purports to be. A statement should be obtained from the person whose signature was forged showing that he had not signed the document himself and that he had not authorized the accused to do so for him. If the name of a fictitious person was used as the purported drawer of the check, proof of falsity may include evidence that the purported drawer of the check had no account in the bank on which the check was drawn. An interview with a bank officer should provide this information. The forged instrument itself should be produced, if it is available.

2) *Legal Liability.* The signature or writing must be of a nature which would, if genuine, impose a legal liability on another or change his legal right or liability to his prejudice. The writing must on its face appear to impose a legal liability on another as, for example, a check or note. It is not forgery to alter or falsely make with intent to defraud a writing which does not operate to impose a legal liability. For example, a falsely made letter of introduction would not be a forgery in the legal sense. For an alteration to constitute forgery, it must effect a material change in the legal tenor of the writing; for example, an alteration whereby an obligation is apparently increased, diminished, or discharged would be material. The date, amount, or place of payment would be material alterations in the case of a note. The change in legal liability or prejudice may be quite obvious, as in the case of a check. In other situations it may be necessary to obtain the testimony of a bank officer or a company officer as to the effect of the writing or alteration.

3) *Identity of the Forger.* It must be shown that it was the accused

who falsely made or altered the writing or who knowingly uttered, offered, or issued the false instrument. This may be established by the confession of the accused, statements of witnesses, or by the testimony of a document examiner.

4) **Intent to Defraud.** The intent to defraud must be shown; it need not be directed toward a particular person nor be for the advantage of the offender. It is immaterial whether anyone was actually defrauded. The carrying out of the intent need not go beyond the false making or altering of the writing. The intent can often be inferred from the act. Evidence of other forgeries is admissible to prove intent to defraud; hence, other business establishments and towns which the suspect has passed through should be visited for the purpose of discovering similar, additional forgeries or attempts at uttering. It must also be shown that the suspect knew that the instrument he was uttering was a forgery. This is not difficult if the forgery is the handiwork of the suspect, but may become a problem when the utterer and the forger are different persons. In fact the most common defense to a charge of uttering a forgery is that the accused had honestly received the forged instrument and believed it to be genuine. Another claim is that the accused was cashing the check for an acquaintance. To meet such claims the investigation should develop all possible evidence to show the existence of guilty knowledge. Evidence of the existence of other similar checks or other attempts to utter forgeries is admissible.

6. Tracing and Apprehending the Forger

Ordinarily the nature of the forged check is not discovered until long after the forger has departed. Hence, the investigator is usually at a disadvantage of a time lapse of several days. The tracing of the forger is not a simple problem. The actual arrest, however, presents no difficulties since this type of criminal is not given to violent action.

a. **Detection by Cashier.** Naturally the most effective method of catching the forger is to detect him in the act. Alert bank cashiers, storekeepers, and hotel clerks can sometimes spot the forger as he attempts to pass the check. Employees who keep abreast of circularized information on forgers can aid greatly in this work.

b. **Plants.** Persons who steal checks from mailboxes can be caught by means of plants or stakeouts. If the police are aware of the general area of his operations, they can send out investigators to cover certain spots on days on which government checks are delivered.

c. *Modus Operandi.* The check passer will usually have his own peculiar way of operating. His "story" or disguise will become well known. Employees can be alerted to the danger and instructed to call the police on the arrival of the suspect.

7. Interviewing the Victim

Three victims are to be considered: the person who cashed the check; the person whose signature has been forged; and the bank on which it was drawn.

a. **Person Who Cashes the Check.** This is usually a bank cashier or a storekeeper. Bank cashiers are often careless in their habits of accepting checks. In a bank in a large Eastern city, the management subjected one of its cashiers to a test. One of the other employees stepped to the window and submitted a rubber check (the check was actually made of rubber). The cashier took the check, stamped it, made the deposit, and placed the check in its proper place. Although this is an extreme case, lesser degrees of carelessness are common among bank employees. Store personnel are similarly careless. Large chain stores make a rule of cashing the checks of government employees. Chain grocery stores may suffer losses running into the hundreds of thousands of dollars annually. The added business resulting from the check cashing service, however, more than compensates for the losses. The interview with the person who cashed the check should develop the following information:

1) *Physical Description.* A detailed physical description of the check passer should be obtained (see Chapter 29). Descriptions should also be obtained from other persons who may have seen the check passer.

2) *Circumstances.* The manner in which the check was cashed,

the story given by the passer; the exact words used; credentials offered; conversation and behavior after the check was passed.

3) *Date and Time.* Date and time of the occurrence.

4) *Number of Persons Present.* Was the store or bank crowded at the time?

5) *Record.* A record of the cashier in regard to cashing checks. History of the establishment with regard to forged checks.

6) *Handwriting.* Did the check passer sign or write the check in the presence of the person cashing?

b. **The Person Whose Signature Appears on the Check.** It is important to interview this person early in the investigation. In military services where fraudulent checks are quite common because of the relative ease with which they may be passed at Officers' Clubs and post exchanges, it is found that in approximately one-third of the cases an error has been made: The person who first alleged that his name had been forged subsequently remembers or is convinced that the signature is his own. The interview should include the following points:

1) The subject should examine and identify the document. The check may be marked for identification by inscribing small initials on a corner of the reverse side.

2) *Authenticity.* He admits or denies that the signature is his.

3) *A Statement* to the effect that he has not given authority to another person to use his signature.

4) *Handwriting Specimens,* signatures, and other writings similar to those forged, should be obtained.

5) *Check Writing Habits.* Does he write many checks? For what purpose? In what amounts? Manner in which he writes his checks, viz., writing of amounts, assigning check number, manner of writing date.

6) *Access to Check Forms.* Where kept? Who has access to the area?

7) *Records of Employees and Associates.* Inquiries should also be made about acquaintances.

8) *Suspects.* He should be encouraged to name any persons whom he may suspect and to give his reasons for his suspicions.

9) *Financial Status.* What is the condition of his credit? Does he have an account at the bank on which the check was drawn? In what

bank does he have accounts. Has he had any bad checks, i.e., complaints of insufficient funds? Has he been connected in any way with a previous forged check case?

c. **Bank.** The bank on which the check was drawn should be visited to ascertain certain facts. Information relating to the proof of the crime must be obtained as well as any clues which they may offer.

1) Is the check invalid?

2) Does the person whose name appears on the check have an account there? Has he ever had an account there?

3) Have they had any forged checks similar to the evidence check?

8. False Identity Papers

Advances in printing and photocopying techniques have made it increasingly difficult to detect bogus or altered birth certificates, resident alien or "green cards," driver's licenses, and Social Security cards. What is more disturbing is the ease with which dealers and aliens themselves are able to obtain authenticated copies of genuine documents such as birth certificates from lax state and local agencies. With a birth certificate, an impressive array of other genuine ID cards can easily be acquired. Birth certificates are the most common means of establishing identity, and birth certificate frauds are among the easiest to perpetrate, according to the Federal Advisory Committee on False Identification. Approximately 10 million certified copies of birth certificates are issued yearly on 1,000 different forms by more than 7,000 local and state offices. More than 80 per cent of them are requested and sent out by mail, sometimes to foreign countries. Even unsigned requests are generally honored, as are requests from supposed relatives or other interested parties. State vital records offices also allow thousands of applicants each year to "create" birth records. (A person born in the United States can claim U.S. citizenship.) The applicant simply states that he was born at a certain location but that his parents did not register his birth. "Evidence" such as an affidavit signed by a friend, relative or minister, a notation in a family Bible, a church census, and other easily forged papers will be acceptable. Because so many different forms are used and because they are generally made by photostat, birth certificates are among the easiest documents to counterfeit or alter.

The widespread use of false identification papers and the consequent "loss" of billions of dollars through their illegal use has led to the establishment of the Federal Advisory Committee on False Identification mentioned above. This is a group of 80 members drawn from federal and state agencies as well as private industry who will assay the breadth of the problem and re-examine more than 400 federal statutes dealing with false identification to determine whether new legislation is needed. According to the committee it is quite easy to obtain the birth certificate of a deceased infant in any one of 15,000 vital statistics offices throughout the country, since births and deaths are registered separately by these agencies. A person can acquire a new identity by simply asking for the birth certificate of someone who was born close to the birthday of the applicant and died soon after. This information is obtainable from the obituary notices.

The Federal panel believes that the United States is losing billions of dollars annually because of the illegal use of easily obtained false identity papers. This extravagant figure includes an estimated $10 billion in earnings sent out of the country by more than six million aliens and at least $100 million in income tax evaded by these aliens. Customs Service Investigations has stated that close to $1 billion in heroin and cocaine had been smuggled into the United States since 1967 by persons using false identity. The FBI maintains that many arrests of underground radicals involve false identification papers. The Post Office has stated that 25 per cent of stolen postal checks are cashed by means of false papers.

9. Physical Evidence in Forgery

The questioned check is part of the *corpus delicti* and should, accordingly, be safeguarded as a valuable piece of evidence. When not under examination the check should be protected by a transparent envelope. For identification, the investigator's initials and the date should be placed on the back of the check.

The examination of the check for physical evidence should be performed by a competent document expert. If an expert is unavailable, a properly trained investigator can perform some of the preliminary work of the examination. The handwriting comparison of signatures of a suspect with signatures on the check should be performed only by a person qualified to testify as an expert witness. Law enforcement agencies should submit the evidence to the laboratory without tampering with it in any way.

a. **Photographs.** One-to-one photographs of the front and back of the check should first be made.

b. **Latent Fingerprints.** If the forgery is detected early and the check has not been handled to any great extent, the possibility of latent fingerprints exists. The check can be dipped in a 5 per cent solution of silver nitrate, dried, and then exposed to bright light (see Chapter 32). The check can be later cleared of the nitrate and restored to its previous condition by immersing in a bath of mercuric chloride and drying. If it is found (by spot testing) that the ink is water soluble, iodine fuming can be used. Checks consisting of heavily sized paper can be processed with black powder.

c. **Forging Methods.** The techniques employed by the forger will depend upon his skill. Some of the most common methods of reproducing a signature are given below:

1) *Free hand.* If the forger is an experienced and skilled penman, he may simulate the signature from the model which he has obtained. This is the most difficult of all methods. If the forger's work is slow and painstaking, an examination under a low-power microscope will reveal the hesitation and the interruptions at points where the pen was lifted.

2) *Tracing.* The signature can be traced from a model. Proof of forgery in this case lies in the fact that the questioned signature is an exact duplicate of an authentic signature. It is practically impossible to write the same signature twice in exactly the same way. The forged signature can be superimposed over the model in front of a strong light. There are two common methods of tracing:

a) Carbon Paper Trace. A piece of carbon paper is placed over the check. The genuine signature is placed over the carbon. With a pencil, the genuine signature is traced and a light carbon outline is produced on the check. The forger then inks in the outline with his pen. This type of trace may be detected by examining under a low-power microscope. Traces of the carbon will be visible in the forged signature.

b) Transmitted Light. The check is placed over the genuine signature and the two are placed over a piece of glass the under side of which is illuminated from below by a strong light. The forger now traces the signature which is visible over the light. This type of trace can sometimes be detected by the abnormal shading and the signs of slow, painstaking movement. Nervousness, retraced lines, varying density, interruptions caused by pen lifts, and tremor may be apparent.

d. **Alterations.** The check may be altered to change the amount, the name, or some other element. The existence of any changes can be discovered by holding the check under an ultraviolet lamp.

1) *Additions.* If the check has been "raised," additional writing is present. The difference in the inks may be apparent to the unaided eye or under the ultraviolet lamp. The use of filter photography or of infrared film will often visibly emphasize the difference in the inks.

2) *Erasures.* When an eraser is used on the paper, the sizing and the fibers are disturbed. The new ink writing placed on the erased area will have a tendency to spread or "feather." If chemical eradicators are used, a bleaching stain usually is apparent. Ultraviolet examination or merely holding the check in front of a light will usually reveal the erasure.

e. **Watermark.** The watermark can be used to trace the source of the check paper. To reproduce the watermarks a photograph can be taken of the check illuminated from the back so as to emphasize the mark. Sometimes, the watermark can be printed directly on photographic paper. When the design cannot be clearly photographed because there is writing or printing in the watermark area, a radiograph can be made using soft x-rays. In this way the writing or printing is eliminated and a picture of the watermark alone is obtained.

f. **Rubber Stamps.** A rubber stamp found in the possession of the suspect often can be related to the stamp impressions on forged checks. In order to give an appearance of genuineness to their work, some forgers stamp the check with the word "CERTIFIED." The stamp may have individual characteristics which are reproduced in each impression. The stamp will, of course, have class characteristics that establish a similarity, but not an identity. The stamp itself should be submitted to the laboratory for comparison with the impressions. Some of the characteristics which may be present are the following:

1) *Mold Defects.* In making a "one-piece" mold, the defects existing in the type of the mold are reproduced in the series of stamps made from the mold.

2) *Accidental Nicks.* Careless use of the mold results in individual nicks in the rubber. These can be distinguished from mold defects.

3) *Mounting Defects.* When a "one-piece" stamp is cut out and mounted on its sponge rubber cushion, characteristics may be observed along the border of the stamp.

4) *Alignment.* Stamps which are made by the forger from individual letters will have a poor alignment because of the limitations of the hand-setting process with rubber letters. The investigator should carefully protect the stamp so that the alignment is not disturbed.

5) *Foreign Matter.* Dirt and other foreign material may become imbedded in the letters of the stamp. The result in use is a defective impression which is highly characteristic. Again, the investigator on coming into possession of such a stamp should protect its original condition and should not disturb any foreign matter by mishandling or haphazard testing.

g. **Checkbook.** If a checkbook is found among the effects of the suspect, it should be examined as a possible source of the forged check.

1) *Perforations.* Particular attention should be paid to the perforated line of the checkbook stub and the check. Sometimes, it can be shown that these match and thus it is established that the check was extracted from the suspect's checkbook.

2) *Watermark.* Sometimes the watermark of the check paper overlaps the stub and the check. A matching of the two parts of the watermark is convincing proof of the source of the check.

10. Obtaining Exemplars

Exemplars should be obtained from each person whose name appears on a questioned check as well as from the accused. The methods for obtaining exemplars are described in Chapter 43. There are several reasons for this procedure:

a. To establish the fact of forgery where it exists.

b. To determine whether an attempt has been made in the questioned endorsement to simulate the genuine signature.

c. To verify the genuineness of the endorsement in cases where the complainant actually endorsed and cashed the check but denies the facts in order to obtain a second payment.

d. To verify the genuineness of the check in cases where the complainant suffers from a faulty memory.

11. Sources of Information

a. **General.** Since the nature of the forger's occupation requires that he change his scene frequently, moving about a great deal, patronizing a variety of stores, banks, hotels, and other businesses, and sometimes leaving a trail of bad checks in his wake, the proprietors of these establishments and their security personnel should be consulted where appropriate. Additional clues to the identity and location of the forger may be obtained in this manner. Further help may be sought from retail credit, protective, hotel, and bankers associations.

b. **FBI Resources.** Because of the travel aspects of the offense, the Federal Bureau of Investigation is in a position to offer considerable help in the investigation of a forgery. This assistance relates both to the materials used by the forger and the identification of the offender.

1) *Standards Files.* The FBI document section maintains the following:

a) Checkwriter Standards File
b) Ink Standards Collection
c) Rubber Stamp and Printing Standards File
d) Typewriter Standards File
e) Watermark File

2) *PROCHEK.* A computerized file of professional check passers, containing information on their description, habits, and methods of operation.

3) *National Fraudulent Check File.* This is a large (about 100,000 specimens) collection of fraudulent checks gathered by encouraging local police agencies to submit copies of fraudulent checks written in excess of a specified amount. The file is said to aid in the identification of forgers and writers of bad checks.

ADDITIONAL READING

Dobrowolski, J.A.: Optical Interference Coatings for the Validation of Valuable Papers and Identification Documents. 5 *Canadian Society of Forensic Science Journal,* 129, 1972.

Federal Advisory Committee on False Identification. *The Criminal Use of False Identification.* Washington, D.C.: U.S. Government Printing Office, 1976.

Flynn, W.J.: Forgery by Phone. 4 *Journal of Police Science and Administration,* 326, 1976.

Hargett, J.W. and Dusch, R.A.: Classification and Identification of Checkwriters. 4 *Journal of Police Science and Administration,* 404, 1976.

Hogan, B.: The Rise and Fall of Forgery. *Criminal Law Review,* 81, 1974.

How Big is the Bad Check Problem? 11 *Security World,* 7, 1974.

Huet, R.: The Check Offenders. 17 *Corrective and Social Psychiatry and Journal of Applied Behavior Therapy,* 31, 1971.

Kelley, J.H. and Morton, S.E.: How Many Forgers? 2 *Journal of Police Science and Administration,* 164, 1974.

Lemert, E.M.: The Behavior of the Systematic Check Forger. 6 *Social Problems,* 141, 1958.

McDonnell, J.B.: Rapid Decline of Privity in the Modern Law of Commercial Paper. 30 *Business Lawyer,* 203, 1974.

Speiser, S.M.: Abolish Paper Money and Eliminate Most Crime. 61 *American Bar Association Journal,* 47, 1975.

Traini, R.: Beating the Forger. 15 *Security Gazette,* 10, 1973.

Whaley, D.J.: Forgery and the Holder in Due Course. 78 *Community Law Review Journal,* 277, 1973.

Williams, G.: Forgery and Falsity. *Criminal Law Review,* 71, 1974.

Chapter 25

HOMICIDE

I. LAW

1. Introduction

THE UNLAWFUL killing of a human being is still looked upon as the classic crime. The detection of the murderer is considered the most severe test of the abilities of the investigator. Considered statistically, however, murder is not a serious problem. The sixteen thousand non-negligent homicides which occur annually are but a small fraction of the total number of felonies with which law enforcement agencies must deal. The annual rate of more than fifty-seven thousand motor vehicle homicides, however, constitutes a serious problem. Whereas the victim of a murder is often a person who is criminally involved, the deceased in a motor vehicle death is ordinarily an innocent, law-abiding citizen, frequently a child. It is for this reason that great stress has been placed in the present treatment on the investigation of motor vehicle homicides, with particular reference to the hit-and-run driver. Of course the problems of murder and manslaughter in general have been given the customary emphasis. The crime of murder permits a discussion of the full resources of the science of investigation. The varieties of physical evidence, the motives of the culprit, and the efforts which he will make to evade detection combine to give this crime an interest, both academic and dramatic, that can be found nowhere else in the whole catalogue of the penal law.

2. Definitions

Homicide is the killing of a human being. Depending on the circumstances, it may be criminal or innocent.

493

a. **Criminal Homicide.** A homicide which is not excusable or justifiable is considered a criminal homicide. The crime is considered to have been committed at the place of the act or omission although the victim may have died elsewhere. The death must have occurred within a year and a day of the act or omission and must have been the result of an injury caused by the act or omission. There are two major categories which will be later discussed in detail:

1) *Murder.* Killing with malice aforethought (premeditation) is considered murder. The law presumes all homicides to be committed with malice aforethought and thus to be murder. The burden is on the defendant to show otherwise, i.e., that there was an excuse, justification, or alleviation.

2) *Manslaughter.* This term is used to describe an unlawful and felonious killing without malice aforethought (premeditation).

b. **Innocent Homicide.** There are two kinds of homicide which do not involve criminal guilt, namely, excusable and justifiable homicide:

1) *Excusable Homicide.* For practical purposes we need only consider two kinds of excusable homicide: first, a homicide which is the outcome of an accident or misadventure while doing a lawful act in a lawful manner and without negligence. For example, a hunter accidentally shoots a concealed man; or a lawful operation, performed with due care and skill, results in the death of the patient. Second, a homicide which is committed in self defense. In order to excuse a person for killing on the ground of self-defense, it is required that he must have believed on reasonable grounds that the killing was necessary to preserve his own life or the lives of those whom he might lawfully protect. If the grounds actually exist, the homicide is justifiable; if the grounds, although believed for good cause to be present, do not actually exist, the homicide is excusable. For example, if a person threatened by an assailant who is armed with an imitation pistol reasonably believes the weapon to be lethal and so kills, the killing, although not authorized by law, is excusable because of the reasonable mistake of fact.

2) *Justifiable Homicide.* A killing is justifiable if it is authorized or commanded by the law. A killing to prevent the commission of a violent felony such as rape, robbery, or other felony against the

person is authorized by the law. Other examples are: killing an enemy on the field of battle in time of war, within the rules of war, and executing a death sentence pronounced by a competent tribunal. The acts of a subordinate performed in good faith in compliance with supposed duty or orders, within the scope of authority and without negligence, are justifiable.

3. Murder

A criminal homicide is murder if one of the following four conditions exist:

a. There is a premeditated design to kill.

b. The accused intended to kill or commit great bodily harm.

c. The accused is engaged in an act inherently dangerous to others and shows a wanton disregard of human life.

d. The accused is engaged in the perpetration (or attempt) of a felony against the person such as robbery, burglary, sodomy, rape, or aggravated arson.

4. Premeditated Design to Kill

The term "malice aforethought" is sometimes used in place of "premeditated design to kill." The taking of the human life must be consciously intended. A well-laid plan is not essential; the slaying may be conceived and executed in a short interval of time.

5. Intent to Kill or Inflict Great Bodily Harm

Since a person is presumed to have intended the natural and probable consequences of an act purposely performed by him, where such an intentional act is likely to result in death or great bodily injury, it may be presumed that the accused intended death or great bodily harm. Premeditation is not required. For example, A accidentally meets B, a person who has previously wronged him, and, on the impulse of the moment, shoots and kills him. Great bodily harm refers to serious injuries such as shooting to break a person's leg.

6. Act Inherently Dangerous

To kill while engaged in an act inherently dangerous and evidencing a wanton disregard of human life can constitute murder. Examples of this behavior are: shooting into a room or train in which persons are known to be present; throwing a live grenade to another person as a practical joke.

7. Felonies Against the Person

Certain felonies have been attended so frequently by death or great bodily harm, even when not intended by the wrongdoer, that they must be classified as dangerous. Hence a homicide committed during the perpetration (or attempt) of burglary, sodomy, rape, maiming, robbery, and aggravated arson is considered to constitute murder, even though the killing was unintentional or even accidental. For example: A robbery victim in attempting to disarm his assailant is killed by the accidental discharge of the assailant's firearm. Another example: A robber orders his victim at gunpoint to throw up his hands. The victim staggers back, fall, dies of a fractured skull. In both examples the robber is guilty of murder.

8. Proof of Murder

In order to prove the crime of murder the following elements must be established:

a. The person named or described is dead.

b. The death was the result of an act of the accused.

c. The circumstances show that the accused had a premeditated design to kill; or intended to kill or inflict great bodily harm; or was engaged in an act inherently dangerous to others and evidencing a wanton disregard of human life; or was engaged in the perpetration or attempted perpetration of burglary, sodomy, rape, robbery, maiming, or aggravated arson.

9. Manslaughter

Any homicide which is neither murder nor innocent homicide is called *manslaughter*. It is the unlawful killing of another without malice aforethought. Manslaughter may be voluntary or involuntary depending upon whether there existed an intention to kill.

10. Voluntary Manslaughter

An unlawful killing, although committed in the heat of sudden passion caused by adequate provocation, is not murder but voluntary manslaughter even though there was an intent to kill or commit great bodily harm. It is recognized that a man may be so overcome by sudden passion that he may strike a fatal blow before he can bring himself under control. The law recognizes that in the light of the provocation such homicide does not amount to murder. The provocation, however, must be such that the law considers adequate to arouse uncontrollable passion in a *reasonable* man. In judging provocation the following requirements are considered: *Adequate* provocation, *sudden* heat of passion, and causal connection between the provocation, the transport of passion, and the fatal act.

a. **Adequate Provocation.** Adequacy is determined by an objective test: What effect would the provocation have on the *average, reasonable* man? If the nature of the provocation is such that it is calculated to inflame the passions of the ordinary reasonable man, it is considered adequate. The following are forms of provocation which commonly occur:

1) *Battery.* An unlawful, hard blow inflicting great pain or injury may be sufficient.

2) *Assault.* The attempt to commit serious personal injury, although not accompanied by a battery, may be calculated to excite sudden and uncontrollable passion and, hence, may constitute

adequate provocation. For example, A fires a gun at B, misses, and runs away. B shoots A in the back as he flees. This is not considered self-defense but sufficient provocation may exist to reduce the grade of homicide to manslaughter.

3) *Mutual Combat.* All the circumstances of the combat must be considered. Who was the original assailant? Was the fight truly mutual or was one person clearly the attacker? Did the original assailant have an intent to kill? Did the counter-attack exceed the requirements of self-defense? If both parties engage in an altercation with unlawful intent to kill, there is no mitigation on either side.

4) *Words.* Insulting words alone are not adequate provocation.

5) *Trespass.* A trespass may be sufficient if it is upon a dwelling house and involves personal danger to the slayer. The consideration here is of a trespass of a nature insufficient to authorize the use of deadly force. If the force used is permitted by law under the circumstances, no question of provocation arises because no crime is committed in the slaying. A purely technical trespass, even in a dwelling house, is not recognized as sufficient for this purpose.

6) *Outrageous Acts.* It is generally recognized by law that certain outrageous acts constitute provocations. For example: Adultery, seduction of the slayer's infant daughter, rape of a close female relative of the slayer, or felonious injury inflicted upon a close relative of the slayer is considered adequate provocation.

b. **Heat of Passion.** The accused must have killed in the heat of passion. It is not necessary that the passion be so great that the killer does not know what he is doing at the time. It is sufficient if the passion is so extreme that the slayer's action is directed by passion rather than by reason. A subjective test must be applied: Did the slayer kill in the actual heat of passion? This is different from the objective test used in determining adequate provocation where the reaction of the ordinary reasonable man was considered. It should be noted here that *both* adequate provocation and heat of passion must be present to reduce the homicide to manslaughter. Either alone is insufficient.

c. **Suddenness.** The heat of passion must be sudden. The time lapse between the provocation and the fatal act should not have presented a reasonable opportunity for the slayer's passion to cool.

An objective test is applied: Would the mind of the ordinary reasonable man have cooled sufficiently so that the act could be considered to have been directed by reason rather than passion? The length of the cooling time will vary with the circumstances. The severity of the provocation and the occurrence of intervening acts are factors to be considered.

d. **Causal Relation Between Provocation, Passion, and the Fatal Act.** It is not sufficient that the provocation, passion, and the fatal act occurred in rapid sequence. It must be shown that the adequate provocation aroused the passion and that heat of passion immediately led to the fatal act. If, for example, the intent to kill existed before the provocation, the fatal act would be a murder since the provocation would not have been the cause of the fatal act.

11. Involuntary Manslaughter

Involuntary manslaughter is defined as an unlawful homicide committed without intent to kill. Negatively, it is an unintentional killing which is neither justifiable nor excusable. Involuntary manslaughter is an unlawful homicide committed without an intent to kill or inflict great bodily harm; it is an unlawful killing by culpable negligence, or while perpetrating or attempting to perpetrate an offense other than burglary, sodomy, rape, robbery, or aggravated arson, directly affecting the person.

a. **Culpable Negligence.** Culpable negligence is a degree of carelessness greater than simple negligence. It is a negligent act or omission accompanied by a culpable disregard for the foreseeable consequences to others of such act or omission. Thus, the basis of a charge of involuntary manslaughter may be a negligent act or omission which, viewed in the light of human experience, might forseeably result in the death or another, even though death would not, necessarily, be a natural and probable consequence of such act or omission. Examples of culpable negligence are: Negligently conducting target practice so that the bullets go in the direction of an inhabited house within range; pointing a pistol in fun at another and pulling the trigger, believing, but without taking reasonable precautions to ascertain, that it would not be dangerous; carelessly leaving poisons or dangerous drugs where they may endanger life.

b. **Legal Duty.** When there is no legal duty to act, there can, of course, be no neglect. Thus, when a stranger makes no effort to save a drowning man, or a person allows a mendicant to freeze or starve to death, no crime is committed.

c. **Offense Directly Affecting the Person.** By an offense directly affecting the person is meant one affecting some particular person as distinguished from an offense affecting society in general. Among offenses directly affecting the person are the various types of assault, battery, false imprisonment, voluntary engagement in an affray, maiming, and the use of more force than is reasonably necessary in the suppression of a mutiny or riot.

d. **Proof of Manslaughter.** The following elements must be proved to establish the offense of manslaughter: That the victim named or described is dead; that his death resulted from the act or omission of the accused, as alleged; and facts and circumstances showing that the homicide amounted in law to the degree of manslaughter alleged.

II. THE IDENTITY OF THE DECEASED

12. Introduction

In the proof of criminal homicide the first element is the establishment of the fact that the victim named or described is dead. To support a criminal charge, it must be shown that someone is dead. Every effort should be made to identify the victim. It is not, however, considered absolutely essential that an identification be made. Convictions have been obtained for causing the death of an unknown person.

13. The Fact of Death

Obviously, one of the first actions of the investigator on arriving at the scene of an allegedly fatal occurrence is the verification of the death. He may not consider a person dead until the fact has been established by a competent person. All deaths will be verified by a licensed physician. In the event that the investigator is the first to arrive at the scene of an apparent homicide, he should summon a physician to examine the victim and determine whether he is dead.

a. **Definition of Death.** An individual is said to be dead in a medical sense when one of the three vital functions is no longer performed by the body, namely, respiration, cardiac activity, and central nervous system activity. In a legal sense, death is considered to have occurred when all three of these vital functions have irrevocably ceased.

b. **Presumptive Signs and Tests for Death.** The following are a few of the signs indicative of death:

1) Cessation of breathing and respiratory movements.
2) Absence of heart sound.
3) Loss of flushing of nail beds when pressure on nail is released.

c. **Suspended Animation.** Death may be superficially simulated. Cardiac activity, breathing, and the functioning of the nervous system may reach such a low level of activity that an observer is deceived into an assumption of death. Although such advice is irrelevant to the topic, the investigator is naturally encouraged to devote his full energies to resuscitation in the absence of obvious signs of death. Intelligently applied first aid may obviate the need of a homicide investigation. Among the conditions which will produce the simulated appearance of death are the following:

1) Electrical shock.
2) Prolonged immersion.
3) Poisoning from narcotic drugs.
4) Barbiturate poisoning.
5) Prolonged exhausting diseases such as typhoid fever.
6) Certain rare mental diseases.

d. **Brain Death.** With the advent of heart transplantation medical experts have stressed the importance of brain death, or the cessation of brain activity, as an acceptable criterion. In ordinary cases brain death usually coincides with the stoppage of heart and breathing and the old criteria are adequate. Beginning in the early 1950s, however, the need arose for better ways of determining brain death independently because respirators were developed which allowed a patient's breathing to be maintained artificially even though the brain was dead. Under these circumstances the heart would often continue beating too because the artificial breathing was giving the blood the oxygen it needed to nourish the heart. For the purpose of a heart transplant, the respirator would be used to maintain the heart's breathing capability (and the heart's condition) even though the donor's body, because of brain death, was no longer capable of spontaneous respiration. In 1972 a court in Richmond, Virginia, accepted the concept of brain death as an adequate definition of death.

14. Identification Procedure

Identifying the victim is obviously a critically important investigative step. First, the identity of the deceased may arouse suspicion in a mysterious death, since the victim may be a person whose life has been threatened or whose death was desired for criminal purposes. Second, the identity of the dead person provides a focal point for the inquiry, since the investigators can then center their attention on the associates and haunts of the deceased. Moreover, police agencies maintain files of missing and wanted persons and the identification of the deceased can sometimes be related to previous convictions, property claims, insurance claims, desertion claims, and similar matters. Several cases must be distinguished, depending upon the condition in which the body was found. The whole body discovered soon after death does not present any serious problems. Drowned, mutilated, and cremated bodies, however, require expert attention. In any case, the clothes and other possessions of the victims, where they are present, provide the simplest clues.

a. **Clothes and Other Articles.** In the absence of the next of kin of a deceased person, a representative of the law enforcement agency having jurisdiction takes possession of all property of value found on the person of the deceased, making an exact inventory and delivering the property to the agency. Subsequently, the property is surrendered to the person entitled to its custody or possession. The medical examiner or his equivalent may take possession of any portable objects useful in establishing the cause of death and deliver them to the agency. The circumstances under which the body is found usually determine the number of identifying clues that are present in the form of possessions. In the deceased's hotel room, an abundance of clues may be found. In other circumstances, there will usually be simply the clothes and a few personal articles. Licenses, Social Security cards, draft cards, ID cards, letters, and similar articles are obviously most helpful. In the absence of such items, the investigator may sometimes establish an identification by means of the clothes alone. If a name or set of initials is in the jacket or hat, the problem is greatly simplified. The clothes may sometimes be traced by one of the following methods:

1) *Tracing by Purchase.* The clothing (and also some other manufactured articles found on the person) will bear some of the following identifying data: brand name; type; model; retail price; size; code number; color; outlet; date; and characteristic marks. It is the aim of the investigator to trace the clothing to the retail store, where an employee may know of the identity of the purchaser.

2) *Laundry and Dry Cleaner's Marks.* One of the best means of tracing the owner of a garment is through the laundry mark on shirts and underwear and the dry cleaner's marks on jackets, trousers, and hats. The law enforcement agencies of large cities and states usually maintain a file of these marks through which the mark can be traced to the launderer or dry cleaner. In some laundries and dry cleaning establishments, a record is maintained of the customer' name and address and the associated clothing marks. Many cases of unknown identity are solved each year by means of such files (see Chapter 34).

b. **Identifying a Whole Body.** The procedure to be followed in identifying a whole body is similar to that for identifying living persons.

1) *Physical Description.* Procedures for describing living persons are given in Chapter 29. In composing a description of a deceased person, the investigator should not be misled by characteristics that are acquired after death. For example, the color of the deceased undergoes certain postmortem changes. The skin tends, with time, to take on a negroid appearance, assuming such colors as blue, blue-black, and brown. The hair is similarly subject to change; brown and red hair becomes lighter and gray and blonde hair darker. Since the color of the hair can be altered, the hair on the head should be compared with that on the other parts of the body. If

the color of the head hair is patchy or if it varies close to the scalp, a dye should be suspected. Samples of the head hair should be requested from the medical examiner for microscopic and chemical examination to determine the presence of coloring matter. A sample of head hair should be preserved in any case in anticipation of the discovery of hairs as a clue. In cases of sexual assault, samples of torso hair should also be taken. Postmortem changes affect even the contours of the body. The features broaden and run together. The body is subjected to swelling. Thus, the weight of the deceased may be grossly over-estimated. The fit of the clothing, however, will give an indication of the degree of swelling.

2) *Fingerprints.* This is the best means of identification. Special techniques must be employed if the fingers have been deteriorated from putrefaction, drowning, mutilation, or burning (see Chapter 31). A set of fingerprints may be forwarded to the FBI with a request for a search. The assistance of other agencies, such as police departments which maintain fingerprint files, should be sought.

3) *Photographs.* Photographs should be taken of the whole body and of the head alone, full face and profile. Significant features such as scars, deformities, and amputations should be photographed. These photographs can be shown to persons who may have known the deceased. They can also be checked against the files of photographs in the identification bureaus of law enforcement agencies.

4) *Age.* The apparent age of the deceased can be estimated only roughly from the teeth and the joining of the bones. The medical examiner, by means of an x-ray examination, can estimate the age from a study of the epiphyses of the bones (the stage of uniting of bones, a condition varying with age). This procedure is helpful only in persons below the age of about twenty-five years. Histological examinations are informative.

5) *Teeth.* Dental structure and dental work provide an excellent means of identification. With the invention of the high-powered drill three decades ago, permitting more sophisticated dental restoration such as tooth capping and root canal work, dentists have been making extensive x-rays and plaster molds, both of which are accurate records of oral anatomy not dependent on the record-keeping ability of the dentist. The forensic dentist is especially

helpful in the identification cases where the corpse is burnt or dismembered. He can determine the approximate age of a person by wear on the teeth, or in the case of preadolescence, by the amount of tooth blood left in the jawbone. The degree of abrasive wear gives a clue to the socioeconomic status of the corpse because it tells something about the diet. Jawbone construction provides anatomical landmarks that never change, no matter how much dental work is performed. Fillings and caps are helpful, since they are highly individual. Probably the most celebrated recent case in which dental evidence played a significant role was the identification of Diane Oughton, as one of the three bodies in the remains of a Greenwich Village town house explosion. A fragment of a little finger and of a jaw with three and one-half teeth were sifted out of the debris. The FBI found a childhood orthodontist of Miss Oughton's and, by comparing the shape of the roots and the bone structure with x-rays taken fifteen years before, was able to confirm the identification they had already made with the fingerprint.

6) **Fractures.** The existence of old fractures may serve as a point of identification.

7) **Blood Group.** Samples of the deceased's blood should be taken for grouping purposes as well as for autoptical reasons. The group and Rh factor provide an additional means of identification. It is the custom of military services to include this information on identification cards.

c. **Mutilated Remains.** To make identification difficult, the criminal sometimes removes or disfigures the head, hands, and feet. Identification then becomes a difficult matter in which the investigator must rely heavily on the medical examiner. Frequently, the assistance of anatomists, dentists, and radiologists is required. The following significant information may be established by the examinations:

1) **Human or Animal.** If a reasonable amount of material is present, this determination is not difficult.

2) **Time Elapsed Since Burial or Death.** A considerable number of years are required for the disappearance of tissue in a buried body. If only bones are discovered, it may be said that they have been buried for a long time. If the organic matter is present, some conclusion can be drawn from the state of decomposition. Again, the

ease of the determination will depend on the amount of material available.

3) *Means Used to Cut Up the Body.* It can readily be determined from a study of the body whether skill was used in its dissection or whether it was cut up without regard for anatomical considerations.

4) *One or Several Bodies.* The examiner can determine usually whether the parts belong to one body or several bodies.

5) *The Sex.* Differences in the weight and structure of the skeleton will indicate the sex.

6) *The Structure.* To form an accurate estimate of the height, it is usually necessary to have the greater part of half the skeleton. A rough estimate can be made from a single bone.

III. THE INVESTIGATION AT THE SCENE

15. Introduction

The proper investigation of a homicide is one of the most exacting tasks with which the investigator can be confronted. He is faced, first of all, with an occurrence of the utmost gravity; hence, the responsibility of competent inquiry is exceptionally great. Secondly, a criminal homicide is a complex crime, since the motives are devious and varied and the methods that can be employed by the criminal are great in number. The variety of physical evidence that may be discovered in connection with a homicide can tax the full resources of the laboratory experts. The investigator arriving on the scene of his first homicide case soon becomes aware of the complexity of the work ahead of him. He is the key man in the investigation; yet he must rely greatly upon the assistance of others. He is, in a way, the coordinator for the various forces that will be brought to bear on the inquiry—the medical examiner, the laboratory technicians, the detective force, the district attorney, and other civilian investigating agencies. To properly utilize these aids the investigator must be aware of the potentialities of the services that are available to him and he must know the appropriate assisting action to be taken. The medical examiner is able to inform him as to the probable cause of death if the body has not been moved or tampered with prior to his examination. The physical evidence may be eloquent in proving important points if it has been discovered by a competent search, collected and preserved according to best practice, and transmitted to the laboratory experts with accurate information. Most important of all, the investigator brings to the investigation, in addition to training, knowledge, fidelity to directions, and adherence to regulations, the invaluable ingredients of good judgment and imagination. Common sense will enable him to establish causal relations between the various elements that are discovered in the course of the inquiry. Imagination will aid him in reconstructing the crime—the process whereby the scene of the crime, the physical evidence, and the information obtained from witnesses are woven together to produce a logical pattern of the course of events that culminated in the fatal act.

16. Preliminary Procedure

On receiving notification or information concerning a possible homicide, the investigator should at once resort to methodical procedure. He should resist impulses arising out of curiosity, a false sense of urgency, or a desire for immediate action. The investigator's initial activities may determine the success or failure of the subsequent investigation. The first step should be the recording of the receipt information. The following data should be recorded:

a. Date and exact time of receiving the information.

b. Method of transmission of the information.

c. Name and other data identifying the person giving the information.

d. Complete details of the information.

17. Action on Arrival

The procedures to be followed with respect to the control, recording, and collecting of evidence at the crime scene have been described fully in Part I. It will be found that the usefulness of the suggestions given there is most fully realized in a homicide case.

IV. BLOOD AND OTHER BODY FLUIDS

18. Introduction

One of the most common clues to be found in connection with homicides is the bloodstain. Homicidal assaults can be especially productive of the victim's blood, traces of which may be carried from the scene on the perpetrator to later connect him with the crime. As an identifying medium, blood possesses limited value. Through a series of tests, it is possible by sampling progressively larger areas of a stain to show first that it is blood; secondly, human blood rather than animal; thirdly, that it belongs to one of four major groups; and finally, under exceptionally favorable conditions of quantity and preservation, that it belongs to one of the many subgroups. Thus, although blood is not a medium of unique identification, varying degrees of probability can be established with respect to the suspect's association with the scene of the crime. To put it more simply, if a bloodstain discovered on the clothing of a suspect is of the same group as the blood of the deceased and different from the suspect's own blood group, there is a strong presumption as to the origin of the stain.

19. The Victim's Blood

In paragraph 14 it is recommended that samples of the deceased's blood should be taken and the blood group determined in all cases of homicide and suicide. The purpose of this procedure is to provide a standard with which suspicious bloodstains on possible weapons or on the suspect's clothing or other possessions can be compared. This precaution is repeated here since experience has shown that in the absence of insistent attention to this point at the time of the autopsy there is a possibility of overlooking this obvious procedure.

20. Bloodstains

By using the four major blood groups, O, A, B, and AB, together with various subgroups, blood types, and factors, it is possible to distinguish a great many different kinds of blood. Under optimum conditions of freshness, quantity, and preservation, however, it is possible to identify a blood stain in only a few of these categories. An old bloodstain, moreover, may have been subject to such deterioration that no more can be done with it than to show that it is human in origin or that it belongs to one of the four major groups. Similarly, a minute stain or a contaminated stain may be severely limited in its grouping potential. In the great majority of blood examinations the laboratory technician cannot go beyond the determination that the blood belongs to one of four major groups. Certain useful conclusions can be drawn on the basis of blood examinations. Although blood cannot be positively identified with an individual, it can be shown definitely that blood could not have come from a certain source. These negative conclusions are often useful in investigations. They are immensely valuable in the settlement of paternity problems. Among the questions that ordinarily can be answered by blood examinations are the following:

a. *Could* this minute stain be blood?
b. *Is* this stain blood?
c. Is it animal or *human* blood?
d. Could this blood have come from the suspect?
e. Is this blood of the same group (and subgroup) as the blood of the suspect?

21. Tests—Preliminary Field Test—Could the Stain be Blood?

In the investigation of a homicide, numerous stains may be brought to the attention of the investigator. The discoverer of the stains may be quite positive that they are blood. On testing it will be found that some are blood and others are lipstick, rust, or one of many substances which appear similar. The investigator should make no conclusions as to the nature of the stain from its appearance. Of course, if the substance is fresh, liquid, and appears to be blood, it can be concluded that it is blood and collected without hesitation. If the stain is questionable, it should be tested by a preliminary chemical test such as the following:

a. **Benzidine.** This is an extremely sensitive test that can be applied to minute stains. If the stain reacts positively, the investigator may presume that it may be blood. Unfortunately, a number of other substances give the same reaction. If the stain reacts negatively, it is not blood. In all cases, the reagent should first be tested with known blood.

1) A small test tube is filled to the height of an inch with distilled water. About ½ gram of benzidine dihydrochloride is placed in the tube and dissolved by shaking. One cubic centimeter of 3% hydrogen peroxide is added and the tube again shaken. The benzidine reagent is now ready for use.

2) A minute part of the stain is scraped or tweezed onto a piece of filter paper. A medicine dropper is used to place a few drops of the reagent on the stain fragment now in the filter paper.

3) If the stain is blood, a blue-green color appears in a short time.

b. **Reduced Phenolphthalein.** This test is an alternative to the benzidine test and shares the same limitations. Two grams of phenophthalein are added to 100 milliliters of 30 per cent sodium hydroxide in a 250 milliliters round-bottom flask. About 20 grams of zinc dust are added to the solution. A water-cooled condenser is attached in an upright position and the solution is refluxed until it is colorless. The solution may then be kept by placing about 10 grams of granulated zinc in the container. In testing, five drops of the reduced phenolphthalein solution are added to 5 milliliters of a saline solution (1.7 grams of sodium chloride in 200 milliliters of distilled water). An equal volume (5 milliliters) of 3 per cent hydrogen peroxide is added to the mixture. A small part of the stain is scraped off and placed in a saline solution in a test tube. A few drops of the reagent are now added to the test tube. If blood is present, a rose color develops immediately.

22. Confirmatory Tests—Is It Blood?

To detemine definitely that the stain is blood, a small portion of the stain is dissolved in the normal saline solution and subjected to one of the following tests.

a. **Teichmann or Hemin Crystal Test.** This is the most common test. It is not effective with heated blood. Identification depends on the formation of hemin crystals upon the application of an appropriate reagent.

b. **Microspectroscopic Test.** A drop of the dissolved stain is placed on the stage of a microscope to which a spectroscope is attached. The appearance of certain lines or bands in the absorption spectrum establishes the fact that the stain is blood.

23. Precipitin Test—Is the Blood of Human or Animal?

With a larger stain, additional tests can be made. The precipitin reaction distinguishes between the blood of a human being and that of an animal. The test is based on the fact that when an animal is injected with the protein of an animal of a different species, an antibody is developed in its serum which causes the latter to react specifically with the protein of any other species. A test animal such as a guinea pig is injected with human blood serum and with whole blood over a period of time. The blood of the test animal provides an antihuman serum. To perform the test, a few drops of the bloodstain dissolved in salt solution are placed in a test tube. A few drops of the anti-human serum are added to the test tube. The formation of a gray precipitation ring at the interface of the two layers within twenty minutes indicates that the stain is human blood.

24. Blood Grouping

A further classification of blood can be achieved by means of certain clumping reactions caused by the presence in human blood of two factors known as agglutinogens and agglutinins. The agglutinogens are found in the red blood cells of all human blood serum of all groups except O. Consequently, when the agglutinogen of a certain group is mixed with its opposing agglutinin, clumping will take place. It is for this reason that care is taken to provide blood of a compatible group in giving a transfusion. By means of clumping properties, it is possible to divide blood into four major groups, namely, O, A, B, and AB. Each person's blood can be placed in one of these groups. The blood group of a human does not change throughout life. The grouping of fresh human blood is a straightforward laboratory procedure. Old bloodstains, however, present difficult problems in blood grouping.

25. Other Group-Specific Substances

A number of other serological fluids which the body contains also have the property of possessing a characteristic group.

a. **Secretors.** It has been estimated that approximately 60 per cent of the population carry in the bloodstream a group-specific substance which makes it possible to determine the blood group of other body fluids such as saliva, semen, tears, urine, perspiration, and nasal secretion. Individuals in this category are known as *secretors*. Studies of innumerable cases have established the following biological conclusions concerning body fluids:

1) The body fluid group of a secretor will always be identical with his blood group.

2) A secretor will never change to a non-secretor (or vice versa) during his life.

b. **Application.** The practical application of the secretor phenomenon lies in the fact that garments and non-blood stains may also provide evidence. The perspiration present in an abandoned shirt or the semen stain on the victim's garment may be sufficient to determine the blood group of the perpetrator. Saliva and urine stains provide similar opportunities. Success in these procedures, however, is infrequent.

26. Location of Stains

a. **Perishable Nature of Blood.** Blood is a type of evidence which undergoes a rapid change in its character with the passage of time, as the process of clotting and drying commences almost immediately on exposure to air. Furthermore, blood offers little resistance to decomposition, especially when exposed to certain conditions and influences which, if prolonged, will cause the specimen to lose its identity. It is, therefore, extremely important that blood samples be sent to the laboratory as soon as possible after their discovery. Prior to a general search of the crime scene, the floor should be examined carefully in order to minimize the danger of loss or destruction caused by being walked upon by persons otherwise engaged in the investigation.

b. **Clothing.** All articles of wearing apparel of the victim and the suspect should be collected for further scrutiny. The shoes, in particular, should be given special attention. No article of clothing should be discarded simply because a superficial examination fails to reveal suspicious stains. Garments which have been washed may still retain sufficient blood to produce a positive reaction.

c. **Fingernails.** It is not unusual to find traces of the blood of the victim under the fingernails of the suspect or under the cuticle at the base of the nail. Similar traces, torn from the suspect, may be found in the same locations on the fingers of the victim. In the latter instance, lacerations of the face and hands of the perpetrator of the crime may have been produced by the victim's instinctive attempts to protect himself. Moreover, the victim would be less likely, and sometimes unable, to wash his hands after the offense in order to remove incriminating traces.

d. **Furniture.** No search for bloodstains on furniture is complete until the *under* sides, as well as the tops, of tables, chairs, desks, radios, and other articles have been examined. This will also apply to the bottoms of all drawers in dressers, vanities, desks, and similar items. It frequently happens that fingerprints in blood are left in these places, and a reconstruction of the movements of the suspect may indicate that such articles have been lifted or otherwise moved during the commission of the crime. Special effort should be directed toward all pieces of furniture which do not appear to be in their accustomed locations.

e. **Motor Vehicles.** The location and amount of blood on the exterior, interior, or in the vicinity of a motor vehicle may often have an important bearing on an investigation. A serious crime such as murder, rape, or assault may have been committed in the vehicle; a body may have been transported from the scene of an offense to another spot for disposition; the automobile itself may have been the instrument of aggression; or the crime may have been of the hit-and-run variety in which the operator of a vehicle has failed to stop after knowingly causing death or personal injuries to another. The search for incriminating bloodstains should be conducted on the exterior as well as the interior of the automobile, with special attention directed to the undercarriage and the front assembly.

f. **Weapons.** Any instrument suspected of having been used to cut, stab, or strike a victim should be forwarded to a laboratory for blood examination. In many cases, it will be found that no attempt has been made to remove telltale stains, particularly when the weapon has been discarded in the immediate area of the offense. It frequently happens, however, that the guilty person will retain possession of the weapon, and at the earliest opportunity, will try to destroy traces of incriminating residue by washing in water or other solvent. In spite of the time and effort expended in this manner, it is sometimes possible to detect bloodstains on certain parts of the instrument, if it has come in contact at any time with the blood of the victim. In his examination, the laboratory technician will devote particular attention to cracks in wooden clubs or handles, to the junction of the blade with the handle of a knife, to the space between the grip and the frame of a pistol or revolver, or in any place where the blood may have seeped while still in a liquid state. It sometimes happens that the stains on exposed surfaces may present an aspect that will deceive the average person. Blood on rusty metal, for example, may appear as a slightly glazed area which blends into the background, or the same reddish, shining, and cracked appearance may be noted in rusty iron when there is no blood present. The possibilities in this phase of investigation are so vast that searches for blood traces cannot be conducted too carefully. It is emphasized that a liberal supply of bloodstained or suspected objects be collected, regardless of the subsequent work entailed in their examination.

g. **Plumbing.** The bathroom and kitchen offer to the criminal a means of disposing of blood, either through the washing of stains from articles of clothing and cleaning rags, or through the use of the bathtub for the dissection of the body of the victim. The mere washing of blood from the hands may leave identifiable traces in a sink or washbowl. When this action is suspected, the towels and washcloths should be collected and submitted for examination, especially if it appears that there has been an attempt to conceal the articles in the laundry or in discarded rubbish. Drain pipes and joints in the plumbing fixtures may be dismantled and examined, sometimes with positive results. The space under the curved rims of certain designs of bathtubs should not be overlooked, as this area is often neglected by the criminal in his attempt to remove traces of blood after the commission of the crime.

h. **Rugs and Similar Material.** Any dark stain, wet or dry, on rugs, upholstery, tapestry, overdrapes, or similar fabrics, should be examined carefully and considered with suspicion, pending a decision concerning its potential value in the investigation.

27. Other Conditions Observed at the Scene

a. **Amount of Blood Near Body.** The average male body of 154 pounds contains approximately 12¾ pints of blood. As soon as a considerable amount of bleeding takes place, a defense mechanism lowers the blood pressure, which has been forcing the blood from a wound, thus decelerating the flow. Some bleeding will occur, therefore, if death is not instantaneous. After death, the blood pressure drops to zero and bleeding ceases. Consequently, it may be said that dead bodies do not bleed; they drain. When a body is found with wounds which indicate that much blood has been lost, but the amount of blood near the body appears to be less than what one would normally expect to find, the logical assumption is that the crime was committed elsewhere. Every effort must be directed to the establishment of the other location. The distance between the two points may provide a clue to the method employed in moving the body, such as by dragging or carrying from a location nearby or by automobile transportation from a more distant spot. The nature of the terrain will indicate the type of search for such evidence as tire tracks, bent or broken bushes, or a trail caused by a heavy object being dragged through grass or some type of soil. A similar search should be conducted if it appears that the body has been moved in an urban area, as, for example, from an automobile to a building or vice versa, from one building to another, from a building to an outside area, from floor to floor, or from room to room. Blood traces may be deposited in the passage of the body between the indicated points.

b. **Clotting of Bloodstains.** The mechanism of blood-clotting is due in part to the existence in the blood of very small, fine-grained particles which are without nuclei and whose origin is unknown. These are known as platelets. On exposure to air, a fibrous coating forms on a bloodstain, generally in three to five minutes, and under normal conditions the entire process of clotting will be completed in ten to twenty minutes, accompanied by a change in the color from red to dark brown. Physically, the blood changes from its liquid state to a mass resembling jelly, surrounded by a wet area produced by the serum, which has separated from the other components. Prolonged clotting and drying of blood in a wound cause the formation of a scab, which acts as a protective seal in the process of natural healing.

c. **Drying of Bloodstains.** A bloodstain begins to dry at the edges and the process continues toward the center of the stain. The length of time required after the complete drying of the stain is governed by many conditions, specifically as follows:

1) *Temperature.* The higher the temperature the greater will be the increase in the speed of drying.

2) *Humidity.* An increased percentage of humidity will slow down the drying speed.

3) *Material.* Bloodstains dry faster on smooth and non-absorbent surfaces.

4) *Exposure to Elements.* Drying is speeded when the stains are exposed to wind and sunlight. Contact with moisture in the form of rain, snow, etc., has a tendency to prolong the process of drying.

5) *Size of Stain.* The larger the stain or pool, the longer it will take to dry.

d. **Direction and Distance of Fall.** A study of the shape and size of a splash or stain of blood, and a comparison with other stains created by a fall at a known angle and from a known height can lead to an approximation of the angle and distance from which the questioned drop of blood has fallen. In this type of experiment, animal blood may be used to prepare standards of comparison.

1) The vertical fall of drops is characterized by a round stain, with or without a surrounding pattern of droplets, depending on the distance of the fall.

2) Drops falling at an angle other than 90 degrees from the

horizontal will form a blot, roughly oval or tear-shaped, with the point extended in the direction of fall. Frequently, droplets will be found in prolongation of or extending from the pointed end, and small splashes from the parent blot will be seen in the area beyond the original point of impact.

28. Collection and Transmission of Blood Specimens

All activities and observations of the investigator pertaining to the evidential use of blood and body fluids must be conducted in a methodical and meticulous manner. Instructions pertaining to the handling of evidence in general are particularly applicable to blood specimens. It frequently happens that blood is overlooked at the crime scene because its familiar characteristics are missing, and it is not recognizable in the form and condition ordinarily associated with blood. It putrefies rapidly at high temperatures and excessive humidity. Specimens submitted for examination are often insufficient for laboratory use. Dried stains are easily cracked, chipped away, and lost through improper handling and packing. The following procedures are suggested as being conducive to the effective preservation of specimens between the time of finding and the ultimate disposition:

a. **Notes.** These should be copious and should be made concurrently with the events described rather than as a result of later recollection. Specific information should relate to the following:

1) Whether the suspect stain is liquid, moist, or solid.
2) The color of the specimen.
3) What photographs were taken and when.
4) When sketches were made.
5) The method of removal.
6) How specimen was marked for identification.
7) The methods used for the protection of the evidence.
8) Facts relating to the transmission to the laboratory, such as the laboratory to which sent and the date of transmission.

b. **Sketches.** A rough sketch should be made of the scene and the immediate area, with measurements and complete information regarding indicated features. In the detailed sketch, small stains may be traced for size and shape, while large stains may be plotted on graph paper. If a sketch of the crime scene has already been accomplished, the detailed sketch will suffice.

c. **Removal of Stains.** If the article on which the stain is found can be sent to the laboratory, it should be submitted intact. In cases where the bulk or weight of the article prohibits its shipment, the stains may be removed using the methods described in Chapter 7.

V. OTHER PHYSICAL EVIDENCE

29. Hairs and Fibers

Hairs from the assailant are sometimes found on the deceased. Fibers from the clothing of the criminal may be found on the clothing of the deceased. Similarly, hairs or fibers from the deceased may be found on the clothing of a suspect. Since these items of evidence are light in weight and difficult to see, great care must be exercised in handling and packaging. The following recommendations will be found useful in collecting hair and fiber evidence and transmitting it for expert examination.

a. Hairs and fibers from different locations at the scene should be placed in separate containers.

b. Hairs and fibers should be placed in round pillboxes or wrapped in druggists' powder paper. The box or paper should then be sealed with transparent tape, marked for identification, and placed in an envelope which is also sealed and marked for identification.

c. Where hairs are found attached to an object, particularly one which has been used as a weapon, such as a hammer or wrench, the object itself should be forwarded to the laboratory for examination without detaching the hairs. In such instances, the area bearing the evidence should be protected by a cellophane or paper wrapping secured with tape before the object itself is packaged for transmittal. Where the object itself is too large to forward to the laboratory, the hairs should be removed and submitted as previously described.

d. **Clothing.** Since the clothing is to be submitted to a laboratory examination by an expert, as described below, there is no need to remove such evidence for separate transmission.

e. **Standard Specimens.** In collecting hair specimens from a suspect and a victim for comparison purposes, obtain several hairs from different sections of each region of the body as may be pertinent to the individual case. For example, in selecting known samples of scalp hair for comparison purposes, at least twelve to fifteen hairs from various areas of the head and preferably full length should be obtained. This precaution is necessary in view of the known fact that the characteristics of hair from one area of the scalp may vary from those of hair taken from other portions of the same head. Where it becomes material to examine the hair of a victim who has sustained a scalp injury, several of the specimens should be taken from the vicinity of the wound. Chapter 41 describes more fully hair and fiber evidence.

30. Shoe and Tire Impressions

Restrictions must be placed on the movements of even authorized personnel until the area has been thoroughly searched for shoe and tire impressions. The approaches to the scene should first be examined. The impressions in earth should be photographed and plaster casts made following the procedures described in Chapter 35.

31. Shoe and Footprints

The violence associated with indoor homicides is often attended by a disturbance of furniture and a scattering of paper. The floor should be searched for the presence of papers which bear shoe prints. In wet weather, particularly, such prints may contain a wealth of detail far exceeding that of an impression in the earth. On tiled surfaces such as bathroom floors, consideration should be given to the possibility of latent footprints which may be developed in the same manner as fingerprints. Foot and shoe prints should be first photographed with the 4 × 5 camera, with the axis of camera perpendicular to the ground.

32. Clothing of the Deceased

a. **Importance.** The clothing of the deceased is an important article of evidence in the investigation of a homicide since it may be part of the *corpus delicti* and can yield valuable information concerning the manner of death. The garments should be described and marked for identification by the medical examiner. The marks and locations of weapons in relation to the body should be studied. Stains, cuts, and holes may be encircled with chalk in patterns which will facilitate repeated location and study without interfering with the examination. It will be found that the deceased's clothing is of great importance in shooting cases. For example, the medical examiner can determine whether the firearm was discharged from a distance or close to the body. Where the bullet has passed through the body, the holes in the clothing aid in establishing the direction of fire under circumstances in which the entrance and exit holes are not readily differentiable.

b. **Disposition of Clothing.** The clothing of a person who is the victim of a homicide should not be given to the family after it has been examined. Ordinarily, it is delivered by the identifying officer to the prosecuting attorney. If the deceased dies in a hospital, the authorities of that institution should be requested to retain the clothes for examination by the medical examiner.

c. **Care of Clothing.** The clothing should be obtained from the morgue or hospital as soon as possible. If moist stains are present on the garments, they should be placed on hangers to dry. After the clothing is thoroughly dry, it should be placed in a large box with as little folding as possible. Each piece should be separated by a layer of paper.

d. **Example of Evidence.** As an example of the importance of an examination of clothing in homicide investigation, a recent case may be cited where the defendant, while admitting the fatal shooting, claimed that it was done in self-defense. The fatal bullet passed completely through the body. In the course of an operation performed on the victim before death, a bullet wound in the front of the abdomen was obliterated. The physician performing the autopsy erroneously interpreted a bullet perforation on the back as an entrance wound and, as a consequence, the plea of self-defense was held in great suspicion despite the presence of strong corroborative evidence. During the trial, it was discovered that the deceased's clothing had not been examined. On studying the garments, it was found that the bullet had perforated all the articles of clothing in front, but not in the back. This fact supported the claim of self-defense.

33. Ligatures and Gags

A careful study should be made of all ligatures, gags, or wads which may be found in the area of the neck and head, or in the mouth and throat in cases of strangulation by ligature or choking. In other cases, ropes, wires, and improvised ligatures and restraining devices may be found on the limbs or body. These articles can sometimes be traced to their source, and their probable ownership can thus be established.

34. Fingernail Scrapings

The fingernails of the deceased sometimes contain indications of an assault. In a struggle with his assailant the victim may scratch him or scrape his clothing. Minute fragments of skin, strands of hair, cloth fibers, and other materials which can serve as useful clues may sometimes be found, particularly in cases of strangulations, smothering, choking, and homicidal assaults with clubs or knives. The medical examiner will ordinarily take fingernail scrapings in these cases. Fingerprinting of the deceased should be postponed until the scraping procedure has been accomplished. The scrapings from each fingernail should be placed in a separate filter paper and appropriately labeled.

VI. POSTMORTEM EXAMINATION

35. General

The term *postmortem* examination is used here to include the procedures followed by the medical examiner, coroner, or other qualified person in the investigation surrounding certain types of death. The procedure includes the examination at the scene of the crime, the identification of the body, the external examination of the body, the autopsy, and subsequent technical examinations, such as toxicological analysis, which the case may require. The postmortem examination may all be accomplished by one physician or it may be performed by a physician in association with a pathologist, toxicologist, serologist, or histologist. The primary purpose of the examination is to determine the cause of death. It is considered the function of the investigator to determine who committed the offense.

36. Qualifications of the Examining Physician

The postmortem examination, especially the autopsy, should be performed preferably by a forensic pathologist. The branch of medicine called pathology is the study of abnormal changes in bodily tissues or functions caused by diseases, poisons, or other bodily affections. By certain techniques, such as .the microscopic examination of samples of tissues from vital organs, the pathologist can draw reliable conclusions concerning the causes of bodily conditions. The forensic pathologist employs special techniques to gather evidence concerning how, when, and where the victim came to his death. His special study is the problem of sudden, unexpected, and violent death. He endeavors to determine whether the nature of the violence employed was suicidal, accidental, homicidal, or other.

37. Availability of Expert Assistance

Since local laws and customs are the determining factors, no definite requirements can be given concerning the qualifications of the physician who will perform the postmortem examination in investigations of homicide. Obviously, an effort should be made to obtain the most qualified persons available. The investigator will, however, be usually restricted to personnel locally available, and to the laws and customs of the community serving such agency. If qualified personnel is not available, the investigator should seek a physician with some experience in postmortem work. Failing this he should obtain the services simply of a person with a degree of doctor of medicine. Where the investigator does not have authority and responsibility in the case, he must abide by local laws and customs. He should, however, remember that the services of the Armed Forces Pathological Institute, FBI Laboratory, and other law enforcement laboratories are available to him for toxicological, pathological, and serological work. Organs and other specimens can be properly collected, preserved, and transmitted over great distances for ultimate examination by qualified persons.

38. When Should an Autopsy be Performed?

As a general rule a postmortem examination including an autopsy should be performed in every death where there is a suspicion of homicide (including suicide). Specifically the following types of death should be the subject of a preliminary examination by a physician: deaths from criminal violence, accidental deaths, suicides, sudden deaths where the person had been in apparent good health, deaths unattended by a physician, deaths occurring in prison, and deaths occurring in any suspicious or unusual manner. The physician should go to the scene of the death and take charge of the dead body. He should then fully investigate essential facts concerning the circumstances surrounding the death. If the cause of the death is established beyond a reasonable doubt, the physician should so report. If, however, in his opinion an autopsy is necessary, this should be performed by a qualified physician. An autopsy is performed when the cause of death is doubtful or when it appears that criminal violence has been employed.

The term *qualified physician* has been used here in referring to the person making the initial examination. Ideally, this person should be a medical examiner, i.e., a doctor of medicine who is a skilled pathologist. Lay persons, whether private citizens, police officers, prosecuting attorneys, or physicians not trained to carry out medicolegal investigations often cannot decide the nature of sudden death, or of death where there has not been any medical attention, and accordingly should not be burdened with that responsibility. Their opinion of any such death should not preclude an investigation by a medical examiner with the authority to decide upon the advisability and necessity of an autopsy and to perform such autopsy. The investigator should not be satisfied with the procedure in practice in some communities of referring only the obviously violent, suspicious cases to the medicolegal department. Laxity in this regard is responsible for the exhumation of bodies which are embalmed and buried too hastily because the violence was not apparent or suspected at the time of death. The later development of new evidence necessitates an exhumation. Often a careful routine postmortem examination in cases first reported as non-suspicious leads to the detection of a number of violent deaths each year in those communities where rigorous medical examiner's laws are in effect.

39. Coroners and Medical Examiners

It should be remembered that the term *medical examiner* is not in universal use even in the United States, nor is the *medical examiner system* (substantially the investigative practice recommended in the preceding paragraph) in widespread use. The term *medical examiner* will be used throughout here on the assumption that the investigator is endeavoring to conform to the best practice in homicide investigation. It is understood that he will frequently find himself in communities and jurisdictions where he must be satisfied perforce with something less than the best practice. The term *pathologist* is used in some communities with the same connotations as *medical examiner.* The title *coroner* is neutral in regard to the degree of education and skill possessed by its owner. This will vary widely with the community; in some states it will be the equivalent of a medical examiner, while in others the coroner may be an undertaker or a barber. In dealing with the latter type of coroner, the investigator may suggest the advisability of further examination by a professional medical man.

40. Removal of the Body

After completing his preliminary examination, the medical examiner orders the removal of the body to the mortuary. An identification tag should first be attached to the body. The transportation of the body must be carefully supervised in order to avoid mutilation and interference with anatomical lesions which may be present on the surface. If the body is handled roughly, new injuries may be produced which are not easily distinguishable from the antemortem injuries. In moving the body it is important to avoid soiling the clothing with foreign dirt or body discharges. Powder marks, hair, dust, and other fragile evidence should not be disturbed.

41. Identifying the Body

The identification of the body to the medical examiner is an obvious and simple procedure which although important may be readily overlooked by the inexperienced. The body of the deceased is identified to the medical examiner by the first representative of the law enforcement agency having jurisdiction who saw it. This identification is a vital link in the chain of evidence. Without it the body autopsied by the medical examiner is not connected to the particular crime of which a suspect will be later accused. The identification may be made at the scene or later at the mortuary. In those cases where the victim survives for a period of time and later dies in a hospital, the identification is of particular importance, since the medical examiner will have first seen the body only at the mortuary. The time and place of identification should be recorded in the investigator's notes and should later become a part of his report of investigation. The manner of identification and the persons to whom it is made should also be made a part of the report.

42. Responsibilities of the Investigator

Obviously, the investigator does not engage in any autopsy work himself. He may, however, be expected to assist in making the necessary arrangements where responsibility has been assumed by another agency. The investigator should be capable of determining whether the medicolegal purposes of the autopsy are being adequately served. He should, moreover, place himself in a position where he can report whether the circumstances under which the autopsy was conducted were proper. For example, he should know whether the body was properly identified to the persons performing the autopsy. He should also make sure that evidence requiring further examination is properly preserved, packed, and transmitted.

43. Procedures in Autopsies

At the time of the autopsy, it is impossible to determine initially all the lines along which the case may develop. Hence, it is desirable that a complete examination be carried out in a systematic manner. The examination is not limited to the region in which the cause of death is supposed to exist and ordinarily does not even begin in this area. The requirements of the case dictate the order of procedure but in all cases a fixed routine governs the operation. This routine is established on anatomical considerations, mechanical convenience, and the general principle that a structure should be examined before it is disturbed. The customary order is as follows: external examination, head and brain, incision of the body, thorax, abdomen, pelvis, extremities, and an examination of the various regions. Microscopic studies of selected portions supplement the unaided visual examinations.

44. Reporting the Autopsy

A record of the findings of an autopsy is called an autopsy *protocol*. The preferred protocol is one which is dictated by the operator as the examination progresses. Negative as well as positive findings are recorded. Many physicians employ a prepared autopsy blank which guides the procedure and assures completeness as well as order.

45. Legal Considerations

An autopsy must be conducted in accordance with the laws of the state or territory governing the conditions under which an autopsy is performed. The investigator should scrupulously avoid any violation of these laws in his efforts to cooperate with the authorities. The following general information will serve as a guide in many situations.

a. **Authorization.** Generally speaking, an unauthorized autopsy is a tort (the offending party is subject to civil suit for damages). Authorization for an autopsy may be made by consent of the person entitled to custody of the body, by the coroner or medical examiner, or by the will of the deceased. Since the dead have no right to privacy, the liability for an unauthorized autopsy is based on the outraged sensibilities of the person entitled to custody. The coroner, or medical examiner, can authorize autopsy only for statutory purposes. It should be noted that unauthorized spectators or unauthorized use of photographs may constitute grounds for damage claims.

b. **Privileged Communications.** Ordinarily the information which is obtained by an autopsy is not privileged.

c. **Property Rights.** A dead body is not property and a person cannot own a dead body or acquire title thereto. Since, however, the duty of burial falls on the next of kin, the custody of the body is given to this person. Interference with rights of custody and interment of the dead may result in recovery of damages for mental pain and suffering.

d. **Disposition of the Body.** The regulations of the state department of health control the embalming, transportation, and interment of a dead body.

e. **Exhumation.** The principle of the sanctity of the tomb controls disinterment. The coroner or medical examiner may request the sheriff in writing to disinter a body for examination.

VII. TIME OF DEATH

46. Importance

One of the first steps in an investigation of a homicide is to determine the time of death. Although it may not be possible to set the time precisely, good estimates within certain limits can be

established by observation of the following changes that take place in the body after death:
 a. Temperature and rate of cooling.
 b. Postmortem lividity.
 c. Rigor mortis.
 d. Putrefaction.
These changes can provide information on the following points:
 a. Time of death.
 b. Alterations in the position of the body after death.
 c. Whether the death was suicide or a murder.

47. Temperature

Normally the temperature of the body is 98.6°F. The rate of cooling depends on the following factors:
 a. Temperature of the air and the manner in which the body is clothed. On cold days the rate of cooling is greater. Heavy clothing will retard the cooling.
 b. The age, size of a person, and the amount of fat on the body. A fat person of 250 pounds will tend to cool slowly. Aged persons with less subcutaneous fat will cool more rapidly.

48. Postmortem Lividity

This is the dark blue discoloration that is observable on the parts of the body which are nearest the ground. The blood settles under its own weight into the lowest parts of the body. This coloring appears about two hours subsequent to death. After the blood has settled, it tends to clot in the tissues. Hence, although the body is moved after death, the lividity remains. If a body is found with postmortem lividity on the upper surface, it can be concluded that the body was moved after death. It is important to differentiate between discoloration due to lividity and that due to bruises. Close observation will reveal distinct differences.
 a. The bruise may have a swelling or an abrasion; lividity does not have these indications.

b. The color of the bruise is variable; that of lividity is uniform.

c. Lividity appears only on the low-lying parts of the body; bruises may appear on any part.

d. In the case of lividity, an incision will reveal the fact that the blood is still in the vessels; in bruises an incision shows that the blood has broken out of the vessels.

49. Rigor Mortis

The muscles of the body stiffen after death, because of the chemical changes that take place within the muscle tissue (the accumulation of waste products causes the coagulation of the myocin in the muscles). Immediately after death the body is limp and relaxed. A relaxing of the sphincters leads to incontinence. With the onset of rigor mortis the body becomes exceptionally stiff. The stiffening process begins at the neck and lower jaw and spreads downward. All the muscles, voluntary and involuntary, including the heart muscle, contract.

a. **Time Required.** Rigor mortis may begin to set in fifteen minutes after death or fifteen hours after. On the average, it commences in about five to six hours after. The upper part of the body is affected within about twelve hours and the whole body within about eighteen hours.

b. **Duration.** Rigor mortis usually disappears within thirty-six hours. The head and neck once more become relaxed and the limpness gradually extends to the lower parts of the body. The process may take from eight to ten hours.

c. **Estimating Time of Death.** Many variables enter into the speed with which rigor mortis sets in and disappears. Great heat will accelerate the process by coagulating the proteins in the muscles. Individual differences such as relative muscular development affect the time. In general, however, the investigator may employ the following rough rule:

1) Rigor mortis should begin within ten hours after death.

2) The whole body should be stiff within twelve to eighteen hours after death.

3) Stiffening disappears within thirty-six hours after death.

d. **Cadaveric Spasm.** Sometimes, stiffening occurs immediately after death. This happens when there is a severe injury to the central nervous system or when there was great tension at the moment of death. The body becomes stiff rapidly and the hand may be found clutching the weapon. In such cases it is strong presumptive evidence of suicide. Ordinarily, the hand relaxes after death and the weapon falls away. If a weapon is subsequently placed in the hand of a dead person, it will lie there loosely. It is not possible to force the hand to grasp the weapon tightly. The tenacious grasp is characteristic of cadaveric spasm; hence, its importance in questions of suicide.

50. Indicative Acts

Logical deductions concerning the true time of death can often be made by careful study of the crime scene and the reports or evidence of the activities of the deceased prior to death.

a. **Acts Performed by the Deceased While Alive.** Certain evidence present at the scene may indicate activities of the deceased and establish the fact that he was alive at a certain time.

1) *Lights.* The fact that the lights in a house are on or off will suggest whether the crime occurred during the day or night.

2) *Collections.* Milk, mail, and newspapers are ordinarily collected within a definite span of time. The presence or absence of these objects from their place of delivery is significant.

3) *Preparations.* Meals prepared or eaten indicate the lapse of time intervals. The shining of shoes, brushing of teeth, bathing, and other actions may be related to a definite time by one familiar with the personal habits of the deceased.

b. **Acts Not Performed.** The failure to perform certain customary acts indicates that death had already occurred. Thus, negative conclusions can be associated with the actions listed in the preceding paragraph.

c. **Correlation of Other Events with Death.** Independent events which affect the crime scene can be used to set certain time limits to the time lapse since death. For example, in an outdoor crime scene the area beneath the body may be found to be unaffected by a rainfall or snowfall. Obviously the body must have been situated on the spot prior to the time set by weather bureau statistics for the beginning of the precipitation.

51. Putrefaction

In cases where the elapsed time interval is a matter of days, the changes of the body attributable to putrefaction become important. The onset and rate of development of putrefaction are influenced mainly by the temperature of the environment. Thus putrefaction may be well developed within a day in tropical surroundings or may be scarcely observable after months of exposure to a freezing atmosphere. The principal perceptible changes are:

a. *Bloating* of the body by gas. With the passage of time the gas escapes and the bloated tissues collapse. Disintegration or desiccation sets in depending on the humidity of the body.

b. *Darkening* of the skin in suspended parts of the body.

c. Green *discoloration* of the skin of the abdomen.

d. Formation of *blisters* filled with fluid or gas.

52. Insects

A competent entomologist can sometimes estimate the time elapsed since death by the kinds of insects present on the remains. The time at which insects attack a dead body is partly determined by the temperature and the accessibility of the body. Flies may lay eggs between the lips or eyelids within a few minutes. Maggots may be present within twenty-four hours. Different kinds of insects are attracted according to the relative freshness of the meat. As long as the temperature exceeds 40°F., insects of one kind or another will infest and feed upon the body.

53. Chemical Changes

Chemical analysis of unputrefied bodies may provide valuable information concerning the time of death. The numerous chemical changes which take place in orderly sequence enable the pathologist to draw some useful conclusions.

VIII. ASPHYXIA

54. Asphyxia

Asphyxia or suffocation is a suspension of breathing due to a deficiency of oxygen in the red blood cells. Among the forms which asphyxia may take are drowning, hanging, strangulation, choking, and smothering. Death results if the oxygen supply to the blood and tissues falls below a certain level. If breathing stops for a period of three to four minutes, movement ceases. The heart, however, will continue to beat for another five minutes.

a. **Forms.** Asphyxia can occur in a number of ways. In all of these forms of death, postmortem examination can yield only the information that death resulted from asphyxia. The following may cause death from asphyxia:

1) Disease such as pneumonia.
2) Cutting off air externally as in drowning or smothering.
3) Cutting off air in the throat by choking or hanging.
4) Breathing certain gases.
5) Poisoning or wounds.

b. **Postmortem Appearance.** Lividity of the mucous membranes is apparent; lips are pale blue to black; blue fingers and toenails can be seen; face is usually calm, but may be distorted; sometimes froth appears at the mouth; postmortem lividity is well marked because the blood is dark venous in color. The postmortem appearance of asphyxia is not an indication that death did not come from natural causes. Death of this kind is due to lack of oxygen in the tissue. It is, then, of extreme importance to discover the cause of asphyxiation.

55. Hanging

Usually, hanging is suicidal; sometimes it is accidental. Rarely is it used as a means of murder. It is not necessary that the body be suspended clear from the ground for death to take place. The body may be half-prone or in a sitting position.

a. **Causes of Death.** There are several causes of this type of death:

1) Asphyxia attributable to the tongue pressing upward and backward. This is the most common cause.

2) Occlusion or tightening of the great vessels of the neck. With the supply of blood to the brain cut off, unconsciousness intervenes. This may take place in a few seconds or in the space of several minutes. This rapidity of occurrence is an explanation of those cases of accidental hanging in which it appears that a minor effort would have freed the person.

3) Inhibition of the heart due to pressure on the vagus.

4) In legal hangings, the fracture-dislocation of the spine is the most common cause of death.

b. **Postmortem Appearance.** The knot is usually on the left side. If a small rope is used a deep groove will be made in the neck, under the jaw bone. Black and blue marks are visible along the edges of the groove. After several hours, the tongue protrudes slightly from the mouth.

c. **Accident, Suicide, or Murder.** The following indications are helpful in distinguishing accident from purpose:

1) *Accident.* Accidental hanging of adults is extremely rare. If a young boy is found dead from hanging or a child is found hung by the cords of the venetian blinds, the occurrence can usually be attributed to accident. Unconsciousness takes place so rapidly that death intervenes before discovery.

2) *Suicide.* Hanging is a common form of suicide. The person may bind his hands or feet. If the body is not completely suspended, it is usually a case of suicide, since a murderer will strive to achieve complete suspension.

3) *Murder.* Hanging, as remarked above, is a very infrequent form of murder. Ordinarily, it would be necessary for the victim to be unconscious from drugs, alcohol, or a blow before succumbing to the hanging procedure.

4) *Hanging After Death.* Hanging may be employed after a murder has been committed by other means in order to give the appearance of suicide. Other signs of violence may be visible about the neck to indicate prior strangulation.

56. Drowning

In drowning, death is the result of asphyxia. The lungs ordinarily are not filled with water. In the process of drowning the person takes some water in the mouth and begins to choke. Irritation of the mucous membranes result in the formation of a great deal of mucus in the throat and windpipe. Efforts to breathe produce a sticky foam which may be mixed with vomit. The foam prevents the passage of air into the lungs.

a. **Appearance.** Drowning presents a characteristic appearance if the body has not been in the water too long. In addition to the fine foam about the mouth and nose, the body is usually pale, although some areas may redden because of the sudden lowering of temperature in cold water.

b. **Diagnosis.** Was the death of the deceased due to drowning or was the person dead before being thrown into the water? This question can sometimes be answered by the medical examiner from an examination of the body. The following indications are looked for in determining true drowning:

1) Articles grasped in the hand, such as seaweed.
2) Swelling of the lungs.
3) Signs of asphyxia.
4) The nature of the water in the stomach.
5) The mouth is usually found open.
6) Comparison of the chloride content and the magnesium content in the right and left ventricles of the heart.

c. **Emergence of the Drowned Body.** Invariably a submerged body will rise again. The bacteria in the body cause the formation of gases which distend the body until it is again buoyant. The time required for emergence depends on the fat content of the body and upon the temperature of the water. Weights attached to the body will, of course, increase the required time. Eventually, the gas escapes from the tissues and the body sinks once again.

IX. BURNING, LIGHTNING, AND ELECTRIC SHOCK

57. General

The finding of a body in a burned building or vehicle presents a number of special problems in homicide investigation. The fire may be incendiary or accidental in origin; the death may be accidental or intended; finally, the cause of death may be other than the fire itself. Combining these possibilities will present the following possible situations.

a. **Accidental Fire and Accidental Death.** The investigation in this situation is centered around the question of negligence. The improper storage of fuel, amateur electrical work, or other careless act or omission may point to negligence. The techniques of arson investigation are applicable.

b. **Accidental Fire and Intended Death.** It is possible that after the commission of a homicide, a fire accidentally broke out. The investigator is faced here with the probem of investigating a homicide in which much of the evidence has been destroyed.

c. **Arson and Accidental Death.** Although the arsonist may not have been aware of the presence of a human being in the building, he can be charged with murder if a death is caused by the fire.

d. **Arson and Intended Death.** A criminal may use fire as the lethal agent or, more commonly, he may employ the fire for the purpose of concealing a homicide. An attempt may be made to conceal a suicide by fire.

e. **Arson and Death from Natural Causes.** It may be desired by the criminal to make death by natural causes appear to be the result of accidental fire in order to collect additional insurance.

58. Cause of Death

From the preceding outline of the problems resulting from the combination of fire and death it is apparent that the establishment of the cause of death is the most significant step in the investigation. Among the more common causative factors in the death of a person in a burning building are the following:

a. **Exposure to Gases.** During the course of a fire noxious gases are generated. The gases can cause death either because they are so searingly hot that they burn the skin and air passages or because they are toxic.

b. **Direct Exposure to Flame.** A vital organ exposed to flames can be completely incapacitated or destroyed to the point where life can no longer be supported.

c. **Falls While Attempting Escape.** In an effort to escape from the flames, the victims of a fire will take extraordinary risks in climbing, often falling to their deaths. Theater and hall fires may result in death from trampling or crushing as a consequence of panic.

d. **Falling Beams and Masonry.** The burning of a building naturally loosens the elements of its structure with considerable hazard to persons trapped within.

59. Mechanisms of Death

The precaution that should underlie the investigator's point of view in the investigation of conflagration deaths is the avoidance of the assumption that death occurring in a fire is necessarily attributable to exposure to the flames. A list of the actual mechanisms of deaths in fires must include the following:

a. **Carbon Monoxide Poisoning.** Obviously, there is a great amount of incomplete combustion in a building fire. The result, which is a source of comfort to relatives, is that the victim dies by asphyxiation or by the incapacitation due to the carbon monoxide in the blood. Persons sitting too close to an ordinary fire in a brazier are sometimes overcome by carbon monoxide and fall face forward into the fire.

b. **Pulmonary Irritants.** Fires in factories or other commercial establishments where certain chemicals are stored are characterized by the generation of great amounts of unusual gases such as pulmonary irritants, the inhalation of which can rapidly cause death. Among the gases sometimes found in fires are oxides of nitrogen; acrolein; refrigerant gases such as ammonia, freon, and methyl chloride; and phosgene, which is generated on burning carbon tetrachloride.

60. Antemortem and Postmortem Changes

The critical question in many investigations of deaths in fires is concerned with whether the deceased was alive at the time of the fire. Often a person desiring to conceal a homicide will look on arson as the only practical solution to his problem. The body, however, does not burn as readily as the arsonist imagines. It resists the destructive forces of fire with astonishing durability, and frequently there is sufficient evidence remaining for the medical examiner to draw some useful conclusions.

a. **Life Probably Present During Fire.** The following signs suggest that the victim may have been alive during the conflagration although unconscious or dying from other causes:

1) Smoke stains about the nostrils, in the nose and the air passages.

2) Carbon monoxide in the blood.

3) Blistering and marginal reddening of the skin.

b. **Life Not Necessarily Present During Fire.** A conclusion of this nature can be made only by an experienced pathologist who is aware of the origin of the anatomical changes that can result from exposure of a dead body to fire. The so-called *pugilistic posture*, in which the arms and wrists are flexed in a boxer's pose, is of no value in this determination, since a body exposed to heat can acquire this attitude as a consequence of heat rigor regardless of the cause or time of death. Similarly, skin splits, fractures, and other signs suggestive of injury will have no significance for the investigator until they are interpreted by the pathologist in terms of their cause and probable time of occurrence in reference to the fire.

61. Lightning

Death from lightning is due either to fibrillation of the heart (marked change in strength and rhythm of the heartbeat) or paralysis of the respiratory center. There is no characteristic appearance. When a person is struck by lightning, he may be thrown into the air for a considerable distance, with consequent fractures and lacerations. Burns may be observed particularly in the areas covered by metal objects worn near the skin, such as religious medals or garter clips. At times, highly typical superficial burns may be observed in the shape of arborescent (treelike) markings caused by variations in skin conductivity. To decide whether lightning is the cause of death, the following steps are useful:

a. Eliminate all other common causes.

b. Determine, by interview, the storm and lightning activity in the immediate neighborhood.

c. Look for signs of lightning strikes on trees and other tall objects near the scene.

d. Look for skin burns under metal objects and for treelike markings.

62. Electrocution

Deaths from electric shock are similar to those from lightning. A combination of small voltage and high current or high voltage and small current may cause death. Potentials as low as 50 volts have been known to be fatal. The electric chair is ordinarily charged with 1700 volts. Most important in determining the danger of electricity is the question of good contact with good ground. Wet hands on plumbing fixtures combined with standing in water cause many deaths in bathrooms; wires falling into pools of water present another hazard. A high voltage will send the heart into a spasm with death rapidly following. Low voltage such as 110 volts can cause death if the person is well grounded, but death does not occur with the same rapidity. Fibrillation of the heart takes place (the strength and rhythm of the heartbeat are altered). As a consequence, there is a failure of blood supply to the brain and the person lapses into unconciousness. If this continues, the heart ceases to beat and death follows.

a. **Skin Appearance.** Although the resistance of the skin causes the electrical energy to be transformed into heat, an electrical injury is not necessarily a burn. Often no mark is apparent where contact was made. The true electrical injury is an elevated, round, grayish-white or yellow, wrinkled area. The dried skin may peel. The surrounding area may be black or may be burned.

b. **Postmortem Appearance.** Ordinarily the appearance is not sufficiently characteristic to exclude all other causes. Pulmonary edema (swelling) and the appearance of asphyxia are usually present. Entrance and exit lesions together with the physical surroundings are helpful in forming a diagnosis.

X. WOUNDS IN GENERAL

63. Classification

For the purposes of investigation, wounds may be classified according to the nature of the instrument used in their production as follows: Wounds due to cutting or stabbing; wounds caused by an instrument having no blade; gunshot wounds. In making the postmortem examination the doctor attempts to answer questions relating to the following points:

a. The nature and extent of the wound and the extent of damage to the organs. From this examination it may be possible to determine the nature of the weapon used.

b. **The Cause of Death.** It should not be assumed that the victim died as a direct result of the wounds. Although the body may bear severe wounds, it is possible that death was caused by a fall or by heart failure.

c. The time elapsing between the infliction of the wounds and death.

d. **The Nature of the Occurrence.** Is it accident, suicide, or murder?

e. The condition of the victim with regard to speech and the use of his limbs after receiving the wound.

64. Stabbing and Cutting Wounds

A common form of homicide is that resulting from the use of a knife, or other instrument possessing a blade.

a. **Nature and Extent of the Wound.** It should not be concluded from a simple visual examination that a wound was caused by a knife. Sometimes gunshot wounds striking the body surface at an angle may have the appearance of a slash. A person falling and striking his head on a curb, radiator, or on ice may suffer a laceration resembling a knife wound. The nature of the wound made by a knife will in general depend on the following:

1) The type of knife used, and the area, shape, and length of the blade, whether single or double-edged, sharpness.

2) The manner in which the knife was used. The action of stabbing, i.e., plunging the knife into the body, is usually accompanied by a cutting motion before it is withdrawn. One result of this motion is that the length of the entry slit or hole is larger than the blade of the knife.

3) *Part of the Body.* The elasticity and thickness of the skin vary in different parts of the body, thus determining in part the size and shape of the wound.

4) *Depth of Stab.* An indication of the length of the knife can be obtained from the depth of the stab. The dissecting surgeon can usually determine the depth of the wound during the autopsy.

b. **Cause of Death.** In determining the cause of death in cases where the deceased bears stab wounds, the doctor does not assume that death resulted from the wounds. The actual cause is determined by means of an autopsy. The following causes are considered:

1) *Primary Causes*

a) HEMORRHAGE. Where the large artery is cut, the death can be attributed to bleeding. The quantity of blood visible is also an indication.

b) VITAL ORGAN. Injury to a vital organ is readily determined by the autopsy.

c) SHOCK. The victim may have been subjected to a number of small injuries, no one of which is sufficient to cause death. In these cases the death may be attributed to shock. Fear, inhibitions, total affected area, trauma, and other considerations assist in the diagnosis of shock.

2) *Secondary Causes.* The victim may not die from the original wounding but rather from an ensuing complication such as pneumonia or tetanus.

c. **Time Elapsed.** By observing the condition of the wound the doctor can estimate within twelve hours the time elapsed between receiving the injury and death. It is possible also to determine whether a wound was received before or after death. Such information is of value when an effort has been made to conceal true causes of death by inflicting stab wounds. If the wound is received before death, it gapes and usually bleeds profusely; if received after death, the wound does not gape and bleeds but slightly.

d. **Accident, Suicide, or Murder.** Usually a death by stabbing or cutting presents a murder or a suicide case. Rarely is it an accident.

1) *Accidental.* Accidental deaths due to cutting or stabbing are ordinarily the result of a fall. For example, if a person falls on a pitchfork, picket fence, or against a long needle the projection may puncture a vital organ.

2) *Suicide.* The throat, left wrist, left chest, and femoral artery are the parts of the body most commonly attacked in suicides by stabbing or cutting. Of these, the most frequently occurring form of suicide is that of cutting the throat with a razor or knife. The razor is usually held in the right hand; the cut is begun below the left ear and drawn under the chin to the right side. One common indication of suicide is the existence of superficial cuts, approximately one inch long, at the point of origin of the wound. These cuts are referred to as *hesitation marks*. They ordinarily indicate that the person tested the razor on his skin before summoning sufficient courage to make the fatal slash. The presence of the razor or knife tightly clenched in the hand of the dead person is also considered strong evidence of suicide. Another indication of suicide is the finding of the body at the point where the cutting or stabbing was done. In cases of homicide the victim in an effort to escape or pursue his assailant runs away from the point of occurrence leaving blood drops and other traces as he goes.

3) *Homicide.* If the victim is awake at the time of the attack, it is difficult to kill him by cutting alone. Stabbing strokes of the knife must ordinarily be employed. In defending himself the victim may receive wounds on the palms of the hands and outer surfaces of the forearms. If the victim grasps the knife, deep gashes may be observed in the palm or under surface of the fingers. The fatal wounds are usually in the neck or the upper chest. Wounds in the back are obviously indicative of homicide.

e. **The Crime Scene.** In addition to the usual matters connected with the crime scene there are certain points of special interest in stabbing and cutting crimes. The investigator should note the condition of the clothing; the photographs should show the position of the hands. If a hand is gripping a knife, attention should be directed to the firmness of the grip, the direction in which the blade is pointing with relation to the hand, and the direction in which the cutting edge is pointing. The presence or absence of defense wounds should be observed. The extent of the bleeding and the condition of the blood should also be noted.

f. **Information Obtained from the Autopsy.** Ordinarily in cases where death appears to be attributable to a knife wound, an autopsy is performed. The investigator may then obtain from the surgeon information such as the following:

1) *The Cause of Death.* It is not to be assumed that the victim died of the knife wounds. The true cause must be ascertained from the surgeon.

2) *The Type of Weapon.* An estimate of the size, shape, and sharpness of the knife or other weapon can be made from an examination of the wounds. The depth of penetration and the dimensions of the wounds are indications of these characteristics of the weapon.

3) *Circumstances Surrounding the Attack.* The character and location of the attack suggest the vigor of the resistance offered by the victim to the assault.

65. Blunt Force or Direct Violence

Under this heading will be placed deaths caused by the application of direct violence, a category including by far the largest proportion of the homicides with which the investigator must deal. Clubbing over the head, kicking in the stomach, and hurling the victim to the ground or into some other stationary object are examples of the work of blunt force. In general, assaults, motor vehicle homicides, and negligent homicides frequently involve the use of blunt force. Although death by direct violence is accomplished in a crude manner, the cause of death may be difficult to establish. The external appearance of bruises is not a reliable indication of the seriousness of the internal damage. The part of the body directly affected, the nature of the instrument used, and the degree of force exercised in the application of the instrument are determining factors.

a. **Head Injuries.** In approximately 45 per cent of the fatal motor vehicle accidents, the cause of death is an injury to the head. Similarly, in death from assaults and falls, damage to the head is the most important factor. The scalp lying over the hard skull is easily lacerated by blunt force with a resulting appearance suggestive of the use of a sharp instrument. Injury to the scalp and a state of unconsciousness are not reliable indications of the extent of serious damage to the brain. The medical examiner by examining the injuries to the skull and brain can make certain deductions as to the nature, extent, and direction of the force and the type of instrument used. His description of the damage to the head employs the introductory term *fracture of the skull*.

b. **Spine.** Fracture of the spine occurs most commonly in falls and motor vehicle accidents. Sometimes spine fractures are due to indirect violence such as a punch on the chin, diving into shallow water, and a fall of a weight on the head.

c. **Neck.** A broken neck in itself is not the cause of death. Death will follow a broken neck if there has been sufficient damage to the spinal cord. A diagnosis of an injury of this type can only be made by an autopsy.

d. **Chest.** Blows or crushing wounds on the chest may fracture the ribs, causing them to pierce the lung or heart and thus resulting in death. In motor vehicle accidents in which the driver is thrown against the steering wheel, the heart becomes squeezed between the sternum and the vertebral column and death may follow from heart failure. If the violence is exceptionally severe, the heart may be crushed, ruptured, or torn out of place.

e. **Abdomen.** An injury to the abdomen may result from a fall, kick, or motor vehicle accident. Although only slight abrasions may be visible externally, the damage to the organs may be fatal. The liver, spleen, and kidneys may be ruptured, resulting in death from hemorrhage. A rupture of the stomach and intestines can follow as a result of crushing against the spine. For example, in a street fight an assailant may drive his knee into the abdomen of the victim, with fatal consequences.

XI. GUNSHOT WOUNDS

66. General

In the investigation of a death caused by firearms the wound is examined for the purpose of determining the nature and type of the weapon employed; the distance and direction of fire; and the relative positions of the victim and the assailant at the time of occurrence. If the bullet is still remaining in the body, the surgeon will recover it. From the fatal bullet additional information can be obtained concerning the character of the weapon. If a gun is discovered which is thought to be the murder weapon, it may be possible to identify or exclude it by means of a comparison between fatal and test bullets. In the investigations of unexpected death all weapons, bullets, and shells should be submitted for expert examination as described in Chapter 7.

67. Nature and Extent of the Wound

The two types of wounds, entrance and exit, are studied with regard to certain characteristics which vary with the kind of ammunition used; the firing distance; ricocheting (striking another object before hitting the body); passage through clothing; and path through the body.

a. **Entrance Wounds.** The shape, size, and appearance of the entrance wound are affected by the distance of discharge, the type of weapon, the nature of the gunpowder, and the affected part of the body. The terms near and far discharge are used below in a relative sense. At one time when black powder was in common use, a gun fired from a distance of a few feet would leave distinct evidence of the closeness of discharge. With modern ammunition this effect is not apparent when the distance of discharge exceeds a few inches. Wounds, however, vary with the discharge distance and some useful conclusions can be drawn from a consideration of certain characteristics of the wound.

1) *Near Discharge.* When a bullet strikes the skin, it pushes against a tough, elastic surface which it stretches and indents. A part of the skin removes the grime from the sides of the bullet and forms a gray ring around the entrance wound. The wound itself is larger than the bullet, since at close distance it is affected by undispersed explosive gases. Powder, clothing, and, in cases of shotguns, a wad may be discovered in the wound. The powder is not completely burned, and small particles of the unburnt powder are driven into

the skin by the explosive gases, resulting in a "tattooing ring." Powder marks and scorching are more prominent on the side from which the bullet came.

2) *Far Discharge.* The entrance wound reveals no discharge products such as tattooing or scorching. Because of the absence of explosive gases the wound is smaller than the bullet. The edges of the skin are usually inverted.

3) *Shotguns.* This type of discharge is recognized by the presence of shot in the wound. The most common type of shotgun found at the scene of a murder is the 12-gauge shotgun. This weapon, when fired from a distance of 1 to 3 feet, will make a hole in the body of 1½ to 2 inches in diameter. When fired from greater distance the gun produces no central hole but rather a number of small wounds. The size of the pattern will depend on whether or not the shotgun is chokebored, i.e., narrowed slightly in the muzzle to concentrate the pattern. A search should always be made for the wadding since it gives an indication of the gauge of the gun. If the discharge distance is less than 10 feet, the wad will usually be found in the body. Outdoors the wadding can usually be found within a radius of 50 feet from the gun.

b. **Exit Wounds.** If the bullet passes through the body unobstructed by bone, the typical exit wound is small and everted (skin edge turned out). Where the bullet strikes bone, it may turn over on its axis, push fragmented matter ahead in its path, and produce a large exit wound. It is difficult to draw useful conclusions from the relative sizes of the entrance and exit wounds. If the gun is fired from a distance, both entrance and exit wounds may be of the same size. At a close distance the relative size will depend on whether the bullet struck bone in its path.

68. Accident, Suicide, or Murder

In the absence of eyewitnesses it is not always a simple matter to determine whether a death from gunshot wounds is an accident, suicide, or murder. The circumstantial evidence is helpful in some cases. Often, however, no conclusion can be drawn.

a. **Accident.** Gunshot deaths attributable to accident are quite common. Pulling a gun through a hedge; carelessly cleaning rifles; pointing guns at other people in jest; untutored handling of guns; and similar misuse of a firearm can result in a fatal accident. Questions of motive and opportunity must be investigated before a judgment of accident can be made. One of the most important factors to be considered in drawing any conclusion is the distance from which the shot was fired.

b. **Suicide.** The determination as to whether a death due to a gunshot wound is suicidal in nature can often be a difficult problem. A suicidal death can be contrived to appear accidental for the purpose of defrauding an insurance company. For the same purpose the suicide may arrange the circumstances surrounding his death so that the conclusion of murder will be drawn.

1) *Location of Wound.* The position of the wound in the body is of great importance. In murder the wound may be found in any part of the body. Certain areas, however, are relatively inaccessible to the suicide. Typically, suicides select an area such as the right temple, the mouth, the center of the forehead, beneath the chin, the left chest, behind the right ear, and in the center of the back of the head. The majority of suicide wounds are inflicted in the head, at the right temple. The gun is usually held against the skin so that the imprint of the muzzle and the front sight may be seen. The next most popular area for suicides is the mouth. The muzzle of the gun is placed in the mouth.

2) *Distance of Discharge.* Without the aid of some ingenious mechanical device a person cannot commit suicide unless the gun is within a few feet of his body. If the gun is fired close to the victim (a distance less than 18 inches), a discoloration is visible on the exposed skin about the entrance wound. Two types of discoloration can be found, namely, smudging and tattooing. These are not visible if the bullet has gone through clothing. Ordinarily, however, the suicide is reluctant to shoot through clothing and bares the skin covering the area in which he intends to shoot.

a) SMUDGING. Burnt powder produces a smoke and powder which is deposited on the skin when the gun has been held at a distance of from 2 to about 18 inches. The result is a dirty, grimy appearance at the entrance. The size of the smudge is a function of the caliber of the bullet, the type of powder used, and the firing distance.

b) TATTOOING. When the gun is fired, unburnt powder and particles of molten metal are also discharged in the blast. On striking the body surface the powder and particles imbed themselves in the lower layers of skin. The effect is known as "tattooing." The size of the tatooed area is a function of the caliber, powder charge, and the discharge distance from the victim. In estimating the distance of discharge the expert fires test shots from varying distances with the fatal gun and similar cartridges.

3) *Position of the Body.* Useful conclusions can often be made from the position in which the body is found with relation to other objects. In some cases it is obvious that the "stage has been set." Before shooting himself the person may have removed a garment to bare his chest and may have so placed himself that he would fall on a bed. Preparations such as these eliminate the probability of accident and point to suicide.

4) *Actions After Receiving Wounds.* Although a person has shot himself fatally, he may still be capable of rational acts. Even a person who has shot himself through the temple may still be able to move and alter the scene of death. The investigator cannot conclude, therefore, that the scene has not been changed since the shots were fired.

5) *Clenching the Weapon.* A strong indication of suicide is the presence of the weapon clenched in the hand. It is said to be impossible to reproduce this tension in the grip by placing the gun in the hand after rigor mortis has set in. If the weapon lies loosely in the hand or if it apparently has fallen away from the hand, no conclusion can be drawn (see paragraph 49d).

c. **Murder.** The conclusion that a particular homicide is a murder is often made by the exclusion of accident and suicide. In murder the wound can be found on any part of the body; wounds in the back are particularly indicative of murder. The position from which the shot was fired can usually be determined from a study of the body wounds. If the shooting took place indoors and the bullet passed completely through the body, the location of the bullet in the wall, floor, or furniture will assist in determining the direction of fire. In making this determination the lodging place of the bullet is aligned with the entrance and exit holes of the body.

1) *The Body.* The body should be photographed from various

angles to show its relationship to doors, windows, and furniture in the room. The distance of the body from these objects should be measured. The exact position of the body should be noted.

2) *The Bullet.* The floors, ceiling, walls, and furniture should be examined for bullet holes, shells, fired bullets, and shotgun wadding. A recovered bullet or shell should be marked for identification as described in Chapter 7.

3) *The Weapon.* The investigator should note the exact position of the gun; the type (automatic, revolver, shotgun, rifle) and caliber or gauge should be recorded together with the make, lot number, and serial number. Chapter 7 describes the procedures to be used in connection with this evidence.

69. Chemical Tests for Powder Residue

The discharge of a firearm may deposit certain gunpowder residues from which useful conclusions can be drawn. Several tests of varying reputation are available for the detection of powder residue on the skin and on the clothing. The dermal nitrate or paraffin test is applied to the hand of the deceased to determine whether his own hand discharged the weapon. It is also used on the hands of suspects. The dermal nitrate test is used to determine the presence of nitrates which are present in the gunpowder blown back on discharge. The Walker test is used to determine the presence of nitrate on the skin or clothing as an indication of powder residue and of the proximity of discharge. Both of these tests are discussed at length in Chapter 38.

XII. POISONING

70. Definition

A poison is a substance which when introduced into the body in small quantities causes a harmful or deadly effect. The emphasis in this definition should be placed on the term "small quantities." The word "small" is used relatively. Many substances such as alcohol become poisons when they are used in excessive amounts. Alcohol, however, is not a substance which would be employed by a murderer. The essence of the poisoner's technique is the administration of the fatal dose surreptitiously. The substance has been consumed before the victim is aware of the noxious presence, and the problem becomes one of detecting traces. Substances which become poisonous when taken in excessive quantities or after being contaminated do not ordinarily present difficult investigative problems. Poisonous materials fatally effective in small quantities are adaptable to the purpose of the murderer. Substances producing lethal effect in large quantities may be found in cases of manslaughter and negligent homicide.

71. Classification

Poisons may be classified in a simple manner according to the following scheme:

a. **Irritants.** This class of poisons produces vomiting and acute pains in the abdomen. The autopsy effects are recognizable by the redness or ulceration of the gastrointestinal tract. An extremely active irritant is termed a *corrosive*. The following are some of the more common irritants.

1) *Mineral Acids and Alkalis.* Among the most common are the following:

a) *Sulphuric Acid* (Vitriol). Deaths from this acid are usually accidental and occasionally suicidal. In assaults motivated by jealousy and revenge, a bottle of this acid may be thrown at the victim.

b) *Hydrochloric Acid* (Muriatic Acid) is the most commonly used poison among the inorganic acids. It is a strong corrosive acid similar to, but less destructive in its effects, than sulphuric acid.

c) *Nitric Acid (Aqua Fortis) is similar to hydrochloric acid.*

d) *Ammonia* is a common cause of death in industrial accidents attributable to the bursting of refrigerators.

2) *Organic Acids.* This group includes three of the quickest and most powerful of all poisons.

a) *Carbolic Acid* (Phenol, Cresote, Lysol®) in its pure state is colorless. For industrial use as a disinfectant, it is mixed with impurities and assumes a darker color. Carbolic acid, sold under the manufacturer's name of Lysol, is one of the more common means of suicidal poisoning. The characteristic smell and the staining about the mouth are indicative of poisoning by carbolic acid.

b) *Hydrocyanic Acid* (Prussic Acid). A colorless liquid, hydrocyanic acid is commonly employed in trades such as photography and engraving. Its use as a gaseous disinfecting agent on ships occasionally results in accidental death. The extreme rapidity of the onset of symptoms discourages its use in murders.

c) *Oxalic Acid* is used extensively in industry as an analytic reagent and as a bleach. Printing, dyeing, cleaning, paper, photography, and rubber are some of the industries in which it is employed. As a poison it is one of the most sure and rapid means of killing. Since it is inexpensive and easily obtained, it is often used by suicides. A burning of the throat and stomach, vomiting of bloody matter, an imperceptible pulse, and a quiet spell followed by death in about twenty minutes are indications. The drinking vessels and vomitus should be examined for characteristic white crystals.

b. **Metallic Poisons.** Two of the most commonly used poisons in murder are arsenic and antimony. In suicides and in deaths from industrial diseases mercury and lead are common. Traces of metallic poisons remain in the body long after death. Occasionally, a body is exhumed long after burial for the purpose of verifying a belated charge of murder.

1) *Arsenic.* This is the most commonly occurring poison in cases of murder. It is also one of the most readily available. Compounds of this metal are used as insecticides for spraying trees, as rat poison, and for medicinal preparations. Arsenic is extremely effective in minute doses. Quantities as small as a one and one-half grains have been known to cause death. For the purpose of murder, the poisoner sometimes avoids administering the large fatal dose and induces chronic progressive poisoning.

2) *Antimony.* This is a less commonly used poison and is ordinarily available in two forms: tartar emetic and butter of antimony, a substance used in veterinary practice. It differs from arsenic in that the onset of symptoms is immediate. The postmortem appearances of death by antimony are similar to those of poisoning

by hydrochloric acid. The body remains in an excellent state of preservation for a period of years after burial.

3) **Mercury and Lead.** These are in common use for industrial purposes. Accidental deaths may occur through the use of certain preparations designed to prevent contraception or to induce abortion. These poisons are not used by murderers and only occasionally are they the means of suicide.

c. **Organic or Vegetable Poisons.** A large and effective group of poisons is extracted from various plants. They may be classified as *alkaloids* and *non-alkaloids*. These are sometimes called *neurotics* because they act mainly on the nervous system. The chief symptoms are drowsiness, delirium, coma, and sometimes convulsion and paralysis. Postmortem examination usually does not reveal any obvious physical effects on the organs as in the case of irritants.

1) **Alkaloids.** These are organic compounds which are alkaline in their chemical characteristics. They are poisonous in small quantities, affecting mainly the nervous system.

a) OPIUM DERIVATIVES. At one time, opium and its derivative alkaloids were extensively used as a poison. Suicidal poisonings were accomplished in the great majority of these cases by drinking laudanum. Although their popularity as poisons has diminished considerably in modern times, opium derivaties are still widely used. Opium itself is a dried juice of the opium poppy. Among the alkaloids which it contains are morphine, codeine, and papaverine. Heroin, a synthetic derivative of morphine, although the most commonly used narcotic in the world of illegal consumption, is rarely used as a poison. Morphine is the most common of these poisons. On absorbing a small amount of an opium derivative, such as morphine, the victim passes through a short period of mental excitement into a phase of nausea and finally into a coma. Convulsions may precede death. The skin becomes blue and clammy, bathed in sweat. Death follows from asphyxia, since the respiratory function ceases. The pin-point pupils, blue skin, gasping breath and the odor of opium on the breath are the chief points in diagnosis.

b) BELLADONNA GROUP. This class includes atropine and scopolamine or hyoscine. Symptoms develop in one-half to three hours. Respiratory failure is the cause of death. The pupils become dilated, the throat husky, and the face flushed. A mild delirium precedes death. Since these drugs are extensively used in medicine and rarely employed in homicides, a strong possibility of accidental death always exists.

c) STRYCHNINE. Poisoning from strychnine is also likely to be accidental, since salts of this substance are used in medicines such as cathartics. Taken in quantities such as a grain, strychnine is a deadly poison which acts rapidly to affect the spinal cord and ultimately results in a cessation of breathing. Characteristic of this form of poisoning is a series of extremely violent convulsions. Within approximately fifteen minutes, muscular twitchings begin, followed by a sensation of suffocation and constriction of the chest. The sudden onset of a convulsion is attended by stiffening of the body and an apparent cessation of breathing. The head and feet are bent backward in a tetanic spasm, the face becomes blue and the mouth is contracted in a fixed grin—the *risus sardonicus*. Within a few minutes, the spasm passes and is succeeded by a relaxed exhaustion, while the victim awaits in terror and dread the onset of another convulsion. After three or four increasingly severe convulsions, the victim dies of exhaustion, the respiratory function becoming completely inactive.

2) *Non-Alkaloids.* Certain soporifics (sleeping potions) are commonly used as poisons. Since their purpose is the inducement of sleep, obviously an overdose may lead to permanent unconsciousness.

a) BARBITURATES. The most common sleeping pills in use today are barbiturates or derivatives of barbituric acid. Since most pharmaceutical concerns produce these drugs with their own trade names, the nomenclature of these substances varies. The most popular of these sleeping pills or sedatives are phenobarbital, Seconal, and Nembutal (see Chapter 18). They may appear as tablets or as white powders in colored capsules. In ordinary dose, a natural sleep is induced. Excessive doses (eight or ten grams) result in profound coma and subsequent death. As a method of suicide, the barbiturates in recent years have achieved an impressive popularity. The barbiturate is an ideal poison; moreover, it is simple to obtain since physicians are not reluctant to prescribe it. Digestion is no problem, for the substance is practically tasteless. The first sensations are pleasant, amounting to an uneventful relaxation in inhibitions. Sleep overcomes the victim and death follows easily. The required dose for poisoning by barbiturates can be considerably lessened by drinking whiskey or strong wine before and after the poison. The coma resulting from an overdose of barbiturates may last several days. (Consequently, prolonged efforts to recall life by stomach lavage and stimulants are justified in the light of the experience.)

b) CHLORAL HYDRATE. Another widely used soporific is chloral hydrate, the active ingredient of the so-called "Mickey Finn." This is a white crystalline substance that is prescribed by physicians for sedation of the nervous system. Again, through overdose the victim becomes comatose and respiration is shallow.

d. **Gases.** 1) *Hydrogen Sulphide.* Sulphuretted hydrogen is the toxic agent in sewer gas. It is found in sewers, cesspools, privies, and other places where decayed animal or vegetable matter is present. In heavy concentrations, it produces immediate unconsciousness. Poisoning from this source is almost always accidental.

2) *Phosgene.* This gas is formed through the decomposition of chloroform or carbon tetrachloride by heat. The use of certain fire extinguishers in confined spaces can result in the decomposition of the carbon tetrachloride and the formation of phosgene.

3) *Carbon Monoxide.* The most common cause of death from chemical asphyxiation is carbon monoxide, a colorless, odorless, and tasteless gas. Deaths are almost always accidental or suicidal. Often a person attempting suicide will use the exhaust from an automobile as the source, closing the garage doors and starting the motor. Obvious suicides are those in which the person lies on the floor with his head near the exhaust pipe. If the person is sitting in the car and the weather is cold, it is difficult to draw definite conclusions. Accidental deaths are sometimes associated with defective gas refrigerators. Since the symptoms of carbon monoxide poisoning are those of asphyxiation, the problem of distinguishing accident from murder can arise.

a) CHARACTERISTICS. Carbon monoxide is the product of the incomplete combustion of carbinaceous materials such as wood, coal, and gasoline. The toxicity of carbon monoxide depends upon the fact that it has a greater affinity for the haemoglobin of blood than oxygen. In effect, by combining with the haemoglobin, carbon monoxide prevents the ordinary diffusion of oxygen to the cell tissues. Thus, the body processes are no longer supported and as a result the victim is suffocated rather than poisoned. The factors on which the effects of carbon monoxide depend are:

(1) *Concentration* of the gas.

(2) *Length* of time exposed.

(3) *Temperature* and *humidity* insofar as they affect blood circulation.

(4) *Individual characteristics*, some persons having greater resistance than others.

(b) INVESTIGATIVE TECHNIQUES. Death from carbon monoxide should be suspected if the skin has a cherry red color. The source of the gas is usually an apparatus such as an automobile or a gas refrigerator in which combustion is incomplete. On arriving at the scene of a refrigerator death, the investigator should inquire about the state of the windows, doors, and transoms. In the excitement of the initial discovery of the body, the windows are usually thrown open and the premises aired. Thus, it is impossible to determine accurately the original concentration of carbon monoxide which was present at the time of death. If tests are to be run with the assistance of a chemist, the original conditions should as far as possible be reproduced. The machine should be turned on and permitted to operate for some time. Tests can be conducted with special apparatus for determining the concentration of carbon monoxide. In lieu of this, air samples can be collected by the chemist and later analyzed. A concentration of forty parts of carbon monoxide to 10,000 parts of air is usually fatal if the exposure takes place in an inclosed room for a period of an hour or more.

4) *Carbon Dioxide.* Another common cause of death from asphyxiation is carbon dioxide. Deaths from this gas may appear to be of a suspicious nature until the cause is determined. In rooms where heating and cooking appliances are being used without proper ventilation, the oxygen is depleted and the carbon dioxide content is built up to a level at which the air of the room can no longer support life. The condition of the windows and other openings to the room at the time of discovery should be ascertained. Usually, the room is well ventilated by the time the investigator

arrives at the scene. In certain situations, however, the gas may still be present in lethal concentrations. In a manhole, for example, the hold of a ship, or a silo, the original concentration will still be present. A sample of the gas can be obtained by filling a gas collector with water and subsequently permitting the water to run out and be replaced by the atmosphere. The sample can be analyzed with little difficulty by a competent chemist.

e. **Food Poisoning.** In civilian jurisdictions, cases of accidental food poisoning are investigated by the local Department of Health or its equivalent. The interest of the police in a case of accidental food poisoning is concerned with the question of negligence. It is possible that acts or omissions amounting to ordinary negligence have led to death from poisoning. The investigation is directed toward the discovery of the origin of the poisoning, the violation of sanitary regulations in food service, and the failure to report existing disease. Naturally, if the poisoning is non-accidental, the case is treated in the same manner as other poison cases. Where a number of persons are afflicted by the poisoning, the possibility of sabotage must be entertained by the investigator.

1) *Physical Effects.* The word *ptomaine* poisoning is a misnomer. Food poisoning is usually a synonym for bacterial food poisoning. The bacilli belong to the salmonella group. The affected food does not yield any abnormal appearance or smell. The diagnosis is not difficult. Proof is established by isolating bacteria from the excreta. In dead persons, the spleen, liver, and intestines are examined for bacteria.

a) ELAPSED TIME. The time of onset is usually between six and twelve hours after ingestion. It can take place as early as half an hour or even twenty-four hours after ingestion, depending on whether the poison was already formed in the food or was formed after eating or drinking.

b) SYMPTOMS. Headache, abdominal pain, vomiting, and diarrhea mark the onset.

c) POSTMORTEM APPEARANCE. The appearance is similar to that resulting from gastrointestinal irritation and toxemia.

2) *Botulism.* Bacterial food poisoning may also be due to eating sausages or canned foods. The bacillus is *B. botulinus*. This anerobic organism produces symptoms slightly different from those of

ordinary food poisoning. There is no fever or pain. Partial paralysis takes place. The respiratory muscles and heart become affected, and the patient finally dies. Loss of consciousness and vomiting do not occur.

3) **Non-bacterial Food Poisoning.** This type of affliction is caused by eating certain plants and animals containing a naturally occurring posion. The following substances are the most common causes: certain kinds of mushrooms such as *Amanita muscaria* and *Amanita pholloides;* immature or sprouting potatoes; mussels at certain undetermined times of the year; grain, especially rye which has become contaminated with the ergot fungus; fruits containing metallic contaminants such as substances sprayed with salts of arsenic or lead and food stored in cadmium-lined containers.

4) **Physical Evidence.** The advice of the attending physician or a forensic chemist should be sought in the collection of physical evidence. Food, vomit, and feces are of basic importance. These should be collected in separate, stoppered jars. Utensils used in the preparation of the food should also be preserved. In some instances, kitchen fixtures such as faucets may be of importance to the case.

72. Investigative Techniques in Poisoning Cases

Ordinarily, the investigator does not enter a poisoning case until the death is an accomplished fact. He is thus presented with an investigation in which there are no witnesses to the crucial events. Often, there will be no "crime scene"; i.e., the exact place where the poison was consumed may be unknown. Further, any immediate association of the victim with the perpetrator may be absent, since the poison may have been planted in an accessible place at some indefinite time prior to its consumption. In cases of poisoning, the link between the criminal and the victim is most commonly established by motivation. Revenge, profit, jealousy, and hate are the seeds of poison cases. The following general procedure is applicable to these investigations:

a. The crime scene should be visited as soon as possible.

b. A detailed history of events immediately preceding the death should be compiled. This chronology will serve two purposes:

1) The physical circumstances surrounding the death and the nature of the antecedent illness may supply useful information to the medical examiner in determining whether a poisoning case exists and, if it does, the type of poison employed. The diagnosis of poisoning is often difficult without this information.

2) A knowledge of the victim's activities may enable the investigator to discover witnesses and suspects.

c. A brief history of the victim's life during the preceding year should be obtained as far as practical from his friends, relatives, and associates in employment. In this way the motive may be established.

d. The report of the physician who first attended the victim should be obtained.

e. The medical examiner performing the autopsy should be interviewed and a complete report obtained.

f. The report of the toxicologist should be obtained and the toxicologist should be interviewed for a more detailed discussion of the poison found, its common forms, its availability, the commercial sources, the techniques of administration, and the probability of accidental absorption. The report is a simple, factual statement of findings. The interview will supply a number of leads and provide the investigator with the necessary background knowledge for the investigation of the poisoning.

g. The investigator should next establish whether the poisoning is a case of accident, suicide, or homicide. He has now assembled a considerable body of data. His interviews with the attending physician, medical examiner, and toxicologist will have explored the possibility of suicide from the point of view of physical evidence and practical experience. The crime scene, if any exists, may have revealed significant clues. The strongest evidence for or against a suicide theory will be available in the information obtained from friends and relatives.

73. Physical Evidence

If there is a reasonable suspicion of poisoning, an investigation should be initiated immediately. Several days or even months may confirms the suspicion. In that time, some or all of the evidentiary traces at the scene will have disappeared. In addition to the regular crime scene search that has been recommended in cases of homicide, the following matters should receive attention:

a. **Excretions.** The victim may have vomited or defecated at the scene. The material should be gathered up and placed in separate containers. Since some poisons are volatile, the containers should be carefully sealed to avoid evaporation.

b. **Refuse.** The remains of meals should be similarly collected and preserved. Garbage and remnants in cooking vessels are important. The pail or vessel should be taken together with its contents.

c. **Medicine Closet.** The entire content of the medicine closet should be collected for examination. It is not advisable to choose from among the medicines present, since the containers may be incorrectly labeled.

d. **Food.** The kitchen should be searched for food that may contain poison. Certain foods need receive little attention if they are found intact. It is difficult to place poisons in food that is large in unit size or which has a readily identifiable surface. For example, vegetables and fruits which appear intact are not likely carriers of poison. Prepared cereals such as corn flakes can usually be rejected after brief inspection. Powdered or granulated foods, however, should be collected without questioning. Flour, baking powder, sugar, salt, and spices, for example can be readily diluted with a poison which is not detectable by visual inspection.

e. **Alcoholic Beverages.** Probably the most common method of administering a poison is to first mix it in an alcoholic drink. The alcohol serves as an excellent solvent and, in addition, the beverage dulls the senses of taste and smell. Thus, whiskey, wine, and beer bottles should be collected as well as any dry soiled glasses that are present.

f. **Insecticides.** Insecticides and vermicides should be collected. Plant sprays, roach powders, and rat exterminators are often employed by the poisoner.

74. Suspect's Residence

If a suspect has been "developed" and it is possible to obtain a search warrant, his premises should be examined for the presence of poisons. The preceding paragraph will suggest the substances to be looked for. If the medical examiner has already given his opinion on the type of poison employed, the search can be greatly simplified.

75. Special Points of Proof

In poisoning cases, the following four points of proof should receive special attention:

a. **Access to the Poison.** It must be shown that the accused had access to the poison. This fact may be demonstrated by showing one of the following:

1) *Common Substance.* The poison may be a common substance, readily available to any person.

2) *Purchase.* The investigator should canvass the places where the poison could have been purchased in that area or in an area which the accused had recently visited. Pharmacies, exterminator companies, garden supply companies, and chemical houses are the likely sources. It should be ascertained whether the seller is required by law or company rules to make a record of the purchase.

3) *Occupation.* In various industrial operations it is necessary to employ poisons. A plater, for example, will use cyanide. The investigator should inquire concerning the industrial uses of the poison and draw up a list of acquaintances employed in such occupations.

b. **Access to the Victim.** It must be shown that the accused had access to the victim. The testimony of friends or neighbors can be used to show that the accused was with the victim prior to death. If the substance was sent through the mails, as, for example, nuts salted with cyanide, it may be possible to associate the package with the sender by various traces. Fingerprints on the package, of course, are excellent proof. Wrapping paper, twine, and boxes can be traced to the suspect's house. The handwriting on the package is of great importance.

c. **Intent.** Aside from the usual questions of motive and the relation of the accused to the deceased, there must also be established as part of the element of intent the fact of the accused's knowledge of the poison. It is necessary to show that this chemical substance, which has caused the death and which was presumably administered by the accused, was known by the accused to be a poisonous substance. This fact may be proved by showing that the education or occupation of the accused presumed such knowledge or by showing that the accused made inquiries or conducted library research concerning poisons.

d. **Clothes.** Garments, sheets, and similar articles should be thoroughly dried before they are packed. In packing, the clothing should not be unnecessarily folded. On folding, stains that may still be moist will produce similarly stained areas in other parts of the clothing. Tissue paper should be used to separate layers of clothing in placing it in a box.

76. Diagnosis of Poisoning

To determine whether or not a poisoning has taken place, an extensive investigation must be made. The events preceding the death must be studied. The manner of death and the nature of the illness that preceded it are important. The symptoms of poisoning can be presented by many other medical conditions. Epilepsy, heart disease, uremia, gastric ulcer, gastritis, intestinal obstructions, diseases of the central nervous system, and other conditions present symptoms similar to those of poisoning. The following conditions should give rise to a suspicion of poisoning:

a. **Acute Poisoning.** The following signs suggest acute poisoning:

1) Shortly after taking food, drink, or medicine.
2) A person in apparent good health.
3) Suffers a sudden attack, accompanied by
4) Vomiting, together with convulsions or coma.
5) More than one person is affected in a similar manner.

b. **Chronic Poisoning.** The perpetrator sometimes conducts the poisoning operation over a long period of time. The victim appears to suffer from malaise and chronic ill health. The following history should arouse suspicion:

1) The medical diagnosis was difficult and inconclusive.

2) The patient's condition improved when he was away from home, but not otherwise.

3) The doctor's instructions were not properly followed in caring for the patient.

77. Toxicology

Toxicology is the science which deals with poisons, their effects and antidotes, and recognition. The method of obtaining conclusive proof of the presence of poison is that of chemical analysis, accomplished by separation, purification, and identification.

a. **Autopsy.** A complete autopsy is always desirable and usually necessary in a case of suspected poison. In the event that the autopsy reveals evidence of poisoning, the organs of the deceased, food, and other substances suspected of containing poison must be subjected to a toxicological analysis. Since poisoning is a crime of stealth and the substance is usually administered surreptitiously, only small quantities of the poison are taken into the body. As a result, only microscopic quantities of the absorbed poison are found in the tissues and fluids of the body. The toxicological analysis requires an examination of the vital organs, viz., the liver, kidneys, heart, and brain. In addition, all the urine in the bladder is collected and a pint of blood is taken. In certain instances, sections of the intestines and lungs are used.

b. **Expert Services.** The medical examiner handling the case in question may possess an adequate knowledge of toxicology. More often, he does not, and the investigator will be required to seek the services of another agency for a toxicological examination. Ordinarily a local agency will provide such services. The FBI Laboratory offers the services of trained toxicologists in the analysis of substances and material sent to them for a determination of the presence of poisons. Organs and substances to be examined for poisons should be packed and shipped with dry ice as described below.

c. **Autopsy Report.** A copy of the autopsy report should accompany the specimens. The observations of the autopsy surgeon or the medical examiner are often useful to the toxicologist. Postmortem appearances such as discoloration of the skin, nails, and blood; unusual odors emanating from the body cavity; charring, corrosion, and staining of tissues are indicative of certain poisons.

78. Postmortem Evidence of Poisons

The pathologist performing the autopsy should be experienced in recognizing the effects of poisons on the body. Naturally, the investigator can contribute little to this phase of the inquiry. He should, however, for purposes of background information, possess some familiarity with the general nature of the evidence which the pathologist and toxicologist look for.

a. **Visual Observation.** Some of the effects of poison are visible to the unaided eye. Corrosion of tissues, perforation of the stomach, gastrointestinal irritation, and marked congestion are some of the more obvious effects. Sometimes, the poisonous substance itself may be found in the stomach. Grains of arsenic and belladonna leaves, for example, may sometimes be discovered. Ordinarily, alkaloidal poisons and the barbiturates do not leave visible signs. The diagnosis in this case rests on before-death symptoms and analysis of the organs.

b. **Chemical Analysis.** It is the pathologist's duty to examine the organs and perform some of the more simple qualitative tests in which he is experienced. Familiarity with the basic tests for oxalic acid, hydrocyanic acid, carbon monoxide, and arsenic are desirable; in rural districts, the pathologist may find it more convenient to perform these tests himself. In urban areas, however, a toxicologist or analyst will be available for the examination of the organs to detect poisons. In the analysis, it will usually be possible to place the poison in one of four groups:

1) *Volatile.* Volatile poisons such as carbolic acid, chloroform, and hydrocyanic acid. These are suspected by smell and are isolated by distilling the suspected fluid in a flask and collecting the distillate. Appropriate tests are then applied.

2) *Non-volatile.* Non-volatile inorganic poisons such as arsenic, mercury, and lead. In this type of analysis the organic matter is broken down and the metal is obtained as a chloride.

3) *Alkaloidal Poisons.* Morphine and other opium derivatives are the most commonly used alkaloidal poisons. The principle used in analyzing is based on the fact that alkaloids unite with acids to form salts which are soluble in water but not in ether.

4) *Miscellaneous Poisons.* This group contains poisons which are not contained in any of the preceding three classifications. Food poisons are an example of this group.

79. Submission of Evidence

Toxicological evidence such as body organs and fluids to be submitted for examination should be treated in accordance with the instructions of the controlling jurisdiction. The following additional recommendations will be found useful:

a. **Containers.** Only glass containers should be used since metals may react with the substances present. Pint and quart jars with clean glass caps and new rubber seals are satisfactory.

b. **Sealing.** Each container should contain but one substance, fluid, or organ. It should be sealed by the investigator or the physician performing the autopsy, and the seal should bear the name of the investigator or the autopsy surgeon. An identifying tag or label should be affixed to each container providing the following information: the name of the investigator, the autopsy surgeon, and the victim; the type of organ or fluid submitted; the date and place of the autopsy; and the case number.

c. **Preservatives and Packing.** No preservatives should be added. The containers should be placed in separate bins in one carton. This should be sealed and initialed on the seal. If practicable, the investigator himself should transport the carton to the toxicologist, obtaining a receipt for the package. If the evidence is to shipped a great distance, a wooden box should be used and a lining of insulating material such as rock wool should be provided. The evidence should then be packed with dry ice.

d. **Letter of Transmittal.** A letter of transmittal should accompany the evidence if it is hand-carried or should be forwarded by airmail if the evidence is sent by registered mail. A carbon copy of the letter should be inclosed with the evidence for purposes of proper identification on arrival. The letter should contain all pertinent facts, including an autopsy report concerning the history of the case. This information should include the following:

1) *Duration of the Illness.* The length of time during which the victim suffered from the ill effects may indicate the type of poison or may suggest chronic poisoning.

2) *Treatment by a Physician.* If the deceased was treated by a physician or if he received any other medical treatment, a statement from the physician should be obtained if possible. A note should be made of drugs administered during the treatment.

3) *Background Information.* Pertinent case information should be made available to the toxicologist. The signs and symptoms observed by witnesses may offer useful information to the toxicologist. Reactions such as dilation or contraction of the pupils, vomiting, convulsions, respiratory rate, and other physiological disturbances suggest the possibility of certain poisons. The toxicologist is also interested in the various clues that may be suggested by the physical circumstances surrounding the victim. Thus, the occupation of the victim, the poisons available to him at work and at home, any suspected medicines or unlabeled materials available to the victim, health habits and peculiarities of the deceased, and similar information should be obtained.

e. **Substances to be Submitted.** The most important tissues and fluids to be obtained at an autopsy will vary with the case. Usually, the following are desirable:

1) The stomach and stomach content.
2) The intestines and their contents.
3) The liver.
4) The gall bladder.
5) Both kidneys.
6) Urinary bladder and its contents.
7) Blood in a quart jar.
8) Brain.
9) Heart.
10) Lungs
11) Bone—Parts of the rib or portions of exposed sections of the spinal column.
12) Hair—This should be taken in generous quantities from the

back of the head and near a head wound if one is present. It should be pulled out.

XIII. SUICIDE

80. Definition and Law

Suicide is the killing of one's self. It is a voluntary and intentional destruction. At one time suicide was considered a felony by common law and was punished by ignominious burial and forfeiture of goods. An attempt at suicide was considered a misdemeanor by common law. Under many of the state laws no specific provision has been made for the punishment of suicide or attempted suicide, but it is considered that the attempt is punishable.

81. The Problem of Suicide

The investigator is often called upon to provide factual information which will assist in deciding whether the death in question is murder, suicide, or accident. Since most injuries can be found in one of these three occurrences, the successful solution of the problem must depend to a great extent on the investigator's experience and fund of information. The problem of distinguishing suicide from accident and murder has been touched upon at various places in discussing the causes of death. In the absence of eyewitnesses, a conclusion of suicide is drawn only after a careful study of the type of injury, the presence of the weapon or instrument of death, the existence of a motive, and elimination of a theory of murder, accident, or natural causes.

82. Type of Injury

The cause of death is one of the best indicators in determining whether the case is one of suicide. The type or nature of the injury is not a conclusive indicator but can establish to a degree the improbability of self-infliction.

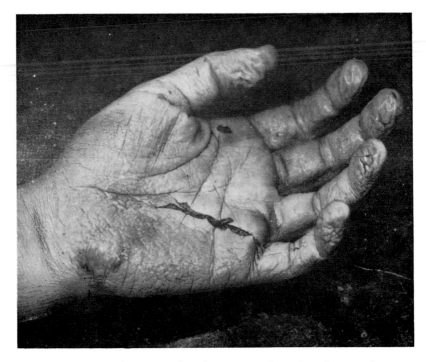

Figure 17. Defense wound, indicating murder rather than suicide.

a. **Position and Awkwardness.** As a general principle, it may be stated that any part of the body accessible to the suicide is also accessible to the murderer; i.e., a wound produced by a suicide could also have been produced by a murderer. Certain types of wounds, however, are readily excluded from suicide; for example, knife wounds in the back indicate murder; cuts on the palms of the hands indicate a struggle against an assailant. Suicides are prone to select the front of the body for attack. With a knife, they will select the throat, wrist, and heart region. With a gun the choice is usually among the temple, forehead, center of the back of the head, mouth, and heart. The position of the wound or the difficulty of self-infliction does not exclude suicide as an explanation. An example of this is a case in which a person shot himself in the top of the head at a range of twelve inches. In another case a man tied a stone to his legs and then bound his arms to his legs to insure death by drowning.

b. **Combination of Methods.** A combination of methods or a choice of several sites is indicative of suicide. For example, a person who is found with a hanging noose or a revolver, while he is actually dead from poisoning, is probably a suicide. Indecision or insurance of one method by another method is characteristic. Cutting of the wrist as well as the throat, for example, is another indication of suicide.

c. **Extent of the Wound.** It is difficult to draw a conclusion from the extent or number of wounds. Often a deranged suicide will inflict very severe wounds in great numbers. Experimental wounds and hesitation marks may be observed in suicides performed with a knife.

d. **Direction of Wound.** In cases of firearms, the investigator can determine whether the person could have fired the fatal shot from a consideration of the direction involved and the limitations of the human body in "positioning" the weapon. In stab wounds, the presence of purposeless incisions is indicative of an assailant trying to discover a vital spot. A series of parallel slashes on the left side of the head and neck would suggest suicide.

e. **Painfulness.** It is logical to expect that a suicide will select the least painful way of dying. The popularity of carbon monoxide and the barbiturates as suicidal agents is attributable to the desire to avoid excessive pain. It must not be concluded, however, because the form of death is too horrible to contemplate from the point of view of self-infliction, that the death must be a murder. The following examples, although obviously illustrating the work of deranged minds, are indicative of the extremes of pain to which suicides may subject themselves:

1) A woman cut off her feet and her left hand before cutting her throat.

2) A woman poured kerosene over her clothes and set fire to herself.

3) A girl enucleated both of her eyes. This is an example of psychopathic self-mutilation.

4) A sexual psychopath killed himself with an axe.

f. **Disfigurement Considerations.** A female suicide will tend to avoid purposely disfiguring her face. Her natural anxiety concerning her appearance extends even to the impression she will make on viewers in her death. Another characteristic of the suicide is the care taken to push aside clothing so that the weapon may be in direct contact with the body. It is difficult to determine whether this action is prompted by a natural reluctance to mark a useful garment or whether it is part of the measures taken to insure the effectiveness of the gun or knife.

g. **Incapacitating Sequence.** Certain combinations of wounds suggest a physical impossibility. To draw a conclusion of suicide, the wounds should be physically not improbable. The existence of two fatal shots at some distance apart does not suggest suicide. For example, shots through the heart and temple are unlikely as the work of self-infliction.

83. Presence of Weapon

The means by which death was accomplished should be apparent. As an obvious example: If the cause of death was a gunshot wound, the firearm should be present. A search for the weapon should be made. If the weapon is not found near the body, a search of adjoining areas must be made since a person, even though mortally wounded, is capable of considerable activity. Persons fatally shot through the head or heart have been known to travel as much as a hundred yards before succumbing.

a. **Concealment.** The weapon is sometimes deliberately concealed by the victim or by others. For example, in one case, a banker arranged for the disappearance of the weapon in order that his suicide should appear to be a murder committed during robbery. In another case, a conclusion of suicide rather than murder was reached after the discovery of a few fragments of broken brick at the fireplace. The victim, by means of strong elastic attached to the gun, had arranged for the firearm to disappear into the chimney after he had shot himself. The possibility of the relatives' concealing the weapon must also be entertained. Among the motives of relatives in concealing the weapon are the collection of insurance and the avoidance of unfavorable publicity.

b. **Accidental Disappearance.** The weapon is sometimes stolen. For example, on finding a man in a deserted house, dead from a bullet wound, a conclusion of murder was first made until it was discovered that the gun had been stolen by neighborhood boys. Sometimes the weapon or instrument may not be apparent. In one case the victim had committed suicide by hanging himself from the cord of a venetian blind. The hanging and death took place quickly and the body slipped away from the unknotted cord. On finding the body on the floor with no obvious means of hanging, it was at first thought that strangulation by garroting was the cause of death.

84. Motive and Intent

The intent to commit suicide may have been evinced by the victim through his oral statements during the period preceding his death or by a statement contained in a death note.

a. **Motive.** Motive is deduced from a study of the victim's behavior during and just prior to the fatal act. It has been found that mental uneasiness or worry is the chief cause of suicide. In fact, there is a general tendency to officially regard suicides as persons temporarily insane. Worry and alcohol, considered together, account for a large percentage of the total number of suicides. Certain occupations which tend to produce anxiety and tension, notably the medical and legal professions, are characterized by a higher incidence of suicides. The investigator should make an inquiry into the state of mind of the deceased by interviewing members of the family, business associates, intimate friends, and social acquaintances. The line of inquiry should be pointed toward discovering the existence of any domestic, business, or financial troubles. It should be noted in this connection that marital harmony, pregnancy, and love are negligible factors when considered as possible motives for suicide. Hence, the deceased's anxiety over his position or work and his financial condition should receive the greater emphasis in this phase of the investigation. The interviews should stress factual information rather than opinions concerning the deceased's state of mind. For example, a history of failures in regard to promotion in rank and the financial statistics in regard to debts should be learned if a witness proffers the observation that the deceased was depressed over professional failure or money.

b. **Intent.** The stated intention of the deceased to commit suicide is of obvious importance. In the course of the interviews, the investigator should endeavor to learn of any statements made by the deceased which would indicate a purpose of self-destruction. A search should be made for a diary, unmailed letters, or other personal writings containing sentiments from which a desire for suicide can be inferred or bearing an explicit statement of the intention. The most typical communication of this nature is the "suicide note." In its classical form, the suicide note contains a clear expression of both the motive and the intent. On finding such a note, the investigator should not accept it at its face value. It must be regarded, at first, with an investigator's skepticism. Is the document what it purports to be? Was it written by the deceased? Was it written voluntarily? To answer these questions the suicide note must be submitted to a qualified document examiner. The note should be picked up with a pair of tongs and placed in a transparent envelope. As a matter of regular procedure the note should be photographed and transmitted to the laboratory or other qualified agency together with adequate samples of the deceased's handwriting. At the same time a request for a comparison of the known writing of the deceased with the writing of the suicide note should be forwarded. Precautions should be taken throughout the handling of the document to avoid contact with the fingers. In the event that the handwriting on the note is found to have been made by someone other than the deceased, it will become necessary to process the note for fingerprints. This conditional request should be included in the original letter.

c. **Young Persons.** It is estimated that between 70,000 and 80,000 young people, between the ages of 15 and 24, will attempt suicide in a typical year. Almost 4,000 will succeed. Fewer than 30 per cent of these young suicides will leave notes. More girls will attempt suicide but more boys will succeed. One explanation offered for this is that the girls will generally use methods (razor and pills) which are less certain than those chosen by the boys (guns and hanging). The sharp increase in young suicides during the past decade has been attributed to an inability to communicate and a feeling of isolation and loneliness.

85. Accidents

A fatal accident which is not witnessed may involve injuries suggestive of suicide. If the injuries are compatible with self infliction and if eyewitness accounts are absent or unreliable, there is a danger that a conclusion of suicide will be made where the subject is in ill health or beset by financial or familial problems. Often the circumstances surrounding a death do not permit any conclusion to be drawn. Cases where persons fall from windows, fall in front of oncoming trains, drown, or are overcome by carbon monoxide often remain mysteries because of the absence of eyewitnesses or of any oral or written statement of intentions. Physical evidence may sometimes be helpful in these cases. For example, in a case involving a fall from a window in a high building, the wall areas at the sides of the windows and the sill area should be processed for latent fingerprints and palm prints which may indicate preparations for a leap. If a carbon monoxide death is intentional, certain precautionary arrangements, such as locked garage doors or a position near the exhaust, may be observed.

86. Natural Causes

A death from natural causes may appear to be suicide in the preliminary stages of any investigation. A person suffering from an unsuspected disease may suffer an attack, fall into an unexpected collapse, and die. Again, deaths from falls or drowning will serve as examples. A man is seen to fall from a ladder which had begun to slip. He is dead when examined and the question arises: Is the death an accident or did he suffer a dizzy spell and lose his coordination? The question is not trivial since on that determination may depend the awarding of the industrial accident insurance indemnity to the estate of the deceased. In suicides these questions sometimes arise when the motive is the escape from a painful disease. For example, in one case, the dead body of a man was found with a revolver nearby. It was apparent that the deceased had killed himself by firing the gun with the muzzle in his mouth. A full hot water bottle was found on the bed. In the autopsy it was discovered that the deceased had suffered a ruptured aorta. To relieve the excruciating pain of this condition he apparently prepared the hot water bottle and, on applying it, had failed to find alleviation. In despair he finally shot himself. The perforating wound in his head, however, was not the cause of his death. The ruptured aorta had supervened and the death was natural rather than suicidal. We may divide "death from natural causes" into two categories: first, a person dies from natural causes, but there is an appearance of violence; and, second, a person dies of violence but the apparent explanation is one of natural causes.

a. **Appearance of Violence.** The possibility of death from natural causes should never be excluded in the initial phase of the investigation because of presence of obvious marks of violence. The appearance of a struggle can be created by the abnormal activity of a person suffering from an acutely painful attack. There are over seventy diseases the onset of which can produce sudden death. A person experiencing such an attack may disarrange his clothing and injure himself severely by falling. Prominent among these diseases are those associated with heart failure. Coronary involvement is precipitated in a large number of cases by a sudden stress resulting from an emotional crisis or undue physical exertion. Where signs of violence and severe injury are present and a fatally diseased condition also exists, a number of questions arise concerning the relationship of the injury and the disease to the death. The autopsy surgeon can provide the investigator with information bearing on the following questions:

1) Has the natural disease any unusual relation to the injury or is it a distinct process?

2) Could the natural disease by itself have caused the death?

3) Had the disease progressed to such a state that death could have been expected?

4) Is the injury sufficiently severe to cause death by itself?

5) Is the disease merely a contributory factor in the death, which is due to the injury?

6) Is the injury merely a contributory factor to the death, which is due to natural causes?

b. **Appearance of Natural Causes.** A death may be a suicide even though it has the appearance of being the result of natural causes.

For purposes of defrauding the insurance company or to protect the family reputation, the person may contrive the circumstances surrounding his death to give the impression of natural causes. For example, a person may kill himself by injecting an adequate quantity of absolute alcohol into his veins. If he has also taken a few drinks to give his breath the odor, the conclusion may be reached that he died from drinking excessively. A more common example is that of a death attributable to an overdose of sleeping pills. The increased and more lenient use of barbiturates is fast making these the drugs of choice among suicides. In a case of this nature or in a similar poisoning case, the investigator should ascertain whether the deceased obtained the drugs legally and whether he was aware of their lethal effect.

XIV. INTERVIEWING WITNESSES

87. Classification

After completing his work at the scene of the crime, the investigator must direct his attention to the witnesses. This phase of the investigation is equal in importance to the examination of the physical evidence. Often the scene of the crime offers only evidence bearing on the *corpus delicti*. The vital question of the identity of the perpetrator will be answered ordinarily by the intelligent interviewing of witnesses. Most witnesses should be questioned as soon as possible since the lapse of time permits a deterioration of the memory and opens the door to the entry of motives for discreet silence. The order in which the witnesses are interviewed will initially depend on their availability. A more logical order will suggest itself as the development of information gives form to the case and meaning to the events. Witnesses may be classified according to the type of testimony they are expected to give. Thus, we may place them in the following categories:

a. **Eyewitnesses.** Persons who saw the fatal act.

b. **Circumstances.** Persons who can give information concerning the circumstances surrounding the crime, as for example, the druggist who sold the poison or the dry cleaner who can identify the jacket left at the scene.

c. **Motive.** Persons who can give information concerning the motive for the fatal act.

d. **Flight.** The persons who can testify to acts of the accused subsequent to the slaying and indicative of flight. The landlady of the suspect's rooming house, for example, may testify to the fact that the suspect failed to return home after the fatal act.

e. **Expert Witnesses.** Persons qualified to give expert opinions on the significance of the physical evidence.

f. **Suspects.** Logical suspects should be interrogated in appropriate order.

88. Witnesses to Circumstances

Interviewing witnesses of circumstances surrounding the crime should consist of a comprehensive examination of details concerning the physical evidence:

a. **Categories of Physical Evidence.** For convenience of discussion, physical evidence will again be placed in the following useful but arbitrary categories:

1) *Corpus Delicti Evidence.* This evidence tends to show that a crime has been committed. In a murder, for example, it must be proved that a person is dead through the criminal agency of another. This kind of physical evidence is ordinarily given by the medical examiner.

2) *Associative Evidence.* This evidence can be used to show that the accused was linked to the crime scene or with the act in general. It includes such diverse matters as the accused's previous possession of the objects left at the scene and the identity of the automobile used in flight. Since lay witnesses are usually the ones who offer such information, it will be the investigator's responsibility to conduct interviews to obtain the evidence.

3) *Identifying Evidence.* This evidence tends directly, from the clues at the scene, to establish the identity of the person who brought about the death. Fingerprints, foot impressions, and quantities of blood are examples of this kind of evidence.

4) *Tracing Evidence.* These are articles and materials that help to locate the suspect. A laundry mark found on his clothing in a

furnished room may assist in tracing the fugitive. His use of a credit card during flight may establish a pattern leading the investigator to his place of incidence. Of course, it may also serve as a means of identifying the suspect.

Since our categories of evidence are simply aspects under which the evidence may be considered for investigative purposes, the student should not be disturbed by an apparent overlapping, i.e., an object of evidence can sometimes be placed in two or more of these classes. The latter three classes are of special interest to the investigator since his concern is to establish the identity and whereabouts of the perpetrator and to link him logically to the scene. For example, botanical material clinging to the suspect's clothing and peculiar to the flora of the crime scene may provide a critical link. In homicide involving a firearm or a poison, the investigator's procedures may include the following.

a) TRACING THE GUN. In cases where the lethal weapon is found at the scene, the investigator must try to trace the history of the weapon. Who is the owner? If it is government property, official records should be consulted to establish the history of possession. Where the weapon cannot be traced through government sources, the inquiry must be conducted by the investigator or by a firearms identification expert. The records of state and municipal law enforcement agencies should be consulted to determine the owner of the gun. Available data concerning the sale and distribution of the weapon must be obtained from the manufacturer. The weapon must then be traced to the distributor, the wholesaler, and finally to the retailer. If the sale of the weapon has been legal, the retailer's books should yield the name and address of the purchaser. It will be found that this information is often incorrect and that the gun has been stolen between the time of its manufacture and the time of the fatal act. An inquiry into the larceny must then be made. If the larceny has been solved, information must be obtained concerning the disposition of the gun. To whom was the gun sold? Was the thief involved in the killing?

b) TRACING THE SOURCE OF POISON. The investigator in this case must canvass drugstores, garden supply houses, hardware stores, chemical companies, and other places where the particular type of poison could be sold. The poison may have been purchased by the accused or by a friend offering the pretext of destroying rodents or a sick animal. The friend is usually innocent and when interviewed will relate the details concerning the poison: from whom it was bought; how he came to buy it; when and where he gave it to the killer; and any conversation relating to poisons that took place. The killer himself may have knowledge of poisons and may have obtained it from available sources at his place of employment. The inquiry must then follow the line of the killer' education in poisons, his opportunities to obtain them, and his possession of them.

(1) The accused's familiarity with the locus of the crime.

(2) The accused's knowledge of the victim, his location, and his habits; or, if the victim is unknown to the accused, the latter's acquaintance with someone who could supply information concerning the victim.

(3) Information concerning the accused's normal style of living; his wealth or lack of it; and his legitimate income.

(4) The accused's financial condition before and after the killing; his activities, lawful and criminal, during this period.

(5) Actions of the accused which indicate an effort to establish an alibi on the day of the crime or to provide an excuse for any change in his financial condition after the crime.

89. Witnesses to Establish Motive

Although it is not necessary for the prosecution to prove a motive in a homicide, such a failure is considered a serious strategic weakness in the presentation of the case. The progress of the investigation will also suffer in the absence of a reasonable motive to give form and logic to the line of inquiry. The investigator, drawing from his ingenuity, experience, and available data, must base his investigation on a theory that rationally explains the fatal act. Among the common motives are revenge, love, degeneracy, financial gain, and robbery. In addition to the many possible motives, the investigator must also consider the fact that the crime may be relatively free from motive.

A brutal, sadistic assault or a reckless expression of drunken rage may provide a seemingly inexplicable problem to the investigator, whose first encounter with the suspect finds him a calm and relatively pleasant person bearing little resemblance to the psychopathic killer. The investigator must be a particularly astute interviewer in questioning witnesses for the purpose of establishing a motive. For example, he must be courteous, sympathetic, and discreet in questioning members of the killer's family who may allege that they were outraged by the victim. In killings resulting from a group conspiracy, he can obtain a great deal of information if he can convey to individual members the impression that he is in possession of the inside facts or create discussion by implying that one of the members has talked. In cases involving an illicit love affair, the third party should be questioned closely and persistently about his or her relations with the accused. Usually, the character of such a person is weak and he will supply the desired information for the purpose of protecting himself.

90. Witnesses to Flight

Flight is a sign of guilt. The absence of the suspect from his home and haunts can be interpreted as flight. A search should be made for the suspect in these places. Someone should be in a position to testify that the accused did not return to his home or visit his usual haunts. If the suspect lived in a lodging house or in a hotel, the cooperation of the landlady or manager can be enlisted to testify to the lodger's absence after the occurrence of the homicide.

91. Eyewitnesses

The investigator must be patient and exhaustive in his interviewing of the eyewitnesses. A background history of the witness should be developed. He should be asked to give a brief history of himself which will include any criminal record or involvement. He should be asked to account for his presence at the scene of the crime and the fact of his acquaintanceship with either the victim or the accused. The witness should then be requested to tell his story in his own way. He should be subjected to detailed questioning concerning the identification of the accused. The following is a list of representative questions which will suggest many others to the investigator in an actual case:

    a. Do you know the accused?
    b. Was this the first time you have ever seen the accused?
    c. How long a time did you observe him?
    d. From what position?
    e. What attracted your attention to the accused?
    f. What attracted your attention to the victim?
    g. Have you identified the accused since his apprehension?
    h. What were the circumstances surrounding that identification?

92. Classifying the Witness

The investigator should observe the witness closely and classify him from a moral, intellectual, and physical point of view. Is he of weak character, one who would be subject to such influences as corruption, intimidation, or the solicitation of a mutual friend? Is he aware of the seriousness of his position as a witness and of the grave responsibility of adhering to the truth in his statements? Is he honest but not of strong character, one who could be easily led into confusion and vacillation? All these mental notes will aid in estimating the strength of the case from the standpoint of the quality of the available witnesses.

93. Physical Competency of the Witness

During the interview the investigator should observe the physical condition of the subject who is a prospective witness. Direct questioning can also be used to acquire information on an aspect of physical condition which may affect his credibility as a witness. If the witness is to testify to what he saw under difficult conditions of visibility, the possession of normal vision, natural or corrected, becomes an important point. Impairment of hearing would affect the reliability of his testimony in regard to things heard. The investigator should be able to make some estimate of the witness's powers of observation and his ability to relate facts briefly, correctly, and clearly without becoming emotionally disturbed. Finally, the physical condition of the witness should be noted with a view to his availability at the time of trial.

XV. TRENDS AND PATTERNS IN HOMICIDE

94. Application

It is decidedly advantageous in the investigation of homicide to possess a general understanding of the patterns and trends of this offense. Cases of murder and manslaughter frequently fit into conventional patterns. The investigator who can readily recognize types of homicide can also mentally classify the offender and shorten the process of locating a logical suspect. Some of the information given below will serve to provide a background in homicide trends in large urban communities of heterogeneous population. The figures given should be considered as rough estimates.

95. Circumstances

a. **Time.** More than half of all homicides are committed over the weekend. Most homicides are committed during leisure hours, particularly between the hours of 8:00 P.M. and 2:00 A.M.

b. **Place.** Usually the highest rates of homicide exist in areas which have the highest delinquency rates, such as low-income residential areas surrounding industrial business areas. A significant number of homicides occur in the home.

c. **Weapon.** There is a growing tendency toward the use of firearms in homicide. More than 65 per cent of all murders are committed with firearms while less than 20 per cent are accomplished with cutting instruments. Knives are often used (as well as guns) in those murders arising spontaneously, while the gun figures prominently in premeditated murder where the perpetrator has time to arm himself. Women are more inclined than men to select a knife or icepick rather than a firearm.

d. **Alcohol.** The majority of the homicide cases involve alcohol as a factor, with the assailant or the victim, or both, drinking heavily.

96. Victim—Offender Relationships

a. **Sex.** Males commit more than three-fourths of the homicides and comprise more than three-fourths of the victims.

b. **Race.** Generally, whites murder whites and blacks murder blacks. Blacks are more likely both to commit murder and to be the murder victim.

c. **Acquaintance.** In over three-fourths of the cases, the victim knows his assailant. In over one-fourth of the cases, the victim is a member of the family.

d. **Quarrels.** 1) *Sexual.* A significant number of murders are attributable to quarrels over a woman. A sexual reason ordinarily lies behind a slaying of a woman by a man. Among the middle-income groups, the slaying is usually of the ordinary sex-triangle type, the man killing his wife or her lover. Where a male kills a female, the victim is usually his wife or his girlfriend. In the lower-income groups, the slaying of a woman by a man may arise out of a sex triangle or out of a orgiastic drinking-sex party.

Occasionally, the cause is trivial and unrelated to sex. The conflict over sexual rights to a woman is much more likely to give rise to murder among the lower-income groups. The unstable marital arrangements and the primacy of physical strength among the very poor are a combination from which murder can easily spring. Slayings by middle-class females are quite rare. The lower-class female is more inclined to defend her sexual rights to a man by slaying him or her rival. In some cases, the woman will slay her husband or lover to protect herself from a beating.

2) *Property.* Quarrels arising out of gambling or from a disputed claim to property are an important source of homicide among the lower-income classes. In fact, the quarrel over property is a more common cause than the sexual factor.

3) *Quarrels of Trivial Origin.* Oddly enough, the most common causes of homicide are trivial in nature. A fancied insult, a jostle, or a choice bit of profanity when properly mixed with alcohol can readily

lead to a fatal struggle. This is particularly true of the lower-income groups, where minor affronts are often greatly magnified and then subjected to the arbitrament of the knife.

XVI. INFANTICIDE AND OTHER INFANT DEATHS

97. Definition

Infanticide is the slaying of a newborn infant. This form of homicide is concerned only with the period from the time of birth until the time when the birth is reported to the authorities as required by law. The general term *homicide* is applied to the killing of an infant after the time of reporting. The destruction of a fetus during labor for the purpose of saving the mother's life is not considered infanticide. An infanticide must be treated as any other homicide. The slaying can be murder, manslaughter, or negligent homicide depending upon the circumstances.

98. Motive

If the death is not accidental, the motive of infanticide is obviously the desire to be rid of an unwanted child. The child can be unwanted for any of a number of reasons. Usually, infanticide is preceded by a secret birth. The mother is unwed and fears the stigma of giving birth to an illegitimate child. Among other reasons for not wanting the child are economic family straits and deformities of the body.

99. Autopsy Determinations

The discovery of a dead infant under circumstances giving rise to suspicion does not justify a hasty conclusion of homicide. Higher probability of accidents is associated with secret births. The many misadventures that are easily avoided or readily corrected under the care of a physician in a hospital can quickly result in the death of an infant born to an inexperienced woman under rigorous physical conditions. A careful pathological examination must form the basis of any conclusion that the death resulted from criminal violence rather than accidental injury. Among the specific questions which the autopsy surgeon can answer in regard to infanticide are the following:

a. **Viability.** Was the infant able or likely to live? It is necessary to show that the infant could have lived under normal care. The accepted criterion is normal formation and a gestation period of at last seven months in the uterus. An infant fulfilling these conditions is considered viable, i.e., capable of survival.

b. **Live Birth.** It must be shown that the baby was born alive. Pathological examination of the lungs will determine whether the infant actually breathed.

c. **Cause of Death.** The autopsy is the only reliable means of determining whether the baby was stillborn or died of natural causes, accidental birth injuries, or criminal violence.

d. **Infanticide.** Is the death due to infanticide? This determination is accomplished in the same manner as in ordinary homicides. The likely methods employed in the criminal act are known from experience: Drowning in tubs, dropping in privies, smothering, and the other simple methods of accomplishing asphyxia that are invited by the helplessness of the infant.

100. Innocent Deaths of Infants

The causes of deaths in children under two years of age are frequently mysterious at the outset of an investigation and often result in erroneous conclusions on the part of the investigators. A knowledge of some of these causes can serve to obviate unnecessary suspicions of homicide.

a. **Common Causes.** The following three classes include most of the common causes of infant deaths requiring autopsies:

1) *Natural Causes.* Illness and disease are the most commonly occurring causes. Involvement of the lungs, particularly interstitial pneumonia, accounts for most of the deaths. Death may occur with

great rapidity. The infant, apparently in good health or at worst suffering from a slight cold, is put to bed and later fed at some period during the night. In the morning the parents find the child dead with little evidence of disturbance other than a spot of blood on the bed clothing or a slight discharge from the nose. Bacterial and viral infection can fatally overwhelm a child in a short time because of the absence of defenses possessed by adults.

2) *Congenital Malformations.* The child may be afflicted at birth with some defect unknown to the parents. The absence of a vital structure, a defective heart, or a poorly functioning kidney or liver may be the cause.

3) *Birth Injuries.* The child may have been injured at birth by the forces of labor and delivery. Most commonly the skull is affected by compression and subsequent release of pressure, and the brain is damaged.

b. **Accidents.** A suspicious injury is sometimes the result of a fall from a bed. Asphyxia may result from food caught in the respiratory passages.

c. **Smothering.** It is a common error of investigators and even physicians to jump to an erroneous conclusion of death from accidental smothering, where the cause is not obvious. As a matter of practical experience, accidental suffocation is rarely the cause of death. It has been stated by competent authority that it is "almost impossible for an unrestrained normal infant, three weeks of age or older, to be accidentally smothered by a pillow or bed clothing. . . . Most deaths attributed to smothering are interstitial pneumonias although they may also be terminal conditions following other serious illness." The self-accusing parent can be relieved of remorse only through the information offered by an autopsy.

d. **Non-bacterial Food Poisoning.** This type of affliction is due to eating certain plants and animals containing a naturally occurring poison. The following substances are the most common causes: certain kinds of mushrooms such as *Amanita muscaria* and *Amanita phalloides;* immature or sprouting potatoes; mussels at certain undetermined times of the year; grain, especially rye which has become contaminated with the ergot fungus; fruits containing metallic contaminants, such as substances sprayed with salts of arsenic or lead, and food stored in cadmium-lined containers.

XVII. MOTOR VEHICLE HOMICIDES

101. General

In the investigation of traffic accidents as in the investigation of all criminal offenses, the objective is to determine all of the facts relating to the incident under examination. However, in motor vehicle accidents, particularly hit-and-run cases, the reconstruction of the occurrence is more dependent upon proper evaluation of physical evidence than upon the statements or testimony of witnesses. Scientific methods of examination and evaluation of physical evidence have become accepted and approved procedure of modern accident investigation. The proper examination and correct evaluation of physical evidence is a responsibility of the technician or expert, who by reason of his training and experience is qualified in the particular field involved. It is not practical to train the investigator in all of the techniques necessary to scientifically examine physical evidence which may come to his attention. He should know, however, what scientific aids are available, and he should be sufficiently familiar with the basic principles of the techniques common to scientific examination that he can perform the following functions in connection with a motor vehicle accident investigation:

a. Isolate and safeguard the scene of the accident.

b. Interview witnesses and obtain statements.

c. Photograph the initial appearance of the accident and significant evidence found at the scene.

d. Evaluate evidence of potential value and transmit it for expert examination.

102. Hit-and-Run Accidents

The classical problem of motor vehicle accident investigation is the establishment of the identity of the hit-and-run vehicle. This is the most difficult problem and consequently the investigative procedures described below will be based on the assumption that the identity of the hit-and-run vehicle is unknown. The solution of lesser problems will follow readily from a study of the techniques employed in this type of an investigation. It should be remembered that a driver who leaves the scene of a motor vehicle accident without properly identifying himself is guilty of an offense under state laws. If a driver remains at the scene he may be found guilty under the state laws of reckless driving or drunken driving, depending, of course, upon the circumstances and his culpability.

103. Scientific Aids

Experience has shown that materials found at the scene of an accident are of great importance in the case, and evaluation of these materials will sometimes involve complicated analyses. It is a safe rule to consider that all materials, traces, or conditions found at the scene which cannot for the moment be satisfactorily explained as having no bearing whatsoever upon the investigation at hand are physical evidence until their relative importance can be definitely determined. Ordinarily the immediate objectives of scientific aids in the investigation of a motor vehicle accident are:

a. To identify a car as having been on the scene of the accident.

b. To establish conclusively that a suspected car has been in an accident.

c. To reconstruct the circumstances surrounding the accident in order to determine the causative factors.

d. To corroborate or to disprove statements of the persons involved.

104. Scientific Techniques

The most common techniques employed in the scientific evaluation of physical evidence may be roughly divided into five general divisions:

a. **Preservation.** Photography is the most important means of preserving the initial appearance of the scene and the evidentiary materials. Casting is used to preserve such traces as tire and foot impressions.

b. **Physical Comparisons.** The most common of these are visual comparisons of missing parts. These may be conducted with magnifiers or low-power microscopes.

c. **Analytical Examinations.** Chemical analysis and spectrographic examinations of paint and soil are the most common analytical procedures.

d. **Physiological Examinations.** These include the facts developed by the autopsy; the examination of the body of the victim with a view to determining facts of the accident; and the analysis of body fluids to determine alcoholic content and blood group.

e. **Psychological Examinations.** These are related to the examination of persons involved in the accident to determine mental condition and superficial evidence of drunkeness. Also included are the techniques of deception detecting by mechanical means or by purely psychological means such as the word association test.

105. Examination of the Scene

The chief responsibility of the investigator at the scene is the discovery and preservation of the evidence. In regard to the other techniques it is expected that he will be aware of their potential value and will avail himself of their use. He must also provide the evidentiary materials to which the investigator can most effectively operate with regard to the physical evidence. The investigation of the hit-and-run accident will be divided into three phases:

1) The scene of the accident.
2) The superficial examination of the injured persons.
3) The examination of the suspected vehicle.

In hit-and-run accidents the scene of the occurrence frequently provides the only clues to the identity of the missing car. The scene moreover may contain sufficient evidence to enable the investigator to prove certain facts concerning the manner in which the accident took place. Traces, conditions, and material objects left at the scene are often more conclusive evidence of what happened than the oral testimony of eyewitnesses. All the factors of faulty perception, varying degree of memory, different levels of intelligence, and emotional stability enter into the testimony of witnesses but the physical facts provide objective evidence for the investigator.

a. **Principles of Searching.** As in the search of crime scene areas, the site of a motor vehicle accident must be subjected to a complete search. Every part of the scene must be examined, attention being given not only to the center of activity but to all the surrounding area as well and particularly to the approaches to the scene. This can be accomplished only if the search is planned and systematized. The particular pattern of search will vary with the individual case. Some of the most important factors to be considered in a plan of search are:

1) The scene should be isolated so that perishable traces are not destroyed.

2) Perishable traces such as tire tracks, foot impressons, and stains should be preserved before attention is given to the less destructible items.

3) No significant area should be overlooked.

4) Notes should be taken as the search progresses.

5) Physical evidence should be scrupulously marked for identification as it is picked up.

b. **Pattern of Search.** In the typical scene of a motor vehicle accident the search can be organized according to the following plan:

1) The point of impact should serve as the center of the search. The area immediately surrounding the center should be searched, and the perishable evidence cared for as the search progresses.

2) The path of the escaping car should be examined for glass particles, metal fragments, and paint flakes that may have fallen from the vehicle.

3) The approach to the point of impact should be examined for skid marks and tire impressions.

4) The path of the wrecked car, i.e., the car of the victim, should be studied. The car itself should be examined for transfer traces which were acquired from the other car at impact. Metal parts, impressions of bumpers, and paint are typical examples of this type of evidence.

c. **Collecting and Marking Evidence.** Evidence should be properly marked for identification as it is collected. The data concerning the evidence should be recorded in the investigator's notebook at the same time. Typical data for recording evidence are the following:

1) The exact position of the article of evidence with reference to fixed objects in the roadway and with reference to the vehicle.

2) Condition of the article, i.e., whether it was broken, dirty, and so forth.

3) Identifying description and information as to its probable source.

4) The names of the investigators who witnessed the finding.

The articles which can be removed should be placed in clean containers, envelopes, or cardboard boxes and properly marked. Large objects should be marked with an identifying mark. A tag should then be attached. They should then be removed to a safeguarded place for later, more detailed examination. Envelopes, containers, and boxes should be sealed and labeled as described in Chapter 7.

106. Photography of Motor Vehicle Accidents

Photographs of motor vehicle accidents are the most common type of court exhibit. Since the photograph is taken outdoors, it appears to be a relatively simple matter to make such a picture. Yet, a great number of traffic accident photographs are unacceptable because of distortion, misrepresentation, or some other inadequacy. The principles for producing accurate traffic accident scenes are complicated. It will be understood in the present discussion that a tripod should be used with the 4 × 5 camera.

a. **Completeness.** A photograph intended as evidence in a motor vehicle homicide should include all significant elements of the scene. Several photos should be taken to insure that all the facts are pictorially present. Contributing factors such as foliage obstructing vision should be shown clearly. Since different impressions of a scene are received from different points of view, the camera should be shifted so as to photograph the scene from several significant angles. Particularly important are the points of view which were available to the drivers of the vehicles and of any pedestrian involved in the accident.

b. **Distance from the Subject.** The camera should be located at a distance from the subject matter that will give a normal perspective for the lens employed. If the viewpoint of the camera is too close, perspective will seem distorted. If the camera is at too distant a point the scene will be lacking in depth and the objects will appear to be too near to each other.

c. **Height of Camera.** As a general rule in photographing traffic accidents, the camera should be at eye level. This is particularly important if it is desired to show the view available to a pedestrian at a given point. There are, of course, situations where other points of view are desirable. For example, if the investigator wishes to photograph an intersection to be used as a chart of the scene on which the approximate course of the colliding cars can be shown, a view from a very high camera position will be better than a photograph taken at eye level.

d. **Focusing.** Since the field of view in an accident photograph is so extensive, it is sometimes difficult to achieve proper focusing of all the significant objects in the scene. The simplest procedure to follow is to focus on the principal object and stop the diaphragm down to the next to the last opening. In this way considerable depth of field can be achieved. Modifications of this procedure must be made when lighting conditions are poor and background movement is present.

e. **Subject Matter.** The scene of the accident should be first photographed to show general conditions, approaches to the point of impact, and the views of the different drivers. These photographs should be taken after the vehicles are moved to show the nature and course of tire tracks and skid marks. Skid marks should next be photographed. The length of the skid mark is an indication of the speed at which the vehicle was traveling. Knowing the coefficient of friction of the roadway and the length of the skid marks, an expert can determine with fair accuracy the minimum speed at which the vehicle was traveling before the brakes were applied. A camera is placed at eye level to photograph the marks. Tire impressions on dirt roads and tire imprints on wet pavements are useful in identifying the unknown car. Photographs should be made of the tire tracks with the camera lens at a distance of approximately 5 feet and with the plate parallel to the surface of the road. A ruler should be included in the field to provide a reference scale for later measurements on the photograph. A plaster cast of tire impressions of the unknown vehicle should then be made. Evidentiary materials, such as glass pieces and metal fragments, lying on the surface of the roadway should be photographed before they are collected. Close-up photographs should be taken to insure a recognizable image. One of the views should include sufficient background to enable the viewer to locate the articles with reference to the scene in general.

107. Evidence at the Scene

The following types of evidence are among the most common clues which the investigator will find at the scene of a hit-and-run accident:

a. **Skid Marks.** These are the black marks left by a deposit of rubber from the tires. They are visible only when the wheels are almost locked by the forceful application of brakes. Skid marks help to locate the point at which the brakes were first applied. The length of the marks is an indication of the speed at which the vehicle was traveling prior to the application of the brakes. On finding skid marks at the scene of a motor vehicle accident, the investigator should photograph them and carefully measure their length. For an interpretation of the skid marks in terms of the original speed of the car, the investigator should request the services of an expert in this type of investigation.

b. **Tire Marks.** Tire impressions in mud, dirt, snow, and tar often contribute useful evidence. If the impression is clear, it may be possible to determine the manufacturer of the tire and the size of the wheel. If a sufficient number of characteristic defects are present it is sometimes possible to identify the tire itself. Tire prints on hard surfaces should be photographed with the plate parallel to the ground and a ruler in the field of view. An overall photograph of the tire print should be made in the same manner. In addition, the tire mark should be cast by means of plaster of paris.

c. **Dirt from Impact.** It is possible to obtain useful evidence from the mud and dirt which become caked on the undersurface of the fenders of an automobile. On collision with another vehicle or, in some cases, with a pedestrian, part of this mud or dirt is loosened and falls on the road. Dirt of this nature is easily recognized in the roadway. Samples should be collected and preserved for a possible later comparison with dirt obtained from the undersurfaces of the fenders of the suspected vehicle. Spectrographic analysis is used by laboratory experts in order to compare samples of this material chemically. In many cases this comparison will yield no evidence of value because the dirt or soil is common in nature and is found over a wide area. If, however, there are some elements or substances in the dirt which are highly characteristic, it is possible through this means to establish the fact that the vehicle passed over the area of the accident scene. Evidence of this nature is seldom conclusive because of the wide variety of soil which a vehicle may travel over in collecting fender dirt. Sometimes the shape of a piece of dirt may be significant. If the impact caused a large piece of dirt to fall intact it may be possible to find a corresponding cavity in the dirt remaining on the fenders.

d. **Cloth.** It is sometimes possible to find small fragments of cloth, usually in the path of the skid marks. When the injured person is run over by the wheels of the vehicle, these small fragments of cloth are removed and left in the roadway. Consequently, in subsequent examinations of suspected vehicles, attention should be given to the tires for the purpose of finding similar pieces of cloth or fibers.

e. **Blood, Tissue, and Hair.** When these substances are found on the roadway at the accident scene the investigator may make certain conclusions concerning the evidence which he may expect to find on a suspected car. It is unnecessary, ordinarily, to collect blood, tissue, or hair that is found at the scene of the accident since samples of these can be obtained from the autopsy surgeon. Sometimes, however, particularly when this type of evidence is found at a distance from the body, it is helpful to preserve the samples since their presence in a particular location is useful in reconstructing the accident. The collection of blood and tissue has been described in a preceding section.

f. **Chipped Flakes of Paint.** When two cars collide it is to be expected that there will be an exchange of paint smears and even that small flakes of paint will shaken loose and fall to the ground. This is particularly true of collisions involving an old car on which the paint has already begun to flake. It is possible from the examination of a flake of paint to determine the make and year of a car. The FBI Laboratory maintains a national automotive paint file which is used to provide such information. In addition, it is possible to state that a certain sample of paint came from a certain car. This is especially true where the car has been repainted several times and has thus acquired a number of individual and characteristic layers of paint. All samples of paint found at the scene of an accident should be collected in order to enable a future spectrographic analysis to be made by a comparison with the paint from the suspected car. If the paint is found in flake form it should be preserved intact so that it will be possible later to establish that the flake fit into the outline of a certain area of the metal surface of the suspected vehicle.

g. **Broken Equipment.** One of the best types of evidence for the purpose of showing that a suspected vehicle was at the scene of the accident is a broken piece of equipment such as the side mirror, headlights, or radiator emblem. These ornaments or accessories are sometimes detached from the vehicle by the shock of the collision. If on locating a suspected car it is found that a corresponding piece of equipment is missing, a photograph should be made which will show the part found at the scene in juxtaposition with the area of the vehicle from which it was detached. By the use of appropriate photographic techniques it is possible to show an exact correspondence between the part and its source.

h. **Headlights.** One of the most common clues found at the scene of a hit-and-run accident is broken headlight glass. From an examination of this glass it is sometimes possible to establish the exact type of lens and from this to discover the year and type of the car which was involved in the accident. The tendency to equip cars with a standard type of headlight, namely the "sealed beam" headlight unit, is a limiting factor. In nighttime accidents the condition of the headlights can be an important element. One of the first steps of the investigator is to check the position of the light switch. The headlights themselves should be examined with special reference to the filaments. If the lamp was on at the moment of impact, the coils may have suffered a deformation. The effects of impact on a headlight will be different for lighted and unlighted lamps.

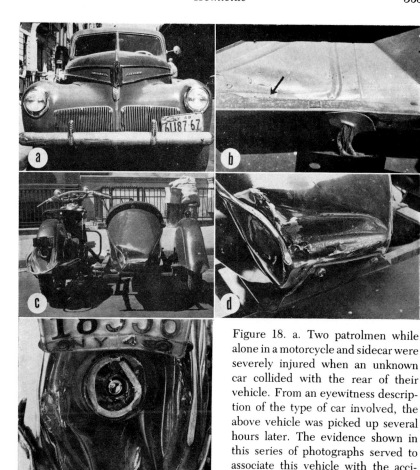

Figure 18. a. Two patrolmen while alone in a motorcycle and sidecar were severely injured when an unknown car collided with the rear of their vehicle. From an eyewitness description of the type of car involved, the above vehicle was picked up several hours later. The evidence shown in this series of photographs served to associate this vehicle with the accident. The car was examined for indications of a collision with the motorcycle and sidecar. Red and yellow paint marks were found on the bumper. b. The grille was removed from the car. In the area in back of the grille pieces of white, red, and yellow glass were found. Some of these are visible in the area indicated by the arrow. c. The motorcycle was damaged in the rear fender and the sidecar was dented in the rear. A cast was made of the car bumper to show that the shape fitted across the dented areas of the motorcycle and sidecar. D. Red paint was removed from the dented area of the rear of the sidecar. This was shown by spectrographic analysis to be of the same composition as the red paint on the car bumper. e. Glass samples removed from the damaged tail light were shown to match the glass found behind the grille of the car. The yellow paint of the license plate of the motorcycle proved on analysis to be the same as that found on the car bumper.

1) *Identifying Make and Model.* When glass fragaments are discovered at a hit-and-run accident scene the investigator should first photograph them as they lie on the gound and should then collect them in an envelope. The pieces may be placed together in the manner of a jigsaw puzzle. Transparent tape will facilitate the procedure by holding together pieces that are found to match. If a sufficient number of pieces of glass are present, it will be possible to determine the trade name of the lens, the name of the manufacturer, and sometimes the make and model of the car.

2) *Matching.* If pieces of headlight glass are later found in an automobile, it may be possible to match them with pieces found at the scene.

108. Examination of the Injured

The deceased may bear marks from the car on either his body or his clothing. Both should be examined carefully for traces.

a. **Clothing.** The clothing should be removed and studied for the following:

1) *Grease* from the understructure of the vehicle.

2) *Tire marks.* These may be irregular because of the yielding action of the clothing.

3) *Paint.* The buttons and sometimes the cloth may retain paint from the car.

b. **The Body.** The chest or back of the deceased sometimes bears a distinct tire mark.

109. Examination of the Suspected Vehicle

The determination of whether a suspected vehicle has been in an accident is by no means simple. Often the body of the deceased is cast aside on impact and leaves no trace on the car. If the car collides squarely with the body, traces may be left.

a. **Dents and Scratches.** These provide a special problem to the investigator. It is not a simple matter to determine the recency of the damage or the exact cause of it. The owner should be questioned

Figure 19a. A hit-and-run homicide on water. Two boys fishing from a rowboat had been killed when their vessel was hit amidship by a fast-moving cruiser which left the scene without being identified. The ship shown above was picked up on suspicion. Its owners denied participation in an accident. The small black marks faintly visible on the port side suggested oarlock impressions. A light smear of paint of the same green as the rowboat was also discernible.

concerning the origin of the damage and the story checked at a later date.

b. **Broken Parts.** Pieces of glass may remain in the headlight or may fall into the grillwork. A broken emblem or side mirror should also attract attention. Questions should be raised concerning the cause of this damage.

c. **Fibers.** Contact with the victim's clothing may leave fibers or even cloth on the vehicle.

d. **Cloth Marks.** If the victim is struck with sufficient force, an outline of clothing pattern may be seen on the paint.

Figure 19b. A closeup of the port of the cruiser showing the pairs of black marks. An oarlock from the rowboat is juxtaposed to show the fit.

Figure 19c. When the cruiser was lifted from the water, pieces of rowboat line and the sweater of one of the deceased were found entwined in the propeller.

e. **Blood and Tissue.** In a particularly violent accident, blood stains and tissue may be found on the radiator, the door handles, and other parts.

f. **Characteristic Soil.** When the accident has taken place on a dirt road, particles of soil may be found adhering to the fenders and the tires. If the chemical composition of the soil is highly characteristic, it may be possible to associate the vehicle with the scene of the accident.

g. **Understructure of the Vehicle.** The car should be placed on a service station jack for the purpose of studying the understructure for various traces such as impressions in the grease or fibers.

ADDITIONAL READING

Adelson, L.: *The Pathology of Homicide.* Springfield, Ill.: Thomas, 1974.

Camps, F.E.: *The Investigation of Murder.* London, Michael Joseph, Ltd., 1966.

Choron, J.: *Suicide.* New York, Scribner's 1972.

Gil, D.: *Violence Against Children.* Cambridge, Harvard University Press, 1970.

Harvard, J.D.J.: *The Detection of Secret Homicide.* London, Macmillan, 1960.

Heaps, W.A.: *Assassination: A Special Kind of Murder.* New York, Hawthorn Books, 1969.

Hendrix, R.C.: *Investigation of Sudden and Violent Death.* Springfield, Ill.: Thomas, 1972.

Hughes, D.J.: *Homicide Investigative Techniques.* Springfield, Ill.: Thomas, 1974.

Macdonald, J.M.: *Homicidal Threats.* Springfield, Ill. Thomas, 1968.

Moritz, A.R. and Morris, R.C.: *Handbook of Legal Medicine*, 3rd ed. New York, Mosby, 1970.

Rushforth, N.B., et al.: Violent Death in a Metropolitan County. Changing Patterns in Homicide (1958–1974). 297 *New England Journal of Medicine*, 10, 1977.

Simpson, K.: *Forensic Medicine*, 7th ed. Maidenhead, Berkshire, England, Arnold Pub., 1974.

Snyder, L.: *Homicide Investigation*, 2nd ed. Springfield, Ill.: Thomas, 1967.

Assault

Cameron, J.M. and Rae, L.J.: *Atlas of the Battered Child Syndrome.* New York, Longman, 1975.

Dimaio, V.J.M.: The Frequency of Accidental Gunshot Wounds. 4 *Forensic Science Gazette*, 3, 1973.

Gil, D.: *Violence Against Children.* Cambridge, Harvard University Press, 1970.

Mulvihill, D.J. (Ed.): *Crimes of Violence—A Staff Report Submitted to the National Commission on the Causes and Prevention of Violence*, vols. 11-13. Washington, D.C.: U.S. Government Printing Office, 1969.

Perkins, R.M.: Analysis of Assault and Attempts to Assault. 47 *Minnesota Law Review*, 71, 1962.

Pittman, D.J. and Handy, W.: Patterns in Criminal Aggravated Assault. 55 *Journal of Criminal Law, Criminology and Police Science*, 462, 1964.

Blood and Other Body Fluids

Culliford, B.J.: *The Examination of Bloodstains in the Crime Laboratory*. Washington, D.C.: U.S. Government Printing Office, 1971.

Examination of Biological Fluids. 41 *FBI Law Enforcement Bulletin*, 6, 1972.

Gramar, L. and Tausch, D.: Determination of ABO Blood-Group in Hair. 72 *Journal of Legal Medicine*, 1, 1973.

Macdonnell, H.L.: *Flight Characteristics and Stain Patterns of Human Blood*. Washington, D.C.: U. S. Government Printing Office, 1971.

Outteredge, R.A.: Recent Advances in the Grouping of Dried Blood and Secretion Stains. In Curry, A.S. (Ed.): *Methods of Forensic Science*, vol. 4. New York, Wiley–Interscience, 1965.

Prokop, O. and Uhlenbruck, G.: *Human Blood and Serum Groups*. New York, Interscience, 1969.

Race, R.R. and Sanger, R.: *Blood Groups in Man*, 5th ed. Philadelphia, Davis, 1968.

Poisoning

Amelink, F.: *Identification Methods in Pharmacy and Toxicology*. New York, Wiley-Interscience, 1962.

Clark, E.G.C.: *Isolation and Identification of Drugs*. London, Pharmaceutical Press, 1969.

Curry, A.: *Poison Detection in Human Organs*. Springfield, Ill.: Thomas, 1969.

Glaister, J.: *The Power of Poison*. New York, William Morrow, 1954.

Hayes, W.J., Jr.: *Clinical Handbook of Economic Poisons*. USPHS Pub. #476. Washington, D.C.: U. S. Government Printing Office, 1967.

Sunshine, I.: *Handbook of Analytical Toxicology*. Cleveland, Chemical Rubber Co., 1969.

Von Oettingen, W.F.: *Poisoning*. Philadelphia, Saunders, 1968.

Motor Vehicle Homicide

Auten, J.J.: *Traffic Crash Investigation*. Springfield, Ill.: Thomas, 1972.

Baker, J.S.: *Traffic Accident Manual for Police*, 4th ed. Evanston, Ill.: Traffic Institute, Northwestern University, 1963.

Collins, J.C. and Morris, J.L.: *Highway Collision Analysis*. Springfield, Ill.: Thomas, 1967.

Greenwald, R.: Scientific Evidence in Traffic Cases. 59 *Journal of Criminal Law, Criminology and Police Science*, 57, 1968.

Lacy, G.W.: *Scientific Auto Accident Reconstruction.* Albany, N.Y.: Matthew Bender, 1964.

McGrew, D.R.: *Traffic Accident Investigation and Physical Evidence.* Springfield, Ill.: Thomas, 1976.

Turner, W.W.: *Traffic Investigation.* Rochester, Aqueduct Books, 1965.

Woods, J.: Headlights are Tools in Traffic Accident Investigation. 25 *Law and Order*, 6, 1977.

Chapter 26

CRIMINAL EXPLOSIONS

1. Introduction

IT IS NOT the purpose of the present treatment to provide detailed descriptions of explosive devices such as bombs, *suspicious packages*, infernal machines, or incendiary devices. Information of that nature should not be made easily available to the general public. The problems associated with bomb threats, unexploded bombs, and bomb scene procedures are basically the problems of the patrol force. The student who wishes to learn about explosives, protective response, and preventive measures against bombs is referred to the series of excellent publications of The National Bomb Data Center of the International Association of Chiefs of Police. It is assumed in this chapter that an explosion has already taken place and an investigative problem exists. The investigator, then, is faced with a scene of wreckage; the physical clues appear either non-existent, irrevocably scattered, or mutilated beyond recognition; even the eyewitnesses may have been killed in the blast.

2. Initial Action

Appropriate attention to routine police tasks is also assumed throughout so that space can be devoted to the special features of an explosion investigation. For example, the injured will have been cared for, measures will have been taken to extinguish fires or prevent their subsequent outbreak, and the possibility of further accidents or explosions from utility hazards or other dangers will have been eliminated. The investigator must determine the nature and cause of the explosion. Initially, he must distinguish between an accidental explosion and one produced intentionally or by criminal negligence.

All persons who witnessed the explosion or observed any significant attendant circumstances should be detained, identified, and interviewed. Observations concerning the number and nature of the explosions, the color of smoke, the presence of peculiar odors and other observations of the senses will be important. Recollections concerning the movements of persons before and after the occurrence should be recorded while they are fresh in the witnesses' memories.

The scene of the explosion should be placed under safeguard as soon as possible by assigning an adequate number of officers to the duty of rigorously excluding unauthorized persons. To preserve the crime scene as far as possible, rescue workers should be cautioned against unnecessary disturbance of the wreckage and the fire chief requested to restrict overhauling to a minimum.

3. Types of Explosions

The investigator should be able to distinguish between the two basic types of explosions. A low explosive results in a *push* effect, leaving a diffuse pattern with no marked progression of effect from a point source. The high explosive incident is marked by a definite *seat* of origin. Movable objects are blown outward from this point, the force of the blast diminishing in intensity with distance.

a. **Low Explosives** are characterized by the relatively low velocity with which the energy wave is transmitted—a few thousand feet per second. Gunpowder, gasoline, and carbon monoxide are examples of low-explosive substances. The explosion is identifiable by two characteristics: a low-frequency sound, which has been variously described as a *puff, boom,* or *pop,* and the absence of relatively severe damage in the area of the explosion.

b. **High Explosives,** on the other hand, such as dynamite and nitroglycerine, have velocities as high as 25,000 feet per second, are accompanied by a shattering high-frequency sound, and reveal a definite crater of explosion. On the basis of these differences it is often possible to identify the character of the explosion even though no traces of the explosives remain.

4. Crime Scene Action

Crimes involving explosions present many of the difficulties usually associated with arson, paramount among which is the partial or total destruction of evidence tending to establish a *corpus delicti*. Hence, although the usual investigative steps are followed at the crime scene, great care must be taken in handling the articles of evidence and interpreting the pattern suggested by their location.

a. **Defining the Scene.** Depending on the severity and location of the explosion, the crime scene area may be restricted to a room or may extend over an area of several acres. Determine the outer limits of the area to be searched and post a guard to prevent the entrance of any unauthorized persons and the removal of any object from the area. The posting of placards marking the limits of the crime scene area is helpful in these situations. Of course, special problems will be presented by certain kinds of explosion. For example, a time bomb exploding on a plane in flight may result in the distribution of wreckage over more than a mile of territory.

The Colorado aircraft disaster of November 1, 1955 provides an example of an exceptionally difficult "crime scene," since the mid-air explosion resulted in the distribution of fragments over a wide area. In this case a twenty-three year old youth had plotted to kill his mother for the sake of the insurance money and the prospect of a major share of a $150,000 estate. The perpetrator had tied together twenty-five sticks of dynamite and attached the timing device connected with a dry cell battery and two blasting caps. The ensemble was concealed in a suitcase which his mother took aboard the plane. In the mid-air explosion forty-four persons were killed. It was found later that the perpetrator had bought $37,500 in vending machine insurance policies on his mother's life before planting the bomb on the DC-6B. Further investigation revealed a previous forgery charge against the bomber. The Colorado explosion was the first known case of successful bomb sabotage in the history of this country's airline operations.

b. **Documenting the Scene.** Because of the significance of the pattern of strewn objects created by the explosion and the importance of tracing the point of origin through this pattern, documentation should be unusually painstaking.

1) *Photography.* Overall photographs of the scene and sectional views of important areas should be taken before anything is disturbed. During the search close-ups of articles of evidence should be taken as they are discovered. If it is helpful to include markers or signs in the field of view, it is advisable to make two sets of such photographs, one with and one without the markers. The use of transparent overlays with unmarked photographs should also be considered. Significant objects and places can be marked on the transparent overlay to correspond to the exact location of such items on the corresponding photograph. The report of investigation should include photographs as a supplement with text references to evidence objects and areas at the scene keyed to the symbolism used in the photographs and sketches.

2) *Sketches.* A representation of the scene should be made by means of sketches—an overall sketch for the whole scene and individual sketches for separated areas such as rooms. Significant items of evidence should be located by symbol and accurate measurements from fixed points. Rectangular coordinates are preferable for indoor scenes, while polar coordinates are more suited to outdoor explosions extending over broad areas. Compass directions, legends, and other essentials should be given in each sketch.

3) *Investigator's Notes.* Although photographs and sketches can be invaluable supplements to the investigative report, they should not be expected to take the place of the investigator's notes. These should contain detailed descriptions of the scene and each important object in it. Identifying data for each evidentiary article should be inscribed in the notebook.

c. **Searching the Scene.** The investigator should enlist the aid of any available technical assistance in his search of the crime scene. Accompanied by a member of the Bomb Squad or Explosives Unit, a police laboratory expert, an explosives specialist, or an arson investigator, he should search the scene for physical evidence. If a point of origin can be located, a spiral method of search can be used effectively. The searchers should begin at the point of origin and progress outward using increasingly larger circles. Limitations on this procedure are naturally set by the extent of the area.

The searchers should look for evidence which will establish a

Figure 20. Bomb squad detectives equipped with protective armor remove a suspected bomb, using a steel mesh bag.

corpus delicti, viz., the fact that an explosive device was used and that there was an intent to injure some object or person. They should, of course, be constantly alert for clues which may lead to the identity of the perpetrator or link him to the scene. Pieces of metal such as pipe fragments, wire, or parts of a timing device; string, paper, leather, wood, and other fragments which may have been used to package the bomb; unexploded materials, pieces of paper that may have been part of the explosives wrapping; and any other trace evidence which may have been part of an explosive device or its container should be carefully collected after its location and initial appearance have been documented as described. This procedure was used in the case of the New York World's Fair bomb with the result that a sufficient quantity of clue materials was recovered to enable the experts to identify the clock, explosive materials, and suitcase, to reconstruct the bomb, and to trace some of its components.

The value of trace evidence in the investigation of an explosion was dramatically shown in a California case in which a dynamite bomb found near the home of a prominent citizen was submitted to a microanalyst, the late Doctor Albert Schneider, dean of the Berkeley School for Police Officers. Doctor Schneider examined every part of the package minutely—burlap, paper wrappings, the dynamite sticks, caps, fuses, and a piece of string. Particles clinging to this latter item provided considerable information under the microscope. Doctor Schneider drew the following conclusions from his examination: "This twine came from a farm upon which will be found a fast-running stream of water, pine trees, black and white rabbits, a bay horse, a light cream colored cow, and Rhode Island red chickens."

On reading this report there was considerable head shaking and exchanging of glances among the more cynical officials; nevertheless, they filed the data for future reference. The dynamite was traced to an explosives dealer in Novato, California, who gave the police details concerning three recent sales of dynamite in the neighboring communities. On investigating the three purchasers, the police officers found that one of them lived adjacent to a farm which matched that of Doctor Schneider's description in every detail. The farmer was innocent of the crime. The dynamite, however, had been stolen from his premises by two farm hands, comparative strangers in his employ, who later proved to be the guilty parties.

d. **Examination of Victims.** Deceased persons should not be disturbed until the medical examiner (or other person serving in a medicolegal capacity) has made his examination to determine such matters as the cause and manner of death, the time of death, and whether death took place before or after the explosion. Where the victims have been mutilated or burned to a degree that prevents recognition by relatives or associates, identification may be made by means of fingerprints, teeth, and bones. The medical examiner can provide information as to age, height, and weight, even though only part of the body is available. He can also provide data on operations, including the length of time since the operation, and pathological

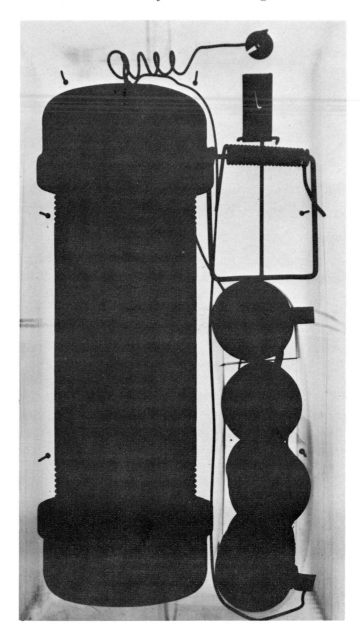

Figure 21. Radiograph of a suspected package, revealing a pipe bomb and trigger mechanism.

findings as to physical ailments which can lead to identification. Further information can be obtained through the laboratory examination of clothing, documents, and personal items, particularly metal articles, such as watches, rings, or cigarette lighters. Since the position of all such articles with relation to the body is important for identification purposes, the exact location of each item should be recorded before it is collected.

e. **Utilities.** A bomb which is set off unknowingly by the action of an occupant of the premises may present a problem in regard to the source of electrical energy required for detonation. Electrical or telephone equipment can be used to supply the necessary power. Check such devices as telephones, electric clocks, heaters, coffee pots, and lamps for breaks or additions in the wiring. The wiring systems of the engines of powered devices, such as lawn mowers, compressors, and pumps, should also be examined. The presence in any of these motors of extraneous wires or fragments of fuses, caps, or detonators should provide a lead. In certain cases, as for example those of suspected sabotage, the entire electrical system including motors, appliances, and other apparatus should be examined for defects such as exposed wires, incorrectly installed wiring or fuses that could result in overheating or sparking. The investigator should enlist the aid of a safety expert or an electrician in this phase of the search for evidence. Experienced assistance of this character is required not only because of the complexity of the investigative problem but also because of the need for expert testimony on the matters in the event of a trial.

In a New York case to which the newspapers gave the garish title "The Case of the Golden Bomber," a pipe bomb was wired to the utility lines so that when the intended victim switched on the cellar light an explosion would take place. The victim survived, however, and assisted in the solution of the case by indicating the motive: $985 concealed in a metal container in the cellar was missing. The perpetrator proved to be an electrician who had access to the cellar for storage facilities. Part of the evidence that linked him to the pipe bomb was a gilt (gold) paint which through some whim he had chosen to decorate the bomb. The search of the cellar in this case required extreme care, since the defendant had stored away 220 pounds of powder, 259 flares, and 115 bombs.

Figure 22. Effect of bombing resulting from labor troubles.

5. Nature of the Criminal

A number of elements in crimes involving explosions render the investigation of these crimes unusually difficult. Particularly significant is the fact that quite often the bomber is not a criminal by record or inclination. Thus we are faced with a disturbing paradox: the perpetrator of one of the most heinous of crimes may not at heart be a professional criminal. In all likelihood he may be a man with a

c. **Storage.** The magazines used for storing explosives are subject to laws, that describe their size, construction and location.

d. **Sale and Use.** Safety regulations are usually established to restrict the sale of explosives to legitimate users such as owners of construction works, mines, quarries, and even farm lands on which it is necessary to blast stumps or perform other clearance operations. Ordinarily it is required that the record of sales be maintained.

11. Dog-Handler Teams

In 1972 a Trans World Airlines jet bound for Los Angeles was turned back to Kennedy Airport on receiving an anonymous phone call warning that a bomb was aboard. After the passengers were evacuated, a German shepherd went to work, sniffing out the bomb within twelve minutes before it was set to detonate. This success has been repeated a number of times in the intervening years. It is estimated that the trained dogs have saved more than 100 lives and prevented millions of dollars in property damage. More than twenty-seven city airports are presently protected by bomb squad dog teams, which spend 40 per cent of their time at airports and the remainder in patrol work and bomb detection work in the city. In non-airport searches the dogs have found sixty-eight explosive devices, including a letter bomb addressed to the former mayor of Los Angeles. In 2,000 airport and aircraft searches, most of them false alarms, the dogs and their handlers have found explosives twenty-one times, seven of them on aircraft. The handlers are local police officers, trained at Lackland Air Force Base, Texas, who use male German shepherds because of their stamina, adaptability, intelligence, and size.

ADDITIONAL READING

Aids to the Detection of Explosives. A brief review of equipment for searching out letter bombs and other explosive devices. 17 *Security Gazette*, 2, 1975.

Brodie, T.G.: *Bombs and Bombing*. Springfield, Ill.: Thomas, 1973.

Chapter 27

RULES OF EVIDENCE

1. General

THE SUCCESS or failure of a criminal prosecution usually depends upon the evidence presented to the court. It is in the court that the investigator must present the evidence which he has so laboriously collected over a period of months. Will his evidence be admitted? Has he taken precautions to obtain evidence that is admissible? Has he observed the rules which govern admissibility? A failure through ignorance on the part of the investigator may lead to the rejection of a vital piece of evidence by the court with the result that a conviction cannot be sustained. Since the investigator is occupied constantly with the business of evidence, it is an indispensable part of his training to understand the purpose of evidence and the rules that control its admissibility. It is only in this way that he can serve the cause of justice efficiently. The rules of evidence lie at the heart of modern judicial systems, and their understanding is necessary for an intelligent participation in prosecutive procedures.

2. Purpose

The term *evidence* includes all the means by which an alleged fact, the truth of which is submitted to scrutiny, is established or disproved. The purpose of evidence is the discovery of the truth of the charge. The laws of evidence are the rules governing its admissibility. This system of rules does not constitute a science of logical proof. From long experience with witnesses, jurors, and litigant parties, it has been found that certain types or forms of

621

information tend to possess risks of irrelevancy and to confuse the issues rather than assist in determining truth. The rules of evidence have as their primary aim the screening out of all evidence having these risks and tendencies from consideration by the jury and court members. There is no universal law of evidence. The rulings of the different states vary. For example, common law exists in some states, while in others, a different law exists or the common law prevails side by side with statutes. In federal courts, the common law has been superseded by procedural rules.

3. Classifications and Definitions

Evidence may be divided into three major classifications:

a. **Direct Evidence.** Evidence which directly establishes the main fact of issue (elements of the crime) is called *direct evidence*. For example, an eyewitness account of a criminal act is direct evidence; the witness is here describing an event which he actually saw.

b. **Circumstantial Evidence.** Evidence which establishes a factor or circumstance from which the court may infer another fact at issue is called *circumstantial evidence*. Where direct evidence is the immediate experience on the part of a witness, the essence of circumstantial evidence is inference. As an elementary example we may consider the following:

> *Example:* X and Y go into a closet together and close the door. A shot is heard and Y rushes out with a smoking gun in his hand. X is found lying on the floor. An eyewitness relating this event would be offering circumstantial evidence since he did not see Y fire the shot. The facts, however, are so closely associated that it may reasonably be inferred that Y shot X.

c. **Real Evidence.** This comprises tangible objects introduced at a trial to prove or disprove a fact in issue. The evidence speaks for itself. It requires no explanation, merely identification. Examples of real evidence are guns, fingerprints, and blood stains. Real evidence may be direct or circumstantial.

4. Admissibility of Evidence

Evidence to be admissible must be material and relevant. The rules of evidence are concerned with the admissibility of facts and pertinent materials and not with their weight. With respect to given evidence, the weight is a question of fact for the judge or jury to determine.

a. **Materiality.** If the fact which the evidence tends to prove is part of an issue of the case, the evidence is material. Evidence which proves something that is not part of an issue is immaterial. To be material the evidence must affect an issue of the case significantly. Example: X is being tried for larceny of a crate of oranges. His attorney discourses at length on the fact that the oranges were yellow in color. Such evidence is unimportant to the trial and is, therefore, immaterial.

b. **Relevancy.** Evidence which tends to prove the truth of a fact at issue is relevant. Example: A murder has been committed with a bow and arrow. It is relevant to show that the defendant did know how to use a bow and arrow. It would be irrelevant to show that he was well acquainted with firearms.

5. Competency of Witnesses

A competent witness is one who is eligible to testify. The competency, both mental and moral, of a witness over thirteen years of age is presumed. Mental competency refers to the ability to see, recall, and relate. Moral competency implies an understanding of the truth and the consequences of a falsehood. The competency of children is not dependent on age and may be shown by apparent understanding and a recognition of the moral importance of telling the truth. A record of conviction of crime is unrelated to competency but may affect credibility.

6. Impeachment of a Witness

Impeachment is the discrediting of a witness. A witness may be disqualified by showing, for example, a lack of mental ability, insufficient maturity, previous conviction of a crime, or a reputation for lack of veracity.

7. Judicial Notice

Certain kinds of facts need not be proved by formal presentation of evidence, since the court is authorized to recognize their existence without such proof. This recognition is called *judicial notice*. The general rule prescribes that the court will not require proof of matters of general or common knowledge. Examples: historical and geographical facts; a state's own laws; weights and measures; and so forth.

8. Burden of Proof

No person is required to prove his innocence. The burden of proof for a conviction rests solely with the prosecution. In criminal cases, the prosecution has the burden of proving the accused guilty *beyond a reasonable doubt*. The accused, however, must prove his own allegations such as alibis, claims of self-defense, and insanity.

9. Presumption

A presumption is a justifiable inference. It is an inference as to the existence of one fact from the existence of some other fact founded upon a previous experience of their connection. Presumptions generally serve the purpose of shifting the burden to the other party to establish the contradictory facts.

a. **Conclusive Presumption.** This presumption is considered final, unanswerable, and not to be overcome by contradictory evidence. The following are examples:

1) Everyone is presumed to know the law.

2) Children under seven years are presumed to be incapable of committing a crime.

3) A boy under fourteen years cannot commit the crime of rape.

b. **Rebuttable Presumptions.** These can be overcome by proof of their falsity:

1) Every man is presumed to be innocent.

2) Presumption of sanity.

3) One intends the natural consequence of his acts.

4) Presumption of good character, chastity, or sobriety.

5) That an officer properly performs his tasks.

6) Legitimacy of children and validity of marriage.

7) Presumption of death after an unaccounted absence of seven years.

10. Rules of Exclusion

Much of the body of the rules of evidence concerns itself with the *rules of exclusion*. These latter deal with the conditions under which evidence will *not* be received. They are often extremely technical in nature with the consequence that their purpose is obscured.

a. **Purpose.** The rules of exclusion were primarily evolved to control the presentation of evidence in a trial before a jury. It was supposed that the juror who decided the facts in controversy was inexperienced in legal matters and would be unable to separate the immaterial and unimportant from matters truly germane to the issue. It was feared that the layman would not discriminate properly between gossip and fact, or between allegation and truth.

b. **Function.** The function of the rules is to limit the evidence which a witness may present to those things of which he has a direct, sensory knowledge. The witness may relate what *he* saw, felt, and smelled. The jury endeavors to put itself in the place of the witness and to judge the reliability of the witness.

c. **General Rule.** All direct and circumstantial evidence, if material and relevant, is admissible except:

1) Opinion evidence.

2) Evidence concerning character and reputation.

3) Hearsay evidence.

4) Privileged communications.

5) Secondary evidence.

There are exceptions as regards admissibility to all of the categories of evidence listed above.

11. Opinion Evidence

a. **The Opinion Rule.** The general rule is that opinion evidence is not admissible in a trial. A witness may testify only to facts, not to their effect or result, or to his conclusions or opinions based on the facts. He can bring before the court only those facts which he has observed, directly through the medium of his senses—sight, hearing, touch, taste, or smell. The reasons for this restriction lie in the fact that it is a function of the jury to weigh the evidence and to draw conclusions. Moreover, where a witness adds opinion to observation, a confusion may arise in the minds of the jurors as to what is the observed fact and what is the witness's derived interpretation of the fact originally apprehended by his senses.

b. **Exceptions to the Opinion Rule.** Several exceptions are attached to the opinion rule. These exceptions recognize first the fact that certain simple judgments based immediately on sensory observation are so much a matter of common practice in the mind of the average man that they may be given with much greater reliability than the word "opinion" ordinarily connotes. Second, the court recognizes that the opinions of certain specialists in regard to their specialty should be treated with greater consideration than mere opinion.

1) *The Lay Witness.* The layman may express an opinion on matters of common observation. This exception arises in cases where an opinion is the only logical way to receive the information concerning the fact, since a recounting of all the facts which caused the formation of the opinion would tend to confuse the jury. Necessity and expediency dictate the exception. These opinions, of course, are permitted only concerning subjects in which the average man has considerable experience and knowledge. The following are examples of matters of common observation in which an opinion may be expressed:

a) Physical properties such as color, weights, size, and visibility.

b) Gross estimates of a person's age.

c) Implications of race, nationality, and language.

d) Emotional states.

e) The apparent physical condition of a person.

f) Intoxication.

g) Speed of vehicles.

2) *Expert Testimony.* An expert is a person skilled in some art, trade, or science to the extent that he possesses information not within the common knowledge of men. Medical doctors, fingerprint

specialists, and collectors may be considered experts. The testimony of an expert can be admitted to matters of a technical nature that require interpretation for the purpose of assisting the judge and jury in arriving at a correct conclusion. Expert testimony is not proof, but evidence that can be accorded its own credibility and weight by each member of the court.

a) Tests of Admissibility. An expert may not testify as such until he has satisfied the court that he has the proper skill, knowledge, and background of experience or education. In other words, he must possess qualifications. He must, moreover, testify concerning a subject on which expert testimony should be received. The facts concerning which he gives an opinion are of such a technical nature that the judge and jury may not be expected to have sufficient knowledge, skill, and understanding of such matters.

b) Examples of Expert Testimony. Among the innumerable examples of subjects on which expert opinion may be received are the following:

1) Medical matters.

2) The direct movement of a car before a collision based on a study of tracks left by the vehicle.

3) Minimum distance required to bring a vehicle to a stop from certain speeds.

4) Extent of damage to a vehicle.

5) The field of police science, viz., fingerprints, photography, casting, etc.

6) Chemical analysis, e.g., drugs, paint, etc.

7) Serology, i.e., the study of body fluids such as blood and semen.

12. Character and Reputation

As a general rule, testimony concerning a person's character and reputation cannot be introduced for the purpose of raising an inference of guilt. This exclusion is based on the difficulty that the jury may experience in separating the fact that a defendant has a previous record of crime from the question of his guilt in the crime under consideration. The following are among the usual exceptions to this rule:

a. **Character.** The defendant may introduce evidence of his own good character and reputation to show the probability of innocence. Such testimony may either be given by himself or by character references. It should deal with specific character traits such as sobriety and chastity. When such testimony has been introduced, the "door is open" for the prosecutor to introduce evidence concerning those specific areas of character treated in the defendant's testimony. For example, if the defendant introduces testimony concerning his sobriety, the prosecution may produce evidence relating to instances of drunkenness.

b. **Exceptions.** Previous acts of crimes of the accused may be introduced in evidence if they tend to show that the defendant actually committed the crime for which he is being tried. Some examples of this type of testimony are the following:

1) *Modus Operandi.* The prosecution may show that the pattern of previous crime is similar to that of the present crime, i.e., they may show that "this is the way the defendant operates."

2) *Previous acts.* These may be brought in to rebut a defense of *mistake* or *ignorance*. Example: A wife claims that the arsenic in the meal which her husband ate and which caused his death was the result of a mistake. The fact that three previous husbands died of a mixture of arsenic in their meals would be admissible.

3) *Identifying Evidence.* The evidence is admissible if it serves to identify the defendant as the perpetrator of the crime. Example: In a case of burglary, it may be shown that the pistol found at the scene was stolen previously by the defendant. This evidence is specifically designed to show that the pistol was in the possession of the defendant before the crime and not to show guilt of a theft.

4) *Guilty Knowledge or Intent.* An example of this would be a case in which it is shown that the defendant had previously been a fence for stolen goods and hence was aware that the goods in the present case were stolen.

13. Hearsay Evidence Rule

a. **Definition.** Hearsay evidence proceeds not from the personal knowledge of the witness but from mere repetition of what the witness has heard others say. It does not derive its value from the credit of the witness but rests mainly on the veracity or competency of other persons. Example: A witness states, "I know X hit Y because Z told me." Hearsay applies not only to oral statements, but also to written matter. Wherever the matter is quoted or is not within the personal knowledge of the witness, it may be adjudged hearsay.

b. **Exclusion.** Hearsay evidence is excluded for the following reasons:

1) The author of the statement is not present and under oath.

2) No opportunity for cross-examination is afforded the defense.

3) There is no opportunity for the court to observe the author's demeanor.

4) No consideration is given to the defendant's right to confront witnesses against him.

5) There is a possibility of error in the passage of information from one person to another.

c. **Exceptions to the Hearsay Rule.** There are numerous exceptions to the exclusion of hearsay evidence. These exceptions are of sufficient importance and of such common occurrence that they should be treated in detail. It will be noted that the circumstances surrounding the exception tend to greatly minimize the possibility of error or fraud.

1) *Confessions.* (See Page 133 for an extended treatment of confessions.) Since a confession is a direct acknowledgment of guilt, it is not likely that a person would voluntarily so commit himself.

2) *Conversations in the Defendant's Presence.* If the defendant is confronted with an accusation of guilt before apprehension and fails to deny it, the circumstances can be offered in evidence.

3) *Dying Declaration.* In a trial for criminal homicide, the dying declaration of the alleged victim concerning the circumstances of the act which induced his dying condition, including the identity of the person who caused his injury, is admissible in evidence to prove such circumstances. The following specific conditions must be fulfilled in order for a dying declaration to be admissible:

a) The evidence must be given in a trial for homicide.

b) The statement must be that of the victim.

c) The statement must concern the circumstances of the act causing his condition, including the identity of the person who caused the injury.

d) The victim must believe he is dying.

e) The victim must in fact have died.

f) The victim must have been competent at the time the statement was made.

4) *Spontaneous Exclamations.* Ordinarily, if a person speaks before he has time to reflect or to fabricate a lie, he will speak the truth. The element of surprise tends to minimize the possibility of design or deliberation.

a) DEFINITION. A *spontaneous exclamation* is an utterance concerning the circumstances of the startling event by an individual in a condition of excitement, shock, or surprise, which warrants the inference that it was spontaneous and not the product of deliberation or design. Such a statement is admissible when made by anyone who heard it. The spontaneous exclamation can be made either in favor of or against the person making it. It can be made by anyone present at the event and not simply by the victim. The term *res gestae* literally means: "things which happened." Thus, testimony concerning spontaneous actions is included in this broader term, but exclamations relate specifically to the hearsay rule.

b) TESTS OF VALIDITY. A spontaneous exclamation must be carefully examined before it is admitted into evidence. The following points should be considered:

1) The statement or action should be close in time to the main act, i.e., it should precede, follow, or be concurrent with the main act very closely in time.

2) The spontaneous character of the statement should be clear so as to preclude the possibility of fabrication or deliberation.

3) The declaration should not have been made in response to a question.

4) The statement should tend to elucidate or explain the character of the act.

5) In general, only a person who committed, participated in, or witnessed the act may be the declarant.

c) FRESH COMPLAINT. In prosecutions for sexual offenses such as rape, carnal knowledge, or sodomy, evidence that the victim made complaint within a short time thereafter is admissible in certain jurisdictions. In fresh complaint only the victim's statement is considered; the statement may relate only to *who* and *what* caused the conditions; the complaint may be made within any reasonable time after the event. These three points differentiate fresh complaint from spontaneous exclamation.

5) *Documentary Evidence.* a) Best Evidence. Documents may be introduced in evidence as an exception to the hearsay rule. Their submission is controlled by several rules, the most important of which is the "best evidence" rule. Basically, this rule requires that a person bring into court the best evidence available to him. Thus, whenever possible, the original of a written document should be produced.

b) Secondary Evidence. This evidence, which includes copies, carbons, and other duplicates of the original, is not ordinarily admissible. Under the following exceptional circumstances, secondary evidence may be admissible:

1) When the original is lost or destroyed.

2) When it is in the hands of the defendant, who refuses to surrender it.

3) When it is of such official nature that its production in court is not deemed advisable.

4) When there is some other valid reason for which it cannot be produced.

c) Official Records. These can be introduced by duly authenticated copies because their maintenance is required by law, regulation, and custom, and they can be attested to by the custodians. It is reasoned that it would disrupt the machinery of government to require the appearance of the recording official at each time the records are required. Moreover, it would be difficult to have the official testify to every record because of distance, death, and changes in office.

d) Investigator's Notes and Memoranda. Notes covering the period of time when the events in question occurred may be used by the investigator to refresh his memory in testifying. They may be entered into evidence under the conditions described in Chapter 2.

e) Former Recorded Testimony. Under certain conditions former recorded testimony may be introduced. The requirements are as follows: The witness who gave the testimony is not now available and the former trial involved the same or similar defendants in substantially the same issues.

f) DEPOSITION. The testimony of a witness who will be beyond the processing of the court at the time of trial may be formally reduced to writing and is ordinarily admissible. Written interrogatories are submitted by both prosecution and defense and the answers of the witness by both parties may be reduced to writing. The right of cross-interrogation is protected, since both parties may use the deposition. Special requirements are placed on the qualifications of the persons taking the depositions.

g) REGULAR ENTRIES IN THE COURSE OF BUSINESS. It is reasoned that an entry made in the conduct of a regular business is sufficiently credible to make it admissible as evidence. Tests of admissibility must be applied:

1) The entry must have been made at a time close to the occurrence of the fact in issue.

2) The entry must have been made with personal knowledge of the person making the entry or the regularity of the bookkeeping system.

3) The entry must have been made within the usual course of business.

4) The original entry in the book must be offered.

6) *Matters of Pedigree.* Formerly, much of our knowledge relating to matters of death, birth, marriage, and family relationships was based on the knowledge of members of the family. Statements relating to pedigree made by a member of the family circle (including old friends and servants) before the beginning of a controversy in which pedigree arises as a question can be received in evidence when the person making the statement has died.

14. Privileged Communications

Information obtained in certain confidential relationships will ordinarily not be received in evidence. The court considers such information to be privileged communication and in the interest of public policy will refuse to receive evidence by the person whom it benefits. The court may, however, receive this evidence from a person not bound by the privilege. The following are examples of privileged communications:

a. **State Secrets and Police Secrets.** 1) Informants to public officers in the discovery of a crime are privileged.

2) Deliberations of petit and grand juries.

3) Diplomatic correspondence.

4) Official communications, the disclosure of which would be detrimental to public interest.

b. **Personal Privileged Communications.** 1) *Husband and Wife.* Neither can divulge in the trial of either confidential information imparted to each other, unless the consent of both is obtained. The person entitled to the benefit is the spouse who made the communication.

2) *Attorney and Client.* The communication is privileged if it was made while the attorney-client relation existed and in connection with the matter for which the attorney was engaged.

3) *Penitent and Clergyman.* The communication is privileged if made as a formal act of religion or while seeking spiritual advice on a matter of conscience.

4) *Doctor and Patient.* Confidential information given by the defendant to a doctor while he is a patient of the doctor is privileged in a few jurisdictions.

15. Real Evidence and Admissibility

The question of self-incrimination arises in connection with certain types of real evidence. The privilege against self-incrimination is based primarily on the Fifth Amendment to the Constitution: No one shall be compelled to be a witness against himself in a criminal case. This privilege is not limited to the person on trial but extends to any person who may be called as a witness. Ordinarily, the prohibition against compelling a person to give evidence against himself relates only to the use of compulsion in obtaining from him a verbal or other communication in which he expresses his knowledge of a matter. In other words, if the fact involved is a *testimonial utterance*, a compulsory answer involves self-incrimination. If the presentation of the fact does not demand the *intervention of the*

f. Negative proof of *corpus delicti* has in some recent cases been permitted. Thus in the offense of arson, it can be shown negatively that the fire was initiated by criminal agency by logically eliminating all natural or accidental causes.

ADDITIONAL READING

Chamelin, N.C. and Evans, K.R.: *Criminal Law for Policemen*, 2nd ed. Englewood Cliffs, N.J.: Prentice-Hall, 1976.

Hanley, J.R. and Schmidt, W.W.: *Legal Aspects of Criminal Evidence*. Berkeley, Calif.: McCutchan, 1977.

Inbau, F.E., Aspen, M.E, and Carrington, F.: *Evidence Law for the Police*. Philadelphia, Chilton Book, 1972.

Entrapment

Hardy, B.A.: The Traps of Entrapment. 3 *American Journal of Criminal Law*, 165, 1975.

Heydon, J.D.: The Problems of Entrapment. 32 *Cambridge Law Journal*, 268, 1973.

Miller, J.D.: The Entrapment Defense, Part I. 42 *FBI Law Enforcement Bulletin*, 2, 1973. Part II. 42 *FBI Law Enforcement Bulletin*, 3, 1973.

_____: Entrapment. 42 *FBI Law Enforcement Bulletin*, 10, 1973.

Park, R.: The Entrapment Controversy. 60 *Minnesota Law Review*, 163, 1976.

Mathematics and Proof

Fairley, W.B.: Probabilistic Analysis of Identification Evidence. 2 *Journal of Legal Studies*, 493, 1973.

Finklestein, M.O. and Fairley, W.B.: A Bayesian Approach to Identification Evidence. 83 *Harvard Law Review*, 489, 1970.

Finklestein, M.O. and Fairley, W.B.: The Continuing Debate over Mathematics in the Law of Evidence. 84 *Harvard Law Review*, 1801, 1971.

Kingston, C.R.: Application of Probability Theory in Criminalistics. 60 *Journal of the American Statistical Association*, 70, 1965.

Mode, E.B.: Probability and Criminalistics. 58 *Journal of the American Statistical Association*, 629, 1963.

Tribe, L.H.: Trial by Mathematics: Precision and Ritual in the Legal Process. 84 *Harvard Law Review*, 1329, 1971.

Chapter 28

TESTIMONY IN COURT

1. General

T HE APPEARANCE of the investigator as a witness before a court of law
is the final and most severe test of his efficiency. The preparation
of the case is made with the goal of ultimate presentation before the
jury constantly in view. The precautions taken at the crime scene,
the meticulous preservation of the evidence, the patient gleaning of
information from scattered witnesses, the dogged search for the
fugitive, the painstaking interrogation of the suspects, the
preparation of exhibits, the detailed report of investigation—all of
these exhausting and time-consuming stages of the inquiry
culminate in the trial. The probative value of the accumulated
evidence depends in no small degree upon the manner of its
presentation to the jury. Finally, the effectiveness of the evidence is
a function of the impression which the investigator makes as a
witness.

Since the reputation of the investigator rests in great part on his
courtroom performance, he should give some heed to the art and
science of behavior on the witness stand. In external demeanor he
should possess dignity and should behave with a decorum consonant
with his surroundings. On the witness stand the investigator
represents the agency which employs him. Deficiencies or
irregularities in his behavior will reflect upon his organization.
Errors of judgment and misrepresentations, moreover, may
unjustly affect the fate of the defendant and thus defeat the aims of
justice.

When the investigator takes the witness stand he is subject to the
most critical censure he will encounter in his career. He is no longer
dealing with the admonitions of a friendly supervisor. He must

contend now with the objective and critical eye of the court and at times with the outright animosity of defense counsel. Regardless of the proficiency with which the investigation was conducted prior to the trial, a failure in the vital task of testifying on the witness stand may render worthless much of the commendable work he has performed in the case. The court trial is the test which is weighed most heavily by the public and by his organizational supervisors. Although the substance of the investigator's testimony is of paramount importance, an almost equally great significance is attached to his conduct on the stand and to his manner of informing the court of the facts discovered during the course of the case. It is not to be expected that the investigator become a proficient witness in his first appearance in court. He can, however, assist his rapid development in this aspect of his profession by complying with the elementary principles of "witnessmanship."

2. Training in Laws of Evidence and Court Procedure

To become trained and skilled in the work of testifying on the witness stand the investigator should first become thoroughly conversant with the laws of evidence. In this way he can guide his investigation so that evidence relevant to the issues receives primary consideration. Through an understanding of the rules of evidence the investigator will acquire a general knowledge of what is taking place in the courtroom at any given time. He will understand what the prosecution or defense counsel is attempting to achieve by means of a particular tactic. Finally, he will be able to avoid the pitfalls and traps of the unscrupulous cross-examiner.

a. **Rules of Evidence.** A knowledge of the rules of evidence is indispensable to the investigator on the witness stand. He must be able to recognize relevant and material evidence. He should know the rules governing the admissibility of evidence, particularly those relating to hearsay, confessions, and documents. He may testify only to facts whose knowledge he has acquired through his own senses, i.e., he may not give opinions but may testify only to facts that are part of his personal knowledge. If he is asked a question by counsel, the answer to which would in his mind be inadmissible, he should pause for a short space to give opposing counsel an opportunity to object. A knowledge of the laws of evidence will suggest many of these small but important points in the technique of testifying.

b. **Knowledge of Court Procedure.** In addition to knowing the jurisdiction of the various courts, the investigator should have an understanding of the court procedure. The positions occupied by the judge and the other members of the bar should be clear to him. He should understand the functions of the court clerk and the court attendants. A familiarity with the terms and operations of the courts will enable him to understand each step in the trial.

3. Preparation

On the stand the investigator should give the impression of being prepared while at the same time avoiding any parrot-like recital which would imply that he has been rehearsed. In preparation, the investigator should review his notes and endeavor to fix in his mind the highlights of the case. He should refresh his recollection on all important happenings in the events which he intends to relate.

Prior to testifying in a case, the investigator should prepare his testimony in anticipation of logical questions. He should be cognizant of the rules of admissibility and of the evaluation factors that govern the probative value of his evidence. The full history of his association with the evidence should be at his fingertips. A careful study of his notes will refresh his memory and enable him to select the significant parts of the accumulated data of the investigation. He should be so familiar with his case that at all times he is prepared to use his wits to his best advantage, expressing his information upon the issues in a fair, convincing, and forceful manner. He must avoid errors, confusion, and inconsistencies which may lead to a loss of poise and composure and thus undermine the confidence of the jury in his credibility.

Although the investigator is permitted to use his notes in court, he will convey a better impression if he is able to narrate the facts without reference to a memorandum book. If a witness must look up each point in his notebook, his testimony loses force and he becomes ineffective. He must know his case well enough to report all facts without reference to notes except data such as numbers, dates, addresses, and the spelling of names. Thus, his appearance on the stand must be preceded by a conscientious, thoughtful review of the facts and the points with which they are involved. A failure to conduct a review of a case will result in misstatements, omissions of material facts, and even contradictions. This is particularly true of those cases which involve events that occurred some months in the past.

4. On the Witness Stand

On being called as a witness the investigator should step up to the stand and permit himself to be sworn in. In sitting he should assume a comfortable but alert posture. He should identify himself and his membership in his organization. His testimony should then be given *slowly, audibly,* and *distinctly.* The court stenographer should be given an opportunity to hear and record every word. The investigator should address his testimony to the jury and not to counsel or judges.

Ordinarily the investigator is asked to relate a series of incidents that he observed. This recital can be accomplished in simple chronological fashion. Using straightforward language, the witness should describe the observed events in the order in which they took place. The narrative should enable the jury to understand clearly the incidents that occurred.

Since the prosecuting attorney is prevented from asking leading questions, the testimony in which he is particularly interested should be anticipated by the investigator. He should endeavor to place appropriate emphasis on the highlights. The narration of events should be designed to present certain elements of proof.

In giving his testimony, the investigator should present a modest demeanor and should display a sincere interest in accuracy and truth of statement. Bias, prejudice, and antipathy should not color the testimony, since they will affect the court adversely. The investigator must give the appearance of an officer whose interest lies not in the conviction of the accused but in the presentation of the facts of a case.

On assuming his position on the witness stand, the investigator should picture accurately his position in the court. Although he may view himself as an objective collector and retailer of the facts, unbiased and unprejudiced because of his official position and professional experience, others in the court will look upon him as an interested party, ready to accuse a person of a crime on slight suspicion or out of excessive zeal for prosecution. The defense counsel will endeavor to portray him as a police officer who is trying to solve a case by seizing the nearest suspect at hand regardless of the dearth of evidence. Thus, the investigator must not display any extraordinary interest in presenting his testimony. He must play the part of the impartial, conscientious public servant endeavoring in his modest way to achieve the aims of justice. His calm and forthright presentation must be designed to win over the judge and jury to a belief in his honesty and integrity. This effect can be accomplished by following a few simple rules:

a. **Personal Knowledge.** The investigator must tell only what he knows from personal knowledge to be the truth. This is the sole function of the witness. It is in this way that he will assist the court in arriving at a just decision in the case, whether the verdict be a conviction or acquittal. The truth is told not only by an accurate choice of words but also by a careful control of emphasis and tone to avoid exaggeration or underestimation.

b. **The Appearance of Candor.** The professional investigator should train himself to give the impression of telling the truth. (No suggestion of duplicity is intended by this statement.) It is the misfortune of some scrupulously honest souls that their appearance does not convey to their hearers an impression of unquestionable honesty. Nervousness and timidity give them an almost evasive manner. Such a deficiency is almost fatal to the investigator whose professional duties include testimony in court. He must school himself carefully so that poise, lack of timidity, and forthrightness are evidenced in his demeanor.

c. **Courtesy.** An attitude of respect must be maintained at all times. The investigator must not engage in sarcasm, witticisms, or ridicule. Even obviously absurd questions should be answered seriously and temperately.

d. **Direct Answers.** The witness must answer the question asked, i.e., his answers must be responsive. He should listen to the question and gather its exact meaning. If he does not understand it, he should request clarification. If he knows the answer, he should offer it without hesitation. The answer should do no more than reply to the question. It should not express a view of the case, draw a conclusion, or present an argument. Further, it should not gratuitously provide "ammunition" for opposing counsel.

e. **Control.** A witness who becomes angry or otherwise loses control of his emotions is an easy prey to astute counsel. Emotional composure is a paramount virtue in a witness. He must ignore insults, badgering, and innuendoes. He should, in other words, take a professional view of the proceedings. Every effort should be made to avoid the impression of being contentious.

f. **Appearance and Manner.** The witness should speak in natural, unaffected tones. His speech should be clear and sufficiently loud to be heard by all concerned parties. It should be directed to the jury or to the judges as the nature of the court may be. The posture of the witness should be erect and comfortable, since slouching or other appearance of carelessness suggests an indifference to the issues.

5. Expert Testimony

Although the investigator does not hold himself to be an expert witness in the sense of a professional laboratory expert, he will occasionally find himself in a position where he is an expert to a limited degree. There are a number of techniques such as photography and casting which are required in the investigator's profession. In testifying concerning these technical procedures, the investigator should know something of expert testimony.

a. **Expert Testimony.** The expert witness deals in opinion testimony. Ordinarily a witness must state facts and may not express his opinions or conclusions. He may testify to impressions of common experience such as the speed of a vehicle, whether a voice was that of a man, woman, or child, or to a person's state of intoxication. Beyond that he is closely limited. An expert witness is one who possesses a special skill, be it an art, trade, or science, or one who has special knowledge in matters not generally known to men of ordinary education and experience. Possessing this knowledge the expert may express an opinion on a state of facts within his specialty and related to the inquiry. Before he expresses such an opinion, however, it must be established that he is an expert in the specialty.

The testimony of the expert is given in a number of ways. He may, for example, be requested to state his relevant opinion based on his personal observation or from an examination which he has conducted without specifying hypothetically in the question the data upon which his opinion is based. On the other hand he may be asked to express an opinion upon a hypothetical question if the question is based on facts in evidence at the time the question is asked or, at the discretion of the court, on facts later to be received in evidence.

b. **Common Experience.** Treated more simply, expert testimony is a valuable means of arriving at the truth; it consists most commonly of experiments conducted to prove or disprove a fact or statement of the defendant or one of the witnesses. The following are some examples which investigators will frequently encounter:

1) Visibility—the possibility of seeing one place from another.
2) The length of time required to go from one place to another.
3) The distance traveled in going from one place to another.
4) The nature and audibility of a sound.
5) The length of time required for a candle to burn.
6) The results of firing with a given weapon.
7) Whether a particular firearm will give a visible flash with certain ammunition.

c. **Evidence of Experiment.** Facts such as those listed above can be proved by experiments conducted by the investigator. These experiments must be made under substantially the same conditions as those existing at the time of the incident in question.

d. **Professional Experts.** In matters requiring a depth and breadth of technical knowledge, the investigator should have recourse to the professional expert. The success of the case is jeopardized if a person of limited knowledge or experience endeavors to give an opinion that is within the realm of the scientific criminologist or other expert. For example, questions relating to microscopy, biology, handwriting, or fingerprint identification should be resolved only by experts. The investigator can assist the expert by acquiring an understanding of the scope and limitations of the expert's scientific knowledge. He should know what can be fairly expected of science and what lies out of the realm of possibility in the expert's field. Thus he will understand the methods of collecting and preserving evidence and of properly transmitting them to the expert so that their full probative value can be realized.

e. **Expert Investigative Techniques.** In relation to the professional techniques in which the investigator, himself, can be considered an expert, he should be able to show on the witness stand that he possesses the necessary training, experience, and knowledge of the literature. Photography, casting, and the development of latent fingerprints are the subjects most commonly mastered by investigators. Before testifying concerning these matters the investigator should review some standard work on the particular technique which was employed in acquiring the evidence. He should inform the prosecutor of his qualifications and, in particular, of instances where he has previously testified in similar matters.

ADDITIONAL READING

Burke, J.J.: Testifying in Court. 44 *FBI Law Enforcement Bulletin,* 9, 1975.

Kuhn, C.L.: *The Police Officer's Memorandum Book.* Springfield, Ill.: Thomas, 1964.

Petersen, R.D.: *The Police Officer in Court.* Springfield, Ill.: Thomas, 1974.

Tierney, K.: *Courtroom Testimony: A Policeman's Guide.* New York, Funk & Wagnalls, 1970.

PART VI
IDENTIFICATION AND REPRODUCTION

Chapter 29

OBSERVATION AND DESCRIPTION

I. OBSERVATION

1. Gathering Information

IN THE ACQUISITION of information the investigator relies mainly on indirect sources, such as the accounts of witnesses, the reports of investigation prepared by associates, photographs, sketches, and the reports of laboratory experts. There are occasions, however, when he must rely on the reports of his own senses. In a surveillance, for example, the appearance of the subject and the persons whom he contacts must be recorded in the investigator's mind. At the scene of a crime, although the assistance of the camera and the sketcher is available, the investigator must ultimately rely on his own observations for a comprehensive and truly significant representation. The accuracy of his observations will depend chiefly upon his training and experience. Their usefulness, however, will often depend on his ability to communicate their purport to others, either orally or in a report. In other words, he must be trained to describe as well as to observe.

2. The Senses in Observation

In recording the data of a scene or occurrence the investigator must employ his senses, primarily that of sight and secondarily hearing, smell, touch, and taste. The eye is the most fruitful source of information, but in the absence of training it is also one of the most unreliable because of the tendency of the observer to fill in the gaps

647

that inadequate observation may leave. Hearing is the most objective sense; nevertheless the observation of a sound is subject to such errors as mistaken estimates of distance and illogical comparisons. The sense of touch is usually unreliable because of the inexperience of most persons in the accurate use of this sense. Smell, the olfactory sense, is considered relatively unreliable because of its susceptibility to suggestion. The sense of taste suffers from the same defect. It has been estimated by psychologists that approximately 85 per cent of our sensual knowledge is gained through the medium of sight; 13 per cent through hearing; and the remaining 2 per cent through smell, touch, and taste. The reliability of the information obtained through the senses may be considered to be in the same relation.

3. Psychological Elements

For the purposes of the investigator the process of observation can be divided into three stages—attention, perception, and report.

a. **Attention.** The psychological process of being brought into the presence of a fact is called *attention*. The observer cannot observe a phenomenon until he is aware of it. A convenient division of attention consists of three phases, namely, involuntary, voluntary, and habitual. Each of these phases is influenced by such factors as size, change, interest, physical condition, suggestion, and repetition.

b. **Perception.** Recognition of the significance of a phenomenon is termed *perception*. In this stage the observer not only *apprehends* a phenomenon but also *understands* it. In understanding the fact to which attention has been drawn the following factors are contributory:

1) *Intelligence.* The mental capacity of the observer is an obvious factor.

2) *Educational Background.* Observation depends upon reference. The educated person is at an obvious advantage in being able to refer observed phenomena to matters which he has learned.

3) *Experience and Occupation.* These elements constitute a frame of reference for the observer.

c. **Report.** The third element of observation is the identification of a fact, i.e., the subject identifies, names, or otherwise subconsciously becomes aware of the significance of a fact.

II. PHYSICAL DESCRIPTIONS

4. Description of Persons

The ability to describe persons accurately has traditionally been highly prized in the investigative profession. Before the advent of fingerprint classification physical descriptions were considered to be the basis of identification files. The art of describing a person in custody was refined to a procedure consisting of a series of measurements of the various features and was accorded the impressive title of anthropometry. During this period great stress was laid on the ability to describe persons after a short period of visual observation. The systematic procedure for such a verbal description was called the *portrait parlé,* a term that is still in general use at the present time. Although the talent for verbal description has lost much of its former emphasis among modern investigators, the logic that underlay the nineteenth century development remains undiminished in its validity for purposes of criminal inquiries.

5. General Information

To fully identify a person, the following background data should be obtained:

a. **Name, Aliases, and Nicknames.** The full name should be obtained and not merely the initials. The varied spellings of the different aliases should be included.

b. **Social Security Number.**

c. **Military Serial Number.**

d. **Fingerprint Classification.**

e. **Present and Former Addresses.**

f. **National Origins.** An exceptionally useful item in a description is the national origin of the person. Thus, Irish-American or Italian-American are more descriptive terms than those used to list the facial characteristics.

g. **Scars and Marks.** Cicatrices, birthmarks, and tattoos are valuable identification points. Both visible (normally dressed) and invisible scars and marks should be reported where known.

h. **Physical Traits.** Significant physical habits are important.

1) *Walk.* The manner of walk is highly individual. Such terms as the following are commonly used: athletic, limping, shuffling, bowlegged, flatfooted, and pigeon-toed.

2) *Voice.* The voice may be high– or low-pitched; loud or soft; or, more typically, it may lie between these extremes.

3) *Speech.* The most obvious trait of speech is the local characteristic of enunciation, viz., southern, midwestern, New York, Boston, etc. Foreign speech should be associated with the country of origin. "Educated" and "uneducated" speech can sometimes be discriminated.

i. **Personal Habits.** Despite any efforts at disguise, the personal habits that characterize an individual are seldom changed.

1) *Dress.* The standard of dress is usually maintained by a well-dressed fugitive as a matter of personal pride, whereas the person used to slovenly attire will remain in that condition out of ignorance or inertia. Tendencies toward sport clothes or loud dress will be retained. Slovenly, neat, expensive, cheap, or conservative are a few of the adjectives that may be employed.

2) *Other Habits.* A number of other personal habits are found useful in identification. A propensity for frequenting bars, theaters, bowling alleys, and other forms of entertainment; a "weakness" for women or other forms of sex diversion; an addiction to narcotics; a desire to engage actively in sports such as fishing or bowling—any of these habits can serve to provide a line of inquiry or search for a wanted person.

j. **Relatives and Associates.** The names, addresses, and occupations of relatives, friends, associates, and acquaintances should be listed.

k. **History.** This should include his education, military history, criminal record, and professional or occupational background.

6. Physical Description

The verbal description or *portrait parlé* is still considered a reliable aid in the field of identification. The degree to which the investigator can place detail in such a description will depend on his training and natural gifts in this direction. The following items are basic in a verbal description.

a. **General Impression.** Type; personality; apparent social status; comparison by name with an actor, political figure, or other well-known person.

b. **Age and Sex.**

c. **Race or Color.**

d. **Height,** estimated within 2 inches.

e. **Weight,** estimated within 5 pounds.

f. **Build.** Thin, slender, medium, and stout.

g. **Posture.** Erect, slouching, round-shouldered.

h. **Head.** Size, whether small, medium, or large; and shape, whether round, long, dome-shaped, flat on top, or bulging in the back.

i. **Hair.** Color; sheen; part; straight or curly; and area of baldness.

j. **Face.** General impression, followed by a description of the features.

1) *Forehead.* High, low, bulging, or receding.

2) *Eyebrows.* Bushy or thin; shape.

3) *Mustache.* Length; color; shape.

4) *Eyes.* Small, medium, or large; color; clear, dull, blood-shot; separation; glasses.

5) *Ears.* Size; shape; size of lobe; angle of set.

6) *Cheeks.* High, low, or prominent cheekbones; fat, sunken or medium.

7) *Nose.* Short, medium, big, or long; straight, aquiline, or flat; hooked or pug.

8) *Mouth.* Wide, small, or medium; general expression.

9) *Lips.* Shape; thickness; color.

10) *Teeth.* Shade; condition; defects; missing elements.

11) *Chin.* Size; shape; general impression.

12) *Jaw.* Length; shape; lean, heavy, or medium.

k. **Neck.** Shape; thickness; length; Adam's apple.

l. **Shoulder.** Width and shape.

m. **Waist.** Size; shape of stomach.

n. **Hands.** Length; size; hair; condition of palms.

o. **Fingers.** Length; thickness; stains; shape of nails; condition of nails.

p. **Arms.** Long, medium, or short; muscular, normal or thin; thickness of wrist.

q. **Feet.** Size; deformities.

7. Voice Identification

The recognition of a human voice is a common experience. Picking up a telephone we may recognize immediately, from the sound of a few words, the voice of a person whom we have not seen for months or even years. Although we may attribute this ability to recognize an individual voice to some special capacity of perception and memory, there is an implicit acknowledgment of the fact that voices are distinctive—that each individual can be uniquely

Figure 24. *Voiceprints* are usual representations of characteristics of the human voice that permit identification by comparison. The spoken word "You," for example, can be recorded to provide "spectrograms" such as these, in which the expert can find an adequate base of similarities or differences for a definite opinion as to the identity of the speaker.

associated with his voice and that the sounds emitted in human speech possess characteristics, such as pitch, intensity, and "quality," which impose a unique pattern upon the human ear.

The investigator, however, is interested not so much in recognizing a human voice as in the problem of proving for court purposes the identity of the voice with relation to its owner. The need for this form of proof can arise in a variety of ways. For example, the identity of the speakers in a taped recording of a conversation during which no names are mentioned can be essential to the prosecution of a conspiracy case. Similarly, the identity of a person accused of telephoning bomb threats can be established from a study of recordings of the voice in question. Voice identification would prove valuable also in kidnapping and extortion cases.

A solution to the problem of objective proof of voice identification has been offered in the form of an electronic recording of the energy output of the subject's voice in producing a specified word (specified for purposes of comparison). The result is a sound "spectrogram" that can be used for comparison purposes. Whenever the person says the word—"you," for example—regardless of pitch, volume, or attempt to disguise his voice, the "spectrogram" or "voiceprint" will be substantially the same.

The consistency is said to arise out of the fact that voice quality is determined by the physical characteristics of the vocal cavities (in the throat, the nasal system, and the mouth) and by the structure and use of more than half a dozen "vocal muscles" such as the lips, the jaw, and the tongue. Since speaking is a randomly learned process, in which the infant tries thousands of vocal combinations before coming up with his own, the end product is a unique voice. The factors used in voiceprint identification are those which are not under speaker's conscious control. Thus, the identification ignores loudness, rapidity of speech, and pitch, since these can be controlled consciously. Even the use of a different language does not affect the identification.

The usefulness of voiceprints can be seen in the following 1970 case of the St. Paul Police Department. Shortly after midnight an anonymous telephone call was received at headquarters, requesting aid for a woman about to give birth. A two-man patrol car arrived at the given address to find only a darkened house. While one patrolman went around to the back door, a sniper opened fire from across the street, fatally wounding the other patrolman. The shooting appeared to be a senseless attack on police in general. The only clue was a taped recording of the telephone call. The investigation sought to identify the voice by interviewing thirteen neighborhood women and recording their voices. As a result of voiceprint analyses, Caroline Trimble, 18, was arrested and later indicted for murder.

Two earlier cases involving voiceprints came before courts in New Jersey (1967) and California (1968), and both times the appeals courts rejected the method as unreliable. In another 1967 case, a voiceprint identification in a grand jury investigation of police corruption was later admitted to be an error. The subject of the voice comparison, a deputy inspector of police, was identified as the owner of a voice recorded in a telephone conversation with a known gambler. The identification, made in 1967, was acknowledged to be an error in 1971 only after the police official, through his own investigative efforts, had found and produced the true owner of the recorded voice.

At this stage in the development of voice identification great care must be exercised in view of the technical uncertainties and the substantial lack of agreement among speech scientists. The method is ill served by excessive claims with respect to specificity and infallibility. Even though a method falls short of 100 per cent reliability, it can still be quite useful to the courts and the police provided the users are aware of present limitations. The actual physical mechanism of voice production is still a dark area of science. The investigator should not be misled by nomenclature such as "voiceprints" and "voice spectrograms" with their implied analogies of fingerprints and spectrography into attributing a comparable degree of scientific reliability to voice identification. He should be aware of the inherent limitations in the method and in the performance of the examiners.

8. Lost or Stolen Property

One of the most effective methods of recovering lost or stolen property is the employment of a central index of articles which have been reported lost, stolen, pawned, or sold at second hand. Many thieves lack the imagination or underworld associations which would enable them to dispose of the property with a reasonable gain and relative safety. Ordinarily they resort to a haphazard sale of the stolen goods and run the risk of detection. They usual modes of disposal of the property are sales to pawnbrokers, secondhand dealers, innocent friends, strangers, or fences.

9. Lost Property Files

Whichever of these channels of disposal is employed, there exists the likelihood that the stolen object will eventually find its way to a pawn shop or a secondhand dealer. In most cities it is required that pawn shops and secondhand dealers daily report the pawning or purchase of certain types of property on official police department forms. These forms are then filed at the central office. A detective investigating a larceny can readily check on property by merely communicating with the lost property office. The following files are usually maintained: lost property; stolen property; property pledged at pawn shops; and property sold in secondhand stores. In one scheme of reporting, these four types of reports are filed together. This system theoretically eliminates the possibility of an object being reported in groups 3 and 4 without the knowledge of the staff. If these are maintained separately, it is possible through carelessness that an object may be reported pawned and not be checked in the stolen property file. The mingling of reports 1 and 2 is logical, since an object which is thought to have been lost may have actually been stolen through a clever larceny.

10. Description of Property

Property is primarily filed according to classification of article, e.g. watches, automobiles, fur. Thus, one set of file cases will be devoted to watches alone, another to automobiles, and so forth. Certain types of property can be readily subclassified according to serial number. Watches, automobiles, typewriters, and cameras, for example, usually bear a stamped serial number. Unfortunately, many owners (and even dealers) keep no record of these numbers. Where they exist, however, they should determine the system of filing. In describing property the following basic data should be included:

a. *Kind* of article (e.g., watch or camera).

b. *Physical appearance* (model, size, shape and condition).

c. *Material* of which it's composed (the more expensive substance, such as gold or silver, should be mentioned where it is applicable).

d. *Brand name*.

e. *Number* of articles or weight.

f. *Identifying marks* such as serial numbers or personal inscriptions.

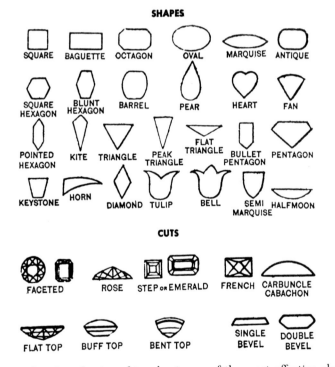

Figure 25. The identification of jewelry is one of the most effective clues in a burglary investigation. Shown above are the various shapes and cuts of stones, together with the terms used in their description.

11. Examples

Listed below are examples of some of the more common types of stolen property, together with the more important identifying characteristic:

a. **Automobiles.** License, motor number, make, model, color.

b. **Watches.** Case number, movement number, make, model, metal, inscriptions, setting.

c. **Jewelry.** Kind; style; metal; setting; kind and number of stones. Rings should be classified according to type: engagement, wedding, cocktail, etc. If no initials or inscriptions are present, the number and kind of stones is the determining factor in filing at the Lost Property Unit. Matching with pawned or purchased property is possible only if the accurate number and size of stones are given. The shape and cut of the stones should also be given.

d. **Fur.** Kind of fur; style; manufacture. (Fur coats can be filed according to manufacturer.)

e. **Cameras.** Kind, manufacturer, model, number; kind of lens including lens focal length, f/number, and serial number.

12. Personal Marking

To facilitate property recovery in the event of theft, a number of police departments are encouraging citizens to engrave their Social Security numbers on their valuables and register them with the police. By means of an electric needle-tipped device the citizen *tattoos* his number on his bicycle, television set, silverware, camera, and jewelry. A record of the numbered article is then registered with the police department's Lost Property Unit. If an item is subsequently stolen and later recovered in a pawnshop or with a secondhand dealer, the department's computer can match the article with the owner in a matter of minutes. Ordinarily the police must check their lists of stolen property or go through a manufacturer's list of serial numbers in a time-consuming procedure that may require several weeks to trace the owner of recovered property. The scheme is especially useful in discouraging bicycle thefts, since a policeman can check a numbered bike with the cyclist's Social Security card in the space of a minute.

III. MODUS OPERANDI

13. Basis of Method of Operation

The criminal aspires to the status of a professional man, trained by experience and instruction in the most effective techniques of his occupation. He is, of course, limited or enhanced by his mental and physical capabilities and influenced by such factors as his fugitive status or the availability of a "fence." Ordinarily he judges the value of his methods solely on the basis of successful accomplishment. Having achieved a few minor successes he is loath to alter his operational procedure, his reluctance stemming from superstition, lack of imagination, and inertia. A summary of the habits, techniques, and peculiarities of behavior is often referred to as the *modus operandi* or MO, a term which means no more than *method of operation*.

14. Purpose

Large law enforcement agencies maintain MO Files to enable their investigators to recognize a pattern of criminal behavior, to associate a group of crimes with a single perpetrator, to enable them to predict, approximately, the next target of the criminal, and to assist complainants, eyewitnesses, and investigators to recognize the perpetrator by means of the recorded information concerning the characteristics of his criminal activity. It has been found that the MO File is most effective in crimes involving personal contact, such as felonies against the person, confidence games, and forgery. Apparently the physical description, mannerisms, and speech of the criminal are important elements in the effectiveness of such a file.

15. Organization

The traditional MO arrangement devised by Atcherley has been found to be still effective a half century after its inception. In the Atcherley system the following were considered the significant elements in the detection of offenders:

a. **Property.** The nature of the stolen property provides an excellent clue in crimes which involve a larceny.

b. **Description.** If the criminal was observed, a verbal description is usually the most important clue to the identity of the perpetrator.

c. **Observations at the Scene.** The data of the senses are important since they may result in a useful pattern. Thus the objects and substances seen, heard, smelled, tasted, or felt will contribute to the complete picture.

d. **Motive.** In addition to the acquisition of property there are many other criminal motives. Thus, in murder, rape, or assault, in general, a pattern of behavior may be discerned in the course of a series of crimes. This observation is particularly true with regard to the crimes accomplished by the psychopath.

e. **Time.** The time at which the crime was committed is an important element in the pattern. Naturally, since the exact moment of occurrence cannot be readily established in many cases, the investigator must endeavor to establish the time of occurrence between determinable limits.

f. **Peculiarities.** From evidence, weaknesses of character will ordinarily reveal themselves in the uninhibited surroundings of the crime. Peculiarities such as partaking of the victim's liquor, psychopathic defecation, and theft of inconsequential items such as ties or cuff links are particularly significant.

g. **Observed Peculiarities.** An observer of the offense may be able to supply valuable clues in the form of personal idiosyncracies. Speech is one of the most important clues. Enunciation, dialect, and diction can be closely described.

ADDITIONAL READING

Observation and Description
Basinger, L. F.: *Techniques of Observation and Learning Retention.* Springfield, Ill.: Thomas, 1973.
Cameron, J. M.: Forensic Dentistry. 2 *International Journal of Forensic Dentistry,* 5, 1974.
Nash, D. J.: *Individual Identification and the Law Enforcement Officer.* Springfield, Ill.: Thomas, 1978.

Penri, J.: *Looking at Faces and Remembering Them. A Guide to Facial Identification*. London, Elek Books, 1971.

Sognnaes, R.F.: Forensic Stomatology. 296 *New England Journal of Medicine*, 79, 1977.

Sopher, I.M.: *Forensic Dentistry*. Springfield, Ill.: Thomas, 1976.

Zavala, A. and Paley, J.J. (Eds.): *Personal Appearance Identification*. Springfield, Ill.: Thomas, 1972.

Voiceprints

Bloch, E.: *Voiceprinting*. New York, David McKay, 1975.

The Evidentiary Value of Spectrographic Voice Identification. 63 *Journal of Criminal Law, Criminology and Police Science*, 349, 1972.

Greene, H.F.: Voiceprint Identification: The Case in Favor of Admissibility. 13 *American Criminal Law Review*, 171, 1975.

Jones, W.R.: Evidence Vel Non: The Non Sense of Voiceprint Identification. 62 *Kentucky Law Journal*, 301, 1973-1974.

Kersta, L.G.: Voiceprint Identification. 3 *Police Law Quarterly*, 3, 1974.

Tosi, O. and Nash, E.: Voiceprint Identification Rules for Evidence. 9 *Trial*, 1, 1973.

Voice Identification Research. Washington, D.C.: U.S. Government Printing Office, 1972.

Voiceprint Identification: The Trend Towards Admissibility. 9 *New England Law Review*, 419, 1974.

Voiceprint Technique: How Reliable is Reliable? 63 *Illinois Bar Journal*, 260, 1975.

Chapter 30

IDENTIFICATION BY WITNESSES

1. Difficulties

THE TYPICAL witness is a layman unskilled in the techniques of investigation and unaware of the special terminology that is used in the *portrait parlé*. In addition, he is not a trained observer. As a consequence, when he is asked to describe a wanted criminal he offers a confusing set of generalities from which it is difficult for the investigator to form a definite picture or even to establish one useful peculiarity. The investigator obviously must assist the witness in describing the criminal, but he must avoid the introduction of errors that may result from suggesting characteristics to an impressionable witness.

2. Identifying Wanted Criminals

The aim of the investigator in questioning a witness concerning the appearance of a fugitive from justice is to obtain a complete verbal description and, with the aid of an artist, a pictorial representation. Two cases are distinguished: the known fugitive and the unknown criminal who was observed by the witness.

a. **Known Fugitives.** The known fugitive belongs to a definite neighborhood. Police records and even photographs may exist. A limited background investigation including a local agency check will develop the desired information. Relatives and other friends can offer a description. Emphasis should be placed on peculiarities and defects. Social acquaintances and barroom companions are more likely to stress odd characteristics and peculiarities of dress. By obtaining copies of all available photographs and by gathering a number of verbal descriptions, it is quite possible to acquire an excellent pictorial and verbal representation of the fugitive.

b. **Unknown Criminal Observed by Witness.** The problem of identifying the unknown criminal by means of an eyewitness must be approached with special caution by the investigator. The fallibility of eyewitness identification was made clear in 1932 with the publication of E. M. Borchard's book, *Convicting the Innocent.* Documenting sixty-five cases of innocent persons who had been convicted of crimes, Borchard showed that twenty-nine were victims of mistaken identity. In one case identification had been made by seventeen witnesses, and later the real offender was found to bear little resemblance to the falsely accused. Convictions are still being obtained on erroneous identifications. One of the more famous cases involved Campbell, a respectable stockbroker, who was identified as a wanted forger by several eyewitnesses. The main point in the identification was his mustache; a minor point was the fact that he used green ink. After Campbell had served a good part of his jail term, the true forger was apprehended and confessed to a series of crimes which included the Campbell offense. The real forger also wore a mustache and used green ink.

3. Identifying Methods

Three methods may be recommended for identifying an unknown criminal by a witness.

a. **The Verbal Description.** The *portrait parlé* may be used. Its inadequacies have been described, and the investigator should judge its worth by the capacity of the witness to describe persons known to the investigator. The description of the known person can serve as a control in judging the reliability of the description of the unknown criminal.

b. **Photographic Files (Rogues' Gallery).** The witness may be taken to the headquarters of the law enforcement agency and requested to examine the photographs in the Known Criminals' File. The *modus operandi* of the crime under investigation should suggest a group of photographs for viewing by the witness. It should be brought explicitly to the attention of the witness that the wanted criminal's photograph may not be contained in the file. The witness should also be instructed to call the investigator's attention to any strong similarity in the photograph of a single feature such as the nose or mouth.

c. **General Photographs.** An additional photographic identification technique employs a variety of facial types which do not necessarily represent criminals. The investigator should make up his own file of photographs representing different features in each photo. The image should be of the same size in all the pictures. The selection of photos should include the varieties of various features such as degree of baldness, length and shape of nose, shape of ear, and so forth.

d. **Artist's Assistance.** Law enforcement agencies have had considerable success in identification by employing an artist to depict a composite of the features as described by the eyewitness. The witness is shown a chart which contains representations of the various types of human features such as noses, eyes, and ears and is requested to select the individual features that most nearly represent those of the unknown criminal. From this selection the artist draws a composite face which may be a close approximation to the criminal. The following steps may be used:

1) *Separation of Witnesses.* If there are a number of witnesses to the appearance of the unknown criminal, they should be separated or advised not to exchange opinions on this matter. A witness who is susceptible to suggestion may readily acquiesce in the opinion of a more forceful person. To retain the value of the witness's initial impression it is necessary to obtain a description before he has spoken at length with others.

2) **Written Description.** After listening to the witness's oral account of the occurrence and his description of the criminal, the investigator should request the witness to reduce his description to writing. The form given in the preceding chapter will be found satisfactory.

3) *The Composite Description.* After studying the written descriptions given by each of the witnesses, the investigator will be able to establish a common denominator for each of the features of the unknown criminal. He should, of course, weigh the description according to his personal observation of the witness's reliability.

4) *Preliminary Sketches.* An artist should be called in at this point to assist the investigator. On the basis of the composite written description, he should make up several sketches which are variants of the common impression. The witnesses are separately requested to examine the sketches, select the closest approximation, and write their suggestions for improvement.

5) *Final Sketch.* On the basis of these suggestions the artist can now draw a second sketch. The witnesses are now called in as a group and may discuss the second and the preliminary sketches with the artist. Suggestions are offered, studied, and incorporated into a final sketch which can be printed on a wanted notice and distributed. It may be noted that a final sketch of this type was employed in the Lindbergh kidnapping and in a number of other prominent cases. In many instances it was found that the sketch was a close resemblance to the suspect.

e. **Identification Kits.** There are presently on the market a number of mechanical and optical systems to aid the investigator or the artist in assembling an image of the suspect corresponding to the witness's description and recollection. The kit consists of a variety of facial features that can be systematically composed into a single face in response to the direction of the witness.

f. **Electronic Aids.** The Supreme Court itself has recently suggested the use of modern technology in identification practice. The following are a few of the technical aids available:

1) *Videotape in Identification.* Videotaping is mechanically simple and requires no expertise or special training for its operation. The actual pre-trial confrontation would consist of having the eyewitness view a series of videotaped "bits," each bit consisting of a sequence of actions, profiles, and spoken words by a single line-up participant. One of the bits, the sequence of which would be identical to the others, would involve the suspect. The identification, if any, would take place during the viewing. A library of available bits with identical sequences can be established by routinely videotaping persons at booking when fingerprints and other information are present. Videotaping for identification purposes offers significant practical advantages over present corporeal identifications. It would eliminate the present difficulty of procuring on short notice a group of line-up participants similar in

age, height, race and other characteristics to the suspect. The risk of an unfairly composed line-up would be minimized. Videotaping would also preserve the confrontation itself for reproduction at trial. This could be accomplished by merely showing the bits used at the identification in court.

2) **Miracode.** This is a computer-like information retrieval system that facilitates the identification of criminal suspects by a witness. Instead of requesting the witness to thumb through mug books, he is seated in front of a screen similar to the kind used to read microfilm copies of a newspaper. Miracode uses cassette cartridges of microfilm onto which have been coded twenty-five characteristics of recently arrested criminals. The viewer is first asked to provide a verbal description of the suspect, which a systems operator translates into numerical symbols that determine what the scanner is to look for once it receives the microfilm cartridge. Each cassette can hold information on 600 suspects.

4. Identification of a Person in Custody

a. **Purpose.** "Is this the man whom you saw at the scene of the crime?" This is the critical question that is asked of the eyewitness after he is permitted to view a suspect in custody. Years of unfortunate experience have instilled in the investigator a deep-seated suspicion of the reliability of eyewitnesses. Mistaken identifications are still common occurrences. The investigator can, however, greatly increase the reliability of identifications by eyewitnesses through the medium of the intelligently conducted "line-up" or "show up." In police work the line-up is often used to present to the view of detectives the recently arrested criminals who are charged with serious offenses. This practice is of questionable value. The line-up is more profitably used as a means of selecting a suspect from a group of innocent persons. The purpose of the line-up is the elimination of the power of suggestion as a factor in identification.

b. **Procedure.** To conduct a line-up, a group of seven to ten persons should be available. The following precautions should be observed:

effective identification medium, namely, permanence, universality, unicity, ease of recording, and simplicity of classification.

a. **Permanence.** The medium should be fixed and relatively unalterable by deformation or replacement. Fingerprints are present at birth and last throughout a person's life. Although cuts, burns, and skin diseases may produce temporary disfigurement of the ridge pattern, the ridges will ordinarily resume their original appearance on healing. Permanent destruction of the ridges is possible but unusual. Disease and injury of the glands in the lower skin level can destroy the ridge pattern. Criminals have occasionally accomplished this destruction by mutilation or illegal operations. The grafting of a new ridge pattern on to a finger is considered surgically impossible.

b. **Universality.** The medium must be found on each person. This is obviously true of fingerprints. Where fingers have been amputated or mutilated, the scars of such destruction serve equally well the purposes of identification.

c. **Uniqueness.** The medium must possess a unique form for each person; the uniqueness can be established in two ways. First, the employment of the empirical method has not revealed the existence of two persons sharing a common fingerprint pattern (for even one print). Secondly, theoretical considerations exclude the probability of such an occurrence. Putting the case at its weakest and simplest, if we consider a print to be made up of approximately twenty characteristics and if we assume that the probability of finding one of these characteristics in a fingerprint to be one chance out of ten, then the probability of finding a fingerprint with a particular set of twenty characteristics is $1/10^{20}$ or one divided by one followed by twenty zeroes. This is a negligible probability if we place the population of the world at two billion.

d. **Simplicity of Recording.** An effective identification medium should be susceptible of being recorded in a simple manner. The fingerprint satisfies this condition, since the record can be accomplished by merely inking a finger and pressing it against paper. So marvelously simple is the recording process that soiled or perspiring fingers leave their own record without the knowledge of their owner. Thus, fingerprints are potentially extremely valuable clues.

e. **Simplicity of Classification.** This quality must be considered from two points of view. First, the classifying process must not be so complex as to require hours for its accomplishment. Obviously, such a system defeats its purpose when a large number of prints must be dealt with. Second, each person should have an almost unique position in the files; that is, there should be a unique correspondence between persons filed and classification formulas. This position should be simple to find by means of the system. The fingerprint classification systems in common use adequately fulfill this requirement.

2. The Nature of a Fingerprint

If we consider the nature of a fingerprint, the remarks previously made concerning the uniqueness of the fingerprint pattern for each person will appear quite obvious. One of the basic principles of criminal identification, whether of prints or handwriting, is that no two objects are alike. Fingerprints, paper clips, sheets of paper, blades of grass, or peas cannot be found in identical pairs, and sufficiently close examination will always reveal differences. If the differences are sufficiently great, the scientific detective can draw useful conclusions. Objects are essentially collections of molecules, which are the bricks with which nature builds its structures. The number and position of all of these elements in an object can never be exactly reproduced. We should as soon expect a builder to construct two identical houses. The fingerprint pattern is a configuration of ridges and intervening depressions or valleys. The ridges are dotted irregularly with pores, the orifices from which perspiration is emitted. These pores can in themselves provide a valid, though perhaps impractical, means of identification, since their position is unchanged throughout life. When the finger is inked and rolled against a white card, the ink from the ridges is transferred to the paper, leaving a picture of the ridge lines separated by white (inkless) lines corresponding to the depressions between the ridges.

3. Recording Fingerprints

In order to provide a permanent record of fingerprints for comparison, identification, and filing in an indexed series, the ridge patterns are covered with a black ink and rolled on a stiff paper form. The procedure appears in description to be relatively simple. Unfortunately, many investigators fail through carelessness to master this elementary technique. As a consequence, many fingerprint cards are submitted daily to identification bureaus with defectively recorded prints that are partially illegible and relatively worthless in a reliable fingerprint file. An hour's practice in the inking and rolling of fingerprints will reward the investigator with a lasting mastery of the basic technique.

a. **Equipment.** The essential equipment for rolling fingerprints consists of a tube of ink, a rubber roller, and a slab of glass. More complete equipment will include the following:

1) **Ink.** Fingerprint ink is similar to printer's ink, containing an admixture of oil which permits the ink to dry rapidly.

2) **Rubber Roller.** A hard rubber roller, 4 inches in length and 1 inch in diameter, is used to distribute the ink evenly on a glass plate.

3) **Slab.** A piece of plate glass, 4 by 10 inches, is used as a bearing surface for the ink. Aluminum, stainless steel, porcelain, and other non-porous substances will serve the purpose.

4) **Card Holder.** A piece of wood with metal strips serves to hold the conventional 8-inch square fingerprint card.

5) **Fingerprint Card-Form.** The standard fingerprint form of the FBI or other law enforcement agency is used. The front is marked with allotted spaces for single fingers and for the grouped fingers. The back of the card provides for descriptive data of the subject.

6) **Table.** A shelf or table 40 inches in height will provide a comfortable surface for fingerprinting.

b. **Inking the Slab.** One of the main causes of illegible prints is an excess of ink on the pad. The exercise of care in two simple operations will eliminate this difficulty.

1) Squeeze four small (⅓-inch diameter) blobs of ink on the slab.

2) Spread the ink evenly over the slab by applying the roller in a back-and-forth motion.

c. **Cleaning the Fingers.** The subject's hands should be cleaned of perspiration, grease, and dirt by wiping with a small cotton ball dipped in carbon tetrachloride.

d. **Rolling the Prints.** The operator must control the rolling process completely. Smooth rolling, even pressure, and relaxed fingers are the key to successful rolling. The following steps are recommended:

1) Place the fingerprint card in the holder and request the subject to sign his name in full in the signature block of the card.

2) Instruct the subject to relax his fingers, look away from the card, and permit the operator to do the work without assistance.

3) Roll each finger of the right hand separately on the glass, placing the finger so that it is inked from below the first joint to a point as close as possible to the tip and from nail edge to nail edge. The thumb should be rolled first.

4) Beginning with the thumb, the finger is rolled in the appropriate space in the card. The right hand of the operator should be used to grip the subject's finger between the first and second joint. The left hand should control the pressure and guide the movement of the finger in rolling. The finger is first rolled on the inked plate through an arc of 180°. The finger is then rolled through the same 180° arc in the appropriate card space. The pressure should be light and the direction of roll away from the operator. The card is moved up to the correct space after each print.

5) At the bottom of the card, a space is provided for inking all four fingers simultaneously without rolling. This serves as a check on the sequence in which the rolled prints were taken. Again, without rolling, each thumb is printed in the proper space. A notation of scars and deformities is made. The subject should then be requested to sign the card. Naturally, each print should be checked carefully for clarity and legibility.

6) A paper towel and detergent should be given the subject to clean his hands. The operator should now fill out the front of the card with the data relating to the subject and should sign the card. The descriptive data on the reverse of the card should be completed. The card should not be folded.

e. **Reasons for Rejection.** The following are the more common reasons given for the rejection of prints when they are submitted for identification:

1) The ink was unevenly distributed.

2) The entire first joint of each finger has not been entirely inked and rolled.

3) Too much ink was used.

4) Insufficient ink was used and the ridge characteristics are indistinct.

5) Some of the impressions are blurred or smudged as though the fingers slipped while being rolled.

6) Moisture or some other foreign substance may have been present on the fingers, as the impressions are blurred and indistinct.

7) The ridge characteristics are not distinct, possibly because they may have been partially effaced due to the nature of the subject's employment, to some skin disease, or to some other temporary cause. In many instances, legible prints can be obtained in cases of this type by retaking the prints after a lapse of several days.

8) The hands have been reversed, i.e., the left hand fingers placed in the spaces provided for the right hand.

9) The impressions of the fingers of one of the hands were taken twice, and the impressions of the fingers of the other hand not at all.

10) One or more of the rolled or plain impressions is missing or partially missing. It is necessary to have the complete impressions of all ten fingers, unless amputations appear. In cases of bent or paralyzed fingers a spoon or similar instrument should be used and the fingers printed individually and then mounted on the card in the appropriate block.

11) The impressions have not been recorded in correct sequence.

12) Printer's ink was not used in recording the impressions. Fingerprints taken with ordinary writing fluid, stamp pad ink, or chemicals are not usually legible or permanent.

f. **Judging Acceptability.** The experienced investigator should judge the recorded prints critically before he forwards them to the identification bureau. If, upon examination, it appears that any of the impressions cannot be classified, new prints should be made. If not more than three impressions are unclassifiable, new prints of these fingers may be taken and pasted over the defective ones. If more than three prints are unclassifiable, a new chart should be made. The following points are to be observed in judging the quality of the rolled impressions:

1) A delta, the point at which the lines forming the loop or whorl pattern spread and begin going in different directions, should be clearly defined. All loops have one delta. Whorl prints have two.

2) Loop prints cannot be classified unless the center of the loop and the delta and the lines between them are clear.

3) Whorl prints cannot be classified unless the two deltas and the lines connecting the deltas are clear.

4) Arch fingerprints can be classified only if a sufficiently clear impression is obtained to permit identification of the pattern as being an arch.

4. Sole Prints

Certain purposes of identification can be served by areas of the body surface (other than fingers) bearing a permanent and relatively complex set of ridges or lines. The palm of the hand and sole of the foot are especially suitable, since their latent prints are sometimes found on crime scene surfaces and evidentiary objects and hence can be used to place a suspect at the scene. Although there is no generally accepted system of classification of these prints, they can nevertheless be identified with comparable prints of a suspect. Identifications of this nature have been accepted in court.

Another important purpose of identification is served by infant footprints. Sole prints of the baby recorded soon after birth can later be used to identify the child in the event of a baby "switch," accidental or otherwise. In both civil and criminal cases the importance of infant footprints has been demonstrated. In two cases of kidnapping a positive comparison of the child's footprint with a hospital record was accepted by the court as conclusive proof of the child's identity.

a. **Infant Footprints.** Both the ridge areas and flexure lines can be used to identify an infant. When ridge areas are present there is a tendency to structure the identification about the ridges. However, no inference should be drawn from this concerning the validity of the flexure lines of the child's foot as a means of identification. Indeed, sometimes the child's foot does not present any legible ridge areas, but the flexure lines of the sole are sufficient in number, complexity, and variance in distribution to permit an identification.

Two kinds of flexure lines are observable on the foot of the newborn child. One group of lines tends to disappear after about seven months. The other group is more permanent; the same set of lines in the same relative location is observable over a period of years. These latter lines form the basis of foot identification in infants, since, like fingerprints, they will remain unchanged during the period in question and the number and distribution of the lines provide a complex sufficiently distinctive for purposes of comparison and differentiation. Naturally, the case can be further strengthened by the existence of a ridge area.

b. **Hospital Records.** The maintenance of adequate footprint records at the hospital is basic in any attempt at infant identification. In some jurisdictions private as well as public hospitals are required to record the footprints of newborn infants. The records of many hospitals, however, have been found inadequate because of unsatisfactory printing technique.

c. **Recording Footprints.** A group of hospital employees should be instructed in the elements of inking and recording footprints. The first lesson for the group should be devoted to the purpose of footprinting, the nature of the footprint, and the recognition of a correctly recorded footprint. Instruction in footprint recording procedure should stress the importance of using a limited quantity of ink and of applying the correct pressure. Finally, to maintain footprint recording technique at a satisfactory level, the records should be inspected regularly by an experienced hospital supervisor.

Police departments can aid greatly in a hospital's identification program by instructing personnel in printing technique, periodically reviewing the hospital's file, and conducting an informal critique of recent records by pointing out examples of good and bad footprinting procedures.

d. **Latent Sole Prints.** By this term is meant a print made with the bare foot, ordinarily at the crime scene. If the sole print is already clearly visible, it should be photographed before further treatment. Occasionally a relatively invisible, or truly latent, sole print can be developed by the methods used for latent fingerprints on comparable surfaces. Large, tile bathroom floors, paper on floors, polished wood, and similar surfaces are receptive to such prints. The friction ridges on the sole of the foot sometimes leave a deposit of perspiration (or, perhaps, moisture) and dirt which will respond to the appropriate methods of development used for fingerprints. The investigator will first become aware of the presence of such prints through the faintly observable outlines of the foot. After development the print should be photographed on a one-to-one scale, using a 3¼ × 4¼″ fingerprint camera, which ordinarily will cover the relevant friction ridge area. A camera of larger film size—such as the 4 × 5″ or preferably a view camera—should be used for larger footprint areas (e.g., where flexure lines may be present in addition to a ridge area) and for the usual overall picture, which will include the background in the field of view. Comparison prints of a suspect should be made using the procedures described above for infant footprinting.

5. Deceased Persons

The investigator in the field occasionally is confronted with situations in which it is necessary to establish by fingerprinting the identity of a deceased person. The technique employed in this type of fingerprinting will depend upon the condition of the corpse. In extreme cases it may be necessary to amputate the hands of the person and forward them to the criminal investigation laboratory. A surgeon or other medically qualified person may perform the operation. Legal authority is frequently necessary before cutting a corpse in order to fulfill the requirements of federal or state law. As a general principle, the action taken by the investigator in printing a deceased person should be guided by the fragility of the skin of the fingers. Non-destructive methods such as photography should precede any removal or printing action that might damage the friction ridges. In severe cases, every effort should be made to preserve the fingers intact until the body can be transported to a place where the services of a physician or laboratory technician are available.

a. **Recently Dead.** If death has taken place within the last ten hours and rigor mortis has not set in, the following techniques may be used: (It should be noted that the presence of an assistant greatly simplifies the operation.)

1) Cut a fingerprint card in such a manner that the five spaces for the fingers of each hand are on two separate strips.

2) Insert the strip for the right hand in a curved holder or "spoon," the strip fitting into the curve of the spoon. With this piece of equipment it is possible to achieve the effect of rolling the finger by pressing against the spoon. The entire pattern can be obtained in this manner.

3) Extend the arms of the deceased forward and ink the fingers by means of a plate or a spatula.

4) If the fingers are clenched, they can be extended by standing behind the deceased's shoulders and lifting his arms as though extending them above the head. Another method is that of massaging the hands or soaking them in warm water until relaxation is felt.

5) If the fingerprinting of the deceased is not accomplished at the crime scene, paper bags should be placed over the victim's hands to protect evidential material during transportation. Traces such as blood, fibers, hair, and debris should be removed from the victim's hands before fingerprinting. Since it is necessary to clean the deceased's hands prior to printing, valuable evidence can be lost if this precaution is not taken.

6) If the fingers are wrinkled from immersion in water, it is frequently necessary to fill out the finger before a satisfactory impression can be made. This can be done by means of a hypodermic needle and a suitable filling fluid such as warm water or glycerin. The fluid is injected in the finger in sufficient quantity to restore its normal contour. A piece of string may be tied around the finger at a point immediately above the hole to prevent the fluid from leaking out.

b. **Advanced Decomposition.** In cases involving bodies that are in a more advanced state of decomposition, the techniques of the laboratory and the medical examiner should be employed. Since these are highly specialized procedures, a full explanation will not be attempted here. The investigator under these circumstances should exercise great care to avoid damaging the remaining evidence. His initial step should be to photograph the fingerprint using careful lighting to emphasize the ridge outlines. In the subsequent steps the state of putrefaction of the fingers will dictate the procedures. The investigator should seek the advice of a qualified technician or a physician, if he himself has not had the training.

With extreme care the fingers should be cleaned with water or with xylene and then gently inked and printed in the usual manner. In some cases the epidermis or outer skin may be destroyed. Since the second layer of skin has the same ridge outline in a less pronounced form, it can sometimes be used in the same manner to obtain fingerprints. Remaining fragments of the outer layer should first be removed. The second layer is then cleaned, inked, and rolled as previously described. If the resulting prints are not satisfactory, it is often because the ridge detail is too fine to record. In this situation, photography should be again employed.

c. **Desiccation and Charring.** Desiccated and shriveled skin presents the problem of smoothing out the print surface. This may be done by first softening the skin and then attempting to fill it out by the previously described methods. Charred skin is quite brittle, depending on the degree of charring, and is best approached by preliminary photography. Inking and rolling should not be attempted if there is any indication that the charring is sufficiently severe to result in crumbling on manipulation.

d. **Drowned Persons.** The prints of "floaters" or persons subjected to prolonged immersion can sometimes be taken by actual removal of the skin. The operator places the removed skin over his own finger (which is first protected by a rubber glove) and proceeds to print as though it were his own finger.

e. **Dusting-Tape Method.** For extremely fine or worn ridge detail the dusting-tape method has been found by some experts to be superior to the inked method of friction ridge impression. Ordinary black fingerprint dusting powder is applied to the cleaned (alcohol or xylene) fingers of the deceased using a fingerprint brush or cotton ball. A piece of white-backed, opaque pressure-sensitive tape is then applied to the dusted ridges of each finger, peeled off and pressed against a piece of glass or transparent vinyl.

Chapter 32

LATENT FINGERPRINTS

1. General

THE SEARCH for fingerprints should be conducted before any of the objects present at the scene are moved. The fingerprints found may be placed in three classes:

a. **Latent Fingerprints.** These, the majority, are "hidden" or relatively invisible and must be developed by one of the special methods described below.

b. **Plastic Fingerprints.** These may be found on such objects as soap, butter, putty, melted wax, etc. Impressions are depressed below the original surface.

c. **Visible Fingerprints.** These are left by fingers covered with a colored material, such as paint, blood, grease, ink, or dirt.

2. Searching for Fingerprints

If the scene is outdoors there will be few articles which are suitable for bearing fingerprints and the order in which the objects are processed will not present any problem. For indoor scenes the search for fingerprints is conducted in accordance with rules which are extremely flexible. Some system must be followed, however, in order to insure complete search and positive results under varying conditions produced by the type of crime, the *modus operandi* of the culprit, and the existence of surfaces capable of retaining fingerprint impressions. A clockwise order can be followed in processing a room filled with articles. In addition, observation should be made of points of entrance and departure, and such objects as doorknobs, window sills, door panels, windowpanes, and porch railings.

a. **Searching for Latent Fingerprints.** Latent fingerprints of value for comparison are not frequently found at the scene of a crime. This is attributable to the delicate nature of the print. To deposit a thin layer of perspiration or grease in the complicated pattern of the friction ridges optimum conditions must be present. The surface must be such that it can retain the print without absorbing and spreading it. Thus hard, glossy objects such as glass and enamel painted walls and doors present ideal surfaces. Dirty surfaces and absorbent materials do not readily bear prints. The fingerprint, moreover, must be deposited with the right amount of pressure. The object must not be touched with an excess of pressure, since this tends to spread the print. A movement of translation of the finger will result in a smear. The fingers of the person depositing the prints must have a certain degree of moisture or should have some body grease on the ridges. When all these requirements are fulfilled a good latent fingerprint is deposited. Despite the infrequency with which a latent fingerprint examination meets with success, the unsurpassed value of a print as evidence warrants the expenditure of effort that this search entails. No general rules can be given concerning the finding of fingerprints. Although it is known that prints are seldom found on certain types of surfaces, the fact that such impressions under unusual circumstances are sometimes discovered should suggest to the investigator the necessity of exhausting all possibilities before abandoning the search for latent fingerprints. Some useful comments can be made on the likelihood of finding prints on certain typical surfaces encountered at the scene of a crime. The following are representative of articles to be examined in serious crimes:

1) Suspected poisoning—glasses, bottles, cups, saucers, spoons, medicine cabinets, bathroom, kitchen, etc.

2) Shooting—firearms, unfired cartridges, ammunition boxes, desk or cupboard where ammunition or firearm was habitually kept, etc. For fingerprints on guns see p. 778.

3) Cutting or stabbing—all sharp pointed or edged instruments, broken glass, or crockery.

4) Automobile used in the commission of a crime and abandoned—rearview mirror, rear deck, edges of doors, radio, all glass, glove compartment, hood, and other accessible, smooth areas.

5) Burglary and larceny—areas necessary for access and containers, closets and objects probably handled in searching for valuables.

b. **Pertinent Techniques.** 1) The beam from a flashlight held at an acute angle with a surface may reveal impressions that are not otherwise visible.

2) The examination of a surface from different angles may produce a like effect.

3) Breathing on a surface may cause fingerprints to be visible on certain types of materials.

3. Developing the Impression

To serve the purposes of investigation the latent fingerprint must be converted into a visible image—a few hundred micrograms of residue left behind by evaporating sweat on a glass or handle must be changed to reveal a legible ridge pattern. Some method of developing latent fingerprints must be used to provide a contrast between the ridge lines and the background. A fairly extensive technology has been created to solve this problem: (1) the use of an adhering powder such as lampblack; (2) the reaction of iodine with the fatty fraction; (3) the reaction of silver nitrate with the chloride ion; (4) the reaction of the amino acids with an organic reagent such as ninhydrin (especially useful for old prints since the amino acids diffuse less rapidly than the salts), which turns the print to a pink color. The term *developing*, used in this sense, should not be confused with the developing of photographic negatives in the darkroom. The nature of the surface, the degree of visibility before development, and the type of camera available should be the deciding factors in the determination of the proper technique in each case. Experiments should be conducted in order to study the effects of the different mediums, but any latent fingerprint which is a part of the evidence should never be used in an experiment. A latent impression should be placed on the same or a similar surface for this purpose. The following methods of development have stood the test of time and are highly recommended: powder, vapor, and liquid.

a. **Powder.** This method is recommended for the development of latent impressions on a hard, dry, and smooth surface. Effective fingerprint powders may be obtained commercially, although there are many acceptable substitutes which lend themselves to this type of investigation.

1) *Qualities.* The powder selected should possess the following qualities:

a) It should be adhesive to the extent that it clings readily to the ridges of the fingerprint.

b) It should not absorb water.

c) It should "photograph" well, i.e., provide good contrast.

2) *Colors.* Powders of many colors are obtainable, but it is believed that the following will take care of every condition that may be encountered.

a) White or grey powder will provide sufficient contrast when used on a dark surface.

b) Black powder is used to provide a contrast against a light-colored surface.

c) Fluorescent powder, such as anthracene, is recommended for the development of latent fingerprints found on a multicolored background. Illumination by means of ultraviolet light causes the powder to fluoresce vividly while the colors in the background remain only faintly visible.

3) *Application.* Of the available methods for developing fingerprints with powder the use of the brush is the simplest and most effective. The others, however, have their special uses.

a) Brush. If haste and haphazard techniques are avoided, the following steps will successfully develop latent prints on suitable surfaces.

1) A good brush is needed. One with soft hairs approximately 1½ inches long with a 3-inch handle is recommended. It is advisable to paint the handle in a color to match that of the powder with which it is to be used. One brush should not be used with powders of different colors.

2) Powder should be used sparingly. A small quantity is placed on a piece of paper and is picked up with the brush as required. It is poor practice to push the brush into the bottles, as this tends to lump the powder and damage the brush.

3) The brush is used to distribute the powder lightly across the fingerprint until the characteristic outlines of the ridge become visible.

4) More powder is added, if necessary, and the desired density built up gradually. As soon as the maximum development is completed, the surplus powder is tapped from the brush, which is now used to "clean" the impression by a continuation of the brushing motion. It is sometimes of advantage to follow the contour of the ridges in removing the surplus powder.

b) ROLLING OR SIFTING. An excellent procedure for latent prints on a surface such as well-sized paper is to sift or place a quantum of powder on the sheet and then, by tilting the paper, roll the powder back and forth over the areas of response. When the print is fully developed, the excess powder is removed by a few sharp taps of the fingers. Black powder is especially effective with this method.

c) FERROMAGNETIC MIXTURES. The Magna-Brush® method achieves the same effect as rolling by using a ferromagnetic powder and moving it across the paper by means of a magnet passed beneath the paper. The excess powder is removed by the magnet when the print is developed.

d) SPRAYING. To process large areas, some identification men prefer the use of a spraying apparatus such as an atomizer. By squeezing the bulb a fine stream of powder is made to pass over the surface under examination. Sprays have a tendency to clog if the powder is not of the proper consistency or if it is affected by moisture.

e) AEROSOL SPRAYING. A few years ago the aerosol can was brought into use as a means of spraying fingerprint powder. Efforts have been made to overcome the problems of clogging and unevenness of distribution. The manufacturers recommend the supplementary use of the brush, at least for the removal of excess powder. In the opinion of a leading expert in the field: Fingerprint spray is mainly useful on large areas. Since the broad and indiscriminate application of fingerprint powder is often demanded by suspicious complainants and nervous supervisors, the spray will do much to improve public and departmental relations for the identification man. However, for the effective development of latents he will rely mainly on the brush to apply powder with discrimination, skill, and purpose.

b. **Chemical Development.** Different methods must be used on absorbent surfaces such as poorly sized paper and wood. Of the many methods that have been suggested for this purpose, fuming

Figure 26a. Developing latent fingerprints by the powder and brush method. b. Using the fixed-focus fingerprint camera to record a developed print.

and immersion enjoy the widest use. Although the processes are described here, the investigator is encouraged to submit the evidence to a law enforcement laboratory whenever possible.

1) *Fuming.* If a sheet of paper is exposed to a flow of iodine vapor, latent fingerprints can be made visible. They can be suspended in a glass case over a crucible containing iodine crystals, which, since they sublime at room temperature, will emit a flow of vapor upward toward the paper surface. The crystals may be heated to hasten the process. A portable iodine fuming apparatus—consisting of an open-ended glass tube containing the iodine crystals separated by means of glass wool from a quantity of calcium chloride, a drying agent—is available for treating objects at the crime scene such as papers and greasy surfaces. The warmth of the operator's breath serves to enhance sublimation and provide a stream of vapor that can be directed as desired. (Since iodine fumes can be poisonous, the use of this vapor should always be managed with care.) The fingerprints should be photographed as soon as it appears that maximum contrast has been reached, since the iodine-vapor image is not permanent.

2) *Immersion.* A variety of substances has been proposed for the chemical development of latent fingerprints on paper and wood. Of

these, silver nitrate and ninhydrin appear to be the most widely used.

a) SILVER NITRATE. A reagent such as silver nitrate can be used to convert the sodium chloride content of the latent print into silver chloride, a photosensitive substance which darkens on exposure to a strong light. The envelope or sheet of paper to be processed is dipped in a 3 per cent solution of this reagent (4 ounces of silver nitrate dissolved in a gallon of water) and hung to dry in a darkened room. On drying, the paper is exposed to sunlight or suitable artificial light until the print areas have darkened sufficiently. The prints are then photographed. If it is desired to preserve the prints, the document should be placed in a light-tight container, such as an empty film box. The paper can be restored to its original color by immersion in a mercuric chloride solution followed by rinsing in water.

b) NINHYDRIN. For the development of old fingerprints, particularly on paper, some identification experts favor the use of ninhydrin, a substance known to react with amino acids. A solution of ninhydrin with ethyl alcohol or acetone (0.2 to 0.4%) is sprayed over the document or other surface by means of an atomizer. Care should be exercised to guard against over-spraying, since the excess may dissolve the prints. After optimal spraying, the document is heated in an oven at a temperature between 80° and 140° C until pink areas are observed. With the passage of time the fingerprints will acquire a deeper shade of pink, improving in contrast for photographic purposes even after several days. Ninhydrin can also be applied by immersing the document in a tray of the solution. Aerosol containers of ninhydrin are marketed for convenience in spraying.

c. **Use of Other Cameras.** The investigator who has a more advanced knowledge of photography may prefer to use a camera other than the fixed-focus fingerprint camera, such as a Speed Graphic which will provide for filters, variable shutter speeds, and "*f* stops" in addition to permitting greater latitude in angles of illumination.

d. **Identification.** A small tab of paper on which is inscribed appropriate identifying data should be placed in the field of view in a manner that will insure its inclusion in the photograph. This suggestion is particularly advisable in order to avoid confusions in overlapping investigations.

e. **Chain of Custody.** If the person who made the photographs permits another person to complete the darkroom processing, the taker should be sufficiently familiar with the operation to enable him to state that the work was performed under his supervision. Courts will generally allow the photographs to be admitted as exhibits if the photographer identifies them properly, even though the darkroom processing was accomplished by a second party.

f. **Plastic Impressions.** Details in plastic impressions may be emphasized by unscrewing two (adjacent) of the bulbs in the fixed-focus fingerprint camera and making an exposure by means of the cross-lighting of the two remaining bulbs. The exposure time must be doubled to compensate for cutting the illumination in half.

g. **Curved Surfaces.** Photographs of latent impressions on a curved surface may be made with the fingerprint camera, provided that the arc of the curve is not too pronounced. Persons who use this camera should familiarize themselves with the restriction in depth of focus imposed by the absence of the iris diaphragm. If it appears that the subject is beyond the capabilities of the fingerprint camera, another type should be used.

4. Handling and Transmission

The removal and transportation of objects bearing fingerprints must be accomplished with great caution. The following procedures will be adaptable in most cases:

a. Gloves may be worn.

b. Articles should be touched only in those places where there is the least likelihood of disturbing a latent fingerprint.

c. Objects should *never* be wrapped in a handkerchief or a towel.

d. Small objects should never be placed in a paper bag.

e. Cellophane sheets or envelopes may be used for protecting papers.

f. Fired bullets and cases should be packed separately in absorbent cotton and placed in a small box.

g. Prior to removal from the scene, the latent print should be photographed one-to-one, or actual size, and also in a way to show relationship with the surrounding area.

h. Articles bearing fingerprints should be marked for identification and packed according to instructions.

i. If it is inconvenient to move an object because of its excessive size or weight, it may be necessary to detach the part bearing the fingerprint. For example:

1) Doors may be removed from hinges.

2) Windows may be removed from frames or panes of glass taken from sashes.

3) Legs and arms may be removed from chairs and tables.

4) Drawers and desks and dressers may be handled separately.

5) Boards may be lifted from floors or paneling from walls.

6) Any part of an automobile may be detached.

j. Under ordinary circumstances, it is advisable to leave the fingerprint impression on the surface where it was found. Its subsequent introduction in court in its original location serves to enhance its evidential value.

5. Elimination of Persons Legitimately at the Scene

When fingerprints are found at the scene of the crime, immediately consideration should be given to the possibility that the impressions may belong to persons whose presence has been legitimate.

a. Rolled impressions should be made of members of the household, the servants, and police officers who may have touched anything carelessly, or in the ordinary course of their activities prior to the commission of the crime.

b. In many cases where there are obvious discrepancies between the patterns being compared, the fingerprints of innocent persons may be eliminated by means of a visual examination of the fingers, thus obviating the necessity of making fingerprint records.

6. Lifting

Lifting is the process which involves the physical removal of a latent fingerprint from its original surface. Under ideal conditions, using the proper equipment, a skilled operator may expect to produce the desired results by employing this method. There are, however, attendant dangers involved, among which the following should be mentioned.

a. **Disadvantages.** 1) Accidental air bubbles under the lifting material, which may be unnoticed by the operator, will leave a blank spot in the lifted impression.

2) If the attempt is not successful, it is generally useless to repeat the lifting process on the same latent impression.

3) The admissibility of lifted impressions in court may be subject to objection on the ground that the evidence has been altered through tampering.

4) Many authorities on the subject of fingerprint identification state that the lifting process should be employed only when it is impossible to secure good photographs.

b. **Techniques.** If a decision has been made to lift a latent fingerprint, there are two types of material which may be used effectively. The choice of one in preference to another will generally be based on personal reasons.

1) *Transparent Tape.* When transparent tape is used as a means of lifting fingerprints, it is necessary that the width be at least 1 inch in order to cover the area to be treated. All subsequent examinations and photographs should be made from the dry or non-adhesive side so that the details of the impression will not be reversed. Direct projections may be made in the enlarging camera by using the transparency as a negative. The adhesive side of the tape should be protected by covering it with a small section of fairly stiff cellophane.

2) *Rubber Lifter.* This material resembles an ordinary inner tube patch. Being opaque, the lifted impression must be examined and photographed on the reverse side only. Under these conditions, it is necessary to print or enlarge photographs with the negative reversed; otherwise, a true picture of the fingerprint will not be obtained.

3) *Application.* The technique of lifting fingerprints is the same for transparent tape and rubber lifter.

a) Press the sticky side of the tape or rubber against the powdered fingerprints, carefully avoiding the production of air bubbles.

b) Insure complete adhesion by rubbing the entire surface with a smooth round object.

c) Beginning at one edge or corner, peel the lifter gently from the surface and cover the sticky surface with cellophane.

d) A small tab or paper, inscribed with pertinent identifying data, may be attached to the lifter by placing it between the lifter and the cellophane cover at one corner.

Latent Fingerprint Development

Property of Print	Method	Operation	Effect	Color	Surfaces
Stickiness	Powder	Brush or Spray	Adhere to Ridges	Color of Powder	Smooth, Glazed or Sized
Fatty Material	Iodine Reagent	Fuming	Darkens Ridges	Brown	Paper and Wood
Chloride Ion	Silver Nitrate	Immersion and Exposure to Light	Sensitive to Sunlight and U. V. Lamp	Dark Brown	Paper and Wood
Amino Acids	Ninhydrin	Spray or Immersion	Organic Reagent	Pink	Old prints on a variety of surfaces

ADDITIONAL READING

Allison, H.C.: *Personal Identification.* Boston, Holbrook Press, 1973.

Bridges, B.C.: *Practical Fingerprinting.* Rev. by C.E. O'Hara. New York, Funk & Wagnalls, 1963.

Brooks, A.J., Jr.: Frequency of Distribution of Crime Scene Latent Prints. 3 *Journal of Police Science and Administration,* 292, 1975.

_____. Techniques for Finding Latent Prints. 54 *Fingerprint and Identification Magazine,* 5, 1972.

Crown, D.A.: The Development of Latent Fingerprints with Ninhydrin. 60 *Journal of Criminal Law, Criminology and Police Science,* 258, 1969.

Federal Bureau of Investigation. *The Science of Fingerprint.* Washington, D.C.: U.S. Government Printing Office, 1977.

Gidion, H.M. and Epstein, G.: Latent Impressions on Questioned Documents. 39 *Police Chief,* 8, 1972.

Lambourne, G.: Glove Print Identification: A New Technique. 48 *Police Journal,* 219, 1975.

Micik, W.: Latent Print Techniques. 56 *Fingerprint and Identification Magazine,* 4, 1974.

Moenssens, A.A.: *Fingerprint Techniques.* Philadelphia, Chilton Book, 1971.

Morris, J.R., Goode, G.C. and Godsell, J.W.: Some of the New Developments in the Chemical Detection of Latent Fingerprints. *1973 Police Research Bulletin,* 21, 1973.

Petersilia, J.: *Processing Latent Fingerprints—What are the Payoffs?* Santa Monica, Calif.: Rand Corp., 1976.

Thomas, G.L.: The Physics of Fingerprints. 8 *Criminologist,* 30, 1973.

Trowell, F.: A Method for Fixing Latent Fingerprints Developed with Iodine. 15 *Journal of the Forensic Science Society,* 189, 1975.

Wilson, J.C.: Developing Latent Prints on Plastic Bags. 56 *Fingerprint and Identification Magazine,* 6, 1974.

Vandiver, J.V.: Fingerprint Procedures. 22 *Law and Order,* 10, 1974.

Chapter 33

CLASSIFICATION OF FINGERPRINTS

1. Introduction

To THE LAYMAN'S eye, the rolled print is a meaningless array of curved and relatively straight lines which are obviously highly individual but which do not appear to lend themselves to any system of ordered filing or indexing. The problem of classification—to convert a fingerprint into a significant label—has challenged many ingenious minds and has been successfully solved by several practical "systems." The most commonly used method of fingerprint classification is the Henry System. The present discussion is directed toward an exposition of this system. The investigator should bear in mind that fingerprint classification is a comparatively simple branch of knowledge. By approaching the study as a practical problem, the various steps of development will suggest themselves as straightforward and logical. Basically, the problem of fingerprint classification is that of representing an array of lines by a formula, consisting of numbers and letters, which can be easily indexed. Three considerations present themselves: The elements or types of ridges; the location of the ridges; and a method of counting the lines. The matter of counting ridges implies a point of reference, that is, a point from which one can by convention begin to count.

2. Ridge Characteristics

The ridges are the basic elements in the system of classification. From a study of the ridge lines, it is found that these lines can be satisfactorily classified by eight types which form the bases for comparing prints. The accompanying illustrations are self-explanatory.

694

3. Basic Features

Certain ridges are basic to the fingerprint patterns in the sense that they either form or locate the pattern frame of reference.

a. **Pattern Area.** This is simply that part of the fingerprint which contains the ridges necessary to determine classification. It is the working area of classification.

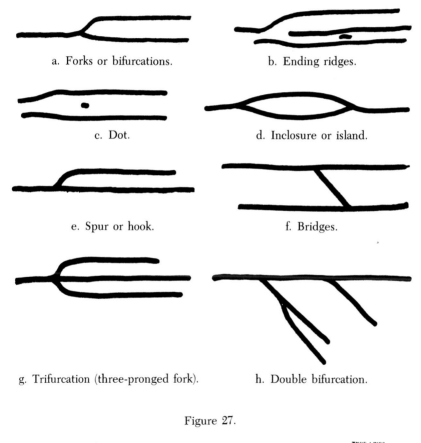

a. Forks or bifurcations.

b. Ending ridges.

c. Dot.

d. Inclosure or island.

e. Spur or hook.

f. Bridges.

g. Trifurcation (three-pronged fork).

h. Double bifurcation.

Figure 27.

Figure 28. Pattern area or working area of classification.

Figure 29. Type lines.

b. **Type Lines.** These lines are the intermost ridges which start as parallel lines, diverse, and bound the pattern area. They define the working area of classification. Type lines may not be continuous and may even be absent.

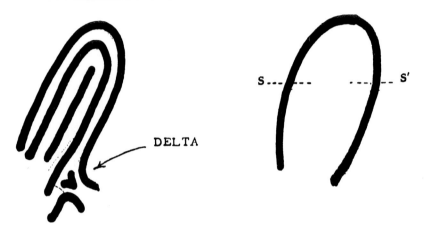

Figure 30. Typical delta.   Figure 31. Loop shoulders.

c. **Delta.** Referring to the figure immediately above, it will be noted that an imaginary point has been indicated where the type lines began to diverge. This is called the center divergence. The delta is defined as the first fork or bifurcation nearest the center of divergence. The delta need not be a fork but may be any type of ridge formation.

Where a choice appears between two formations, either of which seems to fulfill the defintion of a delta, the following rules may be applied:

1) The delta may not be located at a bifurcation which does not open toward the core.

2) If there is a choice between a bifurcation or some other type of delta, the bifurcation is selected.

3) The delta may not be placed in the middle of a ridge running between the type lines, but only at the nearest end of the ridge.

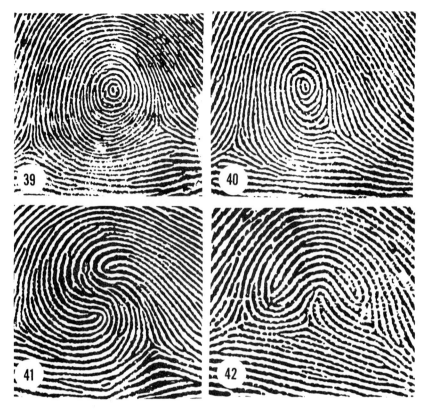

Figure 39. Plain whorl.
Figure 40. Central pocket loop.
Figure 41. Double loop.
Figure 42. Accidental.

c. **Double Loops.** These consist of two separate but not necessarily unconnected loop formations. Two forms are commonly recognized:

1) *Twinned Loops.* In the twinned loop pattern there is a composition of two loops. The entwining of two distinct loops causes the pattern to be so named. This pattern has two deltas. The terminations of the ridges of each loop of the pattern are in opposite directions to each other. One loop enters and terminates *above* a

delta, and the other loop enters and terminates *below* the opposite delta.

2) **Lateral Pocket Loop.** The lateral pocket loop is composed of two distinct loops surrounding each other and is often confused by the inexperienced with the twinned loop. In the lateral pocket loop, both loops flow in a lateral direction and both terminate either above or below the same delta.

d. **Accidentals.** The accidental derives its name from the unusual formation of the ridge pattern which appears to have been formed by accident and does not conform to any of the rules that would apply to the other patterns. This accidental formation is a natural condition and is not caused by any injury to the finger. As most accidentals have two or more deltas, this pattern is classed as a composite.

8. Classification of fingerprints

The goal of a classification system is to assign a formula to a set of fingerprints impressions so that the set can be readily located in a file. This formula consists of letters and numbers written above and below a horizontal line. All ten fingers are used. The formula will include a key and major division and the primary, secondary, subsecondary, and final. The following is an illustration of a typical classification:

Key	Major	Primary	Secondary	Sub-Secondary	Final
17	L	1	U	III	4
	S	1	U	IIO	3

a. **Blocking Out.** After examinaing the rolled impressions to determine by comparison with the simultaneous impressions whether they are in their correct square, the operator "blocks out" or marks the pattern symbol below each pattern. The following symbols are used:

1) **Symbol.**
a) Arch—A, a.
b) Tented Arch—T, t.
c) Radial Loop—R, r.
d) Ulnar Loop—/ (in left hand;\in right hand).
e) Whorl—W, w.

2) **Block Out Rules.** a) INDEX FINGERS. The appropriate *capital* letter is placed under the index fingers for all patterns except the ulnar loop.

b) ALL OTHER FINGERS. The appropriate *small* letter is placed under all other fingers for every pattern except the ulnar loop.

c) ULNAR LOOP. Slanting lines are used for all fingers. The slant should be in the direction of the loop.

b. **Ridge Counting.** The classification of fingerprints depends largely on ridge counting. The method of counting ridges differs in loops and whorls.

1) **Loops.** The following rules apply to loops and whorls.

a) The *ridge count* is the number of ridges counted on an imaginary straight line drawn from the point of the delta to the point of the core.

b) The core and delta are not counted.

c) A white space must come between the first ridge and the delta. This condition defines the first ridge.

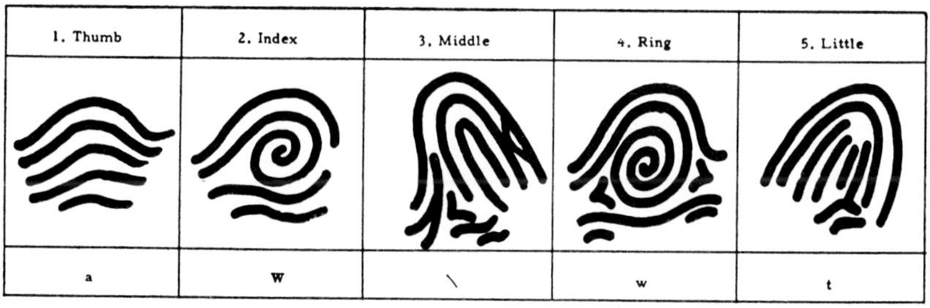

Figure 43. Right hand block out.

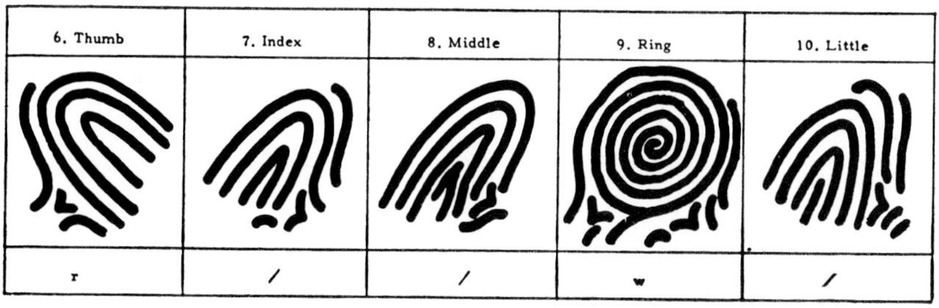

Figure 44. Left hand block out.

d) If there is a bifurcation on the line of count, two ridges are counted.

e) If the line crosses an island, two ridges are counted.

f) Dots and short ridges are counted if they cut by the line and are heavy and thick.

Figure 45. Ridge counting.

2) **Whorls.** To distinguish the various types of whorls the symbols I, M, and O are used for *Inner, Meeting,* and *Outer* whorls. The appropriate letter is placed in the upper right hand corner of a whorl print after being selected by means of the following steps:

a) The deltas are located.

b) A tracing line is established by starting with a ridge at the lower side or point of the extreme left delta and continuing to the point nearest or opposite the extreme right delta.

c) The number of ridges between the tracing line and the right delta is counted.

d) If the traced ridge passes inside or above the right delta with three or more ridges intervening between the traced line and the delta, the whorl is called *inner* and is indicated by the letter I.

e) If the traced ridge passes outside (below) the right delta and there are three or more intervening ridges between the traced line and the delta, the whorl is termed *outer* and is indicated by the letter O.

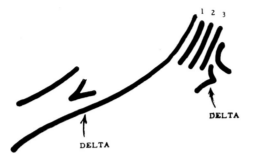

Figure 46. Inner whorl.

Figure 47. Outer whorl.

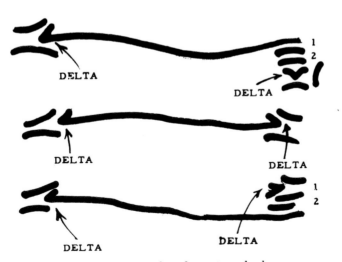

Figure 48. Examples of meeting whorls.

f) If the traced ridge meets the right delta or not more than two ridges intervene when passing inside or outside of the delta, the whorl is called a *meeting whorl* and is represented by the letter M.

g) If the traced ridge forks, the lower branch of the fork is used to continue the trace.

h) If the traced ridge ends abruptly, the trace is resumed on the next lower ridge.

9. Primary Classification

In making the primary classification, certain conventions are assigned in the form of designated numerical values to the fingers in the following manner:

Right Hand	Thumb	Index	Middle	Ring	Little
	16	16	8	8	4
Left Hand	Thumb	Index	Middle	Ring	Little
	4	2	2	1	1

a. It is seen that fixed values are assigned to pairs of fingers.

b. These values are counted only for whorls; when arches, tented arches, or loops appear, they are given no value.

c. Beginning with the right thumb and using every *odd* numbered finger of both hands, each time a whorl appears, the numbers in the corresponding boxes are added. The sum, plus one, is the denominator of the primary classification symbol, i.e., the number is the lower part of a symbol which will be in the form of a fraction.

d. Beginning with the right index finger and using every even numbered finger of both hands each time a whorl appears, the numbers in the corresponding boxes are added. The sum plus one is the numerator (upper number of a fraction) of the primary classification symbol.

Example: Let us assume that whorls have been found on the right index, right ring, left index, and left little finger. These are fingers no. 2, 4, 7, and 10 respectively. To find the denominator, we must first add from the illustrated box the value of 2.

e. The lowest primary classification is 1/1.

f. The highest primary classification is 32/32.

```
Sum for odd numbered fingers  = 2
                     Adding     1
              Denominator      = 3
```

To find the numerator, we add values for the even numbered fingers (2, 4, and 10), thus,

```
Sum for even numbered fingers  =  16 + 8 + 1 =  25
                     Adding                      1
                  Numerator                     26
```

$$\frac{26}{3}$$

Hence, the primary classification is:

10. Secondary Classification

Secondary classification is the assignment of letters to the fingers. The symbols are in the form of a fraction. Symbols representing the right hand are placed in the numerator; left hand symbols are placed in the denominator.

a. **Index Fingers.** The capital letters are used for the index fingers, viz., A, T, R, U and W for Arch, Tented Arch, Radial Loop, Ulnar Loop, and Whorl, respectively.

Examples: A radial loop on the right index and an ulnar loop on the left index would give the secondary classification: R/U. (This is actually only part of the secondary classification.)

If the right index is an arch and the left index a whorl, we have: A/W.

b. **Other Fingers.** Small letters are used when arches, tented arches, and radial loops are found on fingers other than index fingers.

c. Ulnar loops and whorls appearing on thumbs are ignored. If they appear on the middle or ring finger and there is an arch, tented arch, or radial loop to their right, they are represented by a dash.

d. If successive fingers have the same small letter, they are represented by a numerical coefficient and the letter. Thus, r would be 2r.

t	W	a	a	r
u	W	r	t	r

The secondary classification is:

$$\frac{tW2ar}{Wrtr}$$

11. Sub-secondary Classification

The thumb and little fingers are not considered in the sub-secondary classification. Again, right hand fingers appear in the numerator and left hand in the denominator.

a. **Whorls.** The symbols I, M, and O are used for Inner, Meeting, and Outer whorls, which are determined by the procedure described in paragraph 2 above.

b. **Arches** are not considered or represented.

c. **Loops** are represented by letters I and O.

1) *Index Fingers.* A ridge count of 1 to 9 inclusive is represented by I; a ridge count greater than 9 is represented by O.

2) *Middle Fingers.* A ridge count of 1 to 10 inclusive is represented by I. Greater than 10 is represented by O.

3) *Ring Fingers.* A ridge count of 1 to 13 inclusive is represented by I; more than 13 is O.

Example: A sub-secondary classification would be

$$\frac{IOI}{OMM}$$

12. Final Classification

For the identification bureau of a small police department the primary, secondary, and sub-secondary classifications are sufficient. In larger identification bureaus where there are a great number of cards with the same primary, secondary, and sub-secondary classifications, a final classification is used. A number indicating a ridge count on the little finger is the final classification and is obtained as follows:

a. **Loop on Right Little Finger.** The ridge count of this finger is placed in the numerator at the right of the subsecondary classification. The complete final classification is this number.

b. **Loop on Left Little Finger.** If there is no loop on the right little finger, but there is a loop on the left little finger, the ridge count of the latter is the final classification and is written in the denominator.

c. **No Loop on Little Finger.** In this case there is no final classification. Some identification bureaus in treating this case consider the whorl as an ulnar loop and use the ridge count of the whorl. The count is taken from the left delta to the core in the right hand and from the right delta to the core in the left hand.

13. Extension of the Henry System

At times there is a need for further sub-classification of fingerprints and a key and major division are used for this purpose. Their use is recommended by necessity.

a. **The Key.** The key is always placed to the left of the numerator regardless of the finger on which it is found. The key consists of the ridge count of the first loop found in a set of prints beginning with the right thumb but omitting the little finger.

b. **Major Division.** Only the thumbs are considered. The major subdivision is written immediately to the right of the key in the numerator and on the extreme left in the denominator. The right thumb is recorded in the numerator and the left thumb in the denominator.

1) *Both Thumbs Whorls.* The major division consists of one of the symbols I, M, and O, representing the tracing as Inner, Meeting, or Outer.

2) *Both Thumbs Loops.* The ridge count of the left thumb is represented in the denominator by the symbols S, M, and L, representing respectively the words Small, Medium, and Large. Ridge counts 1 to 11 inclusive are represented by S; counts 12 to 16 inclusive by M; and above 17 by L. For the right thumb the ridge counts are represented in the numerator by the symbols S, M, and L, arrived at by the same designation of ridge counts as described for the left thumb. A ridge count of 14 on the right thumb and 9 and on the left would give a major division of $\frac{M}{S}$.

3) **Combinations of Loops and Whorls.** The same system as described in the preceding two paragraphs is employed. Ridge counting is used for the loop, and ridge tracing for the whorls with the appropriate symbols.

14. Identification Records

The function of the identification bureau of a police department is twofold: it must maintain conveniently and efficiently the various files of identification records of criminals, and it must provide for the rapid and reliable searching and filing of these records.

a. **Identification Files.** Typically, the records of the identification bureau can be placed in four or more major classifications such as the following:

1) **The Master Criminal File.** This contains the criminal records and fingerprints in serial-number sequence.

2) **The Fingerprint File.** This contains card-size (8″ × 8″) fingerprint records, together with criminal record sheets.

3) **The Index File.** This consists of 3 × 3-inch cards filed alphabetically and by fingerprint classification.

4) **The "Mug" Shot File.** Identification photos are placed on file, together with the prisoner's record and other useful data, such as his height, weight, age, and a description of his significant characteristics. "Mug" pairs (side and front views) are usually printed on 3 × 4¾-inch paper to be filed in a standard 3 × 5-inch card file.

15. NCIC Fingerprint Classification System

As previously described (p. 172), one of the files in the National Crime Information Center (NCIC) is the computerized Wanted Persons File on individuals for whom federal warrants are outstanding or who have committed or been identified with an offense which is classified as a felony or serious misdemeanor under the existing penal statutes of the jurisdiction originating the entry and a felony or misdemeanor warrant has been issued for the individual with respect to the offense. This includes probation and parole violators.

When a wanted person's fingerprint classification is available, the National Crime Information Center fingerprint classification (NCIC FPC) should always be included in the wanted person's record. While not a positive identifier, the NCIC FPC can be of assistance in establishing the identity of a suspected wanted person. The following information and instructions, which include a modification of the Henry System, have been issued by the FBI to aid police officers in the submission of criminal data and fingerprint records.

In November, 1971, a file known as Computerized Criminal History (CCH) was added to the NCIC data base. The file contains data concerning personal descriptions of those individuals arrested for violations of serious crimes, the nature of the charge, and the disposition of the arrest. This file is meant to service all agencies in the criminal justice system. Developed in conjunction with local, state, and federal NCIC participants, this file was designed to meet the needs of police, as well as those of prosecutors, courts, and correctional institutions for prompt up-to-date information concerning an individual's past criminal history. One field of data which has been provided for and which should be used in the CCH record is the subject's NCIC FPC. The NCIC FPC is not a positive identifier, but it can aid in establishing the identity of an individual, particularly when a subject possesses a common name and the search for his CCH record is being made against a vast repository of computerized data based records.

To alleviate problems existent due to the various methods of fingerprint classification, the following method was devised and should be utilized in classifying fingerprints for entry into the fingerprint classification (FPC) field of the wanted person record format, as well as the FPC of the CCH record. This is a twenty character field.

The fingers are numbered beginning with the right thumb as number 1, and continuing through number 10 with the left thumb being number 6. Two characters are to be used for each finger as shown below:

Pattern Type	Pattern Subgroup	NCIC FPC Code
ARCH......................	Plain ARCH...............	AA
	Tented ARCH..............	TT

LOOP...................... Radial LOOP............... 2 numeric characters. Determine actual ridge count and add fifty (50). E.g., if the ridge count of a radial loop is 16, add 50 to 16 for a sum of 66. Enter this sum (66) in the appropriate finger position of the FPC field.

Ulnar LOOP............... 2 numeric characters indicating actual ridge count (less than 50). If the ridge count is less than 10, precede actual count with a zero. E.g., ridge count of 14, enter as 14; ridge count of 9, enter as 09.

WHORL..................... Plain WHORL............. Enter "P" followed by tracing of whorl.

Inner tracing......... PI
Meeting tracing...... PM
Outer tracing......... PO

Central Pocket Loop WHORL — Enter "C" followed by tracing of whorl.

Inner tracing......... CI
Meeting tracing...... CM
Outer tracing......... CO

Double[1] Loop WHORL. Enter "d" followed by tracing of whorl. In double loop whorl pattern the small letter "d" is utilized when classifying prints in lieu of the capital "D" in order to make the handwritten character more distinguishable from the handwritten letter O. When entered in a computer data base or when the NCIC FPC is otherwise typed or printed out the capital "D" will be used instead of the small letter "d" to avoid the complications involved in having to provide both upper (capital letter) and lower (small letter) case character sets.

Inner tracing.........	dI
Meeting tracing......	dM
Outer tracing.........	dO
Accidental WHORL......	Enter "X" followed by tracing of whorl.
Inner tracing.........	XI
Meeting tracing......	XM
Outer tracing.........	XO

MISSING/AMPU-
TATED FINGER²..................................... XX
COMPLETELY... SR
SCARRED OR
MUTILATED
PATTERN³

---

¹In double loop whorl patterns the small letter d is utilized in lieu of the capital D in order to make it more distinguishable from the handwritten letter O.

²Used only in instances of missing and totally/partly amputated fingers making it impossible to accurately classify an impression according to the above instructions for NCIC FPC. It is recognized that under the Henry System of classifying fingerprints, if a finger is missing or amputated, it is given a classification identical with the opposite finger; however, this should not be done in the NCIC FPC, since the precise identity of the finger or fingers missing/amputated is not preserved.

³Used only in instances in which the fingerprint cannot be accurately classified due to complete scarring or mutilation and a classifiable print cannot be obtained. As in the case of missing and amputated fingers, the procedure for assigning the classification of the opposite finger, as is done under the Henry System of classifying fingerprints, *should not be used* for the NCIC FPC.

It shall no longer be necessary to place a diagonal line through the number zero. The computer program now distinguishes the difference between the number 0 in a loop classification and the outer tracing whorl designation capital O.

An example of the NCIC FPC for a set of fingerprints made up of all ulnar loops might thus read: 12101116141109111713. The same fingerprints with #2 and #7 fingers being radial loops would appear as follows: 12601116141159111713.

Suppose then for an example, a set of fingerprints is classified under the Henry System and contains the following: #1 finger is an ulnar loop with 12 ridge counts, #2 finger has been amputated, #3 finger is a plain arch, #4 finger is a Central Pocket loop with outer tracing, #5 finger is an ulnar loop with 4 counts, #6 finger is completely scarred, #7 finger is a radial loop with 9 ridge counts, #8 finger is a tented arch, #9 finger is a double loop with a meeting tracing, and #10 finger is an ulnar loop with 10 ridge counts. Applying the foregoing rules, the correct NCIC FPC would be: 12XXAACO04SR59TTdM10. (If typed or machine printed, the small letter "d" would be a capital letter "D" in this classification.)

16. Use of Computers

Great files of fingerprints stand mute unless a search process can be limited by some classification easier than print-by-print comparison of details used for final identity. Even with the best available proposed schemes for assigning unambiguous codes to prints, a print-by-print search will require looking at thousands of cards. Machine searching is already used widely, although by no means universally and not for the largest national files. The New York State method involves counts of ridges on each finger and some coded assignment of patterns. Then a punched-card file can be searched for the entire set of numbers, at the rate of seven or eight cards per minute. Fully automatic methods, without human assignment and count, are latent in the technology; like most pattern-recognition problems this one is not yet solved as a practical matter.

The President's Commission on Law Enforcement has recommended two studies leading to the development of a semiautomatic fingerprint recognition system: a basic study of classification techniques and a utility study to assess the value of a latent print searching capability. Positive identification of a person from his fingerprints is presently made by manual file-searching techniques structured around the 10-point classification system. A single fingerprint developed at the crime scene still presents overwhelming difficulties. If a suspect is in custody or if there are a limited number of named suspects on file, a comparison can be made. A general search, however, is impractical. It is expected that modern computer technology will make feasible the search of a file of even millions of prints for comparison with a single fingerprint. Complete automatic recognition capability is desired, but semi-automatic operation, involving a trained operator working together with a machine, presents a more accessible goal with current technology. A brief description of projected and present fingerprint searching capabilities:

a. **Single Fingerprints.** The identification of single fingerprints found at crime scenes has always been a laborious, time-consuming and thankless job for identification experts who through the years have had to manually scan, code, and match individual prints against files. Recently a major breakthrough in the identification of single fingerprints was achieved by the development of computerized equipment. What was formerly the work of weeks can now be achieved in the space of a few hours by means of this system in which microfilmed prints and a laser beam technique permit the electronic data processing and optical scanning of eighty fingerprint images a second. Under the new system, a Polaroid® photograph of the fingerprint is placed in a photo-processing camera to produce a holographic three-dimensional filter that is then fed into an optical scanner that matches the fingerprint with others on file.

b. **Automatic Fingerprint Search System.** The FBI is presently nearing completion of its comprehensive plan for the automation of the fingerprint card processing and related activities carried on at the Identification Division in Washington, D.C. The complete system will be known as the Automated Identification Division System (AIDS). The system will eventually provide for automatic fingerprint searching of the criminal name indices, computer storage and retrieval of arrest record data, and the capability to gather criminal statistics and system performance data.

The new system is far too difficult to describe in detail. Basically it will consist of an analyzer or optical character recognition station where the fingerprint card is broken down into minutiae and ridge direction data to be integrated later into classification data. Another element will be a mass memory system which will be capable of on-line storage of a miniature file of up to 15 million fingerprint cards. Minutiae retrieved from the mass memory system by a search request will be processed through *matchers*, which compare the minutiae of a search fingerprint card with every file set of the same classification and evaluate comparisons.

The final step in the processing is the verification of possible matches. Verification will be performed by a technician. When there is a possible match he will visually compare the hard copy search card with a displayed microfilm or microfiche image of the possible matching file card selected by the matcher. He will either verify or reject using traditional manual comparison procedures.

c. **State-Of-The-Art.** The preceding glowing paragraphs are intended to encourage the fingerprint specialist and not to mislead him with polysyllabic prophecies. Money is being spent and things are being done in high places. In practice, however, the fingerprint technician of the typical police department is very much where he was many years ago, waiting for an improved search and identification capability. On the average about 5 per cent of burglary investigations are productive of significant latent prints. Studies have shown that a more intensive print collection effort will be unproductive unless there is a corresponding increase in fingerprint identification capability. Our discussion hitherto has been designed to indicate the direction that is being taken to alleviate the present condition.

ADDITIONAL READING

Classification of Fingerprints

Allison, H.C.: *Personal Identification*. Boston, Holbrook Press, 1973.

Bridges, B.C.: *Practical Fingerprinting*. Rev. by C.E. O'Hara. New York, Funk & Wagnalls, 1963.

Federal Bureau of Investigation. *The Science of Fingerprints*. Washington, D.C.: U.S. Government Printing Office, 1977.

Field, A.T.: *Fingerprint Handbook*. Springfield, Ill.: Thomas, 1971.

Automated Fingerprint Systems

Banner, C.S. and Stock, R.M.: The FBI's Approach to Automatic Fingerprint Identification. 44 *FBI Law Enforcement Bulletin*, 1 and 2, 1975.

Califana, A.L.: Simplified Version of the NCIC Technique for Coding Fingerprints. Parts I, II, and III. 22 *Law and Order*, 3, 4, 5, 1974.

Levinson, J.H.: Sonic Digitizer Aids in Fingerprint ID. 25 *Law and Order*, 9, 1977.

Kingston, C. R. and Madrazo, F. G.: *Latent Value Study*. Albany, New York State Identification and Intelligence System, 1970.

Snyder, R. E.: Automated Fingerprint Identification. 44 *Police Chief,* 10, 1977.

Stroh, H. D.: The Identification Unit and the Miracode Retrieval System. 56 *Fingerprint and Identification Magazine,* 5, 1974.

Verruso, J. F.: Department of Criminal Justice Service Improves Facsimile Fingerprint Network. 57 *Fingerprint and Identification Magazine,* 7, 1976.

Chapter 34

LAUNDRY AND DRY CLEANER MARKS

1. Introduction

IT WAS a routine house burglary. At two o'clock in the morning the detectives received a call from a couple who had returned from a theater party to find their suburban house burglarized. The detectives visited the house and examined the scene of the crime. Entrance had been made through a kitchen window, which had been unlocked by means of a "shove knife." The dresser drawers had been overturned on the bed. Jewelry and clothes had been taken. The owner remarked that the burglar must have worn one of his expensive jackets, since he had left his own jacket on the floor of the bedroom. The detectives examined the jacket and found a dry cleaner's tag on the inside of a sleeve.

The detectives brought the jacket to the identification bureau of their department. The identification man on duty examined the tag and searched through his file on dry cleaner's marks. He extracted one card which bore an inscription similar to that of the evidence tag. Printed on the card was the name of a tailor who used the mark to identify the clothing of his customers. In the morning the detectives visited the tailor, showed him the tag, and requested information concerning the customer. The tailor gave them the customer's name and address of a house just four blocks away. In a few minutes the detectives were in the room of the burglar. The criminal quickly confessed and showed them the stolen property.

2. Importance

Investigations as simple as that described above occur every month in the police departments of large cities. For every case

718

which is "solved" by a latent fingerprint, there are probably two solved by laundry and dry cleaner's marks. These marks form a direct link between the crime and the criminal. They are attached to his clothing and associate him positively with the garment. The prosaic dry cleaner's mark has fortunately received little publicity, being ignored alike by criminals, fiction writers, and newspaper reporters.

3. Procedure in Brief

Laundries and dry cleaners are faced with a basic processing problem. The retailer receives clothing from the customer, records it, marks it, gives it to the wholesaler for processing, receives it on completion, and returns it to the customer. Obviously he must employ some reliable system of marking the clothes in order to insure the return of the proper garments to each customer. Thus, trousers, jackets, hats, dresses, shirts, handkerchiefs, towels, and similar articles which have been laundered and cleaned become, through the medium of the identifying mark, invaluable clues in a variety of cases that come to the attention of the police. The marks are not infallible clues. Some retailers do not record customers names and addresses. Moreover, there is no uniform system of marking.

4. Cases

Clothing as a clue enters into a large number of police cases, criminal and otherwise. The following list is representative of the more common types of cases:

a. **Crimes of Violence.** In murder, rape, assault, and robbery the elements of physical contact, violence, and rapid escape are present. The criminal may lose his hat, jacket, or shirt in the struggle or may simply forget them in his hurry to escape.

b. **Tracing.** The marked garment may serve as a tracing clue:

1) *Unidentified Persons.* When a dead body is found the clothing provides the most direct clue in the absence of identifying papers.

Unconscious persons, lost children, and persons susceptible to mental disturbance can be identified in this manner.

2) **Wanted Persons.** Often the police are end-stopped in their pursuit of a fugitive when they arrive at his hotel or furnished room. If the fugitive has departed hurriedly, clothing may be left in the closet. By tracing the clothing marks, the detectives will obtain additional leads such as aliases and former addresses.

5. Marking Systems of Laundries and Cleaners

There are two types of numbers used to identify clothing in processing, namely, the *line number* and the *customer's receipt number*. This system has been built up by the laundries and dry cleaners themselves. As yet there is no uniform system imposed on the industry by the police as a control. Such a system would, of course, be invaluable in criminal identification work. The procedure described below is typical of the systems employed by most laundries and dry cleaners.

a. **Line Number.** This is the number used by the wholesaler to designate a particular retail store. The line number is the link between the wholesaler and the retailer. The wholesaler "picks up" clothing from a large number of retailers and lays out routes for the delivery trucks. A wholesaler with five routes will designate these as the 100 route, 200 route, and so forth. The retail stores on the 200 route, for example, will be given line numbers such as 201, 207, 205, and so forth. The system is not necessarily uniform. Some wholesalers may use letters such as MX or LY or even symbols such as triangles or squares. Some retailers may send their clothing to two or more wholesalers.

b. **Customer's Receipt Number.** The retailer must be able to associate the clothing with the customer. To do this he must add a customer's number to the line number. Receipts are issued to the customer and the number of the receipt is placed on the garment. The retailer may maintain a receipt book in which he records the customer's name and address. Some retailers can remember the owner of each garment or bundle and do not employ receipts or numbers. Where a receipt book is maintained, the retailer usually keeps his records for approximately one year before destroying them. The placing of the line number on the article of clothing is done by either the retailer or the wholesaler.

6. Marking Clothing and Other Articles

The methods of marking vary widely with wholesalers, retailers, and with communities. The common methods are described below.

a. **Marking Area.** Certain conventions are commonly observed in regard to the place where the garment is marked or tagged.

1) *Coats and Jackets.* Inside of the sleeve, usually the right sleeve.

2) *Vests.* In the lining, usually under the right arm pit.

3) *Trousers.* Waist band, fob pockets, or right rear pocket lining.

4) *Shirts.* Collar band, shirt tail, or front of shirt (invisible marks).

5) *Sheets, Pillowcases and Towels.* On the edges.

6) *Gloves.* On the inside, near the center.

7) *Hats.* On the sweat band, front or rear, or on the lining.

b. **Marking Media.** There are three common ways in which a garment is marked.

1) *Hand Marking.* Ink or indelible pencil is used.

2) *Tagging.* A small rectangular tag is clipped or affixed by a wire frame to the garment. The tag varies in size, color, material, and marking. It may be printed or hand marked.

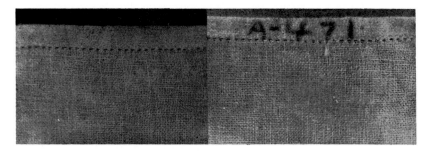

Figure 49. Obliterated laundry mark on a handkerchief.

Figure 50. Rendered visible by photographing with infrared film and a Wratten 87 filter.

Figure 51. Invisible laundry mark on a shirt fluorescing under ultraviolet radiation. Courtesy of George Keenan.

3) **Machine, Stamp, or Stencil.** These methods are employed mainly by laundries. The type varies in size with the individual laundry.

7. Identifying the Mark

The following is typical of the procedure followed in identifying a mark:

a. **Locating.** The mark is located by turning the garment inside out and examining the lining. An ultraviolet lamp is used to search for invisible marks that fluoresce.

b. **Line Number.** A search of the file is made for the line number, and the cards under the given numbers are withdrawn.

c. **Comparison.** The mark is compared with the field numbers until a matching number is located which is made with the same type of printing or with the same handwriting. In cases of tags, the color, size, and material are considered. The comparison of the type or handwriting is the most difficult part of the search. If a successful match is found, the retailer's name and address are recorded.

d. **Visiting the Retailer.** The investigator now takes the garment to the retailer and requests an identification. The retailer may at this point be able to give him the name and address of the customer by means of his records or through memory.

e. **Doubtful Cases.** Quite often the files do not yield a mark which has the same type of printing or handwriting. In these cases the numbers most closely resembling the evidence number are recorded and a visit is made to various wholesalers or retailers for further identification. Dry cleaners' associations can also be consulted.

f. **Illegible Marks.** The difficulties of marking cloth frequently result in illegible marks. In these situations the police laboratory can assist in rendering the mark legible. Photographs made with process or infrared film may provide the contrast necessary for clarifying the number. Sometimes the symbols are strongly impressed on the garment but their identity cannot be established because of the poor writing. The investigator must then visit those establishments using symbols most nearly resembling the evidence inscription.

8. Identification Bureau Files

Separate files are maintained for laundries and dry cleaners in identification bureaus. A standard 3 × 5″ card is ordinarily used. The cards are cross-indexed by means of various possible combinations. The name and address of the laundry or cleaner, wholesaler and retailer, are recorded on the card and a sample mark is affixed thereto. The cards are filed in numerical and alphabetical order. Finally, a file is made of all cards of the establishments according to address. The person assigned to the file must obtain samples of marks and tags by visiting each retailer and wholesaler. Annually, each establishment must be revisited for new marks or marks made by new personnel. The following types of establishments should be included in the files:

    a. Laundries, steam, general, Chinese.

    b. Cleaners and dryers, wholesale and retail.

    c. Overall cleaning establishments.

    d. Hat and glove cleaning establishments.

    e. Pawn shops and secondhand dealers.

    f. Cleaning shops that have their own plants.

    g. State hospitals.

    h. Reformatories.

    i. Welfare houses, county, town, city, and state.

    j. Hotels.

    k. Private institutions, boarding schools.

    l. Furriers, retail, wholesale.

    m. Storage plants.

    n. United States Government hospitals and the branches of the armed services.

9. Sources of Information

The investigator will find that there are a number of agencies which maintain files of laundry and dry cleaner's marks, ranging from the local to the national level. Ordinarily the local agency, usually the municipal police department, maintains the most effective file, since efficiency in this activity requires frequent personal contact. The following are some of the available sources.

    a. Crime laboratories or identification divisions of municipal, county, and state law enforcement agencies.

    b. The Federal Bureau of Investigation maintains a file of invisible laundry mark systems.

    c. Laundry and dry cleaning establishments in the local area.

    d. National Marketing Machine Co., Cincinnati, Ohio. This firm supplies the equipment and materials used in invisible laundry marking systems. A distinctive symbol is assigned to each company using the system. On receipt of an official request this organization will provide the name and address of a launderer or dry cleaner using a particular invisible mark.

    e. The National Institute of Cleaning and Dyeing, Silver Springs, Maryland, although not maintaining a national file, can provide a notification service for the investigator. By circularizing the laundry or dry cleaning mark among the establishments with which it has contact, the necessary publicity can be accomplished.

Chapter 35

CASTING AND MOLDING

1. Application

A NOTHER method of recording the appearance of evidence at the crime scene is to reproduce its external form in the three dimensions by making a cast and, if necessary, a mold. Thus impressions such as those produced by feet, tires, teeth, and tools can be reproduced by casting, and the shape of objects such as weapons, seals, or the features of a dead person can be duplicated by casting and subsequently making a mold. Ordinarily the purpose of making casts is to enable a scientific comparison to be made with the object suspected of having made the impression and to thus establish that the object, and inferentially its owner, was at the scene of the crime.

2. Plaster of Paris

Although a number of materials can be used to make a cast, experience has shown that plaster of paris is the most widely applicable, particularly in outdoor scenes. It is simple to prepare, provides a durable cast, and is capable of reproducing fine detail.

a. **Preparation.** Before the evidentiary indentation or impression is cast it should be photographed from seven points of view. First, an overall photograph should be made to show the impression in its background. Second, close-up pictures should be taken both with and without a ruler in the field of view and with the camera plate parallel to the base surface of the impression. Finally, photographs should be taken from various angles which may reveal significant detail. Relatively large particles of extraneous matter should be removed to prevent the obscuring of parts of the impression.

726

b. **Spraying.** If the receiving surface consists of a soft substance such as dust, sand, or flour, a quick-drying fixative such as plastic spray or shellac should be applied prior to casting. The spray should be directed against a piece of cardboard and permitted to settle over the impression. When the fixative is quite dry, a fine layer of machine oil should be sprayed over the surface to facilitate separation of cast from the fixative.

c. **Mixing the Plaster.** An estimate of the amount of material required for an inch-thick cast should be made and a corresponding quantity of water placed in a glass, porcelain, or rubber container. The plaster is then sprinkled evenly over the surface of the water until sufficient has been deposited to extend in a mound from the bottom of the vessel to the surface of the water. The plaster is not stirred thoroughly until the mixture has the consistency of cream. Plaster or water is added to achieve the proper consistency.

d. **Pouring.** The mixture is poured over the impression at a low level. The fall of the liquid should be broken by means of a flat piece of wood. When a depth of ½ inch is reached, the pouring should be interrupted and the cast reinforced by laying on pieces of fine mesh wire or light, flat pieces of wood. The remainder of the plaster is then poured on the first layer.

e. **Setting.** The cast should be permitted to set for approximately thirty minutes. In hardening, the plaster first becomes warm and subsequently cools on setting.

f. **Identification.** Before the plaster has completely set, it should be marked by the investigator for identification. The date, case number, and initials of the investigator can be scratched on the upper surface.

g. **Cleaning.** After hardening, the cast should be removed and permitted to further dry for several hours. It can then be washed and lightly brushed in water to remove the adhering debris.

3. Moulage

In reproducing the shape of an object such as the face of a deceased person, it is first necessary to make a mold. Subsequently, a cast is made of the mold. Ordinarily a colloidal substance is employed to make the mold and a wax composition is used for the cast. Since the substances employed for this purpose are commercial products possessing individual characteristics, the investigator must rely for guidance on the instructions provided by the manufacturer. The occasions on which the investigator will be required to employ a moulage method are quite rare; hence the practice of this reproduction technique is usually restricted to the law enforcement laboratory.

Figure 52. Making a plastic cast of a shoe impression. The various steps in the casting procedure are readily recognized.

4. Modeling Clay

For small impressions, such as tool marks, modeling clay will be found to be a satisfactory reproduction medium. A cast of the impression is made by simply pressing the clay into the indentation and removing. The form of the clay is now that of the object which made the impression. A positive impression can be made from the clay by immersing it in plaster of paris.

Chapter 36

VARIOUS IMPRESSIONS

1. Impressions in General

THE EVIDENTIAL value of impressions made by a shoe, hand tool, or other article is based on the theory that no two physical objects are alike and hence that impressions made by such objects often are marked by uniquely identifying characteristics which can be detected upon close scrutiny. In general there are two types of characteristics associated with an impression. First, there are the class characteristics which identify the kind, make, or model of the object that produced the impression. For example, the general shape of the tool mark may indicate to the observer that it was made by a screwdriver with a broad blade. The pattern of a tire impression may reflect that the imprint came from a Firestone tire. Secondly, there are *individual* characteristics which serve to identify the specific object which causes the impression. Illustrative of this class are the individual striations in the tool mark which correspond exactly with the defects of the suspect tool, or the nicks and cuts in the tire impression which match the defects in one of the tires on a suspect car. It is readily seen that individual characteristics are of much greater probative value than simple class characteristics. Unfortunately, they are more difficult to discover, and only occasionally are sufficient distinctive features found to permit a fairly conclusive identification of the impression with the object. Class characteristics do have some probative value; in addition, they serve to narrow the field to be searched in the preliminary stages of the investigation.

2. Foot Impressions

a. **Casts.** The process of making plaster casts of foot impressions is described in Chapter 35. Once the cast has been obtained it should be carefully examined for distinguishing characteristics. The fact that shoes are usually mass-produced tends to lessen the probative value of any class characteristics which may be present and, therefore, particular attention should be given to individual characteristics which would serve to identify the impression with a shoe having the same distinctive marks. Marks of wear, protruding nails, and other defects are usually helpful in effecting a comparison.

b. **Walking Patterns.** Where a number of consecutive footprints are found, it is sometimes possible to detect some distinctive characteristics which may be helpful in the course of the investigation. For example, the angle of walk, the length of step, and any infirmities which are characteristic of the person will normally be reflected in the impressions. However, such characteristics are merely indicative and should not be made the basis of positive conclusions with respect to identification.

3. Surface Footprints

The surface footprint is produced by the depositing of material on the surface by the foot or shoe. Whereas the foot impression deforms the surface, the footprint merely deposits a layer of dust, liquid, mud, or perspiration upon it. The most common prints of this type are shoe prints. These are often found in connection with office burglaries where the perpetrator has, in the course of this search, carelessly scattered papers from the drawers or safe and has stepped on the sheets. Usually a heel print can be found on the paper. If the weather is rainy, it may be possible to find excellent imprints of the heel and part of the sole. A shoe print found on any surface should first be photographed. Where it is difficult to see the print, oblique lighting should be used. Wherever possible, the camera should be placed directly over the print with the lens and plate parallel to the surface. A scale should be included in the photograph. If a suspect is found, his shoes should be examined to see if they compare favorably in size and shape with the questioned print. In many cases the investigator can eliminate shoes which do not correspond, particularly if the evidence print bears some class characteristic which is dissimilar. Where it appears that a good match has been obtained, he should endeavor to obtain the shoes of the suspect to forward to the laboratory for comparison with the evidence prints. If the shoes cannot be obtained, sample prints can be secured by coating the shoes with fingerprint ink and pressing them against plain white paper.

4. Sole Prints

Prints made with the bare feet are called *sole prints*. Occasionally such prints can be developed by the usual methods employed in connection with latent fingerprints. Large tile bathroom floors, paper on floors, polished wood, and similar surfaces are receptive to such prints. The friction ridges on the sole of the foot sometimes leave a deposit of perspiration and dirt which will respond to the appropriate methods of development used for fingerprints. The investigator will first become aware of the presence of such prints by faint outlines of the foot. The print should be photographed in one-to-one size after it has been developed. A fingerprint camera of the $3\frac{1}{4} \times 4\frac{1}{4}''$ type will usually include the major part of the friction ridge pattern. An overall picture should be made with the $4 \times 5''$ camera to include the background in the field of view. Comparison prints of a suspect can be obtained by the regular inking method used for fingerprints.

5. Palm Prints

Quite frequently, palm prints are discovered at a crime scene, particularly in burglary cases. The act of climbing in and out of windows and other activities associated with a burlary often involve pressing the palms on the window sills and casements. In the absence of latent fingerprints, palm prints are particularly useful for comparison purposes in the event that suspects are found. The basis of a palm print identification is the same as that of fingerprints. The permanent, unalterable pattern of friction ridges and flexure lines on the palm varies with the individual, and thus, when two patterns are found to correspond in a sufficient number of characteristics, the expert may conclude that they were made by the same hand. Palm prints are developed and photographed in the same manner as fingerprints. Comparison prints of a suspect can be obtained by inking the palm and pressing it on a card. Best results can be realized by placing the card on an appropriate convex surface so that the pattern of the entire palm area will be reflected.

6. Poroscopy

The friction ridges of the palms and fingers of the hand contain an additional means of identification in the characteristic formation of the pores. Each ridge is dotted by pores which differ in position, shape, and size. Thus it is possible to establish a pore pattern in a small area containing only a few friction ridges and to use this pattern as a basis of identification of a suspect. Since the pores are permanent in structure throughout a person's lifetime and since they appear in an infinite variety of patterns, an identification effected in this manner has the same theoretical validity as that attached to fingerprint identification.

a. **Application.** Poroscopy can be used where a latent partial fingerprint is develped and prints of suspects are available for comparison. In order for a latent fingerprint to be of value in establishing an identification it is generally (and loosely) required that there must be at least twelve corresponding characteristics in the friction ridges. When twelve corresponding characteristics cannot be found, the technician may resort to a pore pattern study. The technique is not commonly used because of the fact that outlines of the pores are so delicate, they are generally not clearly visible in latent prints.

b. **Developing Latent Pore Prints.** Since pore prints are extremely delicate and easily destroyed, special care is required in their development and subsequent protection. Iodine fuming has been recommended for development on hard polished surfaces.

Powders such as lead carbonate and mercuric oxide may be used on other surfaces with satisfactory results. When using powder, the brush should be held over the print and tapped gently so that the powder will be sprinkled lightly over the impression. By delicate brushing the powder is subsequently spread and the excess removed.

c. **Pore Prints of Suspects.** Although ink has a tendency to fill the pores and spoil the outline of pore patterns when it is used carelessly, it is possible to obtain a satisfactory reproduction of pores if the ink is applied to the finger lightly and the finger is not pressed too forcefully against the recording card. Special chemical formulae exist for obtaining superior pore prints for comparison purposes; however, their use is generally confined to the laboratory.

7. Tire Impressions

In crimes such as murder, rape, and robbery the criminal usually employs a vehicle to escape from the scene of the crime. If the area of criminal operations is unpaved the possibility of finding tire impressions exists. Often the tire tracks are the only clue left at the crime scene. Unless the car has traveled backwards only the rear tire tracks will be visible. In some cars in which the rear wheels are farther apart than the front, part of the front tire tracks may be visible.

a. **Direction of Travel.** If oil is dripping from the car the shape of the drops will be such that on hard surfaces they will taper toward the direction of travel of the car. On unpaved roads small masses of dirt may be thrown up by the side of the wheels so that they taper in the direction of travel.

b. **Measurements.** The distance between the wheels should be measured as well as the breadth of the tire track. A photograph of the track should be made with the plate and lens board parallel to the tire impression and a rule in the field of view. The impression should then be cast with plaster of paris.

8. Tool Marks

Another form of impression that sometimes provides a valuable clue is the mark left by a tool such as a jimmy applied to a relatively

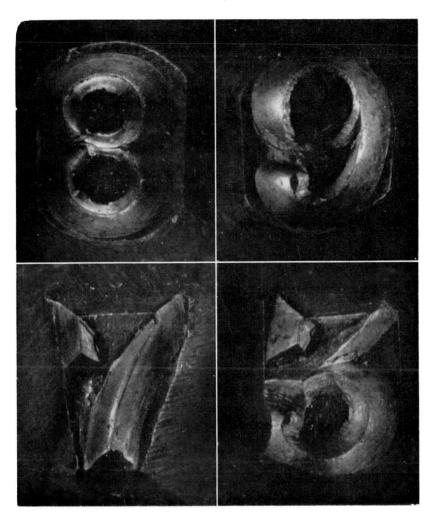

Figure 53. Example of tool defects. These dies were used by automobile thieves to stamp in motor numbers on stolen cars. The defects on the striking edges, visible in these photomacrographs ($\times$ 15), served to identify the work of this gang and associate it with a series of larcenies.

hard surface. The blade or working face of a tool is seldom the smooth, unmarred surface which it appears to be to the eye. Low-power magnification will reveal certain imperfections. If there are a sufficient number of these and if they are sufficiently

Figure 54. A fingerprint in which the pores are visible. The wide variation in the shape of the pore outline is apparent.

characteristic, it is possible for the expert to conclude that the mark was made by a particular tool in question. The theory that underlies the study of tool marks is similar to that applied in firearms identification. A bullet or a shell is quite frequently impressed with the characteristic markings of the gun from which it was discharged. If the evidence bullet is not multilated on contact the expert can usually determine whether it could have been discharged from the suspect firearm. Tools, like guns, differ in size, width, thickness, and general shape. Even where the tools are alike in these characteristics, minute differences will exist which may be attributable to manufacturing, finishing, and grinding; uneven wear; unusual use or abuse; sharpening; or modifications made by the owner. These imperfections are usually visible under a low-power microscope. If the tool is applied to a soft metal surface, these individual characteristics are transferred to the metal. Occasionally the defects are sufficient in number to permit the expert to assert, on the basis of a comparison, that a certain mark was produced by a certain tool.

Figure 55. A tire impression photographed before casting. The careful selection of the right angle of illumination serves to emphasize the pattern.

a. **Findings.** Although positive identifications are relatively rare, the evidence of tool marks is often found useful for one of the following purposes:

1) *Association.* The tool impression found at the scene of the crime may be matched with a tool found on a suspect or a tool found at the scene.

2) *Linking.* A series of burglaries may be linked together to show common authorship by means of similar tool impressions.

3) *Modus Operandi.* The tool marks often indicate the manner in which force was applied to a door, window, or safe. Similar applications of force in separate crimes may point to a common *modus operandi.*

4) **Searching.** The search for the tool used in perpetrating an offense may be greatly limited by determining the type of tool employed, from a study of the tool mark.

b. **Types of Tool Impressions.** Tool impressions will vary depending upon whether the tool was moved along the surface or was merely pressed in. If a tool, such as a screwdriver, is used simply as a lever, the resulting impression may not contain as many identifiable characteristic markings as the impressions from a tool such as a wrench, pliers, or saw which is usually moved along or around the surface. Of course, if an instrument such as a crowbar or jimmy is forced into a narrow space and then used as lever, both types of marks may be imparted to the surface.

c. **Handling of Tool Mark Evidence.** Tool impressions are usually found in burglary investigations. They most commonly occur at the point of the break and, in burglaries involving larceny, on the safe or strongbox which was rifled. The following is a suggested method of procedure at crime scenes of this kind.

1) **Discovery.** Openings, such as doors, windows, transoms, and skylights, should be examined for signs of forcible entry. Broken, forced, or cut locks, latches, and bolts should be studied for marks. Finally, desks, cabinets, safes, and cash boxes are examined. Tool impressions and tools should be carefully noted and included in pictures and sketches of appropriate parts of the crime scene.

2) **Protection.** Arrangements should be made for guards to protect the evidence until the examination or collection is complete. Doors and other openings which have been found to bear tool marks may, in addition, require careful processing for fingerprints and hence should not be touched unless absolutely necessary and then only with extreme care.

3) **Removal.** After appropriate photographs and sketches have been made, the investigator should, if necessary, remove the surfaces bearing tool impressions for the purpose of forwarding them to the laboratory together with any tools which are logical instruments for a comparison. Several precautions should be observed in removing such evidence.

a) MARKING. The item removed as evidence should be marked with the investigator's initials, the date, and if known, the case number. The evidence should also be marked to show the inside, outside, top and bottom surfaces, and the area bearing the tool impression. This marking should, of course, be done after the photographs have been taken.

b) PROPERTY CONSIDERATIONS. The investigator should make arrangements with the owner or custodian of the property for the return of, replacement, or compensation for items to be removed as evidence.

c) BASIS OF A DECISION TO REMOVE. The wholesale removal of property or integral parts of valuable structures and equipment is neither desirable nor necessary. The decision for removal should be based on the importance of the case, the probative significance of the tool impression in comparison with other available evidence, and the distance from the crime scene to the laboratory. Where it is impractical to remove the original evidence, the investigator can photograph and cast the evidence or, if feasible, request the presence of a technical expert at the scene of the crime to perform the comparison.

d. **Photographing Tool Marks.** Before the tool mark is disturbed or altered by casting, molding, or removal it should be carefully photographed to provide a permanent pictorial record of the evidence in its original condition. The photograph will also serve to identify original evidence with any casts or molds that may be made and thus satisfy legal requirements for records of original evidence. Two types of photographs are required: one showing the tool marks together with the background for identification purposes and a close-up photograph (at least one-to-one size) to show minute details of the tool mark. In both photographs a ruler should be placed in the field of view and to one side, in order to provide laboratory technicians with a reference scale for examination and comparison purposes.

e. **Casting and Molding Tool Marks.** A cast or mold of the tool mark should be made only when the investigator is unable to remove the original evidence. The methods described in Chapter 35 are applicable to this work. The investigator should not attempt the casting or molding until he has practiced the particular method on a similar wooden or metallic surface unassociated with the evidence. The most satisfactory method of making a cast of a tool mark is the use of modeling clay or plasticene. The casting material is kneaded between the hands and pressed against the mark until it fills the area and is conveniently shaped in the back. The method is applicable to both wooden and metallic surfaces. The resulting cast is in the shape of the blade or other portion of the tool used to make the impression. A reproduction of the tool mark itself can later be made from this cast by using plaster of paris.

9. Laboratory Findings

The investgator may submit to the laboratory for examination the original tool impression, suspect tools, casts, and photographs. In the ideal situation the investigator is seeking to conclusively identify a suspect tool with the tool mark. A number of lesser but still useful findings may result from the examination. The following are the possible conclusions that can be made in the laboratory.

a. The mark can be compared with a suspect tool to determine whether it was made by the tool.

b. A tool mark from a crime scene can be compared with similar tool marks from the scenes of other crimes. A positive finding can aid in establishing the guilt of, or in obtaining a confession of guilt from, a suspect who may be responsible for more than one crime.

c. Information can be obtained concerning the nature of an unknown tool from a study of the mark, thus narrowing the search.

d. By matching pieces of wire it may be possible to determine whether the pieces were cut from the same wire and whether a given tool or machine was used to make the cuts.

ADDITIONAL READING

Foot Impressions
Abbott, J.R.: *Footwear Evidence.* Springfield, Ill.: Thomas, 1964.
Cook, C.W.: Footprint Identification. 57 *Fingerprint and Identification Magazine,* 6, 1975.
Petty, C.S., et al.: The Value of Shoe Sole Imprints in Automobile Crash Investigations. 1 *Journal of Police Science and Administration,* 1, 1973.

Thomson, M.W.: Photographic Reproduction of Footprints. 2 *Forensic Photography*, 4, 1973.

Vandiver, J.V.: Footwear Marks. 24 *Law and Order*, 9, 1976.

Van Krunkelsven, H.: Improved Photographic Method for Making Hand and Footprints. 2 *Forensic Photography*, 5, 1973.

Tire Marks

Given, B., Nehrich, R. and Shields, J.: *Tire Tracks and Tread Marks*. Houston, Gulf Pub., 1978.

Lloyd, J.B.F.: Luminescence of Tyre Marks and Other Rubber Contact Traces. 16 *Journal of the Forensic Science Society*, 5, 1976.

Vandiver, J.V.: Tire Marks. 25 *Law and Order*, 7, 1977.

Tool Marks

Biasotti, A.A.: The Principles of Evidence Evaluation as Applied to Firearms and Tool Mark Identification. 9 *Journal of Forensic Sciences*, 428, 1964.

Brackett, J.W., Jr.: A Study of Idealized Striated Marks and Their Comparison Using Models. 10 *Journal of the Forensic Science Society*, 27, 1970.

Burd, D.Q. and Gilmore, A.E.: Individual and Class Characteristics of Tools. 13 *Journal of Forensic Sciences*, 390, 1968.

Davis, J.E.: *An Introduction to Tool Marks, Firearms and the Striagraph*. Springfield, Ill.: Thomas, 1958.

Freeman, H.G.: *Tool Dictionary*, 2nd ed. New York, Adler, 1960.

Peterson, J.L.: Utilizing the Laser for Comparing Tool Striations. 14 *Journal of the Forensic Science Society*, 57, 1974.

Townshend, D.G.: Photographing and Casting Toolmarks. 45 *FBI Law Enforcement Bulletin*, 4, 1976.

Vandiver, J.V.: Identification and Use of Tool Mark Evidence. 24 *Law and Order*, 7, 1976.

Palmprints

Alexander, H.L.V.: *Classifying Palmprints*. Springfield, Ill.: Thomas, 1973.

Guide to Taking Palm Prints. Washington, D.C.: U.S. Government Printing Office, n.d.

Wentworth, B. and Wilder, H.H.: *Personal Identification*. Chicago, T.G. Cooke, The Fingerprint Publishing Association, 1932.

PART VII
SPECIALIZED SCIENTIFIC METHODS

THE INVESTIGATOR AND SCIENTIFIC TECHNIQUES

Iᴛ ɪs ɴoᴛ to be expected that the investigator also play the role of laboratory expert in relation to the physical evidence found at the scene of the crime. Obviously his opinions on many aspects of the evidence such as a chemical analysis or a physical test would in great likelihood be rejected by the court. Criminalistics, the work of the police laboratory, is a separate study associated with the main field of investigation. It suffices that the investigator investigate; it is supererogatory that he should perform refined scientific examinations. Any serious effort to accomplish such a conversion would militate against the investigator's efficiency.

Although the investigator may not aspire to the function of the laboratory expert, there does remain for him a great deal of elementary police science that he can profitably master. Photography, physical methods of reproduction, the development of latent fingerprints, and many other simple techniques should be part of the investigator's professional knowledge. In general the investigator should know the methods of discovering, "field-testing," preserving, collecting, and transporting evidence. Questions of analysis and comparison should be referred to the laboratory expert.

A certain degree of medicolegal knowledge should also be part of the investigator's background to assist him in problems of suspicious deaths. A knowledge of the medical examiner's resources will enable him to understand and implement the methods used in determining the cause of death and the lethal agents employed. The investigator can greatly aid the inquiry into a homicide if he is acquainted with the common symptoms of violent death. He should recognize the appearance of typical poisons. Most important, he should know what evidence is significant in the varied circumstances of homicides. This topic has already been treated in the chapter on homicide.

In the following chapters a selection has been made of scientific topics in accordance with the frequency of application of the techniques. Consequently, the subject of document examinations has been treated more extensively than the others. It will be found in practice that the most common use of the laboratory expert is in connection with questioned documents. Unless the investigator has a fair knowledge of the services which the document examiner is prepared to offer and of the procedures in relation to the evidence whereby he can assist the examiner, his effectiveness is seriously limited.

The scientific and technological future is typically described in terms of general benefits deriving from the application of operations research and systems analysis to the various problem areas. Multidisciplinary teamwork is expected to achieve impressive breakthroughs in police science in such areas as communications, information storage and retrieval, police management and operations, and criminalistics. Describing the future capabilities of law enforcement, however, would be to adjourn our main purpose to skirmish with difficulties of desirability and practicality. The interest of the investigator is in the present and the text has held closely to the presently available methods. The reader should, nevertheless, be conscious of the greatly increased rate of obsolescence that has been projected for the present methods of police science.

ADDITIONAL READING

Federal Bureau of Investigation. *Handbook of Forensic Science*, rev. ed. Washington, D.C.: U.S. Government Printing Office, 1975.

Hall, J.C.: *Inside the Crime Laboratory*. Englewood Cliffs, N.J.: Prentice-Hall, 1974.

Kirk, P.L.: *Crime Investigation*, 2nd ed. New York, Wiley, 1974.

Kirk, P.L. and Bradford, L.W.: *The Crime Laboratory: Organization and Operation*. Springfield, Ill.: Thomas, 1965.

O'Brien, K. and Sullivan, R.C.: *Criminalistics: Theory and Practice*, 2nd ed. Boston, Holbrook Press, 1976.

O'Hara, C.E. and Osterburg, J.W.: *An Introduction to Criminalistics*. Bloomington, Indiana University Press, 1972.

Peterson, J.L.: *The Utilization of Criminalistics Services by the Police.* Washington, D.C.: National Institute of Law Enforcement and Criminal Justice, 1974.

Saferstein, R.: *Criminalistics. An Introduction to Forensic Science.* Englewood Cliffs, N.J.: Prentice-Hall, 1977.

Ullyet, K.: *Criminology: The Science of Crime Detection.* London, Franklin Watts, 1972.

Walls, H.J.: *Forensic Science.* New York, Praeger, 1968.

Wisconsin Department of Justice. *Criminal Investigation and Physical Evidence Handbook*, 2nd ed. Madison, Wisconsin Department of Administration, 1973.

(A number of the books listed above should be considered references for the scientific and technical chapters in this work. For reasons of space they will not be found at the ends of the chapters.)

Chapter 37

STAINS, TRACES, AND CHEMICAL ANALYSIS

O NE OF the most common laboratory operations is that of chemical analysis to compare two substances or to establish the constituents of a questioned substance. When large quantities are available to the chemist, the difficulties are naturally diminished. Investigative work, however, frequently leads to situations where the available traces at the scene of the crime consist of a minute sample such as a fragment of glass, a smear of lipstick, or a stained garment. In order to appreciate the potentialities of evidence of this nature and to guide him in the collection of samples, the investigator should have some knowledge of the analytical methods and instruments which are available to the laboratory technicians for this work. The techniques employed in collecting evidence in the form of stains and particles have been described in Chapter 7.

1. Spectrographic Analysis

The classical problem in the treatment of physical evidence is the analysis of minute traces. A faint smear of paint or a minute fragment of glass may constitute the vital link in the chain of evidence. To be able to establish the exact nature of the constituents of the sample and its distinctive impurities may be an essential step in the proof. Because of the minuteness of the evidence sample, ordinary methods of chemical analysis are not effective. The techniques of microanalysis can often be used in these situations, but the difficulties of these methods are sometimes discouragingly formidable. The ideal solution to such problems is the use of optical methods, of which spectrographic analysis is the most familiar and the most generally effective.

748

Figure 56. A small trace, such as that shown above, found on a burglar's tool can be analyzed for its constituents. By means of the trace, the tool and its possessor can be associated with the crime. Courtesy of Dr. James J. Manning.

a. **Advantages.** The spectroscope has been in practical use for over a century. The spectrograph (a spectroscope with an arrangement for recording on film the field of view) has been employed in chemical analysis for some fifty years. In that time its many advantages have become known to the world of chemistry. By means of this instrument it is possible to analyze minute samples in amounts of the order of a small fraction of a gram. Since only a minute part of the available physical evidence is required, subsequent tests may be made by interested parties with the remainder. The spectrograph, in addition, is an extremely rapid means of accomplishing the analysis and provides a permanent photographic record of the findings. In this latter respect, the spectrograph is, to a great extent, an objective method of analysis.

Figure 57. A comparison of the spectograms of a known and unknown substance showing similarities of basic constituents and trace elements.

b. **Nature of the Spectrograph.** The essentials of a spectroscope are remarkably simple in view of the complex problems which it solves. If a substance is burned and the resulting light dispersed through a prism, a crude spectroscope analysis has been performed. The principle of the spectroscope may be understood by reflecting on the common observation that different substances burn with different characteristic colors. When a substance is heated its characteristic atomic arrangement is disturbed; the displaced atoms send out waves of energy which are observed as colors. If this light is passed through a slit and dispersed through a prism, a broad band of different constituent colors can be seen. When an image of this color pattern is focused on a photographic plate, a series of parallel lines is presented to the photographic plate (colored lines, if color film were to be used and black lines of varying density with the ordinary film which is almost exclusively employed.) The short black lines on the film represent different colors or, in the language of physicists, wavelengths. Different lines represent different elements. Variations in the density (heaviness) of the lines correspond to varying proportions of different substances. In summary, the analysis of a substance can be reduced to the study of an arrangement of black lines on a photographic plate. A unique arrangement of lines "fingerprints" a substance for the analyst.

c. **Illustrative Cases.** In general, the spectrographic method is useful in analyzing inorganic substances. Modifications of the instrument are employed for organic substances. Inorganic materials include many common clue materials such as paint, glass, and metals. The following examples will illustrate the application of the spectrograph to criminal investigation:

1) *Hit-and-Run.* A police officer pursuing a criminal fired to the side of him in warning. The bullet struck the fugitive and killed him. The deceased was a member of a politically active minority group, and his death was readily attributed to police brutality since the offense of which he had been suspected was not serious. The police officer claimed that the bullet had ricocheted from a nearby automobile. Laboratory technicians examined the car and found a crease in a significant area. The medical examiner, on examining the bullet recovered from the body of the deceased, found that it bore traces of paint. Spectrographic analysis of this minute sample of

Figure 58. Infrared spectrophotometer. This instrument is especially effective in the chemical analysis of organic substances. Courtesy of the New York Police Laboratory.

paint established that it was identical with the paint on the car, thus verifying the police officer's story.

In a typical hit-and-run case, bits of paint from the missing car may be found on the buttons or belt of the victim. As soon as a car is picked up on suspicion, a sample of its paint is sent to the laboratory for comparison by spectroscope. While in most paints the main ingredients are the same, a specific batch of paint may be identified by its content of trace elements, or impurities. Here the police scientist resorts to the theory of probability. If, to take an over-simplified case, we assume that the probability of finding a specific impurity in a given batch of paint is one in ten, and if we find ten such impurities, the probability that just this combination of impurities will be found in any other batch of paint is only one chance in ten billion. Obviously such a coincidence is far beyond the leeway provided by reasonable doubt; the chances of finding two identical batches of paint of this composition may be even smaller than of finding two human fingerprints exactly alike. In practice the situation is not usually so clear-cut. Some elements are more common than others; some tend to run in groups. The probability calculation is often exceedingly complex, and part of the technician's job is to phrase the results in accurate terms that are comprehensible in the courtroom.

2. The Spectrophotometer

The spectrophotometer also has proved its worth in crime detection. It can detect tiny differences in inks, dyes, lipsticks, and other organic materials. Moreover, it provides evidence in precise, objective mathematical terms and is especially valuable in court. The spectrophotometer was used effectively in a recent mugging case. A woman walking home from the subway was gripped from behind by an assailant who clapped his hand over her mouth, grabbed her handbag, and ran. She screamed for help. A few minutes later a man was picked up by the police three blocks from the scene. The woman had not seen the thief's face, and there was no evidence to link the suspect to the crime except his proximity, his suspicious behavior, and a red smear on the palm of his left hand. But a spectrophotometric analysis showed that the substance on his hand gave the same absorption spectrum as the woman's lipstick. This, with supporting evidence, was sufficient to convict the accused.

3. X-ray Diffraction

When a stain can be made to yield crystals, or at least a substance which is not truly amorphous, it may be analyzed by x-ray diffraction. An x-ray diffraction camera can distinguish substances identical in chemical constituency but differing in atomic arrangement. Not long ago a man was found dead on the ground beneath the

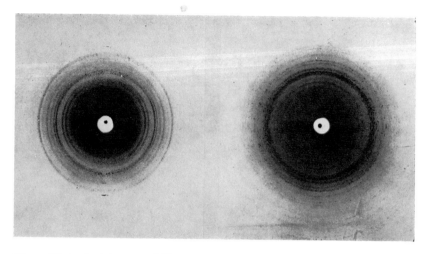

Figure 59. Analysis by x-ray diffraction patterns of (a) phenobarbital and (b) sodium pentobarbital.

window of his garret room. It was supposed that he had committed suicide. But on the low, slanting ceiling near the window were some black smudges. An x-ray diffraction picture showed that the material was the same as that in the heels of the deceased's shoes. The smudges could hardly have been made on the ceiling if he had jumped; he must have been picked up and pushed out. After further investigation two casual acquaintances of the man were arrested, and they admitted they had been with him. X-ray diffraction is used to identify and compare barbiturates, which are ordinarily distinguishable only by their melting points. Grease stains can also be recognized by this device. In one case the prosecution claimed that the stain on a defendant's clothing was kitchen grease from the scene of the crime. The defense maintained that it was auto grease. X-ray diffraction analysis of the sample, less than a milligram, proved that the stain was kitchen grease.

4. The Electron Microscope

The electron microscope promises to yield valuable information from such clue materials as dust, metals, fibers, inks, and other materials whose particle size and distribution cannot be differentiated by less sensitive instruments. It was used effectively in connection with the murder of a woman by a burglar. A suspect was "developed," but the police could discover no stolen property in his possession, nor could they trace his activities on the night in question. They did, however, find in his room a towel bearing a pink stain. The laboratory determined that this small stain was face powder, and under the electron microscope it was identified with powder in the woman's compact. Faced with this evidence, the suspect confessed to the crime.

5. Neutron Activation Analysis

The principle of neutron activation analysis depends on measuring the wavelength and intensity of the radiation given off by the radioactive substances that are induced in the specimen (or evidence sample) when it is subjected to a stream of neutrons. These measurements serve as qualitative and quantitative determinations of the constituents of the sample and as a means of unique identification. The method is a non-destructive, ultra-microanalytical tool of extreme sensitivity. It is anticipated that measurements of the major and minor constituents of hair, fingernails, blood, and other substances, performed by this means, can serve as a means of identification.

At least seventy elements can be readily identified and quantitatively determined in terms of measurements made on radioactive end products resulting from the interaction of their stable isotopes with a neutron source. Each of these end products (induced radionuclides) decays according to a fixed half-life period, emitting a characteristic radiation as it decays. Since many of the radionuclides emit radiation in the gamma region of varying intensities, the technique of gamma scintillation spectrometry is applied to give a graphic picture of the analysis. A plot of the intensity of radiation against wavelength results in a set of photopeaks or, perhaps, in a single photopeak that characterizes a specific radionuclide and, in turn, the stable element of which it is an end product. A measure of the intensity of radiation in the photopeak can be used as a measure of the quantity of the stable element in the sample. Thus, the location and height of the photopeaks can provide a uniquely identifying picture of the sample.

The analytical potential of this method is illustrated by the procedure proposed for the determination of the firing hand by means of powder residue. The failure of the dermal nitrate or paraffin test (p. 771) to achieve widespread acceptance has been attributed by its opponents to its lack of qualitative specificity and by its proponents to an absence of full understanding and technical competence in its application. Neutron activation analysis has been proposed as an effective means of determining the presence of gunpowder residue on the back of the firing hand. Tests performed on such residue indicate that all revolver ammunition leaves readily measurable traces of antimony on the back of the hand; in many cases traces of barium are deposited and in some cases traces of copper can be found. Following the procedure described above, the residue, after being removed from the hand, is subjected to activation for thirty to sixty minutes in a TRIGA reactor; the induced substances (radionuclides) are separated radiochemically; their half-life periods, radiation wavelengths, and intensities are measured. The radionuclides in this examination would be Sb-122 (an isotope of antimony with a half-life of 28 days); Ba-189 (a barium isotope with an 85 minute half-life); and Cu-64 (a copper isotope with a 12.8-hour half-life). Lead is not used in this analysis since the induced activity of Pb-209 is a pure beta radiation.

ADDITIONAL READING

Electron Microscopy

Brown, J.L. and Johnson, J.W.: Electron Microscopy and X-Ray Microanalysis in Forensic Science. 5 *Journal of the Association of Official Analytical Chemists*, 930, 1973.

Microscope and Crime. 236 *Nature*, 427, 1972.

Paplauskas, L.: The Scanning Electron Microscope: A New Way to Examine Holes in Fabric. 1 *Journal of Police Science and Administration*, 362, 1973.

Taylor, M.E.: Scanning Electron Microscopy in Forensic Science. 13 *Journal of the Forensic Science Society*, 269, 1973.

Neutron Activation Analysis

Cason, J.L.: Neutron Radiography with ^{252}Cf in Forensic Science. 17 *Journal of Forensic Sciences*, 79, 1972.

Chan, R.K.H.: Identification of Single-Stranded Copper Wire by Non-destructive Neutron Activation Analysis. 17 *Journal of Forensic Sciences*, 93, 1972.

Hackleman, R.P. and Graber, F.M.: *Applications of Neutron Activation Analysis in Scientific Crime Investigation—Final Report*. Springfield, Va.: National Technical Information Service, 1970.

Lukens, H.R. and Guinn, V.P.: Neutron Activation Analysis. 16 *Journal of Forensic Sciences*, 301, 1971.

Ostroff, E.: Restoration of Photographs by Neutron Activation Analysis. 154 *Science*, Oct. 7, 1966.

Chromatography

Jain, N.C., et al.: Identification of Paints by Pyrolysis-Gas Chromatography. 5 *Journal of the Forensic Science Society*, 102, 1965.

Permisohn, R.C., Hilpert, L.R. and Kazyak, L.: Determination of Methaqualone in Urine by Metabolite Detection via Gas Chromatography. 21 *Journal of Forensic Sciences*, 98, 1976.

Sullivan, R.C., et al.: Evaluation and Selection of Gas Chromatography/Mass Spectrometry Systems for the Identification of Dangerous Drugs. 2 *Journal of Police Science and Administration*, 185, 1974.

Metals

Lingane, J.I.: *Analytical Chemistry of Selected Metallic Elements*. New York, Van Nostrand Reinhold, 1966.

Wilson, M.L.: *Nondestructive Rapid Identification of Metals and Alloys by Spot Test*. Tech Brief 70-10520. Hampton, Va.: NASA Langley Research Center, 1970.

Glass

Cobb, P.G.W.: A Survey of the Variations of the Physical Properties of Glass. 8 *Journal of the Forensic Science Society*, 29, 1968.

McJunkins, S.P. and Thornton, J.I.: Glass Fracture Analysis. A Review. 2 *Forensic Science*, 1, 1973.

Pearson, E.F., May, R.W. and Dabbs, M.D.: Glass and Paint Fragments Found in Men's Outer Clothing—A Report of Survey. 16 *Journal of Forensic Sciences*, 283, 1971.

Reeve, V., et al.: Elemental Analysis by Energy Dispersive X-Ray: A Significant Factor in the Forensic Analysis of Glass. 21 *Journal of Forensic Sciences*, 291, 1976.

Cosmetics

Balsam, M.S. and Sagarin, E. (Eds.): *Cosmetic Science and Technology*, 2 vols. New York, Wiley, 1970.

Barker, A.M.L. and Clarke, P.D.B.: Examination of Small Quantities of Lipsticks. 12 *Journal of the Forensic Science Society*, 449, 1972.

Lucas, D. and Eijgelaar, G.: An Evaluation of a Technique for the Examination of Lipstick Stains. 6 *Journal of Forensic Sciences*, 354, 1961.

Vegetable Materials

Joce, C.R.B. and Curry, S.H.: *The Botany and Chemistry of Cannabis*. London, Churchill, 1970.

Stahl, E. (Ed.): *Drug Analysis by Chromatography and Microscopy*. Ann Arbor, Mich.: Ann Arbor Press, 1973.

Thornton, J.I. and Nakamura, G.R.: The Identification of Marijuana. 12 *Journal of the Forensic Science Society*, 461, 1972.

Soils

Bridges, E.W.: *World Soils*. Wolfe City, Texas, University Press, 1970.

Heinrich, E.W.: *Microscopic Identification of Minerals*. New York, McGraw-Hill, 1966.

Muckman, H. and Brady, N.C.: *The Nature and Properties of Soil*, 7th ed. New York, McGraw-Hill, 1969.

Murray, R.C., and Tedrow, J.C.: *Forensic Geology*. New Brunswick, N.J.: Rutgers University Press, 1975.

Murray, R.C.: Soil and Rocks as Evidence. 24 *Law and Order*, 7, 1976.

Paint

Crown, D.A.: *The Forensic Examination of Paint and Pigments*. Springfield, Ill.: Thomas, 1968.

Haag, L.C.: Element Profiles of Automotive Paint Chips by X-ray Fluorescence Spectrometry. 16 *Journal of the Forensic Science Society*, 255, 1976.

Leete, C.G. and Mills, R.M.: *Reference Collection of Automotive Paint Colors*. Washington, D.C.: National Bureau of Standards, 1975.

May, R.W. and Porter, J.: An Evaluation of Common Methods of Paint Analysis. 15 *Journal of the Forensic Science Society*, 137, 1975.

O'Neill, L.A.: Analysis of Paints by Infrared Spectroscopy. 7 *Medicine, Science and the Law*, 145, 1967.

Paint Examination Techniques Utilized in the FBI Laboratory. 42 *FBI Law Enforcement Bulletin*, 4, 1973.

Reeve, V. and Keener, T.: Programmed Energy Dispersive X-Ray Analysis of Top Coats of Automotive Paint. 21 *Journal of Forensic Sciences*, 883, 1976.

Rodgers, P.G., et al.: The Classification of Automotive Paint by Diamond Window Infrared Spectrophotometry. Part II, Automotive Topcoats and Undercoats. 9 *Canadian Society of Forensic Science Journal*, 2, 1976.

Schlesinger, H. and Lukens, H.R.: *Forensic Neutron Activation Analysis of Paint*. Springfield, Va.: National Technical Information Service, 1970.

Steinberg, H.L.: *Standard Reference Collections of Forensic Science Materials*. Washington, D.C.: U.S. Government Printing Office, 1977.

Tweed, F.T., et al.: The Forensic Microanalysis of Paints, Plastics and other Materals by an Infrared Diamond Cell Technique. 4 *Forensic Science*, 3, 1974.

Trace Elements

Bosen, S.F. and Scheuing, D.R.: A Rapid Microtechnique for the Detection of Trace Metals from Gunshot Residues. 21 *Journal of Forensic Sciences*, 163, 1976.

Krishnan, S.S.: Detection of Gunshot Residues on the Hands by Trace Element Analysis. 22 *Journal of Forensic Sciences*, 304, 1977.

____:Examination of Paints by Trace Element Analysis. 21 *Journal of Forensic Sciences*, 908, 1976.

Obrusnik, I., et al.: The Variation of Trace Element Concentrations in Single Human Head Hairs. 17 *Journal of Forensic Sciences*, 426, 1972.

Trace Metal Detection Technique in Law Enforcement. Washington, D.C.: U.S.Government Printing Office, 1970.

Chapter 38

FIREARMS

1. Introduction

THE WIDESPREAD use of firearms is, perhaps, the most individual characteristic of American crime. The United States, the birthplace of the revolver, has been prolific in its production of firearms and indiscriminate in their distribution. As a consequence, most serious crimes in this country have, as an attending circumstance, the use or at least the possession of a firearm. Quite frequently the crime is solved by tracing or otherwise establishing ownership of a pistol or revolver. The evidence found at the scene is usually one of the following: the bullet, the cartridge case, the firearm, the wound, or indication of the trajectory. A study of these five elements can sometimes lead to the owner of the weapon and thence to the establishment of criminal responsibility. Since a criminally owned weapon is often used in a series of crimes, this type of evidence is of paramount importance. Moreover, in many states the mere custody of small arms without a license is a felony, and the criminal, in the absence of other evidence more intimately associating him with the crime at hand, is charged with illegal possession of a firearm. Every investigative agency should foster a firearms specialist. This is not a difficult matter, since the study of firearms is a popular hobby to which a considerable number of investigators are addicted. Naturally, the firearms hobbyist should not be confused with the firearms identification expert, whose status can be attained only by years of study and experience. Small communities can usually refer the difficult aspects of a firearms identification to an expert in the FBI, state police, or in a neighboring city. There should, however, be locally available a firearms specialist who can properly make an initial examination at the scene of the crime; collect, mark, and label the evidence; establish the possible value of the evidence; and, with reasonable accuracy, indicate the issues in question.

2. Tracing Guns

The problems of tracing guns have been outlined on page 575. Police departments and firearms dealers find difficulty in maintaining accurate records of ownership of handguns. A further complication arises from the great number of unregistered guns that were brought into the country during the World War II and subsequent war periods. Inadequate distribution records of military handguns, variations in state licensing laws, the lack of any central exchange for gun information, and failures to record significant data in describing handguns are additional obstacles. The situation is further complicated by the existence of millions of junk handguns—the *Saturday night specials*. The dimensions of the problem are known: the citizens of the United States own 30 million handguns and 100 million rifles and shotguns. In a typical year guns will be responsible for 3,000 accidental deaths, 7,000 suicides and 10,000 murders. In 1970 over 500 persons were murdered in New York City with handguns, while only three persons suffered this fate in Tokyo.

3. Problems Concerned With Firearms

The services of a firearms examiner can be used whenever a gun comes into the custody of the police under suspicious circumstances, especially in connection with cases of robbery, assault, suicide, and homicide. The classical question raised in a homicide case is: "Who fired the fatal shot?" "This inquiry raises further questions: "Who owned the gun?" "Is this the gun that fired the fatal bullet?" and so on. The subsequent investigation of the firearms problems will center about the following points:

a. **Identification.** 1) From what type of gun was the evidence bullet fired? The type of firearm may often be established through an examination of the bullet or the case.

2) Is this the gun that fired the fatal bullet? Here the questioned bullet is compared with a specific firearm.

3) Is this the gun from which the evidence case or shell was fired?

4) Were these filler wads or top-wads fired by a shotgun such as the one in question?

b. **Trajectory and Distance.** The location and point of view of the person firing the fatal shot are of importance in the investigation of homicide. A knowledge of the discharge distance assists in distinguishing suicide from murder. The approximate discharge distance can be estimated from a study and comparison of powder patterns on clothing and skin or, in the case of shotguns, from an examination of the shot pattern.

c. **Other Problems.** It should be borne in mind that in practice only a small percentage of forensic firearm examinations limit themselves to identification. The firearms examiner concerns himself with a great many other practical considerations (for example the workability or functioning condition of the weapon) too numerous to detail here.

4. Outline of Firearms Identification

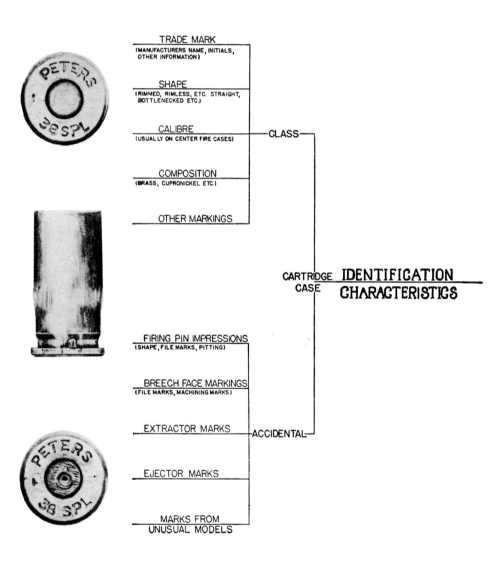

TRADE MARK
(MANUFACTURERS NAME, INITIALS, OTHER INFORMATION)

SHAPE
(RIMMED, RIMLESS, ETC. STRAIGHT, BOTTLENECKED ETC.)

CALIBRE
(USUALLY ON CENTER FIRE CASES)

COMPOSITION
(BRASS, CUPRONICKEL ETC.)

OTHER MARKINGS

CLASS

FIRING PIN IMPRESSIONS
(SHAPE, FILE MARKS, PITTING)

BREECH FACE MARKINGS
(FILE MARKS, MACHINING MARKS)

EXTRACTOR MARKS

EJECTOR MARKS

MARKS FROM UNUSUAL MODELS

ACCIDENTAL

CARTRIDGE CASE

IDENTIFICATION CHARACTERISTICS

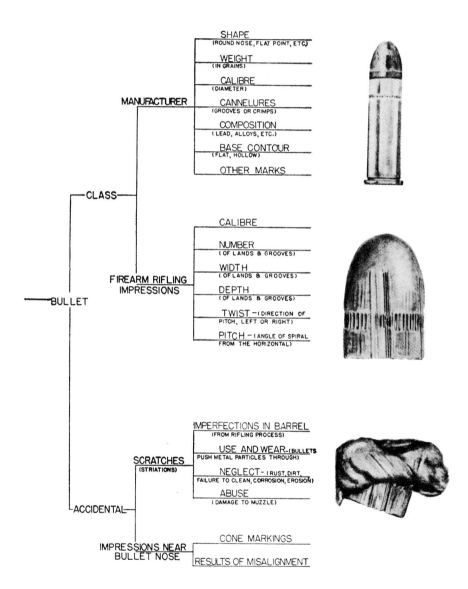

- BULLET
  - CLASS
    - MANUFACTURER
      - SHAPE (ROUND NOSE, FLAT POINT, ETC.)
      - WEIGHT (IN GRAINS)
      - CALIBRE (DIAMETER)
      - CANNELURES (GROOVES OR CRIMPS)
      - COMPOSITION (LEAD, ALLOYS, ETC.)
      - BASE CONTOUR (FLAT, HOLLOW)
      - OTHER MARKS
    - FIREARM RIFLING IMPRESSIONS
      - CALIBRE
      - NUMBER (OF LANDS & GROOVES)
      - WIDTH (OF LANDS & GROOVES)
      - DEPTH (OF LANDS & GROOVES)
      - TWIST — (DIRECTION OF PITCH, LEFT OR RIGHT)
      - PITCH — (ANGLE OF SPIRAL FROM THE HORIZONTAL)
  - ACCIDENTAL
    - SCRATCHES (STRIATIONS)
      - IMPERFECTIONS IN BARREL (FROM RIFLING PROCESS)
      - USE AND WEAR — (BULLETS PUSH METAL PARTICLES THROUGH)
      - NEGLECT — (RUST, DIRT, FAILURE TO CLEAN, CORROSION, EROSION)
      - ABUSE (DAMAGE TO MUZZLE)
    - IMPRESSIONS NEAR BULLET NOSE
      - CONE MARKINGS
      - RESULTS OF MISALIGNMENT

5. Describing The Firearm

If the investigator comes into possession of a firearm in the course of official action, he must mark, label, and describe the handgun so that it can be unquestionably identified in any subsequent legal action. As a minimum the description should contain the following information in the order given: *calibre; make; model; type; serial number;* and *finish*.

a. **Calibre.** The more common are .22, .25, .32, .38 S&W, .38 S&W Spl., and .45. In doubtful cases consult an experienced firearms man.

b. **Make.** The manufacturer's name is usually stamped on the barrel of revolvers and on the slide and frame of automatics. The most common American makers of handguns are Colt, Harrington and Richardson, Iver Johnson, and Smith and Wesson.

c. **Model.** Since two revolvers of the same calibre and make can have identical serial numbers, designation of the model is essential. Some examples are Colt "Official Police"; Smith and Wesson "Military and Police"; Iver Johnson "Trailsman 66"; and Harrington and Richardson "Young America."

d. **Type.** A term describing in general the manner of operation, such as *revolver, automatic, semi-automatic,* and *single shot*. Some knowledge of firearms is required in distinguishing certain types. Several single shot target pistols, for example, resemble automatics and are best identified as to type by the absence of a magazine in the grip.

e. **Serial Number.** These are located in various areas on handguns. Even on guns of the same manufacture, the positions of such numbers may be reversed. On the very old Colt revolvers, for example, the serial number is located in the area where the parts number would be found on the modern Colt. On some handguns the serial numbers are not visible unless the weapon is disassembled. The investigator should not dismantle a gun to find hidden serial numbers, if it is planned to submit the gun later to a firearms expert for examination.

f. **Finish.** This term describes the color and surface of the firearm. The most common examples are *Blue, Nickel,* and *Parkerized* (the dull gray appearance of military handguns).

g. **Additional Data.** If the gun is difficult to describe, include such other characteristics as *barrel length, overall length,* and the number of chambers or magazine capacity. Barrel length of a revolver is measured from the muzzle to the front end of the cylinder. The barrel length of an automatic is measured from the muzzle to the face of the breech. Items such as "ducks-bill hammer," "ramped sights," or a broken trigger guard should be recorded. With foreign-made automatics give any markings stamped on the slide or frame, since these often are indications of the model and place of manufacture. Remember: Too much information rather than too little should be the rule in describing handguns. Why? For the simple reason that size, model, make and serial number do not identify firearms. The description ".32, H. & R., Serial #12345," for example, is inadequate, since the description may fit eight or more different firearms. Finally, consider the Remington .41 cal. Derringer. It has been estimated that about 250,000 were distributed; yet most of these weapons have only *three-digit* serial numbers.

6. Identification Procedure

The term *firearms identification* is concerned primarily with two problems: first, from a bullet or cartridge case found at the scene of the crime to determine the kind of firearm used; second, from the bullet or cartridge case to determine whether an individual, "suspected" firearm was used. The first problem is more commonly solved. The second problem is more difficult and is only infrequently treated with success. The class and individual characteristics of the bullet and case form the bases of the solutions.

a. **The Bullet.** In the manufacture of ammunition, the bullet is produced with certain gross physical properties or general characteristics. Many of these properties remain intact after firing and serve to indicate the nature of the firearm for which they were intended. After being discharged from a firearm, the bullet is stamped with an additional set of general characteristics which more closely identify the types and make of gun. In addition, the firearm may impress upon the bullet a set of individual characteristics which serve to identify the individual gun.

1) **General Characteristics (Manufacture).** Although weight, approximate diameter, and approximate length of a fired bullet are not always proof of calibre, these and other characteristics are unquestionably helpful in determining the nature of the ammunition.

a) *Weight* in grains is characteristic but variations of several grains are within the limits of tolerance and hence not significant.

b) *Material*. Soft-nosed, lead, and other designations.

c) *Diameter* is measured to determine calibre. Obviously this and other dimensions are often greatly distorted in striking hard objects.

d) *Cannelures* are knurled grooves on the curved surface.

e) *Contour* or shape, although subject to distortion from impact, is often retained after firing.

f) *Base*, whether flat or hollow, is another useful characteristic.

g) *Size and weight* serve to identify shotgun pellets.

2) **General Characteristics (Rifling Impression).** a) *Land impressions* slant to the left or right, corresponding to the direction of twist in the bore of the firearm. These impressions are produced by the "lands" of the barrel, which are raised ribs running in a spiral (helix) lengthwise through the bore. The lands are impressed in the barrel by the cutting of grooves. The surfaces of the lands are the original surfaces of the interior of the barrel before the rifling is cut.

b) *Groove impressions* correspond to the grooves or indentations produced by the rifling cuts. They are equal in number to the lands. In different manufacturers they vary in width; depth (usually from .0035 to .005 inches deep); driven edges (whether rounded or not); and angle of spiral. The width of the lands is usually slightly less than that of the grooves except in the case of firearms using small bullets.

c) *Rifling* is the result of cutting grooves in the barrel and serves to impart a spin to the bullet, thus providing the necessary rotational inertia and permitting elongated instead of round bullets to be used. The cutting tools used in the rifling process often produce characteristic marks in a series of guns.

d) *Diameter* is measured in two ways: Bore diameter is the distance from land to land; groove diameter is the distance from bottom to bottom of opposite grooves.

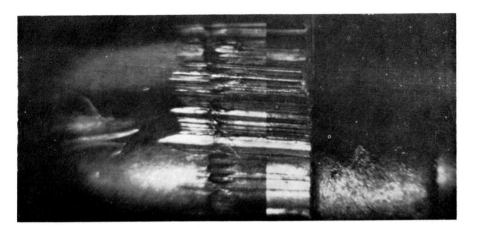

Figure 60. Photomicrograph made with the comparison microscope. The fatal bullet is seen on one side of the fine line near the center and the test bullet fired from the suspect's gun on the other. The striations of one bullet appear to run into those of the other, thus showing that they were discharged from the same weapon.

e) *Number of Lands and Grooves* varies from four to sixteen.

f) *Direction of Spiral or Pitch.* The majority of firearms are made with clockwise (right) direction to the pitch. In the United States the Colt and several other firearms have a left (counterclockwise) pitch.

g) *Pitch,* the measure of the rate at which the direction of the grooves changes is calculated by the quotient of the circumference of the bullet and the tangent of the angle of twist. In practice the pitch is not really constant, is not accurately measurable, and does not in general provide a means of positive identification.

3) **Individual Characteristics.** Imperfections in the barrel are produced in the process of manufacture or may be the result of wear and rust. They are constantly changing in a small degree because of the fragments of lead which remain in the barrel after a discharge. Succeeding bullets push forward the particles and alter the scoring. Imperfections near the muzzle of the barrel produce the most marked effect on the bullet. To answer the question "Was the fatal bullet fired from this gun?" a test bullet, obtained by firing the gun into a box of cotton, is recovered and compared with the evidence bullet. Actual comparison is attempted only after it has been determined that there are no disqualifying dissimilarities in the

general characteristics of the test and evidence bullets. A comparison microscope, consisting of two stages, two matched objectives, and a comparison eyepiece which permits viewing both bullets at the same time, is used to examine the evidence bullet in conjunction with the test bullet. The viewer sees corresponding parts of the two bullets in the same field. If striations are found to match, they can be aligned to appear collinear. The entire circumference of both bullets is studied under low magnification. Striations are found on the groove impressions as well as on the land impressions because of the fact that the bullet diameter is greater than the groove diameter of the barrel. Thus the bullet will be in contact with the entire inner surface of the barrel during passage. Rifling impressions nearer the nose of the bullet will sometimes be parallel to the longitudinal axis of the bullet. These are known as "skid marks" or "slippage." They are considered by some to be produced by worn rifling or by the action of a revolver in which the bullet travels a distance without a spinning motion, due to the absence of rifling in a cylinder.

b. **The Case.** 1) *General Characteristics.* The following class characteristics are common to large numbers of guns:

a) *Manufacture* is indicated by the name or initials stamped on the head for center fire cases and by initial or trademark for .22 calibre. Some makes are not marked.

b) *Shape* can be divided first into rim, rimless, and semi– or Auto-rim, and second into straight, tapered, or necked.

c) *Calibre* is stamped on center fire cases generally.

d) *Composition* may be brass, nickel-plated, copper, plated steel, paper, or plastic.

2) *Individual Characteristics.* The case is ejected in automatics but remains in the cylinder of revolvers until discarded by a separate ejection action. Hence, with automatics, the case is usually found at the crime scene.

a) *Firing pin indentations* are produced when the hammer striker hits and explodes the cap of the cartridge. The tip of the pin produces its own shape and also may leave a record of its file marks and pitting.

b) *Breech face markings* are produced on the case when the pressure of the generated gas drives it against the breech face or, in

Figure 61. Comparison photomicrograph of the firing pin marks on two cartridge cases. The left side of the test shell is merged with the right side of the evidence shell. The fine scratches appear to run continuously from one shell to the other.

rifles, the bolt head. File marks and machining marks are present on the breech face as a result of manufacturing processes or from use in firing and are impressed on the soft face of the primer.

c) *Extractor marks* are produced on the rim of a rimmed case and the flange, as well as sometimes on the groove of a rimless case. The cylindrical surface of the case just below the rim or groove is also marked. These marks are formed from the use of automatic, autoloading, bolt–, pump–, and lever-action rifles and shotguns, and automatic pistols. The extractor, under spring tension, is forced over the rim of the case at the moment of loading the cartridge into the chamber.

d) *Ejector marks* are found on the base of the case, the rim, or the flange. They are usually located on the side opposite the extractor marks. When the fired case is drawn from the chamber by the extractor, the base of the shell strikes against the fixed ejector and receives characteristic marks.

e) *Peculiarities* are apparent in certain gun models. The following are examples of peculiarities of two well-known firearms.

1) *Colt Automatics.* When the fired case is thrown from the firearm by the combined action of the extractor and ejector, the open end of the case strikes against the side of the slide with sufficient force to leave a flat area in one section of the circular opening. When the cartridge is in the chamber of this weapon, in firing position, the entire case is supported by the chamber except for a section near the base. At this point, a ramp has been cut away at the rear of the chamber in order to facilitate the loading operation. The expansion due to the interior pressure is not restricted in this area, so that a noticeable "hump" is left in the case after firing.

2) *Thompson Submachine Gun.* The bolt travels some distance behind the upper cartridge in the magazine. As it moves forward, the face of the bolt strikes a sharp blow against the head of the cartridge, leaving a mark on the head in the shape of a half-moon.

7. Powders

Three types of powder may be used in the ammunition for small firearms, namely, smokeless, black, and semi-smokeless. The use of black powder and semi-smokeless is practically negligible.

a. **Smokeless Powder.** This consists of cellulose nitrate with or without glycerol nitrate. In the trade these substances are called respectively nitrocellulose and nitroglycerine. To act as stabilizers, aid the firing rate, and minimize gun corrosion, substances such as nitrates, bichromates, oxalates, nitrobenzene, graphite, and petroleum jelly (Vaseline®) are added.

b. **Black Powder.** The traditional gunpowder is a mixture of saltpeter (potassium nitrate), charcoal (carbon), and sulphur in the approximate proportions of 75:15:10.

8. Dermal Nitrate Test

The dermal nitrate test (paraffin gauntlet test) is a procedure designed to determine whether a suspect has recently discharged a firearm. Melted paraffin is brushed over the "shooting" hand of a suspect until a thin coat is obtained. The glove can be built up in layers by using thin sheets of fabric until it is about ⅛″ thick. The diphenylamine reagent is prepared by adding 10 cubic centimeters of concentrated sulfuric acid to 2 milliliters of distilled water. To this is added 0.05 grams of diphenylamine. The reagent is dropped on the paraffin mold with a pipette. Dark blue specks appearing on the inner surface of the cast indicate a positive reaction. The reaction may be considered a two-stage oxidation of diphenylamine, first to diphenylbenzidine and this in turn to diphenylbenzidine violet. Theoretically, the diphenylamine reagent is used to test for the presence of nitrates, which are contained in the residue of gunpowder blown back on the hand in discharging the firearm. From the existence of nitrates on the hand and from other indications, it is concluded that the suspect discharged a gun.

a. **Objections.** There are several scientific objections to the test as described above in its simplest form. The role of the nitrate on the hand is that of an oxidizing agent. Other strong oxidizing agents can produce the same effect. Hence, launderers, chemists, pharmacists, and other persons handling bleaches or other oxidizing compounds may have materials on their hands which would yield a positive reaction. Thus the test does not necessarily indicate the presence of nitrates, but establishes merely that an oxidizing substance is present on the hand. In brief, the test is non-specific. Another objection is concerned with the fact that there are many non-incriminating sources of nitrates such as fertilizers, explosives, tobacco, urine, and cosmetics. Certain foods also contain nitrates. Finally, some experimenters have found that it is possible to obtain a negative reaction from the hand of a person who has recently fired many rounds of ammunition. Conversely, a positive reaction can be obtained from the hand of a person who has never discharged a firearm. Thus, in the hands of the uninformed, the test may be not only unreliable but also misleading. Moreover, a report of negative results in connection with a suspect who is indeed the guilty party will provide the defense with arguments that may well confuse the court. In summary, it is helpful to quote the Interpol Seminar on Scientific Aspects of Police Work: "The seminar did not consider the traditional paraffin test to be of any value, neither as evidence to put before courts, nor even as a sure indication for the police officer. The participants were of the opinion that this test should no longer be used."

b. **Proponents.** A number of experts maintain that the test is effective when performed by an experienced and competent person and that its opponents give consideration in their arguments only to the chemical aspect and ignore the physical appearances which constitute the most important part of the test. Some of the proponents place great emphasis on the topographical distribution of the blue specks in the cast, which is a characteristic configuration of gunfire and not merely the result of random contact with various materials. Even more important is the claim that the physical appearance of nitrates from gunpowder is distinguishable from nitrates from other sources when found on the hands because of the fact that the discharge of the gun tends to imbed the particles in the intradermic layers of the skin. In the test as described by Nichols, the hands of the suspect are first washed and scrubbed with cold water to remove nitrates from indifferent sources and any interfering contaminants from the surface of the skin. The hot paraffin is painted on with a sterile cotton swab. A diphenylbenzidine reagent is used on the cast because of its great sensitivity. The cast is examined for minute dark blue specks which become visible within two or three minutes. Under a magnifier these specks appear to be little mounds, as though the hot paraffin had drawn out particles of unburned gunpowder imbedded in the pores. On the basis of these phenomena and also the distribution of the specks, a positive reaction is interpreted as proof that the hand was used in the discharge of a gun.

9. Powder Residue

A positive and reliable test has been devised by Walker for the detection of powder residue on the skin and clothing of a victim of a shooting. The test detects the presence of nitrites and is designed to reproduce the pattern of the powder residue about the bullet hole.

The pattern is useful in estimating distance of discharge, a problem often arising in suspicious suicide cases. Grains of burned and unburned powder are deposited on the skin or clothing of the victim, if the muzzle of the firearm was held within 6 feet in the case of black powder and 24 inches (or even more depending on the load and other factors) in the case of smokeless powder. Ordinary glossy photographic paper (unexposed) is desensitized by immersing in a hypo bath for twenty minutes and washing in water for fifty minutes. After the paper is dried, it is placed in an 8 per cent solution of C-acid (2-naphthylamine-4, 8-disulfonic acid), for ten minutes. The paper is again hung to dry. A towel is laid on a table and the prepared paper placed on it face up. The fabric bearing the bullet hole is placed face down on the paper. Three layers of thin toweling are now placed on top of the fabric. The middle layer is slightly moistened with 20 per cent acetic acid. The other layers are dry. A warm electric iron is pressed on the arrangement for about eight minutes. On removal the prepared paper will be found to have red-orange spots corresponding in position to the partially burned powder grains about the bullet hole. A one-to-one photograph is made of the pattern. The test is specific for nitrites and insensitive to other common chemicals.

As an early example of the application of the powder residue test a

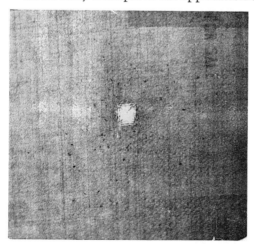

Figure 62. Powder residue about a bullet hole in dark clothing revealed by means of an infrared photograph.

1937 case may be cited in which a special patrol-man, George Schuck, shot and killed an alleged burglar, James Keenan. The special patrolman stated that he had approached Keenan in the act of removing six men's caps from a showcase in front of a hat store. Keenan had wrestled with him and attempted to escape. Thereupon Schuck discharged his revolver, the bullet striking Keenan in the heart. A question

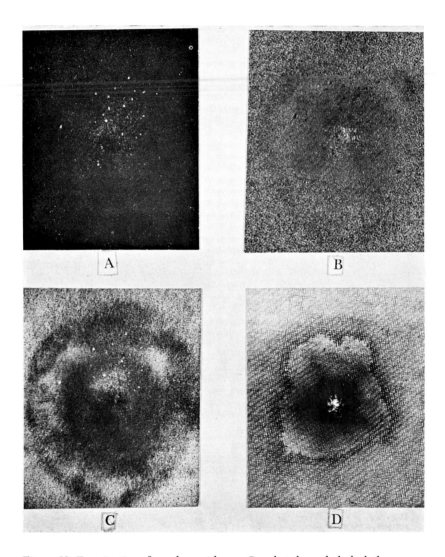

Figure 63. Examination of powder residue: a. Gunshot through dark cloth, as seen by the unaided eye. The white specks are caused by reflected light from unburned powder particles. b. An improvement in contrast and detail through the use of process ortho film. This effect can be further inhanced by means of Kodalith® Film. c. Infrared film with a Wratten 87 filter results in a marked improvement in contrast. d. The use of soft x-rays provides additional detail and tonal differences. (Type M Eastman Kodak® Film, 12 kv peak, 50 ma. 20-inch focus-film distance, 5-second exposure.) Courtesy of James Osterburg.

arose in the minds of the investigators as to the distance that separated Schuck and Keenan at the time of fire. The decedent's overcoat and other apparel were subjected to the powder residue test. From the residue present on the overcoat and from the bullet hole in the coat, it was concluded that the bullet had traveled from 4 to 7 feet before it struck Keenan. Thus, the special patrolman's account of the occurrence was corroborated and the issue of manslaughter was not raised.

10. Other Techniques for Bullet Hole Areas

Photography and radiography should precede chemical testing of bullet hole areas to provide a pattern of the powder residue, lead fouling, or smoke residue left by a discharge of a firearm.

a. **Process Film.** A simple but effective photograph can be taken with process film. The great contrast of the film provides an outline of the residue on light clothing.

b. **Infrared.** By using infrared film and a Wratten 87 filter excellent contrast can be obtained in photographing dark clothing. A fingerprint camera can be used for this purpose.

c. **Soft X-rays.** If a soft x-ray apparatus is available, a radiograph can be made of the bullet hole to reveal the lead fouling or minute particles of metal impregnated in the cloth. The following settings are satisfactory: Distance from tube to cloth, 8 inches; 15 kilovolts; 10 milliamps; and 3 seconds exposure.

11. Trace Metal Detection Technique (TMDT)

This is a technique for determining whether a person's hand or clothing has recently been in contact with a metal object such as a tool or weapon. The surface (usually the hand) to be examined is treated with a test solution and placed under the ultraviolet light, where its fluorescence can be studied and photographed. The traces left by different metals differ in the color of their fluorescence. The pattern left by handling a metal object will be determined by its shape and the way it is used. From a study of the fluorescent pattern on a person's hand the examiner can draw some useful conclusions as to whether or not he had been handling a weapon or tool. The test is not conclusive in the sense of permitting the conclusion to be drawn that the fluorescence could only have been caused by *this* particular weapon or tool. Nevertheless, it does provide additional useful information for the investigator, since a positive test suggests a strong probability.

a. **Equipment.** The TMDT test solution is a 0.1–0.2% solution of 8-Hydroxyquinoline in isopropanol (CP grade). This is applied with a plastic spray-type container, having no metal parts. In the field a battery-powered ultraviolet light source is used together with a shielding arrangement for excluding visible light.

b. **Application.** The area most commonly selected for examination is the palm and undersurface of the hand, since the investigation is usually concerned with the handling of a firearm or other metal weapon. The TMDT test solution is sprayed thoroughly over the area with the test surface held vertically to prevent puddling. After about four minutes of drying time the surface is examined under the ultraviolet lamp.

c. **Examination.** Under the ultraviolet lamp the TMDT solution produces a yellow fluorescent background. Metal trace patterns will be visible against this background in colors that are characteristic of the metal. In the case of a handgun, the examiner will look on those parts of the hand that came in contact with the gun: the index finger, which rested on the trigger; the remaining fingers and thumb which enclosed the gun; the palm; and the degree of protrusion beyond the junction of the thumb and index finger. He looks for any irregularities or distinctive marks in the pattern which may have been made by screws, protrusions, ornamentations, and other markings. A photograph is then made of the pattern produced under ultraviolet light.

d. **"Signature" Catalog.** To facilitate these examinations the police laboratory should maintain a collection of the distinctive patterns or *signatures* which are specific to types, makes, models, and calibres of these signatures. For this purpose a catalog of signatures should be prepared of as many types of specimen handguns as can reasonably be obtained. This will actually be a collection of fluorescent patterns of handguns left on the hand and photographed under the ultraviolet lamp. It should be accompanied by a record of observation of the colors and other characteristics.

e. **Conclusions.** A positive reaction will give confidence depending on the intensity and character of the color and the details of the pattern outline. It will serve as a guide to the investigator, suggesting the preferred line of inquiry.

12. New Weaponry

A number of new weapons of unusual capabilities have recently been marketed. Two of them are described here. Unfortunately there is evidence that both have been used by criminal offenders.

a. **The 180 Automatic Rifle.** This is a fearsome weapon with tremendous impact shock and fire power. Using .22 calibre long rifle ammunition, it is easily aimed and is free of noise, recoil, or other motion in firing. Since the bullet weighs 40 grains and 30 are fired in 1 second, the impact effect is that of 1,200 grains of bullet lead fired into a 2-inch circle at 20 feet in 1 second—an incredible shock. The 180 provides a powerful weapon that is relatively compact, light, and easily handled with a low noise level yet with a high cyclic rate of fire that can be safely handled by anyone with minimum training. Its magazine capacity gives the officer unlimited fire power. The 180 can chop down a telephone pole, blast through sheets of steel and cinder block, punch through a brick wall, or chew through the side of a speeding car. Because of its laser beam lighting system, users of the gun find it almost impossible even in reduced lighting conditions to miss a target. One of the most practical features of the 180 is the Laser Lok sight, an attachment that can project an intense beam of red light at a distance and centered in the middle of the point of impact. The appearance of the red dot is sufficient by itself to discourage a knowledgeable offender.

b. **The Taser.** The Taser or "Electronic Stun Gun," as it is sometimes called, is an instrument shaped like a flashlight that ejects small, barbed electrical contactors trailing up to 500 feet of wire, which attach themselves to the victim's person. A controlled electric charge is administered through the barbs until the electrical contacts are removed or the current shut off. The range of the Taser is reported to be 15 to 18 feet. When the twin triggers are pressed, a charge of gunpowder ignites, firing two missiles that strike the victim and cause him to fall virtually senseless, his muscles thrown into spasms by a supercharged jolt (50,000 volts) of electricity. It stuns without killing. The pain and injury are supposed to be transitory, over in minutes. The relative advantages and disadvantages of such an apparatus are obvious. The legal implications present a number of difficulties. Suffice it to say that the Bureau of Alcohol, Tobacco and Firearms has decided that the Taser meets the definition of a firearm under both Title I and Title II of the Gun Control Act of 1968.

13. Fingerprints on Guns

"Why were no fingerprints found on the gun?" This is a favorite question raised by defense counsel and an effective tactic with a jury whose criminalistics information is drawn mainly from remembered scenes of movies and television. On film it was customary for the evidence technician to develop the latent fingerprints of the perpetrator on the pistol or to draw the firm conclusion that the perpetrator wore gloves. This, of course, is mostly nonsense. Although it is not impossible to find a print on a pistol, it is highly improbable. The point is so important that we have taken the liberty of quoting from the *New York Times* (Mar. 13, 1973) a report of relevant testimony in this matter:

> A police expert testifying at the trial of H. Rap Brown said yesterday that it was virtually impossible to obtain usable fingerprints from a firearm.
>
> Sgt. William Torpey, who has been assigned to the Crime Lab for 18 of his 19 years on the force, was called to the stand in the State Supreme Court where Brown is on trial with three co-defendants in the armed robbery of a West Side bar and the attempted murder of several policemen in a subsequent gun battle on Oct. 16, 1971.
>
> The prosecution apparently introduced yesterday's testimony in anticipation of a defense challenge that would ask why it had not introduced fingerprint evidence linking the defendants to the various weapons that are already in evidence.
>
> Sergeant Torpey testified that during his 18 years at the Police Crime Laboratory he had examined more than 500 firearms for fingerprints and had found only one identifiable print.

"Even when fingerprints are found on a firearm," Sergeant Torpey said, "they are almost always too smudged to be useful. One reason," he said, "is that these weapons are likely to be slightly oily, especially if well kept. Another is that the person using the weapon holds it so tightly that the prints are smeared. And if the weapon is fired," he added, "the jolt smears any prints that might otherwise have been useful."

ADDITIONAL READING

Booker, J.L.: A Method for the Identification of Smokeless Powders and their Residues by Thin-Layer Chromatography of the Minor Constituents. 13 *Journal of the Forensic Science Society*, 199, 1973.

Bosen, S.F. and Scheuing, D.R.: A Rapid Microtechnique for the Detection of Trace Metals from Gunshot Residues. 21 *Journal of Forensic Sciences*, 1, 1976.

Brill, S.: *Firearms Abuse: A Research and Policy Report*. Washington, D.C.: Police Foundation, 1977.

Burrard, G.: *The Identification of Firearms and Forensic Ballistics*. New York, Barnes, 1962.

Cornelius, R. and Timperman, J.: Gunfiring Detection Method based on Sb, Ba, Pb and Hg deposits on Hands. Evaluation of the Credibility of the Test. 14 *Medicine, Science and the Law*, 2, 1974.

Dimaio, V.J.M.: Accidental Deaths Due to Dropping of Handguns. 3 *Forensic Science Gazette*, 5, 1972.

Electronic Dart Gun Immobilizer in U.S. Robberies. 18 *Security Gazette*, 3, 1976.

Fatteh, A.: *Medicolegal Investigation of Gunshot Wounds*. Philadelphia, Lippincott, 1976.

Grove, C.A., Judd, G., and Horn, R.: Examination of Firing Pin Impressions by Scanning Electron Microscopy. 17 *Journal of Forensic Sciences*, 645, 1972.

Hatcher, J.S., Jury, F.J. and Weller, J.: *Firearms Investigation, Identification and Evidence*. Harrisburg, Pa.: Stackpole, 1957.

Hendry, E.B.: Restoring a Heavily Rusted Weapon no Problem—If You Know How. 57 *Fingerprint and Identification Magazine*, 3, 1975.

Krcma, V.: *Identification and Registration of Firearms*. Springfield, Ill.: Thomas, 1971.

Krishnan, S.S.: Detection of Gunshot Residue on the Hands by Trace Element Analysis. 22 *Journal of Forensic Sciences*, 2, 1977.

Maiti, P.C.: Powder Patterns around Bullet Holes in Bloodstained Articles. 13 *Journal of the Forensic Science Society*, 197, 1973.

Martiney, B.J.: Study of Spent Cartridge Cases. 28 *International Criminal Police Review*, 270, 1973.

Mathews, J.H.: *Firearms Identification*, 3 vols. Springfield, Ill.: Thomas, Vols. I and II, 1962, Vol. III, 1973.

Millard, J.T.: *A Handbook on the Primary Identification of Revolvers and Semiautomatic Pistols*. Springfield, Ill.: Thomas, 1974.

Munhall, B.D. (Ed.): Supplementary Bibliography for the Firearms Examiner. 53 *Fingerprint and Identification Magazine*, 1, 1971.

National Institute of Law Enforcement and Criminal Justice. *Your 1976 Guide to Firearms Regulation.* Washington, D.C.: U.S. Government Printing Office, 1976.

Nesbitt, R.S., et al.: Evaluation of a Photoluminescence Technique for the Detection of Gunshot Residue. 22 *Journal of Forensic Sciences*, 2, 1977.

Pillay, K. and Sagans, J.: Gunshot Residue Collection Using Film-Lift Techniques for Neutron Activation Analysis. 2 *Journal of Police Science and Administration*, 388, 1974.

Principe, A.H., Stauffer, J.C. and Verbeke, D.J.: A New Method for Measuring Fired Bullets Employing Split-Image Analyzer. 4 *Journal of Police Science and Administration*, 56, 1976.

Schlesinger, H.L., et al.: *Special Report on Gunshot Residues Measured by Neutron Activation Analysis.* Springfield, Va.: National Technical Information Service, 1970.

Scroggie, R.J.: Firearm Silencers. 46 *FBI Law Enforcement Bulletin*, 5, 1977.

Shaw, W.: The Electronic Stun Gun. 24 *Law and Order*, 8, 1976.

Wolten, G.M. and Loper, G.L.: Detection of Gunshot Residue Status and New Approaches. 11 *Journal of California Law Enforcement*, 3, 1977.

Chapter 39

TESTS FOR INTOXICATION

1. Alcohol and Crime

THE PRESIDENT'S Commission on Drunkenness has observed that arrests for alcohol use account for more than half of all reported offenses in the United States. It has been estimated that 40 per cent of all people who are victims of a homicidal assault and 50 per cent of those who commit fatal assault are intoxicated. A comparable percentage of suicides takes place under the influence of alcohol. The incidence of other crimes is similarly affected. In addition, the mental instability and abnormality of alcohol intoxication predispose to a wide variety of accidental deaths. In fatal motor vehicle homicides, approximately 60 per cent of the responsible drivers have been drinking heavily. Obviously, the person who is investigating a homicide will be seriously interested in the relative sobriety of the victim and his assailant. If a suspect is found soon after the fatal occurrence, it may be possible to determine whether he was intoxicated at the time of the commission of the crime. The most common method of making this determination is to observe the actions of the suspect and to smell his breath. Evidence of this nature is valuable, but is far from conclusive. Shock, disease, and personal traits may suggest a state of intoxication. The odor of alcoholic beverages is deceptive and gives little indication of the amount of the beverage consumed. To present valid evidence of intoxication to a court, the investigator must request the services of persons who are capable of performing the accepted chemical tests for this determination. The investigator should at all times request a physician to take samples of the blood of the deceased for the purpose of determining alcohol concentration. In situations where there is reason to believe that a suspect is under the influence of alcohol, the investigator should endeavor to obtain the voluntary consent of the suspect for submission to a blood sampling by a physician or other qualified person.

2. Effect of Alcohol

On entering the stomach, some of the alcohol (approximately 20 per cent) is absorbed through the stomach walls and passes into the blood vessels of the intestines. At the end of fifteen minutes, the absorption of the liquor is more than half accomplished and, at the end of two hours, it is almost complete. Eventually, a fraction of the alcohol reaches the brain where it upsets the delicate mechanism that guides judgment and controls skills. According to the drinker's emotional makeup, he becomes bellicose, melancholy, friendly, or joyful. Contrary to the popular conception, alcohol is not a stimulant, but a depressant. It has a drugging action on the brain cells, slowing down their activity and affecting coordination.

3. Blood-Alcohol and Intoxication

It has long been known that there is a definite relation between the amount of alcohol in a person's blood and the degree of intoxication which he manifests, i.e., the amount of alcohol in his brain. The relation appears to be fairly simple—the more alcohol in the blood, the more intoxicated the subject. It is found that when the alcohol concentration is greater than 1.5 parts per 1000, the person is under the influence. At three parts per thousand, he is intoxicated; at four parts per thousand, he becomes unconscious, after five parts per thousand he will probably die. It is possible, then, by analyzing a blood sample from the victim of a homicide to determine whether he was intoxicated at the time of his death. It may also be stated, although this aspect of the subject is not the chief concern of this section, that it is possible to determine whether a suspect in a homicide was under the influence of alcohol at the time of the fatal act if samples of his blood are taken soon after the occurrence. Although blood is the most reliable body medium for this determination, other body substances such as urine or breath can be used.

4. Blood-Alcohol Zones

The problem of intoxication has been investigated extensively in relation to its effect on automobile driving. A correlaton between the degree of impairment of a person's mental and physical faculties by alcohol and its concentration as determined chemically in certain body fluids has been established authoritatively by two groups: the *Committee to Study Problems of Motor Vehicle Accidents* of the American Medical Association and the *Committee on Tests for Intoxication* of the National Safety Council. The standards which they have established have been approved by the American Bar Association. In describing the three zones which are commonly employed as measures of intoxication the term *blood alcohol per cent* is used. In this measure the parts of alcohol per thousand are expressed as a percentage. Thus 1.5 parts of alcohol per thousand parts of alcohol per thousand parts blood becomes 0.15 per cent.

a. **Zone 1 (0.00–0.05 per cent).** Blood alcohol values in this zone are considered fairly good evidence that the person is sober. The ordinary person is not affected by this amount of alcohol. To reach this level, the average person must drink approximately two ounces of whiskey or two 12-oz. bottles of beer on an empty stomach.

b. **Zone 2 (0.05–0.15 per cent).** Some persons will be under the influence at this level; others will not. The blood alcohol levels in this zone are inconclusive by themselves. This is the region in which a person has taken from 2 to 6 ounces of whiskey or from two to six 12-oz. bottles of beer.

c. **Zone 3 (above 0.15 per cent).** This concentration of alcohol is *prima facie* evidence that a person is under the influence of alcohol. Unless good evidence to the contrary can be presented, the person will be considered intoxicated. To reach this level, the average person must drink 8 ounces of whiskey or eight 12-oz. bottles of beer.

5. Significance of the Zones

The use of upper (0.15 per cent) and lower (0.05 per cent) limits serves to overcome the objections which are sometimes raised against the use of the concentration of alcohol in the body fluids as an index of intoxication. Zone 1 protects those who might be wrongly accused of being under the influence of alcohol because of certain physical symptoms such as a flushed face, halting speech, alcohol odor, or lack of coordination or who may be suffering from pathological conditions which gave the appearance of intoxication. Zone 3 serves to detect those who after the shock of an accident or the stimulus of an assault may appear to be sober.

6. Sampling from Dead Bodies

In cases of homicide or suicide, the investigator should request the surgeon performing the autopsy to take a sample of blood for the purposes of a blood-alcohol analysis. The blood must, of course, be taken before an embalming fluid is used. The specimens should be taken as soon as possible. Two blood specimens should be reserved for use by the defense in the event there is a request for another analysis. A 4 or 6-ounce size bottle should be used. In order to preserve the sample, 20 to 30 grains of sodium fluoride should be added to each bottle. The specimens should be sealed and labeled in the presence of witnesses. The label should show an identification number, the date, time, and place at which the specimen was obtained and the signature of the person taking the specimen.

7. Intoxication Tests for Persons Living

The question of the sobriety of a suspect in a criminal case has an important bearing on such matters as intent and negligence. This statement is particularly applicable in motor vehicle homicides. In other types of homicide, the problem of drunkenness will also arise. A suspect who is relatively sober may later claim that he was intoxicated at the time of the fatal act. More commonly, a guilty suspect who performed the act in a moment of drunken recklessness may appear to be sober and pretend to have been dissociated from the social events preceding the homicide. In any of these situations, the value of a sobriety test is obvious.

8. Rights Against Self-Incrimination

The constitutionality of compulsory chemical tests to determine alcoholic intoxication has been the object of extensive study in legal circles. At present the taking of samples of blood and urine for intoxication tests is not, in most jurisdictions, considered to be in violation of the suspect's rights, and conclusions drawn as a result of a chemical analysis of the samples may be used as evidence of his intoxication in a trial. In some jurisdictions refusal to submit to the test subjects the driver to the penalty of revocation of his operator's license for a lengthy period of time.

9. Media for Testing

An analysis of a blood sample is the most direct and reliable way of measuring alcohol concentration in a person's blood. Urine and breath are the other body substances used for this purpose. Since intoxication tests are most commonly used in connection with motor vehicle accident investigations, law enforcement agencies have found the breath tests most convenient. The breath sample, collected by means of a balloon, is analyzed for alcohol content by means of an apparatus (such as the "Breathalyzer") designed to give direct readings in blood-alcohol per cent after a few simple operations. Recently some jurisdictions have introduced the requirement of a confirmatory blood test where the breath test gives a positive finding above 0.15 per cent.

10. Taking Blood Specimens

Blood specimens should be taken only by a physician, medical technologist, or other person with similar qualifications. In jurisdictions requiring this condition, they should be taken only with the consent of the person, unless he is in an unconscious condition. When taking the specimen, the skin and the instruments must not be disinfected with alcohol, ether, or other volatile reducing organic fluid. A 1:1000 bichloride of mercury solution should be used as a disinfectant. Two samples of at least 10 cubic centimeters should be taken. The samples should be collected in wide-mouth bottles and closed tightly with rubber stoppers. Approximately five grains of sodium fluoride should be added as a preservative. Each specimen should be sealed with gummed paper in the presence of witnesses. The label should show an identification number, the date, time, and place at which the spcimen was obtained, and the signature of the person taking the specimen. The person who supervises the taking of the specimens should deliver them personally to the chemist, technologist, or physician who is to analyze them. If they are to be sent to a distant laboratory, he should supervise the mailing. If the specimen is to be stored, it should be kept under lock and key in a cool place. The addition of the preservative will maintain the value of the specimen during any considerable lapse of time between the taking of the sample and its analysis.

ADDITIONAL READING

Alcohol and the Impaired Driver. A Manual on the Medicolegal Aspects of Chemical Tests for Intoxication with Supplement on Breath/Alcohol Tests. Chicago, National Safety Council, 1976.

Barnett, C.W.H.: Blood and Urine Alcohol Test Procedures. 120 *New Law Journal*, 949, 1970.

Borkenstein, R.F.: *The Role of the Drinking Driver in Traffic Accidents.* Bloomington, Indiana University Press, 1964.

Bradford, L.W.: Drinking Driver Enforcement Problems. 57 *Journal of Criminal Law, Criminology and Police Science*, 518, 1966.

————: Breathalyzer Experiences under Operating Conditions Recommended by the California Association of Criminalists. 9 *Journal of the Forensic Science Society*, 58, 1969.

Defeating the Breathalyzer. 4 *British Medical Journal*, 745, 1972.

Erwin, R.E.: *Defense of Drunk Driving Cases*, 2nd ed. San Francisco, Matthew Bender, 1966.

————: There is No Danger of a Fair Trial in a Drunk Driving Case. 51 *California State Bar Journal*, 3, 1976.

Landauer, A.A.: The Accuracy, Reliability and Validity of the Breathalyzer. 5 *Australian and New Zealand Journal of Criminology*, 250, 1972.

Little, J.W.: Statistical Relationships between Presumptive Blood Alcohol Concentration Limits of Illegality and Measured BAC's of 278 Drunk Drivers. 63 *Journal of Criminal Law, Criminology and Police Science*, 278, 1972.

Pitchess, P.J.: Sheriff Focuses on Drunk Drivers. 41 *Police Chief*, 11, 1974.

President's Commission on Law Enforcement and Administration of Justice. *Drunkenness: Task Force Report.* Washington, D.C.: U.S. Government Printing Office, 1967.

Randolph, C.C. and Randolph, D.G.: Breathalyzer—Statutory and Constitutional Deficiencies. 9 *Wake Forest Law Review*, 331, 1973.

Chapter 40

TRACING MATERIALS AND DETECTIVE DYES

1. General

A_N IMPORTANT technical aid for the investigation of systematic petty larcenies and, in general, for the detection of unknown perpetrators of localized acts is the use of staining powders such as methylene blue and uranyl phosphate which will temporarily mark a culprit in a recognizable manner. To detect a thief, for example, a planted wallet may be dusted with a methylene blue, a powder. When the thief touches the wallet, the powder clings to his hands and in the presence of perspiration is turned into a deep-staining dye. A surveillance of washrooms and towels will usually reveal the culprit. A more elaborate use of tracing powder is illustrated by the following case in which the problem of trailing a narcotics seller was solved. The narcotics pusher would sell his wares to an addict in the street and disappear into a five-story tenement building where it was believed a ring of sellers had their headquarters. The police planned to conduct a surprise raid to trap the leaders of this group. An addict was employed as confederate. He was given a number of dollar bills which had been dusted with uranyl phosphate, a powder fluorescing brilliantly under ultraviolet radiation. The currency was placed in an envelope. The addict then used the money to buy a deck of heroin from the pusher in a street sale. Before completing the transaction the seller felt within the envelope to count his money. Subsequently he disappeared into the tenement house. The sale had been kept under surveillance by the investigators who now drove up to the tenement and alighted with a portable ultraviolet lamp. The lights on each landing were dimmed and the ultraviolet lamp was played on the doorknobs. Finally, one of the knobs was found to bear some bright, shining particles of the powder. A raid was quickly arranged and the local headquarters of the narcotics ring was discovered.

2. Methods

There are three basic methods of employing tracing powders:

a. **Staining.** In this method a powder is employed which on touching the skin will be converted to a dye by the moisture. The powder is selected for the permanence of its stain and for its color. If a brown wallet, for example, it to be treated, a powder of similar color is selected. The following are some of the powders which have been found useful:

Name	Color-Dry	Color-Wet
Crystal Violet	Green	Violet
Chrysoidine	Maroon	Orange
Malachite Green	Green	Green
Methylene Blue	Dark Green	Blue
Rhodamine B	Brown	Cherry

b. **Fluorescent.** One of the disadvantages of using staining powders is the necessity for maintaining surveillance, since the stain can be removed by persistent washing. To avoid this requirement a powder which fluoresces under ultraviolet radiation can be used. The powder is used in small quantities and is invisible to the culprit. Under the ultraviolet lamp each speck of the substance fluoresces brightly. The following powders can be used for this purpose:

Name	Visible Color	Color in Ultraviolet
Fluorescein	Maroon	Yellow
Rhodamine B	Brown	Orange
Uranyl Nitrate	Yellow	Yellow

c. **Chemical Detectors.** As a tracing material for liquids which are subject to theft or illicit use, a chemical indicator or a fluorescent material can be added. These techniques are discussed more fully below.

3. Application

The investigator will find that tracing materials can be used in a wide variety of cases. A number of these are described below, but the investigator's imagination will readily suggest many others.

a. **Thefts.** Systematic petty larcenies in barracks, dormitories, or locker rooms provide the most obvious use of detective dyes. The object of the larceny, a wallet or pocketbook, is powdered with one of the tracing substances selected for its color in relation to that of the background. A close surveillance should be maintained to note any effort to wash off a stain. The culprit may wipe off the stain with a handkerchief or may wear gloves. These objects should be seized in such contingencies. On apprehension the subject's hands should be examined. Traces of the stain will usually be visible in the borders of the fingernails. If a fluorescent powder is used, a loose surveillance will suffice. An ultraviolet lamp should be brought to the premises where the thefts are taking place. It will be found that particles of the fluorescent powder cling to the clothes of the subject. Hence, it is possible to detect the offender many hours after the occurrence.

b. **Burglaries.** Systematic burglaries can be detected by these methods, if there is a known and limited group of suspects. Fluorescent powders can be used at the areas where a break can be logically expected. Doorknobs, locks, latches, and sills should be dusted with the powder. Care should be exercised so that other persons do not innocently touch these areas without the knowledge of the investigator. A line-up of suspects or, in general, personnel having access to the area should be conducted on the morning after a burglary. In place of powders, which may wash off in the rain, the technique described in the next paragraph is useful in solving some types of burglary.

c. **False Alarms.** An excellent means of detecting persons who have a penchant for pulling fire alarm boxes is the use of a dye which will withstand varying weather conditions. A saturated solution of crystal violet or one of the other stains in oleic acid ("red oil") is painted on a part of the handle which is not in the line of view.

d. **Gasoline Thefts.** By adding a chemical indicator to the gasoline supply, theft of the gas can be detected through a chemical examination of samples taken from the cars of suspects. A quantity of

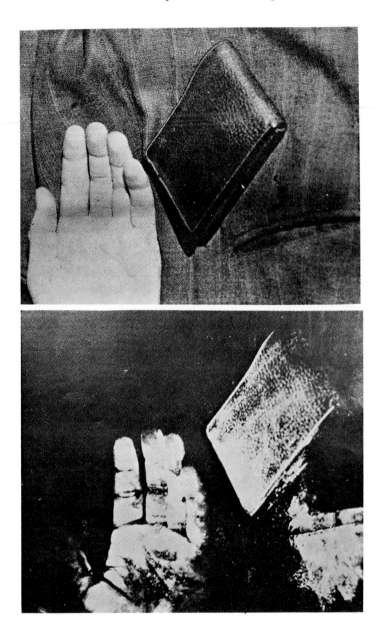

Figure 64. *Fluorescent powder* can be used to detect the perpetrator of a theft. At the top, objects labeled with such a powder are seen under ordinary light. At the bottom the same objects are photographed under ultraviolet light.

fifty-six milligrams of phenolphthalein is used for each gallon of gasoline. If the gas tank has a capacity of 500 gallons, one ounce of phenolphthalein is dissolved in fifteen ounces of isopropyl alcohol and added to the gas reservoir. To detect the phenolphthalein a sample is taken from the suspect's tank. One cubic centimeter of a 5 per cent solution of sodium hydroxide is mixed with 10 cubic centimeters of the gasoline. If a red layer is observed at the bottom, the gasoline contains phenolphthalein. Another technique consists of adding a fluorescent substance to the gasoline. Fluorene or anthracene is satisfactory. A tablespoon of the powder added to a 500-gallon tank will cause the gasoline to fluoresce under an ultraviolet lamp.

e. **Explosives.** The lethal 1975 explosion at New York's LaGuardia Airport revived once more the project of adding innocuous chemicals to explosives to provide trace substances that would survive detonation, leaving vital clues to the source of the explosive. Under a pilot program sponsored by the Treasury Department (Bureau of Alcohol, Tobacco and Firearms) it was proposed to mix small amounts of chemically coded additives with more than 700 million pounds of explosives. These minute additives would remain after the explosion to be collected and traced to the origin of the explosives. It is anticipated that the taggants will provide immediate investigative leads and that the knowledge of their existence will prompt explosives dealers and users to employ greater security measures. The extension of this detection method to ammunition materials, in general, would greatly facilitate the investigation of crimes involving firearms.

4. Radioactive Tracers

With the increasing availability of radioactive substances it is practicable for the investigator to use these materials as tracing substances. Their presence can be detected by means of a survey meter.

ADDITIONAL READING

Hack, F.X.: Trap Substances. 27 *International Criminal Police Review*, 257, 1972.

Chapter 41

HAIR AND FIBERS

1. Significance

THE STRAY HAIR found at the scene of the crime, adhering to the murder weapon or even in the grasp of the victim, has long been considered one of the classic examples of physical evidence. Unfortunately there is little to recommend hair as a medium of identification. It has no unique chemical characteristics; there is little of a special nature in its shape; and its color, although highly characteristic, is not readily subjected to a color (spectrophotometrical) analysis. At best the expert can say that two specimens of hair are similar; in his present state of knowledge he may not say that they are identical in source. Nevertheless, hair specimens provide valuable exclusionary evidence. Although one may not say that the evidence specimen of hair belongs to a particular person, it can at least be asserted that the hair did not come from certain other persons. It is not often that hair is an important contributing factor to a case; such evidence, however, and its potential application to the case under investigation, must never be considered as worthless. A negative finding may serve to disprove erroneous theories. A positive finding, although merely suggesting the implication of an individual, is of importance when it is correlated with other newly discovered facts. The following are the possible findings:

a. **Non-Identity of Sources.** Establishing the fact that the evidence sample and the standard sample did not come from the same source serves the purpose of elimination.

b. **Possible Source.** Establishing that the evidence sample is similar to the standard sample may only indicate that a hypothetical event is possible or probable. In the presence of other evidence this fact may provide valuable corroboration.

2. Laboratory Examination

A number of determinations can be made in the laboratory, chiefly with the aid of a microscope.

a. **The Specimen Is Hair.** This may be established by the three parts of hair: the medulla or core, varying in thickness and continuity; the cortex or body surrounding the medulla; and the cuticle or outer covering formed by overlapping scales which vary in size, shape, and number per unit length.

b. **The Hair Is Human.** Often a suspect maintains that an incriminating hair specimen found on his person came from an animal. The difference between animal and human hair is readily apparent because of the relative diameter of the medulla and the location and distribution of pigment.

c. **Characteristics.** Hair possesses a number of useful characteristics such as the color, length, diameter, dye, or bleach.

d. **Determinations.** In addition to forming an opinion concerning the similarity of the evidence and the standard specimen, the laboratory expert is sometimes able to make some other useful deductions from a hair specimen. The sex of the owner is suggested by the thickness and length; gray hair indicates age; hair from different parts of the body varies; the race is sometimes indicated by the shape of the cross section; foreign matter may give a clue to the occupation of the owner; the nature of any dye present may be revealed by microchemical analysis; in assaults and homicides some clue to the nature of the instrument used to inflict a blow may be derived from the impression left on the hair; arsenic may be found in small traces in the hair of a person poisoned by this substance.

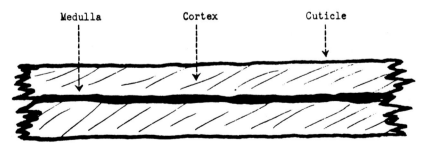

Figure 65. Longitudinal cross section of a hair.

e. **Scanning Electron Microscope.** Hair identification entails many tests, and uncertainties still exist in drawing final conclusions to determine whether a single hair can be identified with an individual. The Scanning Electron Microscope at present provides the most informative studies of hair, greatly simplifying determinations of surface characteristics, such as scale count, hair shape, scale structure, and surface damage, whether physical or chemical, which may be significant in criminal investigations. S.E.M. far surpasses the techniques of light microscopic studies in topographical resolution of hair features and has the advantage over Transmission Electron Microscopy in eliminating the need for replication.

3. Fibers

The clothing of persons involved in crimes of personal violence is a source of valuable clues. The fibers from the clothing may adhere to the person of the victim. In hit-and-run cases fibers from the victim's clothing may be found on the radiator, grille, or tires of the vehicle. Since fibers vary widely in composition, source, color, and shape, they possess many more identifying characteristics than hair. The following examples illustrate the value of these clues.

a. **Rope.** The victim of a homicide had been trussed with a three-strand rope. The probable manufacturer of the rope was located. It was possible to identify the rope by the marks of the machine that had been used during a certain period and by means of the characteristic chemical properties of the substance that had been used for impregnation. An examination of shipping records revealed that a wholesaler in the home town of the suspect and victim had received a shipment of the rope. A search of the garage of the suspect disclosed a length of rope similar in every respect to that used in tying the victim.

b. **Cloth and String.** Parts of the dismembered body of a woman were discovered in different locations of an Eastern city. Each part was found as a package, wrapped in the same type of cloth and tied with string made from twisted paper. It was found after diligent search that the cloth and string had been obtained at a small store devoted to the manufacture of window shades. Further investigation revealed that the suspect lived in a room on the second floor above the shop and could have obtained the cloth and string from piles of scrap in the rear of the building.

4. Types of Fibers

For the purpose of the laboratory expert, fibers may be divided into the following classes:

a. **Animal.** A number of fibers were derived from animal products, the most important being wool, silk, camel's hair, and fur.

b. **Vegetable.** This class includes most of the inexpensive clothing fibers. The familiar types are cotton, linen, jute, hemp, ramie, and sisal.

c. **Mineral.** Minerals provide such useful fibers as glass wool and asbestos. Fibers of this kind are used in safe insulation.

d. **Synthetics.** Applied chemistry has produced a number of fibers among which are rayon, nylon, orlon, and dacron.

5. Fiber Examination

The problems of fiber comparisons should be submitted to the laboratory expert. The investigator should not attempt to make such a comparison for the official record. He may, however, make preliminary examinations which are not destructive to the evidence in situations where the expert is not available. In this way he can avoid the pitfalls of false leads.

a. **Animal or Vegetable.** These fibers can be distinguished by the application of flame. After the flame is withdrawn and the fibers are permitted to continue burning, it is noted that animal fibers will burn for a short time only, emitting a characteristic odor of burned animal matter and assuming a swollen appearance at the ends. On the other hand, vegetable fibers will burn easily with a smell resembling burning wood and with the burned end appearing sharp. This type of experiment should not be considered in an actual case when the amount of evidence is limited to a few fibers.

b. **Microscopic examination** of fibers is made in comparing unknown with known specimens in order to establish similarities and variations. The complete study of woven or spun material will include data on the following characteristics: nature of the fiber; color; method of weaving; number of threads per inch, both laterally and longitudinally (lateral threads are called the filler and the longitudinal threads are called the warp); number of twists per inch in a thread; direction of the twist; position and nature of any stains and marks; nature of any dust or dirt.

   c. **Examination of String and Rope.** String is identified in much the same manner as yarn from cloth or other fabrics. Rope is identified by the "lay" or angle at which the strands are twisted; the circumference; number of strands; number of yarns per strand; number of fibers per yarn; chemical processing involving sizing, lubricants, preservatives, or insect repellents.

ADDITIONAL READING

Hair

Appleyard, H.M.: *Guide to the Identification of Animal Fibers*. Torridon, Leeds, England: Wool Industry Research Association, 1960.

De Forest, P.R. and Kirk, P.L.: Forensic Individualization of Hair. 8 *Criminologist*, 27, 1973.

Forslev, A.W.: "Nondestructive" Neutron Activation Analysis of Hair. 11 *Journal of Forensic Sciences*, 217, 1966.

Ishizu, H., et al.: Scanning Electron Microscope Studies on Surface Structure of Hairs. 27 *Japanese Journal of Legal Medicine*, 113, 1973.

Korda, E.J., Macdonell, H.L. and Williams, J.P.: Forensic Applications of the Scanning Electron Microscope. 61 *Journal of Criminal Law, Criminology and Police Science*, 453, 1970.

McCrone, W.C.: Characterization of Human Hair by Light Microscopy. 25 *Microscope*, 1, 1977.

Niyogi, S.K.: A Study of Human Hairs in Forensic Work. 2 *Proceedings of the Canadian Society of Forensic Science*, 105, 1963.

Obrusnik, I., et al.: The Variation of Trace Elements Concentrations in Single Human Head Hairs. 17 *Journal of Forensic Sciences*, 426, 1972.

Perkons, A.K. and Jervis, R.E.: Trace Element in Human Head Hair. 11 *Journal of Forensic Sciences*, 50, 1966.

Verhoeven, L.E.: The Advantage of the Scanning Electron Microscope in the Investigative Studies of Hair. 63 *Journal of Criminal Law, Criminology and Police Science*, 125, 1972.

Vernall, J.: A Study of the Size and Shape of Cross Sections of Hair from Familiar Races of Man. 19 *American Journal of Physical Anthropology*, 345, 1961.

Fibers

Carter, M.E.: *Essential Fiber Chemistry*. New York, Dekker, 1971.

Himmelfarb, D.: *The Technology of Cordage Fibers and Rope*. Plainfield, N.J.: Textile Book Service, 1957.

Kornreich, E.: *Introduction to Fibers and Fabrics*. New York, Elsevier, 1966.

Martin, E.P.: Wool Fibres as Evidence: Their Probative Value in Criminal Procedure. 30 *International Criminal Police Review*, 288, 1975.

Mauersberger, H.R.: *Matthews' Textile Fibers*, 6th ed. New York, Wiley, 1954.

Pounds, C.A.: The Recovery of Fibres from the Surface of Clothing for Forensic Examinations. 15 *Journal of the Forensic Science Society*, 12, 1975.

Press, J.J. (Ed.): *Man-Made Textile Encyclopedia*, 2 vols. New York, Textile Book Pub., 1970.

Rouen, R.A. and Reeve, V.C.: A Comparison and Evaluation of Techniques for Identification of Synthetic Fibers. 15 *Journal of Forensic Sciences*, 410, 1970.

Snyder, P. and Snyder, A.: *Knots and Lines Illustrated*. Tuckahoe, N.Y.: De Graff, 1970.

Strell, I. and Kennedy, R.W.: *Identification of North American Pulpwoods and Pulp Fibers*. Toronto, University of Toronto Press, 1967.

Chapter 42

INVISIBLE RADIATION

I. ULTRAVIOLET RADIATION

I. Nature of Ultraviolet

ONE OF more common problems of the police laboratory scientist and the document examiner is the decipherment or discernment of the relatively invisible. Thus, a stain on a garment or an obscured writing on a document can be rendered visible by the use of certain techniques. One of these methods is the employment of rays which border the visible, i.e., radiation which is slightly longer (infrared) or slightly shorter (ultraviolet) in wavelength than visible light. The wavelength of ultraviolet light is in the region from 136 to 4000 angstrom units.

2. Effect of Ultraviolet Light

When ultraviolet radiation strikes a surface it is absorbed by some substances and its energy transformed and radiated back in light of different colors. Thus, although the original ultraviolet is invisible, its effects on an object as observed in a dark room are distinctly visible. The object is then said to *fluoresce*. This interesting phenomenon is useful to the investigator who may in this manner detect stains on a garment, alterations on a check, or secret writing in a letter.

3. Sources of Ultraviolet

To obtain ultraviolet light a special lamp must be used. Although the sun is rich in ultraviolet and may be used as a source by filtering out other rays with a Wratten 18A filter, it is customary to employ a portable ultraviolet lamp such as a quartz mercury-vapor lamp which will yield wavelengths from 1800 to 14000 angstrom units. A flashlight form of the ultraviolet lamp is found useful for certain purposes at the scene of the crime. The ultraviolet lamp is used in a dark room to eliminate the effects of visible light. The effects can also be photographed by methods which will be described later.

4. Fluorescence Effects

Ultraviolet light can be used on a wide variety of subjects in investigative work. The most common uses are described below:

a. **Documents.** The widest use of ultraviolet is in the field of document examination. One of the first steps in many document problems is the examination of the evidence under the ultraviolet light.

1) *Paper.* Ultraviolet rays can distinguish between various types of papers. The sizing of one paper may fluoresce green while that of another may appear reddish. The appearance of the paper under ultraviolet is the most rapid method of paper comparison.

2) *Alterations.* If the paper is altered by mechanical erasure or chemical obliteration, the effect on the sizing can be readily observed.

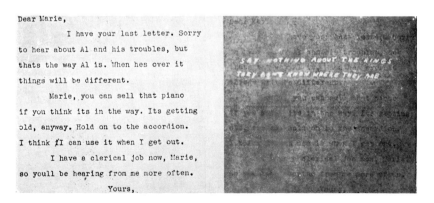

Figure 66. A letter containing secret writing, photographed in the visible light and in the ultraviolet radiator.

3) *Cancellation Marks.* Chemically washed stamps which have been treated to bleach the cancellation mark can be detected after they have been dried and regummed.

4) *Ink.* Aniline inks can be differentiated under the ultraviolet light.

5) *Secret Inks.* One method of secret communication employs physiological fluids such as urine, milk, and saliva, or colorless solutions of fluorescing substances such as quinine hydrochloride. Since these substances are selected for their brilliant fluorescence under the ultraviolet, their detection is a simple matter.

6) *Resealed Envelopes.* An envelope which has been steamed and resealed with a different adhesive will reveal the tampering under ultraviolet.

7) *Counterfeits.* The forgery of tickets and coupons can often be detected by the different fluorescence of the sizing. Some tickets, such as pari-mutuels, are impregnated with a fluorescent substance as a means of identification.

b. **Laundry Marks.** Some laundries use an invisible ink for their marks and identify the garments under the ultraviolet. Clothing found in connection with a crime can often be traced to its owner by means of the laundry mark (Chapter 34). In such cases the garment should always be place under an ultraviolet light to discover any invisible marks.

c. **Stains.** Ultraviolet light provides an excellent means of locating stains preparatory to testing. For example, in rape cases, semen and urine can be readily found on a garment by means of their fluorescence. Fingernail polishes, lipsticks, and rouges frequently contain fluorescent substances.

d. **Gems and Glass.** Fluorescence tests are often useful in differentiating gems that appear similar. As a preliminary or screening test, fluorescence is a useful means of distinguishing between samples of glass found at the scene of the accident and in the subject.

e. **Painting.** Fraudulent imitations of old masters can sometimes be detected by fluorescence tests. Varnishes used on old paintings often fluoresce differently from modern varnishes. Retouching and other alterations can be detected by the appearance of the painting under the ultraviolet.

f. **Fingerprints.** In processing a multicolored surface for latent fingerprints a fluorescent powder such as anthracene, fluoranthene, or uranyl phosphate can be used. The fluorescing fingerprint can then be photographed under ultraviolet light to achieve the desired contrast to the background.

5. Photography of Fluorescent Objects

If positive results are obtained in exposing articles to ultraviolet radiation, it is desirable sometimes to photograph the fluorescent effects. This is particularly true in cases of documents on which alterations have been discovered. The photographic procedure is not difficult, the only problem being the correct estimate of the exposure. Briefly the procedure consists of placing the object under ultraviolet radiation in a dark room and photographing the fluorescence.

a. **Light Source.** An ultraviolet lamp such as a Hanovia quartz lamp or a Cooper Hewitt lamp with a nico tube is adequate as a source of radiation. The source should be close to the object. Two General Electric B-H 4 lamps at 20 inches are adequate.

b. **Camera.** No special camera is required.

c. **Filter.** A Wratten 2A filter is useful in removing the excess of blue light.

d. **Film.** A fast panchromatic film is satisfactory. Process panchromatic can be used if great contrast is desired.

e. **Exposure.** This will vary widely with the intensity of the fluorescence. Exposures as long as thirty minutes at f/11 are sometimes required. In other situations an exposure of twenty seconds may be adequate. A series of test exposures should be made.

6. Photography in Reflected Ultraviolet Light

It is possible to photograph objects in ultraviolet radiations. The visible light, including the fluorescence, is excluded by means of a Wratten 18A filter placed over the lens. Alternatively a filter such as a Corning Violet Ultra No. 5860 can be placed over the lamp to transmit only ultraviolet radiation and the photographs can be made in the dark. Ordinary panchromatic film can be used. For the far ultraviolet region it is necessary to use a quartz lens and a special film. Since the results are unpredictable and rarely justify the work involved, photography by reflected ultraviolet is at present mainly of academic interest.

II. INFRARED RADIATION

7. Nature of Infrared Rays

Infrared, the spectral region of longer wavelengths immediately below the visible range, is another tool employed by the investigator to reveal information hidden from the eye. In that respect it is similar to the ultraviolet. It differs from the ultraviolet region, however, in that it has no fluorescent effects which can be seen by the unaided eye. The appearance of an object in the infrared must, ordinarily, be studied through the medium of a photograph. It is possible to see certain infrared effects more directly by means of a night-viewing device such as the "Snooperscope," an instrument designed primarily for surveillance operations in the dark.

8. Effects

The utility of infrared rays is attributable to the fact that certain substances are opaque or transparent to this radiation in a manner which is independent of their reactions to visible light. For example, two specimens of ink writing may appear identical to the unaided eye, but in an infrared photograph one ink may appear much darker than the other because of their varying capacities to reflect the infrared. The reason for this characteristic reaction to the longer wavelengths of the infrared is not fully understood. It is not possible at present to predict from theory whether an unknown substance will reflect or absorb infrared. From experience, however, it has been learned that substances such as india ink and carbon pencil will absorb infrared.

9. Applications

As in the case of ultraviolet the usefulness of infrared radiation has been learned by experience. The following are some of the typical applications:

a. **Documents.** The most fruitful field to which infrared can be applied is that of documentary evidence.

1) *Inks.* Two inks which appear to the eye to be the same can sometimes be differentiated by an infrared photograph.

2) *Obliterations.* If ink has been used to obliterate writing, it may be possible to determine the nature of the writing by means of infrared photography. If the obliterating ink is transparent to the infrared and the lower writing is opaque, it is a relatively simple matter to render the writing legible. Some inks such as Chinese and india inks, iron tannate inks, and chrome logwood inks are opaque to the infrared. Others, particularly colored inks containing aniline dyes, are transparent.

3) *Erasures.* When writing is mechanically erased, small particles of the ink or pencil sometimes remain in the outline. It may be possible to increase the contrast of the residual writing by means of infrared.

4) *Secret Writing.* Infrared photography is another method of detecting secret writing.

5) *Unopened Letters.* If the paper is transparent to infrared and the ink opaque to this radiation, it is possible to read the contents of the letter without opening it. The letter is placed in contact with an infrared film in a printing frame and exposed to a light filtered through an infrared glass.

6) *Charred Documents.* Burned documents can sometimes be deciphered by an infrared photograph. Success depends upon the nature of the ink or pencil and the degree of charring.

b. **Comparison Tests.** In the course of an investigation it sometimes becomes necessary to compare a known and questioned sample of a substance in an effort to prove identity of source.

Infrared provides a preliminary screening test for certain materials such as cloths and paints. If the two samples reflect infrared to distinctly varied degree, it can be said that they have different sources.

c. **Powder Marks.** Infrared photography is an excellent means of determining the presence of powder marks surrounding a bullet hole. It is particularly useful when the bullet hole is found in a dark suit.

d. **Stains.** Infrared provides an additional method of detecting and differentiating stains.

10. Infrared Photography

A special film such as Eastman Kodak® Infrared film must be used in this type of photography. Filters must be employed which exclude the visible to a great extent and transmit the infrared. The procedures are similar to those of ordinary photography. The following data will be found useful:

a. **Light Source.** A tungsten lamp such as a photoflood is a good source of infrared radiation. Varying the angle of illumination sometimes affects the results. Special flash bulbs can also be used as described below.

b. *Film.* Kodak Infrared film is available in standard sizes. In photographing a small area, such as that of an altered signature, a 2¼ × 3¼-inch film size may be used conveniently with a fixed-focus fingerprint camera in which a filter has been placed.

c. **Filter.** If it is desired to exclude all the visible light a Wratten No. 87 filter should be used. The Wratten No. 25 filter, which transmits visible light also, can be used to obtain a different effect. It is possible to dispense with the filter over the lens by using flashbulbs dipped in a special lacquer and photographing in darkness. A No. 22R lamp is recommended. By using a f/3.5 opening a photograph can be made up to a distance of 20 feet in a dark room. This procedure is useful for surreptitious photography. A dull red glow is visible only by looking directly at the lamp.

d. **Camera.** No special camera is required.

e. **Focusing.** Since infrared rays come to focus in an image plane slightly behind the visible plane, the exposure should be made at about f/16 to allow for any error in focusing. Alternatively the bellows extension can be increased by 3 per cent of the focal length of the lens to compensate for any error.

f. **Exposure.** A filter factor is provided for the Wratten No. 25 filter. For the Wratten No. 87, exposures must be greatly increased. A set of test exposures should be made. A test exposure for photographing a document in the infrared with two No. 1 photoflood lamps at 3 feet from the object is four seconds at f/16 with a Wratten No. 87 filter.

III. X-RAYS

11. Introduction

X-rays provide the investigator with another method of seeing objects invisible to the normal eye. In this respect they are similar to ultraviolet and infrared radiation. Among the situations in which the investigator would find these rays useful are the following: a "suspicious package," i.e. a package which is thought to contain a bomb; a locked suitcase thought to contain contraband; loaded dice; fraudulent paintings; the detection of lead fouling in contact bullet holes on clothing; and, in general, the presence of metallic objects in non-metallic surroundings.

12. Nature

X-rays are similar in nature to light; they are electromagnetic radiations differing from light in that they are much shorter in wavelength, a characteristic which gives them great penetrating power. In the same way as light, x-rays affect a photographic plate. A film exposed by means of x-rays is called a *radiograph*. The technique of making radiographs is relatively simple and need not present any more difficulty than ordinary photography. A few lessons in the manipulation of the x-ray apparatus suffice to provide a

Figure 67. Examination of antiques. The photograph shows what appears to be the original face of the clock.

Figure 68. The appearance of the same clock recorded with infrared illumination. The superimposition of paints is apparent. Note that the paint used for the numbers on the overlayer is not transparent to infrared radiation.

facility adequate for the demands of police radiography. The subtleties of medical x-ray methods are not necessary in this branch of criminalistics.

13. The X-ray tube

The source of x-rays is a vacuum tube containing a cathode and an anode with a potential difference ranging from 20,000 to 60,000 volts or 20 to 60 kilovolts. The apparatus operates from an ordinary 110 volt AC line. A transformer supplies the needed voltage. When the cathode is hot enough, electrons fall from the cathode to the anode at high speeds and strike a target in front of the anode. The target thus bombarded gives out x-rays, which penetrate non-metallic objects. Since they are blocked by metallic objects, these latter produce a shadow on the photographic plate. This shadow picture is the radiograph. The intensity of the shadow and the penetrating power of the rays can be controlled by varying the voltage and current of the tube.

a. **Voltage.** If the voltage is increased, the wavelength of the x-rays becomes shorter and the radiation is more penetrating. X-rays in the range of 4 to 25 kilovolts are called *soft x-rays;* those from 50 to 140 kilovolts are *hard x-rays.* A different x-ray apparatus is required for each type. Hard x-rays of great penetrating power are useful in examining suspected bombs.

b. **Current.** The intensity of the shadow depends also on the tube current, which is measured in milliamperes. When the current is increased, the filament becomes hotter and gives off a greater quantity of electrons. Current does not affect the speed of the electrons and consequently the penetrating power of the x-rays. The greater the current, the shorter the exposure time.

c. **Tube-Film Distance.** To take a radiograph of a suspicious box, the photographic holder containing film is placed under the "head" of the x-ray tube. If the holder is on the level of a table, the x-ray head will be about 2 feet away from it. The box is placed on top of the holder. Since the box is between the head and the holder, metal objects will cast a shadow on the film when x-rays are emitted from the head. It is not necessary to remove the dark slide, since the x-rays penetrate this material. The exposure will depend on the distance of the head or tube from the box. The tube-to-object distance also controls definitions or sharpness of image. The object-to-film distance is also a factor. The definition or sharpness improves as the tube-to-object distance becomes greater. If the object is placed as close as possible to the film, the sharpness is improved.

14. Film and Screens

Practically any film is satisfactory for the exploratory work of police radiography. An ordinary 8 × 10-inch wooden and plastic film holder with commercial film will yield satisfactory results. Metal film holders should not be used. The development procedures are the same as those of ordinary photography.

The above procedures have been described in order to impress the reader with the simplicity of radiography. Naturally, a more

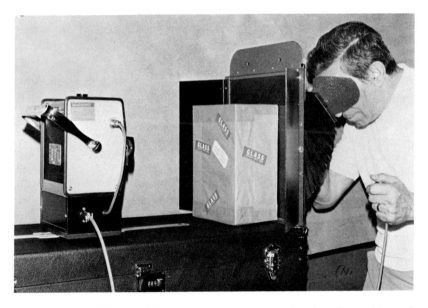

Figure 69a. Field surveillance x-ray unit. A completed radiographic and fluoroscopic unit with a Polaroid® camera attachment for a permanent photographic record. Courtesy of MinXray Inc.

professional technique can be developed by employing equipment specifically designed for x-ray work by the manufacturers. For more exacting work special x-ray films such as Eastman Kodak type F should be used.

Another method of improving x-ray work is to employ cassettes containing x-ray screens. An x-ray cassette is a film holder equipped with intensifying screens. The purpose of the screens is to decrease exposure time. When x-rays strike a film only 1 per cent of the radiation affects the screen, the remainder passing uselessly through. The screen permits more of the radiation to be utilized. The exposure time is greatly decreased, since the screen renders the film approximately thirty times faster. Polaroid backs or film-holding arrangements are available for rapid work in the field.

15. Protection

X-rays, because of their penetrating power and peculiar effect on human tissue, are dangerous if used carelessly. A lead apron and gloves should be used by the operator to absorb the rays. It should be remembered that the effect of x-rays is "summed up" or cumulative. The doses received on different days are additive, and thus a massive dosage can be accumulated by successive exposures over a period of weeks.

16. Fluoroscopy

For quick inspection of an object under x-rays, a fluoroscope is used. The fluoroscope is a small box with a viewing aperture for both eyes on one end and calcium tungstate (or similar substance) screen on the other. X-rays striking the screen fluoresce and present a shadow picture to the viewer.

17. Use of X-rays in Police Work

a. **Soft X-rays.** These rays range from 4 to 25 kilovolts. For most work a potential of 12 kilovolts and a current of 8 milliamps will

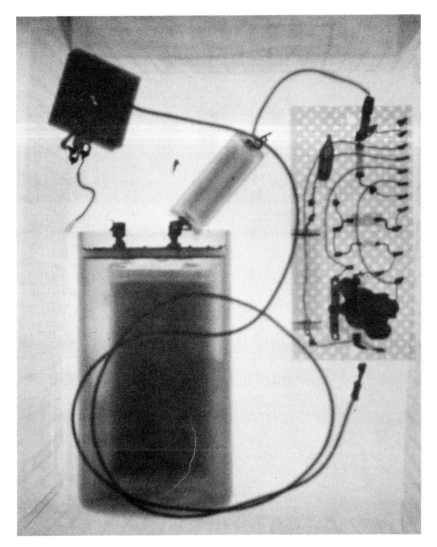

Figure 69b. Radiograph of explosive device. Courtesy of MinXray Inc.

suffice. The distance of the tube to the film can range from 4 inches to 3 feet. An average distance of 20 inches suffices. The exposure time may range from one second to four minutes depending on the other factors.

1) ***Paintings.*** Cases of fraudulent paintings and of superimposed paintings have been solved by the use of soft x-rays. The different compositions of the paints produce different effects on the film under x-rays. Where an old picture, in which paints relatively opaque to x-rays have been used, lies under a new painting with relatively transparent paints, the x-ray will reveal the presence of the older painting.

2) ***Fabrics.*** Two samples of cloth visually similar can be differentiated by means of x-rays.

3) ***Paper.*** The texture of paper can be studied with x-rays and in this way two apparently similar specimens can be distinguished. Handmade papers can be differentiated from machine-made papers because of the differing opacities of the fillers and the fiber structure.

4) ***Jewelry.*** Imitation diamonds such as rutile and zircon can be distinguished from the genuine. Similarly, differences in natural and synthetic pearls can be detected.

5) ***Gunshot Wounds.*** When a gun is discharged at a close distance from the body, lead fouling is distributed about the hole. To determine whether a hole in a garment was made by a bullet and also to acquire information about the discharge distance, x-rays can be used to produce a picture of the lead fouling (see page 775).

6) ***Secret and Obliterated Writing.*** Lead and other metals are sometimes used in the manufacture of paint which is employed in stenciling numbers on clothing. If the letters become illegible through wear, a radiograph may be used to decipher the writing. Barium chloride and lead nitrate can be used to produce invisible writing. Their presence can be detected, however, through the use of x-rays.

b. **Hard X-rays.** The range from 25 to 140 kilovolts is used to detect gross, metal objects. A potential of 60 kilovolts; a current of 10 milliamps; a tube distance of 2 feet; and an exposure of about two seconds will suffice to indicate the desired settings.

1) ***Suspicious Packages.*** If a bomb is hidden in a suitcase or sent through the mails in a box, it is naturally preferable to study the structure without opening the container because of the danger of trigger devices. It is routine procedure with many law enforcement agencies to radiograph such objects before taking any further steps.

2) **Contraband.** To detect hidden guns and other metal objects hidden in luggage or cushions, hard x-rays can be used.

3) **Security Measures.** In a plant engaged in the production of classified items, the use of photographs as an espionage technique can be discouraged by setting up x-ray beams at the gate to fog film concealed on employees. Transmitters hidden in furniture can be detected by fluoroscopy.

4) **Loaded Dice.** In the investigation of assaults and homicides associated with gambling sessions, the presence of loads in the dice may supply a motive. Loaded dice are also significant in the investigation of gambling cheats.

5) **Paintings.** In the examination of a suspected painting, x-rays can be applied to the stud of the materials and processes which the forger may have used to simulate the attributed period and authorship. Both the hard and soft x-ray regions are useful. Most generally helpful is a radiograph taken at about 35 kilovolts. The exposure time will vary with the current as well as the distance, which, in turn, will vary with the size of the area being x-rayed. The information about the structure of the painting obtainable through x-radiography may include the following: the nature of the support and its condition; the existence of damage beneath the visible surface; retouchings; the relative density of the pigments (mass-absorption coefficients); the manner in which the painter has used white lead (and zinc white) and whether a white lead priming coat has been used; the presence of latent images where the artist has painted over an already existing image; and other information relevant to particular cases.

c. **Gamma Rays.** Extremely hard radiation can be obtained by means of radioactive substances such as cobalt-60 or radon. The equipment needed is simply the capsule of radioactive material and the film. The capsule is suspended by a string a few feet above the object. This radiation is useful in dealing with metal boxes which are impenetrable to ordinary hard x-rays.

d. **Electron Radiography.** Secondary radiation produced by x-rays can be used to obtain information concerning the surface and lower layers of an object such as a painting or written document. The blocking effect of the support, e.g., wooden panel or crosspieces, sometimes makes it difficult or even impossible to obtain a satisfactory x-ray picture of a painting. An electron radiograph (i.e., an image made by secondary radiation) is sometimes helpful in these situations; it is a useful supplement in any event to a comprehensive radiographic study of an art work.

A 150-kilovolt source is used to emit x-rays which are too short in wavelength to affect the photographic film but which will excite some of the materials of the painting (in particular, the metallic components) so that they emit a radiation which will be recorded on the film. With the film placed on top of the painting, the x-rays are sent through the film to impinge on the painting and cause it to emit a secondary radiation which will affect the film. Since the emitted electrons are readily absorbed by air, the operation is conducted in a partial vacuum (4mm.) by placing both the painting and the film in a polyethylene bag which can be attached to a vacuum pump. The problems associated with a vacuum can be obviated by displacing the air in the bag with helium, an inert gas which has relatively little absorptive effect on electrons.

Other applications of this radiographic method will suggest themselves. For example, erasures or obliterations of metallic ink writings may be radiographed in this way to obtain a clearer image of residual or latent ink strokes.

e. **Neutron Radiography.** Since neutrons are atomic particles bearing no charge, they can penetrate relatively substantial objects. In neutron radiography a beam of well-collimated thermal neutrons is passed around and through an object. By virtue of spatial intensity modulation, the beam on the far side of the object carries information about the object's internal structure and composition. The spatial flux variation is recorded by an imaging system on standard x-ray film. Since the film is relatively insensitive to neutrons, it is placed under a thin sheet of gladolinium, a converter screen which captures the neutrons and emits low-energy gamma rays, thus exposing the film. Neutron radiographs measuring $14 \times 17''$ are produced routinely by industry in the examination of devices loaded with explosives and pyrotechnics. Although a nuclear reactor is used to achieve a neutron flux of the required magnitude, work is being done on a portable non-reactor neutron source, which should become available in the near future.

1) *Characteristics.* The important difference between neutron

diffraction and the diffraction of x-ray and electron beams lies in the manner in which the scattering power varies with atomic number and scattering angle. The scattering power of an atom increases directly with the atomic number and inversely with the scattering angle. The scattering of neutrons, however, appears to be the same for all angles and indifferent to atomic number. Some light elements will scatter neutrons more intensely than some heavy elements. Elements close together in atomic number may have widely different scattering powers, while elements widely separated in atomic number may scatter equally well.

2) *Effectiveness.* As an analytical tool, then, neutron diffraction is capable of structural analyses that are impossible, or possible only with great difficulty, using x-rays or electron diffraction. For example, in a compound of hydrogen or carbon with a heavy metal, the x-rays will not detect the hydrogen or carbon because of their low scattering power, whereas its position in the lattice can be easily determined by neutron diffraction. The method is particularly applicable where the sample is minute and even its partial consumption is not desired.

3) *Nondestructive Inspection Technique.* In the present discussion our special interest is radiography rather than analysis. Because the absorption characteristics are markedly different from those of x-rays, it is found that the neutron radiograph will yield contrasts between materials vastly different from those available in an x-radiograph. Thus, the neutron radiograph can record information that can never appear on an x-radiograph. Since x-rays are absorbed in the electron shell around the atom, their absorption coefficient is ordinarily (i.e., disregarding the coefficient's dependence on x-ray wavelength) a monotonically increasing function of atomic number. Neutron absorption, however, is almost independent of atomic number, because it involves a nuclear interaction determined by nuclear properties not specifically related to atomic number.

4) *Examples.* The advantages of neutron radiography can be illustrated by the ordinary cigarette lighter. An x-radiograph can show all the metal parts of a lighter and their relationship but not whether there is any cotton or wick. In a neutron radiograph most or all of the parts visible in the x-radiograph are discernible; in addition, the cotton, wick, and flint are clearly visible, since they are

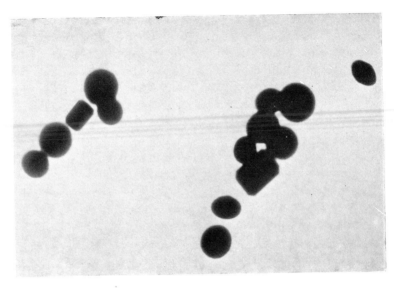

Figure 70. Radiograph that located two packets of smuggled diamonds secreted in a pillow. Lack of sharpness is the result of separation of diamond packets and film by part of the pillow.

Figure 71. A one-to-one photograph of the fourteen diamonds recovered from the pillow. Notice the two emerald cut gems, which may also be identified in Figure 59 by their rectangular shape.

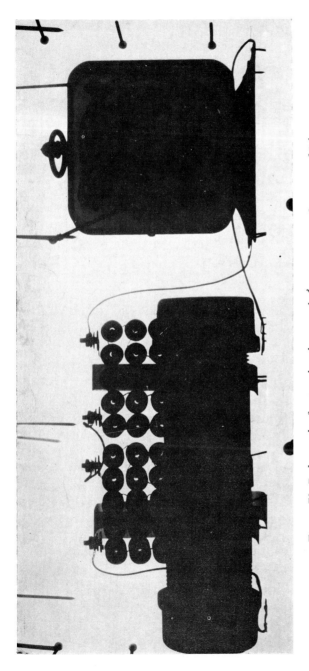

Figure 72. Radiograph of a time bomb concealed in a suitcase. Courtesy of John Bealler.

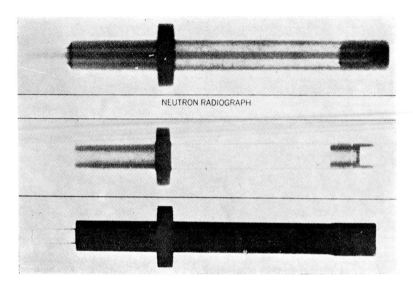

Figure 73. Neutron radiograph and light and dark positive x-radiographs of the same explosive device. The explosive train visible (down the middle of the device) is obscured in the x-radiographs but clearly visible in the neutron radiograph.

highly hydrogenous and thus opaque to neutrons. For the same reason, it can be established even that the lighter has been filled with fluid. Another example is given by Figure 73 in which the packing condition of the increments in an electrically initiated detonator are examined by neutron radiography and x-radiography. For example, two out of the five increments comprising the train can be shown in the neutron radiograph to have been passed together to a higher density, since their images will be darker than those of the other three. The thin layer of case material, offering little resistance to neutrons, will be barely discernible, whereas in the x-radiograph only the case material will be visible.

5) *Applications.* The effectiveness of neutron radiography as a non-destructive inspection technique suggests its applicability to a number of investigative problems. In general, neutron radiography is applicable to the examination of assembled or sealed objects which are beyond the reach of x-radiography because their internal components are transparent to x-rays or their coverings or casings

are opaque to x-rays. Some of the obvious applications are listed below.

a. **Explosive Devices.** A concealed bomb or "infernal machine" can be examined by means of neutron radiography to show the arrangement and condition of the internal components and thus provide a basis for subsequent decisions on its disarming, transportation, and disposal. Although the method is particularly applicable to bombs in metal enclosures or casings, such as pipe bombs, it is also a useful supplement to an x-ray examination, since it will detect the presence of substances such as fluids which will not be shown by an x-radiograph.

b. **Contraband.** The search for illegally possessed objects or substances can be aided by this inspection technique where the materials are visually inaccessible or undiscernible by x-rays because of their own nature or because of the nature of their protective covering.

c. **Espionage Materials.** A recent spy case will serve as an example. Faced with the problem of transmitting a copy of highly classified security information which had been made on 8 mm film, an enemy agent conceived the scheme of inserting the tightly rolled, undeveloped film segment into a small hole drilled into the edge of a half-dollar piece. Fortunately, the laboratory examiner, on detecting the plug placed over the hole to protect the film and conceal its hiding place, had the foresight to remove the plug in the darkroom, using only a green safelight to determine the condition of the film. Neutron radiography is especially suitable to an examination of this nature, particularly when the method of concealment is not easily detectable and film is readily spoiled by x-rays.

d. **Art Objects.** It has been said by Burroughs that in an x-radiograph "one studies the use of white in painting." The effect of pigments containing white lead predominates in x-radiographs of the work of early Renaissance painters, who used white lead to raise the tone of pure colors and to provide highlights and greater luminosity. X-radiographs of the fourteenth, fifteenth, and six-teenth centuries are characterized by the clarity, delineation, and almost modeling of the figures, attributable in great part to the use of white lead in the colors and of non-attenuating materials for the ground. In the latter half of the sixteenth century, however, the use of white lead as a priming coat came into general use with the result that the x-radiographs of paintings after this period tend to be thin and lacking in the clear delineation of the figures. We have seen the application of secondary radiation as a means of acquiring information concerning a painting which is not amenable to x-ray methods. Similarly, neutron radiography can be used on works of art that present special problems. The blocking effect of the support or other background material can sometimes be overcome in this manner. The author has found neutron radiography especially useful in exploring the internal structure of a figurine or other small object of art. For a small metal figure such as the famous horse of the Metropolitan Museum of Art this would appear to be the obvious method of choice.

ADDITIONAL READING

Costain, J.E. and Lewis, G.W.: A Practical Guide to Infrared Luminescence Applied to Questioned Document Problems. 1 *Journal of Police Science and Administration*, 209, 1973.

Graham, D.: *The Use of X-Ray Techniques in Forensic Investigations*. Edinburgh, Churchill Livingstone, 1973.

Lundquist, F. (Ed.): *Methods of Forensic Science*, vol. 2. New York, Wiley-Interscience, 1963.

Reeve, V., Mathiesen, J. and Fong, W.: Elemental Analysis by Energy Dispersive X-ray: A Significant Factor in the Forensic Analysis of Glass. 21 *Journal of Forensic Sciences*, 291, 1976.

Richards G.B.: The Application of Electronic Video Techniques to Infrared and Ultraviolet Examinations. 22 *Journal of Forensic Sciences*, 53, 1977.

Schwartz, S. and Woolridge, E.D.: The Use of Panoramic Radiographs for Comparisons in Cases of Identification. 22 *Journal of Forensic Sciences*, 145, 1977.

Chapter 43

DOCUMENTARY EVIDENCE

I. INTRODUCTION

I. Importance

THE IMPORTANCE of documentary evidence can scarcely be overemphasized. The investigator will find that documents in one form or another will account for approximately 70 per cent of the physical evidence which he will encounter. Checks, claims, marriage certificates, various types of executed forms, record cards, sworn statements, and many other forms of writing may be encountered as evidence in the course of an investigation. The investigator should understand the various types of questioned documents, the proper submission of documentary evidence, and the ways in which he can assist the document expert.

2. Document Problems

The most common document problem is that of questioned authorship. The origin, contents, and circumstances of preparation may also be questioned. The following are typical document problems:

a. The identity of the writer of a document.

b. The determination, removal, or decipherment of erasures, interlineations, deletions, additions, and other alterations.

c. The age of a document.

d. The source of the paper.

e. The source and age of typewriting.

f. Comparisons of handwriting and typewriting.

3. Investigtor and the Expert

The technical information contained here is given in order that an investigator may understand the potentialities of expert document examination. The investigator may aid the examiner by properly collecting, preserving, and transmitting the evidence. The opinions or views formed by an investigator concerning a questioned document should not be included in an investigative report. When document examinations are relevant and material to the case, the documents should be submitted only to a recognized expert qualified to make such examinations. The value of a document diminishes with careless treatment. Although a certain amount of handling is necessary in any document examination, the document can be carefully preserved throughout the proceedings. The following rules are useful:

a. Preserve the document initially by handling with wooden or plastic tongs.

b. Retain the document in a transparent envelope or protected by thin tissue paper unless it is under examination by an expert.

c. Determine initially if a fingerprint processing is required.

d. Do not alter the document unnecessarily by chemical treatment.

e. Preserve the document from dampness, heat, and sunlight.

f. Do not fold the document along new lines.

g. Do not make a tracing on the document.

h. Mark each document for identification by writing the case number, investigator's name or initials, and the date in some neutral area on the back of the document. If the document must first be processed for prints, the identification should be placed on the protective envelope.

i. Record relevant data such as the circumstances surrounding the acquisition of the document, the name of the person submitting it, the date, and a brief description of the paper.

4. Document Examination

There are two phases of the document examination—the investigator's and the expert's.

a. **Examination by the Investigator.** The investigator may perform a limited examination of the evidence document in cases, such as those involving anonymous letters, where the authorship is questioned. He should study the document and compare it with any available standards. His attention should be directed to the contents of the letter, similarities in writing, typing, spelling, locutions, punctuation, and the type of paper. Immediate precautionary action or investigative leads may be indicated as a result of this study. Conclusions concerning the document should remain within the province of the expert.

b. **Laboratory Examination.** At the laboratory the expert employs scientific techniques using appropriate instruments. Microscopy, chemical analysis, micrometry, colorimetry, photomicrography, ultraviolet and infrared photography are among the available techniques.

II. HANDWRITING IDENTIFICATION

5. Importance

The majority of questioned document cases are concerned with proving authorship. Samples of a suspect's writings are obtained and compared with questioned writing. The following determinations may be involved in comparisons of handwriting:

a. Whether the document was written by the suspect.

b. Whether the document was written by the person whose signature it bears.

c. Whether the writing contains additions or deletions.

d. Whether a document such as a bill, receipt, suicide note, or check is a forgery.

6. Basis of Handwriting Comparison

The principles underlying the comparison of handwriting are similar to those on which the science of fingerprint identification is based. No two products of man or nature are identical, and differences are perceptible if a sufficiently close study is made. Through years of practice each individual acquires permanent habits of handwriting. The group of characteristics which form his script constitutes an identifiable picture. In comparing two specimens of handwriting the expert searches for characteristics which are common to both the questioned and standard writing. If the characteristics are sufficient in kind and number and there are no significant unexplainable differences, he may conclude that the writings were made by the same person.

7. Handwriting Characteristics

Although document examiners may differ in their interpretation of the significance of various characteristics of handwriting, they usually concentrate on the same elements. The following characteristics provide the basis of the examination.

a. **Quality of Line.** The lines which form the letters will vary in appearance with pen position, pressure, shading, rhythm, tremor, continuity, skill, and speed.

b. **Form.** The formation of letters is highly characteristic. Slant, proportions, beginning and ending strokes, retracing, and separation of parts will vary with different persons. Ornamentation and flourishes at the beginning and end of the words and sentences are peculiarly individual.

c. **Spacing.** Letters, words, and lines are separated in a consistent fashion.

d. **Spelling and Punctuation.** The degree and kind of education will determine these elements.

8. Conclusions

It is a common misconception of the layman that a conclusion can be reached by the expert in the majority of handwriting cases. Unfortunately this belief is far from true since, in many cases, the available questioned writing is too limited in quantity or may contain few individual elements. The problem of the examiner is a

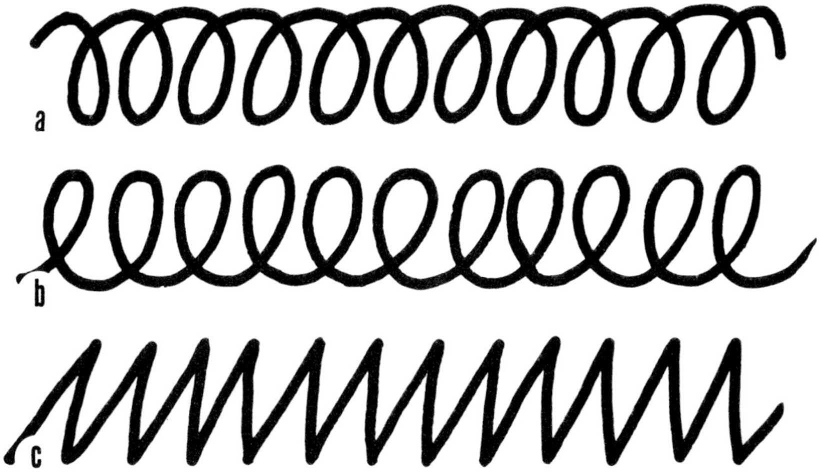

Figure 74. Basic movements in handwriting. It is convenient to consider handwriting as composed in three basic motions: (a) clockwise motion; (b) counter-clockwise motion; and (c) straight line motion. These movements suggest the direction as well as the curvature of the motion. Strictly speaking, an individual handwriting encompasses all directions and curvatures; it will be found, however, that there is a characteristic tendency toward certain shapes and slopes, which assists in identification.

difficult one, particularly in forgery cases; he is limited not only by the nature of the evidence but also by the degree to which the investigator can assist him in providing standards of comparison.

9. Preliminary Examinations

It is not the purpose of this treatment to train the investigator to be a handwriting expert. A certain amount of technical knowledge, however, should be mastered so that while examining a file or record during an investigation, his suspicions may be aroused regarding the validity of certain documents. It is a great convenience for an investigator to be able to segregate the genuine documents from the suspicious ones in order that he may submit the questioned ones for technical examination and report. The following illustrations should provide him with the basic knowledge for this differentiation.

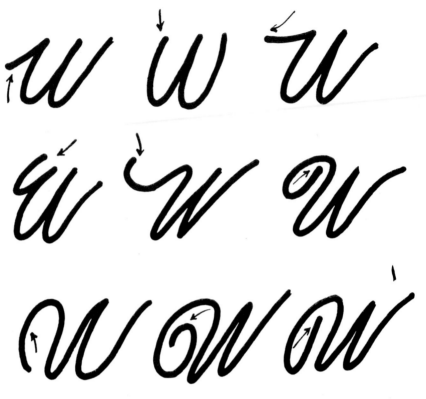

Figure 75. Initial or approach strokes. It is found that approach strokes are highly individual. The direction of the motion, the relative position of the beginning, and its height above the writing line serve to characterize an individual handwriting. The more common variations are shown above.

Figure 76. Curvature. The manner in which certain letters, particularly those with loops, are curved provides an important characteristic.

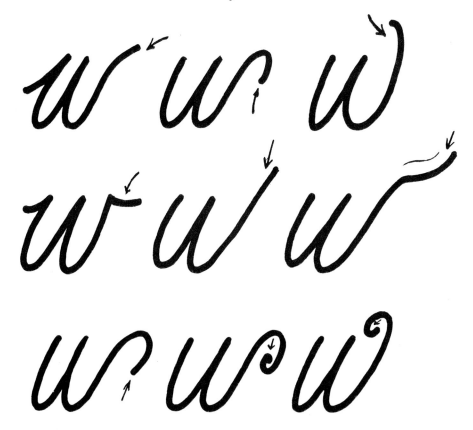

Figure 77. Terminal strokes. The manner in which an individual ends a word or letter is significant. Again, the direction, relative position of the terminal point, and its height above the base line are important.

III. STANDARDS OF COMPARISON

10. Definitions

One of the most important functions of the investigator in relation to a questioned document examination is the provision of suitable exemplars or standards with which the questioned writing or typing can be compared. An exemplar is a standard of writing of known authorship which can be used by the expert in a comparison. The exemplar may be in the form of writing, printing, typing, a stamp or seal impression. Request standards are exemplars which have been prepared at the request of the investigator; non-request standards are usually specimens which have been prepared prior to the investigation.

11. Genuineness

In order that an exemplar be admitted in evidence, its genuineness must first be established. It must be shown that the exemplar is directly and unquestionably connected with the suspect. At the time of obtaining the exemplars the investigator must, by appropriate measures, lay the groundwork for the formal proof of authenticity which may be later required at the trial.

12. Writing Instruments

For suitability an exemplar should be prepared with the materials similar to those apparently used for the questioned document. The appearance of writing depends on the kind of pen or pencil employed; consequently, arrangements must be made to permit a suspect to use a similar writing instrument in preparing a request standard. Naturally, if it is thought that he used his own pen, he should be asked to prepare the exemplar with it.

a. **Pens.** If fountain or dip pen and ink were used, the suspect should not be permitted to use a ball-point pen. From an examination of the questioned writing some conclusion can be drawn concerning the nib. If it appears that a fine, medium, broad, or stub point was used, a comparable nib should be provided. The ink used should be similar in color and tint to that on the questioned document.

b. **Ball-Point Pens.** Unless it is obvious that the perpetrator used such a pen, a ball-point pen should not be employed in preparing an exemplar. The ball-point pen obscures the writer's ability to exhibit his characteristic habits of quality, rhythm, shading, and skill. It fails to reveal pen position or the angle at which the instrument was held

Figure 78. Line quality is the term used to describe the relative smoothness of line. The hand of a normal person accustomed to writing is shown in (a) where the lines are flowing and free from hesitation. In (b) tremor or hesitation is indicated. Certain types of forgery are detected by defective line quality.

Figure 79. Pen pressure and shading. Some persons tend to vary the pressure of the pen in certain strokes. The degree to which variations in pressure are visible depends also on the flexibility of the nib. A similar effect can be obtained by varying other factors such as the degree of intentional shading with a broad nib, the selection of pen position, and the intensity of applied pressure.

Figure 80. Proportion and alignment. The relative size of the various parts of the letters and the ratio of the lengths of capital and minuscule letters are significant.

with relation to the body and the paper. Often it does not respond to normal pressure. Finally, unusual writing habits are created by the use of these pens.

c. **Pencils.** The hardness of the lead and the sharpness of the point affect the appearance of pencil writing. By testing with pencils of different numbers and varying degrees of sharpness, the investigator can choose an appropriate pencil for the production of exemplars.

d. **Crayons, Chalk, and Brushes.** Since these media vary widely in color and composition, the likely one should be selected after experiment. Naturally, the choice can be narrowed by considering the availability of specimens and also the types in the suspect's possession or area of activity. The problem of brushes will arise in oriental countries where ideographic writing is used.

13. Handwriting Standards

The most important phase of a typical document case is concerned with obtaining suitable handwriting standards. The subsequent examination by the expert will depend for its success upon the submission of satisfactory specimens of the suspect's writing or handprinting.

a. **Kind.** The exemplars should be suitable in word and form. Ordinarily, the suspect should be required to write the actual text of the questioned document. In some instances it may be desirable to avoid divulging the exact text of the document; it will then be necessary to use a different text which includes, however, the key words and letter combinations appearing in the questioned writing. Correspondence in form means the use of similar writing materials in preparing the exemplars. Thus, if the questioned document is an anonymous letter, paper of the same size, texture, and quality should be used together with a similar ink and pen. It is especially important that correspondingly lined paper be used where appropriate.

b. **Writing Requirements.** The suspect should be required to use the same type of script as that found on the questioned document. He should write on only one side of the paper unless, of course, he is writing exemplars of a check and an endorsement on the back is desirable.

c. **Procedure.** The suspect should be first seated and provided with writing materials. The investigator should then dictate the comparison text. He should not, ordinarily, suggest the punctuation, spelling, or paragraphing. The material should be dictated several times, the speed of dictation being increased each time so that the suspect will be inclined to lapse into his normal writing habits. Each sheet should be removed as soon as it is completed. In this way the suspect will not be able to imitate the first exemplars which he has prepared and thus maintain any disguise he is attempting.

d. **Number of Exemplars.** If the questioned writing consists only of a signature or a few words, twenty specimens prepared by the suspect will suffice. Where the questioned writing consists of a few paragraphs, five exemplars will usually suffice. If the text is longer, fewer standards will be required. In addition to using the same type of writing instrument for these exemplars, in cases where a ball-point pen or a pencil was used in the questioned writing, the suspect should also be required to prepare several specimens using a fountain pen.

e. **Identification.** The exemplar sheets should be identified by writing on the back of them the case number, date, investigator's initials, and the writing instrument used. If there are several suspects, each suspect should be designated by a letter of the alphabet and his exemplars should be numbered in order as they are prepared. Where different hands are used in different exemplars, a notation should be made to indicate whether it is the right or left.

f. **Auxiliary Request Standards.** When the text of the questioned writing is obscene or contains classified information, it should not be reproduced unless it is so limited in length that the exact wording is unavoidable. Similarly, the text should not be repeated if it is thought that the subject's awareness of the purpose of obtaining the exemplars will lead him to attempt to disguise his handwriting. In these situations auxiliary request standards, that is, specimens which do not repeat the questioned writing, should be used. A little imagination will suggest a suitable text that includes many of the words and the apparently characteristic letter combinations. As an alternative the investigator may use a paragraph in which the words include all the letters of the alphabet and most of the punctuation marks.

g. **Handprinting.** If the questioned text was handprinted, the suspect should be required to use the same style of printing. The exemplars should be written completely in capital letters when the text was thus prepared. If minuscule and capitals were used, the same arrangement should be followed. Because of the difficulties presented to the expert by handprinting, a greater number of exemplars is usually desirable.

h. **Check Exemplars.** Check standards should be prepared on a blank check similar to the one under investigation. If regular check blanks or printed forms are used, the word *void* should be marked on each in the view of the suspect. In forwarding fraudulent checks to the laboratory, the letter of transmittal should state whether any part of the evidentiary check is genuine, whether any of the signatures on the check are those of actual persons, and whether any of the suspects are presently in custody.

14. Rights of the Suspect

The Supreme Court, in *Gilbert v. California*, held that a suspect may not decline to provide a handwriting sample. Hitherto many organizations (e.g., the military investigative units), guided by the theory of handwriting being a testimonial utterance, that is, a conscious act of the mind and body, had required their agents to first obtain the assent of the suspect to the making of standards. It was considered best practice to obtain from the suspect, if possible, a statement to the effect that the specimens were prepared voluntarily (see p. 667).

15. Non-Request Standards

If the subject is absent or refuses to provide specimens of his handwriting, it is obviously necessary to obtain exemplars from other sources. Non-request standards are also desirable even where request specimens are given, because they are free of intentional disguise and indicate whether the request standards reflect the suspect's normal writing habits and characteristics. Good judgment will suggest in a given case the number and kind of non-request documents that should be submitted. Ordinarily all available specimens that can be found should be forwarded to the document examiner.

a. **Sources.** The sources of non-request standards are numerous. In addition to documents such as motor vehicle registrations and personal records which may be discovered among his possessions, a number of agencies will be found to possess files containing specimens of his writing. Most of these agencies are included in the list given in Chapter 13. In addition, school papers, letters to the suspect's family, personnel and finance records will usually provide satisfactory exemplars.

b. **Proof of Authorship.** If the non-request standards are to be admitted in evidence in court, it will be necessary to provide proof of the fact that the suspect is the author. If the suspect does not admit writing the standards, persons who witnessed their preparation may testify to the fact. Witnesses who are familiar with the suspect's writing can also offer testimony.

16. Letter of Transmittal

Suggestions for the protection of documentary evidence are given in Chapter 7. The questioned documents should be placed in a cellphane envelope which is then labeled "Questioned." The standards should be placed in a separate cellophane envelope and labeled "Known Writings" or "Standards." Both can now be placed in a third envelope and forwarded with a letter of transmittal identifying the case and the offense, describing the evidence by exhibit numbers, and specifying the type of examination desired or the nature of the information which is sought. The investigator should furnish the document examiner with any additional information which he thinks will be helpful to him. For example, he should give the reasons why the document is thought not to be genuine, or describe the circumstances under which the document was stored if the appearance of the paper shows signs of exposure or wear. The nature of such additional information will obviously depend on the case at hand.

IV. SPECIAL PROBLEMS IN HANDWRITING

17. Disguised Writing

a. **Techniques.** Writers of anonymous letters and unwilling suspects producing request writings are among those who will attempt to disguise their own handwriting. Forgers may disguise their writing in two ways: they may imitate the handwriting of another person or they may endeavor to invent an entirely new style of writing. The success achieved by a person attempting a disguise is naturally dependent on his skill and imagination. Among the physical methods used in disguising are the following:

1) *Slant.* Changing the direction of the slant is the most common disguise. The forger may employ a distinct backhand slant instead of the usual forehand slant.

2) *Speed.* By writing very rapidly or very slowly a different appearance is achieved.

3) *Irregularities.* Deliberate carelessness will disguise the writing by producing an inferior style.

4) *Size.* The letters may be written unusually large or small.

5) *Printing.* Handprinting may be substituted for script.

6) *Change of Hand.* The forger may use the left instead of the right hand.

7) *Inverted.* The writing may be made "upside down."

b. **Detecting.** Since handwriting is the result of a lifetime of practice and is actually a collection of muscular and nervous habits, it is not a simple matter to disguise all the characteristics of one's hand. The reader may be convinced of this by experimenting with the left hand or with a different slant. Although it is theoretically possible to disguise successfully, as a matter of actual practice it is found that, where the writing is abundant, a sufficient number of characteristics appear through the disguise to permit an identifica-

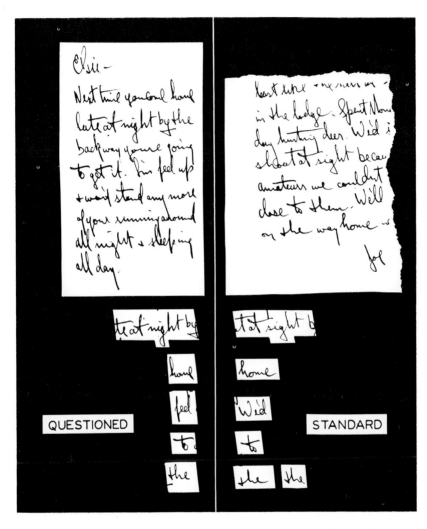

Figure 81. Handwriting comparison. This is an example of an effective choice of a non-request standard. Line quality, curvature, proportion, and other qualities are similar in each specimen, and there are no important unexplained differences. The most characteristic portions have been selected for comparison. Courtesy of Joseph McNally and Francis Murphy.

tion. When the disguised writing is limited to a few signatures, the problem of identification becomes practically impossible. The document examiner will probably be successful in dealing with a long anonymous letter but will often fail when confronted with only one or two forged checks.

c. **Unaccustomed Hand.** The use of the unaccustomed (usually the left) hand in disguising can ordinarily be detected. Since the same mind dictates the action and since little care is given to style, design, and other qualities, the characteristics present in the normal writing can be detected. The major changes will be a difference in slant and a general deterioration of the style. If the examiner has standard specimens prepared with the left hand, his task is greatly simplified.

18. Guided Writing

A person weakened by sickness or age may require assistance in writing his signature. The result will be an unnatural appearance marked by misalignment, abnormal letter formations, abrupt changes in direction, and poor spacing of the letters. If the writing does not show these defects but appears to be fluid in style and well controlled, it can be safely concluded that the hand was not guided.

19. Illiteracy

The writing of an illiterate is marked by an absence of style and the appearance of unorthodox designs. If an attempt has been made to forge the handwriting of an illiterate person, the deception can be detected in the grammatical errors, misspellings, and peculiar phrasing. It is difficult for the forger to know the form which the illiterate's expressions will take. If other samples of the illiterate's writings are available, it is possible to compare the peculiarities of the phrasing in the more common locutions of letter writing.

20. Handprinting

A very common method of disguise is the use of handprinting. In filling out a false automobile registration blank, for example, the criminal often resorts to handprinting in the belief that it is an unfailing disguise. Handprinting can, however, be successfully identified, if the questioned specimens are sufficient in quantity.

The request writings must, of course, be handprinted. Since most persons do not habitually or even occasionally employ handprinting, their rare attempts at it are marked by distinct peculiarities. The design and form of the letters and the choice of small or capital letters will reveal characteristics.

21. Family Similarities

Since each person inherits part of his mental, muscular, and nervous make-up from his parents and since, further, he is exposed to environmental influences including, at times, the same form of education, it should be expected that family resemblances will appear in handwriting. The existence of such a possibility is of interest to the investigator in cases where several members of a family may be logical suspects in a case. The existence of certain similarities in the writing of members of the same family does not seriously affect the examiner's problem of detecting the individualities.

22. Foreign Handwriting

The examination of handwriting made in a European language is accomplished by means of the same principles employed for English. Certain Asiatic languages such as Chinese and Japanese which employ ideographs or picture writing present less difficult problems, since there is an absence of standardization of symbols. The writing of these Oriental languages reflects the individual mind more closely than European handwriting.

V. TYPEWRITING IDENTIFICATION

23. Applications

The typewriter also possesses characteristics which can serve to identify the source of documents. The following are the most common objectives of a comparison of typewritten materials:

a. To identify the manufacturer and model of a typewriter.

b. To identify a specific typewriter.

c. To prove that changes in a document were made with a typewriter other than the one used to type the original document.

d. To establish a limit that can be placed on the age of a document by showing that the machine was not manufactured before a certain year.

24. Obtaining Typewriter Standards

As in the case of handwriting, the success of a typewriting examination will often depend on the manner in which the standards are prepared and the number submitted to the laboratory. In obtaining standards the investigator should make an inquiry to determine whether the typewriter was repaired since the date when the questioned documents were believed to have been typed. The following problems are representative of cases involving typewritten documents.

a. **Age of Document.** To determine the maximum age of a document by establishing the make and model of the typewriter, only the questioned document itself should be submitted to the laboratory.

b. **Make and Model of an Unknown Typewriter.** This determination is usually a preliminary step in the search for the particular typewriter which was used to prepare the questioned document. The document itself should be submitted to the examiner.

c. **Identification of a Typewriter.** To determine whether a particular typewriter produced the questioned document, the latter must be compared with standards prepared with the typewriter. Samples of typing made with the machine in question should be submitted together with the evidentiary document. In cases where it is suspected that the evidentiary typing was recently made, it is sometimes possible to detect portions of the text on the ribbon of the typewriter. Hence, if the ribbon is obviously new, it should not be used to prepare the samples but should be removed and submitted for examination. Two types of standards should be prepared as follows:

1) ***Regular Specimen.*** The text of the questioned document should be copied exactly. A paper similar in quality and color should be used. Ten such copies should be made, if the text consists of approximately fifteen lines. If the text is lengthy only the first ten or fifteen lines need be copied. Each copy should be made on a separate sheet of paper. The ribbon used in preparing the standards should be selected to produce inked impressions of approximately the same intensity and depth as those of the questioned document. Finally, the entire keyboard, including the shift and non-shift positions, should be typed to provide a copy of each letter and character for the examiner.

2) ***Carbon Specimen.*** To enable the document examiner to detect dirty, defective, or scarred type, a carbon specimen of a page of the text should be typed on the machine in question. The ribbon should first be removed or the ribbon guide set in stencil position. A piece of white paper and a fresh piece of carbon paper are inserted in the machine with the carbon facing the white paper in such a manner that the keys will strike directly upon the carbon paper, leaving a carbon impression on the white paper.

25. Identifying Typewriter Standards

To identify standards prepared with a typewriter the following information should be typed on the face of each sheet:

a. Name of the person typing the standard.
b. Manufacturer and model of the typewriter.
c. Serial number of the machine.
d. Date of preparation.
e. Case number.
f. Exhibit number, consisting of a letter of the alphabet to identify each typewriter and a number to identify each exemplar prepared with the typewriter.
g. Additional information for the examiner, such as the date on which the typewriter was last repaired.

26. Procedure in Comparing Typewriting

Typewriting identification is based on the same principles that form the basis of the identification of handwriting. A sufficient number of characteristics may be found present in a specimen of typewriting to enable the expert to state that the typing could have been done on only one machine. The methods for identifying typewriting are similar to those of handwriting. A specimen is obtained from a known typewriter and compared with the typing specimen of unknown origin with respect to certain class and accidental characteristics. Class characteristics such as the design and size of the letters will enable the examiner to determine the make and model of the typewriter, while accidental characteristics such as alignment, slant, and other acquired defects will help in identifying the individual machine within the class. Thus, known specimens are collected as previously described and compared with the questioned typewriting with respect to the following major qualities:

a. **Design and Size.** The design and size of the letters and figures vary with different makes and different models of typewiters. Naturally, if the typewriting was made on a relatively rare model of a machine, the examiner's task is simplified. The following points of comparison will aid the examiner in determining whether the known and unknown specimens were made on the same model of typewriter.

1) Overall size of letters.

2) Lengths of serifs (small bars at the top and bottom of strokes).

3) Length and curvature of endings, in *f*, *g*, *m*, *t*, and *y*.

a) *f*—length of horizontal lines; curvature at top.

b) *g*—proportion of area of upper oval to that of lower; space between ovals; relative positions; shape and position of joining line; and ending at upper right.

c) *m*—relation of height to width; length of serifs and upper left and lower right.

d) *t*—curvature at lower extremity; length and location of crossbar; ratio of lengths of divided vertical line.

e) *y*—angle found in center; relative lengths of parts; length of serif; curvature.

4) Size and design of figures.

a) 8—relative areas and shapes of ovals.

b) 5—the design of this figure is particularly characteristic.

c) 4—proportions of component lines.

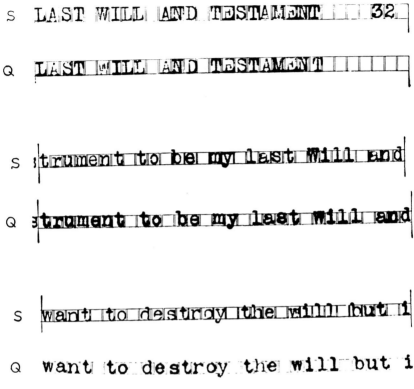

Figure 82. Typewriting comparison between standard (S) and question (Q) specimens in a case of a contested will. The specimens represent the work of several typewriters. It may be seen from the characteristic defects present in each pair of specimens that the same typewriter was used in each case. The ruling of the spaces emphasizes the misalignment of the type. Courtesy of Joseph McNally.

d) 2 and 3—characteristic shape.

e) 6, 7, and 9—length.

b. **Alignment.** If a typewriter is in perfect alignment, a letter will fall in the middle of an imaginary space. All letters and figures occupy the same area. The machine is designed so that a set number of characters occupy a given length. Approximately 90 per cent of the older typewriters have pica type, in which ten characters occupy an inch length of the paper. Many machines have elite type, in which there are twelve characters to an inch. It should be noted also in a page of typing that the characters are aligned vertically as well as horizontally. The lines in a single space sheet of typewriting are spaced six to the inch. Thus, each character should fall in a fixed position in an area of $1/10 \times 1/6''$. With extended use or maladjustment, the character may acquire a tendency to fall in a different position. The misalignment of a letter can be detected by means of a glass plate ruled in one direction at intervals of $1/10''$ and in the perpendicular direction at intervals of $1/6''$. By placing the plate in an appropriate position, the alignment of many letters can be checked at a glance. For example, the alignment of the bottoms of all small letters should be the same except for *g, j, p, q,* and *y*; for the tops of small letters also, except for *b, d, f, h, k, l,* and *t*. A misaligned letter can be determined in this manner, and the extent of its misalignment with respect to an imaginary line can be measured.

c. **Slant.** An aberration in the slope of a letter can be considered as another form of misalignment. Loosely speaking, the letter should be perpendicular to the base line. However, even new machines will be defective in regard to the slant of some of the letters. Older machines develop these defects. The typebar becomes twisted so that the character no longer prints perpendicular to the line of writing. The defect is more readily detected in the tall letters such as *l, h, f, d, b, k, t,* and the capitals.

d. **"Off Its Feet."** In a new machine, the typeface should be adjusted to strike with equal pressure over the entire surface. Divergences frequently occur through maladjustment, use, or wear. The typeface no longer strikes the roller with equal pressure on all parts and variations in the density of the ink impression can be observed. The typeface is then said to be "off its feet." The fault is more readily observed in the broader small letters such as *g, m, o, s,* and *w* and in the capitals.

e. **Other Defects.** A typewriter is made of hundreds of small parts which may become loose, bent, or broken. The resulting small defects provide combinations of characteristics that definitely identify a machine as the source of a typewriting sample. Broken typefaces in which a letter prints with a part missing and worn typewriters which cause characters to print with varying density on successive strokes are among the most common defects.

f. **Electric Typewriters**. The document examiner is faced with additional problems in examining typescript made on a single-element typewriter. In regard to the class characteristics he must, in addition to the make and model of the machine, identify the type element used. Although IBM has dominated the electric typewriter market for years, there are more than a dozen single-element machines available. Different type-style single elements are interchangeable on different machines.

In identifying the individual type element the examiner must rely on acquired characteristics and imperfections in manufacture such as damage to type characters, broken detent (a stopping and releasing mechanism) teeth, and electroplating peeling from the surface of the character. This last characteristic is acquired during manufacture in the course of the molding and electroplating process. Small plastic particles may be accidentally electroplated on the type-character faces in the form of raised beads, randomly placed or distributed. Depending on its size and shape, the bead will indent or even puncture the paper on impact, in some cases leaving an embossed impression on the back of the type sheet. Since the beads are randomly produced, the spacing, size, and shape of the punctures may provide a recognizable and even individual pattern for the examiner's eye. The defects are even more apparent both on the paper and the ribbon if a one-time carbon ribbon was used in producing the questioned typescript.

27. Determining the Age of a Typed Document

It is possible to set a limit to the maximum age of a typewritten document by determining the model of the typewriter. For example, if the typing was done with a model that was first made in 1967, obviously the document must have been made since that date. The FBI and other large law enforcement agencies maintain a reference file of typewriter specimens. If a specimen of typing is submitted to these agencies, the expert can determine the make and model of the typewriter and also can provide information concerning the year of manufacture of a particular model of a typewriter.

28. Determining the Typist

The ideal solution to a problem involving the determination of the source of a typewritten document is to specify not only the particular typewriter, but also the typist who performed the work. This latter determination is of great importance in cases of anonymous letters. Sometimes, the typewritten document contains a sufficient number of clues to permit such identification. The following points are noted by the examiner:

a. **Language Habits.** If the typist composed as well as typed the letter, certain errors of the other characteristics of language will be present. Errors of punctuation, spelling, diction, and grammar may be present in the text. If sample writings of the suspect are available, similar errors may be detected.

b. **Mechanical Habits.** The general appearance of the typing is characteristic. The pressure used in certain letters, margins, length of lines, spacing, indention of paragraphs, and many other points may reveal habits of the typist that can readily be checked by means of comparison of samples of typewriting.

29. Alterations to a Typewritten Document

Questions sometimes arise concerning suspected additions to a typewritten document. If an erasure and a misaligned addition are present, the problem is not difficult. If the addition has been made with great skill, a close examination by means of measuring devices and a low-power microscope is necessary. The following procedure will be found practicable:

a. **Machine.** The examiner may determine whether the addition was made by the same machine or at least by the same make and model of typewriter. The success of this examination will depend on the amount of typing in the added text.

b. **Ink Density.** If the suspected text was truly part of the original text, no difference in the density of the ink impression should be observed since a similar part of the ribbon was used. The examiner will examine the addition under a microscope and compare the inking with that of the accepted part of the text.

c. **Alignment.** It is exceedingly difficult to replace a sheet of paper in a typewriter and perfectly align added letters with those previously made. The examiner tests the suspected additions for alignment by means of a glass plate. It can readily be determined whether a given letter is falling in its proper place in the $1/10 \times 1/6''$ rectangle.

VI. EXAMINATION OF PAPER

30. Application

The origin of paper may arise as a question in the course of an investigation. Cases of anonymous letters, for example, are sometimes solved by discovering the source of the paper. One of the clues to the operations of a forger is the source of his blank checks. Papers can often be identified and distinguished by means of their composition, processing, and marking. In addition, the handling of papers subsequent to manufacture may result in identifying marks. The following are the typical objectives of a comparison with paper standards:

a. To determine whether the standard is similar to the paper bearing the questioned writing.

b. To determine whether a sheet of paper was taken from a particular pad or tablet. For example, it can be shown by matching the partially perforated edges that a questioned check was taken from a particular checkbook. Again, by matching perforated edges, it is sometimes possible to show that the stamp on a questioned envelope was removed from another stamp or a sheet of stamps found in the possession of a suspect.

c. To show that one document was in contact with another. This may be established by the shape of a blot, for example, which had seeped through the questioned document and stained some of the underlying sheets of a tablet. In a recent narcotics case it was possible to show that the glassine envelope containing the morphine found in the addict's possession had been removed from a stack of envelopes on the counter of a suspected pharmacy. The glue with which the lower end of the envelope was sealed in the process of manufacture had, in drying, caused the envelope to adhere to the next lower one in the stack. On separating, the fibers of the lower envelope had been disturbed in a recognizable outline.

31. Standards of Comparison

Standards will be required whenever the source of paper becomes a point of interest in the investigation. It is found that forgers and writers of anonymous letters often exercise great care in selecting a suitable paper, even making a special purchase to suit their needs. The investigator may discover paper standards in the suspect's quarters or place of business, or he may be required to search for the place of purchase. In the latter event the advice of a stationer or a paper manufacturer should be sought on the problem. At least five sheets should be submitted as standards. Each sheet should be identified by writing appropriate case information on the back. In addition, there should be included any appropriate information concerning the circumstances surrounding the discovery or location of the sheets.

32. Examination by the Laboratory

The chemical and physical processes to which paper is subjected in its manufacture often provide identifying characteristics which permit the expert to distinguish one sample from another. By comparing the characteristics of two samples, the analyst can readily determine dissimilarities and eliminate the possibility of identity of source. In some cases, it is possible for him to definitely conclude that two specimens came from the same source. Some of the methods listed cause a physical change in the document and ordinarily are not used by the document examiner without obtaining specific authorization from the contributor.

a. **Physical Tests.** The following physical characteristics and measurements serve to differentiate paper: thickness, measurement of length and width; weight per unit area; color; finish, such as bond, laid, smooth, or glossy; opacity, i.e., capacity of the paper for the transmission of light; folding endurance as determined instrumentally by the number of alternate folds the paper will stand before breaking; bursting strength as determined by the measurement of the pressure necessary to burst a hole in a sheet of the paper; accelerated aging tests performed by means of high temperatures or strong artificial light.

b. **Chemical Tests.** Chemical tests may be conducted to determine the fiber composition, loading material, and the sizing used in the manufacture of the paper. Like the physical tests previously described, chemical tests are of little value unless a side-by-side comparison can be conducted between the paper in question and the known standards submitted for comparison. The use of the chemical tests causes a small change or alteration in the document; hence, extensive testing may consume a part of the evidence, and the investigator should indicate to the expert the degree to which the testing may be carried. The following tests are commonly employed:

1) *Sizing Tests.* By the use of a few drops of chemical reagent, the sizing of two different specimens of paper can be compared. A small perceptible stain results from these tests.

2) *Loading Materials.* This test is performed by burning and ashing the greater part of an ordinary sheet of paper, then analyzing the ash. Obviously, where only a limited sample of evidence is available, this test is not recommended.

3) *Fiber Composition.* Chemical reagents are applied to small sections of the paper in order to determine the nature of the constituent fibers.

4) *Absorption.* Strips of the paper are suspended in liquids to determine either the rate of absorption or the total absorption of the paper.

c. **Watermark.** The chief characteristic indicating the source or origin of paper is the watermark. It is a distinctive mark or design placed in the paper at the time of its manufacture by passing the paper under a *dandy* roll. Several designs are present on the dandy roll, similar to each other, but bearing individual characteristics, particularly if the roll has been subjected to wear or damage. By examining the watermark, the examiner is able to identify the paper as the product of a particular manufacturer.

VII. REFERENCE FILES

33. Use

An investigation involving the source of a questioned document is often quite general in nature, with no logical suspects from whom standards may be obtained for comparison. In this situation a reference file can assist in narrowing the area of investigation and drawing up a list of possible suspects. Thus, a file containing fraudulent checks may serve to identify a questioned check with the work of a known forger. A file containing samples of type from all known machines will aid in identifying the manufacturer of the machine that was used to prepare an anonymous extortion letter.

34. Files of Law Enforcement Agencies

Described below are some of the reference files maintained by law enforcement agencies. The number and extent of the files will usually vary with the size of the agency. Organizations such as the Post Office, the Treasury Department, the FBI, and the New York Police Department maintain a number of these files to suit their special needs.

a. **Typewriting Standards.** This file contains impressions of all the type faces of machines of various manufacturers. Their most common application is in determining the make and model of the machine that was used to produce a questioned document submitted for examination.

b. **Watermarks.** Individual paper manufacturers use characteristic watermarks to identify the source, period, and sometimes the quality of their product. A watermark appearing on a questioned document may be compared with those in the reference file to determine its origin and approximate date of manufacture.

c. **Paper.** The paper reference file contains samples of the manufacturer's product with data relating to weight, color, composition, and quality. It is particularly useful in determining the manufacturer of papers which do not bear watermarks.

d. **Check Writers.** A file of checkwriter and protectograph standards of the machines of various manufacturers is maintained to determine the make and model of the machine used on a questioned check.

e. **Rubber Stamps.** This file is used to trace documents bearing stamped impressions.

f. **National Fraudulent Check File.** This file consists of photostatic and photographic copies of fraudulent checks in excess of a specified amount. Law enforcement agencies throughout the country forward such copies to the FBI, which maintains the file and provides document examination services in connection with the file. Police agencies may forward copies of fraudulent checks for a search and comparison with the files. By means of this centralized collection it is possible to identify the work of professional forgers who travel through the country passing fraudulent checks. With the information obtained from this file a police department can communicate with other communities where a particular forger has operated to obtain a physical description of the suspect and information concerning his *modus operandi.*

g. **Anonymous Letters.** Files of anonymous letters are maintained by the FBI, the Protective Research Section of the U.S. Treasury, located in the White House Annex, and municipal police departments. In this way threatening, obscene, and annoying letters can be classified and, in some instances, the work of a habitual anonymous letter writer can be identified.

35. Private Firms

Law enforcement agencies can often obtain the assistance of manufacturers of writing materials in tracing the source of paper, ink, pens, and pencils and in making comparisons with materials used in questioned documents. Many manufacturers maintain extensive reference files of their own products and employ technical experts with a broad knowledge of the industry.

VIII. AGE OF DOCUMENTS

36. Introduction

A question of the age of a document may arise in connection with papers such as wills or contracts. Documents which impose an obligation, give a title, or grant a benefit may depend for their effectiveness or validity on their date; hence, they are susceptible to the work of the forger. A document can be treated by a skilled forger so that it appears to be fifty years older than it actually is. An experienced document examiner can often detect the falsity of such a document.

37. Methods of Aging

To give the document an appearance of age, it is subjected to chemical and physical treatment. Among the techniques employed are the following:

a. **Heating.** The document may be treated in an oven or over a hot stove to give it the brittleness and discoloration of age. Baking and scorching are variations of this method.

b. **Sunlight.** Exposure to sunlight produces the yellow color of age. Carbon arc and ultraviolet lamps can be used for the same purpose.

c. **Abuse.** The paper may be crumpled, smeared, or discolored to give it the appearance of neglect that is associated with age.

d. **Chemical Treatment.** The document can be subjected to one or more of the many chemical processes that will simulate the appearance of age.

38. Determinations

It is not a simple matter to determine the age of a document. Obviously, the fixing of an exact date is an impossibility in the absence of eyewitnesses to the making of the document. Among the problems which the examiner can sometimes answer successfully are the following:

a. **Purported Age.** Is the document as old as the date or other signs would indicate?

b. **Probable Date.** What is the approximate date on which the document was made? This can be answered by setting a maximum or a minimum age to the document. For example, if the model of the typewriter used to produce the document was not made before 1921, a minimum age can be set. Similarly, if the watermark of the papers was not used by the manufacturer after 1940, a probable maximum can be fixed. The use of a ball-point pen would likewise limit the age.

c. **Several Documents.** A question may arise concerning the priority of production of several documents. Was one document produced before or after another document?

39. Age Indicators

To determine the appropriate age of a document, a study must be made of the physical and chemical properties of the paper and the writing and of the text and its meaning. Among the indicators that can assist the examiner are the following:

a. **Ink.** The age of inks is discussed on page 872.

b. **Typewriting.** Makes and models of typewriters are associated with definite manufacturing dates. The typewritten paper *must* have been produced after the particular model of typewriter was first put on the market by the manufacturer. Another indication of date is a physical defect in the type faces, the existence of which can be associated with a date by another independently made document which bears a date. If another document bearing a date exhibits the defect in the type, then the defect is *at least* as old as the document. The date of the questioned document can now be related to the fixed date by a determination of the existence of the defect. A plurality of defects will obviously serve to narrow the date limits.

c. **Dated Mechanical Styles.** The use of certain styles of mechanical impressions is associated with the date of their first appearance. The following mechanical impressions can be used to set a date limit by their period of manufacture or by the first appearance of defects: printing; lithograph, multigraph, multilith, and mimeograph work; seals and watermarks.

d. **Stamps.** Rubber stamps can be referred to a date by their manufacture or by the appearance of defects on other dated paper. Cancellation stamps on envelopes; bank stamps; certification stamps; and date stamps are useful for this purpose.

e. **Textual Contents.** The document may contain information that suggests a date limit. The letterhead, names of officers on the letterhead, address, titles, and similar matters relate to the history of an organization and thus set a date.

f. **Writing Media.** The chemical or physical properties of the media used to produce the document can be referred to manufacturing periods. Thus, copying pencils, colored pencils, blotters, typewriter ribbons, and pens produce impressions or traces that can be associated with dates. (Ink and typewriting have, because of their importance, been placed in separate categories.)

g. **Physical Characteristics.** If the document consists of several pages, additional evidence of age may be present. Binding method; eyelets; fasteners; staples; and punch holes are among the physical characteristics that may set a date. Thus, if they were dropped from use after a certain date or have been in continuous use after a certain date, an age limit can be specified.

h. **Style.** The very term *style* suggests a date. There are fashions in the arrangement of the various elements of a letter. The disappearance of old styles and the innovations of the new place a date on a letter or other document. Among the elements and details to be noted are the following: the address, heading, form of salutation and complimentary close, abbreviations, and indentation of paragraphs.

i. **Paper.** The composition, size, and condition of the paper are important factors in age determination. The manufacturer of the paper can often be determined from the watermark. The manufacturer's technical employees can then be interviewed in regard to the date of production of certain types of paper. In this way, a maximum age can be set to the document.

40. Procedures

The methods of age determination have been suggested in the preceding section and in the section treating of inks. The details of the procedure and additional points of examination are suggested below:

a. **Storage Conditions.** How was the document kept? Was it stored in the basement or attic? What was the climate?

b. **Paper.** The paper is examined and tested for brittleness, undue soiling, and mutilation. Is the discoloration even or uneven? Is the paper yellow with age, especially near the top and the edges?

c. **Parts.** If the document is soiled, the examination should determine whether the inside or folded portion is more soiled on the inside than on the outside. Such a condition suggests a simulated aging.

d. **Books.** Where the document is in book form, the bindings and torn portions should be studied. Evidence of the removal of pages is significant.

e. **Clips and Marks.** The conditions of areas where clips, pins, fasteners, staplings, and punch markings have been used should be studied to determine if these articles or markings were recently added. For example, if a paper clip has been attached to a document for a long period of time, evidence of discoloration about the edge of the clips should be apparent. The area under certain types of clips will exhibit less discoloration than other areas.

IX. PHOTOGRAPHY OF DOCUMENTS

41. General

The document examiner is necessarily a photographer. Although the volume of his cases may prevent his personally doing the photographic work, he understands its need at each stage of an examination and gives specific directions concerning its accomplishment. He must employ photographs as a record, as a means of examination, as a method of discovery, and as a form of demonstration in court. Many phases of photography are employed. Copy and photostat work, filter photography, photomicrography, photomacrography, ultraviolet, infrared, and even x-ray techniques constitute his basic photographic knowledge.

42. Reproduction for Record

On receiving a case the investigator or document examiner photographs the front and back of the questioned documents to preserve their original appearance as part of the case. A one-to-one copy is made using a reproduction camera such as the "Identiscope." A fixed-focus camera is considered a great convenience for this work. A ruled scale is sometimes placed in the picture to show the exact size and to facilitate later enlarging procedures.

43. Photostats

The use of photostats is quite limited in document work. The photostat is at best an inferior reproduction. It cannot serve as an adequate substitute for the original in any but the crudest type of examination.

44. Substitutes for Handling in Examination

Document examiners handle the questioned documents as little as possible. Every effort is made to avoid the unnecessary touching of the evidence materials. The questioned documents are placed in transparent envelopes and subsequently referred to in this state. Since a document examination requires a great deal of handling of specimens, the expert often uses the photographs as substitutes for the originals.

45. Photomicrography and Photomacrography

To demonstrate certain minute details that are important in the evidence the examiner must make enlarged pictures of the significant areas. To demonstrate, for example, the sequence of strokes, the crossing must be greatly enlarged to show the paper fibers. To make an ordinary enlargement is an unsatisfactory procedure, since there is no great resolution in the original negative. Photomacrography, the process whereby an enlarged image is achieved on the negative, is the most commonly used technique. The use of a 32 mm lens usually supplies all the magnification that is required. Sometimes, particularly where a magnification of over 10 × is needed, photomicrography must be employed. In this technique the photograph is made with a microscope objective and eyepiece.

46. Transparencies

To demonstrate in forgery cases the exact superimposition of writings such as the genuine and the traced signatures, a set of transparencies is made. A film is used instead of a sheet of photographic paper.

47. Filter Photography

In obliterated writing it is often necessary to discern writing that lies beneath other writing. If the two writings were made with different colored inks, a photograph is made using a filter of the same color as the upper ink. Thus, the upper layer of writing is rendered transparent and the lower becomes visible. This is but one of the many uses of filters in document photography. The filter is often employed to provide contrast in preparing exhibits. For example, if the questioned writing is found on a green registration form, a green filter will be used to give the form an appearance of whiteness.

48. Ultraviolet

The use of radiation slightly shorter in wavelength than that of visible light is quite common in document photography. Inks and papers which appear similar in the visible light often are strikingly different under ultraviolet light. Under the ultraviolet radiations some substances transform the energy into fluorescent light. Thus, a document will take on a different appearance under the ultraviolet lamp. The following are some of the uses of this form of radiation.

a. **Inks.** To emphasize differences in inks.

b. **Invisible Writing.** A fluid such as lemon juice or milk can be used to produce writing invisible to the naked eye. Under the ultraviolet light the fluid fluoresces in a highly legible fashion.

c. **Erasures.** Chemical erasures are sometimes made visible.

d. **Identification of Papers.** The fluorescent quality of paper is highly characteristic.

e. **Tampering.** Alterations in seals, checks, and other documents can be readily seen.

f. **Counterfeits.** Invisible markings are used to identify pari-mutuel tickets and lottery receipts. A counterfeit can be detected by means of its fluorescent qualities.

g. **Resealing Envelopes.** Differences in mucilage can be seen in the ultraviolet.

49. Infrared Photography

Some of the dyes used in inks are transparent to infrared radiations, others are opaque and, consequently, are recorded on infrared film. This phenomenon is useful in dealing with obliterations. A filter such as a Wratten 87 is used with infrared film and the photograph is made with incandescent light. As in other forms of filter photography, the lower layer of writing may be seen. The infrared properties of ink, pencil, and paper are used in a number of ways:

a. **Erasures.** Residual ink or pencil in an erasure will appear in contrast to its surroundings, thus giving a more legible appearance.

b. **Burned Documents.** Charred or burned documents can sometimes be made legible.

c. **Faded Writing.** Illegible writings such as old, discolored, or soiled documents should be photographed in the infrared. Obliterated matter on embossed seals, faded stamp cancellations, or postmarks can often be restored.

d. **Sealed Envelopes.** It is sometimes possible to make a legible photograph of a document in a sealed envelope by using infrared film. If the paper is transparent to the infrared radiation and the ink opaque, ideal conditions exist. Electron radiography can also be used.

50. Soft X-rays

The texture of paper takes on a new appearance in a radiograph made with soft x-rays. Chapter 42 deals with this technique in detail.

Obliterated watermarks and, in some cases, erasures can be made legible in this way.

51. Court Exhibits

In order to demonstrate his findings to the court, the document examiner must use enlarged, mounted photographs. In handwriting comparisons he must juxtapose the standard and questioned writing so that the similarities are apparent at a glance. In cases of obliterated writing or erasures he must show the document as it appeared normally as well as its appearance with the concealed elements made legible. Normal size photographs as well as enlargements should be submitted.

X. VARIOUS DOCUMENT PROBLEMS

52. General

In addition to the major problems of documentary evidence such as handwriting and typewriting comparisons and forgery determinations, there are numerous other questions that may arise in relation to documents. The present section endeavors to present the more common of these problems and to indicate in some places the methods applied by the document examiner in their solution. The purpose of this section is to acquaint the investigator with the potentialities of certain types of evidence, which might otherwise be neglected.

53. Sequence of Line Strokes and Paper Folds

In tampering with a document the criminal will often perform some operation which affects the writing or the paper and which can be determined as having been performed after the original document with its writing had been completed.

a. **Sequence of Line Strokes.** An interlineation (writing between the original lines), qualifying statement, or signature may be placed on the document after other writings have been made thereon. It is of great importance in some instances to show the order in which signatures were written on a document. If the spuriously added writing crosses the original writing, the document examiner by examination under the microscope can sometimes determine which writing was made first. If ink was used in both cases the determination is not too difficult. With ink writing and typewriting the determination of sequence is more difficult. The sequence of two rubber stamp impressions or of writing and a rubber stamp impression can also occasionally be determined.

b. **Punch Marks.** Was the writing prepared before or after the area had been perforated with a "paid" or "cancelled" punch? The edges of the punch holes should be examined for the presence of ink stains. If the punch was made after the writing, the edge will not reveal an ink stain, whereas if the writing was made later, the ink will run into the broken surface. Another indication may be present in the form of a tearing or bruising of the paper as the pen catches in the new edge formed by the punch. If it is obvious that the writer studiously avoided the holes, it can be assumed that the writing was made later.

c. **Sequence of Paper Folds.** When a paper is folded the fibers will be affected in the broken area, the extent of the breaking or changing depending on the number of times it is folded and the force employed in the action. If ink writing is added after the folding, the ink will flow or "bleed out" into the crease. Where a pencil has been used, carbon particles will adhere to the disturbed fibers. These effects are not visible when the writing existed prior to the folding. The quality of the paper as well as the extent of the folding treatment will determine the degree to which these phenomena are observable.

54. Alterations of Documents

The significance of a document can be materially altered by changing a number or a word. If the alteration is made by the author of the document, it is simply a correction and, as such, may serve as additional proof of authenticity. The problem of alterations, substitutions, interlineations, and additions is concerned with carefully executed work that would escape ordinary perusal. The alteration of a check, draft, money order, or other negotiable instrument can result in the loss of thousands of dollars. The mere addition of a zero to a number on a check can increase its value tenfold. This process is called "raising" the check. An alteration is detected by the difference in handwriting, typing, or ink or by the presence of an erasure. The document is examined under ultraviolet light for differences in the characteristics of the ink. Photographs are made with filters and process film. Differences may be discovered in the infrared region by photographing the document under incandescent lamps using a Wratten 87 filter and infrared film.

55. Indented Writings

One of the most common document problems is the so-called "indented writing." If the original writing is made on a pad of paper, indentions are produced on the bottom sheets. Thus, although the top sheet is removed, it may still be possible to decipher the writing from the sheet that lay immediately under it. If pencil was used in the original writing, the task is made simpler since a greater degree of pressure has been employed. A number of methods are recommended for the purpose of making such writing legible.

a. **Photography.** The pad is illuminated from the side so that the indentions are placed in relief. A photograph is made using commercial film. A series of photographs should be made, if necessary, varying the angle of illumination. This is the preferred method.

b. **Iodine Fuming.** The pressure applied in the writing process affects the paper fibers and makes them different from the untouched fibers. If the paper is fumed with iodine vapors, this difference is emphasized. A photograph is taken since the fumes further sublime. The fuming process should take place in a glass container with the document suspended over a crucible of iodine crystals. The process is accelerated by heat.

Figure 83. Indented writing. By oblique illumination the indentations on a lower sheet of a bookmaker's pad are made legible. Courtesy of William Stackpole.

c. **Indented Writing Solution.** Another method of emphasizing the alterations in the fiber structure is to dab the document with a piece of cotton dipped in the following solution:

Water	8 cc
Potassium iodide	4 gm
Iodine	1 gm
Glycerin	20 cc

The document can be restored to its original condition by dabbing with a 1 per cent solution of hypo ($Na_2S_2O_3$).

56. Sealed Envelopes

Has the envelope been opened and resealed? This question may arise in connection with money or confidential documents transmitted in sealed envelopes. To detect such tampering the investigator should be familiar with the common techniques employed in the surreptitious opening of envelopes and with the effects of such tampering on the envelope.

a. **Transmitted Light.** The envelope is held before a strong light. Alterations in the paper can be observed where the flap has been opened and resealed. To make a photographic record of the evidence, the envelope is used as a negative and printed onto photographic paper of good contrast. The variation in opacity is thus vividly reproduced.

b. **Postmarks.** If postmarks appear on the flap of the envelope, the resealing process will result in a slight misalignment.

c. **Mucilage.** In resealing, mucilage is usually added. The excess of and difference in the mucilage can be observed under a low-power microscope. A clever operator will reseal the envelope by using another envelope of the same type to provide mucilage by wetting its flap and placing it in contact for a few seconds with the flap of the old envelope.

d. **Raising the Stamp.** Another technique of surreptitiously opening mail consists of loosening and rolling back the stamp and then cutting out the area beneath the stamp. The contents can thus be removed and the stamp replaced in its original position.

e. **Rolling.** A thin rod can be inserted between the flap and the body of the envelope in the loose area near the top. The paper within can then be removed by rotating the rod until it catches the sheet and rolls it up tightly so that it can be withdrawn with the rod.

XI. ILLEGIBLE WRITINGS

57. General

Writings may become illegible through use, mishandling, or exposure to the elements. Someimes an incriminating writing is rendered illegible by intentional obliteration or erasure. Illegible evidentiary writings submitted to a document examiner can often be rendered legible or be deciphered.

58. Alterations of Evidence

Some of the methods employed in rendering a writing legible may alter the appearance of the writing; therefore, the document examiner does not employ such techniques without the permission of the contributing agency. This permission should not be given without thought, since at trial, a valid objection may be made to the admission of evidence on the grounds that it is not in its original condition, or that it has been tampered with. Photographic copies should be made by the document examiner before the examiner in order to show the original appearance of the document at the time he received it.

59. Existence of Erasures

One of the simplest types of inquiries is that of determining whether or not an erasure was made. Visual observation of the surface of the paper will usually reveal an alteration of this type. Pencil writing on good grades of paper can escape casual observation, but ink erasures are difficult to conceal. Physical inspection under ultraviolet light and iodine fuming are additional techniques.

60. Obliterated Writing

Writing may be obliterated by mechanical action; by covering with an overlaying substance; by eradication with a chemical ink remover; or by a combination of these methods. Physical and chemical methods are used in restoring such writings to a state of legibility.

61. Used Carbon Paper

One of the traces that is sometimes overlooked by a criminal is the carbon paper which was used to make a duplicate copy of some message or record used in illegal activity. Frequently, it is possible to decipher the complete original text by a careful examination of the carbon. If a carbon which has been used often is submitted to a laboratory, a legible copy of the desired writing can sometimes be made by the use of special photographic techniques. In handling or shipping the carbon paper, care should be taken to avoid folding or wrinkling.

62. Burned or Charred Documents

Documents which have been accidentally burned in a fire or which have been purposely destroyed in this manner may sometimes be deciphered in the laboratory. If a paper has been subjected to intense heat, reducing it to ashes, it is practically impossible to develop any of the original writing. If the combustion is incomplete, some success can be realized when the pieces are large enough to form a coherent message. Great care must be exercised in packing and shipping evidence of this type. The pieces should be placed between layers of cotton and shipped in a strong, rigid box.

XII. ANONYMOUS LETTERS

63. General

In any large city the anonymous letter writer poses a peculiar problem to the detective division. He may be a harmless crank, a sexual psychopath, an extortionist, or simply a troublemaker. The last mentioned is the most insidious of this type of offender. With a few lines on paper he can disrupt the harmony of a home, create dissension in a business organization, or undermine the structure of an established career. Eminent figures in public life become accustomed to receiving letters traducing their own reputation or casting suspicion on their trusted subordinates. These persons usually follow the simple rule of ignoring the letters or referring them to an investigative agency for the purpose of discovering the identity of the author rather than with any intention of testing the truth of the contents. Persons with less confidence permit the anonymous letter to create doubts and suspicions in their own minds; thus, they grant to the writer the mean success to which he aspired.

Figure 84. Charred documents. In order to destroy evidence the suspect threw the incriminating bonds into a fire. The charred remains were collected and photographed with infrared film and filter. In this way the printing and writing were made legible. Courtesy of John Stevenson and Dominic Paolo.

64. Types

Anonymous letters lend themselves to classification. Four convenient categories may be used to include the person with information, the person with criminal intent, the malcontent, and the crank.

a. **Information.** 1) *Reliable Informer.* A person may write to the police department to inform them of the identity of a criminal. Sometimes the "tip" will be a reliable one. A person witnessing a crime or knowing of the existence of a conspiracy will, out of public spirit or out of personal dislike for the criminal, inform the authorities of the name and address of the perpetrator and of the circumstances surrounding the crime. There is no problem connected with such a letter. The investigator may avail himself of the information with gratitude and test its reliability by discreet preliminary inquiry. It is understandable that the informant does not wish to expose himself or his family to possible recriminations. The most common example of this type of letter writer is the informant on tax delinquencies.

2) *Crank Informants.* A crime which receives a great deal of publicity will inspire a number of slightly unbalanced minds to write letters conveying their suspicions. The writer will usually be obsessed by some *bête noire* and will accuse it of the most heinous crimes including the one under discussion. The language of accusation is appropriately wild and can be readily recognized and profitably ignored.

b. **Criminal Intent.** This is the threatening letter of the extortionist. The writer usually demands a sum of money. Alternatively the receiver of the letter must accept the punishment which is threatened.

1) *Kidnapping.* The criminal may threaten to kill the captive unless a stipulated sum of money is delivered under stated conditions. Wealthy persons are the usual receivers of such letters. The bitter history of such cases points to the advisability of immediately referring them to the police. The Lindbergh case and the more recent Greenlease affair suffice to illustrate this lesson. The captive is, in some instances, dead before the letter is sent. If he has not been killed by that time, the criminals ordinarily have no intention of carrying out their threat.

2) *Extortion and Blackmail.* Blackmail is a form of extortion. In committing the crime of extortion the criminal obtains property from another with his consent induced by the wrongful use of force of fear. In blackmail a letter is used to convey the threat. The blackmailer sends, or causes to be sent, for the purpose of extorting money, a letter or writing which threatens one of the following:

a) To accuse a person of a crime.

b) To do any injury to any person or property.

c) To publish or connive at publishing a libel.

d) To expose or impute a deformity or disgrace.

Again, it is usually unwise to accede to the blackmailer's demand. The payment of the sum does not deprive the blackmailer of his weapon. He reasons logically that, if his criminal method was successful once, he has grounds for greater faith in the outcome of the second trial. The victim by repeated acquiescence finds himself hopelessly enmeshed. He must inevitably take the stand that his conscience originally dictated.

c. **Malcontents.** This is the most common type of anonymous letter writer. In some communities his action is called "dropping a letter." Typically, he is associated with a large organization, in private industry or civil service. His merits have not received true recognition. A rival has been preferred to him and has risen to a relatively high station. He has observed improper behavior in the office or in his rival's private life. He wishes to bring this behavior to the attention of the proper authorities. In police departments the letter writer will accuse his victim of accepting graft. In other civil service work and in private industry he will usually accuse his victim of taking undue credit for work done by others, of petty thievery, or of preferring his friends for promotion.

d. **Cranks.** This term covers a wide range of letter writers. Some of them are harmlessly insane and can be ignored. Others may give violent vent to their feelings and are potentially dangerous.

1) *Attacking Public Figures.* This is the religious or political crank. He addresses anonymous letters to persons in public office or at the head of a large private organization. He recognizes the fact that the public figure is in reality at the head of a conspiracy to promote some political or religious doctrine. The writer is usually a victim of the *idée fixe*, and little can be done to disabuse him of his

illusions. He is often a fanatic of a familiar stripe—anti-Semitic, anti-Christian, anti-Negro, a believer in a white conspiracy, anti-Communist, or pro-Red. Sometimes he is simply an utter fool giving voice to his convictions in confused implications and vilifying. On the other hand, he may be the insidious master of the smear, with just the right touch of truth in each stroke to prevent outright denunciation. Since he is usually not associated with the public figure under attack, he is difficult to identify. However, he is not to be considered a serious problem except in those rare cases where he convinces himself of his destiny to relieve the world of an oppressor by assassination.

2) *Obscene Letters—the Sex Deviate.* Some persons derive great satisfaction, usually sexual in nature, from writing obscene or scurrilous letters to a person of the opposite sex. A neighborhood youth may select a physically well endowed girl for his epistolary attention and send her anonymous letters informing her of his sexual ambitions. An office worker may send letters to the girl who sits three desks away. In a recent case, which is not atypical, a female school teacher was writing obscene letters to herself and complaining to authorities of the receipt of the missives. Characteristic of these letters is the description of abnormal sexual activity. The writer describes his desire for the woman; he relates how this ardency affects him privately and causes him to seek relief; he outlines his amorous ambitions; he writes in detail of the deviations from normal sexual relations which he intends to pursue. Ostensibly he is seeking acquiescence on the part of the woman. Actually he makes no arrangement for her to communicate with him. The letter is scurrilous and only rarely imaginative. The writer may, however, be dangerous; hence the investigator should, if possible, refer the letter to a psychiatrist in order to determine whether the unknown author is potentially a menace. The writer can sometimes be identified by questioning the victim concerning her acquaintances.

65. Identifying the Writer

In cases involving a complainant, the identity of the author may sometimes be established if he is writing a series of letters and if he is within the circle of the complainant's associates, acquaintances, or neighbors. One or more of the following methods may be used:

a. **Latent Fingerprints.** The complainant should be instructed to submit each suspected letter unopened so that it may be processed for latent fingerprints.

b. **Handwriting.** Often a generous sample of the culprit's handwriting is present. Occasionally he resorts to hand printing or pasting together of words cut from newspaper headlines. If it is suspected that the letters were written by a member of a business or other organizations with which the complainant is associated, handwriting standards of selected suspects can be obtained for comparison.

c. **Typewriting.** If a typewriter is used, the make and model of the machine can be determined from the anonymous letter and the search can be limited to the offices and quarters containing similar typewriters. A little ingenuity will be required to obtain samples from these machines or to obtain standards known to have been produced on them. In this way it may be possible to identify the individual typewriter and the persons using the machine. If more than one person uses the typewriter a study of personalities, habits, education, and typing peculiarities should precede an interrogation. Alternatively a trap may be set by arrangement with the predetermined innocent users.

d. **Paper and Ink.** The writing materials in general should be examined for peculiarities which would serve to identify the source.

e. **Plants.** If one or more suspects have been identified, the investigator may obtain conclusive evidence by means of a plant. The use of marked stationery and ink is recommended. If the type of stationery used in the anonymous letters is fairly common or in general supply from a common source, the investigator can arrange to place a small invisible number in fluorescent ink on a corner of each sheet of stationery. Each suspect should be assigned a definite number. On receiving a subsequent letter it should be possible to determine the guilty party by the fluorescent number revealed under ultraviolet light. Another method applicable to a situation in which there is a limited number of suspects is the use of fluorescent ink. Using a substance such as that described in Chapter 40, the suspect's source of ink is contaminated with a tracing material.

When the complainant receives a subsequent anonymous letter, the missive is placed under the ultraviolet lamp to detect any fluorescence. To hasten the procedure, where it is desired to test a number of suspects, variations can be made in the color of the fluorescence by the selection of appropriate materials. If a typewriter is used for the letters, a plant can be made by impregnating the ribbon with a fluorescent liquid which will not interfere with the normal inking properties of the ribbon.

XIII. INKS

66. Inks

In the examination of questioned documents it is sometimes necessary to investigate questions concerning the ink used in the writings. For example, if it is alleged that alterations have been made, it is advisable to compare the type of ink used in the undisputed original writing with that of the alleged alteration. If the chemical examination shows that two different types of ink were used, the inference to be drawn is obvious. Another point of interest lies in the question of the age of inks: is the writing as old as the date it bears; were the writings of chronological business entries all made at the same time or over a period of time as would be natural in the course of business? Finally, it is sometimes of great interest to learn whether a particular bottle of ink was used for the writings on two different documents, e.g., the ink bottle that may be the common source for the ink used on a series of anonymous letters.

67. Types of Ink

The determination of the specific type or age of ink is a very difficult problem for the document examiner because of the number of uncontrollable variables, namely, insufficiency of available ink sample in any writing; inadequate quality control in manufacture; and mass production by a few large manufacturers. The chief concern of the manufacturer is viscosity rather than the quantitative mix of the ink. With the widespread use of the ball-point pen the specific identification of ink has become an even more elusive problem.

The general problem of differentiating between the inks used in two specimens of writing depends for its solution on an understanding of the physical and chemical characteristics of the major classifications of inks. The following types of ink are most frequently encountered in document work:

a. **Iron Gallotannate Ink.** This type of ink has long been used for entries in record books and for business purposes in general. Iron gallotannate or nutgail inks are true solutions and not merely suspensions of solid coloring matter in a liquid medium. Hence the ink is capable of penetration into the interstices of the fibers of the paper, thereby inscribing the writing in the body of the paper and not on the surface alone, thus rendering its removal more difficult. The general constituents of black and blue-black nutgall inks are gallic acid, tannic acid, and ferrous sulfate. These produce a colorless solution which will oxidize and darken when exposed to air. Upon contact with paper, this solution reacts to form a black iron compound in the fibers. A dye material such as Soluble Blue is added to render the writing immediately legible. Iron ink remains on the paper indefinitely if the paper is undisturbed. It is considered the best permanent ink for document purposes. Some organizations require that this ink be used in maintaining records.

b. **Logwood Inks.** From the wood of the logwood tree a natural coloring material (haemotoxylin) is obtained by extraction with water. The color of logwood inks depends upon the inorganic salt which is added; but, on drying and standing, they turn black. The addition of chromium salts will yield the deepest black. At the present time logwood inks are practically obsolete, although they are reported to be still in use in Germany.

c. **Nigrosine Ink.** This is a water solution of a synthetic black compound prepared from aniline and nitrobenzene. This synthetic type of ink is usually referred to as *Nigrosine ink* but is also known as *induline ink* and *black aniline ink*. No new compound is formed by oxidation after this ink is applied to the paper, so that lines are merely deposited organic solids that were in solution before the ink dried. It should be expected, then, that water would affect this ink by redissolving the nigrosine. Hence, inks in this class are easily smudged, affected by moisture, and washed from the paper with little difficulty, regardless of the length of time they have been on the document.

d. **Chinese, India, and Carbon Writing Inks.** Inks containing carbon are the oldest writing substances known. Chinese and india ink are the most common forms. In modern times finely divided carbon held in colloidal suspension is used to produce deep black drawing and writing ink. Since carbon is chemically inert to the usual testing reagents, it will resist all attempts at oxidation or reduction, and will remain uninfluenced by changes in acidity. This type of ink, however, does not penetrate deeply into the fibers of the paper and hence may be washed off.

e. **Ball-Point Ink.** Because of the differences in construction of the ball-point pen, a different type of ink is required. In place of the fluid type of ink, a thick, pasty substance is used which will present suitable dye to the ball-point but which will not flow readily. The permanency of these inks is not known with any accuracy. It has been noted that many ball-point inks have a tendency to fade. One approach to the analysis of ball-point ink samples is the use of the Aminco-Bowman spectrophotofluorometer to obtain a "fingerprint" of the dye components. Thin-layer chromotography (TLC) is used to separate ink components. The TLC plates are automatically scanned spectrophotometrically to determine the proportion of dyes in the ink sample.

68. Comparison of Inks

To determine whether two documents were written with the same type of ink various physical and chemical methods are available. The inks are compared visually for color. The naked eye, color filters, and infrared photography usually reveal differences in color. A 5 per cent solution of hydrochloric acid is the most generally useful chemical reagent. The reagent may be applied with a sharpened wooden toothpick to a small area of the writing. When hydrochloric acid is placed on iron nutgall ink, the color disappears or turns a light blue; on logwood ink a red color developes; on nigrosine or carbon ink there is no reaction. To distinguish nigrosine from carbon ink a 10 per cent solution of sodium hypochlorite (acidified) is used. Nigrosine ink turns brown with this reagent, but carbon ink is unaffected. It should be noted that these reactions sometimes take place over a period of hours. The investigator should test inks only as a screening procedure where a number of suspected documents are available.

69. Age of Inks

It may be said, in general, that under ordinary circumstances it is practically impossible to determine the age of inks. A limit can sometimes be placed to the age by color matching with standards to determine the degree of fading and by chemical reactions which depend on oxidation. The chemical methods are not applicable to nigrosine and carbon inks, which are not oxidized after being deposited on the paper. In any case, age determination will depend on the composition of the ink, its condition with respect to fluidity and impurities, the nature of the paper used in the writing, and the conditions under which the paper was preserved.

ADDITIONAL READING

Bartha, A. and Duxbury, N.W.: Restoration and Preservation of Charred Documents. 1 *Canadian Society of Forensic Science Journal*, 2, 1968.

Bates, B.P.: *Identification System for Questioned Documents*. Springfield, Ill.: Thomas, 1970.

_____: *Typewriting Identification*. Springfield, Ill.: Thomas, 1971.

Baxter, P.G.: Classification and Measurement in Forensic Handwriting Comparison. *Medicine, Science and the Law*, 166, 1973.

_____: Handwriting: Principles and Practices. 7 *Criminologist*, 25, 1972.

Bradford, R.R.: Obtaining Exemplars from All Arrestees. 55 *Fingerprint and Identification Magazine*. 6, 1973.

Browning, B.I.: *The Analysis of Paper*. New York, Dekker, 1969.

Buquet, A.: New Techniques for the Detection of Alterations in Documents. 10 *Forensic Science*, 185, 1977.

Caywood, D.A.: Decipherment of Indented Writing—A New Technique. 1 *Journal of Police Science and Administration*, 50, 1973.

Chodrow, M.M. and Bivona, W.A.: *Study of Handprinted Character Recognition Techniques*. Springfield, Va.: National Technical Information Service, 1966.

Conway, J.V.P.: *Evidential Documents*. Springfield, Ill.: Thomas, 1959.

Crown, D.A.: Landmarks in Typewriting Identification. 58 *Journal of Criminal Law, Criminology and Police Science*, 105, 1967.

Crown, D.A., Brunelle, R.L. and Cantu, A.A.: The Parameters of Ballpen Ink Examinations. 21 *Journal of Forensic Sciences*, 917, 1976.

Edwards, J.: Preliminary Document Screening. 25 *Law and Order*, 7, 1977.

Fryd, C.F.M.: Examination of Inks on Documents. 14 *Medicine, Science and the Law*, 87, 1974.

Gupta, S.A.: A Scientific Analysis of Typewriting Identification. 28 *International Criminal Police Review*, 265, 1973.

Harrison, W.R.: *Suspect Documents: Their Scientific Examination*. London, Sweet & Maxwell, 1958.

_____: *Forgery Detection: A Practical Guide*. London, Sweet & Maxwell, 1964.

Hilton, O.: Some Practical Suggestions for Examining Writing from Electric Typewriters. 3 *Journal of Police Science and Administration*, 1, 1975.

_____: *Scientific Examination of Questioned Documents*. Chicago, Callaghan, 1956.

Leslie, A.G.: Identification of the Single Element Typewriter and Type Element. Part I—Type Elements. 10 *Canadian Society of Forensic Science Journal*, 87, 1977.

Leukens, H.R. and Settle, D.M.: *Forensic Neutron Activation Analysis of Paper*. Springfield, Va.: National Technical Information Service, 1970.

McAlexander, T.V.: The Meaning of Handwriting Opinions. 5 *Journal of Police Science and Administration*, 43, 1977.

Muehlberger, R.J., et al.: A Statistical Examination of Selected Handwriting Characteristics. 22 *Journal of Forensic Sciences*, 206, 1977.

Olson, K.: *The Ball-Point Rip-Off: A Forgery Investigator's Handbook*. Santa Cruz, Calif.: Davis Pub., 1975.

Osborn, A.S.: *Questioned Documents*, 2nd ed. Albany, N.Y.: Boyd Printing Co., 1929.

Patterson, P.: The Chemistry of Inks for Writing, Printing and Copying. 4 *Journal of the Forensic Science Society*, 200, 1964.

Purtell, D.J.: Obtaining Questioned Document Standards for Comparison. 5 *Police Law Quarterly*, 4, 1976.

Tewari, S.N. and Tripathi, S.S.: Paper Chromatographic Identification of Ink Dye-Stuffs and its Importance in Document Examinations. 28 *International Criminal Police Review*, 278, 1974.

Witte, A.H.: The Examination and Identification of Inks. In Lundquist, F. (Ed.): *Methods of Forensic Science*, vol. 2. New York, Wiley-Interscience, 1963.

Appendix 1

WHITE-COLLAR CRIME

WHITE-COLLAR crime was first given substantial recognition in 1949 by the publication of Edwin H. Sutherland's book, in which he introduced the definition: "white-collar crime may be defined approximately as a crime committed by a person of respectability and high social status in the course of his occupation." The definition was consideraly broadened in 1970 by Herbert Edelhertz in his paper, "The Nature, Impact and Prosecution of White-Collar Crime," published by the National Institute of Law Enforcement and Criminal Justice. Edelhertz expanded the idea of white-collar crime beyond restrictions of class and occupation by defining it as: "an illegal act or series of acts committed by nonphysical means and by concealment or guile, to obtain money or property, to avoid the payment or loss of money or property, or to obtain business or personal advantage."

Throughout this text white-collar crime has been touched upon lightly, without imparting proportionate emphasis to an area of crime that many experts consider as costly to society as street crime. Employee theft, for example, is estimated at $10 million a day by Norman Jaspan Associates, an organization that specializes in the detection and prevention of white-collar crime. Dishonesty is considered to be prevalent at all levels—from the warehouse loading dock to the executive suite. Since 1949 the problem has expanded in scope and deepened in complexity.

It is not part of the purpose of this book to treat the investigation and prosecution of white-collar crime. The student will, however, find the following outline of Edelhertz highly informative:

Categories of White-Collar Crimes

In the list given below, white-collar crimes have been classified by the general environment and motivation of the perpetrator.

Comprehensive (except for the exclusion of organized crime) and distinctive, these categories are intended to provide the following benefits: (1) to assist the study of motivation as an aid in preventive programs; (2) to suggest a basis for altering environments which may give rise to criminal violations; and (3) to give insight into the psychology, susceptibility, and other exposed weaknesses of victims.

a. **Personal Crimes.** These are crimes by persons operating on an individual, *ad hoc* basis for personal gain in a non-business context.

1) Purchases on credit with no intention to pay; purchases by mail in the name of another.
2) Individual income tax violations.
3) Credit card frauds.
4) Bankruptcy frauds.
5) Title II home improvement loan frauds.
6) Frauds with respect to social security, unemployment insurance, and welfare.
7) Unorganized or occasional frauds on insurance companies (theft, casualty, health, etc.)
8) Violations of Federal Reserve regulations by pledging stock for further purchases, flouting margin requirements.
9) Unorganized "lonely hearts" appeal by mail.

b. **Abuses of Trust.** These are crimes committed in the course of their occupations by persons operating inside business, government, or other establishments in violation of their duty of loyalty and fidelity to employer or client.

1) Commercial bribery and kickbacks, i.e., by and to buyers, insurance adjusters, contracting officers, quality inspectors, government inspectors and auditors, etc.
2) Bank violations by bank officers, employees, and directors.
3) Embezzlement or self-dealing by business or union officers and employees.
4) Securities fraud by insiders trading to their advantage by the use of special knowledge or causing their firms to take positions in the market to benefit themselves.
5) Employee petty larceny and expense account frauds.
6) Frauds by computer causing unauthorized payouts.
7) "Sweetheart contracts" entered into by union officers.

8) Embezzlement or self-dealing by attorneys, trustees, and fiduciaries.
9) Fraud against the government
   a) Padding payrolls.
   b) Conflicts of interest.
   c) False travel, expense, or per diem claims.

c. **Business Crimes.** These offenses are incidental to and in furtherance of business operations but not the central purpose of the business.

1) Tax violations.
2) Antitrust violations.
3) Commercial bribery of another's employee, officer, or fiduciary (including union officers).
4) Food and drug violations.
5) False weights and measures by retailers.
6) Violations of Truth-in-Lending Act by misrepresentation of credit terms and prices.
7) Submission or publication of false financial statements to obtain credit.
8) Use of fictitious or over-valued collateral.
9) Check-kiting to obtain operating capital on short-term financing.
10) Securities Act violations, i.e., sale of non-registered securities to obtain operating capital, false proxy statements, manipulation of market to support corporate credit or access to capital markets, etc.
11) Collusion between physicians and pharmacists to cause the writing of unnecessary prescriptions.
12) Dispensing by pharmacists in violation of law, excluding narcotics traffic.
13) Immigration fraud in support of employment agency operations to provide domestics.
14) Housing code violations by landlords.
15) Deceptive advertising.
16) Fraud against the government:
    a) False claims.
    b) False statements:
       (1) to induce contracts

(2) AID frauds

(3) Housing frauds

(4) SBA frauds, such as SBIC bootstrapping, self-dealing, cross-dealing, etc., or obtaining direct loans by use of false financial statements.

 c) Moving contracts in urban renewal.

17) Labor violations (Davis-Bacon Act).

18) Commercial espionage.

d. **Confidence Games.** White-collar crime considered as a business or as the central activity of a business takes the form of the systematic frauds which are referred to as *con games*.

1) Medical or health frauds.

2) Advance fee swindles.

3) Phony contests.

4) Bankruptcy fraud, including schemes devised as salvage operation after insolvency or otherwise legitimate business.

5) Securities fraud and commodities fraud.

6) Chain referral schemes.

7) Home improvement schemes.

8) Debt consolidation schemes.

9) Mortgage milking.

10) Merchandise swindles:

 a) Gun and coin swindles

 b) General merchandise

 c) Buying or pyramid clubs.

11) Land frauds.

12) Directory advertising schemes.

13) Charity and religious frauds.

14) Personal improvement schemes:

 a) Diploma mills

 b) Correspondence schools

 c) Modeling schools.

15) Fraudulent application for, use and/or sale of credit cards, airline tickets, etc.

16) Insurance frauds:

 a) Phony accident rings.

 b) Looting of companies by purchase of over-valued assets,

phony management contracts, self-dealing with agents, inter-company transfers, etc.
c) Frauds by agents writing false policies to obtain advance commissions.
d) Issuance of annuities or paid-up life insurance, with no consideration, so that they can be used as collateral for loans.
e) Sales by misrepresentation to military personnel or those otherwise uninsurable.
17) Vanity press and song publishing schemes.
18) Ponzi schemes.
19) False security frauds, i.e. Billy Sol Estes or De Angelis type schemes.
20) Purchase of banks or control thereof with deliberate intention to loot them.
21) Fraudulent establishing and operation of banks or savings and loan associations.
22) Fraud against the government:
a) Organized income tax refund swindles, sometimes operated by income tax "counselors."
b) AID frauds, i.e. where totally worthless goods are shipped.
c) FHA frauds through home improvement schemes or by obtaining guarantees of mortgages on multiple family housing far in excess of the value of the property with foreseeable inevitable foreclosure.
23) Executive placement and employment agency frauds.
24) Coupon redemption frauds.
25) Money order swindles.

ADDITIONAL READING

Carey, M. and Sherman, G.: *A Compendium of Bunk or How to Spot A Con Artist.* Springfield, Ill.: Thomas, 1976.

Chamber of Commerce of the United States of America. *White Collar Crime, Everyone's Problem, Everyone's Loss.* Washington, D.C.: U.S. Government Printing Office, 1974.

Edelhertz, H.: *The Nature, Impact and Prosecution of White-Collar Crime.* Washington, D.C.: U.S. Government Printing Office, 1970.

Finn, P. and Hoffman, A.R.: *Exemplary Projects: Prosecution of Economic Crime.* Washington, D.C.: U.S. Government Printing Office, 1976.

George, B.J., Jr.: *White-Collar Crime: Defense and Prosecution.* New York, Practicing Law Institute, 1971.

Investigation of White-Collar Crime. Washington, D.C.: U.S. Government Printing Office, 1977.

Lipman, M.: *Stealing—How America's Employees are Stealing Their Companies Blind.* New York, Harper's Magazine Press, 1973.

Miller, C.A.: *Economic Crime: A Prosecutor's Hornbook.* A Project of the National District Attorneys Association, July, 1974.

Ogren, R.W.: The Ineffectiveness of the Criminal Sanction in Fraud and Corruption Cases. 11 *American Criminal Law Review*, 959, 1973.

Oughton, F.: *Fraud and White-Collar Crime.* London, Elek Books, 1971.

Rosefsky, R.S.: *Frauds; Swindles, and Rackets.* Chicago, Follett Pub., 1973.

Smigel, E.O. and Ross, H.L. (Eds.): *Crimes Against Bureaucracy.* New York, Van Nostrand Reinhold, 1970.

Sobel, L.A.: *Corruption in Business.* New York, Facts on File, 1977.

Appendix 2

ARREST, SEARCH, AND SEIZURE

1. Arrest

THE POWER of a criminal investigator to make an arrest depends upon the federal law and the local state laws of arrest in the area in which he is operating. A criminal investigator possesses, of course, the same right as the private citizen to make an arrest. He may arrest for a felony or a breach of the peace committed in his presence and for a felony not committed in his presence if the felony has in fact been committed and he has reasonable cause to believe that the person arrested committed the felony. In making arrest under other circumstances the investigator ordinarily first obtains a warrant. A military investigator may arrest persons subject to military law for violation of the Uniform Code of Military Justice or as otherwise provided by regulation.

a. **Police Arrest.** This term describes the act of taking an offender into custody and imposing restraint upon him with formal notification that he is "under arrest." Military law employs the term *arrest* to mean a moral restraint imposed on a person by oral or written order of competent authority limiting his personal liberty pending disposition of charges and binding upon the person arrested, not by physical force as in the police arrest, but rather by virtue of his moral and legal obligation to obey such an order of arrest.

b. **Police Restraint.** In addition to the police arrest, criminal investigators also employ the other specific types of physical restraints which involve the deprivation of liberty by taking into custody. These restraints are usually called "detaining for questioning," "protective custody," and "holding on a short affidavit."

2. Technique of Arrest

The manner in which the arrest is accomplished will naturally depend on the circumstances in which the investigator finds himself. He can in some cases exercise control over these conditions. In other situations, he must take advantage of his opportunities. The safety of bystanders and of himself should be a primary consideration. The force employed should be sufficient to overcome resistance. The use of excessive force is subject to censure and, if employed to a marked degree, renders the investigator liable to prosecution. In any event such an abuse of authority is prejudicial to the case.

a. **Behavior in Making an Arrest.** The arrest should be made in a straightforward manner whenever possible. The suspect should be notified of the fact that he is being placed under arrest. The investigator should then display his credentials or badge to establish his authority. An inconspicuous, courteous manner should be employed. The investigator must, however, convey the seriousness of his intention by his demeanor, voice, and movements. He should, at all times, control the situation. There should be no show of nervousness or indecision. A preliminary search can be accomplished in an inconspicuous manner. The subject can then be removed to a place where a more thorough search can be made without the danger of interference and without attracting a crowd.

b. **Employment of Force.** Unnecessary force or violence is to be avoided. The degree and kind of force should be calculated only to overcome the resistance offered and will depend on the nature of the case, that is, whether the case involves a misdemeanor or a felony.

1) *Misdemeanor.* In misdemeanor cases the investigator may not use force calculated to cause grave bodily harm. Although a law enforcement officer need not, under any circumstances, retreat in the face of resistance, it is preferable to permit a person accused of a misdemeanor to escape rather than inflict serious injury in effecting his apprehension. Firearms should not be used in arresting for a misdemeanor.

2) *Felony.* Deadly force may be used when required in felony cases, but only such force as is necessary to accomplish the arrest or prevent the escape of the suspect. Since a law enforcement officer is

characterized by his capacity to use judgment in extraordinary situations, it is expected that his decision to use force will not rest solely on the simplistic distinction between a misdemeanor and a felony. He will not, that is to say, decide to use deadly force simply because he is dealing with a felony case. The kind of felony should also be taken into consideration. For example, the few dollars that may distinguish a grand larceny from petty theft may not justify the use of a deadly weapon simply to prevent an escape. Similarly, a person wanted for armed robbery and a person who has forged and cashed a check for $500 may both be guilty of a felony, but the investigator, in planning an apprehension, would assign widely differing values to the potential of each offender for resistance to arrest and would be prepared to act accordingly.

A general principle of minimum violence should guide the investigator's tactics in making an apprehension so as to provide maximum safety for innocent persons in the area, suitable precautions for his own protection, and necessary, but not excessive, force in overcoming resistance.

3. Search of the Person

A search of a person is conducted to discover weapons or evidence, or to determine identity. Taking custody of property found by searching is called seizure, a term which implies a forcible dispossession of the person arrested. A preliminary search of a person ordinarily is made at the time and scene of an arrest; its primary purposes are the discovery of concealed weapons and the seizing of incriminating evidence which might otherwise be destroyed. At the place of detention (usually a station house) a more complete search is made. A suspect is stripped, and his clothing and other possessions carried on his person thoroughly examined. Female investigative personnel search women prisoners.

The Supreme Court has traditionally interpreted the Fourth Amendment's prohibition against "unreasonable searches and seizures" to mean that policemen could not search unless they had either a search warrant or enough evidence to arrest the suspect and take him into custody. In 1968 the Supreme Court announced a rule of reasonableness that authorizes the police to detain subjects for questioning and search them "when a reasonably prudent man in the circumstances would be warranted in the belief that his safety and that of others was in danger." If a legal search turns up a weapon or any other evidence, it can be used in court. With this ruling the Supreme Court clarified the "stop and frisk" situation, in which the policeman stops a person whom he suspects but could not legally arrest and whose clothing, if he looks dangerous, the officer pats down for weapons before questioning. Concerning the subjective test of "reasonableness" the Court concluded that "no judicial opinion can comprehend the protean variety of the street encounter," and that local judges would have to be trusted to judge the reasonableness of each one on a case-by-case basis (*Terry v. Ohio*, 392 U.S. 1 [1968]).

4. Search of the Area

The investigator should not, in the busy moments of taking the prisoner into custody, overlook the possibility of evidence being in the area. When the arrest has been made, and the prisoner has been subjected to a preliminary search and secured, the area surrounding the place of arrest should be searched for weapons, narcotics, or other evidence. The prisoner may have taken the advantage of the moments elapsing between his being surprised and his apprehension to throw evidence away. If the prisoner was in a vehicle, both the vehicle and the area should be searched. In a hotel room or house, the premises should be searched. In a train or bus the seat and its surrounding area should be examined.

5. Seizure of Evidence

In gathering evidence from a premises, especially from the subject's home, the investigators should be guided by the Fourth Amendment's prohibitions against unreasonable searches and seizures. In general, officials cannot seize in a search, or use as evidence, any items except illegal articles or contraband, such as narcotics, or the instrumentality of a crime, such as a weapon, or the fruits of a crime. Prior to the Supreme Court decision of 1967 *Warden v. Hayden,* 387 U.S. 294 (1967) all other items had been declared "mere evidence" and could not be used in court, even if the search had been made with a valid search warant or incident to a lawful arrest.

This "mere evidence" rule had been the outgrowth of an early judicial belief that the Fourth Amendment's prohibition against unreasonable searches and seizures was designed primarily to protect property from seizure. Thus, the government was permitted to seize only property that the suspect had no legal right to retain. This view has been discredited in recent years. It is now recognized that the primary object of the Fourth Amendment is the protection of privacy rather than property.

Accordingly, in the decision cited, the Court ruled that clothing seized in a lawful search should not be excluded from evidence against a defendant simply because it is "mere evidence" and not the contraband or a fruit or instrumentality of the crime. The demise of the "mere evidence" rule, however, does not necessarily permit the seizure of written documents, which would constitute compulsory self-incrimination, nor does it authorize the seizure of articles that are not related to the crime that prompted the law enforcement agents to make the search. In the case cited, police officers in hot pursuit of Hayden, after the robbery of a Baltimore taxi office, found him at home and took items of clothing of the type that the robber was said to have worn. The clothes were introduced in evidence and Hayden was convicted.

6. Reasonable Searches

The laws governing searches and search warrants are in some ways quite explicit. The area to be searched and the search itself must be reasonably calculated to find the object. In other ways the laws are found to be loosely worded and prone to conflicting interpretations.

The investigator must be guided by the court decisions and policy of his own state, jurisdiction, and department. It is expected that the scope of the search be in proportion to the specific information that the police have and to the seriousness of the offense. For his own protection where a major search is anticipated, the investigator should request that this be specified by the judge in the warrant. He should, of course, be prepared to show probable cause, an element that may be defined as more than mere suspicion but less than proof beyond a reasonable doubt.

In matters of property damage and extent of search the investigator should permit official caution to temper his personal zeal. Moreover, he should not be discouraged by the absence of more definite guidelines, since these matters are in the hands of judicial officials more familiar with such problems and competent to make the relevant decisions. When there is doubt in the investigator's mind concerning the nature of a search, he should consult the prosecuting attorney or the judge empowered to issue the warrant. Acting intelligently and in good faith, the investigator should feel assured of the support of the courts.

ADDITIONAL READING

Cohen, S.: A Criminologist Looks at Search and Seizure. 2 *Police Law Quarterly*, 2, 1974.

Creamer, J.S.: *The Law of Arrest, Search and Seizure.* Philadelphia, Saunders, 1968.

Fischer, E.C.: *Laws of Arrest.* Evanston, Ill.: Traffic Institute, Northwestern University, 1967.

Klotter, J.C. and Kanovitz, J.R.: *Constitutional Law For Police*, 3rd ed. Cincinnati, Anderson, 1977.

Models Rules for Law Enforcement: Warrantless Search of Persons and Places—With Commentary. 9 *Criminal Law Bulletin*, 645, 1973.

Nedrud, D.R.: *The Supreme Court and the Law of Criminal Investigation.* Chicago, Law Enforcement Publishers, 1969.

Ringel, W.E.: *Searches and Seizures, Arrests and Confessions.* New York, Clark Boardman, 1972.

The Warrantless Search of Motor Vehicles. 40 *FBI Law Enforcement Bulletin*, 3, 1971.

Appendix 3

SUGGESTIONS FOR
LAW ENFORCEMENT AGENCIES
TRANSMITTING EVIDENCE
TO THE F.B.I. LABORATORY

PROPER SEALING OF EVIDENCE

The method shown below permits access to the invoice letter without breaking the inner seal. This allows the person entitled to receive the evidence to receive it in a sealed condition just as it was packed by the sender.

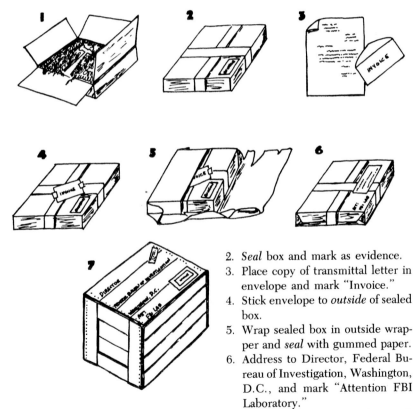

2. *Seal* box and mark as evidence.
3. Place copy of transmittal letter in envelope and mark "Invoice."
4. Stick envelope to *outside* of sealed box.
5. Wrap sealed box in outside wrapper and *seal* with gummed paper.
6. Address to Director, Federal Bureau of Investigation, Washington, D.C., and mark "Attention FBI Laboratory."
1. Pack bulk evidence securely in box.
7. If packing box is wooden—tack invoice envelope to top under a cellophane cover.

CHART[1] FOR LAW ENFORCEMENT AGENCIES SU

Specimen	Identification	Amount desired	
		Standard	Evidence
Abrasives, including carborundum, emery, sand, etc.	On outside of container. Type of material. Date obtained. Agent's name or initials. Case and number.	Not less than 1 ounce...	All........
Acids........	........do........	1 pint........	All to one pint........
Adhesive tape........	........do........	1 foot........	All........
Alkalies—caustic soda, potash ammonia, etc.	........do........	{ 1 pint liquid........ { 1 pound solid........	All to 1 pint........ All to 1 pound........
Ammunition........	........do........	2	
Anonymous letters, extortion letters.	Place in cellophane envelope, seal with evidence sticker; place date and agent's initials on sticker; make detailed notes describing letter.		All........
Blasting caps........	On outside of container. Type of material, date obtained and agent's name.		........do........
Blood:			
(a) Liquid........	Use adhesive tape on outside of test tube. Name of victim or subject, date taken, doctor's name, agent's name.	⅙ ounce (5 cc.) collected in a sterile test tube or Sheppard (vac) tube.	........do........
(b) Drowning cases........	........do........	2 specimens: 1 from each side of heart.	
(c) Small quantities: 1. Liquid........	........do........		All to ⅙ ounce (5 cc.).....
2. Dry stains........	On outside of pill box, powder or druggist fold. Type of specimens, date secured, agent's name, case and number.		As much as possible........
(d) Stained clothing, fabric, etc.	Use string tag or mark directly on clothes. Type of specimens, date secured, agent's name, case and number.		As found........

[1] This chart is not intended to be all inclusive. If evidence to be submitted is not found herein consult the specimen list for an item most similar in nature and submit accordingly.

Preservation	Wrapping and packing	Transmittal	Miscellaneous
None............................	Use containers such as ice cream box, pill box, or powder box. Seal to prevent any loss.	Registered mail, railroad or air express.	
......do......................	All glass bottle. Tape in stopper. Pack in sawdust, glass or rock wool. Use bakelite or paraffin lined bottle for hydrofluoric acid.	Railroad express only.	Label acids, glass, corrosive.
......do......................	Place on waxed paper or cellophane.	Registered mail..............	
}......do......................	Glass bottle with rubber stopper held in with adhesive tape.	Railroad express only...	Label alkali, glass, corrosive.
......do......................	Pack in cotton, soft paper or cloth in small container. Place in wooden box.	......do.......................	If standard make, usually not necessary to send. Explosive label.
Do not handle with bare hands.	Wrap securely........................	Registered mail..............	Include original envelope. Advise if search of anonymous letter file desired and if letter should be treated for latent fingerprints.
Should not be forwarded until advised to do so by the Laboratory. Packing instructions will be given at that time.			
Sterile tube only. No preservative. No refrigerant.	Wrap in cotton, soft paper. Place in mailing tube or suitably strong mailing carton.	Air mail, special delivery. Registered.	
......do..............	......do..............	......do..............	
......do..............	......do..............	......do..............	Collect by using eyedropper or clean spoon transfer to sterile and chemically clean test tube.
Keep dry......................	Tops, ends and all folds sealed to prevent leakage.	Registered mail..............	
If wet when found, dry by hanging. Use no heat to dry. No preservative.	Each article wrapped separately and identified on outside of package. Place in strong box packed to prevent shifting of contents.	Registered mail, air or railroad express.	

Specimen	Identification	Amount desired	
		Standard	Evidence
Bullets (not cartridges)	On base. Agent's initial or other individual identifying character.		All found
Cartridges	On outside of case near bullet end. Agent's initial or other individual identifying character.	2	do
Cartridge cases (shells)	Preferably on inside near open end or on outside near open end. Agent's initial or other individual identifying character.		All
Charred or burned paper.	On outside of container indicate type of material, date obtained, agent's name or initials, case and number.		do
Checks (fraudulent).	See anonymous letters		
Check protector, rubber stamp and dater stamp sets, known standards.	Place agent's name or initials, date, name of make and model, etc. on sample impressions.	Obtain several copies in full word-for-word order of each questioned checkwriter impression. If unable to forward rubber stamps, prepare numerous samples with different degrees of pressure.	
Clothing	String tag or mark directly. Type of evidence, agent's name, date, case and number.		All
Codes, ciphers, and foreign language material.	As anonymous letters		do
Drugs: (a) Liquids	Affix label to bottle in which found including agent's name, date, case and number.		All to 1 pint.
(b) Powders, pills, and solids.	On outside of pill box. Agent's name, date, case and number.		All to ¼ pound.
Dynamite and other explosives.	Consult the FBI Laboratory and follow their telephonic or telegraphic instructions.		

Preservation	Wrapping and packing	Transmittal	Miscellaneous
None.........	Place in cotton or soft paper. Place in pill, powder or match box. Pack to prevent shifting during transit.	Registered mail..........	
......do.......	......do.......	Railroad express only...	
......do.......	......do.......	Registered mail..........	
......do.......	Pack in rigid container between layers of cotton.	......do.......	Added moisture, with atomizer or otherwise, not recommended.
......do.......	Wrap securely.......	......do.......	Advise what parts questioned or known. Furnish physical description of subject.
......do.......	Wrap securely.......	......do.......	Do not change the ribbon or alter the inking.
......do.......	Each article individually wrapped with identification written on outside of of package. Place in strong container.	Registered mail or railroad or air express.	Leave clothing whole. Do not cut out stains. If wet, dry before packing.
......do.......	As anonymous letters.......	As anonymous letters...	Furnish all background and technical information pertinent to examination.
......do.......	If bottle has no stopper, transfer to glass stoppered bottle and seal with adhesive tape.	Registered mail, railroad or air express.	Mark "Fragile." Determine alleged normal use of drug and if prescription, check with druggist to determine supposed ingredients.
......do.......	Seal to prevent any loss by use of tape.	......do.......	

Specimen	Identification	Amount desired	
		Standard	Evidence
Firearms....................	Attach string tag. Name of weapons, caliber, serial number, date found, agent's name, case, and number. Serial number in agent's notes.		All................................
Fuse, safety.................	Attach string tag or gummed paper label, agent's name, date, case, and number.	1 foot..........................	........do.............
Gasoline.....................	On outside of all metal container, label with type of material, agent's name, date, case, and number.	1 quart.......................	All to 1 gallon...............
Glass fragments..........	Adhesive tape on each piece. Agent's name, date, case, and number on tape. Separate questioned and known.		All................................
Gunpowder tests: (a) Paraffin.............	On outside of container. Type of material, date, agent's name, case, and number.		........do.............
(b) On cloth.........	Attach string tag or mark directly. Type of material, date, agent's name, case, and number.		........do.............
Hair and fibers...........	On outside container. Type of material, date, agent's name, case, and number.	Several hairs. Must be a representative specimen from different parts of head or body.	........do.............
Handwriting, handprinting and forgeries, known standards.	Agent's name or initials, date, and from whom obtained should be written on the back. Voluntary statement written by suspect if included, may appear on either side of samples.	Obtain several samples in full word-for-word order from dictation, including some with hand not commonly used.	
Matches.....................	On outside of container. Type of material, date, agent's name, case, and number	1 to 2 books of paper. 1 full box of wood.	All................................
Medicines. (See Drugs.)			

[2] Reproduce the original writing conditions as to speed, slant, size of paper, size of writing, type of writing instruments, etc. Do not allow suspect to see questioned writing. Give no instructions as to spelling, punctuation, etc. Remove each sample from sight as soon as completed. Suspect should fill out blank check form in check cases. In handprinting cases, both upper and lower case samples should be obtained. In forgery cases, sample signatures of the person whose name is forged should be forwarded.

Preservation	Wrapping and packing	Transmittal	Miscellaneous
Keep from rusting.....	Wrap in paper and identify contents of package. Place in cardboard box or wooden box. Label "Fire-arms."	Under 4 pounds—Registered mail. Over 4 pounds — railroad express.	Unload all weapons befor shipping.
None............................	Place in manila envelope, box or suitable retainer.	Registered mail, railroad or air express.	
Fireproof container....	Metal container packed in wood box.	Railroad express only....	
Avoid chipping............	Wrap each piece separately in cotton. Pack in strong box to prevent shifting and breakage. Identify contents.	Registered mail, railroad or air express.	Marked "Fragile."
Containers must be free of any nitrate-containing substance. Keep cool.	Wrap in waxed paper or place in wax sandwich bags. Lay on cotton in a substantial box. Place in larger box packed with absorbent material.	Registered mail..............	Use "Fragile" label. Keep cool.
None............................	Fold fabric flat and then wrap, so that no residues will be lost.	........do............................	Avoid shaking.
........do............................	Druggist fold or pill box. Seal edges and openings with scotch tape or adhesive tape.	........do............................	Envelope not satisfactory.
........do............................	Enclose in manila envelope..	........do............................	(²)
Keep away from fire...	Metal container and packed in larger package to prevent shifting. Matches in box or metal container packed to prevent friction between matches.	Railroad express or registered mail.	"Keep away from fire" label.

Specimen	Identification	Amount desired	
		Standard	Evidence
Metal............................	On outside of container. Type of material, date, agent's name, case, and number.	pound............................	All to 1 pound.............._____
Oil..................................	............do............................	1 quart together with specifications.	All to 1 quart................
Obliterated, eradicated, or indented writing.	See anonymous letters..........		All..................................
Organs of body............	On outside of container. Victim's name, date of death, date of autopsy, name of doctor, agent's name.		All to 1 pound..............
Paint: (a) Liquid..............	On outside of container. Type of material, origin if known, date, agent's name, case and number.	¼ pint................................	All to ¼ pint.............._
(b) Solid (paint chips or scrapings).	..........do............................	At least ½ sq. in. of solid.	All. If on small object send object.
Plaster casts, tire treads, footprints.	On back before plaster hardens. Location, date, and agent's name.		All..................................
Powder patterns. (See gunpowder tests).			
Rope, twine, and cordage.	On tag or container. Type of material, date, agent's name, case, and number.	1 yard................................	..........do............................
Safe insulation or soil.	On outside of container. Type of material, date, agent's name, case, and number.	½ pound........................	All to 1 pound..............
Tools............................	On tools or use string tag. Type of tool, identifying number, date, agent's name, case, and number.		All..................................
Tool marks..................	On object or on tag attached to or on opposite end from where tool marks appear. Agent's name and date.	Send in the tool. If impractical, make several impressions on similar material as evidence using entire marking area of tool.	..........do............................

Preservation	Wrapping and packing	Transmittal	Miscellaneous
Keep from rusting.....	Use paper boxes or containers. Seal and use strong paper or wooden box.	Registered mail, railroad or air express.	Melt number, heat treatment, and other specifications of foundry if available.
Keep away from fire....	Metal container with tight screw top. Pack in strong box using excelsior or similar material.	Railroad express only...	Do not use dirt for packing material.
None..........................	Wrap securely..........................	Registered mail..............	Advise whether bleaching or staining methods may be used. Avoid folding.
None to evidence. Dry ice in package not touching glass jars.	All glass containers (glass jar with glass top).	Railroad or air express....	"Fragile" label. Keep cool. Metal top containers must not be used. Send autopsy report.
None..........................	Friction top paint can or large mouth screw top jars. If glass, pack to prevent breakage. Use heavy corrugated paper or wooden box.	Registered mail or railroad or air express.	
Wrap so as to protect smear.	If small amount, pill box or small glass vial with screw top. Seal to prevent leakage. Envelopes not satisfactory.	.......do....................	Do not pack paint chips in cotton or secure with scotch tape or adhesive.
None..........................	Wrap in paper and surround with suitable packing material to prevent breakage.	Registered mail..............	Use "Fragile" label.
....	Wrap securely..........................	.......do....................	
....	Use containers such as ice cream box, pill box or powder box. Seal to prevent any loss.	Registered mail, railroad or air express.	Avoid use of glass containers.
....	Wrap each tool in paper. Use strong cardboard or wooden box with tools packed to prevent shifting.	.......do....................	
Cover ends bearing tool marks with soft paper and wrap with strong paper to protect ends.	After marks have been protected, wrap in strong wrapping paper, place in strong box and pack to prevent shifting.	.......do....................	

Specimen	Identification	Amount desired	
		Standard	Evidence
Typewriting, known standards.	Place agent's name or initials, date, serial number, name of make and model, etc., on same side as samples of typewriting.	Obtain at least 1 copy in full word-for-word order of questioned typewriting. Also include partial copies in light, medium and heavy degrees of touch. Also carbon paper samples of every character on the keyboard.	....
Urine or water...........	On outside of container. Type of material, name of subject, date taken, agent's name, case, and number.	Preferably all urine voided over a period of 24 hours.	All.............................
Wire (see also tool marks).	On label or tag. Type of material, date, agent's name, case, and number.	1 foot.................................	........do.................................
Wood.............................	........do.................................	........do.................................	........do.................................

Preservation	Wrapping and packing	Transmittal	Miscellaneous
None................................	Wrap securely............................	Registered mail.............	Examine ribbon f o r evidence of questioned message thereon. For carbon paper samples either remove ribbon or place in stencil position.
None. Use any clean bottle with leak-proof stopper.	Bottle surrounded with absorbent material to prevent breakage. Strong cardboard or wooden box.	........do................................	
....	Wrap securely............................	........do................................	
....	........do..	........do................................	

BLOODSTAIN CHART

CONDITION OF STAIN

Surface bearing stain	FRESH MOIST STAINS		DRIED STAINS	
	Small Quantities	Large Quantities	Small Quantities	Large Quantities
Fabrics (Clothing, sheets, blankets, rugs)	Allow stain to dry at room temperature. Transmit fabric to laboratory with clean, white paper inserted to protect stain from rest of material.	With clean eye dropper transfer blood to a clean test tube, and insert stopper. For the remainder of the stain follow the directions given for small quantities.	Remove entire fabric to laboratory, interlaying white paper to protect stain.	If permitted, cut portion size of a square 2 in. on edge and place in a test tube and stopper. If possible remove remainder of stain on fabric to laboratory in original condition, interlaying white paper to protect blood stains.
Solid objects (Stove, linoleum, cement, plaster, wood, automobile)	Remove as much blood as possible with eye dropper, place in test tube, and insert stopper. If none can be removed with eye dropper, remove object to laboratory, if possible; otherwise, scrape off stain with scalpel and place in pill box.	Remove as much blood as possible from object with an eye dropper, place in a clean test tube, and insert stopper. Allow remainder of stain to dry and remove object to laboratory, if possible.	First remove any crusts. Place them intact in a test tube or pill box. Avoid breaking crust by rough handling. Remove object to laboratory. If impossible, scrape off as much as possible and place in clean test tube, stopper and remove to laboratory.	First remove any crusts. Place them intact in a test tube or pill box. Avoid breaking crust by rough handling. Scrape off all remaining blood possible. Place in a test tube or pill box.

INDEX

899